Goldwater

Goldwater

The Man Who Made a Revolution

Lee Edwards

Foreword by Senator Trent Lott

REGNERY PUBLISHING, INC.
An Eagle Publishing Company
Washington, D.C.

First paperback printing 1997

Library of Congress Cataloging-in-Publication Data

Edwards, Lee.
Goldwater / Lee Edwards.
p.   cm.
Includes bibliographical references and index.
ISBN 0-89526-471-4 (acid-free paper)
1. Goldwater, Barry M. (Barry Morris), 1909-   . 2. Legislators—
United States—Biography. 3. Presidential candidates—United
States—Biography. 4. United States. Congress. Senate—Biography.
I. Title.
E748.G64E38 1995
973.92'092—dc20
[B]   95-13283
                                                       CIP

Published in the United States by
Regnery Publishing, Inc.
An Eagle Publishing Company
422 First Street, SE
Washington, DC 20003

Distributed to the trade by
National Book Network
4720-A Boston Way
Lanham, MD 20706

Printed on acid-free paper.
Manufactured in the United States of America

10 9 8 7 6 5 4 3 2 1

Books are available in quantity for promotional or premium use. Write to Director of Special Sales, Regnery Publishing, Inc., 422 First Street, SE, Washington, DC 20003, for information on discounts and terms or call (202) 546-5005.

For Elizabeth

—

Contents

PART IV
Legislator

PART V
Paradox

Foreword

By Senator Trent Lott

NOT MANY POLITICIANS can be said to have prophetic vision. Barry Goldwater is one of the great exceptions.

As we know, to be a prophet is not necessarily to receive honor from one's countrymen. So has it been with Senator Goldwater. He has been attacked, demonized, and caricatured for his beliefs and for his bravery, especially during the 1964 presidential race.

Goldwater lost that race in a landslide. His landslides would come later. The forceful conservative viewpoints he espoused—most eloquently described in his book, *The Conscience of a Conservative*—propelled Republican victories during the Eighties and, with last November's elections, the Nineties. This book, *Goldwater: The Man Who Made a Revolution*, is an engaging portrait of this great man, Barry Goldwater.

I had just graduated from the University of Mississippi when Republicans gathered in July 1964 at the Cow Palace to proclaim Barry Goldwater their choice for president. Then, conservatism was considered a fringe movement by the media and the ruling radical social engineers. A fog of turmoil and uncertainty had fallen upon the nation. The centralization of all power in the federal government was not opposed.

Into this era of liberal intolerance came Barry Goldwater. A peddler's grandson, Goldwater had been a successful businessman, a distinguished serviceman, and a local official in Phoenix, Arizona, before he became a U.S. Senator. In that role, he challenged Presidents and his colleagues in the Senate, opposing reckless expansion of the federal government.

Barry Goldwater believed, with his hero Thomas Jefferson, "that government is best which governs the least, because its people discipline themselves." It was the West in Goldwater, the undying glow of individual and mass manifest destiny, that animated his faith in people and their abilities instead of in the state. It was his view that man, a great wonder created by God, should be the source of power, ingenuity, and effort, and that this idea had made America the greatest nation on Earth.

Goldwater was, thus, a classical liberal, influenced by traditional values, and steeled by a moral faith in America's rightness. His liberalism was the liberalism of the Founders, with all men equal in their infinite worth. Modern liberalism, though, is an ideology of all men as pawns: hapless children playing among the ruins of their society in the shadow of the mega-state.

When Barry Goldwater during the 1964 Republication Convention proclaimed, "I would remind you that extremism in the defense of liberty is no vice! And let me remind you also that moderation in the pursuit of justice is no virtue!" many people turned against him. The we-know-best politicians and the collectivism-boosters in the press painted Goldwater as a dangerous man with dangerous ideas.

What was dangerous were the people and forces, both internal and external, that came to infamous prominence during the next sixteen years. The liberal democracies around the world found themselves powerless to limit discord and riots. The welfare state ballooned. Communism, not adequately checked, was on the march. The extremists for liberty were very much outnumbered, it seemed.

The American people, though, began searching for these extremists. In the late Seventies, President Carter said there was "malaise" in the land. The Kremlin was razing Afghanistan. Gangster-mullahs held Americans hostage. Under these circumstances, the country found Ronald Reagan—a Goldwater supporter—who won the presidency.

President Reagan ran on essentially the same ideas—limited government, individual freedom, anti-communism—that had been called extreme in 1964. In 1994, a growing, ideologically-attuned electorate that had seen Communism collapse wanted to see more freedom and opportunity here, in America. They saw more freedom and opportunity in the Republican proposals than the Democratic; the GOP gained control of the Senate, and took over the House for the first time in forty years.

So, today, we realize that the Goldwater of 1964 foresaw his vindication, and the vindication of the American ideal, in the political realm. There have been many heroes of the conservative movement—Goldwater is preeminent.

There are some, though, who, hearing the recent statements of Barry Goldwater, now question Goldwater's place of prominence. Lee Edwards in this wonderful book talks about these statements. Senator Goldwater, it seems on first glance, has become stridently pro-abortion, pro-gay-agenda, and anti-traditionalist. Liberals, having very little to cheer about these days, have cheered on Goldwater, claiming him as one of their newly-converted.

But liberals and former admirers of Senator Goldwater shouldn't be too hasty. Mr. Edwards points out that Goldwater still calls himself conservative. And, Goldwater's new liberal acolytes have neglected a main element of Goldwater's thought that they constantly forget: responsibility.

For it was responsibility that forced Goldwater into public service. It was responsibility that strengthened his lone voice in the wilderness against excess government. Goldwater, as he stated so well in *Conscience*, believed that if an individual's responsibility was taken away, "we take from him also the will and the opportunity to be free."

I personally disagree with Senator Goldwater on several issues, but on this we agree: Freedom cannot long last without limits, moral and legal. We suffer in this age a loss of responsibility, the spread of victimhood, the plague of passing the buck. I think part of the reason why people want less government, why there is still uncertainty in the land, is because people sense that we are less free. Our energies are not harnessed enough, because the government has taken over functions that used to be the purview of communities, ordinary citizens, parents, and preachers. People want to take responsibility; they want to be fellow-builders in the American Dream. The Dream seems so distant and unachievable now, because Americans are barred from putting their own hands to the plow.

That sense of responsibility is something most people believe in, and Barry Goldwater believes in it most deeply. He believed in it so much, he crusaded for a better vision for America, a vision not widely shared at the time. That crusade seemed ill-fated at the time, but it actually gave birth to a future movement that is ascendant today.

Introduction

ON NOVEMBER 3, 1964, Lyndon Baines Johnson, thirty-sixth president of the United States by reason of succession, got what he wanted more than anything else in the world—a landslide election as president in his own right. He received 43.1 million votes to only 27.2 million votes for his conservative challenger, Senator Barry M. Goldwater. Johnson carried forty-four states and the District of Columbia (voting for the first time in a presidential election) for a grand total of 486 electoral votes. Goldwater won only his home state, plus the five Deep South states of Mississippi, Alabama, Louisiana, South Carolina, and Georgia.

It was the most lopsided victory in presidential politics since 1936 when President Franklin Delano Roosevelt carried every state but Maine and Vermont against Governor Alfred M. Landon of Kansas.[1] It was not just an electoral landslide but a political debacle that, almost everyone agreed, buried Goldwater and his antigovernment, anticommunist brand of conservatism forever.

American politics could return to normal, with sensible Eastern liberals like Nelson Rockefeller leading the Republican party, and responsible liberal Democrats like Lyndon Johnson creating a Great Society that would solve most if not all of the country's economic and social problems. James Reston of the *New York Times* summed it up neatly: "Barry Goldwater not only lost the presidential election . . . but the conservative cause as well."[2] By all the normal laws of politics, 1964 should have marked the end of Barry Goldwater as a national leader and the end of conservatism as a meaningful electoral force in America.

xiii

And yet, on November 4, 1980, only sixteen years later, conservative Ronald Reagan, who got his start in national politics with a televised speech for Barry Goldwater in the 1964 campaign, was elected president of the United States, handily defeating the incumbent Democratic president, Jimmy Carter, by 43.9 million votes to Carter's 35.5 million while third-party candidate John Anderson received 5.7 million votes. Reagan received 489 electoral votes to Carter's 49, losing only six states and the District of Columbia, very nearly mirroring Lyndon Johnson's "historic" win in 1964.

But this time it was an unabashed conservative, promising to "get the government off our backs and out of our pockets," who swept to victory. Echoing the major Goldwater themes of 1964, Reagan called for tax cuts, less welfare spending, fewer governmental regulations, and a balanced budget. He promised to challenge not just contain communism around the world, proclaiming a policy of peace through strength.

Reagan's conservative victories in 1980 and 1984 were not political aberrations as President George Bush's defeat in 1992 suggested to many observers, including some on the right. Far from being a burntout case, the Republican party came roaring back in the 1994 elections to capture the U.S. House of Representatives for the first time in forty years, take back control of the U.S. Senate (after an interim of eight years), and wind up with thirty governorships—representing 70 percent of the country's population—giving Republicans their first majority of state houses since 1970. The mood of the electorate was unequivocally anti-Bill Clinton and anti-Democratic. Not one Republican incumbent lost in the Senate, the House, or a state capital.

It was, as the *New York Times* wrote, "a political upheaval of historic proportions." The change that the American electorate called for, according to the *Washington Post*, was "almost uniformly in one direction . . . against liberalism and toward the right."[3]

Conservatives were giddy. Richard Brookhiser, senior editor of *National Review*, declared that the voters had set in motion "the second stage of the Reagan Revolution, which will make the one-term presidencies of George Bush and Bill Clinton seem like political hiccups." David Brooks of the *Wall Street Journal* wrote that the elections were "another step in a long cultural revolution, the rise and maturity of . . . the Conservative Counterestablishment." Commentator (and presidential aspirant) Pat Buchanan suggested that "a second dawn of conservatism may be at hand."[4]

Liberal political reporter David Broder and conservative columnist George Will agreed that the 1994 results did not just happen. Broder wrote that they "may have put the finishing touches on the thirty-year-old effort to make the South [the GOP's] new foundation." Republicans now held 16 of the 28 Southern and Border Senate seats, 7 of the 14 governorships, and 73 of the 139 representatives. Will stated flatly that "conservatism's long march . . . began thirty years ago with Barry Goldwater's capture of the Republican party."[5]

Goldwater himself was characteristically more modest, content to say that 1994 "was just a coming to life of conservatism." But he conceded that the renaissance "probably did get its start around 1964."[6] One week after the election, House Speaker-to-be Newt Gingrich, a former professor of history, declared that "it signaled the end of the New Deal and Great Society eras."[7] And House Majority Leader-to-be Dick Armey stated that Goldwater's "eloquent defense of freedom has altered our country forever."[8]

What happened to bring about such an epic change in American politics—to produce what has been called the Reagan or, more properly, the Goldwater-Reagan Revolution? Part of the answer lies in the decline and fall of American liberalism, which lost its way between the New Deal and the Great Society, Korea and Vietnam, Harry Truman and George McGovern. Another part can be found in the maturation of American conservatism that learned how to integrate classical thought and modern technology and to combine traditionalists, libertarians, and neoconservatives; the South, Midwest, and the Far West; and blue-collar Catholics and Protestant evangelicals into a winning political force.

The 1980 election, like all presidential elections, was a referendum on the two candidates. The voters rejected Carter, an arrogant, inept president who blamed everyone but himself for the soaring inflation, the persistent unemployment, the double-digit interest rates, and the American hostages in Tehran. They embraced Reagan, who offered a message of hope and optimism and explained on election eve: "America is still united, still strong, still compassionate, still clinging fast to the dream of peace and freedom, still willing to stand by those who are persecuted or alone."[9]

The 1994 election was also a referendum—between Reagan's limited government policies of the 1980s and Clinton's expanded government plans of the 1990s. When Democrats, led by President Clinton, launched an all-out assault on Gingrich's Reaganite "Contract with America" (balance the budget, cut taxes, reduce regulations, pass a line-item veto), they ensured a national debate and their crushing defeat. In his 1992 campaign, Clinton promised that he would govern on a "New Democrat" agenda, but the first two years of his presidency were defined by a gigantic, government-run health care proposal and broad tax increases. One prominent exit poll in 1994 revealed that 52 percent of the voters considered Clinton a "liberal," 30 percent a "moderate," and 6.2 percent a "conservative."[10]

Terming the 1980 Reagan victory a "tidal wave" and the 1994 Republican sweep a "sea change," the *Washington Post* commented that nothing of their size and force "could have been created over a weekend or even a week or two by the assorted mullahs and miseries of our times."[11] The forces that placed Ronald Reagan in the White House and then gave Republicans a majority in Congress and state houses were decades in the making.

And while there are many who played important parts in their creation, one man, more than any other, ignited the conservative revolution that altered the course of American politics. One politician first raised the domestic and foreign policy issues that have dominated the national political debate for thirty years. One presidential candidate inspired a generation of young men and women to commit themselves to mastering the political process and making conservatism the dominant political philosophy of the United States. Yet this man set out only to pay back his country for what it had given him. And he often wondered whether he was smart enough to make a good president.

The same man, by reason of his willingness to speak out regardless of the political consequences, became the conscience of the Senate. This man was the one upon whom other senators depended to do the difficult, unpleasant jobs they shunned: accusing President Eisenhower of "fiscal irresponsibility"; urging President Johnson not to make a political issue out of the Vietnam War; informing President Nixon that it was time for him to resign; taking President Carter to federal court for violating the U.S. Constitution; telling President Reagan that he had violated international law by mining harbors in Nicaragua; insisting that the Pentagon had grown too bureaucratic and unwieldy to fulfill its mission.

The man, the politician, the candidate, the senator was Barry Goldwater. He was an unlikely revolutionary: the grandson of a Jewish peddler who became a millionaire; a college dropout whose book *The Conscience of a Conservative* has sold over 3.5 million copies (it was once required reading for History 169b at Harvard University); a master mechanic and ham radio operator whose K7UGA MARS station patched more than 200,000 calls from U.S. servicemen in Indochina to their families back home during the Vietnam War; a man who never smoked a cigarette or drank a cup of coffee but kept a bottle of Old Crow in the refrigerator of his Senate office for after-five sipping; a gifted photographer whose sensitive portraits of Native Americans and scenes of Arizona have hung in galleries around the world; an intrepid pilot who during World War II ferried a single-engine P-47 Thunderbolt over the Atlantic to Britain and four-engine C-54s over the Himalayas and subsequently flew more than 170 different planes, including the latest jets.

He was tall, lean, muscled, with a chiseled jaw, blue eyes, and curly prematurely gray hair that swept back from a high forehead. He wore carefully tailored suits in the Senate (his father had been one of the best-dressed men in Phoenix) and faded blue jeans and tattered plaid shirts at home.

He was a man of contradictions: inspiring and infuriating, courageous and cantankerous, profane and profound, impulsive and stubborn. He delighted in saying the unexpected, in challenging conventional wisdom, but with the Constitution always as his guide. He insisted that doing something about the farm problem "means— and there can be no equivocation here—prompt and final termination of the farm subsidy program." He declared that welfare ought to be "a private concern . . . promoted by individuals and families, by churches, private hospitals, religious service organizations, community charities, and other institutions."[12] Sam Nunn, who served with him on the Senate Armed Services Committee, affectionately remarked, "Barry Goldwater's motto has never changed: Ready! Fire! Aim!"[13]

He was a man of plain tastes (a cheeseburger supreme with a slice of raw onion and a chocolate shake for lunch) and old-fashioned virtues (patriotism, hard work, faith in God). He was a man of enormous charm, pungent speech, and self-deprecating humor. On the wall behind the desk in his Senate office was a framed inscription, lettered in black ink, that read, *Noli Permittere Illegitimi Carborundum* ("Don't let the bastards get you down"). Asked how he would respond to a Soviet nuclear attack, he said the first thing he would do would be to circle the wagons. He once called a press conference to announce that a movie would be made about his life, produced by "18th Century Fox."

He affected American politics more than any other losing presidential candidate in the twentieth century. Theodore White has written: "Again and again in American history it has happened that the losers of the presidency contributed almost as much to the permanent tone and dialogue of politics as did the winners."[14] Like a stern, unyielding prophet of the Old Testament, Goldwater warned the people to repent of their spendthrift ways or reap a bitter harvest. Anticommunist to the core, he urged a strategy of victory in the Cold War by a combination of economic, political, and psychological means as well as military strength. He was dismissed as a madman, literally, in 1964, for counseling a quick end to the Vietnam War, but the trauma of that conflict, our first and only lost war, scars our nation to this day.

American politics is filled with "what ifs," but if Barry Goldwater had been elected president in 1964, we can be certain of two things: The Vietnam War would have been won in six months or President Goldwater would have brought the troops home; and America would not have embarked on the multitrillion-dollar experiment in welfarism known as the Great Society.

Barry Goldwater laid the foundation for a political revolution and led a generation of conservatives to understand that theirs was a winning as well as a just cause. In his memoirs, he insists that he did not start a revolution, that all he did in 1964 was to begin "to tap . . . a deep reservoir [of conservatism] that already existed" in the American people.[15] That is like Samuel Adams saying that he was not responsible for the Boston Tea Party, that all he did was to tap a deep reservoir of discontent in the citizens of Boston. Or Tom Paine claiming that he wrote *Common Sense* without any notion of trying to bring about the American Revolution. Goldwater draws closer to the truth when he adds that neither he nor Reagan *is* the conservative movement but are *symbols* of the movement. For millions of conservatives, Goldwater and Reagan are not symbols but icons.

But what if an icon becomes an iconoclast—if he seems to change and even contradict what he once stood for? Today, Goldwater backs gays in the military and warns the Republican party not to take an adamant anti-abortion stand. In the spring of 1994, he urged Republicans to "get off [Clinton's] back and let him be president," and some angry Arizona Republicans demanded that his name be removed from the Barry Goldwater Center in downtown Phoenix.[16] Distraught conservatives ask, "What's happened to Barry?" Some wonder, "Are there *two* Barry Goldwaters—the traditional conservative of 1964 and the radical libertarian of 1994?"

I wrote this book to answer those questions and to give this American original his true place in our times and in our history. My biography of Barry Goldwater (the first in thirty years) is based on interviews with the senator and his family and some 170 of his friends, assistants, and colleagues, Democratic as well as Republican. I also spent considerable time reviewing the Goldwater papers at Arizona State University as well as visiting six presidential libraries and private collections at other libraries.

Whether you agree with everything the old man on the mountain says or not, there is little dispute that his presidential candidacy in 1964 marked the true beginning of a fundamental shift in American politics from liberalism to conservatism that continues to this day.

PART I

Popularizer

1

Peddler's Grandson

AT THE CLOSE OF WORLD WAR II, political change was in the air. As historian Eric F. Goldman wrote concerning the 1946 congressional elections: "A nation which had quite enough of inflation and the Russians, of strikes, shortages, and the atom bomb, of everlasting maybe's about peace and prosperity, rose up in a hiss of exasperation and elected the first Republican Congress since the far-distant days of Herbert Hoover."[1]

One group of euphoric Republicans, emboldened by the results, proposed to cut $10 billion from the budget, lower taxes, and abandon "the philosophy of government interference with business and labor."[2] Led by Senator Robert A. Taft of Ohio, Republicans decided that a strongly partisan line in domestic policy would accentuate the differences between the two political parties and win them the White House in 1948. But external events like the communist seizure of Eastern Europe converted their partisan plans into bipartisan cooperation in the field of foreign policy, although not without heated disputes.

Still, the American intelligentsia were predominantly liberal. But the Left was jolted by the intellectual power and mass appeal of a little 240-page book, *The Road to Serfdom*, that appeared in the fall of 1944. Written by Friedrich A. Hayek, an emigré Austrian economist living in

3

London, its thesis was devastatingly simple: "Planning leads to dictatorship," and "the direction of economic activity" inevitably means the "suppression of freedom."[3]

Hayek proposed a different road, the road of individualism and "classical" liberalism, which he insisted was not laissez-faire but based on government, carefully limited by law, that encouraged competition and the functioning of a free society. Although Hayek stated that his work was "not intended for popular consumption," *Reader's Digest* condensed the book in late 1944 and arranged for the Book-of-the-Month Club to distribute more than a million reprints.[4] Hayek became the center of a fierce controversy, with the *New York Times Book Review* calling *The Road to Serfdom* "one of the most important books of our generation" and *The New Republic* dismissing it as the darling of "reactionary" business interests. Young American servicemen like Robert Nisbet and Russell Kirk read Hayek and other classical liberals, along with libertarian mavericks like Albert Jay Nock, who titled one of his works, *Our Enemy the State.*

Convinced that traditional liberals should unite, Hayek convened a group of forty prominent European and American scholars in Mt. Pelerin, Switzerland, in April 1947. The mood of the conferees was somber, for socialism and statism dominated European governments and was on the march in the United States, despite the recent Republican capture of the Congress. Declaring that the "central values of civilization are in danger," the group defined its central goal as "the preservation and improvement of the free society" and named itself the Mt. Pelerin Society. Although the meeting was not reported on the front page of the *New York Times*, it demonstrated, as member and future Nobel Laureate Milton Friedman put it, that "we were not alone."[5]

Six thousand miles from the snow-peaked mountains of Mt. Pelerin, in the middle of America's Southwest desert, a man who seemed to have everything knew that he did not. At age thirty-seven, Barry Goldwater was president of the most popular department store in Phoenix, blessed with a loving wife, four handsome children, and robust health, and surrounded by old friends in a sun-filled climate that drew tens of thousands of tourists and new residents every year. His days were a whirl of community activities—Chamber of Commerce, Boy Scouts, YMCA, Masons, Community Chest. And he indulged himself in his myriad hobbies—flying a plane, operating a ham radio, photographing the people and places of his beloved Arizona.

When asked to help city or state, Barry Goldwater rarely said no: he organized the Arizona Air National Guard, served on the Colorado River Commission to help bring water for power and irrigation to central Arizona, and led a referendum for right-to-work legislation in the state. Goldwater was living the American dream to its fullest. Why, then, was he so dissatisfied? Why couldn't he settle down to the good life he had led before going off to war?

The Goldwater men had always been restless. His grandfather Michael left family and friends and an easy, secure life in London to search for his destiny in the gold fields of western America. His father Baron willingly exchanged the comforts and luxuries of San Francisco for the challenges and uncertainties of frontier Arizona.

MICHEL GOLDWASSER was born in October 1821 in the central Polish town of Konin, one of twenty-two children. His father, Hirsch Goldwasser, was an inn- and storekeeper; little is known about him other than that he could not write. There had been Goldwassers in Konin for generations and a Jewish community in the town as early as 1412.

Michel showed an early interest in reading and politics, but he was deprived of formal education by Russian laws that forbade schooling for Jews. The young man became involved with a group of anti-Russian dissidents and decided to leave Poland rather than risk arrest or conscription into the czarist army. Michel traveled first to Paris where he worked as a tailor until the bloody revolution of 1848 drove him to London. There he learned English, changed his name to Michael Goldwater, and established a prosperous tailoring business.

One day, while walking a London street, Michael Goldwater, tall, muscular, and fair-haired, met Sarah Nathan, pretty and strong-willed, who managed the family fur-processing factory. After a short courtship, they were married in the Great Synagogue of London in March 1850. They soon had two children, Caroline and Morris, who was to play so important a part in the life of Barry Goldwater.

At this point, Michael's younger, free-spirited brother, Joseph, arrived from Poland and began talking about the wealth and adventure in the gold fields of California.[6] Sarah, who much preferred her comfortable life in London, protested strongly, but Michael could not resist. Sarah finally relented when her two brothers promised to support her and the children until Michael was able to send for them.

In August 1852, thirty-one-year-old "Big Mike" Goldwater and his brother Joe, with one trunk between them, sailed from London. Like millions of immigrants in the nineteenth century, they arrived in bustling, crowded New York City, but immediately set off for San Francisco via ship and the isthmus of Nicaragua, the cheapest way at only $180 each. Many of their fellow passengers died during the hard trek across the 212-mile isthmus, much of it jungle, or of tropical diseases. But the two healthy Goldwater brothers arrived in San Francisco in November 1852 and found themselves among thousands of other newcomers lured by the glittering promise of the Gold Rush of 1849. Everything was new and raw and untamed in this two-year-old state of California.

Mike and Joe listened intently to the get-rich-quick stories of the gold camps and at last picked Sonora, located in the foothills of the Sierras, 100 miles east of San Francisco. They started a business that required a small investment and minimal space and that appealed to nearly every miner—a saloon. They rented space on the ground floor of a two-story wooden building, the upper floor of which housed the town's most popular bordello. Contrary to rumors that circulated in Barry Goldwater's political campaigns a century later, the Goldwaters never ran a whorehouse; the two businesses were separately owned.[7]

The brothers worked hard, as Goldwaters always did, and within fifteen months, Mike had saved enough money to bring Sarah and the two children to California. Although she tried, the London-bred Sarah never adjusted to the rough life of Sonora. During her first six months there, there were twelve murders; Mike himself was accidently wounded, although not seriously, by an errant blast from a shotgun.

At last, Sarah announced that the wild ways of a gold rush town were not for her and the children, now numbering four. It was the beginning, biographer Dean Smith writes, of a thirty-year period during which Mike and Sarah were separated for months and years at a time. They loved each other but could not reconcile Mike's search for fortune on the untamed frontier and Sarah's wish for security in California.[8]

Mike's problems multiplied. After several years of success, he fell into heavy debt when the gold mines around Sonora became exhausted, and he moved to Los Angeles where Joe was living. Approaching forty and close to penniless, Mike Goldwater in no way resembled the future founder of a business empire. But he was not a man to give up or in; he remained confident that somewhere, somehow, in this boundless new world where you could be anything, he would find success.

And soon. The Goldwater brothers heard about the gold strikes on and near the Colorado River. They speculated that an enterprising peddler with a wagon full of "Yankee" notions and specialty goods could prosper in the mining camps and towns. Mike, they decided, would take a wagon of goods to sell to the miners on the Gila River, 18 miles east of Fort Yuma. It was a 276-mile trip through barren desert and high mountain passes on a rough wagon road littered with the skeletons of cattle and broken spring wagons. After several weeks of hard travel, Mike crossed the river by ferry to Arizona City (now Yuma) on a fall day in 1860 and headed east to Gila City, the first Goldwater to set foot in Arizona, not yet a territory.

Gila City was a typical mining town, filled with "over a thousand hardy adventurers" who turned the earth upside down looking for gold. They gambled, drank, and bought fancy and not-so-fancy wares. The city had everything, as historian J. Ross Browne describes, "but a church and a jail, which were accounted barbarisms by the mass of the population."[9] Mike Goldwater quickly exchanged everything in his wagon for gold dust at a greater profit than expected and returned to Los Angeles with the good news.

In the early 1860s, Mike was peddling in Arizona, Joe was selling tobacco and candy in the Bella Union Hotel in Los Angeles, and both were running the hotel's bar and billiard parlor. The Goldwater brothers seemed on the edge of achieving solid success when suddenly a San Francisco creditor demanded immediate payment on a note totaling $6,500. Other creditors began clamoring for their money and soon Mike and Joe were stripped of all assets. After days of anger and fear, a good friend and fellow merchant, Bernard Cohn, who had started a general merchandise store in La Paz, 70 miles north of Fort Yuma, invited Mike to join him in the booming new town where the gold nuggets were as big as rocks. Mike started as an employee, soon became a partner, and five years later bought Cohn out.

During this period Mike made a significant political commitment— he became a citizen of the United States on July 29, 1861. Although many residents of southern California favored the Confederacy, Mike supported the Union soon after news of Fort Sumter's fall arrived.[10] On the home front, despite the heavy demands of business in Arizona,

Mike frequently traveled to Los Angeles to visit Sarah and the children and was present in May 1866 for the birth of their last child, Baron, who, forty-three years later, would father Barry Goldwater.

Brimming with confidence and with plenty of money in his pockets, the ever-restless Mike Goldwater branched out into other areas of business. With Cohn, he invested in a mine and undertook contracts to haul supplies to military posts in the interior of Arizona, which was proclaimed a Territory by President Lincoln on February 24, 1863. He added a freighting business and extended credit to a business they established in Tucson, many miles to the south.

In 1868, the Colorado River changed course, isolating La Paz. Undaunted, the Goldwater brothers moved their business downstream and named the new community Ehrenberg, after a close friend, Herman Ehrenberg, an early Arizona pioneer who had been murdered by Indians. A political precedent was established when Joe Goldwater became postmaster of Ehrenberg and a member of the first school board.

The Goldwaters established a grain hauling business that grew steadily, despite frontier dangers. One fine June day in 1872, Mike, Joe, and a Dr. Jones were returning from a business meeting in Fort Whipple, near Prescott, when a band of about thirty Mohave-Apaches ambushed them. During a wild four-mile chase, two Indian bullets hit Joe in the back and shoulder. Escape was looking dim for the fleeing trio when three ranchers appeared around a bend and began firing at the Indians, who abruptly disappeared into the surrounding hills. Dr. Jones extracted both bullets, and Joe returned to San Francisco to recover his health. He had the rifle ball from his back made into a charm for his watch chain, which he wore until his death seventeen years later.[11]

These Indian raids came with the territory and did not end until the famed chief Geronimo, who led bloody raids throughout Arizona and New Mexico, was banished in 1886. By then the Goldwaters, looking for a supply source closer to the interior towns and military posts, had decided to open a branch store in Phoenix, located in the Salt River Valley, which was becoming an important agricultural area for the territory.

THE GOLDWATER STORE in Phoenix opened in December 1872, the year that President Ulysses S. Grant was reelected by the largest popular vote since Andrew Jackson in 1828. The manager of the new store was

Mike's twenty-year-old son, Morris, who had come to Arizona after several years with a prominent hat company in San Francisco. Morris was a skinny young man with a flowing walrus mustache and sharp wit; he was energetic, ambitious, and shrewd. When he learned that a new telegraph line to Prescott was going to bypass Phoenix, he made the government an offer it couldn't refuse: he donated part of the Goldwater store as a telegraph office and offered to serve as a telegraph operator without pay. He introduced the first automatic telegraph recording instrument into the territory, demonstrating an affinity for electrical things that flowered in his nephew, Barry Goldwater.

Morris also displayed an early interest in community affairs, serving as deputy county recorder and running, although only twenty-two, for the territorial legislature as a Democrat. He and his Republican opponent tied, and when it seemed likely that he would be defeated in the runoff, Morris withdrew in favor of a well-known Arizonan; the alternate Democrat won handily. Morris's vote-getting ability and his graciousness in stepping aside were both noted by Democratic party leaders.

Meanwhile, the profits of the Phoenix operation did not meet Mike Goldwater's expectations, and in 1875 the first Goldwater store in Phoenix was closed. The Goldwaters were convinced that the center of Arizona trade and commerce was moving north to Prescott, the future capital of the territory.

The Prescott store was an immediate success. It was the first Goldwater store to carry a line of high-fashion goods and to adopt the motto, "The Best Always." At the insistence of Morris, who became manager in 1879, it began catering to ladies. Home furniture, furnishings, and fancy goods rivaled liquor, tobacco, and flour. Among the store's best customers were the bordello girls, who frequently purchased champagne at $40 a case.[12] Morris soon became as indispensable to the community as to the store, practicing what he often said—that successful people had the moral duty to repay, by whatever means, the communities that had helped make them.[13] It was a belief that Barry Goldwater would take seriously seventy years later when he pondered how best to repay his city of Phoenix for what it had given him.

Biographer Edwin McDowell points out that Morris and his father Mike, now fifty-five and referred to as the "old gentleman," set a high standard of community service. They were the first to pledge $5,000 in bonds for a railroad into Prescott, and Morris and two partners helped finance the construction of a railroad to Phoenix. Morris later helped develop mines and real estate throughout the territory and served as secretary of the Prescott Rifles, which protected the people from Indian attacks.

And then there was politics. Although only twenty-seven, Morris was elected mayor of Prescott in 1879 by an almost 2 to 1 margin. It was the first of his ten terms as mayor over the next forty-eight years. He also helped organize the Arizona Democratic party in the 1880s when the territory was under the control of a Republican administration. Known as a Jeffersonian or conservative Democrat, Morris later served as president of the twentieth Territorial Council and vice president of the crucial 1910 Constitutional Convention, which led to Arizona's statehood in 1912. Following statehood, he was president of the Senate in the second Arizona legislature. He often said, and later repeated to his favorite nephew Barry, that if a man believed firmly in an issue, he should stay with it no matter what the odds or how heavy the criticism.[14] He was only 5 feet 4 inches tall and weighed less than 140 pounds, but he was determined to succeed at whatever he tried.

By the mid-1880s, Big Mike was talking about retiring. Then a group of Prescott citizens urged him to run for mayor. Flattered, he accepted and won. He launched a series of reforms that nearly rivaled the first hundred days of a future president. His measure to ban "B" girls from the bars of Whiskey Row was strongly supported by professional prostitutes who did not welcome the competition. He also supported building a wooden fence around the courthouse square to keep out stray cattle and backed a regulation that required wooden crossings at the downtown street corners.

Encouraged by the public response, Mike pushed through an ordinance requiring all property owners to put board sidewalks outside their property. Absentee owners protested—in many cases the cost of the sidewalks would have exceeded the value of the property. But Mike would not budge, even when urged by old friends. (The same stubbornness would often surface in his grandson Barry.) The man who had "spent a lifetime conquering strange languages, strange customs, marauding Indians, and countless other hazards" could not adjust to the independent ways of a frontier town whose citizens would not be dictated to by anyone, even one of their founding fathers.[15]

Mike pressed forward, and soon went one step too far. He had an altercation with Police Chief James Dodson and the city council and resigned. Within a year, Mike sold the business to Morris and retired to San Francisco, where he lived contentedly as a respected patriarch in the Jewish community until his death in 1903.[16]

THE FORTUNES of the Goldwaters received an important lift in October 1882 when sixteen-year-old Baron, wearing a suit from Wannamaker's and smelling of cologne, arrived from San Francisco to take his place in the family business. His one-color outfits were the talk of the town: he was always in all gray, all brown, or all blue. But, as biographer Stephen Shadegg put it, "Baron may have been a dude, but he was no dunce."[17] He quietly went to work as a clerk and spent a year analyzing the changing tastes and growing wealth of Prescott and the territory. Morris and Henry Goldwater were impressed, but they waited a decade before making Baron, at age twenty-eight, a full partner in Goldwaters. Meanwhile, Baron Goldwater, like his father before him, was looking for new lands to conquer.

By the mid-1890s, Prescott and Tucson had both been eclipsed in growth and economic importance by the farming community of Phoenix. The capital, which had been moved from Prescott to Tucson and back again, was shifted to Phoenix in February 1889. Baron became convinced that there ought to be a Goldwaters store in the most important city in the territory, but Morris was not so certain. Baron pressed his brothers until, the story goes, he challenged Morris to a game of casino to settle the matter and won. Henry wanted to manage the Phoenix branch, but Morris picked Baron because of his flair and steadiness; he would be able to weather the ups and downs of a new enterprise.

Goldwaters, however, was successful from opening day in March 1896; women in particular enthused over Baron's sophisticated taste. Mike and Morris's store in Prescott had met the pioneer need for everything "from shovels to sunbonnets." The Phoenix store offered not only reliable merchandise at low prices but the latest fashions from New York and Europe. Baron decided that pleasing the ladies was the way to economic success. Once he had the new store running smoothly, Baron became active in the civic life of his adopted town. He was soon elected a director of the Phoenix Chamber of Commerce and saw the Sisters' Hospital (now St. Joseph's) through some financial difficulties. He helped establish the Phoenix Country Club, the Arizona Club and was a founder of the Valley National Bank.

In his late thirties, still trim and good-looking, Baron became the town's most eligible bachelor. His parents hoped that all their children would marry in the Jewish faith, but Mike's death in 1903 followed by Sarah's death in 1905 allowed them to marry whomever they wished.

Within two years, both brothers were wed, Morris to his Protestant landlady, Sarah (Sallie) Shivers Fisher, and Baron to a remarkably independent young woman from the Midwest, green-eyed, auburn-haired, Episcopalian Josephine Williams, on January 1, 1907. Neither man ever renounced his faith; Morris, in fact, stipulated in his will that he would have preferred a Jewish burial but since no rabbi was available, he would settle for a Masonic burial.[18] They were sons of Moses who had found their Promised Land, after only twenty years in the wilderness of Arizona. Since there was little or no organized Jewish religion in those early days, Baron followed the Jewish custom of allowing his children to be raised in the faith of their mother.

BARON AND JO Goldwater were an unusual couple. Here is how Dean Smith describes them:

> Baron: devoted to his business and community, sartorially impeccable, carefully conservative, conscious of his public image, reluctant to get his hands dirty or leave the niceties of civilization. . . . Jo: peppery, loving the outdoors, willing to experiment with almost any new idea or device, casual in dress, a bit too profane for the tastes of some Phoenix matriarchs, so honest and direct that she sometimes strained the bounds of diplomacy.[19]

When people write and reminisce about Jo Goldwater ("Mun" or "Mungie" to her children, "Jo-Jo" to her grandchildren), adjectives pop like Chinese firecrackers. She was "a spunky individualist" who refused to "conform to the stuffy moral code of her day."[20] Thin as the proverbial rail, she smoked and swore and wore trousers and liked her drinks. She was a registered nurse (trained in Cook County, Illinois) who moved to Arizona at the turn of the century because she had tuberculosis, a fatal disease in those days, but she lived to see her oldest son run for the presidency in 1964. She took her patriotism seriously, inspired by her father, Robert Williams, a direct descendant of the founder of Rhode Island. Tiny and frail-looking, Jo was tough as rawhide.

She was a crack shot, a champion golfer, and loved to go camping with her three children. Each summer, Phoenix's upper class escaped the city's searing heat by vacationing in cottages along the beaches of southern California. Most made the trip by train, but Jo and her three kids traveled in an open touring car filled with tents, sleeping bags, and camping gear. When the sun began to set, they pulled off the road and set up camp. "Never mind the rattlesnakes, the scorpions, or the Gila monsters—the Goldwater family was on vacation and the wild creatures would have to move over."[21]

Jo Goldwater was a deep-dyed patriot who, with her children beside her, would drive three miles in the hot Phoenix sun to the Indian School to stand in "silent respect as the flag came down." She was a woman of strong opinions and traditional American values who taught her children "what was right and what was wrong and I told them I'd rather they'd steal than tell a lie."[22] As her younger son Bob put it, lying "was the ultimate sin."[23] That lesson stuck. Barry Goldwater could never forgive anyone, particularly a president, who lied.

ON JANUARY 1, 1909, two years to the day after Baron and Jo were married and three years before the Arizona territory became the forty-eighth state, Barry Morris Goldwater was born in his mother's bedroom on the second floor of their home at 710 North Center Street (now Central Avenue). A Phoenix newspaperman wrote, in the ornate language of the time, that the baby boy "promises to add luster to a family name already distinguished in the annals of Arizona."[24] Two other children soon followed: Robert Williams in July 1910 and Carolyn in August 1912.

The Phoenix of 1909 was a typical Southwestern town, leisurely, comfortable, content with life and itself, but still close in time and place to the old frontier. In February, Geronimo had died in an Oklahoma military prison. The paving of city streets and sidewalks began the following year. It was a new town (its first house was built only forty years earlier), but its location in the Salt River Valley and the arrival of the Southern Pacific Railway in 1887 made it a potential center of commerce in the Southwest. That potential was realized in 1911 when the Theodore Roosevelt Dam was dedicated. The state's golden era in farming had begun.[25]

The son of the city's number one entrepreneur and the heir of a prominent Arizona family, Barry Goldwater was a young man with the freedom and means to do almost anything he wanted, and he did precisely that, setting a pattern for the rest of his life. He was daring, athletic, handsome, curious about anything mechanical, but indifferent to books. "I don't think he ever read a book growing up," said his sister Carolyn, "and I don't think he ever missed an issue of *Popular Mechanics.*"[26] He was a leader of the Center Street Gang, played football, basketball, baseball and boxed.

He was a very good boxer, but not so good as he thought. One day, watching Kid Parker, a professional boxer, work out in a downtown gym, Barry cockily agreed to step into the ring and landed a hard punch that rocked the professional. Parker unleashed a string of jabs and punches that had the young man groggy at the end of their one-sided one-round contest. "Sonny," said Parker, "don't ever do that again." But he did. Goldwater never backed away from a tough fight.[27]

He was a more successful swimmer, becoming captain of the swimming teams of his military school and the University of Arizona. And he was a good golfer. Years later he won the Phoenix Open Pro-Am tournament with golfing legend Sam Snead. But even then he went his own way: he showed up for the match dressed in faded blue jeans, a stained sweatshirt, and dirty sneakers. Snead was appalled until Goldwater began firing pars and then a birdie on a handicap hole for an eagle.[28]

Barry's independence was encouraged by his indulgent parents. He had the first radio crystal set on his block, the first and most expensive model train set, and, naturally, the largest wardrobe. At twelve, he received the first factory-made radio set sold in Arizona. He built his own transmitter, operating his amateur radio station, 6BP1, from the garage loft. He became so fond of Dixieland music that he taught himself to play the trombone, although he was never a threat to Tommy Dorsey.[29]

Baron was indifferent to religion, but Jo was a devout Episcopalian and insisted that all the children attend Sunday school and church at Trinity Cathedral. Barry served as both altar boy and acolyte, although theology was not his strong suit. Asked at Sunday school what monogram he wanted on his sweater, he replied that he wanted a "P"—for "Piscopal." The only dances the Goldwater children were allowed to attend were held in the parish hall on Friday night.

Dean William Scarlett, future bishop of Missouri, was a favorite of Barry, Bob, and Carolyn, who liked his open, friendly manner. Scarlett, Goldwater declared, was never "sanctimonious," a deadly sin in the senator's book, and helped to make "God a part of our everyday life when we were kids."[30] God was an essential part of Goldwater's life, although he never felt he had to worship Him in church when He could be found everywhere.

Barry was not a model of deportment at any age. He once fired a miniature cannon at the steeple of the Methodist church. On another occasion, he installed a microphone and loudspeaker in the Goldwater bathroom and delighted in embarrassing female visitors by asking them as they went about their business: "Hi, there, honey. What's new?" He used his photographic skill to capture friends in compromising poses at parties. He was Tom Sawyer, Huck Finn, and Peck's Bad Boy all in one.[31]

In the fall of 1923, when he entered Phoenix Union High School, Barry was pampered, self-centered, and charismatic. He was elected president of his freshman class. He made both the basketball and football teams, but flunked two courses and wound up with two academic credits out of a possible total of sixteen. The school principal suggested that the young man might benefit from a change in school, and Baron selected a military school 3,000 miles away—the celebrated Staunton Military Academy in Virginia. Mun protested, but Baron insisted that Barry needed a different kind of lesson—discipline.

Barry did not take readily to military discipline: he was late for formation, his rifle was dirty, he was not present at bed check. "There were times," remembered Major Alexander M. (Sandy) Patch, his head military instructor, "when we thought we would never get him through the school."[32] But Goldwaters didn't quit. Barry repeated his freshman year and was elected president of his class. He was captain of the swimming team, which won the Virginia state championship in 1927, and was promoted to commander of Company C. In his senior year, he won the school's Kable Medal, awarded to the best all-around cadet, although his marks were only average.[33] He was encouraged to apply to West Point, but his father wasn't well and his mother wanted him home in Phoenix.

Many years later, Goldwater mused: "I should have gone to the Point."[34] As his later service suggested, he almost certainly would have had a distinguished military career.

In the fall of 1928, Goldwater enrolled as a freshman at the University of Arizona in Tucson, arriving on campus in a Chrysler roadster with a trunk full of expensive clothes. He planned to major in business administration and, as he put it, "to have a good time." Once again, he was elected president of his freshman class. He made the football and basketball teams and pledged Sigma Chi fraternity but, or so the story goes, he had trouble because of his Jewish background. Barry is said to have told the fraternity brothers: "I'm half Jewish and half Irish, boys. Why not pledge the Irish half and everybody can be happy." Then there was the time he tried to play golf at a private eighteen-hole course and was turned down because of his name. "I'm only half-Jewish," Goldwater said, "so I promise I'll just play nine holes."[35] Actually, his brother Bob made up the story about himself and told it at a golf banquet, but Barry liked it so much he appropriated it.

At the university, Barry found it difficult "to give my attention to a subject which didn't particularly appeal to me." It didn't seem to matter that much in a world where Herbert Hoover had just been elected, the Twenties were still roaring, and he didn't need a Phi Beta Kappa key to run the family store. Still, he proved he had flair. In a display of fundraising talent that flowered later in the U.S. Senate, he coaxed $5 from each student—a month's spending money—to build a sports stadium.[36]

Life was sweet and lovely for the 6-foot, 180-pound athlete and budding campus leader. But the following spring, his father suddenly died of a heart attack and, after the funeral, he and his brother decided that Bob should continue at the University of Illinois (and later Stanford University) and Barry should leave college and prepare to take his place at the family store.

Goldwater claimed that dropping out of college "was the biggest mistake of my life. . . ."[37] His ensuing feelings of intellectual inferiority led him to remark to a reporter the summer before he announced his candidacy for the Republican presidential nomination, "You know, I haven't got a really first-class brain."[38] Although he made up for his lack of formal education by reading voraciously in later years, he held intellectuals in awe throughout his life.

While Barry was preparing to run the family business, Goldwaters was in the capable hands of Sam Wilson, who had been with the store since 1909 and was "far more qualified to steer the store through the difficult days of the Depression than ex-college freshman Barry."[39]

Wilson started the young Goldwater at the bottom, as a clerk in piece goods at $15 a week. Barry was a natural salesman. "He could sell anything," recalled his brother Bob, who handled the business side. "He still can."[40] As he made his way up, he sparked such innovations as an electric eye door and Little Pedro, the store's advertising symbol. And he had plenty of time left over for practical jokes. One day, he stuck a live mouse in one of the tubes that went whooshing through the pneumatic system. When it arrived at the station of the chief cashier, Clara Mains, she took the temporarily stunned mouse for a toy, which suddenly came alive. Wriggling mouse in hand, Mains chased Goldwater through the store, shouting, "I'm going to get you for this, Barry!"[41]

Although the young merchant prince usually got what he wanted, Margaret (Peggy) Johnson of Muncie, Indiana, was quite another matter. Barry first met Miss Johnson, brown-haired, blue-eyed, and petite, in December 1930 when she was shopping in Goldwaters. She and her family (her father, Ray Prescott Johnson, was executive vice president of the Borg-Warner Company) were wintering in Phoenix, hoping the climate would help Peggy's older brother who had bronchitis.

Peggy thought Barry "extremely handsome" while Barry found her "quite attractive but reserved." But she was only twenty and went back to Mt. Vernon Seminary in Washington, D.C., where she was studying art and design. After graduation, Peggy went to New York City and worked for the highly regarded David Crystal organization. She soon received the plum job of clothes designer, quite an honor for a young and relatively inexperienced woman. In her social moments, she dated several eligible young men, including G. Mennen Williams, later a liberal governor of Michigan and assistant secretary of state for African affairs in the Kennedy and Johnson administrations.

But in the fall of 1932, her father suffered a stroke while in Phoenix, and she was back in Arizona, liking it less than ever. She saw Barry several times at the country club and store, but they did not date as she was focusing all her attention on her father. After her father died, Peggy spent the summer in the Johnson place in Charlevoix, Michigan, where Barry Goldwater found her and came calling. He had planned to stay one weekend but remained for two weeks. He proposed to Peggy the night he left, but "I wasn't ready for marriage," she recalled, and "told him so."[42] Undaunted, Barry stepped up his courtship by letter, telephone, and in person, sending her gifts that displayed the creative

Goldwater touch—a caged lovebird delivered by hand at an airport, a box of apples on a train full of doctors.

In December 1933, Barry arrived in Muncie to spend Christmas with the elusive Miss Johnson. Just before midnight on New Year's Eve, he suggested they call her mother and wish her a happy New Year. They found a telephone booth off the hotel ballroom and, in the midst of the call, Barry closed the door and again proposed, warning her that he was running out of patience and money. "There wasn't any escape," remembered Peggy. "I said yes."

Impetuous as always, Barry wanted an early wedding, but Peggy had promised to go with her mother on a cruise around the world and wouldn't budge. The young man took no chances. While she was on her four-and-a-half month trip he arranged to have a packet of love letters and gifts waiting for her at every port. Finally back in a New York hotel room, she was given a small box with her engagement ring—the wedding ring of Barry's grandmother. Sarah had worn it in 1854 on her trip from London across the Isthmus of Panama to San Francisco, where Big Mike and a new life in a new world awaited her.[43]

Barry and Peggy were married in Grace Episcopal Church in Muncie on September 22, 1934. Peggy, who wanted to share every aspect of Barry's life, took instructions from Dean Scarlett and was confirmed in the Episcopal Church shortly before they were married. They would have four children over the next decade: Joanne, in January 1936; Barry, Jr., in July 1938; Michael, in March 1940; and Margaret ("Little Peggy"), in July 1944.

The 1930s were happy years for the young couple. Whatever Barry loved, Peggy grew to love as well. They went exploring, hunting, fishing, and searching for Indian ruins. She washed photographic prints in his darkroom, cooked over a campfire, and slept on the ground in a bedroll. The one thing she never completely accepted or shared was his life in politics. She worried that the demands of politics, of being in Washington, D.C., or on the road would change him and affect their children. In 1962, when rumors about her husband running for president were mounting, she told Stephen Shadegg, "Not long ago I read . . . that President Kennedy doesn't joke any more, doesn't have time for laughter, doesn't have time for his friends, and it frightens me to think this might happen to Barry. It's bad enough now." But then she quoted her husband, " 'We have to pay rent for the space we occupy,' " and she said, "I guess he's right," adding ruefully, "Barry won't let the rent go unpaid."[44]

THERE WAS ALSO one nonpolitical passion of Barry's that Peggy did not share—flying. "He was a rare natural," commented Ruth Reinhold, one of his early flying instructors who later piloted Goldwater all over the Southwest on campaign trips. "He did everything right almost from the beginning—by instinct. If anyone was born to fly, it was Barry Goldwater."[45] He soloed in 1929 in a Great Lakes biplane, the beginning of a lifelong affair with planes of all kinds and speeds. Part of the fascination was in the mechanics, measuring and balancing airspeed, lift, and pressure altitude. Part of it lay in the exhilaration of flying at night when the stars and the sky seem infinite and freedom is on the wing. For Barry Goldwater, all history is the record of man's quest for freedom, and flying an airplane was "the ultimate extension of individual freedom."[46]

In the 1920s, Barry tried to enlist as an aviation cadet but failed the vision test. In 1930, at age twenty-one, he was commissioned a second lieutenant in the Army Reserve and simultaneously received a commercial pilot's license. During the 1930s, he accumulated over four hundred flying hours. Most of his flying was limited to the valley or the state, what he called "pooping around," but he found time to fly supplies to snowbound Navajos during the winter. While he was running Goldwaters with his brother Bob and raising a family with Peggy, he "never gave up hope of wearing . . . wings" in the armed forces. As he put it, "the store work meant only eating—flying with the corps would be living."[47]

During this time Goldwater discovered history. In the mid-1930s, he began buying dozens of books, poring over old newspapers, and talking with his uncle Morris about life on the frontier. His transformation into a serious student of Arizona history and culture began when, as a store clerk, he discovered a pile of old ledgers from the Prescott store, dating back to its founding in 1876. The young man persuaded his uncle, still lively in his eighties, to make a nostalgic trip to Ehrenberg, now a ghost town. They found the old Goldwaters store, its adobe walls crumbling, its wooden doors rotting. "Well," remarked the young merchant, looking at the tiny room, barely as big as a modern kitchen, "the Goldwaters started small enough!"[48]

Barry began visiting Emery Kolb, who had taken his first trip down the treacherous Colorado River in 1911. Inspired, he began taking boat trips himself down the Colorado. Finally, in July 1940, he and eight others (including three women) set off down the Green River in Wyoming for a six-week, 1,463-mile ride to Boulder Dam. Barry kept a diary of the trip that he privately published; it revealed a great deal about the man who, a quarter of a century later, would run for president.

The temperature never dropped below 100 degrees during the day, with mayflies so thick that ears and mouths and eyes were filled with them. But Goldwater's affinity for nature shone through the pages as he described the rapids and rocks, the canyon and rivers, and sketched the history of the regions they passed through. He respected the rapids, but "if one forgets the[ir] roar . . . and their awesomeness . . . they present nothing but a physical problem that can be easily overcome."[49]

As with most of his experiences, he personalized the journey: "This Sabbath will be our last on the river, and while I will not use such a holy day for a prayer that such a trip be repeated, still I will thank the Lord for the friends I have had the honor to travel with these six weeks past." He was far more thankful to see Peggy and his "beloved" daughter Joanne waiting for him: "Nothing in God's world gives one such an appreciation of home and family as does a prolonged absence."

Yet this was only one of many adventures that would take this restless man from home and family over the next five decades. The last line in the journal was quintessential Goldwater, proud and patriotic: "I said goodbye to the Colorado . . . glad I had seen its wonders in the AMERICAN WAY."[50]

ANOTHER OLD ARIZONAN, John Rinker Kibby, took Barry when he was only seven on his first trip to an Indian reservation. They visited the thousand-year-old Hopi village of Oraibi. Over the years, Barry visited most of the state's tribes, especially the Navajos and the Hopis, eating with the chiefs, talking with the squaws, playing with the children around the hogans. He became a silent partner in a trading post at the base of Navajo Mountain, located in the Navajo reservation in the northwest corner of Arizona. The post sold canned goods, shoes, clothing, hats, gasoline, tires, and tubes, much as his grandfather and uncle had done in La Paz and Erhenberg in the Arizona territory fifty years before. In the early 1930s, he purchased a half interest in Rainbow

Lodge, which could accommodate five hundred guests and offered mule-back tours to the spectacular Rainbow Bridge and Indian cliff ruins. He also built a 2,000-foot runway strip so that he could fly in and out at will.

A Navajo medicine man once warned Goldwater not to fly his airplane around Navajo Mountain, a sacred place for the tribe. Goldwater shrugged off the warning until one day, in 1946 his small plane stalled in flight and hit the side of the mountain. He escaped uninjured but the plane was demolished. As he sat on a rock looking at the wreckage and thanking God that he was alive, several Navajo medicine men appeared. Without a word, they collected pieces of the tinted windshield and placed them in their charm bags. The elder then turned to the bruised pilot and said, "You may now fly the mountain in peace. The gods have proven their medicine stronger than the white man's medicine."[51]

Over time, what began as a "simple interest and historical hobby became an inner conviction and commitment." Later, as a political leader, he would always be an advocate for Indian causes. As Goldwater put it, "from my first campout in Indian country, the red man always seemed as much—if not more—a part of Arizona and America as any white or black person. . . . They'll always be my brothers and sisters."[52]

AFTER PROVING that he could sell with the best of Arizona, Goldwater spent a year at the store's buying office in New York City learning the art of merchandising. He also learned about the East's disdain for the West. "They wouldn't take a check on a bank outside the city," he recalled angrily. "They didn't think Arizona *had* banks. That's when I first said, 'Let's cut off the whole Eastern Seaboard and turn it loose in the ocean.' "[53]

On his return, with a renewed sense of pride in the West, he strove to shape the taste of Phoenix women. One of his ideas came from his collection of Western branding irons, another of his hobbies. In short order, Goldwaters was offering women's blouses, men's sports shirts, and window draperies with branding iron designs. Sales were so good that in the 1930s he placed a series of advertisements in the *New Yorker*—the first national advertising ever done by an Arizona department store—and was soon filling orders around the country and outside it as well. He brimmed over with ideas: a brand of cologne named "Gold Water," and "antsy pants"—men's shorts, covered with a design of red ants, which became a national fad.

But the curve was not always up. Because of the Depression, sales dipped alarmingly low. Goldwater worked day and night, grew short-tempered, and slept fitfully. Finally in 1936, pressured beyond endurance, he had what biographers Rob Wood and Dean Smith called a "mild nervous breakdown." After a long rest, he returned to work, only to have another breakdown, again mild, two years later after being named president of Goldwaters. "His nerves broke completely," Peggy Goldwater was quoted as saying about the second incident in *Good Housekeeping* magazine in 1964. "He couldn't sleep nights." She later said that her choice of words was wrong, that her husband had suffered from simple exhaustion. Goldwater was typically candid when asked about the episodes in a 1959 interview: "I just blew my stack" after five straight days and nights of work.[54] His physician warned him that he must learn to relax, or else.[55] The young executive took the warning seriously—he found that several bourbons in the late afternoon did wonders for his peace of mind and body—and never again had any serious trouble with his nerves.

When Sam Wilson finally retired in 1937, Goldwater was named president of Goldwaters, at twenty-eight, one of the youngest chief executive officers in the nation. He was proud that throughout the Great Depression, no employee was ever let go although everyone, including the two Goldwaters at the top, took cuts in pay.

Goldwaters was a good place to work. The store paid hospital and life insurance for its workers, and during the war years, Barry began putting aside 25 percent of the store's profits each year for a workers' pension plan. In 1942, with the advent of World War II and rationing, Goldwater bought a twenty-five-acre farm on the outskirts of Phoenix, built a clubhouse, swimming pool, and walk-in refrigerator, and put cattle out to graze—a place where workers could go for vacations.[56]

Barry Goldwater and the employees were friends, members of an extended family. When Mrs. Mains (the victim of many of his practical jokes like the live mouse in the pneumatic tube) was injured in an automobile accident, Goldwater made arrangements for her care. When an office manager with no relatives was in a hospital waiting to die, Goldwater visited her faithfully and arranged for her funeral. In 1940, he reassured a longtime employee who had to retire early because of illness that she would continue to receive a monthly check of "$50.00 until such time as you are eligible for Social Security benefits."[57] One December, he noticed a little, poorly clad boy looking longingly at the wonders in the toy section and asked him what he wanted most for Christmas. "If only I could have a red wagon like that one there," the youngster pointed, "I couldn't ask for anything more." The red wagon was under the boy's stocking on Christmas morning.[58]

Goldwater could be tough with presidents, prime ministers, and majority leaders, but not with ordinary people whom he knew and considered his friends. His secretary at the store, Kay Lindner, could never keep him on schedule. "He would set up an important conference in his office," she recalled, "and make me promise not to let a soul in the door until it was over. Then a hungry Indian, or a bunch of kids looking for a baseball team sponsor would ask to see him. Before I could say 'no,' Barry would usually hear them and yell out, 'I'll see them.' He just couldn't seem to refuse."[59]

The remarkable loyalty this sparked taught Goldwater a lesson he carried with him into politics: "Loyalty is an endless circle." But then again, if loyalty takes precedence over matters like competence and wisdom it can create problems, as it did in his presidential campaign, when only loyal friends wound up making many of the important political decisions.

Goldwater liked to say that he led two lives—the "straight life" as son and student, husband and father, businessman and (later) politician, and the "sweet life" as athlete, ham radio operator, pilot, car buff, photographer, gadgeteer, and all-around tinkerer. He was a quintessential American in his abiding curiosity about tomorrow, but different in his deep respect for yesteryear, for the history of Arizona and America. He learned about the West from his family and their early struggle against desert, snakes, hostile Apache Indians, and the searing sun as they sought a foothold in the territory of Arizona. And like them he was grateful. Whatever it took, he would always pay the rent.

EARLY ON, before World War II broke out in 1939, Goldwater recognized the threat of Nazi Germany. He read Hitler's *Mein Kampf* and was appalled by its rabid antisemitism. He hoped that Charles Lindbergh's warnings about the real purpose of the technological superiority of the new German aircraft "would awaken our nation to its peril." Instead, the press characterized Lindbergh as a Nazi sympathizer. Goldwater would be the butt of similar ad hominem attacks by the media in 1964 when he tried to tell the truth about Vietnam. As war drew closer in the late 1930s, Goldwater wondered why the West had failed to maintain its military strength after World War I. "Perhaps," he later wrote, "my commitment through the years to maintaining weapons systems superior to any potential enemy is only the natural outcome of my frustrations and disappointments in this period just prior to World War II."[60] He was convinced that if the United States and other Western nations had remained militarily strong in the 1920s and 1930s and had been prepared to use their strength, Hitler would have backed off.

In July 1941, as chairman of the Armed Service Committee of the Phoenix Chamber of Commerce, a determined Goldwater called on the commander of Luke Air Force Base. He told Lt. Colonel Ennis C. Whitehead that he was a reserve first lieutenant in the infantry and knew something about how to get things done in Arizona. Despite his bad eyesight and age, thirty-two, Goldwater was signed onto a one-year tour of active duty. Lieutenant Goldwater was not sent into the wide blue yonder, but became an airplane gunnery instructor.

While at the base in Yuma, Goldwater, along with Captain Walter Clark and Group Captain Teddy Donaldson of the Royal Air Force, developed a new firing technique called the curve of pursuit. It was based on the theory that all bullets fired at an enemy aircraft, starting at 90 degrees and following through to zero, will hit the target. Before this discovery, only 10 percent of the Yuma cadets were graduated as proficient in aerial gunnery; afterward 94 percent were qualified. The technique was picked up by the training command and is still used in the military.[61]

When the Japanese attacked Pearl Harbor on December 7, 1941, Goldwater had about two hundred hours of unofficial flying time in the AT-6 trainer. At last, Goldwater was given a slot in the Air Transport Command. He was a member of the Over-the-Hill Gang, which delivered aircraft and supplies to every American theater of the war. Promoted to captain, he became operations officer of the 27th Ferry Squadron at New Castle Army Base, Delaware, and was chief pilot of two operations—one from the East Coast to the Azores, across North Africa to Karachi, then the capital of Pakistan; the other from Miami to Brazil, on to Lagos, Nigeria, and across central Africa to Karachi. For months, he was stationed in the China-Burma-India Theater, ferrying aircraft over the Himalaya Mountains in some of the most treacherous weather and terrain in the world.

As always, there were lighter moments. One night in Calcutta, he was drinking with a friend, Major Hap Carswell, when a radiogram arrived with instructions to "return by first available aircraft" to the United States. Elated at what he knew was the long-awaited order to join a B-29 bomber command, he sobered up, called in a crew, and took off on a three-day, 13,000-mile flight to New York—where he learned that the radiogram had been intended for his friend, Major Carswell. He was told to return immediately to India. His 26,000-mile round trip may have been, as Wood and Smith suggest, the longest unnecessary trip of the war.[62]

GOLDWATER WAS a very good pilot, which is why he was selected as one of ten pilots to ferry the first and only group of single-engine P-47 Thunderbolts across the North Atlantic to American units in Britain in August 1943. During their 3,750-mile flight, they touched down in Newfoundland, Greenland, and Iceland before landing in northern Scotland. Goldwater never forgot the briefing they received before taking off. The officer explained how to use the life raft if they went down, about their warm clothing, and the protection the accompanying aircraft (two B-24s) would provide. Then he said, "Well, fellas, if you have to bail out or if you have to put her down in the ocean, don't worry too much. You'll have about twenty minutes to live, and there's no way we can rescue you."[63]

Goldwater kept a thirty-six-page diary of the flight, describing the billowing clouds and the rich blue sea and mountains "flecked with white snow." The fjords of Greenland were covered with large and small ice floes that had broken loose from the glacier; against the rocky coast they "looked like salt on a dark cloth." And of course, he named his plane after his sweetheart: "I am naming her *Peggy G.* after you know who. She has led me thru the best part of my life, so I figured I may as well follow her namesake across the Atlantic. . . . She is the sweetest, smoothest-running airplane ever made, and she and I will get along as famously as her namesake."[64]

The diary recorded his careful attention to detail, his intimate knowledge of every part of his plane, his calm acceptance of the dangerous nature of the mission: "I said the Lord's Prayer and asked Him to do right by all of us, then touched my Flying Saint Christopher Peggy gave me." Returning home in a C-87, he summed up his historic experience in the P-47: "It was the first time in history that a single engine army plane had been flown across the ocean and while my pride in being part of the flight is great I think my pride in a country that can make engines and planes that will stand such a trip is greater."[65]

2

In the Ring

BEFORE WORLD WAR II, Phoenix was an agricultural community of about 65,000 citizens who praised the mild winters and endured the sizzling summers during which the normal temperature ranged between 105 and 115 degrees. The Chamber of Commerce published brochures filled with pictures of grizzled prospectors and desert "rats" with long beards and wide-brimmed hats.

But after V-J Day, thousands of ex-servicemen who had been stationed in Arizona returned to Phoenix to make it their home, nearly doubling the city's population to 107,000 by 1950. Manufacturing began to challenge farming as the primary source of income. The little desert town was rapidly becoming a minimetropolis, and whose family had more experience at helping to run a boom town than Barry Goldwater's?

Although a nonpartisan city council had governed Phoenix well enough in the past, it was clearly not up to the many demands of an expanding modern city. The five council members who managed the city's affairs elected one of their own as mayor. The mayor, with the approval of two council members, could hire or fire anyone, from city manager to bus driver. Not surprisingly, political coalitions came and went, and in the thirty-five years prior to 1950, the city changed managers thirty-one times. Prostitution and gambling flourished, flouting city ordinances and state laws. When one city manager demanded that the city council take action against the brothels, he and the police chief were fired.

Prostitution was only one of the serious problems. None of Phoenix's basic services—police, fire, sanitation—was working well. There were continuous deficits. The city clearly needed to reform its old-style, small-town government.

At last, in early 1947, Mayor Ray Busey, a Democrat, appointed a citizens' committee to revise the city charter. Among the forty citizens he named was businessman Barry Goldwater, who was anything but a political novice. As a small boy, the most important people in the city had dropped by his father's home for a drink. His uncle Morris would often visit, bringing along his friends, many of them politicians. One frequent visitor was Ned Creighton, the Republican leader of Phoenix; another was George Wiley Paul Hunt, six-term governor of Arizona between 1913 and 1928. Robert Creighton, Ned's son and a boyhood friend, remembered that, young as he was, Barry would jump into the discussions. "He would never call them 'sir' or 'mister.' He always used their first names, to the horror of his brother and sister. He would debate with them and never hesitate to ask questions. . . ."[1]

In his teens, Barry often chauffeured Uncle Morris and his Republican opponent as they debated the future of Prescott. They would attack each other on the platform as though "they were mortal enemies" and then pile into the car with their arms around each other and share "a bottle of [illegal] hootch"—it being in the midst of Prohibition.[2] Barry carried the trait—fight hard but don't bear a grudge—to the Senate where even those who strongly disagreed with him admitted they liked him.

Inspired by his uncle, Goldwater began to read authors he had neglected, including Edmund Burke; Thomas Jefferson, a favorite of his uncle; and James Madison, "author of the Constitution," his political bible in the Senate. And he discovered that he didn't like what President Franklin D. Roosevelt was doing. When he was invited by the *Phoenix Evening Gazette* in June 1938 to write a guest editorial, he was ready. "A Fireside Chat with Mr. Roosevelt" is Barry Goldwater's first recorded political statement—a revealing preview of the major themes that concerned him through his long public career.

Goldwater began by recalling that Roosevelt, when first running for president, had called for "economy in government and a reduction in taxes," but that in his first five years in office he "spent more than this government of ours spent in its entire history before 1932." Taxes, moreover, had increased "over 250 percent and I fear greatly that I ain't seen nothin' yet." Roosevelt had promised to better the conditions of the working man, and while hours had been shortened and therefore wages raised, the working man was "making about the same, or a little less, than he did before." As for the unemployed, despite all the promises, millions of men were still out of work. He criticized Roosevelt for "jumping down" the throats of everyone in business and dismissed his talk of "priming the [economic] pump," asking, "Isn't that money really going to prime a few votes?"

His conclusion was pretty good political rhetoric for a twenty-nine-year-old who had never held public office:

> I would like to know just where you are leading us. Are you going further into the morass that you have led us into, or are you going to go back to the good old American way of doing things where business is trusted, where labor earns more, where we take care of our unemployed, and where a man is elected to public office because he is a good man for the job and not because he commands your good will and a few dollars of the taxpayers' money? I like the old-fashioned way of being an American a lot better than the way we are headed for now.[3]

Here are all of the themes, except for anticommunism, that Goldwater would tirelessly promote as senator and presidential candidate: a belief in free enterprise and limited government, a strong dislike for taxes and organized labor, the need for public service in place of professional politics, a commitment to tradition and the permanent things. Although he did not use the word—it wasn't around in those days and would not be for another twenty years—he was a conservative.

A few weeks after Goldwater was mustered out of the Air Corps in November 1945, Governor Sidney Osborn, a Democrat, asked him to organize the Arizona Air National Guard. One of his first recommendations, soon approved, was that the unit be desegregated. Goldwater's integration of the Air National Guard took place more than two years before President Truman, by executive order, integrated the U.S. armed forces in the summer of 1948.

An impressed Governor Osborn asked Goldwater to take on a bigger job: serving on the Arizona Colorado River Commission, whose goal was to secure U.S. congressional funding for the Central Arizona Project, which would divert the Colorado River to central Arizonans. At stake was the most precious resource in the parched lands of the Far West, water. Goldwater, the master salesman, was delighted to take on the challenge.

But California effectively stonewalled the diversion until June 1962, when the Supreme Court decided in favor of Arizona. (Asked in later years how he, a conservative, could actively seek federal funds for a state project, Goldwater replied that he had never opposed federal reclamation projects and had in fact hailed President Theodore Roosevelt's reclamation acts as "invaluable steps in the march of progress.")[4]

While on the Colorado River Commission, Goldwater worked with someone who would play a major political role in his life, Stephen Shadegg. A fluent writer, Shadegg was the most successful campaign manager in the state. He was a new kind of political professional, one who applied the methods of demographics, advertising, and the mass media to politics, anticipating the political strategists of the 1980s and 1990s (men like Roger Ailes, Lee Atwater, and James Carville).

Shadegg had handled the campaign for every winning candidate for sheriff of Maricopa County (which included the city of Phoenix) since 1936 and would manage U.S. Senator Carl Hayden's successful reelection effort in 1950. He was a registered Democrat but like most Arizona Democrats a strong conservative who believed in limited government and free enterprise, the freer the better. Goldwater and Shadegg, both conservative, strong-willed, and direct, hit it off immediately.

Barry Goldwater became more and more involved in the nonpartisan politics of the community. He urged the Phoenix Chamber of Commerce not to approve dog racing, warning that if the city did not take a firm stand against "evils" like racing and crooked politics, it could become another Las Vegas.[5] On another front, organized labor had been trying to expand its influence in Phoenix for years and there were occasional incidents of violence. But unionism, particularly compulsory unionism, had little appeal in Arizona. In the fall of 1946, the Arizona legislature passed a right-to-work law, and the following spring Goldwater was asked to head the retailers' part of the campaign to implement the legislation.

He bought space in the *Phoenix Gazette* to announce that Goldwaters would be closed on July 4th so that its employees "can appreciate more how darned lucky we are being American." Mayor Busey liked the ad so much ("The 4th is a good day to look out over the mountains, the city, or your home and say to yourself, 'Am I doing my best to be the kind of American that made America?' ") that he recited it over local radio.[6]

In 1948, Goldwater became general chairman of the Community Chest Campaign and threw himself into it with his usual energy. The campaign raised $317,313, a record sum. Goldwater was unconsciously gaining invaluable experience in the key elements of a political campaign—money, organization, campaigning, issues, and the media.

The previous year, Mayor Busey had appointed forty Phoenix leaders, including Barry Goldwater, to study possible revision of the thirty-four-year-old city charter. The committee recommended a special election to approve a new charter with the following changes: expand the five-member council to seven; authorize the council to make policy and the city manager to implement it; and choose the manager "solely on the basis of his executive and administrative qualifications" and remove him only for cause.

The intent of the changes was clear: insulate the city manager from local politics and pressures and make the city's department heads responsible to him, not the council. Phoenix's old guard fiercely resisted the reforms. The *Phoenix Gazette*, which would play a crucial role in Goldwater's political career, strongly supported the changes and published a pro-charter editorial four days before the public referendum. In those pretelevision days, newspapers, especially in small cities like Phoenix, made a difference in politics.[7]

The referendum passed. The new revised charter became law, but the vice and corruption continued. The new mayor, Nicholas Udall, brother of Morris Udall, later a Democratic congressman from Arizona and presidential candidate, tried to implement the changes, but the new enlarged council preferred the old political system. Goldwater later remarked ruefully, "We had been naive. We had thought it necessary only to reform the charter; in truth, no written document is of much value unless the people elected to power are faithful to that document."[8]

The eye-opening lesson remained with him all his life. He saw the same syndrome in national politics where executive orders, congressional actions, and Supreme Court decisions radically altered the intention of the Founding Fathers as set forth in the Constitution about the kind of government America should have.

Angered by the stonewalling of the city council, more than one hundred prominent citizens, including Goldwater, formed the Charter Government Committee and determined to elect a city council that would honor the new city charter. To make sure, the committee decided to run its own slate of candidates in 1949. At long last, citizens revolted against political manipulation, inefficiency, and rising costs, and appointed a nominating committee, including Goldwater, to choose the seven candidates for the city council. Pleading political inexperience and his responsibility to the family business, Goldwater declined to run. Seven candidates were chosen, but two days before the filing deadline, two suddenly withdrew. One new candidate was selected, but the other slot remained open. Barry Goldwater, the obvious choice, had already said no. Harry Rosenzweig, his oldest and closest friend and one of the candidates, said, "I'll get him," and invited Goldwater over for dinner. He placed a bottle of his friend's favorite bourbon on the table, and they talked and reminisced late into the evening. At last, Goldwater said, "All right, Harry, what the hell do you want?"

"The boys want you to run for city council."

"What the hell, I'll do it."[9]

Goldwater later admitted that his fast draw was deceptive. He had been thinking for months about whether to get into politics, nonpartisan politics. He recalled his Uncle Morris's belief that prosperous citizens were morally obliged to repay, by whatever means, the communities that had helped make possible their success. By this time public questions rather than business questions occupied his mind. Although he had no intentions of devoting his life to politics and had no exaggerated idea of his competence to serve on the council, he was angry at the people who had betrayed the people's trust. He liked to quote Edmund Burke: "All that is necessary for evil to triumph is for good men to do nothing."

Goldwater's somewhat vague plan, if he won, was to serve two years, perhaps four, and then return to the store. Partisan politics seemed a very unlikely profession. After all, he was a registered Republican, and Democrats outnumbered Republicans in Arizona by about five to one. Since statehood in 1912, only two Republicans had been elected governor and only one had been sent to the U.S. Congress. The Democratic winner in the primaries in September was the de facto winner in the general elections in November.

Given these political odds and the fact that his Uncle Morris had been a Democratic leader most of his life and his father a registered Democrat, why was he a Republican? It was not, as he insisted in his 1979 memoirs, because his mother was a staunch Republican nor was it that his brother Bob was a Democrat and he a Republican for business reasons. Rather, he was a Republican because the Democratic party "had ruled Arizona with an arrogance that offended me. My decision to register as a Republican [in 1928] was an act of defiance."[10] Barry Goldwater always liked to enlist on the side of the underdog. His Republicanism was reinforced by 1930s Rooseveltian programs like the National Recovery Act, "which gave the federal government the power to impose its will on private business." His resentment of the New Deal, he admitted, was "an instinctive rather than a reasoned reaction."[11]

The new candidate tapped out a letter to his brother Bob and Bill Saufley about his decision to seek public office, a letter rightly described as "classic" Goldwater:

Willie and Bob:

You both will probably think me seven kinds of a dirty bastard when you hear that I have decided to run for councilman with Harry and the rest and I dont blame you much. . . .

However I dont think a man can live with himself when he asks others to do his dirty work for him. I couldn't criticize the government of this city when I myself refused to help. . . .

I dont know if we can win but if we do then I know Phoenix will have two years of damned good government that I hope will set a pattern for the coming years and the coming generations.

There has always been one and sometimes two Goldwaters damned fools enough to get into politics and they always did it with service in their minds which is the way I approach this thing. . . .

The city needs help more than any of our governments . . . maybe we can give it to them . . . maybe we will suffer doing it but in our mi[n]ds we will be doing what Americans should always be doing . . . helping each other.

Dont cuss me too much . . . it aint for life, and it may be fun. . . .[12]

B.

He was wrong about one thing: his decision *was* for life, because it was in public service, in politics, that he finally found what he had been searching for—himself.

Goldwater campaigned as he did everything, all out. He and Harry Rosenzweig rang doorbells, shook hands, and spoke at every opportunity: it seemed as though wherever two or three were gathered, there were Goldwater and Rosenzweig. As it turned out, he was a natural politician, especially for Arizona—warm, friendly, plainspoken. He was at his best, it was noted, on the Southside, with its heavy concentration of what were then called Negro and Mexican-American voters.[13] His enthusiasm was infectious, and soon all his fellow candidates were campaigning hard.

Civic activist Margaret Kober remembers one hectic night when the candidates left a rally and Goldwater, despite the tight schedule, stopped to talk with some awestruck boys. "I can see him in the headlights of the car," says Kober, "talking to those little boys about airplanes. It impressed me then that he was a big-hearted man."[14]

On November 8, 1949, forty-year-old Barry Goldwater led the field of twenty-seven candidates and was elected to his first political office, receiving three times as many votes as his nearest rival. The reformers won every precinct when more than 22,000 voters, a record high, cast their ballots.

The following month, Goldwater was elected vice chairman of the new city council, which set about cleaning up the city and straightening out its finances. An audit showed that the city would wind up $400,000 in the red if it adopted the previous administration's budget; after a series of spending cuts and economy moves, the new council announced a surplus of more than $275,000 a year later. City contracts were awarded on the basis of competitive bidding, the police department was reorganized, and vice took a beating.[15]

The conscience of the council was Goldwater, who raised hell, Cain, and various other things at meetings. He could not stand long-winded bores. To make his point, he bought a toy set of windup teeth and set them to clattering whenever a particularly annoying colleague opened his mouth. He was just as direct with someone who would not admit to doing wrong, like a businessman who denied he had overcharged the city for library furniture. Goldwater looked at him and said flatly, "You're a liar." And then there was the underdog. When city housing officials tried to oust a woman from her home to clear the land for a subsidized housing project, he exploded, "You're using Gestapo tactics. Get the hell off this woman's property."[16] During all these council sessions, he was as relaxed as though he were in his living room, even shedding his shoes.

But he was deadly serious when it came to spending the taxpayer's money, including "contingency funds" that he felt ought to be returned to the people. He never hesitated to take on big business, such as criticizing the Southern Pacific railroad because it was blocking the expansion of the city limits. He stunned downtown merchants, of which he was still officially one, by stating that the city had no intention of providing public parking lots. Jack Williams, who served on the council, became mayor of Phoenix, and then governor of Arizona, recalled that before Goldwater and his charter colleagues took office, every city official received a pile of Christmas presents. "They got whiskey, cigars, hams, sides of beef, crates of oranges." But soon "no one was sending anything in."[17] In 1950, only one year after the Goldwater council was swept into office, Phoenix won an All-America City award from *Look* magazine and the National Municipal League.

In February 1951, while still in his first term, Goldwater showed that he meant it when he said he believed in strictly limiting the role of government. A group of angry citizens protested against a beer and wine license being granted to a supermarket 1,200 feet from West Phoenix High School—it would contribute to the delinquency of minors. They were stunned when councilman Goldwater told them they should do a better job of teaching their children to resist temptation. Why penalize the store for the failure of the parents?

This was libertarian Goldwater speaking, the man who insisted you could not legislate morality. It was the first recorded confrontation between Goldwater and what might be called the Christian Right. Goldwater won: the liquor license was granted by a vote of four to three.[18]

BADLY OUTNUMBERED, Republican candidates in Arizona usually received between 30 and 40 percent of the votes in a general election, making the state one of the most Democratic in the nation outside the Solid South. Old Republicans were resigned, but new Republicans—those who had moved in since World War II—did not know they were not supposed to win.

At the spring 1950 meeting of the Republican party organization (which included Barry Goldwater), Charles Garland stood up. He represented the historic shift of political and economic power from east to west and from north to south that was taking place in America. An Arizona resident for only five years, Garland came from Illinois where he had been the Republican mayor of Des Plaines and a congressional candidate. Garland said that the party should fight hard to elect a Republican governor that fall, the first time since 1928. He also proposed that the party draft Howard Pyle, a well-known radio personality, as its gubernatorial candidate. Pyle was young, forty-three, a superb speaker, and a former war correspondent, with only one drawback: he had no political experience. But then neither did any other Republican in one-party Arizona.

Randolph M. J. Evjen, the Republican state chairman, realized that Pyle needed a campaign manager to make the run more than the usual perfunctory effort. The choice was obvious—Barry Goldwater, a well-known figure liked and respected by men and women of both parties.

Pyle was "drafted" by the Young Republicans at their annual convention, and the next day Goldwater called on Pyle. "You got your mouth open too wide, didn't you?" he said and offered to manage Pyle's campaign.[19] The two men made a decided contrast. Pyle was slight, short, and bald. Goldwater was tall, lean, and Hollywood handsome. Pyle was careful and thoughtful, weighing all the alternatives, Goldwater was impulsive and daring, a man of action. Asked which was which, a stranger would have probably said Goldwater was the candidate and Pyle the manager.

Before the two Republicans could take off on what Goldwater had conceived as a unique aerial campaign, the Democrats jubilantly announced that State Auditor Ana Frohmiller, a popular vote-getter whom no one had dared challenge for years, would be their candidate for governor. Republican enthusiasm "wilted like a young flower in the desert sun," and there was talk about waiting until 1952, of canceling the opening Pyle rally. The famous Goldwater temper exploded. "If you guys are going to be scared out by this woman," he told fellow Republicans at a strategy meeting, "I'm through with you. I may even pull out of the party. Where's your guts, anyway?"[20] The rally was held.

The two men set out on a backbreaking, twenty-hour-a-day campaign that covered more than 22,000 miles in Goldwater's red, white, and blue Beechcraft Bonanza. Pyle was a smooth and effective speaker, but Goldwater provided the common touch. Entering a bar to shake some hands, Goldwater would say, "Just put the governor's drinks up here on the bar. If the governor doesn't get to the drinks, I'll personally look after 'em. No waste in this administration!" Day after day the crowds grew larger and more enthusiastic.[21]

Goldwater did more than manage Pyle's campaign and counsel him on political strategy; he breathed new life and purpose into a party that had been asleep for decades. Arizona had never witnessed such a campaign. The Democrats campaigned as always, traveling by automobile and caravan, visiting the county courthouses, dispensing gifts and literature, behaving like visiting royalty. Pyle and Goldwater dropped out of the sky, filled with fire and enthusiasm, young crusaders who promised they would make state government the servant of the people.

In November, Republican Howard Pyle was elected governor of Arizona by a thin plurality of 2,991 votes, a major political upset. The new governor generously credited Goldwater with his success, while his manager coped with postcampaign depression.

But national politics quickly occupied him. More and more people told him they did not like the way things were going in Washington. They were particularly unhappy with the no-win war in Korea. When President Truman relieved General Douglas MacArthur of his command in April 1951, Goldwater realized, as he put it, that "the future of freedom was in the hands of the Washington politicians. I didn't question the president's right to fire MacArthur. I believe in the commander in chief and that civil authority is and should be paramount to any military commander. What troubled me was the apparent loss of our once-strong commitment to defend freedom at any cost."[22] Why not victory?

Goldwater did what he could as a citizen. An ex-GI recalled that the week before Christmas in 1950, during the Korean War, he was at the Los Angeles airport trying to get a ride home to Arizona. But there were no seats. Then he heard over the loudspeaker: "Any men in uniform wanting a ride to Arizona, please go to runway such-and-such." There he and his fellow servicemen found Barry Goldwater sitting in his plane. Every day, all day long, during the Christmas season, Goldwater filled up his twin-engine Beechcraft, flew to Arizona, and then returned to Los Angeles for another load of GIs.[23]

BUT SUCH PERSONAL gestures were not enough. Deeply dissatisfied with American policy, foreign and domestic, he began to think seriously about running for the U.S. Senate. The idea seemed quixotic, even for Goldwater. After all, the two men occupying Arizona's seats in the Senate were Carl Hayden, an Arizona icon and national institution who had served in Washington, D.C., since 1912, and Ernest W. McFarland, who had proved his vote-getting ability when he defeated the popular Henry Fountain Ashurst in the 1940 Democratic primary and was now Senate majority leader. Both, of course, were Democrats as were about 85 percent of the registered voters in the state.

McFarland was up for reelection in 1952 and seemed unbeatable, or at least most professionals thought so. Goldwater was not so sure. President Truman's popularity had declined sharply (down to the mid-twenties, according to Gallup), and McFarland was a Truman man who had backed the Fair Deal, Truman's prolongation of FDR's New Deal, at every opportunity. People were unhappy with the scandals rocking Washington, D.C., the no-win policy in the Korean War, and the lackluster economy. Change was in the air and on the way, even in staunchly Democratic territory like Arizona. Still, friends warned Goldwater that if "I ever opposed [McFarland], he'd saw me in half."[24] But Goldwater had a political itch that could be satisfied only one way—by running.

Goldwater was still weighing his options when Senator Everett McKinley Dirksen of Illinois came to Phoenix in the late fall of 1951 to address a state convention of Republicans. During the cocktail reception, Dirksen took Barry and Peggy Goldwater aside and urged Goldwater to run against McFarland. "I felt overwhelmed," Goldwater remembered. "Here was a veteran national politician coming into my home town, and he not only knew my name but suggested I run to help him in the Senate."[25]

Goldwater talked things over with Peggy. She said, he wrote, that "I was too direct and candid to be successful in politics" and that "I'd get hurt and disillusioned with the endless promises and compromises needed to survive." And she was reluctant to move the family into what she called "the twenty-four-hour whirlwind of Washington politics," thousands of miles from friends and the informal outdoor life of Arizona. But, having had her say, she asked, "Are you really sure you want to do it?"

"Yes," Goldwater said.

"All right, Barry, if that's what you want."[26]

It was indeed. Because he was a Goldwater, and Goldwaters always paid the rent, and a little more for the land they occupied. Because he was bored with the store and even the city council. Because managing the Pyle campaign had been a six-month high, and his own ought to be even more fun. Because he was genuinely disturbed by the foreign and domestic policies of the Truman administration.

But, unlike a young politician from Massachusetts who was also preparing to challenge a distinguished incumbent senator, Goldwater did not view the U.S. Senate as a stepping-stone to higher office. He had no all-consuming ambition to be president; he just hoped he would make a good senator for Arizona. But first he had to get elected, and he went about planning his campaign with his usual thoroughness.

GOLDWATER WON reelection to the Phoenix City Council in November, but his thoughts were already on McFarland. In early December 1951, Governor Pyle asked Goldwater to accompany him to a speaking engagement outside Phoenix. During the twenty-minute ride, Pyle challenged his friend to run for senator. "You've been doing a lot of talking about what the rest of us should be doing about good government. . . . Now, how about getting in there yourself?"[27] Goldwater told a delighted Pyle he was through talking and ready to start running.

Goldwater called on an old friend, Ned Creighton, the Republican boss in Phoenix whom he had first met in his family's living room decades before. "What makes you think you can win?" asked a skeptical Creighton.

For one thing, Goldwater said, "I can call ten thousand people in this state by their first name." For another, he said, "I've heard McFarland talk. I've heard Roosevelt talk. I've heard Truman. I've heard all our state governors and sheriffs and local officials. But they never say what they're really thinking. You see them on the golf course or for a drink and they'll give you a whole different story. I think a guy running for office who says exactly what he really thinks would astound a hell of a lot of people around the country."

"Well," said Big Ned, "it would be refreshing anyway."[28]

Goldwater knew how important a manager was, and he knew whom he wanted: Steve Shadegg. In late February 1952, he visited Shadegg at his office and said he would run for the Senate if Shadegg would handle his campaign. For two hours, a skeptical Shadegg and an enthusiastic Goldwater talked politics and policy. Shadegg revealed that he had been asked to run McFarland's campaign, but had said no because he didn't like McFarland's support of the New Deal and the Fair Deal.

Goldwater did not close the sale that afternoon. But a couple of days later, overwhelmed by Goldwater's energy, his sincerity, and his personal assurance there would be no shortage of money (he could depend on Harry Rosenzweig to shake the money trees), Shadegg agreed to take on the "impossible" assignment of helping to defeat one of the most popular Democrats in Arizona.

"I knew," recalled Shadegg, "that to win we'd have to get 90 percent of the Republicans to the polls and get support from 25 percent of the Democrats. If either fell short, we'd lose. We both realized that there was only an outside chance we could make it."[29]

Shadegg made one stipulation: Goldwater would have to agree not to make any off-the-cuff speeches or adopt any positions that had not been discussed and agreed to in advance. "Oh, you think I'll pop off?" Goldwater asked. That is exactly what Shadegg thought, and Goldwater accepted the condition.[30] Thus began one of the most successful political partnerships in Arizona politics.

Over the next thirty years, with Shadegg as his campaign manager, speechwriter, advertising consultant, resident philosopher, and overall amanuensis, Barry Goldwater would be elected to the U.S. Senate five times, become a nationally syndicated columnist, publish a series of best-selling books, and become the most popular conservative politician in America. During this period, he lost only one election: the presidency in 1964—the only time Steve Shadegg was not his campaign manager.

Goldwater decided that he would make his official announcement as candidate for the Senate at the Arizona Republican Convention in May and stepped with both feet into the middle of a controversy. The party's old guard, strongly in favor of Robert A. Taft, tried to ram through a motion sending all fourteen Arizona delegates to the GOP convention pledged to the Ohio senator. But they were opposed by a small but determined group of Young Republicans who backed General Dwight D. Eisenhower. Goldwater admired Taft and believed he would win the nomination, but the railroad tactics of the senior Republicans so angered his sense of fair play that he suddenly jumped to his feet. "I'm for Eisenhower," he shouted, to the astonishment of all present, and backed it up with an impassioned speech.

The convention rejected the proposal for an all-Taft delegation and wound up approving ten delegates for Taft and four for Eisenhower. Furious pro-Taft Republicans hit back at Goldwater by tearing up several nominating petitions they had been circulating for him and dumping them in his lap.[31]

Goldwater later admitted that he had made "a political blunder which might have damaged my own chances for election."[32] The bitter resentment of those Taft Republicans might have lasted through the fall campaign if Taft had not urged all his supporters to help make Ike the next president.

But it was not just a blunder, an off-the-cuff remark made in anger. Goldwater thought that either man, Taft or Eisenhower, would end the welfare state policies of the Roosevelt-Truman era, but, as he revealed in his 1979 memoirs, he had "some natural leanings toward Eisenhower, acquired during my five years in the military service." Goldwater was more of a practical politician than is generally understood. He believed that "Ike would be a stronger candidate." In his 1988 memoirs, he put it more succinctly: "I felt that Ike was a fresh political personality, he could win, and the party needed a new beginning."[33]

This was, in fact, Goldwater's first of several swerves from the conservative position in presidential contests. He would support the least conservative man for his party's nomination in 1968, 1976, and almost in 1980. (See chapters 18 and 19.)

On May 31, 1952, William Matthews, the Democratic editor and publisher of the influential *Tucson Daily Star,* asked a question that was on the minds of many Arizonans: "What kind of a Republican are you, Mr. Goldwater?" A few days later, Goldwater answered with a letter to the editor and a radio talk broadcast throughout the state. It was the first full public statement of Goldwater's political philosophy. Although carefully crafted by Shadegg, the statement echoed the Jeffersonian themes of limited government and individual freedom in Goldwater's

open letter to FDR in 1938 and his public talks over the years. It began
crisply:

> I am not a "me too" Republican.
> I am not a "Fair Deal" Republican.
> I am a Republican who believes all Republicans and all Democrats must
> practice in their personal and business lives those principles of honesty,
> integrity, devotion, and thrift which all of us long to see reestablished in
> our national government.

The references to honesty and integrity were calculated to remind
people of the ongoing Democratic scandals in Washington. In March,
Goldwater had charged that although Senator McFarland was "a clean,
honest American," he had succumbed to pressure and condoned dis-
honesty in government. "How can Senator McFarland defend the
president," he had asked, "when Harry Vaughn [Truman's military
aide and longtime friend who was a prominent figure in the White
House scandals] sits in his lap?"[34]
The statement continued:

> I am a Republican opposed to the super-state's gigantic, centralized
> authority, whether it be administered by Democrats or Republicans.

This was political boilerplate, but in his blunt way, Goldwater was
serving notice that if elected he would oppose Big Government no
matter who proposed it. He kept his promise, sometimes to the irrita-
tion of President Eisenhower.

> I am a Republican [said Goldwater] who is opposed to appeasement, who
> is shocked and saddened at the failure of our "now do nothing—now do
> anything" State Department, whose vacillating policies have resulted in
> a deterioration of world affairs and the loss of prestige and respect for the
> flag which I hold dear.
> I am a Republican opposed to communism and particularly to the
> communist-inclined sympathizers and communist-inclined policy-
> makers and their companion wishful thinkers.

In 1952, the cold winds of the Cold War were blowing across the
world, Alger Hiss was in jail for denying that he had once been a

communist spy, Senator Joseph McCarthy of Wisconsin was at the peak of his power, and every Republican candidate was waving the red, white, and blue flag of anticommunism. Goldwater was unquestionably anticommunist, but his anticommunism was based on more than the obvious military threat of the Soviet Union and Red China. In the years to come, he would develop the argument that America was a special nation with a special mission: "to preserve and extend freedom" around the world.[35]

I am a Republican [Goldwater continued] who gives more than lip service to a balanced budget. I believe individuals and local governments ... must reassert their independence and their responsibility. ...

Federal spending was increasingly out of control: the last Truman budget was billions of dollars in the red.

I am a Republican who believes that management and labor must work together. ...

Shadegg's moderating influence was clear here. Gone was the anti-labor rhetoric of the past. Many of the 300,000 registered Democrats were union members.

I am a Republican who believes that free men, working freely together, free of the coercion of federal bureaucratic interference and the compulsion of high federal tax demands, can and will work out their own salvation.

Here was the independent Westerner talking, the man who believed with heart and soul that any American could be anything if only government would get out of his way.

The statement would not have been true Goldwater without a reference to his political patron saint, Jefferson:

I am a Republican who has a profound respect for those principles of individual responsibility and limitation of the power of the central government first expressed by Thomas Jefferson and now ignored by the Fair Dealers and the New Dealers.

And it would not have been Goldwater without a nod to the centrality of God in government and society, a notion emphatically shared by Shadegg, a devout Episcopalian:

> I am a Republican who believes that man's freedom comes from Almighty God; that man possesses an important human integrity and an immortal soul. . . .[36]

One omission in the statement stands out starkly—the word "conservative." First, because there was as yet no organized conservative philosophy or movement in America. Liberal critic Lionel Trilling lamented in 1950 that "liberalism is not only the dominant but even the sole intellectual tradition" in America.[37] Second, because in the Arizona of the 1950s, to be a Republican was to be a conservative. Goldwater did not have to distinguish between the two until he came to Washington, D.C., and for the first time met liberal Republicans.

ALTHOUGH SHADEGG wrote almost every word uttered by Goldwater in the campaign, the two men were never ventriloquist and dummy. In July 1952, Goldwater took time out from speaking to tell Shadegg where he stood on the major campaign issues; characteristically, he did it in one page. His positions were to change remarkably little over the decades. Shadegg, a good editor as well as writer, incorporated much of the letter's language in Goldwater's speech in September, which marked the official opening of his campaign. Goldwater wrote:

Spending: The federal budget "must be cut to stop the dangers" of inflation and deficits.

Foreign Aid: "I don't like the idea of sending any amount of money that is asked for out of this country without sound, logical reasons for its use." (Throughout his career, Goldwater would cast more votes against foreign aid than any other federal program.)

Labor: "I believe in the Taft-Hartley Law." (His belief in equal treatment of management and organized labor would earn him the enduring enmity of union leaders like Walter Reuther and win him a national reputation while still a junior senator.)

Military Spending: "The military is the greatest waster of money and manpower we have." (Although he supported the funding of many weapons systems as a senator, he opposed many and spent his last year in the Senate on legislation to reorganize the Pentagon for the first time in forty years.)

Korea: "I say win any war this country ever enters." (He would say the same thing in 1964 when he was running for president and would be pilloried for it.)

Corruption in Government: "Man must conduct himself in office on even a higher plane than he would conduct his own personal affairs." (Nixon's failure to do so during Watergate led Goldwater to characterize him as "the most dishonest individual I have ever met in my life" — an extraordinary statement when one considers that Goldwater also knew Lyndon B. Johnson, Robert McNamara, and Spiro T. Agnew.)[38]

Social Security, Old Age Pensions, and Welfare: "I believe in these programs but I believe in proper and honest administration of them." (He was not a *no* government but a *limited* government Republican, much like the senator he admired so much, Robert Taft.)

Bureaucratic State: "The federal government should get out of the states and municipals as fast as they can." (Here was Goldwater's heartfelt federalism that misled some in the 1960s to call his advocacy of states' rights racist.)

Indian Affairs: "The Indians have made no progress under the Indian Bureau in a hundred years. . . . I believe the Indians can conduct their own affairs better under a state government. The Indian is still not a full citizen and we must make him one." (No issue so engaged Goldwater's passionate commitment as that of the American Indian.)

Foreign Policy: "I believe in a strong foreign policy that will enforce the desires of this country and protect its citizens." (The three key words here are "strong," "enforce," and "protect," all part of the emerging Goldwater code that the United States should worry less about winning world public opinion and more about winning the Cold War.)[39]

In more than one thousand speeches that year, Goldwater said over and over that the choice was clear—the "American Idea" as championed by himself versus the "Socialist Idea" favored by his opponent. That McFarland was not a socialist but a Fair Deal Democrat did not trouble Goldwater, who delighted in "painting McFarland as a collectivist bent on smothering all free enterprise through an all-powerful federal government."[40]

Goldwater liked to tweak his often pompous opponent. One time McFarland boasted that he was "one of the four most important men in the Government of the United States." That being so, Goldwater said, the senator must assume "25 percent of the blame" for the Truman administration. He twisted the knife adroitly: "Will the junior senator from Arizona," he asked, "take 25 percent of the credit for increasing your taxes? Will the junior senator—will this Fair Deal spokesman . . . accept his share of the responsibility for the more than 117,000 American boys who have been killed, wounded, or captured in Korea?"[41]

McFarland's initial strategy was to ignore Goldwater as a fleeting phenomenon. He had won reelection in 1946 in a walkaway, and he saw little reason to doubt that 1952 would be a repeat. He stayed in Washington while his spokesman, attorney Frank Beer, went around dismissing Goldwater as a "country club Republican" totally unprepared for high office. In fact, few Arizonans, even among his friends, thought Goldwater could win; Rosenzweig admitted that a McFarland man had offered to give him a twenty-thousand-vote handicap for a sizable bet, but he had turned it down.[42]

Undaunted, Goldwater campaigned away, attacking "Trumanism," the coddling of communists in government, federal intrusion into the affairs of states, organized labor's growing power, and mounting federal spending.[43] He made frequent and effective use of radio and a new campaign medium, television—he looked even more handsome and rugged on television than in person. Slowly, his fluent delivery of Shadegg's carefully prepared speeches convinced more and more voters that the upstart businessman from Phoenix with the old Arizona name might make a pretty good senator.

Even in 1952, television and radio time was not cheap. Harry Rosenzweig approached friends all over Phoenix and the state for contributions to the campaign. Vic Armstrong, another Goldwater friend and fundraiser, remembered that well-known Democrats would come up to him on the street and shove bills into his pocket, saying, "I'm for Barry, but if you tell anybody I contributed to his campaign, I'll call you a liar." Approximately half the money raised came from outside Arizona. Besides the $5,000 from the Republican Senatorial Campaign Committee (for which Goldwater would one day set a fundraising record), donations came from wealthy businessmen like H. L. Hunt of Dallas, who gave $3,000. In all, the Goldwater campaign raised

$44,721, a modest sum compared with today's million-dollar senatorial contests but not bad for the time.[44]

The campaign organization was a deliberate reflection of the candidate: simple and uncomplicated. Mel Harris, Goldwater's longtime personal secretary, kept the campaign schedule. Hoyt Pinaire, comptroller for the Goldwater stores, was responsible for keeping track of expenditures. Strategy, Shadegg recalled, was decided in a campaign "headquarters" that included one secretary, a telephone, and two typewriters.[45]

Shadegg came up with a political variation of one of the oldest devices in American advertising—the famous roadside Burma Shave sign. In the forty days preceding the general election, the following jingle could be seen on eye-level signs up and down the highways of Arizona:

Mac is for Harry
Harry's all through
You be for Barry
'Cause Barry's for you
Goldwater for Senator

Some analysts have argued that the 1952 Senate campaign was decided when Goldwater gave his formal kickoff speech in late September from the steps of historic Yavapai County Courthouse in Prescott. He surprised the crowd of some seven hundred and a statewide radio audience in two ways. The first was when, determined not to be caricatured as a neanderthal Republican, he praised "the social gains which have been made in the past twenty years"—the Securities Exchange Commission, the Social Security system, unemployment insurance, old-age assistance, and aid to dependent children and the blind. "They were created by the Congress of the United States and no responsible Republican and especially not this Republican has any intention or any desire to abolish any one of them."[46]

Goldwater then proposed a four-part program for reform: putting an end to waste; overhauling and revising the machinery of government; putting into office people who regard public service as "a public trust, not a mandate for private looting"; and establishing a foreign policy that would bring peace.

Here was no knee-jerk, anti-New Deal Republican who wanted to turn the clock back, but a Jeffersonian Republican who believed in limited, responsible government. Here were themes that would occupy him as a senator over the next thirty years and as a presidential candidate in 1964.

The second surprise came in the final five minutes of his speech when he put aside his prepared manuscript and revealed that the cautious McFarland had at last spoken out on one issue—Korea. The people of Arizona were entitled to know, Goldwater said, his voice low and controlled, that in the past week "the junior senator described our Korean War as a cheap war. 'Cheap,' he said, because we're killing nine Chinese for every American boy. And to justify his participation in this blunder of the Truman administration, he added to his statement these words: 'It is the Korean War which is making us prosperous.'

"I challenge the junior senator from Arizona," declared Goldwater, "to find anywhere within the borders of this state, or within the borders of the United States, a single mother or father who counts our casualties as cheap—who'd be willing to exchange the life of one American boy for the nine communists or the nine hundred Red communists or nine million communists."[47]

Shadegg made McFarland pay dearly for his callous remark by producing a radio spot filled with the sound of diving airplanes, firing machine guns, and shouting men while a voice said with understated disgust: "This is what McFarland calls a cheap war."[48]

Realizing that he had seriously erred in taking his reelection for granted, McFarland counterattacked hard, ridiculing his opponent's political inexperience. Frank Beer read over the radio a letter that Goldwater had written to McFarland during the war asking the senator to help him transfer from the infantry to the air force; Beer called it "influence peddling." But the implied slur—that Goldwater had tried to avoid combat—backfired when an angry Goldwater, who had said nothing about his military service, detailed how, denied combat duty, he had still flown many risky missions, including piloting a single-engine P-47 across the North Atlantic, for which he was awarded the Air Medal.[49]

Now desperate, McFarland brought in top Democratic guns from Washington. Veering close to antisemitism, Senator Robert Kerr of Oklahoma referred to Goldwater as "Mr. Silver Stream" and "Mr. Branch Water." Goldwater coolly responded that "If my name were Kerr, I wouldn't think I would fool around with somebody else's name."[50]

With two weeks to go, the polls showed McFarland narrowly ahead, 48.9 percent to 45.1 percent, but Goldwater closing fast. Everything jelled in the last several days. Goldwater rode with Dwight D. Eisenhower in an open car when the general visited Phoenix to give a speech. Eisenhower was comfortably ahead of Adlai Stevenson and expected to carry Arizona by a wide margin.

Shadegg made certain that Arizonans knew that Ike wanted Goldwater in Washington by placing an advertisement in the Phoenix and Tucson newspapers with the headline, "Arizona Needs a Republican Senator in a Republican Administration," right above a large photograph of a broadly smiling Eisenhower shaking the hand of a no-less happy Goldwater. The Monday before election day, another advertisement appeared with the tag line: "GIVE IKE a man he can work with—GIVE ARIZONA a man who can work with Ike for Arizona and America—Vote for BARRY GOLDWATER."[51]

To no one's surprise, the *Arizona Republic* endorsed Goldwater and urged all who wanted Eisenhower in the White House to put Barry Goldwater in the Senate and John Rhodes in the House of Representatives "for the sake of America."[52]

ON ELECTION EVE, the candidate made his last appeal to the people with a half-hour television program called "An Evening with the Goldwaters" that featured all six Goldwaters: himself, Peggy, Joanne, Barry, Jr., Mike, and little Peggy. More than one "fence-hanging voter" moved into the Goldwater column because of it.[53] About 75 percent of the state's population was concentrated in Maricopa County, where Phoenix is located, and in Pima County, which surrounds Tucson, site of the state capital. Goldwater was confident that he would do well in his home county but was concerned about Pima, many of whose citizens resented the increasing economic and political power of Phoenix.

On election night, Goldwater sat down with his family and friends in his home to watch the returns. He was soon smiling. Eisenhower was easily winning Arizona while Pyle and Rhodes moved ahead and remained there. Goldwater was winning by a larger margin in Maricopa than even he had hoped, and McFarland was not doing as well in Pima and the outlying areas as he had expected.

The final tally was Goldwater, 132,063; McFarland, 125,338—a slim majority of 6,725 votes. Eisenhower beat Adlai Stevenson in Arizona by 152,042 to 108,528, giving him a margin of 43,514 votes, almost six times larger than Goldwater's edge over McFarland. Goldwater often declared that in 1952 he was "the greatest coattail rider in history" and that he had "no business beating Mac, and I never would have done it without the help of Eisenhower's popularity and Mac's overconfidence."[54]

But this simply wasn't so. He did all the things that a candidate should do to win: he raised the necessary money to hire Steve Shadegg and a small but competent staff and to pay for a comprehensive advertising campaign; he put together his own organization, using the Young Republicans and the contacts he had made over the years through his many civic and charitable activities; and he campaigned unceasingly and effectively.

Goldwater's campaign was helped in two other critical areas, issues and the media. The paramount national issue was the Truman record, and Goldwater tied his opponent fast to all of it—the military stalemate in Korea, the political scandals in Washington, and the economic stagnation in America. As for the media, television had not yet monopolized the news and information; newspapers could make a decisive difference in a close race. Goldwater was not only endorsed by the most important newspaper in the state, the *Arizona Republic*, but received abundant and front-page news coverage. And as it turned out, he was a natural on television, articulate and relaxed.

He was delighted that he was part of a three-way triumph for Republicans: Pyle had been reelected governor, and Rhodes was elected to the U.S. House of Representatives, where he would serve for three decades, eventually becoming minority leader. As Goldwater later said, "Arizona had indeed become a two-party state,"[55] in large measure due to his efforts. He had persuaded Rhodes, as well as a number of candidates for the state legislature, to run. It was not an exaggeration to call him a, if not the, founding father of the Republican party of Arizona.

3

Mr. Goldwater Goes to Washington

ON JANUARY 3, 1953, two days after his forty-fourth birthday, Barry Morris Goldwater was sworn in as the junior senator from Arizona. Normally confident, he was awestruck, doubtful. As he later wrote, he was not a scholar or an experienced legislator. He was neither a big city politician from the North nor a shrewd country judge from the South. He was a successful entrepreneur who had grown tired of the family business, had entered politics, and had wound up defeating a Truman Democrat with a lot of help from his friends and a national hero named Eisenhower.

As he swore to support and defend the Constitution of the United States, it occurred to him, as he put in his memoirs, that if he did nothing more than keep that oath, he would make a pretty good senator. He revered the Constitution, and he resolved to make it his rock.[1] As he would put it in his most famous book, *The Conscience of a Conservative:* "My aim is not to pass laws, but to repeal them."[2]

Goldwater sat down with Taft, who as Senate majority leader made all the key decisions, to talk about committee assignments. He hoped to land a seat on either Interior, which was important to his state, or

Armed Services, where his experience in the military could be put to good use.

Taft shook his head: Republicans wanted a businessman on the Senate Labor and Public Welfare Committee to counteract the liberals, and Goldwater filled the bill nicely. The freshman senator protested that he knew little about labor relations because he had never had any difficulty with his employees. Union organizers had twice tried and failed to form a union at Goldwaters because they could not offer the employees more than they were already receiving—a liberal benefits package and an hourly wage of $1.75 when the national retail store average was $1.52 an hour. He had campaigned for Arizona's right-to-work law, but that was the extent of his knowledge of national labor law.

But Taft insisted, and Goldwater, for one of the few times in his life, meekly accepted an assignment that, far from burying him politically, helped make him a national figure in his first term. The Labor Committee dealt not only with labor legislation, but with education, the minimum wage, and other social welfare issues that directly touched the life of every American in the 1950s. His highly effective service on the Labor Committee led to his appointment to the famed McClellan Rackets Committee, which investigated and exposed the corrupt activities of union leaders Dave Beck and Jimmy Hoffa.

Goldwater later said that he was "forever indebted to Bob Taft . . . for his insistence that I serve on the Labor Committee."[3] Goldwater was also assigned to the Banking and Currency Committee, and named chairman of its subcommittee on economic stabilization, which handled price, wage, and rent control issues.

Although Goldwater and Taft served together for only seven months before Taft died of cancer in July 1953, the senator who was known as "Mr. Republican" had a profound impact on his younger colleague. Jack Bell, a veteran political reporter for the Associated Press, wrote perceptively of the similarities and differences between the two conservatives. Both men, he said, tended to black-and-white thinking: "to them, a principle was a principle . . . they were, in short, men of convictions with the courage to fight for them." They were against centralized government, socialism, and foreign aid; they were for balancing the budget and preserving states' rights. But, Taft, the veteran legislator, had become reconciled to the role of government in several areas whereas Goldwater, the newcomer, was adamantly opposed. As he put it years later, "I didn't take an oath to make sure every factory [in Arizona] got a little cut of mustard."[4]

While agreeing that some government programs like Social Security were needed, Goldwater disagreed with Taft about federal aid to education, which he argued was the responsibility of the states and not the federal government. He went so far as to suggest that Taft was "quite a liberal if you study his legislation and his debates." But Taft's was a classical liberalism based on government as the agency of last rather than first resort, on government that encouraged competition and the functioning of a free society.

Taft was "a genuinely brilliant man," Goldwater asserted, "whose brilliance was actually overshadowed by his character, his convictions, and the courage which fortified him against the assaults inevitably made upon men to whom principle is more sacred than profit."[5] That is, Taft was too principled for his own political good. Others would say the same thing about Goldwater, particularly when he was running for the presidency. Taft, Goldwater continued, "was the only member of the Senate that I ever knew that could literally tell you what was in every bill on the calendar. Senators by the dozen would come up and say, 'Bob, what the hell's this all about?' and he'd tell them. . . . He was one of the last of our 'chiefs'—men like Walter George and Dick Russell," two legendary Senate leaders.[6]

Goldwater described himself as a "Jeffersonian" from his first days in the Senate (once again reflecting the influence of his Uncle Morris), by which is meant that he adhered to five basic principles: (1) individualism, stemming from a belief in the sufficiency of human reason and the ability of man to govern himself; (2) republicanism, reflecting faith in the people and a conviction that government should be kept as close to the people as possible; (3) anticentralism, based on a distrust of executive power and on the protection of the rights of the states against the federal government; (4) strict constructionism, holding that the federal government can only exercise power delegated to it and enumerated in the Constitution; and (5) frugality and simplicity, calling for economy in government, the payment of debts, and the cutting of taxes.[7] Throughout his public career, Goldwater did his best to apply these Jeffersonian principles.

When Taft died, many conservative Republicans wept for the man who had led them tirelessly in the Senate for two decades and for the seeming end to their chances of nominating one of their own for president. Three times, in 1940, 1948, and 1952, they had put forth Taft, and three times they had collided with the political fact that at convention time, Eastern liberals ruled the Republican party.

They remembered what Senator Dirksen, a Taft stalwart, had said at the 1952 Republican Convention during the heated debate over whether to seat the Eisenhower or Taft delegations. Pausing during his emotional address, Dirksen directed a few words "to my good friends from the Eastern seaboard." Asking the delegates from New York and Pennsylvania to raise their hands and looking directly at Thomas Dewey, he reminded everyone of 1944 and 1948. "Reexamine your hearts," he told the Easterners, "before you take this action [of seating the Eisenhower delegation from Georgia]. . . . We followed you before and you took us down the road to defeat."[8]

Conservatives believed with all their hearts that Taft should have been nominated in 1952, that he deserved to be nominated, and that if he had been nominated, he too would have defeated Adlai Stevenson and been elected president. Now he was dead and MacArthur had faded away and the only champion left was Joe McCarthy.

FROM THE HEADY perspective of 1995, it is difficult to imagine how small, how insignificant, how irrelevant conservatism was forty years ago. In that far-off year, *National Review* did not exist, the future editor of *The American Spectator* was barely out of short pants, *Human Events* was a six- or sometimes eight-page weekly newsletter, and *The Freeman* was almost broke. There were no conservative think tanks— no Heritage Foundation, no Cato Institute, no Center for Strategic and International Studies.

And there were only a handful of conservative intellectuals and their works. Hayek's *The Road to Serfdom* was sometimes quoted. Richard Weaver's *Ideas Have Consequences*, with its trenchant argument that the West was in decline because of the rise of bad ideas, had long since been dismissed by the ruling elite. Philosophers Eric Voegelin and Leo Strauss, in their books and articles, challenged liberal shibboleths but seemingly to little effect.

In 1951, a young Yale graduate named Bill Buckley aroused liberals with his accusatory *God and Man at Yale*, but little had been heard from him since. The first conservative youth organization, the Intercollegiate Society of Individualists, had just been formed, but its purpose and future were uncertain. The religious world was symbolized by the powerful National Council of Churches; the secular world, by reigning liberal columnist Walter Lippmann.

In short, it seemed as though liberalism, the dominant ideology in the universities, churches, unions, media, and public policy institutions, would continue to dominate for many a year.

THERE ARE CERTAIN rites of passage for a freshman senator: his first vote, his first major speech, his first important bill. Six weeks after becoming senator, Goldwater spoke on the Senate floor for the first time, briefly stating his opposition to federal price supports for the cattle industry. On May 12, 1953, four months after taking office, he delivered his first major speech, an attack on federal price controls.

In that speech Goldwater pointed out that such controls were first tried under the Code of Hammurabi, around 1750 B.C., and were a failure. They were tried again during the Roman Empire and in the Middle Ages and failed both times. And they were certain to fail in modern times. He used statistical tables, charts, a consumer price index, a wholesale price list, and personal observations, filling up fifteen pages of the *Congressional Record*. The best way to stop inflation, he argued, was in the halls of Congress, which should stop its deficit spending. Price controls would curtail production, impose heavy burdens on business and industry, and lower moral standards by encouraging black markets. The solution, he insisted, was to balance the budget and "stop living at a Cadillac pace on a Ford income."[9]

Although his one-hour-long maiden speech did not materially affect the Senate's decision to reject price controls, people began to notice the handsome young senator from the West who did not hesitate to speak his mind. President Eisenhower sent him a three-word accolade through a White House aide, "Atta boy, Barry." Theodore Sorensen, who had just been hired as legislative assistant by freshman Senator John F. Kennedy, remembered Goldwater's "energy, his forcefulness. . . . [I]t was [clear] that here was a leader." And Vice President Richard Nixon solicited his advice about changes in the Taft-Hartley Act that Secretary of Labor Martin P. Durkin, former president of the American Federation of Labor plumbers union, had proposed. Goldwater did not like them and neither did Nixon, and the Durkin reforms were never submitted to the Senate.[10]

The first major legislation that Goldwater co-sponsored with sixty-three other senators in the spring of 1953 was the Bricker Amendment, which would have amended the Constitution to prevent the abuse of executive (i.e., presidential) power in making treaties and other international agreements.

The tripartite amendment, authored by Republican Senator John W. Bricker of Ohio, was one of the most controversial measures of the Eisenhower administration. Section 1 stated that any part of a treaty that conflicted with the Constitution would be invalid. Section 2 stated that a treaty could become effective as internal law in the United States only through legislation that would be valid in the absence of a treaty. And Section 3 stated that Congress should have power to regulate all executive and other *agreements* [emphasis added] with any foreign power or international organization, and that all such agreements should be subject to the limitations imposed on treaties by that article.

Supporters claimed that the amendment would protect the United States from unfriendly international organizations like the United Nations. Opponents, like Secretary of State John Foster Dulles, charged that it would alter the nation's traditional treaty-making power and hamper the president's constitutional authority to conduct foreign affairs.[11]

Goldwater felt that the Bricker Amendment would prudently curb the ability of the president, whether Republican or Democrat, from committing America to possibly dangerous and unconstitutional agreements. But President Eisenhower strongly opposed the resolution. A diluted substitute amendment was offered the following year, but even it still failed by one vote to obtain the necessary two-thirds for passage. A classic confrontation between the executive and legislative branches was averted, but the question of who is responsible for the conduct of foreign policy would reemerge during the Vietnam War.

"I favored the Bricker Amendment from the start," said Goldwater, "and I was sorry to see it defeated. If I had it to do over again, I'd still vote for it."[12] For Goldwater, the issue was simple: a president should not make or break a treaty without the appropriate constitutional approval of the Congress. More than a quarter of a century later, he took President Jimmy Carter to federal court when Carter unilaterally severed a mutual defense treaty with the Republic of China on Taiwan.

From his very first days in the Senate, Goldwater displayed a political independence, rarely hesitating to put principle above party. The day that Eisenhower appointed Governor Earl Warren of California as Chief Justice of the Supreme Court, Goldwater did not hesitate to express his misgivings.

"While I have every respect for Governor Warren as a governor," he said, "I don't feel his experience qualifies him for this post." In a clear reference to Warren's crucial support of Eisenhower over Taft at the Republican National Convention the previous summer, he went on, "The Supreme Court of the United States should be composed of the outstanding judicial brains of the country, regardless of politics."[13] Ironically, Eisenhower came to agree with Goldwater, once remarking to him, "The next time I have a vacancy on the court, I'm going to name a man to it with some good, common, horse sense."[14]

In his Senate votes, Goldwater tried to follow the dictum of Edmund Burke, who told his constituents, "Your representative owes you his judgment as well as his industry. He betrays your best interest if he sacrifices his judgment to your opinion."[15] When the Senate debated the administration's request to increase the debt limit in July 1953, Goldwater brought up the need to balance the federal budget. But, he said vividly, the Congress's efforts to do so over the past year "have been pretty much like a man trying to tattoo a bubble."

Congress must do better. "I suggest," he said, "that the Congress should be the banker of this country and say to the administration, 'Mr. Administration, you cannot spend this money because the people do not have it.' " He warned his colleagues of the consequences of deficit spending: "The day of reckoning is going to be dreadful. As an American, I would rather go through one or two bad years now than to wait in my grave for my children to pay the debts we are piling upon their shoulders."[16]

Goldwater's remarks, simple but forceful, struck a chord in the minds of many. The *Congressional Digest* reprinted his speech, as did several newspapers across the country. Fellow Republicans began "to look upon him as a potential spokesman of the conservative point of view" in the Senate and across the country.[17]

His early impact, unusual for a freshman senator, can be laid to his charisma and his willingness to speak his mind regardless of whose sensibilities might be bruised. He was one of the most liked members of the Senate on both sides of the aisle, but he was never regarded as a *legislative* leader who could control or sway a bloc of votes. It was not until his very last year in the Senate that he authored what could be called a major piece of legislation.

Through the years, Goldwater's most significant votes were usually *against* rather than *for* a particular bill. His greatest impact came from outside the Senate, from the thousands of speeches he delivered about the domestic and foreign policy issues that mattered most to him and, he was convinced, to the nation.

IN THE 1950s, a key element of good government and good politics was anticommunism. Goldwater's strong anticommunism had evolved from his anger over the gobbling up of Eastern Europe by the Soviet Union and the invasion of South Korea by North Korean troops armed with Soviet weapons and led by Soviet tanks. When he said in his 1952 Senate campaign that we should "win any war this country ever enters," he was referring not only to the Korean War but to the Cold War.

It was natural for the straight-talking freshman senator to become friendly with the most outspoken anticommunist of them all, Senator Joe McCarthy of Wisconsin. In fact, he already knew McCarthy, who had often vacationed in Phoenix and had campaigned for Goldwater in the fall of 1952.[18]

MCCARTHY'S METEORIC career began in February 1950 with a speech in Wheeling, West Virginia, about communists in government and ended abruptly with his censure by the Senate in December 1954. His decline began in the late summer and fall of 1953 when he took on the Eisenhower administration and the Pentagon by objecting to the promotion of an army officer named Irving Peress.

A commissioned army captain, Peress had invoked the Fifth Amendment when given a loyalty form asking about communist party membership. While McCarthy was investigating the case, Peress was promoted to major and given an honorable discharge. Brigadier General Ralph W. Zwicker, Peress's commanding officer, was summoned and asked to explain the army's action. Angered by the general's platitudinous responses, McCarthy declared that Zwicker, a highly decorated veteran of World War II who had received the Silver Star, the Legion of Merit, the British Distinguished Service

Order, and the French Legion of Honor, was "not fit" to wear his uniform.

President Eisenhower, who had publicly commended Zwicker for his wartime service, was furious. At a White House meeting on January 21, 1954, it was decided that McCarthy would have to be confronted. Charges were filed in the Senate alleging that the McCarthy committee had pressured the Pentagon to secure favorable treatment for an army private, David Schine, who was an unpaid consultant on the staff of the McCarthy committee and a close personal friend of its chief counsel, Roy Cohn.

The result was the celebrated Army-McCarthy hearings, which were televised live in the spring of 1954 before an estimated daily audience of 20 million people.

McCarthy's foes, and they were numerous in and out of the Senate, had found the key to bringing about his downfall—play up the clash between him and an overwhelmingly popular president. As the hearings continued, punctuated by McCarthy's constant cries of "Point of order!" and the smooth performance of the prosecuting attorney, Joseph N. Welch, opinion polls showed a sharp decline in approval of the senator—51 percent disapproved, while only 36 percent approved.

In short order, a resolution of censure was drafted by a committee headed by Senator Arthur Watkins (R-Utah), whom McCarthy publicly called stupid and cowardly, and was debated in a lame-duck session of the Senate after the 1954 November elections. McCarthy's loose language was the despair of his supporters, including Barry Goldwater.

While the resolution was being debated on the Senate floor in November, Senator Price Daniel of Texas, a Democrat, approached Goldwater and told him that if McCarthy would write letters of apology to the two Republican senators (Watkins and Robert C. Hendrickson of New Jersey) who felt that he had insulted them, Southern senators would be persuaded to vote against censure.

Goldwater immediately contacted Edward Bennett Williams, McCarthy's lawyer, and the two men drove to Bethesda Naval Hospital where McCarthy was being treated for an infected hand. To avoid being seen, they walked up thirteen flights of stairs, slipped past the nurses' station, and entered McCarthy's room. Goldwater gave his sick friend the two letters of apology that Williams had drafted, explaining that if he signed one of them, he might win valuable support; if he signed both, he had Senator Daniel's word that the Southern senators would

stand by him. The letters were "short, mild in their language, and
regretted a discourtesy without really conceding any substantive error
on McCarthy's part."

Goldwater and Williams argued that the letters were not any retreat
from principle and then warned that the other side probably had enough
votes to pass the censure resolution. Goldwater recalled that they
thought they had convinced McCarthy, who had taken pen in hand,
when "all of a sudden, he started to howl and scream at us for being
traitors to the cause" of anticommunism. He threw the pen across the
room and pounded on the table, making so much noise that a nurse
came running in, followed shortly by the admiral in charge of the
hospital. The admiral declared he was going to call the shore patrol and
have the two visitors arrested for trespassing. "You can't do that,"
Goldwater protested, "I'm a United States senator."

"I don't give a damn who you are," shouted the admiral, "you get
out of here."[19]

The two men left, probably taking with them McCarthy's only
chance of avoiding censure, and of surviving.

Despite that scene, Goldwater never stopped trying to help the man
whom he described as the "most contentious, controversial, and stubbornly cussed character that I ever met in my life."[20] Taking the Senate
floor, he attacked those Republicans who wanted to censure one of their
own. Such an action seemed almost heretical to Goldwater, who had
worked so hard to build a Republican party in his state and would labor
unstintingly for the party in the decades ahead.

He accused his colleagues of cannibalism: "We find the Republican
party busily chewing on itself." Rather than splitting hairs over techni-
calities and legal trivialities, the Senate ought to concentrate on the key
question: "What will happen to America's fight against communism if
the efforts of a man who has been active in the fight against this evil are
repudiated?" The campaign to censure McCarthy, he said, was not an
isolated incident but part of a larger effort intended to "weaken"
America. His voice heavy with sarcasm, Goldwater described the anti-
McCarthy propaganda as dripping with "idealism, high-mindedness,
and lofty sentiments" when in fact "all of the discredited and embittered figures of the Hiss-Yalta period of American dishonor have
crawled out from under their logs to join the effort to get even."

McCarthy, he said pointedly, had been willing to challenge the
powerful men who "were making decisions which were weaken-

ing America and strengthening Moscow." It might not be "good politics on the senator's part, but it is inspiring and heart-stirring Americanism."[21]

Goldwater's words, weighed and dismissed as the predictable rhetoric of a freshman senator, had little impact on his colleagues, a majority of whom were now prepared to condemn a man who had lost so much support among the public and his own party that it was safe to strike at him. But Goldwater would not turn his back on a friend. When a giant rally for McCarthy was held at Constitution Hall, he joined Republican Senators Herman Welker of Idaho and Karl Mundt of South Dakota on the platform. Censure, he said, would amount to a "global victory for communism." A few days later, he traveled to Milwaukee with McCarthy and his wife Jean for a testimonial dinner.[22]

On December 2, just before the final vote, Goldwater tried one last time, asserting that the Senate was afloat on "a sea of human emotions" and blind to what "we might do to the Senate for censuring the junior senator from Wisconsin on this count."[23] But no one was listening, not even McCarthy, it seemed; he repeatedly said that he hoped the vote would take place soon so that he could get back to exposing subversives in government.

That same day, December 2, 1954, the Senate voted 67 to 22 to "condemn" McCarthy for contempt and abuse of two Senate committees. All of the forty-four Democrats present, including Lyndon Johnson, voted for censure while the Republicans were evenly divided— twenty-two on each side. Goldwater voted against censure as did Majority Leader William Knowland and Everett Dirksen, both of whom would play important roles in his 1964 run for the presidency. With the Senate's repudiation, McCarthy all but disappeared from public view; he was never again on the front page until his death, from cirrhosis of the liver, on May 2, 1957.

AT A SPECIAL Senate memorial service held shortly after McCarthy's death, Goldwater inserted into the *Congressional Record* a brief but eloquent statement. It ended:

> Do not mourn Joe McCarthy. Be thankful that he lived, at the right time, and according to the talents vested in him by his Maker.
> Be grateful, too, that when it came his time to die, he passed on with

the full assurance that, because he lived, America is a brighter, safer, more vigilant land today.[24]

The defiant words were drafted by a young conservative named Brent Bozell, who with his brother-in-law William F. Buckley Jr. had written in 1954 an apologia, *McCarthy and His Enemies*, which described McCarthyism as "a weapon in the American arsenal" and a movement "around which men of good will and stern morality can close ranks."[25] Goldwater liked Bozell's way with words and called on him for writing assistance in the next several years. In 1960, he and Bozell would collaborate on a little book that became the most widely read political manifesto in twentieth-century America.

Twenty years after McCarthy's death, Willard Edwards, a well-known conservative journalist, trying to sum up the Wisconsin senator's appeal, wrote that even liberal newspapermen who opposed his politics liked him personally. "One cause of their sometimes reluctant admiration," he wrote, "was the way he dared to take on anybody and anything in sight—the entire establishment—without a moment's hesitation. . . . [A]gain and again, he had outfought, outwitted or outrun antagonists stronger than himself, and he had never cried uncle."[26]

There was much of that same pugnacious, quixotic quality about Goldwater. Thus, when those who had supported Joe McCarthy for his anticommunism and Robert Taft for his Republicanism and Douglas MacArthur for his patriotism began looking for another leader, their eyes fell, inevitably, on Barry Goldwater.

4

Big Labor and Big Government

SINCE PASSAGE OF THE NATIONAL LABOR RELATIONS ACT (the Wagner Act) in 1935, labor unions had flourished politically as well as economically in America. Their political party of choice was the Democratic party. After his amazing come-from-behind presidential victory in 1948, Truman had proclaimed, "Labor did it," and his narrow win in industrial states like Ohio, Illinois, and California, which he carried by only 58,000 votes out of 10.6 million cast, substantiated his analysis.[1]

With power came arrogance, and then corruption. In the first full year after World War II, nearly 5 million men struck at one time or another, and over 107 million man-days were lost. The Republican 80th Congress reacted by passing the Taft-Hartley Act, which union leaders denounced as the "slave labor act," but most Americans accepted as a reasonable restraint on organized labor.

Among its provisions was Section 14(b), which permitted states to outlaw all forms of union security, including the union shop. By 1954, fourteen states, including Arizona, had implemented this provision. It allowed a worker to hold a job without joining a union, creating one of the most controversial issues of the 1950s.

The following year, the Senate Subcommittee on Permanent Investigations of the Government Operations Committee uncovered examples of kickbacks and other abuses of union welfare funds by union officials. Congressional concern intensified when in February 1955 leaders of the American Federation of Labor (AFL), led by George Meany, and the Congress of Industrial Organizations (CIO), dominated by Walter Reuther, agreed to form one giant international federation, the AFL-CIO.

Formally ratified in December, the new organization embraced 135 national or international unions claiming a total of 14 million members and creating a formidable force in American politics.[2] The two federations soon meshed their separate political organizations into the most powerful political action committee in America, the Committee on Political Education (COPE). By 1957, unions had increased their membership to 17.5 million, 26 percent of the civilian work force.

Enormous sums of money, thousands of skilled organizers, all of the AFL-CIO formidable sources were brought to bear on American politics from the precinct to the White House. In 1958, twenty-five senatorial candidates backed by COPE won; only seven lost. Of the 294 House candidates supported by COPE, 183 were elected. One observer wrote, "No pressure group in history ever had such immediate impact."[3]

Knowing relatively little about organized labor, Goldwater spent his first two years on the Senate Labor Committee listening and learning from older and more experienced colleagues, men like Democrat John L. McClellan of Arkansas and Republican Irving Ives of New York. But he had one advantage over his fellow senators: he had personal knowledge of the close connection between leaders of organized crime and some leaders of organized labor.

His indisputable source was a reclusive, law-abiding resident of Phoenix, William Nelson, who was in fact Willie Bioff, ex-racketeer and ex-convict. In the Hollywood of the 1930s, Bioff had been a special representative of George Browne, president of the International Alliance of State Theatrical Employees and Motion Picture Operators, from which post Bioff forced union members to kick back 10 percent of their salaries. He also pressured motion picture studios into paying him off to keep wages at a lower level. Finally exposed and convicted of extortion in 1941, Bioff was released from prison after serving only part of a ten-year sentence when he turned state's evidence against five members of the Capone gang. His life now in danger, Bioff was permitted to change his name; he took up residence in Phoenix as William Nelson.

In 1952, Nelson decided to contribute $1,200 to the Senate campaign of a promising young politician, Barry Goldwater, who gave him an autographed picture in return. As Goldwater recalled, Nelson walked into his office three days later with the photograph and asked, "Do you know who I am?"

"Sure," replied Goldwater, "William Nelson." The one-time labor racketeer revealed his true name, and over the next three years, the two held about half a dozen extensive meetings during which Nelson/Bioff told Goldwater "how unions could and did abuse power. . . . He described for me how goons posing as labor leaders used illegal and coercive practices. . . . I've never forgotten the lessons he taught me."[4]

Goldwater's direct mentor on the Senate Labor Committee was Michael Bernstein, the Republican counsel, whom Goldwater described as "the person who knows more about labor law than any man I know."[5] Another key adviser was Dr. Jay Gordon Hall, who represented General Motors (GM) in Washington, D.C.

Hall first met Goldwater around 1950 when he flew to Phoenix to meet the young Arizonan and upon his return told friends that the Phoenix councilman was destined to become a national figure.[6] A trained political scientist, Hall became a close friend and confidant of Goldwater, providing him with inside information about organized labor's illegal activities in the Midwest, and broadening his political philosophy by bringing him together with conservative intellectuals like Russell Kirk.

Some time after Goldwater's arrival in Washington, Hall introduced the senator to William Baroody, Sr., head of the American Enterprise Institute (AEI), a Washington-based think tank whose activities GM generously supported. AEI added Goldwater to its list of senators for whom it drafted speeches, particularly on economic issues. Hall himself was a skillful writer who often wrote for Goldwater, including his pivotal "Grow up, conservatives" speech at the 1960 Republican convention in Chicago.

Next to Steve Shadegg, Jay Hall had the greatest political influence on Goldwater during his first two terms in the Senate. Goldwater called Hall "Secret Agent X-9" because of his penchant for meeting people in crowded places like Union Station and turning on the radio in his suite in the Hay-Adams Hotel during conversations to prevent eavesdropping. Hall thought caution was necessary around people like Jimmy Hoffa and Walter Reuther. Carl Curtis, who served on the Senate Labor

Committee, believes that "Jay Hall did more to make Barry Goldwater a national figure than anyone else."[7]

In the fall of 1955, Hall and Bernstein began working on an address that Goldwater was scheduled to give before the Republican National Committee School in Washington, D.C., determined that it would be more than one more political speech. Goldwater's remarks would carry extra weight since he had been appointed chairman of the Republican Senatorial Campaign Committee, a rare honor for a virtual newcomer in the Senate.

Goldwater was picked because of his capacity for hard work, his unflagging energy, his firm faith in the Republican party's philosophy, and his remarkable ability to raise money. He was not shy when approaching wealthy Republicans, bluntly telling them, "Private enterprise depends on the Republican party. If we lose, the end result is socialism—the destruction of individual freedom. Fork over."[8]

He was also selected because no one else wanted to be constantly on the road and away from the Senate campaigning for someone else. But it was an important post. Even with Ike in the White House, Republicans had lost control of both Houses of Congress in the 1954 elections after only two short years in power. The chairmanship was also, Goldwater said years later, "a good opportunity to get to know our grassroots leaders, our problems and strengths, and see if we could move the party in a more conservative direction."[9]

The last is a bit of personal revisionism: in 1955, he rarely used the word "conservative" on the Senate floor. As chairman of the Senate Campaign Committee, Goldwater was expected to and did campaign for all Republican candidates, whether conservative or liberal; white or black; Catholic, Protestant or Jewish; rich, middle class, or poor.

He did not take the job to build a national grassroots organization or to collect political IOUs for the future. Unlike Nixon, a master of such political minutiae, the thought of compiling the names of people who might later be useful never occurred to him. He complained about "the endless travel, tasteless meals, and lonely hotel rooms," but in truth he liked being on the road giving speeches, meeting people, and selling the Republican party.

After a year or two in the Senate, he realized there were two kinds of Republicans: Eastern liberals and everyone else. Like liberals everywhere, Republican liberals believed that big was better, whether it was big government or big business, and they controlled the Republican party. Where did that leave Republicans like himself who favored limited government and individual responsibility? As Goldwater later said, "the mid-1950s were very tough days for a conservative." What kept him going, he added, was "mostly the young people I met along those highways and byways" who hungered for new ideas instead of "the old handouts in social thinking and public programs." The sentence he used that always got the longest, loudest applause was "Any government which can promise you everything you want can also take away everything you have."[10]

WHEN HE CAME to the Senate, Goldwater began a working routine that he followed, with few variations, for the next three decades. Rising at around 5 A.M. in his apartment in Northwest Washington, he reviewed his dictation from the night before, read the "latest liberal line" of the *Washington Post*, brought coffee to Peggy in bed, and was usually in his Senate office by 7:30 A.M. He drove himself, first in a Thunderbird and then in a black 1969 Javelin AMX two-door sports car. He eventually spent an estimated $110,000 on the Javelin, adding more than sixty features, including an altimeter and exhaust temperature gauge from a jet fighter; a musical horn that played sixty-four preprogrammed songs; the first auto cellular phone in America; the first voice-activated phone; an ear-splitting alarm system; and a unique fire extinguisher.

Then there was his ham radio, or rather radios. Beside his radio shack in Arizona, he had his own small rig in his office. And there was a larger rig for the amateur radio club station he organized on Capitol Hill, which had the call letters W3USS. He was the only senator in the group; the others were Hill staffers.[11]

In between committee hearings and Senate floor business, he would lunch at his desk, the same meal every workday: a cheeseburger with everything on it and a chocolate milk shake. He did not vary this meal (his campaign plane in 1964 had strict orders to serve it) until his triple coronary bypass operation in 1982.

He also liked his liquor, and he handled it well. As he put it, he did not smoke or drink coffee because his mother had told her children that smoking and coffee would stunt their growth. "The three of us have always said we were lucky she didn't say anything about booze," he often remarked.[12] Goldwater would have a bourbon in the late afternoon wherever he was and several drinks in the evening if he was at a party or even when he was not. He kept a bottle of Old Crow in the refrigerator in his Senate office and would offer it to visitors or staffers when they gathered there after work to relax and talk over the day's work.[13]

Goldwater as senator and presidential candidate was frequently criticized for having a weak staff. It is true that in the beginning he hired only Arizonans who were unfamiliar with the way Washington works and who followed a casual, Western style of doing things. Henry Zipf, a large, affable lawyer from Tucson, was his first administrative assistant, followed in less than two years by Charles Farrington, who was succeeded in turn by an intense, intelligent young Arizonan lawyer, Dean Burch. But as his political responsibilities increased, Goldwater called on experts in and out of the Senate, including Michael Bernstein, Jay Hall, and Bill Baroody, the man who brought him into contact with AEI's network of distinguished academics. Although he did not hire a press secretary until 1960, Goldwater picked a seasoned, adept reporter when he did—Tony Smith. Bernstein, Hall, Baroody, Shadegg, and Bozell gave Goldwater intellectual firepower equal to that of any other senator, with the possible exception of John Kennedy.

ALTHOUGH HE WAS often on the road and could not be with his four children as much as he wished, Goldwater tried to fill the vacuum with a stream of letters, as part doting father, part exasperated parent, but always grounded in what Russell Kirk calls the permanent things. He wrote his oldest son at nineteen:

> All I've ever expected of you is that you try, that you do your best at that trying, and that you maintain a sound belief in the fundamental good things of life. . . . Grades are not everything in life. The chief thing in college is to learn how to apply yourself and how to study. If you do that, then you're going to pass everything in school and, more importantly, you'll pass everything in life.[14]

A few years later, when Barry Jr. was a senior in college, Barry Sr. wrote about how much they were alike and yet different:

> You are sort of a block off the old chip. It can't be the other way because you are too darned big, so when you look in the mirror what you see is not

just you but a part of me—a part I want to see go way past me, a part I want only the best for, but a part I want to see built on his own decisions and his own counsel, aided, where it is proper, by the advice from the other part who has learned, as you are learning, that the things we want in life we fight and work for—that this fighting and working puts the muscle of confidence and faith where the fat flabbiness of depending on others for everything can grow if we aren't careful. . . .[15]

Goldwater was enormously proud when Barry Jr. was elected to the House of Representatives from California in a special off-year election in 1969, and he hoped that one day he and his son would serve in the Senate together. When Barry Jr. ran for the Republican senatorial nomination in 1982, although an early favorite, he ran a poor campaign and finished third, with only 18 percent of the vote. He was devastated but seemed, in the words of one politician, "more upset about telling his father than about the loss itself."[16] Barry Jr. gave up the House seat that he had held for fourteen years to run for the Senate and dropped out of politics.

Reflecting on his famous father in the wake of his nomination defeat, the younger Goldwater said, "I respect him and I love him and I want him to look proudly upon my accomplishments."[17] He was speaking literally. A decade later, when reminiscing about his years in Congress, Barry Jr. said nothing about his legislative record but only that his father had never visited his congressional office and only telephoned him once for advice. "It was like I wasn't even there," he said.[18]

IN THE SENATE, Goldwater challenged conventional wisdom more and more often, displaying his love of freedom and his patriotism. In one debate in 1955, he referred to the Tennessee Valley Authority (TVA) as "socialistic." He pointed out that when it was started, TVA was a flood and navigation control facility but soon became such a major supplier of power that it prevented any private competition. "I do not believe," he said, "that [kind of monopoly] was envisioned by members of Congress." Perhaps there ought to be a national plebiscite on whether the people "want the government to engage in the production of power."[19]

Senator Henry Jackson of Washington and other liberal Democrats took turns mocking such an absurd notion, but Goldwater stood firm: TVA had strayed far from its original charter and many of its operations ought to be sold to private companies.

In 1964, when he ran for president, he paid a heavy price for his skeptical views about TVA. Twenty years later he was vindicated when the Reagan administration reduced the authority's work force by one-third and proposed that most of TVA be converted into a government corporation. A Democratic Congress rejected the proposal.

In a prophetic speech the same year about the central role of air-power in U.S. strategy, Goldwater displayed his grasp of history and his willingness to challenge shibboleths, even among the military. He traced the different kinds of weapons systems that had been developed through the centuries from Alexander the Great (land-based) through Admiral Mahan (sea-based) to the present—the age of air.

Airpower, he said, had given new meaning to such principles of war as economy, flexibility, security, surprise, and control. It required new thinking on the part of the professional soldier "who has always been reluctant to give up his old weapon for the new or to give up old strategy for the new." Certainly, he believed in tradition, but "we must be willing," he stated, "to take from the past only those things which will be useful today and tomorrow."

Here was a modern conservative, willing to experiment and change. He lauded Secretary of State Dulles for his controversial speech, delivered the preceding year, in which he revealed that President Eisenhower had decided to "depend primarily upon a great capacity to retaliate, instantly, by means and places of our choosing"—the doctrine later called brinkmanship. Goldwater pointed out that most people failed to notice Dulles's following sentence: "Now the Department of Defense and the Joint Chiefs of Staff can shape our military establishment to fit what is our policy instead of having to try to meet the enemy's many choices." That is, instead of reacting constantly to Soviet initiatives in places like Greece, Berlin, Korea, and Indochina, the United States was creating, in Dulles's words, an "international security system" of deterrence with airpower at its core.

Goldwater was not suggesting that surface forces be done away with. But he wanted the new political and military reality to be recognized. "We must accept the influence of powerful air forces upon international behavior," he insisted. "An understanding of the implications of this new weapon is not a matter of choice; it is the very condition of national survival."[20]

This perceptive speech was the first of many he would give in the Senate over the next thirty years about the vital importance of airpower in the protracted conflict with the Soviet Union.

Goldwater carried his militant anticommunist message everywhere. In 1955 at the Michigan Christian Endeavor Convention, he declared that the United States was engaged in a "basic struggle which must inevitably occupy the minds of all the world until total victory." This great contest, he said, was not at its root political or military or economic, but philosophical. It was a clash of beliefs—the communists asserting that man is essentially an economic being and Christians insisting that "man is not merely a social, economic, and physical animal but a spiritual animal as well." Freedom, he went on, is not the product of a political system "but the necessary state of man . . . who is the child of Almighty God."

He ended with a prayer: "Oh God, who are the author of peace and lover of concord, in knowledge of whom standeth our eternal life, whose service is perfect freedom, defend us, Thy humble servants, from all assaults of our enemies, that we, surely trusting in Thy defense, may not fear the power of any adversaries, through the might of Jesus Christ, our Lord. Amen."[21] (A different Goldwater said in 1993 over ABC's "20/20" that "the Religious Right scares the hell out of me."[22])

He happily defended the free enterprise system before friendly and hostile groups because he believed that "it provides the greatest freedom and opportunity for all people, both rich and poor, both worker and executive, regardless of race, color or creed, of any system yet devised by man."

Picking up on the charge that he was "reactionary," Goldwater told a Minneapolis audience that year that he was in truth "a true progressive." The reactionary wanted to break up American business and adopt "big central government"; the progressive stood for the free enterprise system that produces a more abundant living for every segment of society.[23]

Goldwater was, of course, engaging in rhetorical wordplay. He was more comfortable calling himself a conservative. The first instance of his doing so in the *Congressional Record* was in July 1955 when he inserted the Constitution of the Harvard New Conservative Club and remarked, "It is indeed heartwarming to one who prides himself upon being called a conservative that this great seat of learning in the United States is now nurturing conservatism among its young men."[24]

This occurred three years after being elected to the U.S. Senate and, not uncoincidentally, two years after the publication of Russell Kirk's *The Conservative Mind* and the same year as the birth of *National Review*. He was becoming a conscious, articulate member of a movement that had not existed when he entered politics in the late 1940s but which emerged and blossomed in the 1950s.

Once he had adopted the word "conservative," Goldwater used it in a variety of ways, as in his speech, a year later, about "The Liberal Versus the Conservative Today." He pointed out the differences between two stark and unbridgeable philosophies: freedom versus socialism, spirituality versus materialism, God versus man. The modern liberal, he argued, was a far cry from the classical liberals who founded the United States. The new liberals eschewed liberty in favor of bigger government, stricter controls, and a regimented economy. Over and over, he said, "The government gives nothing to its citizens that it does not first take from them."

Then, in conclusion, he asserted proudly, "I am a conservative." But he quickly added, with a nod to the libertarianism that was always so close to the surface, "Yet in the true historic sense of the word, I am also a liberal, for I will never, either in private or public life, accept the terrifying philosophy that the dark shadows of regimentation and control must inevitably blot out the sunlight of freedom."[25]

Throughout his years in Washington, Goldwater never forgot his Western roots. Before and after all things, he was a man of the West, independent, outspoken, generous, confident. Indeed, for him, the West *was* the future. Speaking to a group of advertising executives in Phoenix, he traced the remarkable growth of the eleven Western states, whose population had increased 41 percent between 1940 and 1950 and another 11.6 percent in the past five years—twice the national average of 5.1 percent.

The West's phenomenal growth from 1940 through 1960 began shifting the political and economic center of the United States from the East to the West. Goldwater ran as the first true Western presidential candidate in 1964 (Nixon was a Californian, not a Westerner). He was able to win the nomination and defeat the Eastern liberals of the Republican party—to their astonishment—in large measure because of this historic shift in power.

ALWAYS HAPPIEST when on the move, Goldwater learned to juggle life as chairman of the Senate Campaign Committee and as a member of the Senate, especially his responsibilities on the Labor Committee. His concern about the abuse of power by the leaders, but not the members, of organized labor deepened as the AFL-CIO moved toward its formal merger in the fall of 1955, and it showed in his remarks before the Republican National Committee School.

"I am not directing my remarks against the laboring people of America," Goldwater began, "but against certain politically ambitious leaders in the labor movement." He attacked the compulsory contributions exacted by the unions of members—Republicans and Democrats alike—that were used, in almost every case, to elect Democrats. He criticized organized labor's undue influence on legislation and its threats of political reprisal against those members of Congress who voted the "wrong" way, and spoke witheringly of the violence, instigated by some unions, that had erupted in recent strikes.[26]

He later explained his basic theme: the union movement in America was sound and democratic, but some of its branches had been diverted into dangerous channels by a few bad leaders. "Unionism," he said, "in its proper sphere, accomplishes a positive good for the country. . . . But the pendulum has now swung too far in the opposite direction and we are faced, as a people, with the stern obligation to halt a menacing misappropriation of power."[27]

Goldwater kept up the attack. He knew he was drawing blood when a director of the Labor League on Political Education told a convention of the Arizona State Federation of Labor that he, Goldwater, was "one of the most hated men in the United States," and the convention adopted a resolution calling for the end of his political career.

But, as he told the Senate, he was not hated by working people but by labor bosses like Walter Reuther because he favored right-to-work laws. Nor would he be deterred from opposing illegal weapons like secondary boycotts "one iota" by the hatred of "revolutionists." And he was confident of the final outcome because, sounding one of his favorite themes, "the majority of the people of this country are [not] yet in revolt against the institution of individual liberty."[28]

When three Republican members of the United Automobile Workers (UAW) in Michigan complained that they were being compelled by the UAW's shop rules to pay dues used repeatedly to elect Democrats, Goldwater joined Republican Senator Carl Curtis of Nebraska in a novel ploy: they staged an informal hearing for the union members in the Senate Caucus Room, to which the news media were invited. The hearing, held on December 15, 1955, with Curtis in the chair, drew more than fifty journalists who bombarded the witnesses with questions about abuse of their voting rights.

This foreshadowed the large-scale investigation of labor-union rackets that opened in January 1957 when an eight-member Select Committee on Improper Activities in the Labor or Management Field was appointed.[29] The purpose of what came to be called the "McClellan Rackets Committee" was to investigate union and management racketeering to determine whether changes were needed in federal laws. Goldwater was one of the eight, joining Republicans Joseph McCarthy, Irving Ives of New York, and Karl E. Mundt of South Dakota, and Democrats Sam J. Ervin of North Carolina, John F. Kennedy of Massachusetts, Pat McNamara of Michigan, and John L. McClellan of Arkansas. Robert F. Kennedy was named chief counsel. When McCarthy died, he was replaced on the committee by Carl Curtis, who with Goldwater and Mundt formed a powerful Republican troika.

Throughout 1957, the committee focused on the illegal activities of Dave Beck, West Coast boss of the International Brotherhood of Teamsters, and the financial dealings of Teamster President James R. Hoffa and other Teamster officials. Network television, in daily installments, showed how Beck had stolen hundreds of thousands of dollars from the union treasury, controlled gambling and taverns in several Northwest cities, and exacted kickbacks from large corporations. Beck was later sentenced to jail on graft and corruption charges.

The committee attempted to link Hoffa with beatings, intimidation, even killings. Goldwater, along with other senators, questioned Beck and Hoffa at length, but the real battle was between the committee's counsel, Bobby Kennedy, and the man who ran the Teamsters, Jimmy Hoffa. At last, after several Teamsters officials took the Fifth Amendment during the hearings, Hoffa's powerful union was expelled from the AFL-CIO in 1957.

Goldwater and the other Republicans on the McClellan Rackets Committee now demanded that the committee take an equally hard look at the political activities of the UAW and Walter Reuther, an ardent supporter of Democrats. Charged with being "political," Republicans pointed out that Chief Counsel Kennedy waited until after Beck and Maurice Hutcheson, leader of the Carpenters Union, had declared they would support President Eisenhower's reelection before deciding to investigate their two unions.

Like every other member of the Rackets Committee, Goldwater received thousands of letters from rank-and-file union members calling for help against what Chairman McClellan called "racketeering and . . . totalitarianism." He was appalled that organized labor had the power to commit these crimes unscathed. "My objection," he said, "is not to the worker, but to the boss—the powerful union official who takes advantage of him and, under the guise of fighting 'for the little man,' takes advantage of every other American."[30]

He agreed with Robert Kennedy and others that the graft and corruption they had exposed were an indictment of society, the same society that allowed union leaders to amass tremendous economic and political power, but whom, in this case, Democrats for political reasons would not challenge. Goldwater quoted F. A. Hayek: "The whole basis of our free society is gravely threatened by the powers arrogated by the unions."[31]

This power, and the arrogance that went with it, were epitomized in Walter Reuther, president of the UAW. When no one else would, Goldwater publicly called Reuther "the most dangerous man in America."[32]

Goldwater deliberately used this strong language because Reuther effectively controlled COPE, the AFL-CIO's muscular political arm. And Reuther's political goals, he believed, were diametrically opposed to those of the overwhelming majority of Americans. The senator charged that Reuther was dedicated to central government planning and hostile to free enterprise.

Indeed, Reuther had been a member of the Socialist party in the 1930s and, although he currently declared on every possible occasion that "I no longer share that point of view,"[33] in his many utterances Reuther revealed that he had not changed much from his early socialist years. In the years following World War II, he called for continuing price controls, a giant government public works program, and the institution of tripartite labor-management-government councils to oversee the nation's economy.

The liberals were always ready to come to Reuther's defense, as did *The New Republic* in November 1957 with an article entitled "Goldwater's Racket," which claimed that Goldwater was out to "hunt down Reuther." "Public outrage at the Hoffas and Dios can be used," warned the liberal journal, "and the Goldwaters hope to undermine confidence in Meany and Reuther."[34] Such wild charges (Goldwater frequently praised Meany for his determination to clean up the unions) only served to persuade Goldwater to step up his attacks on the UAW leader.

More than happy to take his case against Reuther and his brand of American socialism anywhere, Goldwater invaded Detroit, the heart of the enemy camp, in January 1958 and delivered a stinging address in which he accused Reuther of using the UAW and the union movement to further his personal political creed. Quoting from Michigan newspapers, he said that organized labor had taken over the Democratic party in the state with the aid of armed squads and baseball bats. Michigan's financial and economic problems, he went on, could be traced to Reuther and his socialist philosophy.

Outraged Democrats swiftly counterattacked. Governor G. Mennen Williams led off by criticizing Goldwater for coming into Michigan and making "unfounded charges against Walter Reuther and the labor movement." Delighted at having drawn blood, Goldwater riposted, "Reuther's not the property of Michigan, he's a national labor leader and a national menace." With characteristic sarcasm, he added, "I don't want to wish him on Michigan, but I would be happy if Michigan could contain him and keep his menacing tactics from overflowing into the other forty-seven states."[35]

But Goldwater went one step too far when he charged that "Walter Reuther and the UAW are a more dangerous menace than the Sputniks, or anything Russia might do." Enraged, Reuther went before a UAW convention and declared that Goldwater was "this country's number one political fanatic, its number one antilabor baiter, its number one peddler of class hatred." Flushed by the roars of approval from the union members, he added that the Arizona senator was "mentally unbalanced and needs a psychiatrist." (Reuther's suggestion may have inspired one of the most infamous incidents of the 1964 presidential campaign: the assertion by more than a thousand psychiatrists that Goldwater was not "psychologically fit" to be president.)

Although Reuther never apologized for his language, Goldwater did; he acknowledged that he had gone too far, explaining that his speech, which was being broadcast on radio, had run thirty seconds short and he had improvised to fill the time. "If I had it to do over," he admitted, "I never would say it."[36]

The Goldwater-Reuther feud continued in and out of Washington, D.C. In late February 1958, Reuther held a news conference in the large caucus room of the Old Senate Office Building, only one floor above Goldwater's offices. The union leader said he wanted to be the first witness at the hearings of the McClellan Rackets Committee on the UAW-Kohler strike but said he was being blocked from appearing by Goldwater and other Republican members. The reason, Reuther explained, was that Goldwater intended to smear him and his union at the start of the hearing and wanted to keep Reuther out until the television cameras had gone and "it didn't matter" whether, or what, he testified. He charged that Goldwater was trying to harass his union just before it began contract talks with General Motors and other automakers.

"Goldwater is trying to immobilize us in the negotiations," snapped the red-haired Reuther, "but he won't get away with it. I believe all of this exposes Goldwater for what he is—a political hypocrite and a moral coward."[37]

Reuther's attack swiftly appeared on the Associated Press news ticker (these were the days before C-SPAN and CNN) and was picked up by Senator William F. Knowland of California, the minority leader, in the Senate cloakroom. Striding onto the Senate floor, Knowland denounced Reuther. He was joined before long by a grim-faced Goldwater, who said slowly, his voice tight with emotion:

> Mr. Reuther accused me today of being a moral coward. In my section of the country when one calls a man a coward, he smiles. I could not tell whether Mr. Reuther was smiling or not, because he is such a coward he locked the door and would not let anyone in except members of the press. . . . So I say that this man, before he casts aspersions on others, should look into the mirror and see who is the coward.[38]

He then told his colleagues that he would be willing to debate Reuther anywhere, adding, with a bit of Goldwater rhetoric, even though "he doesn't know the truth from his left foot or his right foot."[39] The following month, on CBS-TV's "Face the Nation," he challenged Reuther to a public debate in Phoenix, "where warmth and sunshine can get into his soul." He proposed that the subject be the right-to-work law or unions in politics, and that the proceeds be given to the Samuel Gompers Clinic in Phoenix.[40]

And then at last, in March 1958, Goldwater and Reuther met when the union leader arrived to testify before the McClellan Rackets Committee. Each was icily polite to the other. During his testimony, Reuther's answers were so prolix that a journalist was heard to mutter, "I'll bet there's one thing that Mrs. Reuther never says to Walter at night: 'What did you do at the office today, dear?' " At the beginning of his testimony, the UAW president was quick to admit that his union had made mistakes in the strike against the Kohler Company of Wisconsin; there had been an estimated eight hundred instances of violence and threats of violence. He then went on the offensive, charging at one point that Republicans had a "philosophy that Reuther has got to be destroyed because his union is active in politics." Goldwater, who had opposed calling Reuther to testify precisely because he knew he would use the time to push his political goals, said grimly that Reuther was "going to continue to be attacked by me because I don't believe in his economic and political philosophy."[41]

At one point, the standing audience of more than three hundred cheered and clapped when Goldwater said levelly to Reuther, "Some day you and I are going to get together and lock horns."

"We're together right now, Senator," Reuther said with a tight smile.

Goldwater reminded the witness that they were in a place where "I'm asking the questions" but said he hoped they might debate in the "fresh sunshine of Arizona."[42]

Reuther later agreed to a radio debate in Detroit, and a date was set, with Goldwater insisting that he pay half the cost of the thirty-minute program, about $150. But two days before the debate, Goldwater was told that Reuther couldn't make it and that the program would be on television rather than radio. The senator showed up, debated the nationally unknown Leonard Woodcock, a UAW vice president, and paid $750 for his half of the program. Goldwater later said that the man who called "me a moral coward ran out on me."[43]

At the conclusion of the hearings, Reuther claimed that the UAW had been exonerated, but the four members of the Republican minority strongly disagreed. In a separate report, the four accused Chief Counsel Robert Kennedy of distancing himself from the inquiry into the UAW and of providing an inadequate investigative staff. Unlike the committee's investigation of the Teamsters, which was "vigorous and productive," the Republicans charged that Reuther and the UAW had gotten off easily, that "a double standard" had prevailed. If Reuther had truly wanted a "clean bill of health," they said, he would have submitted to a penetrating scrutiny of the UAW's use "of dues moneys on a wide variety of political activities."[44]

Robert Kennedy denied the Republican charges, arguing that although Reuther and the UAW made mistakes, "as a general proposition the UAW is an honest union and Walter Reuther is an honest union official who attempts to run an honest union."[45]

Kennedy was dissembling, and deliberately so. No one, not even Goldwater, had ever claimed that Walter Reuther was a dishonest union leader who was enriching himself with union dues and pension funds as other union officials had. Reuther's modest salary and lifestyle were well known. What Goldwater and his fellow Republicans were disturbed about was not how Reuther spent union dues on himself, but how he spent them on political activities; i.e., always favoring Democrats. The reason the Kennedy brothers whitewashed Reuther was obvious to Goldwater: "Their plan was to make Jack president. Reuther and the UAW could help them gain that objective."[46] And, in fact, organized labor's support turned out to be essential in 1960 when Kennedy carried heavily unionized states like Michigan, West Virginia, New Jersey, New York, and Pennsylvania.

Clark Mollenhoff, the Pulitzer Prize-winning journalist whose reporting on Teamsters corruption helped spark the Senate probe, corroborated, at least partially, Goldwater's claim of a UAW whitewash. Mollenhoff wrote that the Kennedys and their adviser, Kenneth O'Donnell, treated the UAW differently from other unions. "There were certain areas of the United Automobile Workers where, if you were using any kind of fairness, you would look into [them]," said Mollenhoff, but "Bobby and particularly Kenny O'Donnell didn't want to."[47]

GOLDWATER'S OUTSPOKEN criticism of organized labor (not since Robert Taft a decade earlier had any senator been so willing to challenge the political power of the unions), his widely publicized public tangles with Walter Reuther, a union leader admired and even eulogized by the liberal elite, and his constant speech-making on behalf of the Republican party and what he increasingly called conservative principles, all combined to make him, quite suddenly, a national figure. The *Saturday Evening Post* described him as the freshman with "more leadership potential" than any other Republican Senator during the past ten years. Paul F. Healy, a veteran reporter for the feisty *New York Daily News*, called him "aggressive, articulate, colorful" and stated that at a time "when conservatives are retiring and subsiding and dullness is settling over the Senate generally, Goldwater stands out."[48] He was a frequent guest on the radio and television news programs, like "Reporters Roundup" and "Meet the Press." Speaking engagements, many from business groups, poured in from around the country.

Goldwater welcomed the opportunity to speak out on the issues he thought important—and to strengthen his reelection campaign. He needed all the help he could get for he was being challenged by the man he had narrowly defeated in 1952, Ernest McFarland, who had since been elected governor of Arizona twice by wide margins and was determined to take back his Senate seat. And then there was the AFL-CIO's formidable Committee on Political Education, which made his defeat a top priority in 1958.

What would be the major theme of his campaign? As he had held from the beginning and as he would until his final day in public office, Goldwater was against the concentration of power in any hands, whether government, organized labor, or business. Speaking in Prescott, Arizona, the ancestral home of the Goldwaters, he told an attentive audience of Republican and Democratic supporters that there was a growing and evil concentration of power in the American business community. While conceding that some mergers increased productive capacity and lowered unit costs, "when size no longer contributed to a better product or a lower price, size became desirable solely for the establishment of power alone." That kind of power is "an intoxicant . . . it gives its possessor a feeling of omnipotence," he said, and it was bad for business and bad for America.

Goldwater, moreover, predicted that if the trend of the past twenty-five years continued, the independent businessman would disappear, replaced by "gigantic corporate structures"; the independent craftsman would disappear, becoming a member of a "union organization";

and the federal government would expand its activities and increase its power through "paternalistic benefits."[49]

Here was Goldwater, the independent Westerner, the small government Jeffersonian, the libertarian conservative, warning the people, as very few politicians would, that any government big enough to give them everything they wanted was big enough to take away everything they had. Here was a man with a message, and he would not stop delivering it whatever the consequences, even if it meant offending the man most responsible for his being in the Senate, Dwight D. Eisenhower.

5

Becoming a National Leader

WHEN GOLDWATER DELIVERED his Senate speech on April 8, 1957, he knew he was crossing a political Rubicon. During his first four years as a senator, he had been a good and faithful Republican, voting with his president the great majority of the time, rarely breaking with his party on important questions. He had served energetically as chairman of the Senate Republican Campaign Committee, raising money and seeking voters for any and all Republicans, regardless of their philosophy.

And, like almost everyone else in America, he liked Ike and had campaigned for the president the previous fall when Eisenhower swept to a triumphant reelection victory over Adlai Stevenson. He freely acknowledged that he would not be sitting in the U.S. Senate had it not been for Ike's coattails in 1952.

But he had been taught that a man should keep his word, and in October 1952 presidential candidate Eisenhower had said, "This crusade . . . will eliminate deficit as its first step toward bringing down taxes and making the dollar sound" and promised he would reduce federal expenditures to $60 billion by fiscal 1955. Goldwater also remembered that Bob Taft, whom he admired more than any other senator, once said, "If you permit appeals to unity to bring an end to criticism, we endanger not only the constitutional liberties of our country, but even its future existence."[1]

Goldwater's decision to criticize the president was not made any easier when that very morning an Eisenhower aide telephoned and invited him to have lunch at the White House. "The president wants to discuss ways he can help you," the aide offered, "in your coming campaign for reelection."

The senator knew that Eisenhower's enthusiastic backing could make a difference, perhaps a significant one, in his campaign, but he also knew that if he sat down with the president, he could not make the speech he had been working on. "No," he told the aide, "I don't think I should accept." The speech, he later explained, "was something I felt I had to do. After all, we Republicans had promised a change from the big-spending policies of the Democrats, and we were simply promising more of the same."[2] The Eisenhower administration had posted deficits in 1954 and 1955 although it did manage to balance the budget in 1956—an election year. Now Ike had sent to Congress a $71.8 billion budget for fiscal 1957—the largest any president had submitted in peacetime.

In mid-January, only four short months before, Goldwater had accompanied the president on an aerial inspection of the drought areas of the West and Midwest during which Ike had talked enthusiastically about how the states wanted to take care of themselves. It was snowing at almost every stop as the presidential plane, the *Columbine*, touched down in areas long parched by lack of rain. As Goldwater recounted the trip:

He would talk to the farmers and the local businessmen and the Agriculture Department officials who had turned out. He would ask them what they wanted and the farmers would say, "We can take care of this situation through our local and state agencies. We can get along without help from Washington."

Well, Ike would come back on the plane, smiling and rubbing his hands. He would say, "By golly, that's the spirit I like; the states should do it, they say they can take care of themselves." All during the trip, he was just bubbling over with this "states could do it" stuff.

I thought he was sold on the idea, but three days after we got back to Washington, he sent down to Congress a $79 million drought relief bill.[3]

Eisenhower's act of charity, at the taxpayers' expense, confirmed what Goldwater had already concluded: the president talked a good brand of conservatism, period. The senator was reluctant to voice his disappointment publicly, and thus his official report to his constituents about the trip accentuated the positive. Aside from foreign aid, he stated, he and the president had agreed on everything, including the principles of the Republican party.

Goldwater emphasized that "President Eisenhower is just as solid a Republican as you or I are, but I don't think some of the people who are around him have even any right to call themselves Republicans." Here was the 1950s' version of the 1980s' "Let Reagan be Reagan." Goldwater was convinced that liberals around Ike, like Secretary of Health, Education and Welfare Arthur Fleming and speechwriter John Emmett Hughes, were leading him astray. His theory was seemingly confirmed when Eisenhower wrote him in January 1956, after reading his analysis of the difference between modern and classical liberals:

I am glad [said the president] . . . to see this emphasis . . . on a point that every one of us can usefully stress— that historically a liberal system has been one which accords maximum freedom to the individual. One of the greatest political distortions in our history took place when "liberalism" became identified in the public mind with an ever growing, even more powerful central government. I hope we are making progress in dispelling that dangerous illusion.[4]

But when Goldwater read the details of the FY 1957 budget, he stopped trying to excuse Eisenhower. With great reluctance, and aware of the political risks, he explained to his Senate colleagues on that April afternoon that just as he had campaigned "against waste, extravagance, high taxes, unbalanced budgets, and deficit spending" under a Democratic administration, he would battle against "the same elements of fiscal irresponsibility in this Republican administration." Until recently, he said, he believed that the administration was committed to a strong domestic economy, essential to maintaining world peace. "Now, however," he admitted, "I am not so sure."

It was not only the record size of the budget, $71.8 billion, that disappointed Goldwater but that it contradicted many previous assurances of the administration. His criticism, Goldwater made clear, was not personally directed at the president but at the policies of his administration that he felt were inconsistent with traditional Republican principles. He would stand or fall on his position, adding that if he did not survive the 1958 election, "it will not be because [I have] broken faith with either the American people or the principles of the Republican party in this almost frenzied rush to give away the resources and freedoms of America. . . ."[5]

He was a traditional Republican, a conservative, his voice rang out, not one of those "modern Republicans" seemingly obsessed with the notion that the government had a right, even a duty, to interfere in and to direct the lives of the American people. "I have heard discussed on the floor," the senator said, "something about the rights of American citizens. The question is asked, 'What rights have we lost?' Let me name one right we have lost," he went on, his voice now rough-edged. "We have lost the right to decide for ourselves how to spend about 30 percent of our income, because that is about what is going into [federal] taxes today." He then argued:

We can begin the long march to the restoration of that right and every other privilege of American citizenship which has been submerged beneath these outrageous federal spending programs. It is my earnest hope that the president and my colleagues in the Congress will give serious and penetrating thought to this question. We may not, any of us, be here to witness the ultimate consequences of a continuation of this trend, but history would not forget that ours was the challenge forfeited.[6]

At a presidential news conference two days later, when Eisenhower was asked to comment on the Arizona senator's characterization of his budget as a "betrayal" of public trust, he said, "Of course these people have a right to their own opinion"; American politics "is a history of the clash of ideas." But, he added, "In this day and time we cannot . . . limit ourselves to the governmental processes that were applicable in 1890," a variation on the old line that Goldwater and other conservatives were more comfortable with the last than the present century.

Eisenhower said he believed "profoundly" that the programs proposed were "necessary for the country," and there was "no chance of reversing them." He added a few conciliatory words, but there was no mistaking the meaning of his response: big government was here to stay, and the task of the Republicans was to demonstrate they could manage it better than the Democrats.[7]

Eisenhower and Goldwater were looking at each other across a divide—philosophical, political, geographical. Encouraged and surrounded by Eastern liberals—Arthur Fleming, James P. Mitchell (the former secretary of labor), John Emmett Hughes, Paul Hoffman (the former administrator of the European Recovery Program), and his own brother Milton—the president committed himself to a modern Republicanism that endorsed government partnership and guardianship of the nation's economy.[8] Such a philosophy required large federal outlays, which was why Eisenhower was proposing to spend an historic $71.8 billion.

Goldwater and fellow conservatives from the Midwest and the West determined to resist the policies of the "modern" Republicans, or "Me-Too" Republicans. A "Me-Too Republican," the senator explained, was someone who trailed in the wake of Democrats as they promised more and fatter giveaways, yelling at the top of his lungs, "Me too, me too."[9]

Goldwater later asserted that his falling out with Ike and "moderate" Republicans like Senator Jacob Javits of New York and Governor Nelson Rockefeller led to three significant developments: his presidential nomination, the shift of Republican party power "from the Eastern seaboard to west of the Mississippi River," and the "full flowering of the conservative movement during the two terms of President Reagan."[10]

Goldwater's analysis was correct, but his remarks at the time were not part of a calculated, long-range strategy to advance a political philosophy or himself. As he did throughout his life, Goldwater was reacting spontaneously to something he did not like: in this case, a bloated federal budget.

Normally, a single speech by a freshman senator from a small Western state, no matter how critical of the president, would not have drawn much interest in Washington, D.C. It was a measure of Goldwater's growing importance as a Republican leader and the spreading influence of the conservative movement that Goldwater's remarks sparked strong reaction in and out of the nation's capital. Newspapers blared that Goldwater, who had just finished a term as chairman of the Senate Republican Campaign Committee, had "broken" with Eisenhower. Followers of Bob Taft and Joe McCarthy noted yet again the courage of the senator from Arizona who stood up for his beliefs, regardless of who was irritated or offended. They needed a leader, they wanted a leader, they demanded a leader. The thought began to occur: Could Goldwater do what none of their earlier champions had been able to do—capture the White House?

TYPICALLY, GOLDWATER'S thoughts were far from the White House or even Washington, D.C. Making speeches in the Senate that stirred up the troops and stung the establishment was all well and good, but he had an election to win—his own. In February 1956, he wrote Steve Shadegg asking him to handle his 1958 reelection campaign, starting right away. Shadegg immediately agreed. He had been thinking about the race and their likely opponent, Governor McFarland. It would be "a tough campaign," he said, because McFarland had been given credit "for things which he did not do, and no one has taken the trouble to point out the things he hasn't done."

In order to win, they would need "an adequate supply of campaign money and an honest press." Shadegg warned his friend that "people have short memories in politics." Goldwater's solid work for the state since 1952 notwithstanding, "the '58 election will be won by the campaign waged in '58."[11]

Goldwater always understood that the worst campaign manager any candidate could have was himself and thus put himself in Shadegg's hands. In a June letter to Shadegg, he admitted that he had not thought very seriously about campaign themes, but he was

> absolutely convinced that there is a tremendous swing toward conserva-
> tism in America and that the politician who thinks he is going to be
> elected trying to be all things to all people is going to have a rude
> awakening. I regret that our party doesn't sense this and follow a more
> conservative line than we are doing at the present time.[12]

Shadegg emphatically agreed. Over the next four years, he played a central role in Goldwater's accelerating political career—managing his successful reelection campaign in 1958, ghostwriting his popular newspaper column that began in 1960, serving as a major collaborator for speeches in and out of the Senate. Shadegg initially dominated in the interplay of words and ideas, suggesting books and articles the senator ought to read, proposing themes for a column or speech. But gradually Goldwater became more intellectually confident and assertive—like a student who one day realizes that he knows as much as his professor—until finally it was he who was suggesting what Shadegg ought to read.

Their close relationship continued until 1962 when ambition misled Shadegg into seeking the Republican senatorial nomination to run against the venerable and venerated Democrat Carl Hayden. In Goldwater's eyes this was an unforgivable breach of political etiquette against his longtime colleague in the Senate. Goldwater let his unhappiness show, but Shadegg was determined to prove that he could defy political history and be as good a candidate as he was a manager. However, he was roundly defeated for the Republican nomination by Evan Mecham, who in turn was beaten in the fall by Hayden. Goldwater remained angry at his political adviser, ignoring him until early 1964 when he gave Shadegg a limited role in his presidential campaign.

Until that break, Goldwater did not hesitate to contact Shadegg when he had something on his mind, as he did in January 1957, shortly before Eisenhower requested standby authority to send American troops into the Middle East. The request would become the Eisenhower Doctrine—a declaration that the United States considered the preservation of the independence and integrity of the Middle Eastern nations vital to American security and that it would use armed force to assist any nation or nations "requesting assistance against armed aggression from any country controlled by international communism."[13]

Goldwater was a more determined anticommunist than most senators, but, he asked Shadegg in a recorded telephone conversation, was such a request not similar to Harry Truman's concerning Korea, a move strongly criticized by Republicans? And that wasn't all, he told Shadegg, "Who determines what the emergency is? Who says how many boys? What kind of equipment? What kind of forces?"

He realized that Eisenhower was sending a signal to the Soviet Union to stay out of the Middle East, and he trusted Ike not to get the United States into a war. But Eisenhower would not always be president. "Now, we gave him that right in Formosa," said Goldwater, "but that was a specific case, one island that we were defending against one enemy. Here is a case of giving that authority over a large portion of the world."

Shadegg agreed that it sounded like a bad deal "unless he only wants it to have a stronger club to put in Russia's face."

"He's got the strongest God-damned club we'll ever have," retorted Goldwater, "and that's the Strategic Air Command."

Throughout his career, Goldwater opposed the use of U.S. land forces in overseas conflicts unless they were deemed absolutely essential—as, he would argue, they were not in Vietnam. He did not like the president's request, but he hated "like hell to start out voting [in 1957] against the boss."

"All you can do," said Shadegg, "is vote your conscience."

"That's the thing I want to stick to," agreed Goldwater, but the liberals were probing his every action and were "out to get every conservative in the next election. The drive is on. You can feel it."

"You ain't going to get beat," said Shadegg flatly.

"No, I know I'm not," Goldwater said, with perhaps more conviction than he truly felt, "but I don't want to be back here by myself."[14]

IN THE FALL of 1958, as the 85th Congress was drawing to a close, most political observers agreed that Barry Goldwater should be worrying about his own chances of reelection rather than those of his fellow Republicans. After six years in the Senate, he was generally described as charming, personable, hardworking, a man of strong if often "ultra"-conservative convictions (i.e., his backing of a national right-to-work law). He was admired and even praised for his principled positions and willingness to attack sacred cows and popular presidents. But few in Washington, Republican or Democrat, were willing to bet that this maverick could be reelected from a solidly Democratic state like Arizona, particularly when facing a popular governor and one-time senator like Ernest McFarland.

At first glance, the 1958 campaign seemed to mirror the 1952 contest except with Goldwater as the incumbent and McFarland the challenger; but this time the odds favored the challenger. Goldwater and Shadegg had their work cut out for them.[15] As governor, McFarland had given dozens of speeches throughout the state and had often criticized Goldwater's record and performance.

Unlike 1952, Goldwater would not be running on the same ticket as Eisenhower and, in fact, could not even be certain of Ike's unqualified support; Democrats delighted in pointing out that the junior senator was so headstrong that he had gone out of his way to criticize the president of his own party. But he also had powerful allies. Clarence Buddington Kelland, the noted author and prominent Republican leader, had warmly defended Goldwater after his Senate attack on Eisenhower's

$71.8 billion budget, saying, in his typically flamboyant way, "New Republicanism betrays every historical tenet and principle of our Republican party."[16]

Conservative frustration with Eisenhower and modern Republicanism manifested itself in the formation of the John Birch Society in 1958 by Robert Welch, a soft-spoken but autocratic Massachusetts businessman. John Birch was a missionary to China who had served in the U.S. army in the Far East during World War II and had been murdered by the Chinese communists a few days after Japan surrendered. From its beginnings, the John Birch Society specialized in shock tactics, declaring "Impeach Earl Warren!" and "Get the U.S. out of the U.N. and the U.N. out of the U.S."

Welch subscribed to the conspiracy theory of history, arguing that a small but powerful group of bankers, industrialists, publishers, and others were responsible for the spread of collectivism in the twentieth century. In his book, *The Politician,* he went over the edge, asserting that President Eisenhower was either "a mere stooge" for the communist cause or "has been consciously serving the communist conspiracy for all of his adult life."[17]

Before he formed the John Birch Society, Welch visited Goldwater in Phoenix and asked him to read *The Politician.* After leafing through the manuscript, Goldwater told Welch that his theory about Ike being either a dupe or a conscious agent of worldwide communism was inaccurate and that printing the work would harm not only Welch personally but the anticommunist cause. "Welch never sought my advice again."[18]

Once the Birch society was formed, Goldwater would often disagree with its statements but refused to engage in any wholesale condemnation of its members. The last thing conservatives needed in the late 1950s and early 1960s when they were building a movement was "to begin a factional war by reading small minorities or individuals out of our ranks," he said.

In point of fact, the John Birch Society's membership, concentrated in the South and the West, never amounted to more than sixty thousand; it was always more important to the liberal media as a target of opportunity than to most conservatives as a source of information and inspiration. For years, liberals used the society's more extreme statements to stigmatize the entire conservative movement, referring to everyone from Welch to Goldwater to Buckley as part of "the radical Right." In 1962, when *National Review* formally condemned the John

Birch Society, it published a letter from Goldwater, who described Welch's views as "irresponsible" and called on him to resign as president of the society.[19] Despite this statement, the Left continued to link Goldwater and other conservatives with the "radical Right"—using the same tactics of guilt by association and slander for which they had so roundly condemned Joseph McCarthy.

IN 1958, however, the Birch Society was not yet an issue, and did not affect Goldwater's reelection campaign. What did was the Phoenix press. At a time when television was not yet the dominant news medium, the *Arizona Republic* and *Phoenix Gazette* made a critical difference in a close campaign.

From his days as a member of the Phoenix City Council, Goldwater had received editorial support and friendly coverage in the two Phoenix dailies whose conservative Republican owner, Eugene Pulliam, enjoyed his role as an Arizona kingmaker. The pattern continued in 1958. In fact, the *Republic* and *Gazette* quoted Goldwater so often and so admiringly that one opponent remarked in deep disgust, "If Goldwater recited 'Mary Had a Little Lamb,' the Pulliam press would make it the banner story of the day."[20]

Also in Goldwater's favor was the demographic makeup of Arizona. More than half of the state's population was located in the Phoenix area, many of them retirees who opposed excessive federal spending. A large percentage of the many thousands who had migrated to the Grand Canyon State came from the Republican Midwest and were instinctively conservative. In the smaller counties, as biographers Wood and Smith point out, many of the voters were cattlemen, "possibly the most rigidly conservative single group in the nation." In northern Arizona, Indians, particularly the Navajos, accounted for a large share of the voters, and Goldwater was a familiar and respected name on most reservations. Although there had always been industry in the state, unions were not so tightly organized and monolithic as in other states.[21]

Whether an Anglo, Indian, or Mexican-American, a recent migrant or a third-generation Phoenician, a small businessman or a union member, a Democrat or a Republican, all Arizonans had a strong streak of individualism and independence, which was good news for Barry Goldwater, who personified both.

Always a strong believer in market research, in 1957 Goldwater approved a series of informal public opinion polls to determine the major concerns of each Arizona community. Voters, it appeared, were nervous about the economic recession—the severe unemployment and a sharp slump in sales across the nation, although less so in Arizona. Citizens were also displeased by the Sherman Adams and Bernard Goldfine scandals that had tainted the Eisenhower administration. Drawing upon this information, Goldwater targeted three groups: union members, whom he hoped to separate from the shop stewards and union hierarchy; nominal Democrats capable of independent thinking and action; and every registered Republican.

Goldwater did not have one 1952 advantage; McFarland, no longer overconfident, had hired specialists to work on all aspects of his campaign. The expertise was apparent in the McFarland television commercials, which were handsomely filmed and crisply written. In contrast, the initial Goldwater TV commercials were amateurish, made too hurriedly upon Goldwater's belated return from Washington. The poor commercials had one positive result: Goldwater supporters resolved to do all they could to make up for any lost political ground.

Shadegg dictated a campaign timetable based on his belief that the voters who decided an election—those who did not belong to a political party or who did not have any firm political convictions—did not begin to make up their minds about whom to vote for until three or four weeks before election day. Because they rarely attended political rallies or read newspaper accounts of the campaign, they had to be reached by a wide variety of advertising techniques. In Arizona, the state of long distances and highways, one of the most effective was the billboard.

In December 1957, the Goldwater organization rented all the billboards in Arizona; the entire population was sure to see the Goldwater message sometime during the campaign. And in May 1958, Goldwater's advertising company began to buy half-hour TV segments that would appear on every channel in the state. Some in the Goldwater organization objected to the simulcasts, suggested by advertising expert Ivan Shun, on the ground that they might antagonize viewers who would be unable to watch their favorite program. But as Shadegg said later, the simulcasts "proved to be the most effective advertising of the entire campaign."[22]

The Goldwater half-hours were action-packed, filled with film clips of the senator's accomplishments. The first TV program showed less than ten minutes of Goldwater on camera. The rest of the time was given to excerpts from the filmed proceedings of the McClellan Rackets Committee, featuring angry, emotional testimony by Hoffa, Reuther, and others in the form of a network documentary program. Goldwater was the TV anchorman, commenting on the proceedings.[23]

Another television program dealt with a key campaign issue: Goldwater's proposals to provide the union member with statutory protection, including accountability for the spending of union dues; secret votes for strikes; the right of a union member to express his opinion without reprisal; and the elimination of "telephone booth" meetings, where policy decisions were made against the majority will of the members. Following this simulcast, more than one hundred union members visited a Goldwater headquarters outside Phoenix to let him know that "for the first time, they understood what he had been talking about."[24]

What Goldwater had been talking about—the central issue of the campaign—was that organized labor had become too powerful in American politics through the use of union dues, and it was time for reform. Since union leaders violently disagreed, they were trying to shut him up by unseating him. As he put it, the question "is whether a United States senator must . . . accede to their every demand."[25]

One reporter estimated that organized labor might be spending as much as $500,000 in cash, time, and services to unseat Goldwater. Some rather unusual outsiders, like Al Green, a COPE organizer from California with a police record for criminal violence, were actively working against him.

The most bizarre attempt to influence the election was the "Joe Stalin cartoon." During the noon hour on Friday, October 31, four days before the election, an unidentified man distributed hundreds of handbills in the shopping areas of Phoenix. A little before 2 P.M. the first handbill was brought to Goldwater headquarters. It was a drawing of a smiling Joseph Stalin, the late Soviet dictator, smoking his pipe and giving a knowing wink. Just above and to the right of Stalin were the words: "Why not vote for Goldwater?" A caption below the drawing read: "GOLDWATER fully endorsed by Pulliamism and lauded by Mine-Mill-Smelter Union which was expelled from organized labor for Communist domination. Politics makes strange bedfellows!" There was no authority line as required by federal law.

The flyer made little sense: Goldwater could be accused of many things but being soft on communism was not one of them. The Mine,

Mill and Smelter Workers Union moreover had long since purged itself of its communist elements. And rather than "lauding" Goldwater, the union had formally endorsed McFarland.

Who could have distributed so provocative a piece of political literature in the closing days of a hard-fought campaign whose outcome was still in doubt? (After trailing in the beginning, Goldwater had pulled even with McFarland, and momentum now favored him.) The Goldwater people knew they were not responsible, and McFarland was certainly too careful a campaigner to sponsor a "dirty trick" that could boomerang if he were exposed as its author.

Each side quickly moved to take advantage of the Stalin cartoon. The next morning, Saturday, Democrats in Washington announced that James H. Duffy, a majority staff member of Senator Theodore Green's Select Committee on Privileges and Elections, was already en route to Arizona to investigate the distribution of the handbill. Curious about the rapid reaction, the Goldwater office contacted the minority counsel of the Select Committee who revealed that Duffy had planned to leave for Arizona on the Thursday *before* the first handbill appeared in Phoenix on Friday. Did Duffy, and other Democrats, have some advance knowledge of the leaflet? As it turned out, some handbills had been distributed in Yuma on Wednesday, and Governor McFarland, without informing his opponent, had requested a formal senatorial inquiry.

Goldwater headquarters got going. Late Friday afternoon, before Duffy arrived, it mailed copies of the Stalin handbill with a cover letter to officials of the Mine, Mill and Smelters Workers Union; handcarried copies to the *Arizona Republic* and the wire services in Phoenix; and mailed about thirty other leaflets along with a statement condemning the cartoon to the senator's Arizona newspaper list.

On Monday morning, November 3, the day before the voting, Duffy released a statement to the news media stating that while he had found no evidence of either McFarland or Goldwater having "anything to do with the leaflets . . . Stephen Shadegg, campaign manager for Sen. Goldwater, has admitted that he received 400 or 500 copies of the leaflets which he sent to everyone on the senator's mailing list. This is the only evidence of a large-scale distribution of the leaflets that I have discovered."[26] McFarland supporters immediately went on television and radio with Duffy's statement and suggested that Goldwater campaigners had manufactured and distributed the Stalin pamphlet in an attempt to smear McFarland by reverse inference.

The polls would open in exactly eighteen hours. Goldwater was poised to gain a remarkable victory. "Would all this now be swept away," Shadegg later recalled asking, "in a moment of last minute hysteria?"

Taking the offensive, Goldwater appeared on statewide television Monday night and told the people of Arizona what he insisted was the truth about the Stalin cartoon. Why had Duffy, he asked, purchased his airline ticket before anyone in Phoenix even knew about the existence of the cartoon? What kind of inquiry had Duffy conducted during his two brief days in Phoenix? How could he accuse Steve Shadegg of "large-scale distribution" of the cartoon when copies had been mailed to only about thirty newspaper editors around the state?

Warming up, Goldwater fired off a round of pointed questions: "Why didn't Duffy question me? Why didn't he question the people who found the handbill in the first place? And where is Duffy now? . . . I'm here. Shadegg is here. Where is Duffy?" Now angry, Goldwater charged that the smear and subsequent investigation had "been planned for a long time, deliberately planned, by those outside forces who have been here since long before the beginning of this election. The union bosses have to get Goldwater, and this is their last desperate attempt."[27]

It was riveting television seen simultaneously on all of the Phoenix and Tucson stations. That Duffy had not tried to conduct either a thorough or an impartial inquiry was confirmed when Shadegg and Dean Burch cornered the Democrat at his motel after midnight. When they pressed Duffy, he exploded, "Hell, Burch, you know what this is all about. You're a Republican, I'm a Democrat. I came out here to do a job and I did it." Later, Duffy readily admitted to a newspaper reporter that "of course I'm a Democrat, and I hope McFarland is elected."[28]

THREE MONTHS LATER, Frank Goldberg, a former official of the International Association of Machinists (IAM) and a county Democratic committeeman, and Earl N. Anderson, Grand Lodge representative of the Machinists Union, with headquarters in Los Angeles, and former Arizona state chairman of the Machinists Nonpartisan Political

League, publicly admitted personal and sole responsibility for the leaflets.

They claimed that neither McFarland nor Shadegg nor the IAM nor COPE had had anything to do with the Stalin cartoon. They had arranged to have fifty thousand copies printed in a union shop in Santa Monica, California, but deliberately omitted the union label because they did not want to inject California into an Arizona election. Goldberg admitted that an Arizona Democratic leader had asked them to put the blame for the leaflets on Shadegg, but they had refused. The leaflets were not aimed at Senator Goldwater, they explained, but at the "unwanted influence" of the Pulliam newspapers in Arizona politics. This did not of course explain the reference to the Mine, Mill and Smelter Workers Union. Although they had worked in many political campaigns, Goldberg and Anderson insisted they did not know that distributing literature without an authority line was illegal.

In June of 1960, both were found guilty of distributing unidentified campaign material and of transporting the cartoon interstate. They were fined $1,000.

The Stalin cartoon was not an isolated incident. According to Goldwater, campaign telephones were tapped, his campaign office was burglarized, his life was threatened, and an attempt was apparently made to sabotage his airplane. He laid the machinations—several of which were repeated in 1964—at the door of organized labor. Ironically, COPE's all-out efforts to defeat him not only failed but attracted the attention of the national media and "did as much as anything else to make me a national figure."[29]

Although the Joe Stalin cartoon captured the Arizona media's and the public's interest in the last few days of the campaign, the Goldwater-McFarland race was determined by less sensational matters. Goldwater spent $202,717, five times his 1952 figures; McFarland raised only $125,951, as against $24,455 six years earlier. Once again, Harry Rosenzweig was Goldwater's very efficient finance chairman, coaxing money far and wide, from such well-known personalities as Hollywood producer Cecil B. DeMille ($1,000) and Time-Life's Henry Luce ($500).

The Arizona Republican party had become a significant popular force ever since Howard Pyle's seemingly quixotic gubernatorial campaign in 1950. Women volunteers and Young Republicans filled Goldwater headquarters around the state, attracted by the senator's conservative convictions and personal charisma. McFarland was left to depend upon old cronies, state employees, and COPE professionals.

As he had in 1950 for Pyle and in 1952 for himself, Goldwater campaigned eighteen hours a day, visiting every corner of the state in a leased twin-engine Beech Bonanza with his old friend, Ruth Reinhold, at the controls.

On one typical day, he began by speaking in Tucson, 120 miles south of Phoenix, then flew to Nogales on the Arizona-Mexico border, and wound up in Kingman, an hour from Lake Mead and the Nevada border. Night after night, he was on television and radio, campaigning the only way he knew how: "Meet the people, tell them how you stand, answer their questions directly. They may not like what you say, but they'll respect you for it. That's what Americans want, somebody that speaks up."[30]

That was Barry Goldwater, straightforward and stubborn, a man who would not change his style of campaigning or his beliefs for any man or any office.

GOLDWATER ALWAYS tried to keep campaign issues simple. In 1952, he had run against Harry Truman and the New Deal and narrowly won with the help of Eisenhower. In 1958, he ran against the political power of organized labor and corrupt union bosses. McFarland tried to engage Goldwater in a debate about the Eisenhower recession and his legislative record, but to no avail. The Senate Labor Rackets hearings, the stormy confrontations between Reuther and Goldwater, and COPE's vow to defeat Goldwater turned the senatorial campaign into an epic battle between Barry Goldwater as David and organized labor as Goliath.

IN THE END, Goldwater carried eleven of fourteen counties, including Maricopa and Pima, the two largest in the state: Graham, dominated by Mormons, and Navajo, encompassing the giant Navajo reservation, whose people remembered the senator's many acts of friendship through the years. The final tally was Goldwater, 164,593; McFarland, 129,030—a decisive 56–44 percent victory, making him one of the few prominent Republicans, along with Governor Nelson Rockefeller of New York, to win reelection that day.

The next morning, Rosenzweig and several other exuberant friends dropped by the Goldwater home to celebrate. "Where the hell is Barry?" yelled Rosenzweig.

"He's in the swimming pool," Peggy Goldwater said calmly. The friends went outside, but no senator.

"He's not here, Peggy," Rosenzweig shouted.

"He's at the bottom of the pool," answered an unconcerned Peggy.

They peered down and there, stretched out on the bottom of the pool, lay U.S. Senator Barry Morris Goldwater, a weight belt across his stomach and a snorkel tube sticking up an inch above the water. Goldwater waved at his old friend. "Come on up," Rosenzweig yelled. Goldwater shook his head from his watery seclusion.

Rosenzweig went inside and asked Peggy, "This, I'm sure, is a silly question. But what's he doing on the bottom of the pool?"

"He can't hear the telephone there and he needs to rest."

Goldwater had the knack of keeping victory, and defeat, in perspective.[31]

HIS STUNNING reelection in a tough year for Republicans and his willingness to outrage even Eisenhower over deviations from conservative principle had made Goldwater, two months before his fiftieth birthday, the leading conservative political leader in America. Looking ahead to 1960 and the Republican National Convention, some conservatives pondered whether they should try to challenge the almost certain nominee, Vice President Nixon, with a true conservative.

BACK IN WASHINGTON, D.C., Goldwater was upset. His colleagues seemed bent on passing what he was convinced was a bad piece of legislation—the so-called Kennedy-Ervin antiracketeering bill, named after John Kennedy of Massachusetts and Sam Ervin of North Carolina.

He had strongly attacked a similar bill the year before, arguing that what was needed was legislation to cure "a shocking series of actions on the part of some of the labor leaders of this country . . ." whereas Kennedy had produced only a "feeble sham of a bill." He went on to mock Kennedy, whose book, *Profiles in Courage,* had become a bestseller: "I hope more profiles in courage develop as we attempt to make of this weakling the strong, workable, meaningful legislation the people of the United States are demanding."[32]

The previous year the Senate had passed the Kennedy bill, but the House of Representatives had rejected it. Now it had been resurrected with the co-sponsorship of Ervin, a key Southern senator.

Although he knew he was part of a very small minority, once again Goldwater spoke out. The measure, he said, was "loaded with misleading phrases and gimmicks and . . . leads you to believe there's something underneath when in fact there isn't." He declared that it would "never do the job" of ending union corruption. Kennedy sharply replied, "It should be clear by now that our purpose is to curb labor racketeering and that Senator Goldwater's purpose is to weaken labor at the bargaining table."

Goldwater offered eighteen amendments to the Kennedy-Ervin bill, but all of them were defeated. As his frustration increased so did the sharpness of his rhetoric. In terms of its effect "on the evil conditions it professes to cure," he said, the bill "is like a flea bite to a bull elephant."[33]

His efforts to defeat Kennedy-Ervin were prototypical Goldwater. Taft or Arthur Vandenberg, another former giant in the Senate, would have tried to put together a coalition of traditional Republicans and Southern Democrats, but Goldwater had little interest in coalition-building. After seven years in the Senate, he was not yet a member of the Club that quietly ruled the Senate.

Lyndon Johnson or Everett Dirksen would have been busily horse-trading pork for votes. Joe McCarthy could command ideological support from his colleagues, and Hubert Humphrey could win votes by the sheer force of his rhetoric. Barry Goldwater was just one man, one voice, standing up for what he believed in. And one of the things he deeply believed was that sometimes politics was the art of the impossible.

On April 25, 1959, after weeks of debate, the Kennedy-Ervin legislation came to a vote. Goldwater was the only senator to vote "nay"; the other ninety-five members present voted "aye." The following Monday, he was summoned to the White House for an early morning meeting with Eisenhower, who wanted to know why he had voted against a measure that was badly needed to correct the abuses of organized labor. Did he think, the president asked sarcastically, that everybody in the Senate was out of step but him?

"Mr. President," replied Goldwater bluntly, "this bill is a sham and a farce. Have you read the bill?" Ike said that he did not have time to read every bill before Congress but that his staff had told him it was good and apparently ninety-five Senators thought so too. Goldwater did not retreat an inch; he told the president that either he had been deliberately deceived or his staff was "too damn dumb" to understand English.

When Ike's ears began to turn red, Goldwater knew he was in trouble and had to speak quickly. "Mr. President," he said, "please listen to me for just a minute." He proceeded to list his objections: the bill would not prevent "blackmail picketing" or secondary boycotts or "union bosses from looting union treasuries." And the bill ignored the fundamental right of union members to have a strong voice in the affairs of their union's operations.

"It's a bad bill, Mr. President, and that's why I voted against it."

The president had been listening closely and now he grinned. "Thank you, Barry, you've given me a lot to think about, and I'm going to think about it."[34]

Ike was as good as his word and within a week ordered a new team to make a study of the Kennedy-Ervin bill. Three months later, the president went on national television to catalogue all the deficiencies of Kennedy-Ervin and called on Congress to pass truly effective labor reform legislation. On September 3, 1959, the Senate reversed itself and by a vote of 95–2 passed the Landrum-Griffin labor reform bill, casting aside the Kennedy-Ervin measure.

Goldwater was not totally satisfied with the new bill because it did not go to the heart of the union monopoly problem, but he voted for it, knowing there was no hope of getting a stronger bill out of Congress. He later said that "if I had to select the vote I regarded as the most important of my Senate career, it would be the one I cast [against] the Kennedy-Ervin 'Labor Reform' bill."[35] He had proven once again that one man, standing up for principle, can make a difference.

His fellow Republicans in the Senate thought that he could make a difference as chairman of their campaign committee, the post he had held from 1955–1956. He knew that they were impressed by his decisive win in a year when many good Republicans went down to defeat, but he also understood that they wanted him because he could raise lots of money for their campaigns in 1960. He, however, was not at all sure he wanted the responsibility. "It's a heavy job, and I would like to coast," he said, "and get caught up with my other duties."[36]

But when Jake Javits of New York, a card-carrying member of the Eastern liberal establishment, objected to Goldwater's becoming chairman because it would "alienate" liberals in the party, Goldwater got mad. He had campaigned for Republicans of every philosophical stripe before, and no one had ever questioned his loyalty to the party. He saw Javits's opposition, correctly, as one more manifestation of liberal hostility to the growing power of conservatism. Abandoning his ambivalence, he fought for the post and was easily elected.

Other Washington insiders were impressed by Goldwater's reelection and decided he was worth cultivating, people like Bill Baroody of the American Enterprise Institute. Baroody had met Goldwater through Jay Hall and was already supplying him with speeches written by his roster of conservative academics. But now Baroody began inviting Goldwater to his home for small dinners and bringing him into contact with leading policy analysts like economists Milton Friedman and Paul W. McCracken, who would later serve as chairman of the Council of Economic Advisers under President Nixon. Michael Baroody recalls his father saying, "This guy is going to be the president some day." Goldwater repaid Baroody for his intellectual help by raising money for AEI, introducing him to wealthy conservatives, such as J. Howard Pew of the Sun Oil Company.[37]

One other significant political event in 1959 alerted political observers to the fact that Barry Goldwater was now a major figure in national Republican politics.

In November, Goldwater and Governor Nelson Rockefeller of New York, an unannounced but active candidate for the presidential nomination, appeared before the Western Republican Conference in Los Angeles. No greater contrast between politicians and philosophies could have been offered: Rockefeller, the quintessential Eastern liberal, supporter of much of the New Deal and the Fair Deal, a glad-handing multimillionaire who believed that the best "approach to any problem was to spend more money"; Goldwater, the archetypical Western conservative, opponent of the welfare state whether proposed by FDR, Harry Truman, or Dwight D. Eisenhower, a strong, straight-talking man who believed with Edmund Burke that "we can't make heaven on earth."

Rockefeller went first, and the partisan audience responded politely to his call for a modern Republican approach to the nation's problems. When Goldwater was introduced, the crowd clapped loudly, and it became more and more enthusiastic as he presented the case for modern American conservatism.

"For the past twenty-five years," Goldwater said, "the apostles of the welfare state, some Republican, some Democrat, have been transforming that stern old gentleman with the top hat, the cutaway coat, the red, white, and blue trousers, from a symbol of dignity and freedom and justice for all men, into a national wet nurse, dispensing a cockeyed kind of patent medicine labeled 'something for nothing,' passing out soothing syrup and rattles and pacifiers in return for grateful votes on election day."

The political rhetoric would have delighted Morris Goldwater, and it set the Western Republicans to cheering. Goldwater went on to note that John Kennedy, busily campaigning for the 1960 Democratic presidential nomination, had recently said, "Americans have gone soft," and commented, "These people, like the overindulgent guardians who spend the child's inheritance catering to adolescent whims and desires, are now naively amazed at what their overindulgence has produced."

The crowd rocked and roared and cheered. Goldwater then described his kind of Republican party, a party committed to a free state, limited central power, a reduction in bureaucracy, and a balanced budget.[38]

When Goldwater finished, he received a standing ovation, prompting Earl Mazo, the shrewd political reporter for the *New York Herald Tribune*, to remark to a friend that Goldwater had just challenged Rockefeller for his party's presidential nomination.[39]

But Goldwater had come to California to campaign for an idea, not an office. A realist, he knew that Vice President Nixon was almost certain to be the nominee, and running for president was the last thing on his mind.

But the possibility of a Barry Goldwater candidacy was very much on the minds of a group of prominent conservatives who were not happy with the prospect of a President Nixon and were terrified by the possibility of a President Rockefeller.

PART II

Conscience

6

The Conscience of a Conservative

THE 1958 ELECTIONS were a disaster for the Republican party: it lost twelve seats in the Senate, forty-eight seats in the House of Representatives, and thirteen of twenty-one gubernatorial contests. William Knowland, the Senate Republican leader, ran for governor of California and was defeated. John Bricker, a Senate pillar since 1946, failed to win reelection. For the first time in 106 years, a Democrat represented Vermont in the House. Nixon summed it up: "It was the worst defeat in history ever suffered by a party having control of the White House."[1]

The prospects for a Republican presidential victory two years hence ranged from difficult to impossible.

Three victors attracted national interest and speculation: Senator John F. Kennedy of Massachusetts, Governor Nelson Rockefeller of New York, and Senator Barry Goldwater of Arizona. It was clear that these three men, plus Vice President Nixon, would dominate 1960s presidential politics. Only one was acceptable to conservative Republicans, and they resolved to act. In May 1959, Clarence Manion, former dean of the Notre Dame Law School, moderator of the popular weekly radio program, "The Manion Forum," and one of the most influential

105

conservatives in the country, and Hubbard Russell, an old California friend of the senator's, called on Goldwater in his Washington office to discuss the formation of a national Goldwater for President organization. According to a confidential memorandum that he wrote after the meeting, Manion argued that the nomination of either Nixon or Rockefeller would not only lead to defeat in 1960 but "shatter the last chance of survival of the Republican party." Goldwater, and only Goldwater, was acceptable to conservatives.

The senator repeated his public position: he supported Nixon over Rockefeller but was disappointed with the vice president's recent endorsement of the World Court. His visitors sensed that Goldwater was worried about what Nixon might "say or do next." Manion and Russell pressed on. Knowing of Goldwater's passionate commitment to his party, they emphasized that not only could neither Nixon nor Rockefeller win in 1960, but with either of them at the head of the ticket, the Republican party would be "done" and "the country's last chance dissipated." Goldwater agreed—only conservatives could generate enough Republican enthusiasm to win, and then acknowledged that "if anyone should say that he would not be willing and pleased to accept the presidential nomination, he would not be telling the truth."

Goldwater revealed that he had also been approached about the presidency by Southerners, including Democratic Senator Strom Thurmond of South Carolina, who had run as a third party Dixiecrat against Truman in 1948. But he said that he had to be honest, with himself as well as with those who wanted him to run. He had drawbacks, like his Jewish name. And he truly felt that he was unqualified for the job because of his meager education. Manion later wrote in the margin of his memo: "This may be asset." He did not mention whether he reminded Goldwater that Truman had had even less education.

They then asked Goldwater if he had any objection to their plan. He "seemed to be more or less pleased and said, of course, he could not prevent us from going forward." They specifically asked him not to block them, and "he assured us that he would not at any time repudiate the move."[2]

The two conservatives left Goldwater's office elated: the plan to nominate a real conservative as the Republican party's presidential nominee in 1960 had taken a giant step forward.

Manion immediately began contacting prominent conservatives, asking them to join a Committee of One Hundred to draft Barry Goldwater for the Republican nomination for president. As he put it in one letter, "The Goldwater movement will establish a position to the right of 'the middle of the road' around which conservative popular sentiment throughout the country can rally with enthusiasm. The middle of the road is all right in theory but after six years of Eisenhower and Nixon, the road itself is now running along the left field fence and the expression is a complete misnomer."[3] In another letter, Manion declared, "I honestly believe that [Goldwater's] nomination for president by the Republican party is the *one* thing that will prevent the complete disintegration of that party once and for all in the 1960 election."[4]

Such enthusiasm was flattering but potentially embarrassing to Goldwater, who was, after all, chairman of the Senate Republican Campaign Committee. He did not want to encourage any effort that would divide the party. He met with Frank Cullen Brophy, a longtime personal friend and political adviser, who wrote Clarence Manion, summarizing their discussion. First, Brophy said, there was "a good possibility" that the platforms and candidates that would emerge from the conventions would be "unacceptable."

Second, under such circumstances, "the senator would be willing to spearhead whatever movement seems appropriate and is agreed upon by the interested parties at that time." Although Brophy did not elaborate, he meant that any "movement" would have to be within, not outside, the Republican party, consistent with Goldwater's loyalty to the GOP.

Third, "the senator does not want his name linked with this or any similar movement at this time" because then his usefulness in the Republican party "would be greatly curtailed." Brophy also pointed out that going public at that moment would give "the hatchet men a full year to chop him down before the conventions meet." Given the "destructive powers" of those who dominated both parties, he said, "a movement of this sort must proceed with utmost caution."

The memory of what had happened to Taft in 1952 was still fresh in his mind, as in that of all conservatives. Brophy was saying that Goldwater was willing to consider going presidential, but that the timing of his entry was crucial. As he put it, "the dark horse should be kept as dark as possible until he is ready to start."

The contrast between then and now, when a presidential aspirant, with access to the mass media and funding outside the Republican party, often goes public years before the national convention, shows how dramatically American politics has changed. Brophy was also reflecting the inherent doubts in Goldwater's mind as to whether he should even be thinking about running for president. Then, and in 1964, Goldwater rationalized a presidential candidacy by saying that even in failure it could advance conservative ideas and principles.

Fourth, Brophy agreed with Manion that a "skeleton organization" must be built but without linking Goldwater's name to it. He went so far as to include an organization plan.

Fifth, he reported that the senator would continue to "expound the political, social, and economic philosophies that have become identified with his name," particularly in the South "where such a man should acquire a substantial following if he were to appear as a candidate at the right time." Brophy said he agreed with Goldwater's low-key approach but regarded him "as a very definite potential candidate later on."

And finally, that "those of us who are interested in such a movement will have to use patience and tact, while at the same time we must carry on an organizational job of no small proportions."[5]

One significant aspect of the letter was the constant reference to a "movement" rather than the Republican party. Brophy and Manion represented a philosophical movement as much as they did a political party. Particularly for Manion, the Republican party was a means, not an end, to the goal of a more conservative America. He and like-minded conservatives were willing to work with men and women of any party and any geographical region to attain that goal.

But Goldwater was a politician, not a philosopher. He had made the Republican party a real political force in Arizona and had campaigned for Republican candidates of all persuasions across the country. He wanted America to be more conservative, but he believed that the Republican party was the best vehicle to achieve that end.

Manion telephoned Brophy to reassure him: he and his colleagues would never do anything to embarrass Goldwater, and they would not go public with any presidential campaign without the senator's consent. He added that he already had the names of over fifty-five individuals, "men of considerable importance as well as financial worth who are very enthusiastic about supporting [Goldwater] when and if the opportunity arises."

Brophy said that, for their part, they were considering asking people in Alaska, Alabama, and Arizona about placing Goldwater's name "in nomination at the Republican convention." They had picked Alaska because it would be represented at a national convention for the first time, Arizona because it was Goldwater's home state, and Alabama because it stood for "states' rights and traditional America."

In the course of their conversation, Manion suggested something that Brophy thought was "a fine idea, and has great possibilities."

"I hope you agree," Brophy wrote Goldwater and included a copy of his letter to Brent Bozell:

June 18th, 1959

Dear Brent:

I was talking on the phone with Clarence Manion this morning and he spoke of the possibility of having Barry do a pamphlet entitled "What Americanism Means To Me." As you know, Barry writes much of his own stuff and I presume would do it all if he had the time. As a rule, I think it is very effective. In this instance, he might need some help, since I think a good deal of thought and time would be required to get this just right. I am sending a copy of this letter to Barry, since I am writing it with the idea that perhaps you and he can collaborate on the effort.

Clarence Manion seemed to think that many corporations which are not permitted to make political donations, could, nevertheless, legally buy large quantities of this pamphlet and see that they are widely disseminated. If the job is well done and properly handled, I think this would be a most profitable effort for Senator Goldwater to make at this time. This will advance his cause, keep his name in the minds of hundreds of thousands of people, and yet will not put him in the position of being a contender for the presidential nomination at this time.

With best wishes,

Sincerely,

Frank Brophy[6]

Manion's idea of a "pamphlet" about "Americanism," perceived by
him and Goldwater advisers like Brophy as a way of advancing the
senator's presidential prospects in 1960, would become the most
widely read political book of the twentieth century, *The Conscience of
a Conservative*, rivaled in American political history only, perhaps, by
Thomas Paine's *Common Sense*. The suggestion that Brent Bozell act
as a collaborator was logical for he had already written speeches for
Goldwater. And his conservative credentials were impeccable.

Bozell was a founding and senior editor of *National Review* and
brother-of-law of Bill Buckley, whom he met at Yale where he had
converted to Roman Catholicism and anticommunism. He was not only
a brilliant writer and original thinker (some mutual friends said that he
had a better mind than his brother-in-law) but a political activist. In the
fall of 1958, he had run, unsuccessfully, as a Republican for a seat in the
Maryland Assembly (that state's lower house). The following spring
when it was announced that Nikita Khrushchev had accepted
Eisenhower's invitation to come to the United States, Bozell spear-
headed the conservative campaign to make Khrushchev's visit as unpleasant as possible for the Soviet dictator and the American president.
His deep involvement in the anti-Khrushchev effort along with his
intrinsic procrastination when writing would create problems, but at
the moment the energetic Manion included Bozell in his ambitious
plans for 1960.

In late June, Manion informed Frank R. Seaver, a prominent California conservative, that the Committee of One Hundred already had over
sixty "most important" members, including Herbert Kohler of Wisconsin, Colonel Archibald Roosevelt of New York, businessman Fred C.
Koch of Kansas, and former Ambassador Spruille Braden. And he
revealed that Roger Milliken, the prominent Spartanburg industrialist,
was certain that "the South Carolina delegation will be for Goldwater
and that Goldwater can expect *at least* one hundred Southern delegates
by convention time."

Why were so many Southerners for Goldwater? Manion was explicit: "Nixon is loathed in the South because of his affiliation with the
NAACP [National Association for the Advancement of Colored Peo-
ple]," whereas Goldwater was liked for his "forthright advocacy of
constitutional states' rights." Either Manion was not aware of Goldwater's long affiliation with the NAACP and other civil rights organizations in Arizona, or he chose to emphasize the senator's support of

states' rights, leaving the problem of reconciliation for another day. He was candid about his political objective: "If it is impressively launched, the Goldwater movement will be an appeal to the millions of frustrated conservatives who have been driven into defeatism or apathy since 1952."[7]

This one sentence contained several of the beliefs that would sustain conservatives for the next two decades: (1) there was a viable conservative movement in America; (2) it needed a nationally known articulate leader to be effective; (3) there was a sizable bloc of conservatives (more than forty million eligible voters stayed away from the polls in 1956) who needed only the right appeal to vote for and elect a conservative president.

Although Manion did his best to keep his plans confidential, *Human Events* led off its July 1, 1959, issue with an item entitled, "Goldwater to the Fore," which reported that various Republican professionals were giving serious thoughts to a Goldwater candidacy. The arguments for Goldwater included his "smashing" victory the previous fall, his stand on organized labor, and his Westerner heritage—he carried "no taint of New York or Tom Dewey." GOP pros were impressed, the weekly conservative newsletter stated, with Goldwater's warm, infectious personality and his ability to arouse enthusiasm among average citizens. Conceding that the nomination of a candidate from a small state with a limited number of delegates was unprecedented, *Human Events* pointed out that in a time of "political flux and the crumbling of party traditions" precedents could well be broken.[8]

Although these factors did not carry the day, nor the nomination in 1960, they had a significant impact on Goldwater's winning the presidential nomination in 1964.

One of the early members of the Committee of One Hundred, and a good friend of Manion's, was Robert Welch, who, although he had ignored Goldwater's blunt advice not to publish *The Politician*, much preferred the senator to either Nixon or Rockefeller as the standard-bearer of the Republican party. Since Barry Goldwater "is the only prospective candidate on the national scene whom I could support with confidence and enthusiasm," Welch wrote William J. Grede, "I intend to do so to the best of my small ability." A visible show of strong conservative support for Goldwater, he argued, would have a "salutary" effect, even if he were not nominated; and it would increase his influence on the conduct of the campaign and on affairs after the election.[9]

Although Welch undoubtedly hurt American conservatism with his conspiratorial theories and intemperate rhetoric, his endorsement of the Draft Goldwater effort helped Manion to expand the Committee of One Hundred and put in place a national structure to distribute what was now described as "a one-hundred-page book" by Goldwater on Americanism. In a note to another committee member, dated July 17, Manion reported that Bozell was "at work with Goldwater preparing the senator's book . . . which will appear at the year's end."[10] But over the coming months, he learned that dealing with authors was like dealing with home remodelers: it took them at least twice as long to finish their work as they said it would.

Manion had the opposite problem with the Committee of One Hundred, which grew so quickly that he and Bozell found it necessary to meet with a concerned Goldwater in Washington in late July to discuss its future. The committee, they decided, would not be announced until "Barry says the word, but will work like Hell in the meantime."

For his part, Goldwater promised not to endorse anybody for the nomination, using his position as chairman of the Senate Republican Campaign Committee as an excuse. They also agreed that work should proceed on the book, which would serve as "a fine recruiting piece for patriots everywhere."[11]

Soon thereafter, Bozell had a constructive talk with Goldwater about the contents of the book. They agreed to a 50-50 split of the royalties, although neither anticipated there would be much to divide. In a letter to Manion, Bozell foresaw one possible problem: "the way [Goldwater] apparently wants to state his views—a little poetic and corny. But that, most likely, can be worked out." The main obstacle, Bozell told Manion, was not Goldwater but Khrushchev, about whose visit to the United States "I have never felt as strongly as anything in my life." He was trying to get a national committee against the Khrushchev visit "off the ground and operating," and all other obligations would have to be secondary.[12]

Manion, who had lined up a small publishing company (Victor Publishing Company of Shepherdsville, Kentucky) and sent Goldwater $1,000 as an advance against royalties, was understandably worried about an extended delay. In late September, he wrote his old friend, Bill Buckley, about the work of the Committee of One Hundred and the plans to publish a twenty-thousand-word book by Barry Goldwater which for the first time he called *The Conscience of a Conservative* (the title was his, not Bozell's or Goldwater's).[13]

Goldwater, Manion said, had accepted Bozell's outline regarding both domestic and foreign policy. The book would be made available to the committee at cost for resale to corporations in quantity for profit; the net proceeds would be used for further distribution of the book. "Our present problem," he admitted, "is to get the manuscript out of Barry and Brent. The latter, as you know, has been completely absorbed by Mr. Khrushchev." (Buckley was a very visible member of the anti-Khrushchev organization which Bozell had helped to form.) "I hope now that his release is imminent."

Buckley's response, although cordial, was not what Manion had hoped for: he said only that he would "take up what you have to say with Brent," and then added in a postscript: "I doubt there's much money to be made by mass sales of a Goldwater manifesto, recalling the difficulties Taft had in 1952 peddling his foreign policy book."[14] Manion was almost the only person connected with the project, including Goldwater and Bozell, who kept saying that the response to a manifesto would be "considerable."

Why was an "old" conservative like Manion better at gauging the reaction of the conservative movement to Goldwater than a "new" conservative like Buckley? Perhaps because Manion had experienced in a more personal way the bitter defeats of Taft in 1948 and 1952 and knew that people badly wanted a new Bob Taft. Perhaps because he shared more deeply the frustration and disappointment of conservatives about the Eisenhower administration and its modern Republicanism. Perhaps because he saw Goldwater as a true presidential possibility while Buckley and other senior editors of *National Review* (particularly James Burnham, always a strong influence on Buckley) had serious reservations about Goldwater's intellectual capabilities and even his policy positions.

Buckley told Manion that while he admired Goldwater, "it remains true that he has no foreign policy to speak of, and this in itself is a serious deficiency." At first glance, this seems a peculiar statement to make about a senator well known for his insistence that the United States and the West should not simply contain but defeat communism and his unflagging support of a strong national defense.

But recall, this was before the publication of *The Conscience of a*

Conservative and *Why Not Victory?* (in 1962) and before Goldwater had spelled out his views on foreign policy and national security in his newspaper column, speeches, and debates leading up to his 1964 run for the presidency. What Buckley was saying was that he and other *National Review* editors, particularly Burnham, considered Goldwater's foreign policy to be too simplistic for the times. Buckley also engaged in some labyrinthine logic by arguing that since Goldwater was "irrevocably entangled in the Nixon operation," any buildup of Goldwater would contribute to the ascendancy of Nixon—which Buckley emphatically opposed.[15]

Frustrated in his attempt to enlist Buckley's help in spurring on his brother-in-law, Manion urged fellow conservative Hub Russell, *"Keep after Bozell."* Russell passed the buck back; he said he hoped that Manion would "prod Bozell into action." In early December 1959, Manion told Russell that he had talked to Bozell twice by telephone, and "he tells me that he is at work on the manuscript but I haven't seen any copy yet. This is maddening to say the least. Either one of us could have written two books like the one we have in mind while we have been waiting for this one." He dashed off a note to veteran conservative Bonner Fellers, who lived in Washington: "What's the word from Brent Bozell?"[16]

The word was that Bozell was in fact working hard, but unlike his brother-in-law Bill Buckley, who could dash off a sparkling 750-word column in less than an hour, he wrote slowly, with painstaking perfection, chipping away at the manuscript like a sculptor, glad to produce 750 good words in one day. He had read most of Goldwater's speeches and articles and knew how he stood on the issues they had agreed to address: the role of the federal government, states' rights, agriculture, organized labor, taxes, education, welfare, national defense, and communism. He was in frequent telephone contact with Goldwater and every week or so would visit his Capitol Hill office with the draft of a chapter. Goldwater's secretary, Judy Eisenhower, recalls that the senator would scribble his comments on the manuscript or dictate corrections into his Dictaphone, and so it went.

Bozell took approximately six weeks to write *The Conscience of a Conservative*.[17] By late December, he was close to finishing a first draft when Nelson Rockefeller shocked the political world by announcing that he would not be a candidate for the presidency in 1960.

Roger Milliken immediately wrote Manion to reassure him that

South Carolina was "still very much of a mind to push hard for Barry Goldwater" and asked him "to give some thought as to how you think this might best be handled." Greg D. Shorey, chairman of the South Carolina Republican party, also wrote Manion, arguing that "nothing can be lost" if support for Goldwater became "more vocal." Indeed, Shorey said, if a man of "Goldwater's stature and philosophy" did not appear on the Republican ticket this year, he predicted either the emergence of a third party movement that would "sap our ordinary strength" or a decision by "the great majority of thinking citizens" not to "participate or even vote." Nixon, now the all but certain Republican presidential nominee, "still is not trusted by the South." Shorey added that he hoped to attend a Chicago meeting of the Committee of One Hundred planned for late January.[18]

As it happened, neither Shorey nor Milliken was able to attend the January 23, 1960, meeting of the Goldwater committee, held at the Union League Club in downtown Chicago (the same city where Clif White and his band of youngish Republicans would hold their first Draft Goldwater meeting almost two years later). Manion chaired the all-day meeting of twenty-nine prominent conservatives, the majority of whom were highly successful, self-made businessmen who believed in God, country, and free enterprise, although not necessarily in that order. One attendee, Joseph Meek of Chicago, had run for the U.S. Senate from Illinois in 1954, but he was an exception.

Also in attendance was Brent Bozell, who had good reason to be smiling. He had at last finished *The Conscience of a Conservative* and had flown to Phoenix over the holidays to show the manuscript to Goldwater. The senator read quickly the less than two hundred pages, pausing here and there, and then handed it back to Bozell, saying, "Looks fine to me. Let's go with it."[19]

With these few words, Goldwater approved a manuscript that would establish him as not just the leader but the *conscience* of a political movement. Perhaps if he had known how irrevocably the book would change his life, how heavy a responsibility it would impose on him, how people would henceforth look to him to make judgments about everything under the political sun from abortion to Zaire, he might have spent a little more time poring over its contents and its title. But, then, being Barry Goldwater, he probably would not have. However seriously other people took it, even referring to it as their Bible, to him

The Conscience of a Conservative was an "unpretentious introduction to conservative thought, not a dissertation."[20]

Goldwater and Bozell sat and talked for a while. They were incongruous collaborators: the calm, easy-going Westerner and the passionate, high-strung Midwesterner; the college dropout and the Yale law graduate; the Jewish Episcopalian and the Roman Catholic convert; the principled politician and the activist intellectual. But they shared a Jeffersonian conviction that that government is best which governs least; they looked to the Constitution as their political North Star; and they were absolutely convinced that communism was a clear and present danger and evil. They were apostles of conservatism, a new political movement in America, and what they produced was touched with a fire common to all followers of a new movement, religious or political. And most definitely, in the year 1960, American conservatism was a political crusade.

There was no mention of Brent Bozell's essential role in the first or many succeeding editions of *The Conscience of a Conservative.* But in his next book, *Why Not Victory?* (based in large part on a foreign policy speech written by Bozell), Goldwater talked openly about the many people who had "contributed to my thinking, writing, and speaking." He began with his uncle Morris and ended with Gerhart Niemeyer of Notre Dame University. Among the eighteen people he mentioned was Bozell, "who was the guiding hand of my last book," i.e., *The Conscience of a Conservative.* In his 1979 memoirs, Goldwater minimized Bozell's contribution, writing, "I drew on my earlier speeches for much of the content of [*Conscience*] and put it together with the help of L. Brent Bozell and others." He was more forthcoming in his 1988 autobiography, stating that *The Conscience of a Conservative* "was adapted by Brent Bozell . . . based on speeches I'd given and his own research."[21]

Following his retirement from the Senate, Goldwater became progressively more open about Bozell's authorship (widely known within the conservative movement for many years), once saying at a Washington meeting, "Hell, I didn't write *The Conscience of a Conservative*— Bozell did."[22]

Manion began the January 23rd meeting in Chicago by reviewing the activities of what he called the Goldwater "Committee of Correspondence" over the past six months. He reported that more than one hundred "resourceful" people, many of them Republican party officials, were cooperating with the committee and opined that "the one hope for regeneration of the Republican party in 1960 would be the nomination of Senator Goldwater for president." But he agreed with Goldwater that any public announcement at this point "would make the Senator look ridiculous and destroy every prospect for the success of the venture."

Manion therefore proposed the following strategy: start the ball rolling by publishing a book by Senator Goldwater, titled *The Conscience of a Conservative*, setting forth his position on "communism, labor bossism, foreign aid, inflationary federal spending, and states' rights." Although the book contained no overt reference to any presidential ambitions, his "forthright approach to these vital issues in a presidential year is bound to cause a sensation."

All committee members would be asked to help get the book widely distributed and favorably reviewed and to persuade prominent people to commend Goldwater for writing it and urge him to become a candidate for the Republican presidential nomination. This combined activity would "stimulate a popular movement for Senator Goldwater," including the organization of Goldwater Clubs. "If the book results in this stimulation of popular sentiment and all goes according to plan," Manion summed up, "Senator Goldwater will then be willing to permit the public announcement of the formation of a National Committee to secure the Republican presidential nomination for him."[23]

As a strategy for capturing the most important political prize in Republican politics, Manion's proposal was exceedingly naive. There was no discussion of how many delegates were needed to nominate (666), whether and how Goldwater might enter any primaries, the relative standings of Nixon, Goldwater, and others in the GOP and among the public. There was no mention of a campaign budget other than the hope that $100,000 might be raised through sales of the book. Compared with Taft's well-organized and well-financed major league effort in 1952 (and 1948), the Manion committee looked like the Canton Bulldogs of the Ohio League. But the plan did make sense for the national promotion of a book.

Clearly speaking for the senator, Hub Russell reported that "at this time Barry does not want to get out and be picked to pieces," revealing Goldwater's understandable caution about challenging the vice president of the United States without adequate backing and resources.

W. W. Wannawaker, Jr., the Republican national committeeman

from South Carolina, and the only party official at the meeting, offered
to commit all thirteen convention delegates to Goldwater when South
Carolina Republicans met at a state convention in late March. Since
some people feared an "early Southern endorsement" and would
prefer that "the movement start in some other part of the country," he
and his colleagues "would do whatever the committee decides."[24]

Robert Welch unsurprisingly thought "we should fight for principles
and not wait for the political climate to develop"—South Carolina
should declare for Goldwater at its state convention. Goldwater, moreover, would assume national prominence, he said, if he were to "take
the lead in the Senate in opposition to the [Eisenhower-Khrushchev]
Summit Conference."

Also speaking for Goldwater, Frank Brophy explained that the senator was "in a difficult position and doesn't want to destroy his position
or the good which he has done." Furthermore, despite all the newspapers reports, Goldwater had not endorsed Nixon, and explained why.

Nixon, Brophy related, had privately told Goldwater that he thought
inviting Khrushchev to visit the United States was a "mistake." When
Goldwater quoted the vice president, Nixon immediately telephoned
him, protesting that Goldwater had misstated his position. Pressed by
Goldwater, Nixon admitted that his remark was not intended for publication. When Goldwater told Nixon to "get off the hook the best way
he could," the vice president responded by telling the press the next
day that Goldwater was virtually a liar.[25] The incident helped solidify
Goldwater's opinion that Nixon was the most devious politician he had
ever met.

Making no reference to his ghostwriting *The Conscience of a Conservative,* Bozell declared that the committee would be useful in both
the short and long term. If it helped Goldwater get only fifty votes at the
Republican Convention in July, "it would be worthwhile for the future
of the country." If Nixon were nominated, as seemed likely, Bozell
hoped that he would lose in November in order that we "build a
conservative organization so that in 1964 the candidates will be Rockefeller and Goldwater." For Bozell and like-minded conservatives, the
Republican party always came second to the movement.

Meek, a former senatorial candidate, agreed with Welch that Goldwater "should establish himself as a man of principle, a leader against
communism, and that favorable public opinion would be aroused by
such a stand," and Goldwater could do that "for the time being without

running for president. Taft did exactly that. He became a symbol." Republicans like Meek clearly saw Goldwater as Taft's political heir.

The committee unanimously adopted a resolution offered by Welch that was part endorsement and part prophecy. It read in part:

> It must be expected that Senator Goldwater will be heavily attacked and even viciously smeared by the "modern" Republicans and by other "liberals," both within and without the Republican party, but we believe that he will gain far more political strength than he will lose. We believe that ... he will even more quickly emerge as the outstanding rallying point, standard bearer, and recognized leader of the tremendous number of disgruntled Republicans, party-less Independents, and despairing Democrats in this country today. Especially can he rapidly take over, and continue to fill a place with the increasing approval and applause of millions of friends of Senator Taft who are still loyal to Senator Taft's memory and principles, the position of leadership once held by Taft— and which position has now been left almost completely vacant.[26]

The enduring pro-Taft sentiment reflected in the resolution, and in much of the Republican party, would be a critical factor in Goldwater's winning the Republican presidential nomination four years later. Meanwhile, all agreed that when South Carolina Republicans met in March, they should instruct their entire delegation to commit to Goldwater at the national convention in Chicago.

Manion closed the meeting by outlining how corporations could buy 100,000 copies of *The Conscience of a Conservative* at approximately $2.00 each, giving the committee a projected profit of "at least $100,000 to start moving the Goldwater campaign for delegates."[27]

The Committee of One Hundred did not make political history by starting a prairie fire that swept across the country and nominated Barry Goldwater in 1960; almost everyone knew that the nominee would be Nixon. But the committee did change history by publishing a book that began as a pamphlet on Americanism and ended as the most popular political primer of modern times.

Before *The Conscience of a Conservative,* Barry Goldwater was an attractive, forthright, often controversial senator from a small Western state, a political comer who might one day become chairman of a major Senate committee, a long-shot vice presidential possibility.

After *The Conscience of a Conservative* appeared, Goldwater became the political heir to Taft and McCarthy, the hope of disgruntled Republicans, partyless Independents, and despairing Democrats, the spokesman of a national political movement destined to change the course of the nation and the world.

By mid-February, Bozell had finished all but the last few pages of his final rewrite of the manuscript that an excited Manion called "sensational. I predict that it will be a real bolt of political lightening." Writing to Roger Milliken, he declared that "if this book doesn't save the Republican party for the conservative cause, then there is little hope for either the cause or the party."

On February 22, an enthusiastic Shadegg wrote Goldwater, who had asked his friend to review it, that "the manuscript . . . is terrific." He admitted that he found himself saying, "I wish I had said that." Goldwater sent Shadegg's letter, which included a few minor suggestions, to Bozell with the rather patronizing comment: "I thought you would like to see what Steve Shadegg thinks of the book, and I am sure it will give you a sense of satisfaction not too often felt by people devoted to the conservative cause."

Bozell, already a veteran editor and writer in his midthirties, knew that he had written a very good book although neither he nor anyone associated with the project, with the possible exception of Manion, suspected that it would become a political classic. In early March, Bozell wrote Manion that Goldwater's interest was "very high" and that he had called several times to ask how the book was "coming along." He suggested that Manion telephone the senator and give him a full report.[28]

WHAT HAD BOZELL wrought? First and foremost, *The Conscience of a Conservative* presented a vision of the nation and the world as it should be, not a compromise with the world as it was.

Second, it was an original work of politics and philosophy, not a rewrite of old Goldwater speeches and remarks. It was, in fact, a remarkable fusion of the three major strains of conservatism of 1960: traditionalism, classical liberalism or libertarianism, and anticommunism.

Third, although it did not always sound precisely like Barry Goldwater, the book was faithful to his stated positions on issues ranging from foreign aid to organized labor to education. In every respect, it reflected his emphasis on freedom and responsibility.

Fourth, *The Conscience of a Conservative* was a book by a conservative for conservatives at a time when conservatives were beginning to realize how much power they had, if not how to use it effectively. The idea that America was fundamentally a conservative nation and that the American people yearned for a return to conservative principles had arrived.

And so Goldwater declared on the very first page of *The Conscience of a Conservative,* but he then proceeded to blame conservatives for failing to demonstrate "the practical relevance of conservative principles to the needs of the day." He would try in this work, he said, to bridge the gap between theory and practice.

He began by dismissing the notion that conservatism was "out of date," arguing that it was like saying that "the Golden Rule or the Ten Commandments or Aristotle's *Politics* are out of date." The conservative approach, he said, "is nothing more or less than an attempt to apply the wisdom and experience and the revealed truths of the past to the problems of today."[29] (Many have tried and failed to offer a more succinct definition of conservatism's role in politics.) Believing that theory must always precede practice, in no hurry to set forth specific solutions for what ailed America, Goldwater described what conservatism was and what it was not.

Unlike the liberal, he said, the conservative believed that man was not only an economic but a spiritual creature. Conservatism therefore "looks upon the enhancement of man's spiritual nature as the primary concern of political philosophy." Indeed, Goldwater stated, the first obligation of a political thinker was "to understand the nature of man."

He then proceeded to list what the conservative had learned about man from the great minds of the past: (1) each person was unique and different from every other human being—therefore, provision had to be made for the development of the different potentialities of each man; (2) the economic and spiritual aspects of man's nature "are inextricably intertwined"—neither aspect can be free unless both are free; (3) man's spiritual and material development cannot be directed by outside forces—"each man," he declared, with all the conviction of his Jeffersonian, libertarian soul, "is responsible for his own development."

Given this view of the nature of man, Goldwater stated, it was understandable that the conservative "looks upon politics as the art of achieving the maximum amount of freedom for individuals that is consistent with the maintenance of social order." But, he said, the delicate balance that ideally exists between freedom and order had long since tipped against freedom "practically everywhere on earth." Even in America, the trend against freedom and in favor of order was "well along and gathering momentum." For the American conservative, therefore, there was no difficulty in "identifying the day's overriding political challenge: it is to preserve and extend freedom."

Goldwater did not qualify his statement, leaving the clear implication (reinforced in the final one-third of his book, entitled "The Soviet Menace") that the American conservative had an obligation to preserve and extend freedom not only in America but around the world.[30]

Freedom was in peril in the United States, he said, because government had been allowed, by leaders and members of both political parties, to become too powerful. In so doing, they had ignored and misinterpreted the single most important document in American government, the Constitution, which was an instrument, above all, "for limiting the functions of government." The result was "a Leviathan, a vast national authority out of touch with the people, and out of their control."

While deeply concerned at the tendency to concentrate power in the hands of a few men, he was convinced that most Americans wanted to reverse the trend. The transition would come, he said, when the people entrusted their affairs to men "who understand that their first duty as public officials is to divest themselves of the power they have been given."

This was a radical and some would say unrealistic statement. Did not every public official enjoy power, seek power, use power? What public official, what politician, would relinquish rather than seek more power? In one of the most famous and eloquent passages of *The Conscience of a Conservative*, Lincolnian in its rhetoric, Goldwater said that the turn toward freedom would come when Americans in hundreds of communities throughout the nation decided to put in office those who pledged to enforce the Constitution and restore the Republic and who proclaimed:

> I have little interest in streamlining government or in making it more efficient, for I mean to reduce its size. I do not undertake to promote welfare, for I propose to extend freedom. My aim is not to pass laws, but to repeal them. It is not to inaugurate new programs, but to cancel old

ones that do violence to the Constitution, or that have failed in their purpose, or that impose on the people an unwarranted financial burden. I will not attempt to discover whether legislation is "needed" before I have first determined whether it is constitutionally permissible. And if I should later be attacked for neglecting my constituents' "interests," I shall reply that I was informed their main interest is liberty and that in that cause I am doing the very best I can.[31]

This was undiluted conservatism, a radical vision of government that aimed to restore the ideas of the Founding Fathers and throw back the welfarist proposals of the New Deal, the Fair Deal, and the still unnamed New Frontier. It was what conservatives believed was still possible in America; it was what liberals believed was hopelessly anachronistic and even dangerous.

Having laid down the philosophical foundation that "the laws of God, and of nature, have no dateline," Goldwater became specific, beginning with states' rights and civil rights. The first was really quite simple: as recognized by the Tenth Amendment, "States' rights means that the states have a right to act or *not* to act, as they see fit, in the areas reserved to them." States' rights recognized the principle that "essentially local problems are best dealt with by the people most directly concerned," problems like slum clearance and school programs. Nothing could advance the cause of freedom more, he stated, than for "state officials throughout the land to assert their rightful claims to lost state power; and for the federal government to withdraw promptly and totally from every jurisdiction which the Constitution reserved to the states."

The concept of civil rights, Goldwater asserted, had been shamelessly misused by people who knew better. Civil rights, he said, had been equated with human rights or natural rights when in fact a "civil right is a right that is asserted and is therefore protected by some valid law." In the field of racial relations, some rights were clearly protected by law and were therefore "civil" rights, such as the right to vote under the Fifteenth Amendment and the "equal protection" clause under the Fourteenth Amendment.

But it was otherwise with education. "Despite the recent holding of the Supreme Court," Goldwater said, referring to *Brown v. Board of Education,* "I am firmly convinced—not only that integrated schools are not required—but that the Constitution does not permit any inter-

ference whatsoever by the federal government in the field of education."[32] He was not impressed by the claim that the Supreme Court's
decision on school integration was "the law of the land" when it was in
fact the Constitution and the laws "made in pursuance thereof" that
are the "supreme law of the land."

If we condoned the practice of substituting our own intentions for
those of the Constitution's framers, he warned, we were endorsing "a
rule of men, not of laws." He therefore supported all efforts by the
states, excluding violence, to preserve their rightful powers over education. It was a brave and principled position, but it persuaded many
blacks, not knowing his many personal actions in Arizona on behalf of
integration and against segregation, that Goldwater was a racist and a
bigot.

Few blacks were aware that in *The Conscience of a Conservative,*
Goldwater also stated that he was in agreement with the Supreme
Court's *objectives* as stated in the *Brown* decision. He believed it was
both wise and just for black children to attend the same schools as
whites and that to deny them this opportunity carried with it "strong
implications of inferiority." But he was not prepared, he said, to impose
his judgment on the people of Mississippi or South Carolina or to tell
them how and when to reach that goal.

In a statement that summed up his libertarian feelings against government interference in all social and cultural areas, he said, "I believe
that the problem of race relations, like all social and cultural problems,
is best handled by the people directly concerned. Social and cultural
change, however desirable, should not be effected by the engines of
national power.... Any other course enthrones tyrants and dooms
freedom."[33]

Goldwater stood fast against intrusion, governmental or nongovern-
mental, into social and cultural issues in 1960, even when the issue was
the integration of public schools, and continued to do so throughout his
career. He did so again in 1980, when the Moral Majority was promoting a social agenda, and once again in 1992, when the issue was the
inclusion of an anti-abortion plank in the Republican platform. In both
of the latter cases he ran counter to many of his conservative allies.

In the next five chapters of the book Goldwater dealt with agriculture, organized labor, taxes and spending, the welfare state, and education. With regard to the first, he pointed out that the teaching of the
Constitution was perfectly clear, i.e., "no power over agriculture was

given to any branch of the national government." Besides, like any other production, farm production was "best controlled by the natural operation of the free market." In short, the only solution to the farm problem was "the prompt and final termination of the farm subsidy program." This was not something the usual politician, let alone presidential candidate, would say, but Barry Goldwater delighted in the unusual, to the mutual joy of supporters and adversaries.

More than any other, the chapter on organized labor hewed to the public record of Barry Goldwater, its language bound by his many pronouncements. He attacked the enormous economic and political power concentrated in the hands of a few union leaders and advocated (1) enactment of state right-to-work laws, but not a national right-to-work law as he had once contemplated; (2) the limitation of contributions to political campaigns by individuals alone—"I see no reason for labor unions—or corporations—to participate in politics"; and (3) the elimination of industrywide bargaining, applying the principle of anti-monopoly to unions as well as corporations.[34]

Next, echoing the proposals of Nobel Laureate Milton Friedman, he declared that "government has a right to claim an equal percentage of each man's wealth, and no more."[35] He described the graduated tax as "a confiscatory tax." The only way to curtail government spending, he said, "is to eliminate the programs on which excess spending is consumed," including social welfare programs, education, public power, agriculture, public housing, urban renewal, and "all the other activities that can be better performed by lower levels of government or by private institutions or by individuals."

He did not suggest that the federal government drop all these programs "overnight" but that it establish "a rigid timetable for a staged withdrawal," encouraging the process by reducing federal spending in each field by 10 percent each year. Reducing spending and taxes (in that order) would guarantee the nation "the economic strength that will always be its ultimate defense against foreign foes."[36]

In the chapter on "The Welfare State," Goldwater conceded the strong emotional appeal of welfarism to many voters and therefore many politicians. But it was the duty of conservatives, he said, to demonstrate the difference between being concerned with welfare problems and believing that the "federal government is the proper agent for their solution." He again demonstrated his remarkable prescience by arguing that the welfare state eliminated "any feeling of responsibility [on the part of the recipient] for his own welfare and that of his family and neighbors"—the argument and finding of Charles Murray and other welfare critics twenty years later. It was one of the great evils of welfarism, Goldwater declared, that "it transforms the individual from a dignified, industrious, self-reliant *spiritual* being into a dependent animal creature without his knowing it."

More than three decades and several trillion welfare dollars later, Goldwater's words limn only too accurately the unhappy state of America's permanent underclass. Against the notion that only the federal government should care for the needy and less fortunate, Goldwater urged that welfare first be "a private concern," and that public intervention be done by local and state authorities "that are incapable of accumulating the vast political power that is so inimical to our liberties."

He restated a fundamental truth for conservatives: the "material and spiritual sides of man are intertwined." If we take from someone "the personal responsibility for caring for his material needs," he warned, "we take from him also the will and the opportunity to be free."[37]

After listing the several evils and dangers of federal aid to education, Goldwater, sounding much like Russell Kirk, stated that the proper function of the school was to transmit "the cultural heritage of one generation to the next generation" and to train the minds of the new generation so they can absorb "ancient learning" and apply it to the problems of today. The function of our schools, he insisted, was not to educate or elevate *society* but to educate *individuals*.[38]

THE LAST THIRD of *The Conscience of a Conservative* was devoted to the Cold War, which, he said, the enemy was determined to win while the United States and the rest of the free world were not. We have sought 'settlements,' " he stated, "while the Communists seek victories." He proposed a seven-point program to achieve victory:

1. The maintenance of defense alliances like the North Atlantic Treaty Organization (NATO), Southeast Asian Treaty Organization (SEATO), and the Central Treaty Organization (thereby setting himself apart from his one-time mentor, Robert Taft, who, for one, voted against the establishment of NATO);

2. The elimination of economic foreign aid as ill administered and ill conceived; aid should be limited to "military and technical assistance

to those nations that need it and that are committed to a common goal of defeating world communism";

3. A far more skeptical approach to diplomatic negotiations that the Soviets view as "an instrument of political warfare" (although he did not come out explicitly against the forthcoming Eisenhower-Khrushchev summit);

4. A recognition that educational, cultural, and other exchanges are a "communist confidence game," and the reexamination of the question of diplomatic relations with "communist regimes," including the Soviet Union;

5. The achievement of superiority in all weapons, military, political, and economic, necessary to produce victory over communism;

6. A drastic reduction in U.S. support of the United Nations, but (disappointing Welch and other members of the John Birch Society), "withdrawal from the United Nations is probably not the answer" to solving its problems;

7. The cessation of U.S. aid to Communist governments that have used the money "to keep their subjects enslaved." Rather (foreshadowing the Reagan Doctrine of the 1980s), the United States should recognize that "the captive peoples are our friends and potential allies" and encourage them "to overthrow their captors."

And, summing up, America's objective "is not to wage a struggle against communism, but to win it."[39]

While conceding that such a hard policy involved the risk of war, he argued reasonably that any policy short of surrender carried the risk of war. Risks were inevitable, but the future, as he saw it, would unfold along one of two paths: either the communists would retain the offensive, ultimately forcing us to surrender or to accept war "under the most disadvantageous circumstances," or Americans would "summon the will and the means for taking the initiative and wage a war of attrition against them," hoping to bring about "the internal disintegration of the communist empire." The former course ran the risk of war and would lead to probable defeat while the latter ran the risk of war but held forth the promise of victory.

Goldwater ended his manifesto with these words: "For Americans who cherish their lives, but their freedom more, the choice cannot be difficult."[40] It was the latter course that President Reagan, with the backing of the American people, chose in the 1980s, leading the nation and the world to what Goldwater had predicted: the disintegration of the Soviet empire and victory in the Cold War—both without firing a single nuclear shot.

THE CONSCIENCE OF A CONSERVATIVE was published in April. It changed American politics, created a new national spokesman, and proclaimed a major new factor in Republican and national politics— conservatism. In a review in the *Chicago Tribune*, George Morgenstern, chief editorial writer for that key Midwestern newspaper, declared that there was "more harsh fact and hard sense in this slight book than will emerge from all of the chatter of this year's session of Congress [and] this year's campaign for the presidency." *Time* wrote that *The Conscience of a Conservative* served notice that "the Old Guard has new blood, that a hard-working, successful politico has put up his stand on the right of the road and intends to shout for all he is worth." Iconoclastic columnist Westbrook Pegler asserted that "Senator Barry Goldwater of Arizona certainly is now the successor to Senator Taft of Ohio as defender of the Constitution and freedom."

Writing for the *Wall Street Journal,* respected reviewer John Chamberlain said that "Goldwater's conservatism is not isolationism, nor is it a cold-blooded commitment to the 'haves' as against the 'have-nots.' It is the creed of a fighter who has both a warm heart and a clear mind." Conservative thinker Russell Kirk wrote that "if a million Americans would read his book carefully, the whole future of this nation and of the world might be altered for the better. In *The Conscience of a Conservative*, [Senator Goldwater] gives promise of becoming a statesman who can save and reform as well as denounce." *Barron's*, the influential weekly published by Dow-Jones, predicted that while his "uncompromising credo" was unlikely to make much headway in 1960, Goldwater had "raised an [inspiring] standard to which the wise and honest may repair." Even the Soviet Union's *Pravda* had its say, stating ominously that the senator's hard-line anticommunism was "a dangerous, unwise affair . . . a sortie against peace . . . [Goldwater] will end up in a pine box."[41]

The first run was for 5,000 copies followed quickly by runs of 10,000, 20,000, and then 50,000—a total of 85,000 copies in the first month. The very first five hundred copies were grabbed from the bindery in Shepherdsville, Kentucky, and flown to the South Carolina Republican state convention just twenty-four hours before Goldwater delivered the keynote address.

Goldwater did not want to be nominated for president, but state chairman Shorey convinced him that it would strengthen the party's chances in November by demonstrating to Nixon that the conservative sentiment had to be respected. As Goldwater later wrote: "From a philosophical standpoint they were practicing what I had been preaching. . . . I decided to let it stand."[42]

The convention pledged all thirteen of its delegates to Goldwater. Richard Kleindienst, chairman of the Arizona Republican party, and Congressman John Rhodes had already committed that state's delegates to Nixon, but the South Carolina vote changed things. It would have been humiliating to Goldwater if his home state were to commit to Nixon after South Carolina had endorsed him. As he later commented, "I'd be like a scarecrow, left in the field after the corn was plowed under, if Arizona allowed South Carolina to carry the [conservative] ball."[43] And so it was that at its April 23rd state convention, Arizona Republicans pledged all fourteen delegates to their favorite son, Barry Goldwater.

Copies of *Conscience* were sent to every senator and member of the House of Representatives. Advertisements were placed in the *Chicago Tribune* and the *New York Times*, featuring the *Time,* Pegler, *Barron's,* and *Pravda* quotations. Some Americans shared *Pravda's* view of the book. Three cartons containing two hundred copies were shipped to Goldwater in Washington but were missing for three days until they were discovered in a warehouse with all the labels removed. An incensed Goldwater wanted to contact the FBI, but cooled off when the books were finally delivered to his office.[44]

Doffing his writing hat for that of political activist, Bozell took charge of the Washington office of "The National Committee for the Goldwater Book." Promotional flyers were sent to five thousand Republican county chairmen, national committeemen and committeewomen, and other Republican officials. In June, Manion began negotiating for a paperback edition. On June 26, *The Conscience of a Conservative* made its first appearance on the "Best Seller List" of the *New York Times*, placing fifteenth.[45]

Its immediate and continuing success flew in the face of conventional publishing wisdom that political books did not sell, that a New York publisher was essential, and that if the review in the *New York*

Times was negative, the book was dead (the *Times'* reviewer called the senator "as true a conservative as a stage coach or a buffalo").[46] Manion stated publicly again and again that the nomination of Barry Goldwater for president in 1960 was possible, but privately he had his eye on the next convention, writing a friend in Arizona that "nothing but a surrender to communism in the meantime can prevent the nomination and election of Barry Goldwater for president in 1964."[47]

Goldwater was delighted at the surprising success of his book and flattered by all the talk about being nominated for president, but he was more immediately concerned about the wording of the Republican platform. Because of the extraordinary impact of *Conscience*, he was in a stronger position than ever to fight for a conservative platform and against any compromise with the man who was anathema to all right-thinking Republicans, Nelson Rockefeller.

7

"Let's Grow Up, Conservatives"

ALTHOUGH MOST POLITICAL ANALYSTS, including the redoubtable Theodore White, insist that party platforms are a meaningless ritual and few Americans pay any attention to them, the writing of a platform is given significant thought and attention by both Democrats and Republicans every four years. A platform is particularly important to conservative Republicans because, committed as they are to the proposition that ideas have consequences, they believe that the rhetoric and recommendations of a platform can materially affect the outcome of nominations and general elections.

It so happened that in 1960 liberal Republicans agreed with conservatives. Their champion, Nelson Rockefeller, had been insisting for a full year (even after his formal withdrawal as a candidate for the presidency in December) that bold new policies had to be adopted in such areas as care for the aged, civil rights, foreign affairs, and, most of all, national defense.

Rockefeller insisted that America was entering the era of the missile gap and proposed spending at least $3 billion to speed up the construction of missile bases. In so doing, the New York governor was in effect recommending that Republicans repudiate the administration and policies of the man, Dwight D. Eisenhower, who had brought them national victory eight years before.

A fierce battle was joined between conservatives and liberals over what the platform would and would not say. The man in the middle was Nixon, who needed the support of both groups—not to win the nomination (nearly everyone agreed the vice president could not be denied), but to win the presidency. Goldwater made his position clear: as critical as he had been of the Eisenhower administration on more than one occasion (referring to a proposed medical care for the aged program that would cost $600 million as a "dime store New Deal"), he did not accept Rockefeller's across-the-board criticism and certainly did not endorse his bigger-government and increased-spending remedies.[1]

Goldwater arrived in Chicago on July 19th with two prepared statements drafted by Shadegg: his remarks before the platform committee proposing a Declaration of Republican Principles and his formal withdrawal as a candidate for the presidential nomination. Although not matching the simple elegance of *The Conscience of a Conservative,* the proposed declaration offered a list of solid conservative principles.

On defense, Goldwater said, "We declare it is our intention to keep the defensive and offensive military forces of this nation superior to the attacking power of any potential aggressor or aggressors, regardless of the costs in dollars and manpower, to the end that liberty and freedom may be maintained." "*We must,*" he insisted, "*proclaim for victory in the Cold War.*" He condemned deficit spending, "federal tinkering and interference in the lives of the American farmers," the "concentration of power in the hands of a few unconscionable men who have invaded the American labor movement," and the "concentration of power in the hands of business where it is used in a manner inimical to the best interests of the public."[2]

While the platform committee was considering the recommendations of Goldwater and others, and its chairman, Chicago businessman Charles Percy, was desperately seeking compromise language acceptable to conservatives, liberals, and pragmatists, Nixon decided to meet secretly with Rockefeller in his apartment at 810 Fifth Avenue in New York City to resolve their differences. If Rockefeller had gone to Washington to meet with Nixon, most Republicans would have approved; but when Nixon, the vice president, went kowtowing to Rockefeller, most Republicans were shocked and angered. Goldwater felt betrayed.

In the spring, Goldwater had visited the vice president in his capacity as chairman of the Republican Senatorial Campaign Committee. After discussing the electoral chances of the various candidates, Goldwater told Nixon bluntly that "a number of people I've talked with are disappointed with your failure to take a strong stand on some conservative issues—federal spending, a balanced budget, the growing bureaucracy."

Nixon replied that he had said nothing so far because it could have been taken as a criticism of the Eisenhower administration, but he assured Goldwater that he would demand a reduction in spending, a balanced budget, and a halt to bureaucratic growth. As for John Kennedy's constant references to "a missile gap," Nixon said, "I could explode that phony in ten minutes by displaying our high-altitude reconnaissance photographs and explaining the quality of information we are getting. I can't do that without destroying our sources, and Kennedy, the bastard, knows I can't."

Goldwater said that he thought Rockefeller had recruited "substantial support" among the more liberal Republicans, but Nixon laughed, remarking scornfully, "Yes, he's real big with the Ripon Society." And then added, "What the governor really wants is to be on the ticket—to be my vice president. I won't take him."[3]

The two men shifted their discussion to the work of the platform committee, which Nixon knew meant a great deal to Goldwater. As he was wont to do throughout his career, Nixon told his visitor what he thought the visitor wished to hear: "Rockefeller wants to talk to me [about the platform]. I am treating him very politely, but, I promise, I'm not going to visit with him until after the convention."[4]

That was good enough for Goldwater: the vice president of the United States, his party's future presidential nominee, had promised that he would take a conservative position on key issues like spending and national defense and would not meet with Rockefeller until after he had been nominated.

On Saturday morning, July 23rd, Goldwater was about to address the Republican Finance Committee when an aide to Leonard Hall, Nixon's campaign manager, interrupted to say that Hall had to see Goldwater immediately. When Goldwater said he could not snub the finance committee, the aide told him there were reports of a secret rendezvous between Nixon and Rockefeller in New York at which they had discussed the platform and the vice presidency.

Goldwater was stunned. "If Nixon had gone to New York, it was a direct repudiation of the promise he had made to me."[5] Hall, who had not known of Nixon's plans, "was as angry as any man I have ever seen," Goldwater recalled. "His language was blunt and profane [and] I didn't blame him. 'This won't cost Nixon the nomination,' Hall said, 'but it might cost him the election.' " He threatened to resign as campaign manager but quickly cooled off.

GOLDWATER DID NOT. He had scheduled a news conference that morning at which he intended to read his withdrawal statement. Now he stuffed the statement in his pocket and let fly at Nixon and Rockefeller. He called the New York meeting "an American Munich" and a "surrender." He was adamantly against letting the platform be "dictated" by two men a thousand miles away. Of all people, he said, Republicans should follow democratic processes and let the convention write the platform. He predicted that the convention delegates supporting Nixon would never accept Rockefeller on the ticket.[6]

When the details of the Compact of Fifth Avenue became public, and it was learned that Nixon had acceded to Rockefeller on civil rights, medical care for the aged, and foreign affairs (approving proposals already rejected by the platform committee), the anger of the delegates swelled, and Goldwater suddenly found himself at the center of a Republican rebellion. Because he dared to speak out when others were silent, he became the conscience of a convention.

Goldwater was helped by the current issue of *Newsweek*, on display in every Chicago hotel and convention site, which contained a guest column by him on how to win in 1960. He argued that the path to victory lay in proclaiming devotion "to a limited government which is the servant and not the master of the people" and opposing "the superstate socialism advocated by Senator Kennedy." Republicans will win, he asserted, "by offering [the American people] a clear-cut choice; by resisting every temptation to compromise on welfare-state proposals."[7]

In *Six Crises,* Nixon argues that by going to see Rockefeller in New York, "I was able to insure his support for the Republican ticket." But it was Goldwater, not Rockefeller, who delivered 126 speeches in twenty-six states in the fall; Rockefeller's apathy showed up throughout the campaign such as the boxes of Nixon-Lodge campaign literature that were often left standing in GOP headquarters in New York City instead of being distributed. Nixon states that it was Rockefeller, not he, who did the "surrendering" on his proposal to require "forced" economic growth of 5 or 6 percent annually.[8] But he fails to point out that the compact rewrote the moderate civil rights language drafted by the platform committee.

Goldwater later insisted that the original plank would have produced a Republican victory in 1960 by drastically undercutting LBJ's Southern appeal. His analysis was borne out by the Louisiana delegate who said, "We've lost Louisiana, I tell you. Lyndon Johnson's going to come across the border now and talk 'magnolia' to them and they'll vote Democratic." Republicans did lose Louisiana as well as Alabama, Georgia, Mississippi, and South Carolina—Kennedy narrowly carried Louisiana by 50.4 percent of the popular vote.[9]

AMID THE POLITICAL turmoil surrounding the "American Munich," the Texas delegation that had come to Chicago pledged to Nixon began reexamining its position; Goldwater was invited to address it. Arizona started to take its favorite son candidate more seriously as delegates from different states demanded to be released from their commitment to Nixon. A group of Young Republicans, led by an energetic young organizer named Robert Croll, staged a lively street parade, carrying signs that read "Youth for Goldwater for Vice President."

Croll had been lining up state chairmen among his Young Republicans contacts and raising money for the operation (membership $1 a head) since April. Knowing how sensitive Goldwater was about anyone using his name, Croll had called on the senator while he was visiting Chicago in the spring and received permission to proceed with his operation, demonstrating again how difficult it was for Goldwater to say no to any young person.[10]

Manion and Brophy opened an office for Americans for Goldwater in downtown Chicago three weeks before the convention began and were counting delegates and lending logistical support to Croll and others. The telephones into Goldwater's suite in the Blackstone Hotel were jammed as well-meaning friends and frustrated delegates urged him to "get in there and fight." They insisted that he could command the support of 287 delegates, far short of the 666 needed to win the nomination, but enough to remind Nixon that conservatives were a force to be counted and even that their hero deserved a vice presidential nomination.

Goldwater estimated that, including the twenty-seven from Arizona and South Carolina, he had perhaps fifty solid delegates, no more. But fervent supporters kept pressuring him so hard that finally he said, "All right, you go out and get those delegates you say are willing to vote for me. I'll sit in this room all night. You bring them in. I want them to sign a paper saying they'll vote for me." Goldwater sat patiently, and skeptically, in his suite in the Blackstone Hotel as he had promised, "and not a damned delegate came in."[11]

But there was still plenty that Goldwater could do to affect the course of the convention. He had been invited to introduce the senatorial candidates on Monday night and to make some brief remarks. Hall also asked Goldwater if he would second Nixon's nomination and received a succinct answer: "No, I can't do that in good conscience."[12]

In order to present the right image to the American people, he suggested that rather than having the candidates all lined up on the podium, like so many job applicants, each eager to be seen and to hold the microphone as long as possible, they be introduced on the floor surrounded by enthusiastic supporters from their delegations. "Let's give the people of the nation, who watch this show on television, an exciting picture."[13] The television networks quickly endorsed the idea and the initially reluctant committee made the necessary changes.

When Senator Thruston Morton of Kentucky, the convention chairman, introduced Goldwater on Monday night, the convention delegates showed where their hearts were by grabbing banners and parading up and down the crowded aisles for eight minutes, ignoring the entreaties of the chairman and the speaker. Although not a classical orator like Representative Walter H. Judd of Minnesota, who delivered the keynote address that brought the delegates to their feet again and again, Goldwater held his listeners' attention as he raised the standard of conservatism and confronted the "me-tooers" head on.

Goldwater began by equating the "true Republican philosophy" with the "unquenchable spirit of the American Revolution," founded on freedom, creative opportunity, and limited government. The New Frontier, he declared, was nothing more than "a new slogan to dress up a shopworn, outmoded, outworn idea." Republicans were needed in Congress, he said, to protect the nation against "the reckless spenders" and the world against "the apostles of appeasement," and it was the task of the delegates to provide the American voter with a real choice between the two philosophies competing "in our world, the philosophy of the *stomach* or the philosophy of the *whole man.*" [14]

But when the cheering stopped, the Nixon forces still controlled the convention. Working around the clock Monday and Tuesday, they forced the 103-member platform committee, meeting in the Conrad Hilton Hotel, to integrate the Nixon-Rockefeller agreement into the 1960 Republican platform (the committee was nudged into surrender by Dr. Martin Luther King Jr., who was leading a march outside the hotel demanding a strong declaration on civil rights). By noon, Wednesday, it was clear to even the most die-hard conservative that Nixon would be the presidential nominee.

Goldwater met in the morning with Shorey and Milliken of South Carolina, Albert Fay of Texas, Manion, and Paul Fannin of Arizona. Shorey and Milliken declared that with or without his permission, they were going to place his name in nomination. Goldwater argued that this would not affect the outcome but could hurt the political standing of his supporters. He reminded them of how badly Taft delegates had been treated in 1952 for backing him. "Your willingness to put your necks on the line for me is a very humbling experience," he said, "but I'm not going to let you do it." [15]

It was Jay Hall who suggested a way out of the impasse. He proposed that Arizona nominate Goldwater; after some seconding speeches Goldwater would take the podium, withdraw his name, and urge all delegates supporting him to vote for Nixon. Goldwater promptly endorsed the idea, pointing out that if everyone handled his part skillfully, "we might unite the party." [16] Hall began drafting the senator's remarks.

Permission was sought and reluctantly given to bring in pro-Goldwater demonstrators from outside the arena, after Goldwater bluntly told convention Chairman Morton, "You better give my people those tickets."

After Nixon was nominated with the usual "spontaneous" fanfare, Fannin took the podium as planned and called on Republicans to pick Goldwater "as the voice of conscience speaking for the conservatives of the nation." This man, said Fannin, "enjoys the love and affectionate regard of millions of Republicans who have never seen him. This man has challenged the imagination of America." [17]

Pandemonium broke out as the banners of Arizona, Arkansas,

Louisiana, North Carolina, South Carolina, Texas, Mississippi, Georgia, Washington, Nevada, Wyoming, Utah, Idaho, and Puerto Rico snaked through the hall, proclaiming that Goldwater was the favorite of the South and the West, and sending premonitory shivers down the spines of the Eastern liberals. Delegates and demonstrators tooted horns, whistled and shouted, and the band played "Dixie." The demonstration continued for eleven tumultuous minutes and would have gone on and on. But, moving quickly, floor ushers directed many Goldwater demonstrators through doors that deposited them outside the hall, and George Murphy, Hollywood film star and future Republican senator from California, appealed to Goldwater, "We're running overtime. This must be stopped."

At last, the silver-haired conservative signaled for quiet and said what had to be said, "Mr. Chairman, delegates to the convention, and fellow Republicans, I respectfully ask the chairman to withdraw my name from nomination." A ringing cry of "No!" rose from the floor and was echoed by the galleries, "No! No! No!" That cry echoed the bittersweet memories of Taft and Dewey and Eisenhower, of narrow defeats and public humiliations at previous conventions. It signaled the continuing struggle for the sovereignty of the Republican party between East and West, North and South, big city banker and small-town businessman, the Council for Foreign Relations and the Daughters of the American Revolution, liberal powerbrokers and conservative activists.

But at this convention, the liberal establishment had the overwhelming majority of the votes, and Goldwater was no kamikaze conservative. He continued, "Please. I release my delegations from their pledge to me, and while I am not a delegate, I would suggest they give these votes to Richard Nixon."

The few shouts of "No!" were drowned out by the roar of the Nixon supporters. Knowing that many thought he had let them down, Goldwater talked directly to the true believers who had placed his name in nomination.

We are conservatives. This great Republican party is our historical house. This is our home. Now some of us don't agree with every statement in the official platform of our party, but I might remind you that this is always true in every platform of an American political party. . . .

We can be absolutely sure of one thing. In spite of the individual points of difference, the Republican platform deserves the support of every American over the blueprint for socialism presented by the Democrats![18]

Goldwater was putting it bluntly to conservatives: either support the Republican party or let the socialists occupy the White House and run the country. Echoing Robert Taft, who had stayed with the party in 1952 despite his bitter disappointment over losing a (much-deserved) presidential nomination to Eisenhower, Goldwater warned what would happen if conservatives walked out of the GOP: "If each segment, each section of our great party were to insist on the complete and unqualified acceptance of its views, if each viewpoint were to be enforced by a Russian-type veto, the Republican party could not long survive." He added that "radical Democrats" were watching the Chicago convention with the hope that Republicans would split into factions.

"I am telling them now that no such split will take place!" he shouted, and thunderous applause shook the convention hall. He had been campaigning for Nixon for six years "and I see no reason to change my mind tonight," although he admitted that he and the vice president disagreed on a few points. But, he added, "I would not want any negative action of mine to enhance the possibility of a victory going to those who by their very words have lost faith in America."[19]

He concluded with the words that completed the transformation of a junior senator from Arizona into the leader of the American conservative movement, a metamorphosis that began with his remarkable re-election in 1958 and crested with the publication of *The Conscience of a Conservative*, now number six among nonfiction best-sellers:

This country is too important for anyone's feelings.

This country, and its majesty, is too great for any man, be he conservative or liberal, to stay home and not work just because he doesn't agree. Let's grow up, Conservatives. We want to take this party back, and I think some day we can. Let's get to work.[20]

Congressman Morris Udall, a liberal Arizona Democrat and long-time friend, described Goldwater's "Grow up, Conservatives!" speech as the finest he ever made and the beginning of the nation's conservative "upsurge." Political reporter David Broder agrees that the speech was one of the most important of his career, but makes the distinction that Goldwater's "commitment to the party was absolutely clear. It wasn't just an ideological crusade. He was a Republican."[21]

The final tally for the presidential nomination was Nixon, 1,321, Goldwater, 10. Ten stubborn Louisiana delegates refused to vote for Nixon and affirmed their support for the grandson of a Jewish peddler born in Poland a century before. Walter Trohan, political columnist for the *Chicago Tribune,* wrote that Goldwater left the convention "wearing the mantle of the late Sen. Robert A. Taft of Ohio as the leader of the conservative wing of the [Republican] party, which is numbered by the millions in the Midwest."[22]

Some ultraconservatives did not agree. Radio commentator Dan Smoot accused Goldwater of "betraying" conservatism and advancing "the socialist-communist cause" when he withdrew his name from nomination and endorsed Nixon. Reminded of Smoot's harsh words many years later, Goldwater said, "I didn't realize until later there were some conservatives you can never satisfy."[23]

As PROMISED, Goldwater campaigned hard and long for Nixon, particularly in Southern states like Georgia, South Carolina, and Florida, where his message was always the same: "Don't kid yourself that Jack Kennedy has any love for the South. Don't vote for the Democrats just because your grandfather did. Vote Republican! Just try it once—you've no idea how good you'll feel in the morning." They liked what he had to say: Republican headquarters received more Southern speaking requests for Goldwater than for anyone else with the exception of Nixon and his running mate, Henry Cabot Lodge.

Goldwater was unapologetically partisan, personal, and hard-hitting in his speeches. He dismissed Johnson, the Democratic vice presidential nominee, as "the forgotten candidate" and said of Kennedy, "Sometimes I wonder how Jack gets that sailboat back to harbor." He called for a tougher foreign policy, going well beyond Nixon's carefully measured proposals: "If it takes force to remove the Castro government, then we should use force. We cannot have a communist country 90 miles off our shore." As for federal medical aid to the aged, he commented, "If my kids don't take care of me when I'm old, I'll whale the tar out of them."[24]

He sent a constant stream of memos, letters, and telegrams to Nixon, reporting on his travels and offering advice. He urged Nixon to hit harder on the issues and at his opponent, arguing, "I do not find any enthusiasm among the Kennedy followers, but by the same token, your own campaign needs more fire in it, so don't hesitate to campaign as Dick Nixon knows how to campaign."[25] Goldwater's concern about Nixon's lack of aggressiveness was confirmed by his first television debate with Kennedy. After it had aired he wired Leonard Hall: "Kennedy did not appear immature. Nixon did not make his points strong enough. I repeat what I told you before. He must swing harder at his opponent, pointing out the consequences if the New Frontier becomes an actuality. This is not the Nixon campaigning that we know."

Although more than a month remained in the campaign, a frustrated Goldwater was beginning to realize that Nixon might lose, turning the country over to New Frontiersmen like Walter Reuther. In late October, shortly after the fourth and last television debate, which did not produce the knockout he had hoped for, a somber Goldwater wrote Hall:

> I need to tell you that as of this day our man is in trouble and I see two possible helps for him.
>
> (1) The president [Eisenhower] must campaign for him. He must get off the golf course to do this. He retains millions of followers who will listen to him.
>
> (2) Conservatives of both parties are now speaking of staying home. They are being prodded in this by Dan Smoot and Bob Welch, each of whom has a large following.[26]

A day later, he wrote to Nixon directly, proposing that he "get the approval of the president to accept a position as a sort of senior adviser or president emeritus who will help you in the fields in which he is most expert—foreign policy and military." Although it was late in the day and "bad" mistakes had been made, he had hopes of Nixon's chances if he reverted to his old tough self:

> What this nation wants is firmness in its president. It wants to hear more statements like you made in Chicago about wanting victory in the cold war—not just peace.

They want to hear a tough attitude toward Russia—an attitude that might run the risk of war but which would guarantee us a fight for our freedom instead of the slow dribbling away such as the Democrats have been doing at Versailles, Potsdam, Yalta, Tehran, and Korea.[27]

What Goldwater was proposing was that Nixon sound more like Goldwater.

But Nixon stuck to the script he had personally written for his campaign, including a vainglorious promise to campaign in all fifty states rather than in states like Illinois and Texas with the most votes. And he lost to Kennedy by a mere 114,673 votes out of 68,335,642 votes cast. In one of the closest presidential races in American history, Kennedy won by only .17 percent of the popular vote. His electoral margin was substantial, 303 to 219, but depended upon his very narrow victories in two key states, Illinois and Texas.

In Illinois, where Chicago's Democratic boss Richard Daley reigned, Kennedy's popular vote margin was only 8,858 out of 4,746,834 votes cast, less than two-tenths of 1 percent. In Texas, home of Lyndon Johnson and the "yellow-dog Democrat" (such Democrats boast that they will vote for even a yellow dog if it runs on the Democratic ticket), Kennedy won by 46,000 out of 2,289,000 votes, a difference of 2 percent.

Newspaper articles about vote fraud in Illinois and Texas appeared almost immediately, and Goldwater, along with Dirksen and other Republican leaders, pressed Nixon to demand a full-scale investigation.

But Nixon refused to demand a recount because, he later wrote, such a challenge might drag on for months and delay "the orderly transfer of power from the old to the new." He also felt that the "bitterness that would be engendered" would have done "incalculable and lasting damage throughout the country." Finally, he foresaw the possibility "that there would be open-season shooting at the validity of free elections throughout the world."[28]

However great his future political sins, Nixon acted like a statesman in 1960. Driven by his fear of what Kennedy and Company would do to the nation and outraged by the cheating, Goldwater strongly disagreed with Nixon: he felt that tombstone voting ought to be resisted and exposed, regardless of how long the investigation might take.

Goldwater rejected the joy of some conservatives over Nixon's defeat but agreed with their sharp criticism of the Nixon-Lodge campaign. The most crucial strategic error, he said, was Nixon's failure to give Ike a more prominent role. Eisenhower was eager to refute Kennedy's criticisms of his foreign policy. But Nixon never talked politics with him, Ike later told Goldwater, never sought his advice, and did not request his participation until the final week or so—when it was too late.[29]

A second serious error was the failure of Nixon and Lodge to give the voters "a clear-cut choice." Among other things, they appeared reluctant to question "the legitimacy of the expanding federal establishment." Goldwater was also disappointed with the "prejudiced attitude" of the national press, which made Kennedy into a "Galahad" while constantly portraying Nixon in a "harsh and unflattering way."[30]

Goldwater's perception that the Washington press corps had been less than even-handed in its coverage of the 1960 campaign was corroborated by Willard Edwards, veteran political correspondent for the *Chicago Tribune,* who covered both Nixon and Kennedy. Summing up his travels with his colleagues, Edwards wrote that "the great majority of the newspapermen assigned to report the Nixon campaign were openly hostile to him and openly favored Kennedy" and "this animosity crept into [their] dispatches to the detriment of Nixon's candidacy."[31]

Goldwater concluded that above all else, Nixon lost because Republican voters had failed to support him as they had the last two Republican nominees. The figures were persuasive: Eisenhower carried Illinois, Michigan, Texas, and Massachusetts in 1952 and 1956, but Nixon lost all four states. In 1948, Dewey won Pennsylvania, Michigan, Connecticut, Delaware, the District of Columbia, Maryland, New Jersey, and New York; Nixon lost all of them. While not discounting Kennedy's charm and skill, Goldwater was convinced that Republican voters were "turned off by Nixon" and that "the disillusionment commenced in Chicago" where Republican delegates were forced to accept the Munich-like Compact of New York.[32]

If Goldwater ever ran for president, he would not make the same mistakes Nixon had made. Of course, he was *not* interested in running; he loved being a senator. As he told *Time* about the 1964 presidential race: "I have no staff for it, no program for it and no ambition for it."[33]

8

A Genuine Draft

IF BARRY GOLDWATER HAD WANTED TO BE PRESIDENT, he would have sought the chairmanship of the Republican Senatorial Campaign Committee and carefully collected political IOUs for himself as he campaigned across the country; he would have arranged to become a member of the Senate Rackets Committee and won national publicity by calling to account power-hungry union bosses; he would have befriended the head of a Washington think tank and tapped into its wide-ranging intellectual and analytical resources; he would have hired a brilliant writer and intellectual and asked him to ghost a best-selling book about American politics; he would have challenged Nixon for his party's presidential nomination and positioned himself as a major contender at the next Republican convention.

But Barry Goldwater was not Jack Kennedy, and he did not initiate any of these things, although all of them happened. They happened because people saw in him a man who would answer the call of duty and honor. They knew he would undertake the most difficult task with little thought to personal gain. And thus, although there was almost no personal calculation in any of his decisions, their cumulative impact made him a presidential possibility.

Everyone knew that Goldwater hated to say no to friends and colleagues whom he trusted. So when Michael Bernstein, his longtime aide on the Senate Labor Committee, approached him about issuing a "Statement of Proposed Republican Principles, Programs and Objectives" that he and others had drafted, he readily agreed.

The manifesto focused on the "Forgotten American," the individual "whose interests were not represented by existing political pressure groups and whose voice was drowned out amidst the cries of big government, big labor, and big business." At first glance, the statement seemed to be an application of the principles of *The Conscience of a Conservative* with its promises to wage total war on inflation, seek victory in the Cold War, and protect workers against abuses of union power. But the document contained no reference to right-to-work laws or states' rights, and its criticism of Social Security, foreign aid, and the United Nations was muted.

What disturbed limited-government conservatives most about the manifesto was that it proposed an active rather than a passive role for the federal government by substituting conservative for liberal programs. The *Wall Street Journal* described the approach as "progressive conservatism." It rested on the conviction that Republicans needed a fourth approach (different from "me-too" Republicanism, "Neanderthal" conservatism, and the Eisenhower-Nixon middle road) that would be "acceptable to most Republicans and able to capture Democratic votes without imitating Democratic policies."

There was another, more personal objective of the new doctrine in the minds of Bernstein and its other authors: to transform Goldwater's image as "an intractable reactionary who would abolish Social Security and destroy labor unions" to a more progressive version. They were aware that any retreat from rigid conservatism could alienate "the extreme conservatives outside the party who have been his most ardent admirers," but they believed that this would do him more good than harm in 1964. What they hoped was that this "new" conservatism would win active presidential backing from conservatives inside the party "who admire the senator personally but consider him too intransigent and dogmatic to be taken seriously as a White House hopeful."[1]

Even before Willmoore Kendall attacked the manifesto in *National Review* as "neo-Nixonism" and a retreat from conservatism,[2] Goldwater was wondering how he could forget all about "The Forgotten American." Although he liked many of the statement's ideas, particularly its trenchant anticommunism, its emphasis on the need for law and order, and its antitax and antispending rhetoric, he was uncomfortable with its calls for "federal law and the exercise of federal power" to redress wrongs in American society.

And he was very unhappy with all the speculation about 1964 and how the manifesto could win him "support" for an office he had no intention of seeking. If Goldwater had been a candidate for the presidency, the statement would have been a shrewd piece of political strategy, but he was a salesman for conservatism, pure and undiluted, and the subtleties of "The Forgotten American" were of little use to him if they confused conservatives. He wrote Bill Buckley that he had been "misunderstood" and hoped to find time to rebut Kendall, but in the end he quietly let "A Statement of Proposed Republican Principles, Programs and Objectives" fade away.[3]

REGARDLESS OF GOLDWATER'S PERSONAL WISHES FOR 1964, a group of young but experienced conservative Republicans collaborated to produce "the first authentic presidential nomination draft in the history of American political parties."[4] The three ringleaders were close friends and former leaders of the Young Republicans: F. Clifton White, a tall, bow-tied professional politician from New York who had taught politics at Cornell and gone on to work in the presidential campaigns of Dewey and Nixon; Representative John M. Ashbrook of Ohio, former chairman of the Young Republican National Federation and a rising political star in the conservative movement; and William A. Rusher, the erudite publisher of *National Review* and kingmaker extraordinaire of Young Republicans and Young Americans for Freedom. All three men were activists and intellectuals; they not only knew what to do but why they were doing it. The inspirational leader of the trio, according to Rita Bree, White's assistant, was Rusher, without whose unflagging optimism the Draft Goldwater effort would soon have disintegrated.[5]

In late spring of 1961, Rusher felt that a leadership vacuum had developed in the Republican party and was waiting to be filled. Nixon had been defeated, Eisenhower had retired, Rockefeller was too liberal, and Goldwater was too conservative for some. But, Rusher noted, the senator had (1) been selected by his fellow Republicans to be chairman once again of the Senatorial Campaign Committee; (2) campaigned successfully for an unknown Texas professor, John Tower, who had just been elected the first Republican senator from Texas since Reconstruction; and (3) appeared on the cover of *Time,* which described him as "the hottest political figure this side of Jack Kennedy."[6]

Rusher traveled to Washington, D.C., in mid-July to try out his thesis on his old friend and fellow Harvardite, John Ashbrook. As the two talked over lunch, Rusher remarked that "if we held a meeting of our old YR crowd today, I'll bet it would be about the third largest faction in the Republican party." Only Rockefeller, he thought, could have fielded a larger organization than theirs.

Ashbrook not only agreed but back in his office showed Rusher the folders of correspondence from all over the country that he had accumulated since retiring as Young Republican chairman two years before. The names were a national network of former Young Republicans who had taken leadership roles in the senior party while retaining the team spirit and loyalty of their old days in Young Republican politics. Like Rusher and White, most of them had grown steadily more conservative, inspired by journals like *National Review*, books like *The Conscience of a Conservative*, and events like Eisenhower's New Republicanism and Kennedy's New Frontier. Rusher had no doubt that if invited to a reunion and asked to help draft Barry Goldwater for the 1964 Republican nomination, "these old friends of ours would be overjoyed at the chance to work together again."[7]

Back in New York City, Rusher took White to lunch three days later and, after describing his meeting with Ashbrook, suggested that the time was right for a conservative takeover of the GOP. White said that he too had been thinking about the future of their party and revealed he also had files of Young Republicans as well as other regular party contacts. They talked of merging the Ashbrook-White files and starting a nationwide organization committed "to the nomination of a conservative candidate, or at the very least the drafting of a conservative platform, at the 1964 convention." White says that they "went no further than that" but Rusher insists that they specifically talked about Goldwater.[8]

Subsequently, White met with Charles Barr, an astute political observer and lobbyist for Standard Oil of Indiana, who remarked that in his opinion grassroots support for a conservative candidate in 1964 was increasing rapidly. Barr said he would help any way he could with the draft operation, a pledge that helped persuade White that the idea was not so "farfetched" as he had first thought.[9]

The leadership vacuum in the Republican party had been noted by other conservatives, including Steve Shadegg, who in fact had arranged a meeting of half a dozen key Republicans with Goldwater in a Washington, D.C., hotel in December 1960 after Nixon's defeat by Kennedy. Goldwater thought they were there to talk about how to revive the GOP after the Democrats' narrow victory, but Shadegg was working toward the nomination of his friend for president in 1964.

Present, in addition to Shadegg and Goldwater, were William R. Spear, former state chairman of Nebraska; Roger Milliken, an original member of Dean Manion's Committee of One Hundred, who was very active at the 1960 national convention for Goldwater, and now national committeeman from South Carolina; oil executive Charles Barr; R. L. "Dick" Herman, president of an Omaha trucking firm who had helped Senator Carl Curtis in his reelection campaign the previous fall; and G. R. Herberger, a wealthy Minnesota businessman who spent his winters in Arizona and had long been active in Republican finance operations.

But, when Shadegg began turning the discussion toward the 1964 presidential race, Goldwater shook his head and cut him off. He insisted that they focus on more immediate political problems, and a chastened Shadegg allowed the meeting to run its course.[10]

Shadegg's political acumen was confirmed, however, when two men who attended his meeting—Milliken and Barr—became part of Clif White's ad hoc group. In addition, Herman became a regional political director of the Goldwater for President Committee as well as of the presidential campaign, and Bob Herberger served on the finance committee of both.

If White had invited Shadegg to participate, it is likely that Goldwater would have been more sympathetic to the draft effort. But White did not know Shadegg, at least in the way that White, Rusher, and Ashbrook knew each other, as friends and co-conspirators in the Young Republicans wars, and he never brought him on board. Ironically, these men who were responsible for so much of Goldwater's political success—Shadegg as manager of his two winning senatorial campaigns, White as de facto manager of his successful presidential nomination campaign—would play peripheral roles in the biggest campaign of his life, his run for the presidency against Johnson.

But that was in the future, and when White, Rusher, and Ashbrook met in New York City on September 7, 1961, shortly after the Berlin Wall had been erected virtually unchallenged by the United States, they were filled with a sense of urgency as they began selecting the "hard core" of the national political organization that would "ultimately capture control of the Republican party for the conservative camp."[11] They settled on twenty-six people, including themselves, picked a date, October 8th, and a geographically convenient site, Chicago, where Abraham Lincoln had been nominated president by a nascent Republican party a century before.

MEANWHILE GOLDWATER, unaware of the ambitious plans being laid for him, had been doing what he liked best—campaigning for a full-bore conservative Republican, John Tower, who was running in a special Texas election to fill the Senate seat vacated by Vice President Lyndon B. Johnson. Tower, a college professor, who had amazingly received almost a million votes and 42 percent of the vote against Johnson the previous November, now faced William Blakley. Although Republican Tower was a long shot in deeply Democratic Texas, he had several things in his favor, among them Barry Goldwater, who "went all out . . . stumping across the state. The Goldwater magic was potent in Texas, and conservatives—no matter what their party affiliation—responded."[12]

Tower won by only 10,343 votes, about 1 percent of the total. It was not a landslide, but it was more than the 87 vote majority Lyndon Johnson got when he was elected to the Senate in 1948. John Tower became the first real "Goldwaterite" in the United States, a living, breathing, voting testimony to the power of conservatism.[13]

Goldwater was an exceptional chairman of the Senate Campaign Committee. Over six years, he traveled more than one million miles, averaged almost two hundred speeches a year, and raised over $2 million for the party and candidates. Always the party loyalist, he helped every Republican who asked him, from conservative Karl Mundt to liberal Jacob Javits to moderate Ted Stevens.

Stevens has never forgotten how Goldwater came all the way to Alaska in 1962 to help him in his first campaign for the Senate—nor has anyone else in the audience that night. In those far-off, pre-PC days, visiting male speakers would often be given a special memento of their trip to the frontier state—the petrified penis of a walrus. Stevens handed the rigid but lifeless *oosik* to Goldwater, who looked at it and said, "I don't know why, but this makes me think of Lyndon

Johnson."[14] The mostly male audience roared with laughter at this jab at the vice president's political impotence after his years as powerful Senate majority leader.

Victor A. Johnson, the committee's executive director who often traveled with Goldwater, said that they "never had a chairman like Barry. If anybody would ask him to come and give a speech, he'd go." When Governor William Scranton pleaded for help, Goldwater went to Pennsylvania and nearly made up the state committee's $600,000 deficit in one appearance. When Rockefeller was scheduled to speak at a fundraising dinner for Senator Roman L. Hruska of Nebraska and conservative Republicans threatened to boycott the event, Goldwater persuaded them, via a special loudspeaker telephone hookup, to put the party and the reelection of Hruska first and accept Rockefeller.

Such party loyalty came naturally to Goldwater. It added to his surprise and then anger in 1964 when Rockefeller and other liberals failed to unite behind him and the party after he had won the presidential nomination in a fair and open contest.

He never used his position as chairman to advance any presidential goals. Vic Johnson once remarked to Goldwater as they returned from a successful appearance, "Why don't you see about tying this thing up? They go wild over you; you shake thousands of hands, then you get back to Washington and you've got nothing, not even a list of who they are. Why don't you get the names together? They might come in handy." Goldwater shrugged and said, "Well, look how far I've got just pooping along."[15]

The simple truth, although Johnson and all the other Washington pols would not believe it, was that Goldwater did not want to be president. Besides, he thought he had little chance of being nominated with powerful men like Nixon and Rockefeller hungry for the honor.

Time did not agree. In a glowing cover story published in June 1961, the weekly newsmagazine pointed out that in the past three months, Goldwater's office had received 650 written invitations to speak; his mail was running a remarkable eight hundred pieces a day; *The Conscience of a Conservative* had sold more than 700,000 copies and the paperback edition was going into its twelfth printing; and his three-times-a-week newspaper column was syndicated in 104 papers. Four years ago, reported *Time,* Goldwater seemed little more than "an attractive spokesman for a minority on the right edge of the GOP";

today, he stood "not as the leader of a die-hard sect" but as "one of the Republican party's top two or three figures."

The reason for the surge, *Time* continued, was that "Goldwater's unabashed, unapologetic conservatism has struck a responsive note. . . ." The message of "the less government, the better" was reinforced by the man himself: "a tanned, trim (185 lbs.), six footer with searching blue eyes behind his dark-rimmed glasses, and a thinning shock of silver hair . . . Goldwater has more than his share of political sex appeal." Commented one Republican woman after listening to Goldwater: "If Nixon had his looks, we never would have lost."[16]

In the last paragraph of its admiring profile, *Time* said that Goldwater insisted he had no ambition for the White House. *Time* then stated a political truth:

Whether as candidate or merely as Republican conscience, Arizona's Barry Morris Goldwater—GOP salesman supreme and the political phenomenon of 1961—will have plenty to say about the tone and spirit of his party's next platform, and even more to say about who will be standing on it.[17]

Time was not alone. Earlier in the spring, *Newsweek* devoted six pages to the "leading spokesman" for conservatism in the United States, stating that Goldwater had "become the American politician most sought by [college] student bodies." It too spoke of the "Goldwater phenomenon," and of a charm that led one political enemy to say, "The trouble with the s.o.b. is that even the people who hate him like him."[18]

In August, *U.S. News & World Report,* the third weekly newsmagazine, asked "Where is Barry Goldwater headed?" and examined the political potential of Goldwater, Rockefeller, and Nixon in 1964. It concluded that Goldwater's greatest strength lay in the South, the Middle West, and the Rocky Mountain states and that he would enter the national convention with 25 to 35 percent of the delegates. Drawing on the language favored by its predominantly business audience, it reported that the "Goldwater stock is swinging up in a bull market." Capturing the evangelical nature of conservatism in the early 1960s, the magazine reported that his supporters called Goldwater "the savior of constitutional government." Summing up, *U.S. News* stated, "next to

President Kennedy, Mr. Goldwater has become the most publicized political figure in the nation."[19]

Coronet asked William F. Buckley Jr. to write about his fellow conservative in its July 1961 issue, and he described, in the most provocative way, what Goldwater would do if he were president: "get the government out of agriculture and welfare altogether"; "abolish the progressive income tax"; "eliminate foreign aid"; and "be prepared to undertake military programs against vulnerable communist regimes." His point was that Goldwater was a "radical conservative" in that he wanted to return to the roots of America's founding, to the political philosophy of "the men who forged this country and hammered out its Constitution."[20]

And then there was the thoughtful piece in *Fortune*, which outlined Goldwater's basic philosophy—his belief in "the whole man" and the Constitution as the protector of freedom—and his positions on issues like school segregation, foreign aid, and the Cold War. Arguing that "many of his views would be liabilities in a presidential candidate," the author nevertheless concluded that "Goldwater had struck a blow against the faceless neutralism that has been infecting both parties, and restored a sense of party definition."[21]

THE TELEVISION NETWORKS also recognized Goldwater's ascendancy into the higher political realms and frequently called on him as the spokesman for American conservatism. In January 1962, CBS News sponsored a one-hour televised debate between him and Democratic Senator Eugene McCarthy of Minnesota in the old Supreme Court Chamber in the Capitol, which had long served as the meeting place of the U.S. Senate.

The topic was "Does a big federal government threaten our freedom?" Goldwater confidently defended the conservative position against his verbose opponent whose questions were often longer than Goldwater's answers. On federal aid to education, Goldwater suggested that rather than sending direct aid with all of its inevitable strings to the states, the federal government should provide a tax credit that "would enable the states to have about $3 to $4 billion more available" for school bond purposes. It was an example of creative legislative thinking that anticipated the Reagan reforms of the 1980s.[22]

He was again a guest of CBS-TV on its "Washington Conversation" program in April of that same year. Always prepared to define the conservative position, he proposed a "long-range" phasing out of farm subsidies, an "adjustment" of the graduated income tax, and the prohibition of the use of union dues for politics. In 1964, his opponents would grossly distort these views by charging that he favored an immediate, overnight end to agricultural subsidies and a radical rewriting of the federal income tax to help the rich. Asked directly whether in view of the conservative resurgence among Republicans he was not the "logical medium for its expression" at the 1964 convention, he replied, "I would certainly hope not. I would hope that they could find someone who could do it much better than I. I feel that the best job I can do for my country is in the Senate."[23]

In early August, he was paired with Senator Jacob Javits of New York, a liberal Republican, on ABC's "Issues and Answers," with much of the discussion centering around foreign aid. And again, when the question of 1964 came up, as it inevitably did, he repeated, "I am not interested at all in 1964 in any way."[24]

Three years later, when the national news media were describing him as a warmonger, an extremist, and psychologically unfit to be president, Goldwater would recall the earlier glowing words of *Time* and *Newsweek* and his respectful treatment on CBS and other television networks and wonder what had happened to change their rhetoric so radically, when his had not changed at all. One major reason: the media, like every other part of the liberal establishment, did not believe that Goldwater could win the nomination. Therefore, there was no real danger of his being able to implement his radical ideas.

Goldwater's uncompromising commitment to conservatism, and their personal ties to White, Rusher, and Ashbrook brought nineteen busy, conservative Republicans to Chicago on October 8, 1961, to discuss how they might translate the political passion that the senator from Arizona aroused into actual delegates and a presidential nomination at the next Republican national convention.

There were two representatives from New York, three from New England, ten from the Midwest, five from the South, one from the Southwest, and one from the Far West. There were two congressmen, Ashbrook and Don Bruce of Indiana, and three state chairmen: David Nichols of Maine, Charles Thone of Nebraska, and Greg Shorey of South Carolina. There were several well-off businessmen but only one genuine "fat cat"—Roger Milliken of Spartanburg, South Carolina.

During the discussion, there was unanimous agreement that the principal goal should be "to reestablish the Republican party as an effective conservative force in American politics." Several urged that the effort be geared toward nominating Barry Goldwater in 1964, but White argued that it "was still much too early to tie ourselves and our program to any specific candidate. In the end, everyone concurred."[25] Although the point was probably obvious, White warned that those who had controlled the Republican party for more than two decades "would fight us tooth and nail every inch of the way once they discovered what we were up to."[26]

White was asked to draw up a plan of action and a budget; the date for the next meeting was set for December 10th. In the meantime, White was to call on Goldwater and advise him of the group and its purpose, that is, to turn the Republican party in a more conservative direction. Since White knew the senator only casually, Rusher, as publisher of *National Review,* wrote Goldwater for an appointment.

On November 17th, White and Charles Thone met with the senator in his office on the fourth floor of the Old Senate Office Building (now the Russell Senate Building). Cheerful and relaxed, Goldwater chatted with Thone, whom he had known as the administrative assistant to Senator Roman Hruska, about Nebraska politics, and then turned to White, who made the following points: (1) the Chicago group had not been formed to work for his candidacy or that of anyone else; (2) any decision about a presidential candidate should wait until after the 1962 congressional elections; and (3) they intended to concentrate on setting up an organization and rounding up Republicans throughout the country who agreed that "the party should be forged into an effective conservative instrument."

A delighted Goldwater interrupted, "This is the best thing I've heard of since I became active in the Republican party on the national scene. I wish you fellows a lot of luck." Then he added, "Is there anything I can do to help you?" White said he would welcome any suggestions from Goldwater and that they would like to keep in touch with him. He asked for a copy of the senator's travel schedule so that members of the group could get hold of him when he visited their state.

Goldwater agreed, and the talk shifted to national politics during which the senator, according to a surprised White, "seemed to feel that [Rockefeller] had the 1964 nomination all but sewed up and that there was no one on the horizon who might head him off." White later

learned that Rockefeller was in fact spending considerable time courting Goldwater, trying to persuade him that he was not all that liberal.[27]

White and Thone were delighted that the man "who had become the
symbol of the conservative cause in America" had given them the
green light, although it would have flashed a bright red if Goldwater
had known the true intentions of the Chicago group.[28] Strictly speaking, White had not lied: he and the others were not committed at that
time to a Goldwater nomination, but the goal—turning the Republican
party into a more conservative channel—would inevitably depend
upon the presidential nominee in 1964, and the only conservative
candidate was Barry Goldwater.

That may have been clear to White and the others, but not to
Goldwater, who meant it when he said that he had no plans, no staff, no
program, and no ambition for the presidency. White was confident that
he could provide the plans, the staff, and the program, but the wish, the
hunger to be president was another matter, and it would create serious
problems over the next two years between the senator and what would
become the National Draft Goldwater Committee.

Twenty-eight men gathered for the December 12, 1961, meeting in
Chicago, including newcomers Governor Donald J. Nutter of Montana;
Albert J. Fay, national committeeman from Texas; Congressman John
Rousselot of California; and Elton E. "Tad" Smith, the Texas state
chairman. While all geographical sections of the nation were represented, no women were present as well as no blacks or other minorities,
reflecting the almost all-white nature of the conservative movement in
the early 1960s.

After reporting on his successful meeting with Goldwater, White
presented a budget—$65,000 for 1962, including a modest salary of
$24,000 for himself and one for his secretary, Rita Bree—and then
turned to a large wall map of the United States, which he had divided
into nine regions. He suggested a part-time director for each region who
would organize his state down to at least the congressional and where
possible the precinct level. No state, he emphasized, would be over-
looked or written off. As Rusher wrote, "We knew that there were
conservatives, and therefore potential allies, in the Republican organizations of even the most liberal states."[29]

White's vision of how to conservatize the Republican party contrasted sharply with Rockefeller's traditional "back-room" method of
obtaining the 1964 presidential nomination. Top Republican officials

were approached in every state where Rockefeller was thought to have a chance of winning delegates. If he were sympathetic, he would be flown to New York in one of the Rockefeller's private planes, meet personally with the governor, and be plied with inducements, political and financial. The view from the top of the Rockefeller mountain was intoxicating, and a number of leading Republicans committed themselves to the New York governor.[30]

White and his colleagues could not match Rockefeller's money or organization, but they had something the New York governor did not have: a philosophical vision for their party and the nation that transcended normal party politics. They understood that the only way they could defeat Rockefeller and his powerful liberal cohorts was to launch an all-out grassroots effort based on the new political and economic forces in the Midwest, the South, and the West. And they succeeded.

In his professorial way, White spelled out for his fellow conservatives how they could triumph against seemingly insurmountable odds. Two years before each national convention, precinct caucuses were held in almost every state to name precinct, community, and county committeemen. In most cases, the committeemen served through the spring meetings two years later at which delegates were picked for the state conventions or candidates for delegate were selected to run in the primaries. "Our job," White emphasized, "[will] be to assure the selection of *conservative* precinct committeemen and committeewomen in 1962 and 1963 who [will] then have a major voice in picking delegates dedicated to our principles in 1964."

White stressed that most delegates were picked from congressional districts, which made it all the more important to have "strong congressional district organizations with firm roots at the precinct level." Many older Republican professionals had lost touch with the grass roots and were ripe for replacement by well-disciplined conservatives. But White cautioned the others not to incite insurrection unless necessary and to work with party officials, if they were conservative, wherever possible.

The objective was to secure a majority of the delegates for a first ballot nomination in San Francisco.

IN THE EARLY 1960s, until the assassination of President John F. Kennedy on November 22, 1963, American politics operated on several different levels. The Kennedy administration chartered an erratic course, veering wildly from the dark days of the Bay of Pigs fiasco and the uncontested building of the Berlin Wall in 1961 to the peaceful resolution of the Cuban missile crisis in the fall of 1962 and the careful nurturing of the civil rights movement. Barry Goldwater spoke out for conservatism around the country and soared in Republican party popularity while Rockefeller, hampered by his divorce, remarriage, and defiant liberalism, went from a strong first to a distant second behind Goldwater.

Throughout those years, the conservative movement grew steadily in numbers and confidence with the youth group, Young Americans for Freedom, going so far as to sponsor a rally in New York City's famed Madison Square Garden for its hero, the man from Arizona. The Clif White group quietly went about its business of lining up pro-Goldwater delegates for the 1964 national convention. Each level operated independently, and each was affected by the others.

WHILE KENNEDY STAYED in the White House, fretting about the coalition of conservative Democrats and Republicans that blocked many of his legislative proposals, Goldwater took happily to the road and continued to popularize conservatism. In June 1961 alone, he made twenty-three speeches away from Washington without ever missing an important roll call vote.

His mobility was aided by a private plane and crew provided by Curtis Steuart, an old friend and Washington businessman. His travels and writings generated a large, adulatory flow of mail, more than eight hundred letters a day, about 80 percent of them from outside Arizona. He brushed aside all questions from the media about 1964 with his standard response: "I tell them that I am not seeking the presidency—and I'm not." But as President Kennedy struggled to implement the New Frontier and Governor Rockefeller faltered, Goldwater increasingly added, "But that's not a position you have to promise to hold right down to the wire. You never know in this business what you may have to do."[31]

FOR YOUNG CONSERVATIVES in particular, the 1960s was the decade not of John F. Kennedy but Barry M. Goldwater, not Students for a Democratic Society but Young Americans for Freedom, not *The New*

Republic but *National Review,* not Herbert Marcuse but Russell Kirk, not Norman Mailer but Ayn Rand, not a meaningless civil war in Vietnam but an important battle in the protracted conflict against communism. They were for Barry Goldwater because he gave them the blunt, honest, black-and-white answers to life and its problems that young people always look for.

In March 1961, only six months after its birth, Young Americans for Freedom held a wildly enthusiastic rally in New York City's Manhattan Center, which featured William F. Buckley Jr., Russell Kirk, and Barry Goldwater, the three men who made the American conservative movement.

Addressing the subject of "The Conservative Sweep on the American Campus," Goldwater declared that the young conservatives whom he had met at numerous colleges were "the national leaders of tomorrow. They are concerned with their future, and they don't want it mortgaged by political persuasions with which they are not in sympathy."

That was strong stuff but not strong enough for *The New Guard,* YAF's monthly magazine, which stated in its first issue that young America was "sick unto death of collectivism, socialism, statism, and the other utopian isms which have poisoned the minds, weakened the wills, and smothered the spirits of Americans for three decades and more."[32]

The Goldwater fever was also being caught by traditional Young Republicans, a critically important part of the GOP. Unlike the Democrats, older Republicans depended heavily upon their young members as workers and future leaders. Thus, at its national convention three months later, the Young Republican National Federation approved a platform that opposed federal aid to education in any form, rejected any federally administered health insurance plan, called for an immediate resumption of nuclear testing, and supported a total trade embargo of the communist bloc. Hundreds of delegates wore Goldwater buttons, sported Goldwater hats, and carried Goldwater attaché cases. When the senator began to address the meeting, a cheering throng of three thousand repeatedly interrupted his remarks. That same day, New York newspapers published photographs of Governor Rockefeller playing pool at a Brooklyn Boys Club.

James Harff, a Northwestern University student and avowed conservative, was elected chairman of the National College Young Republicans over two liberal candidates. When Harff proclaimed that "the conscience of the conservative has spoken at this convention," the delegates went wild. When the cheering stopped, one of Rockefeller's middle-aged observers said, "These aren't real Republicans . . . they're young zealots."[33] Indeed they were "zealots," radicals fighting for a renewal of Republican principles.

YAF's leaders were so new to national politics that they did not know what could not be done, like scheduling a rally with the theme, "Victory Over Communism," in New York City's Madison Square Garden. The very thought had young liberals in the Ripon Society and elsewhere laughing, but they fell silent when 18,000 conservatives filled the huge arena to the uppermost galleries, eager to hear Senator Strom Thurmond of South Carolina, still a Democrat, Senator John Tower, and Barry Goldwater. Brent Bozell, red-haired and fiery-worded, warmed up the crowd by issuing orders: "To the commander in Berlin: Tear down the Wall!" If there had been transportation outside, there would have been a march on Berlin and beyond.

By the time Goldwater was introduced, it was late, past eleven o'clock, but people had been waiting for that moment since Robert Taft had lost the presidential nomination in 1952, since Joe McCarthy had been censured in 1954, since Kennedy had stolen the election from Nixon in 1960. They had endured all the insults, slurs, and smears— extreme right, radical right, far right, ultra right—and now they beat their hands together and raised their voices high, creating a cataract of sound and praise that lasted for five . . . ten . . . fifteen . . . twenty minutes without faltering.

Goldwater stood at the podium, at first patiently, then impatiently, then puzzled, and finally resigned. The people, lifted up and beyond themselves, were transported into a state of ecstasy familiar to all true believers. They chanted their mantra over and over, "We want Barry!", "We want Barry!", "We want Barry!" until at last, their hands stinging, their voices hoarse, they reluctantly subsided—not into silence but into a new game in which one part of the crowd shouted, "Viva!" and the other chanted back, "Olé!" This was not an audience so much as a multitude that moved and swayed and surged like a Pentecostal congregation on Sunday morning. At last, Goldwater brought the people back down to earth by leaning into the mike and saying, his low deep voice cutting through the scattered "We want Barry!" 's—"Well, if you'll shut up, you'll get him." Like chastened children, the people cheered their hero one more time and at last fell silent.[34]

He told the people what they wanted to hear but also what he and his audience believed: "Conservatism is the wave of the future," it "has come of age at a time of great national need." "No wonder," he said, "that the proponents of the Welfare State are becoming alarmed. . . . They are beginning to read the handwriting on the wall and it spells the twilight of radical liberalism . . . in this country." The crowd roared.

Addressing the central theme of the evening, the senator declared, solemnly and without any flourish, that "we must—for the sake of survival—recognize communism for the enemy it is and dedicate ourselves once and for all to a policy of victory." It was an unconditional call for action because in the spring of 1962 the barbarians were at the gates of Florida and Berlin and a hundred other outposts of freedom around the world.

The following morning, the *New York Times* published a front-page article (and a three-column photograph) about the Madison Square Garden rally, signaling that the voice of the East was taking Goldwater quite seriously.[35]

MEANWHILE, FROM the winter of 1961 until the fall of 1963, Clif White traveled more than a million miles on behalf of the Draft Goldwater effort, visiting old political friends, enlisting political neophytes, steadily building an organization in every state and congressional district, and discovering that conservatives had more political muscle than they realized.

Political money was another matter. Rusher called the first half of 1962 the draft movement's "Valley Forge." By April the money Roger Milliken had raised was nearly gone, and White was reduced to making long-distance telephone calls rather than flying to see people in Texas, Illinois, or the West Coast; he spent $6,000 of the money he had set aside for his son's college education. By September, creditors had become so insistent that he and Rita Bree lunched with Rusher in New York City to tell him that "we would have to fold the tent."[36] Rusher refused to quit. He argued so persuasively that White and Bree agreed to keep going for at least another month.

At almost the last moment, old friends came to the rescue. Robert R. (Randy) Richardson arrived in New York, moved into Suite 3505, and began sharing the rent. Businessmen J. D. "Stets" Coleman and R. Crosby Kemper wrote generous checks, and J. William Middendorf II and Jeremiah Milbank, Jr., who would hold key financial positions in the Goldwater for President Committee, provided enough funds to sustain the operation until after the November elections. Middendorf and Milbank became so proficient at producing urgently needed cash that they were nicknamed "The Brinks Brothers."[37] Rarely before in American politics has so much been accomplished with so little: in its first twelve months of operations, the draft effort raised a total of $43,195, about as much as Rockefeller paid his top speechwriter.[38]

Convinced that the odds for nomination favored Rockefeller, Goldwater continued to tell friends, like Wirt Yerger, chairman of the Mississippi Republican party, that he was not a presidential candidate. Money and organization were worrisome, but also the fact that "I have yet to be approached by a single delegate, let alone leaders of any of the larger states, except Texas." He stressed that more than his personal future was at stake. He dreaded the thought that any decision of his would "kill" the "conservative cause."[39]

In early December of 1962, the hard core again met in Chicago. They had eighteen months to go before the presidential nomination convention, and they agreed that they had only one choice—Barry Goldwater. Their central problem remained: Would the senator approve what they were doing and actively run for the nomination?

White reported that the previous month he had spent several hours with Goldwater in New York City during which he had showed him "the state-by-state organizational chart I was recommending to the group, a proposed budget, a timetable for the state conventions and primaries to be held in 1964, and my estimates of how many Goldwater delegates we could expect to win in each state." White said he had held his breath but all he got out of Goldwater as he scanned White's "black book" was, "This looks good." He promised to read it more carefully the first chance he had.[40]

As far as White was concerned, Goldwater planned to run for the nomination and even wanted White to help him. He later admitted that he was searching too hard for clues that "pointed to [Goldwater] doing what we all wanted him to do." At this point, Goldwater still intended to run for the Senate, not the presidency, in 1964. But when he said, "This looks good" and did nothing to stop White and his colleagues from trying to draft him, a die was cast.

In political fact, Goldwater's chances of winning the nomination were improving. Rockefeller had just won reelection as governor of New York, but with nothing like his resounding triumph four years earlier, due in large measure to David H. Jaquith, the candidate of the newly formed Conservative party of New York. The governor was the favorite in the Gallup Polls and the establishment press, but not among the party rank and file. A recent poll of delegates to the 1960 Republican Convention revealed that Goldwater was their first choice: 264 preferred Goldwater while 203 wanted Rockefeller and only 127 picked Nixon, who had lost, embarrassingly, to Governor Edmund (Pat) Brown of California.

Lyle Wilson, the veteran Washington columnist for United Press International, wrote a much-quoted article that pointed out that with "me-too Republicans" in command, the Republican party had lost thirteen of seventeen national elections since 1940. What the GOP needed, Wilson wrote, "is a commitment to a set of courageous political principles that clearly distinguish it from the Democratic party."[41]

In high anticipation, nearly fifty-five conservatives met in a downtown Chicago motel on December 2, 1962, to launch what would be called the National Draft Goldwater Committee. Among the expanded group were three additional state Republican chairmen, Peter O'Donnell of Texas, John E. Grenier of Alabama, and Wirt Yerger of Mississippi; Congressman William Brock of Tennessee; two national committeewomen, Ione Harrington of Indiana and Hazel Barger of Virginia; Hayes Robertson, Republican chairman for Cook County (Chicago); Jerry Milbank; and Bill Middendorf.

After opening with a brief prayer (reflecting the crusade-like air of the Goldwater movement), White presented a proposed budget for the preconvention period totaling $3.2 million, with some $1.27 million allotted for the primaries.

In *Suite 3505*, White writes that "Negro organizations" were placed high among those to be contacted because blacks "would contrast the obvious sincerity of Barry Goldwater's interest and sympathy with their legitimate aspirations with the patently phony play for their votes being made by many other politicians in both parties." It was thought, he went on, that blacks "would reject the patronizing approach of the Left, which seeks to deal with them as a mass voting bloc, and that many of them would embrace the true equality of conservatism, which welcomes [blacks], like all other citizens, as individuals worthy of respect."[42]

It was not to be. Goldwater's constitutional defense of states' rights plus his principled vote against the Civil Rights Act of 1964 the following summer would enrage black leaders and produce an almost monolithic black vote against Goldwater in November 1964.

To win the nomination, White stated, Goldwater needed 655 delegate votes. Their goal would be to obtain seven hundred votes before the national convention was called to order in July 1964, and he proceeded to explain how it would be done. First, 451 delegates would come from twenty "solid" Goldwater states: Alabama, Arizona, Arkansas, Colorado, Florida, Indiana, Louisiana, Maine, Mississippi, Missouri, Montana, Nebraska, New Mexico, North Carolina, Oklahoma, South Carolina, Texas, Utah, Virginia, and Washington. Next, eighty-one votes from four states that were "leaning" toward Goldwater: Georgia, Kentucky, South Dakota, and Tennessee. Three more states—Illinois, Iowa, and Ohio—would yield 142 votes with "extra-hard work." The remaining twenty-six votes would be picked up from split delegations in states like Michigan, New Jersey, Pennsylvania, and Connecticut. For insurance, Goldwater would run in the California primary; its eighty-six delegates would offset any unexpected defections.

As for the general election, White argued that the same Midwest-South-Far West strategy would bring a victory over President Kennedy. Needing a total of 270 electoral votes, White estimated that Goldwater would receive 179 votes from the so-called "solid" states in the South, Midwest, and West. He would pick up thirty-six votes from states leaning toward him, and he would go over the top with sixty-one votes from the traditionally Republican states of Illinois, Iowa, and Ohio. California, with its forty electoral votes, would again ensure victory. White in effect wrote off the big Northeastern states, the property of "Democratic big-city machines."

In short, White's formula required that Goldwater win all the states, mostly in the Midwest and South, that Kennedy had carried with 51 percent or less of the vote in 1960, such as Illinois, Michigan, Missouri, Pennsylvania, and Texas. Goldwater would also have to hold all of the states that Nixon had captured in 1960, such as California, Ohio, and Wisconsin.

Not everyone present agreed that Goldwater could win all the Nixon states, and California was a question mark because of Nixon's gubernatorial defeat. But the consensus was that "hard work on the part of the troops and a fighting campaign by the candidate" could bring a Republican victory in 1964, because the Democrats' hold on the South was clearly slipping.[43] It was decided to unveil the National Draft Goldwater Committee publicly in March 1963.

The money men met separately and had just begun discussing how to raise three million dollars when "Stets" Coleman, a gravel-voiced, roly-poly Virginian, said bluntly, "Look, everybody's been talking about how we need all this money, but who's going to put some up? I pledge $25,000." Middendorf insists that Coleman's pledge "had more to do with the success of the Draft Goldwater Committee than anything else I know" because it "not only got the other boys off their tails" but it guaranteed an institutionalization of their efforts. By the end of the hour, there were pledges of $250,000, and the National Draft Goldwater Committee was truly in business.[44]

Coleman, Middendorf, and Milbank agreed to serve as trustees of the Finance Committee until a national finance chairman could be found. White was elected chairman and instructed to report to Goldwater the plans to launch the Draft Goldwater Committee. He was not to request the senator's overt approval but to obtain his pledge not to disown the draft or repudiate his own possible candidacy. The meeting was all and more than most of its participants had hoped, and they left Chicago feeling they may have helped to make a little history.

Less than eighteen hours after the Chicago meeting adjourned, White was called by an AP correspondent who revealed that information about the get-together of pro-Goldwater conservatives had been leaked, and he was going to write a story. Reluctant to discuss the private affair, White told the reporter that the meeting was pro-Goldwater rather than anti-Rockefeller.

But conflict makes news, and the *New York Herald Tribune* headlined the report: "Goldwater '64 Boom: Move to Block Rocky." CBS was so taken with the story that it called dozens of Chicago motels and finally discovered where White had been registered over the weekend. It dispatched a camera crew to the Essex Inn where a reporter, standing in a room, dramatically announced that this was the *very* spot where "a group of prominent Republicans had met to plot a presidential campaign for Barry Goldwater." The *New York Times* went one step further and accused the draft committee of "splintering" the Republican party.[45]

White and others were furious at being called conspirators and splinterers for simply participating in the political process. Their true crime, as White put it, was their refusal "to pay proper obeisance to the liberal pantheon and the dogma of the welfare state."

The strong reaction of the liberal forces, including the mass media, indicated how potentially powerful Goldwater and conservatism had become within the Republican party. The double agent who leaked information about the Draft Goldwater Committee clearly intended to sink Goldwater's candidacy in a wave of publicity, but in fact he gave added buoyancy to the movement.

White, for his part, was relieved that the operation was at last out in the open, and looked forward to briefing the senator about the committee's plans in early January.[46] What he did not know was that Goldwater had met over the holidays with Arizona friends and advisers to discuss his political future.

Some of the senator's advisers insisted that it was "within the realm of reasonable possibility" for the senator to win the Republican presidential nomination. After evaluating Goldwater's delegate strength in various states, they decided that he had a potential total of 761 delegates, an estimate similar to White's. Should he seek the presidential nomination and lose, Goldwater was reassured, "you would not be jeopardizing your re-election to the Senate." Some advisers were as direct as he: "Whether you like it or not, you owe an obligation to millions of Americans who believe firmly in the principles you have enunciated and who look to you for affirmative leadership."[47] But their emotional appeal did not prevail, at least not at this time.

Although no formal minutes were kept of the December 27th meeting at the Phoenix Country Club, Dean Burch summarized the discussion in a letter to Goldwater. Four major questions were addressed: (1) Could President Kennedy be beaten in 1964? (2) Should Goldwater run for the Senate and the presidency at the same time? (3) If Goldwater ran and was defeated, what political role would he then be able to play in his state and the nation? and (4) Could all the practical demands of a national campaign, especially financial, be met?

The consensus of those present was that it would be very difficult for anyone to defeat Kennedy in 1964. They were not impressed by arguments that Goldwater had to run or there "may not be a United States in

1968"—things would not become "so critical [under Kennedy] as to justify taking a gamble against miserable odds."

Second, there was universal agreement that after mercilessly criticizing Lyndon Johnson in 1960 for running for vice president and the Senate at the same time, Goldwater could not do the same only four years later.

Third, if he were defeated, Goldwater would not have a large enough forum to give his public pronouncements any weight.

Fourth, while there was nothing "insurmountable" about either the finances or organization of a presidential campaign, it would be important to "check the hole card, however, of anyone who blithely suggests that there is more than enough money . . . to carry on such a campaign."[48]

A week later, Goldwater wrote Burch that his letter "coincides exactly with my thinking." For these very reasons he had stated that he would not make a decision about 1964 for at least a year, hoping thereby to "slow down the almost hourly pressure to seek the nomination *which I assure you I do not want*" "emphasis added." By the end of 1963 or early 1964, he said, "I feel that either Rockefeller will have developed an overwhelming lead or somebody promoted by the kingmakers will have been offered as a sacrificial lamb, and I can go my way happily seeking a third term in the Senate."[49]

He was in this frame of mind (Kennedy probably could not be beaten, Rockefeller was the very likely Republican candidate, and Eastern "kingmakers" still controlled the Republican party), when Clif White came calling on him on January 14, 1963, with the good news that the National Draft Goldwater Committee was going public.

Even if someone other than White had been the messenger, the senator would not have been happy with the message. That it was F. Clifton White of New York City ensured a negative response. Although Goldwater admitted in his 1988 memoirs that he "probably would not have won the nomination without the work of White," and that he had made "a mistake" in not naming White chairman of the Republican National Committee in the summer of 1964, Goldwater always saw White as an "upstate New York public relations man" without any "deep conservative conviction."[50] He never made White a confidant as he had non-Arizonans Jay Hall and Bill Baroody.

William Rusher has speculated that far from being too arrogant, White was too deferential and inhibited when dealing with someone whom he admired, like Goldwater, Ronald Reagan, or James Buckley. He must have seemed, Rusher suggests, like "a particularly nerveless operator with some undeniably useful political abilities."[51] In addition, some people had hinted to Goldwater that White was trying to enhance his political stature, and his income, by associating with a potential president. The suggestion had its impact on Goldwater, who was ultra-sensitive about people using his name to enrich themselves. In truth, the outspoken, outdoors senator from Arizona and the cool, cerebral political operator from New York had little in common, aside from their strong commitment to the Republican party.

White's visit was also ill timed because that very day, new assignments to Senate committees had been made, and Goldwater had been ousted from the Republican Policy Committee, which determines GOP strategy in the Senate, a move engineered by Jacob Javits and several other liberals.

Goldwater was still seething and White had barely begun reporting the decisions made in Chicago when the senator held up his hand and said flatly, "Clif, I'm not a candidate. And I'm not going to be. I have no intention of running for the presidency." White tried a light touch: "Well, we thought we would have to draft you." Goldwater was in no mood for banter and said sharply: "Draft, nothin'. I told you I'm not going to run. And I'm telling you now, don't paint me into a corner. It's my political neck and I intend to have something to say about what happens to it."

Seeing all the work, sacrifice, and hopes of the last eighteen months going down the drain, White retorted somewhat heatedly: "Senator [no "Barry" now], I'm not painting you into a corner. You painted yourself there by opening your mouth for the last eight years. You're the leader of the conservative cause in the United States of America, and thousands—millions—of people want you to be their nominee for president. I can't do anything about that and neither can you."

Somewhat subdued, Goldwater answered, "Well, I'm just not going to run." And added rather lamely, "My wife loves me, but she'd leave me if I ran for this thing."[52]

White had no answer for that and left within a few minutes, trying to assimilate the fact that Goldwater had slammed the door in their faces and given the key to his wife.

Taking the first shuttle flight back to New York City, White relayed the disastrous news to Rita Bree and Randy Richardson, who remarked, "Never run a reluctant horse," and waited for Rusher. When his old friend asked how the meeting with Goldwater had gone, White said bluntly, "I'm going to give up politics and go back into business." A stunned Rusher pressed White, "What did Goldwater say to our proposal for a draft?" "It's no use," White said. "He won't permit a draft. He said he wasn't going to run under any circumstances and that's that."[53] Even the perpetually optimistic Rusher was discouraged and seemed to agree, in White's words, that "you couldn't take a grown man by the scruff of the neck and force him to run for president of the United States."[54]

Over the next month, White, Rusher, and other members of the Chicago group constantly conferred with each other, searching for some way around the near Shermanesque resistance of their candidate.[55] Rusher wrote an emotional letter to Goldwater, pleading, not for his blessing, but to be allowed to go ahead on their own. "The organization we have built in the past year," he said, "is very probably the last one that will ever seek, in a serious and systematic way, to turn the GOP into more conservative channels." Goldwater responded that "any overt action at this time [regarding a presidential nomination] could do me irreparable damage, because I plan to run for the Senate in 1964 and do not want anything like this to happen."[56]

Refusing to accept that as a final answer, Rusher, in February 1963, used the pages of *National Review* to assert that "Goldwater, *and Goldwater alone* (for in this respect Scranton and Romney are in no better position than Rockefeller), can carry enough Southern and border states to offset the inevitable Kennedy conquests in the big industrial states of the North and still stand a serious chance of winning the election."[57] He later learned that Goldwater was impressed by his analysis.

The senator might even have believed there was a conspiracy afoot at *National Review*. For at the same time Frank Meyer wrote the senator that it was "your duty" to become a candidate because "1964 may be the last opportunity to bring into being a responsible and sober conservative alternative to the ruinous liberal leadership which is quite literally carrying the United States to the verge of disaster." Goldwater had "a very good chance of winning," argued Meyer, "but even defeat would leave a powerful conservative opposition."

Goldwater promptly replied that he doubted that "I am the only man who can give leadership at this moment, but if that be true, it will be proven, and I don't think I have ever ducked anything in my life, but I am hoping fervently that I will never have to take this step." Tellingly, he added, "I have never been much of a leader, but more of a pusher."[58]

White, along with Charlie Barr, again met with Goldwater in his Senate office on February 5. Prior to their meeting, White had written the senator a three-page, single-spaced letter in which he reviewed the origin and development of the draft organization and concluded by saying that only Goldwater could lead the Republican party "for the first time in its history" to becoming "a truly national party."[59]

But the senator would have none of it. He told White and Barr that all he wanted to do was to stay in the Senate as long as the people of Arizona wanted him to represent them. When Barr shot back, "It's a free country. We're free to draft a candidate if we choose and there isn't much you or anyone else can do about it," the senator smiled at Barr's spunk but said they would discover what he could do if they pushed him too far.[60]

Barr later confided to White that Goldwater had been even more vehement during a private talk. "He was throwing cold water on the whole idea," said Barr. "And he was throwing it by the bucketful— with ice cubes in it." Their only consolation was that Goldwater had not pulled a "Sherman"; he had not said he would not accept the nomination if chosen.[61]

A disconsolate White decided to hold one more, perhaps the last, meeting of the draft group in Chicago in mid-February. Beside White, Rusher, and Barr, those in attendance were Frank Whetstone, Robert Matthews, and Robert Hughes of Indiana, Tad Smith and Peter O'Donnell of Texas, Congressman Ashbrook, and Andy Carter of New Mexico. As White recounts, they examined and discarded a dozen different ways to get Goldwater, the only possible candidate for conservatives, to run.

At long last, after hours of talk and many pots of coffee, there was an unusually long silence that was finally broken by Hughes, who growled, "There's only one thing we *can* do. Let's draft the son-of-a-bitch."

"What if he won't let us draft him?" someone protested. "He's already told Clif he wouldn't sit still for a draft."

"We'll draft him anyway," Hughes persisted. "I mean *really* draft him."[62]

Once the idea had been aired, it was clear that it was the only way

out of their dilemma. They had all mesmerized themselves into thinking that you could not *force* a man to seek the presidency. But in the
absence of a flat repudiation, they decided that you could *draft* someone with the hope that he would accept it for the good of the party and
the nation.

Hughes' proposal was adopted unanimously, and they moved to the
next problem: naming a chairman whose stature was so high in the
party that Goldwater could not publicly repudiate him. Because of
Goldwater's coolness toward him, White could not be the man, although all agreed he would steer "the bandwagon we were building
right into San Francisco." They had, in fact, a very logical and present
candidate: Peter O'Donnell, chairman of the Texas Republican party,
who asked for twenty-four hours to think it over and then accepted.

A meeting that had begun in a slough of despond ended with the
Chicago group confident, against all the odds, that they could nominate
and then elect Barry Goldwater the thirty-sixth president of the United
States of America.[63]

9

Making Up His Mind

WHEN PETER O'DONNELL, Ione Harrington, and Judy Fernald formally announced the birth of the National Draft Goldwater Committee on April 8, 1963, at a crowded news conference in the Mayflower Hotel in Washington, D.C., Clif White was upstairs in his suite. He had determined to keep out of sight because of Goldwater's apparent antipathy toward him, but he had helped O'Donnell draft a statement and gone over every possible question a reporter might ask.

The conference was an unquestioned success with O'Donnell a confident, often witty spokesman. After explaining that the committee had been formed to "mobilize the tremendous, spontaneous enthusiasm for Senator Goldwater that is sweeping the country," O'Donnell outlined a 1964 presidential strategy that anticipated Nixon's Southern strategy in 1968. "The key to Republican success," he said, "lies in converting a weakness (the paucity of Republican votes in the South) into a strength and becoming a truly national party."

He estimated that Goldwater would receive 280 electoral votes, 10 more than needed to win, as follows: the North and East, 11; border states, 17; the South, 100; the Midwest, 106; mountain states, 30; and Pacific states, 16. He stressed a "choice" theme, the theme Goldwater would use in his formal announcement nine months later. The way to victory, said O'Donnell, was to provide the American people with "a clear-cut choice between the New Frontier of the Kennedys and Republican principles" and, he added, the opportunity to provide that choice "is now open" with the nomination and election of Barry Goldwater.[1]

Asked what would the committee do if Goldwater said "I want it to stop," O'Donnell adroitly sidestepped, "I would like to see what he says before I would comment on that." That afternoon reporters found the senator at a Republican reception and pressed hard for a reaction. At last, he said, "I am not taking any position on this draft movement. It's their time and their money. But they are going to have to get along without any help from me." As White later revealed, everyone at the draft committee "breathed a collective sigh of relief. Our gamble had paid off. Goldwater had refused to deliver the knockout punch we had feared so long. We were in business at last!"[2]

A week later, in an interview with the *New York Times,* Goldwater gave them a little more space in which to operate:

I don't want the nomination. I'm not looking for it. I haven't authorized anybody to look for it for me. But who can tell what will happen a year from now? A man would be a damn fool to predict with finality what he would do in this unpredictable world.[3]

Why was Barry Goldwater so reluctant to seek the presidency? As he admits in his 1979 memoirs (ghosted by Steve Shadegg), part of the reason was "purely personal." The notion of becoming a "prisoner" in the White House, surrounded by sycophantic advisers, the Secret Service, and the press, "was repulsive to me." He just did not want to surrender his privacy. Then too, having watched Eisenhower and now Kennedy for a decade, he understood the magnitude of the problems confronting the nation and how difficult they were to solve, given Congress and a "stubborn" bureaucracy. Both institutions would fiercely resist the limited-government, states' rights reforms that he felt were necessary to repair the Republic. And finally, he was simply overawed by the presidency: "Having no lust for the power of the office, I just could not conceptualize a Barry Goldwater presidency."[4]

There were also political reasons for his hesitation. He was an outsider, a Westerner, a senator from a state with only five electoral votes. The odds were enormous against his winning the nomination and then winning the presidency. He was proud of his senatorial victories and did not want to make a fool of himself by losing badly running for president. Nor was it just himself he was thinking of; there was conservatism, too. As he once remarked:

> Suppose I get in and then get the living hell beaten out of me by Kennedy? What would that do to conservatism? It would hurt it—it might even kill it. But if after looking it over I figured that I could make it a real horse race, then that's something else again. If I could come within 5 percent of a majority [i.e., 45 percent], that would be really a victory for conservatism even if we lost. It would enhance conservatism, and make the Kennedys take in their sails.[5]

He had every right to be skeptical about his chances. He remembered how he had sat all night in his Chicago hotel room at the 1960 national convention, and not one single delegate had showed up to pledge his support. The experience had made him extra careful about people who promised they could deliver the political equivalent of the moon—the White House.

Another factor was his friendly relationship with Nelson Rockefeller. Starting in 1962, the two men began discussing party and policy problems on the telephone and at breakfast and dinner meetings at Rockefeller's home in Washington, D.C. Goldwater discovered they had much in common: "a distrust of Nixon as a politician, general agreement on greater fiscal restraint by the federal government (although Rockefeller was far from a fiscal conservative), and a tough stand against communism."[6]

Always willing to think the best of people, Goldwater became convinced that *the* symbol of Eastern liberalism had moved to the right. As indeed he had, in a calculated attempt to persuade Goldwater to support his nomination or at the very least not to oppose it actively.

The Rockefeller strategy worked so well that by early 1963 Goldwater had decided that among the possible candidates—Rockefeller, Nixon, and Governor George Romney of Michigan—"I preferred Rockefeller." But because the vast majority of conservatives did not share his charitable views about the New York governor, "I did my best to keep my mouth shut."[7] That Mr. Conservative would favor Mr. Liberal over Mr. Pragmatic and Mr. Businessman is only one instance of Goldwater's lifelong tendency to personalize his political decisions.

Most of the media and many Republican leaders continued to list Rockefeller as the front-runner for the nomination although the Gallup

Poll, in March 1963, gave Kennedy a long lead, 63–32 percent, over the New York governor.[8] One potential problem—his divorce of Mary Todhunter, his wife of thirty-one years and the mother of their five children, and his open relationship with a much younger, married woman, Margaretta "Happy" Murphy—seemed to have disappeared from the news and the public's mind. And Rockefeller's aides kept emphasizing the governor's new conservatism. But Rockefeller's fundamental beliefs—that government had a crucial role to play in society and that U.S. foreign policy required a big defense stick—mirrored the welfare state neoconservatism of the 1980s rather than the limited-government conservatism of the 1950s and 1960s.

Another factor in Goldwater's decision regarding the presidency was his friendship with President Kennedy, whom he had served with in the Senate for eight years. He liked Jack and thought he might make a decent president, although he had been shaken by his meeting with him in April 1961 just prior to the Bay of Pigs invasion in Cuba.

On that occasion, Goldwater recalled that Kennedy seemed preoccupied as they sat in the Oval Office, bantering back and forth as they had so often in the Senate.

"So you want this fucking job, eh?" asked Kennedy.

Goldwater laughed and said, "You must be reading some of those conservative right-wing newspapers."

The president then got down to business. The first phase of the Cuban operation, he revealed, had not gone well, Castro's air force had not been destroyed as planned. As the tale unfolded, it seemed that the anti-Castro exiles were supposed to have had sixteen B-26 bombers, but the State Department had persuaded Kennedy to cut the number in half to make more believable the official story that the United States was not involved.

As he listened in disbelief, Goldwater realized that Kennedy was having second thoughts about the entire operation. The president asked his Senate friend what he would do. "I was stunned," remembered Goldwater. "The president was not a profile in courage . . . he projected little of the confidence and lofty resolve of his eloquent speeches. . . . He did not seem to have the old-fashioned guts to go on."[9]

For Goldwater, the situation was simple. Nearly 1,500 men would soon be on the beaches at the Bay of Pigs, and the United States had a professional and moral responsibility to help them. He reminded the president that the navy and its fighter planes were standing by and that there was still time to launch another wave of bombers to destroy Castro's planes on the ground, which would enable the exiles to execute their invasion plan. He argued heatedly that action was "moral and legal and would be understandable to the entire free world."

In his 1988 memoirs, Goldwater goes on to say that the United States had to demonstrate its strength because it "could not tolerate nuclear missiles in Cuba." Writing about events that happened more than a quarter of a century earlier, Goldwater clearly confuses the Bay of Pigs invasion of April 1961 with the Cuban Missile Crisis of October 1962. There was no threat of nuclear missiles in Cuba in the spring of 1961.

As the two men continued to discuss what could be done to salvage the anti-Castro invasion, Goldwater realized for the first time that "I had the toughness of mind and will to lead the country."[10] Others might be more educated or have better speaking and other skills, but he felt he had something that those with greater talents did not have: "an unshakable belief in, and willingness to defend, the fundamental interests of my country."[11]

The essential point, Goldwater insisted, was not world opinion but American "self-interest," which justified action against a communist dictator in its backyard.

"I would do whatever is necessary," he told Kennedy, "to assure the invasion is a success." And he repeated, "Whatever is necessary."

He did not recommend the use of nuclear weapons because they were not necessary; the United States had sufficient conventional air power to get the job done. His voice rising, Goldwater concluded that the American people and every free nation would thank Kennedy "for ridding the world of Castro." The president seemed to relax, and he replied, "You're right."[12]

Goldwater left the Oval Office thinking that enough U.S. air cover would be provided to allow those early freedom fighters to land at the Bay of Pigs and ultimately make their way to Havana. He was grievously mistaken. Kennedy granted permission for the first air strike of B-26s but canceled any follow-up, aborting the planned attack by U.S. navy jet fighters stationed on the nearby USS *Boxer*. "Kennedy," Goldwater concluded, "clearly had lost his nerve." And with tragic result: the anti-Castro brigade was routed, three hundred men were killed, and the rest were imprisoned.[13]

Kennedy's indecisiveness during their private meeting in the White

House prompted Goldwater to begin reevaluating his unwillingness to run for the presidency, although he told no one. He was also influenced by the course of events in Vietnam where Kennedy again equivocated by (1) dispatching 17,000 U.S. troops but with orders not to shoot and (2) praising and then undercutting President Ngo Ding Diem, who was murdered in a United States-sanctioned military coup the same month that Kennedy was assassinated.

By the summer of 1963, Goldwater was convinced that "because of his wavering on foreign policy and his worn-out domestic spending programs, Kennedy was vulnerable and could be defeated in his bid for reelection." [14]

But he was still undecided about his own role when Nelson Rockefeller shocked most Republicans and upset American politics by suddenly marrying Happy Murphy on May 4, 1963, one month after she divorced her husband, Dr. James S. Murphy. From the perspective of the 1990s, with the salacious details of John Kennedy's ongoing adultery, Lyndon Johnson's eye for women, and Bill Clinton's lurid extramarital affairs, Rockefeller's desire to marry someone he had been sleeping with seems almost Victorian. But Kennedy, Johnson, and Clinton are Democrats; Republican presidents and would-be presidents are expected to keep their affairs private and their lusts tucked away in their hearts.

Republican distaste for Rockefeller's decision to discard his wife of several decades and marry his mistress hardened into cold disdain when Dr. Murphy asked for and was given custody of the four small Murphy children. When the governor, accompanied by a beaming Happy in an enormous picture hat, addressed the annual luncheon of the National Republican Women's Club in the grand ballroom of the Waldorf Astoria, an entire table of elderly ladies deliberately rose and slowly walked out on an embarrassed Rockefeller while two thousand stony-faced women watched their exit approvingly. At the end of his remarks, he was greeted with the sound of four thousand gloved hands barely touching, making no more noise than a gravedigger throwing dirt on a coffin. As columnist Stewart Alsop wrote, Rockefeller could have remarried or run for president, but he could not do both. [15]

Rockefeller had been leading Goldwater by about 2-to-1 among Republicans in the Gallup presidential poll, but a month after his marriage in June, Rockefeller plummeted from 43 to 30 percent while Goldwater jumped from 26 to 35 percent. A few days later, Gallup reported Kennedy 60 percent, Goldwater 36 percent in a national trial heat. A month earlier, Kennedy had led Goldwater by 67 percent to 27 percent.[16] Most conservatives saw the controversy over Rockefeller's marriage as a heaven-sent disaster for the Republican party's number-one liberal, but Goldwater was uncomfortable with the shift of emphasis from public issues and policies to personalities and private lives.

The senator was still unsure whether he should run although he told a reporter in mid-June, "I don't want this nomination but it may be forced on me. If I'm put in the position where I have to take it, I won't be a reluctant tiger. I'll get out and fight." Ironically, his determination to delay any announcement was reinforced by advice that President Kennedy had once given him: "Don't announce too soon, Barry. The minute you do you will be the target. If you give them eighteen months to shoot you down, they will probably be able to do it."[17]

Two events during the month of July finally helped him make up his mind: a savage anti-Goldwater speech by an accusatory Rockefeller and a roaring pro-Goldwater rally in Washington, D.C.

The more important occurred on July 14, 1963, when Rockefeller declared that the Republican party was "in real danger of subversion" by the radical Right who rejected the "fundamental principles of our heritage," including equal opportunity for all, freedom of speech and information, fiscal integrity, and the free enterprise system. Republicans, he said, could not stand by idly "in the face of this threat. . . . One must be either for or against these forces." In an obvious reference to a favorite Goldwater theme, Rockefeller agreed that in the next presidential election, the voters should be given "a choice." But that choice, that alternative, he said, could "never be found in a party of extremism, a party of sectionalism, a party of racism, a party that disclaims responsibility for most of the population." The Republican party stood at "the crossroads of its destiny," he declared. "Its destiny is to save the nation by first saving itself."[18]

Rockefeller's prime example of the radical Right at work within the Republican party was the recent Young Republican national convention. He spoke of the deeply disturbing proceedings in San Francisco where "tactics of totalitarianism" were used by "Birchers and others of the radical Right lunatic fringe." In fact, it was the outgoing chairman, moderate Leonard Nadasdy, who had employed crude, antidemocratic tactics, so much so that the convention rejected his hand-picked successor, Charles R. McDevitt, and elected Donald E. "Buz" Lukens, an ardent Goldwater supporter, as the new chairman.

Lukens' victory was assured when the featured speaker of the convention, Senator Barry Goldwater of Arizona, launched a slashing attack on "the self-styled 'liberals' of today." Goldwater brought the Young Republicans to their feet again and again with his unrelenting assault on the "cynical alliance between the politicians who call themselves 'liberal' and the corrupt big-city machines whose job it is to deliver the bloc votes of the big Northern cities." His voice sharp with scorn, he declared that the modern "liberals" were "not only morally bankrupt but they are also intellectually bankrupt. They have not had a new idea in thirty years. They are dead and finished."[19]

Striking back, Rockefeller, in his Declaration of July 14th, indicted conservatives and insisted that real Republicans had to save the party, and the nation, from the radical Right lunatic fringe. Gone was the cordial host of the issues-oriented breakfasts and dinners at his palatial Foxhall mansion in Washington. Gone was the moderate eager to forge philosophical links with Goldwater and other conservatives. Here was a militant, uncompromising Inquisitor determined to destroy the dark forces of the radical Right and ultraconservatism within his party.

At first, Goldwater believed the governor was acting out of frustration and anger, lashing out at conservatives in an emotional response to the strong criticism he was receiving in the media and his sharp fall in the polls.

But Rockefeller was engaged in Machiavellian politics. As revealed by Michael Kramer and Sam Roberts in their investigative biography, Rockefeller realized that he needed an issue to counter the conservative challenge to him and "the extreme Right was it." The Young Republican convention served as a handy excuse "to abandon his neoconservatism" and to attack the radical Right within the GOP. While party harmony had been necessary for his presidential ambitions before his remarriage crippled his prospects, party discord was now the word. His purpose was twofold: to terrify Republicans about "the radical Right" to such an extent that they would turn to him to save the party and recapture the White House in 1964 and to turn Republicans' attention away from his marital twists.

As part of his calculated strategy, Rockefeller followed up his speech with a news conference at which he challenged Goldwater to debate, declaring, "The great threat is whether the radical wing, part of Senator

Goldwater's following, will be able to capture its leader." The man who had preached party harmony when he seemed the certain nominee now sought to divide and conquer the party. All the while he was giving aid, comfort, and ammunition for the 1964 campaign to the real enemy, the Democrats.[20]

Goldwater was first shocked and saddened by Rockefeller's Declaration of July 14, with its wild and divisive charges. Then he was angered by Rockefeller's news conference at which the governor implied that Goldwater was a puppet of the radical Right. Goldwater shot back that the nation ought to be more concerned about "the radical Left" inside the government than anyone outside it. He was finally driven into action by Rockefeller's arrogant assertion in early August that he would not support Goldwater as the Republican nominee against President Kennedy if he were "a captive of the radical Right."[21]

Quite clearly Rockefeller had declared war on conservatives in general and Goldwater in particular. And there was one thing that Goldwater had never backed away from: an important fight on matters of principle and character. Immediately at stake was control of the Republican party that had been dominated by Eastern liberals for decades. It was time to take the GOP away from them and entrust it to the great coalition of West-South-Midwest conservatives who were now a majority of the party.

He looked forward to the battle; for too long, the West had been a colony of big Eastern money. Eastern companies, syndicates, and banks had bled the West of its natural resources and then abandoned it. It was time to pay back the East for its arrogance and injustice.[22]

BENEATH HIS COOL, Harvard-trained exterior, Peter O'Donnell was a Texas wildcat oil gambler. To prove that the National Draft Goldwater Committee was a force to contend with, he decided to hold a giant Fourth of July rally in Washington, D.C. Clif White was opposed, arguing that it was probably the worst day in the whole year to hold a mass meeting in the nation's capital. Official Washington, especially members of Congress, would be riding in parades and making speeches in their hometowns. Less important residents would be at the beach or in the mountains, as far as they could get from Washington's stifling heat.

Since the city did not have a natural conservative constituency, being 10-to-1 Democratic and 75 percent black, the committee would have to transport people in by bus, train, and plane. Yet O'Donnell persisted, adding to the quixotic nature of the event by picking as a site the cavernous National Guard Armory, which seated 6,500 and had been filled only three times in its history—for Ike's inaugural ball in 1957, Kennedy's inaugural in 1961, and a Billy Graham crusade.

"Rally Don" Shafto, a protégé of Marvin Liebman, who had produced YAF's Madison Square Garden extravaganza the year before, was brought in to coordinate the details. There was one critical difference between the New York and Washington rallies, however. In keeping with his hands-off policy, Goldwater would not be a speaker in Washington. The cost of the rally soared to more than $60,000, an enormous sum for the fledging committee, but O'Donnell persisted.

The Fourth of July dawned cool and clear. The planes and trains and buses were on time. Senators and congressmen like John Tower, Carl Curtis, and John Ashbrook, and Hollywood stars like Efrem Zimbalist, Jr., and Walter Brennan agreed to speak. More than seven thousand waving, raving patriots crowded into the old, un-air-conditioned Armory, alarming the fire marshals and the liberal elite.

It was a typical Goldwater crowd. There were little old ladies in tennis shoes, truck drivers with tattoos, professors who read Mises rather than Keynes, right-wingers convinced that Wall Street and the Kremlin were conspiring to run the world, Southern whites who had faith in the Cross and the Flag, retired people on Social Security worried about inflation, Westerners tired of catering to Easterners, anticommunists demanding action against Cuba and Khrushchev, small businessmen fighting a losing battle against government rules and regulations, readers of *The Conscience of a Conservative,* high school and college rebels looking for a cause—all of them believing that it was possible to solve problems as America had in its past, through the First Baptist Church and the Rotary and Kappa Kappa Gamma and the Salvation Army and in their towns, cities, and communities without federal bureaucrats.

They loved America as they loved their family, without reservation, and they did not like what was happening to it. They loved Barry Goldwater because it was plain that he too loved America. They hoped and they believed that he would lead a crusade to make their country strong and whole and right again.

When the evening was over and the cheering had stopped, O'Donnell's gamble had paid off—thanks to grassroots conservatives from forty-four states who staged an old-fashioned patriotic rally that put the Draft Goldwater Committee on the front pages and the evening news telecasts from Washington to Los Angeles.

Under an eight-column banner, the *Baltimore Sun* began its front-page story: "The friends of Senator Barry Goldwater (R., Ariz.) tonight tossed his hat into the 1964 presidential ring." A Democrat was quoted as saying, "Last month they were just a faction. But tonight it looks like they've become a political party."[23]

Within the month, Goldwater asked Denison Kitchel, a close friend and a senior partner of a leading Phoenix law firm, to open a campaign office in Washington, D.C., ostensibly to help plan his reelection run for the Senate in 1964 but in reality to help him determine when he should announce his intention to run for the presidency. It was still possible to reverse course, but Goldwater, like it or not, was headed for a campaign against President Kennedy. He was encouraged by the August Gallup Poll, which gave Goldwater an amazing 16 percent lead over Kennedy in the once-solid Democratic South—54–38 percent.[24]

Kitchel had no political experience beyond several years as general counsel to the Arizona Republican party, but he did have Goldwater's total and unqualified trust. Born in Bronxville, New York, and a graduate of Harvard Law School, Kitchel had moved west while a young man and had become an ardent Arizonan.

A one-time New Dealer, Kitchel had grown so disenchanted with Democratic big government policies that he joined the John Birch Society in 1960 at the invitation of Frank Brophy, who, it will be recalled, had been a member of Clarence Manion's Committee of One Hundred in 1959–1960 (suggesting why Goldwater often remarked that "some of the finest people I know in Phoenix are members of the Society"). But Kitchel resigned in June 1960 after reading Robert Welch's anti-Ike diatribe, *The Politician.*[25] Kitchel's JBS membership never came to light in the 1964 campaign. If it had, the screaming headlines would have destroyed his usefulness.

Before bringing him to Washington, Goldwater instructed his old friend, who was quick to admit that he had little knowledge of national politics, to talk to everybody but to make no commitments.

One of the first people he met was Jay Hall, who introduced him to Bill Baroody. Kitchel and Baroody immediately took to one another, perhaps because each was an intellectual, preferred to operate behind the scenes rather than center stage, and had become a conservative after a youthful fling with New Deal liberalism. Hall had good reason to believe that he, Kitchel, and Baroody would form a triumvirate that would make many of the important campaign decisions over the next year. But Hall was gradually eased out of any key role by Baroody, who came to be called "The Grand Vizier."

The first indication of the new order came in September 1963 when Hall arranged a meeting with Bill Buckley and Brent Bozell in Washington to discuss Buckley's proposal to form a group of leading academics who would advise the senator on public policy and provide him with intellectual support.

When Buckley and Bozell arrived at Hall's suite in the Hay-Adams Hotel, they discovered to their surprise that Denison Kitchel and Bill Baroody were also present. As the meeting proceeded, every suggestion that the two *National Review* editors made was turned aside or challenged by Baroody. At last, Bozell had had enough and politely but firmly "put Baroody in his place." Although nothing was decided that evening, there was agreement that an academic committee should be seriously considered.[26] A committee of distinguished professors was ultimately formed and placed under the supervision of Edward A. McCabe, a Washington lawyer and former White House aide to Eisenhower, who was brought on board as Goldwater's director of research—by Bill Baroody.

It was an all too familiar story in presidential politics. He who has access to the ear of the "king," i.e., the candidate, controls not only the candidate but his campaign. Since Goldwater's reelection in 1958, Baroody had helped him become an increasingly influential spokesman for conservatism, bringing him into contact with leading intellectuals through private dinners at his home and suggesting people for his staff like his press secretary, Tony Smith.

Now Baroody was determined to play the major role in shaping the intellectual content of the candidate's speeches and positions. He conceived the idea of feeding all of Goldwater's public statements into a computer, under the direction of Margita White, so that whenever a question was raised about the senator's position, the research team would be able to call up Goldwater's actual statement immediately and expose any distortion. Although appreciative, a skeptical Clif White commented that "no one ever quite figured out how you could get the press to disseminate this vast store of information to the public."[27]

In his determination to be the number one adviser to Goldwater, Baroody was capable of playing political hardball. A few days after the Hay-Adams meeting, the *New York Times* carried an exclusive story that began: "[The] Goldwater for President ship has just repelled a boarding party from the forces who supposedly occupy the narrow territory to the right of the Arizona senator." The article claimed that Buckley and Bozell had "cornered some Goldwater aides" and expressed their desire "to join the campaign organization . . . on the policy-planning level."[28]

Who leaked the "boarding party" story? It could not have been Buckley or Bozell, badly damaged by its misleading contents, or Hall, so concerned about secrecy that he would turn on the radio during meetings to deter bugging. It could not have been Kitchel, who did not know a leak from a leek and who in fact assured Buckley that he had not talked to anyone, let alone a reporter from the *New York Times*. That left Baroody, who, when questioned, suggested that the room had been bugged but who, in the opinion of Goldwater, Kitchel, and Buckley, was himself the culprit. Buckley says flatly, "Baroody kept us away."[29]

Although Goldwater later claimed that he would have welcomed them with open arms, Buckley, Bozell, and Rusher were all prevented from making any significant contribution to the 1964 campaign. Describing them as men "of the highest integrity and solid conservative views," Goldwater acknowledged that they should have been able to talk with him and others in the campaign about issues, strategy, the media, and other matters. In his 1988 memoirs, the senator comments:

Later, realizing what had happened, I was heartsick about the matter. But what could I say? What could I do? It was too late.[30]

There were several things he could have done to involve (1) the man who wrote the book that helped make him a national political leader, (2) the editor of the most important conservative journal in America, and (3) the man who had been instrumental in creating the Draft Goldwater Committee without which the senator would not have been nominated for president. He could have asked Bozell to research and write speeches; he could have melded Buckley's contacts with Baroody's list to produce an outstanding academic committee; he could have directed Kitchel and Dean Burch, who was hired in September as Kitchel's administrative assistant, to include Rusher in their strategy sessions. But he did none of these things, offering only the unconvincing excuse that it was "too late."

The maladroit handling of Buckley, Bozell, and others showed that Goldwater was guilty of the biggest mistake any candidate, particularly a presidential candidate, can make—not naming an experienced campaign manager and letting him make the major decisions. If Shadegg had been the campaign manager, he would have included Buckley and the others in the campaign, accepting or rejecting their suggestions and using their presence to satisfy Goldwater's conservative constituency. But Shadegg was still outside the pale as a result of his failed 1962 attempt to win the Republican senatorial nomination from Arizona.

In truth, the addition of Bozell, Buckley, Rusher, and other conservative intellectuals like Russell Kirk—all of whom were denied any serious role in the campaign by a turf-conscious Baroody, abetted by Kitchel and Burch—would not have materially affected the final outcome of either the nomination drive or the general election. Goldwater would have still bested the liberals and won the Republican nomination, and he would have still been crushed by the combined weight of the White House, the Democratic party, the media, organized labor, blacks, senior citizens, and others, most of whom had been convinced that he was a combination of Huey Long, George Lincoln Rockwell, and George Patton.

Kitchel later explained that he had agreed to exclude Buckley and *National Review* because they were believed by many to be on the far right fringe of politics, and he did not want any of this to rub off on Goldwater.[31] To characterize the magazine that had, only the year before, read Robert Welch out of the conservative movement as "far right" is hardly convincing. Only someone like Baroody, dead set on eliminating any possible competitor, would have come up with such an argument, and only someone like Kitchel, unfamiliar with the makeup of American conservatism, would have accepted it.

Goldwater tried to make amends after the *New York Times* article appeared by writing Buckley a note asking for his opinions and later making a symbolic visit to *National Review*'s offices in New York City.[32] But in the end, Buckley and Goldwater, the two men who, along with Russell Kirk, were chiefly responsible for creating the modern

American conservative movement, had little contact throughout the nomination and presidential campaigns.

IN THE FALL of 1963, the political news got better and better for Goldwater and worse and worse for Rockefeller. When Nelson and Happy Rockefeller visited a Republican picnic at the Ogle County Fairgrounds in Illinois, they were greeted with a sea of Goldwater buttons and bows. One political columnist wrote: "There was a smell of political death about the day in Ogle County. It was like observing a political corpse who did not realize that he was dead."[33]

In contrast, nearly fifty thousand enthusiastic people jammed Dodger Stadium in Los Angeles to hear Goldwater deliver a stirring address written by Karl Hess, a new speechwriter who had been suggested by Baroody and whom the senator nicknamed "Shakespeare." It was the biggest Republican rally in Los Angeles since Thomas E. Dewey came to town for a campaign speech in 1944. By the time he was through, Goldwater had been interrupted by cheers and applause forty-seven times. The senator declared that "America needs a change" and "freedom needs a chance," and both required an end to "rocking-chair leadership." Mixing equal amounts of conservative and anticommunist rhetoric, he said that the United States was "a shield for freedom everywhere" and left his audience with the announcement that he was flying back to Washington later that night to vote against the Nuclear Test Ban Treaty.[34]

In October, *U.S. News & World Report* published a survey of national leaders that showed that 56 percent of Republican senators and congressmen favored Goldwater while only 10 percent wanted Rockefeller. Among members of the Republican National Committee and Republican state chairmen, the percentages were 56 percent and 71 percent for the senator from Arizona. One party official put it bluntly: "There is no one man in sight who looks strong enough to stop him."[35]

And then there was the poll of New Hampshire Republican voters, which revealed that 58 percent would vote for Goldwater in the nation's first primary as against a distant 20 percent for Rockefeller.

The National Draft Goldwater Committee kept lining up delegates in the wake of Goldwater's triumphant appearances. The entire fifteenth floor of the Mark Hopkins Hotel on top of Nob Hill in San Francisco was reserved for the Republican National Convention.[36] There were of course a few clouds in the sky. Columnist Walter Lippmann warned that because of its right-wing extremism, a Goldwater candidacy "strikes at the heart of the American party system," rejecting "the process of conciliation." If Goldwater were elected, predicted Lippmann, "we should face dangerous days of reaction at home and jingoism abroad."[37] It was a low but not unexpected blow from someone who openly favored President Kennedy.

At the same time, Goldwater kept saying things that did not need to be said. While traveling with writer Stewart Alsop, Goldwater volunteered, "You know, I think we ought to sell TVA." What he meant, and what he had said many times during his years in the Senate, was that certain parts of the authority, like its steam-generating plants and its fertilizer-production program, ought to be sold to the private sector.

But when pressed for an explanation by Congressman Richard Fulton, a Tennessee Democrat, Goldwater simply replied that he was "quite serious" about his proposal and that TVA "would be better operated and would be of more benefit for more people if it were part of private industry." When a group of Southern Republicans, whose states were served by TVA, visited Goldwater to protest, they were told, "You either take Goldwater or you leave him." Knowing Goldwater, they shrugged off the blunt language and asked him to explain, which he did.[38] Republicans were satisfied, but Democrats carefully noted what he had said and filed it away for future use.

The TVA flap prompted Peter O'Donnell to write Goldwater a confidential memorandum in which he urged the senator not to kick sleeping dogs. "A series of TVA-type statements," he warned, "could greatly weaken your position. . . . We must continually be on the offensive in the fight for the nomination and the general election."[39] It was good advice, and a prophetic warning, but Goldwater brushed it aside and Kitchel and Baroody viewed the warning as gratuitous and even disloyal. As a result, O'Donnell was pushed further into the background, left finally with only a minor fundraising role in the 1964 campaign.

At Baroody's suggestion, Ed McCabe, who had been an administrative assistant to President Eisenhower and worked in the congressional liaison office of the White House, was brought in as director of research. Thoughtful and even-tempered always, particularly in a crisis, McCabe frequently traveled to Gettysburg to brief the former president.

At their first meeting in the early fall of 1963, Eisenhower told McCabe that he would not "take a position in favor of *anyone* prior to the convention." Despite unrelenting pressure from Eastern liberals over the ensuing months, Ike stood firm, as McCabe knew he would. Eisenhower went on to say that he did not think that "anyone could head off Barry for the nomination" but then dampened McCabe's spirits by adding that he did not think that any Republican "could head off Kennedy for the election."[40] Kitchel and Baroody were delighted to receive the important news—that Ike would not intervene in the nomination campaign—and waved aside his opinion about Kennedy's strength.

These were golden days for Goldwater and the men around him. *Time* published a state-by-state survey that suggested that one Republican in particular, Barry Goldwater, "could give [President] Kennedy a breathlessly close race." While the president could easily beat any other Republican candidate, he could only be rated even against Goldwater, who could count on carrying states with a total of 266 electoral votes.[41]

Kennedy conceded at an early October news conference that "we are going to have a hard, close fight in 1964." Of Goldwater's chances of being nominated, he said, "I think he can do it. I think it is possible for him to do it. But he has a long road to go. . . ." Previously, Kennedy had usually mentioned Rockefeller as his likely opponent. Asked about a statement by Eisenhower that he, Ike, was unclear about Goldwater's views on certain major issues, Kennedy replied, grinning, "I don't think Senator Goldwater has ever been particularly deceptive. I think he has made very clear what he is opposed to, what he is for. I have gotten the idea. I think President Eisenhower will, as time goes on."[42]

On October 31, when President Kennedy was asked to comment on a Goldwater charge that the administration was slanting the news to stay in office, he said that the senator had had such "a busy week selling TVA, and giving permission to or suggesting that military commanders overseas be permitted to use nuclear weapons, and attacking the president of Bolivia while he was here in the United States, and involving himself in the Greek election. So I thought it really would not be fair for me this week to reply to him." It was witty and dismissive, but as columnist James Reston of the *New York Times* wrote, "The president was light-hearted about the prospects of meeting Goldwater, but privately his associates are not so sure."[43]

Pierre Salinger, however, recalls that Kennedy was confident that
Goldwater would win the nomination but equally confident that he
would be reelected.[44] According to Theodore Sorensen, the man closest
to the president other than his brother Robert, "We regarded Barry
Goldwater as a likely but not yet certain Republican candidate. We
would have welcomed a race with Goldwater because it would have
presented a very clear choice for the voters." In fact, Kennedy
"thought that he would have a better chance of defeating Goldwater
than any other Republican" because of his positions on civil rights and
other issues. Arthur Schlesinger, Jr., believed that Kennedy wanted to
run against Goldwater "to dispose of right-wing extremism once and
for all and win an indisputable mandate for his second term."[45]

But as Clif White pointed out, Goldwater's public appeal was expanding rather than contracting in the last quarter of 1963 as his views
became better and better known.

Southern voters liked him, not only because he insisted on states'
rights as well as civil rights, but because he accepted them as equal
partners in shaping the nation's destiny rather than as second-class
citizens. Western voters basked in Goldwater's independence and pioneer spirit. Midwestern voters saw in him a champion of traditional,
middle-class values. Voters in big cities like Chicago, Cleveland, and
Detroit, many of them union members, were drawn to him because of
the excesses of some civil rights and union leaders. As labor columnist
Victor Riesel wrote, "For the first time since John Kennedy took over
the White House there is an open break on the New Frontier's labor
front over support of the president for reelection in 1964."[46]

The first, and only, planning meeting for Kennedy's reelection was
held on November 13 in the White House. The president's approval
rating in Gallup polls had dropped from 76 percent to 59 percent.
Richard Scammon, director of the Bureau of the Census and a longtime political analyst for Democrats, traced most of the drop to
defecting Southern conservatives who thought Kennedy was too pro-
civil rights. He was also losing support among Northern liberals who
wanted the president to move faster on civil rights. But when paired
against Barry Goldwater, the current favorite to win the Republican
nomination, Kennedy was ahead 55 percent to 39 percent, a comfortable margin.

According to biographer Richard Reeves, the president said, "This
could be fun, if it's Barry." He was so anxious to run against his old

Senate colleague that he commented, "Don't waste a chance to praise Barry. Build him up a little. Don't mention the others."

The "others" were, of course, Nelson Rockefeller, whom Kennedy dismissed as not having "the guts" to sustain a presidential effort, and George Romney, who he thought "could be tough." Although Kennedy is usually described as a shrewd political analyst, his insights into Rockefeller and Romney were off the mark. If there was one thing that Rockefeller had lots of (beside money) it was guts, an unwillingness to give up despite seemingly impossible odds. Romney, on the other hand, was a businessman who seemed to have little taste for the rough give and take of political campaigning. "Give me Barry," Kennedy concluded with a laugh." I won't even have to leave the Oval Office."[47]

That was political bravado, and the Kennedy team knew it. There was no need to build up Goldwater, who was the unquestioned favorite of the Republican rank and file. An Associated Press poll of GOP state and county leaders in early November showed that only 56 of 1,404 respondents, less than 4 percent, thought Rockefeller would make a good candidate. An overwhelming 1,194—more than 85 percent— voted Goldwater the party's "strongest candidate" against President Kennedy. More and more nervous Democrats were warning Kennedy that he faced serious reelection problems. Some had already written off the Deep South, and Vice President Johnson urged the president to start visiting Texas to rebuild political fences and challenge the Goldwater phenomenon.

During his last news conference in November before leaving to campaign in Florida and Texas, an irritated Kennedy attacked the Democratic Congress for its failure to take swifter action on his tax cut and civil rights bills. But when he spoke in Fort Worth on the morning of November 22, 1963, not even a *Houston Chronicle* poll that showed Goldwater leading him in Texas by 52 to 48 percent could dampen his high spirits and good humor. Smiling happily, with his beautiful wife Jackie beside him, he climbed aboard Air Force One for the short flight to Dallas.

FOR BARRY GOLDWATER, things looked so promising that the only question was when, not whether, he would "go all the way." In October, he invited White to meet with him, Kitchel, and Jay Hall in his

Senate office where they discussed the coming campaign and who would fill which key positions. "Although he didn't come right out and say so," White later wrote, "I got the definite impression that he wanted me to serve as his director of organization." White was pleased, and so was Hall, who had arranged the meeting and had been urging the senator to give the man who had already done so much a prominent post in the formal nomination effort.[48]

Discussion then ensued among members of the inner circle as to who might run with Goldwater. High on the list was Governor William Scranton of Pennsylvania, whom Goldwater liked personally from their service together in the Air Force Reserve and who often took a conservative position on economic issues. Goldwater had urged Scranton to run for public office and had helped raise money for him and the Republican party of Pennsylvania on more than one occasion. Because he was popular with the Eastern liberal wing of the Republican party and was a personal favorite of Eisenhower, Scranton would balance Goldwater geographically and philosophically. He was a strong possibility for vice president right up to the national convention in San Francisco.[49]

In that golden autumn month of November 1963, Goldwater was looking forward with genuine pleasure to challenging Kennedy and waging a campaign of issues not personalities, an approach equally favored by the president. On one occasion, the two men went so far as to talk briefly about appearing before the same audiences, as Lincoln and Douglas had done in their historic senatorial debates of 1858. Sorensen confirms that Kennedy was prepared to debate Goldwater or whomever the Republicans nominated, but does not recall any serious discussion of details, such as subjects and sites.[50]

Goldwater, on the other hand, believed there was an agreement, and he intended to talk about the need for a national will and direction that would replace Kennedy's vacillation and pragmatism. "It was my hope," he recalled, "that our direct confrontation would make it clear to the American people that genuine commitment and principles are necessary to sustain all great countries." Even if he lost, he felt the race would be worth running because the conservative cause would gain by exposing its ideas and beliefs to the American people.[51]

Much of the political speculation that fall was about the possibility of Kennedy, not Goldwater, losing. The mid-October Gallup poll reported that Kennedy topped Goldwater in the East (63–37 percent) and the Midwest (also 63–37 percent) but was behind in the South (45–55 percent) and only twelve points ahead in the Far West (56–44 percent). The momentum seemed to be shifting from Kennedy to Goldwater, who registered his strongest national showing yet, receiving 39 percent to Kennedy's 55 percent, with 6 percent undecided.[52] Growing in confidence with every new poll, Goldwater told a Chicago audience that all the New Frontier had produced was "1,026 days of wasted spending, wishful thinking, unwarranted intervention, wistful theories, and waning confidence."

But the old reluctance, the old feeling of inferiority, had not totally disappeared. As late as mid-November he commented to a reporter, "God knows I haven't sought this position. I'm still wishing something would happen to get me out of all this. It's all a little frightening. . . ."[53]

When Rockefeller formally announced on November 7 that he would seek the presidential nomination, Goldwater and the inner circle decided tentatively that he would announce his candidacy toward the end of the month. But the death of Peggy Goldwater's mother in Phoenix and the decision to fly her body to Muncie, Indiana, for burial made that impossible. Allowing for a reasonable period of mourning took them to mid-December, which was too close to Christmas for a political announcement; the best date, it seemed, would be early January.

Meanwhile, Goldwater had good reason to be pleased by everything around him: the favorable national polls, the remarkable progress that White and his group had made toward accumulating 655 convention delegates, the professional campaign organization that Kitchel and Baroody were building (there were gaps, like a finance chairman, but these could be easily filled), his personal conviction, after months of uncertainty and vacillation, that he could run a strong campaign against an incumbent president, and the solid evidence that American conservatism had come of political age and was poised to capture the most sought-after prize in American politics—the presidency. What could possibly go wrong?

PART III

Icon

10

A Choice, Not an Echo

ON THE MORNING OF NOVEMBER 22, 1963, Senator Barry Goldwater, the leading but still unannounced Republican candidate for president, was on his way to Muncie, Indiana, to bury his mother-in-law. F. Clifton White, the architect of the draft Goldwater movement, was in St. Louis attending the Midwest regional conference of the Republican National Committee. Peter O'Donnell, head of the National Draft Goldwater Committee and chairman of the Texas Republican party, was flying home to Dallas. Denison Kitchel and William J. Baroody, Sr., the most important members of Goldwater's inner circle, were in Washington, D.C., discussing, among other things, when their man should make his formal announcement for the presidency. Former Vice President Richard Nixon had just left Dallas and was en route to New York City, having missed President Kennedy's arrival by two and a half hours. Kennedy was in Texas, along with Vice President Johnson, seeking to unite a divided Democratic party and determine how serious a threat Goldwater was in that key Democratic state. He had his work cut out for him. A page two headline of that day's *Washington Post* read: "Texas Democrats Spat As JFK Begins Tour."

At 1:30 P.M., Washington time, Merriman Smith of United Press International dictated the first bulletin over the pool car's radiophone: "Three shots were fired at President Kennedy's motorcade in downtown Dallas." A half hour later, in Parkland Memorial Hospital, the president was pronounced dead. At 2:35 P.M., Washington time, UPI sent out a flash bulletin, with bells ringing, that would change America forever: "President Kennedy Dead."[1]

The immediate reaction of many conservatives, including Clif White, was, "Oh, my God, it must have been one of our crazies."[2] Most Americans had the same thought, and there were many references on network television and radio (even over the Voice of America) to Dallas as the center of the extreme right wing and the heart of "Goldwaterland." Television repeatedly showed a clip of Adlai Stevenson, U.S. ambassador to the United Nations, being shouted at and spat upon by "conservatives" in Dallas one month earlier.

In the Washington headquarters of the National Draft Goldwater Committee, polite young women tried to cope with an unceasing stream of angry, emotional telephone calls while people banged on the locked front door and shouted "Murderers!" When a highly distraught man vowed on the phone that he would blow up the headquarters, office manager James Day, on the advice of the Washington police, closed the office and turned off the lights.[3]

For two hours, the nation watched and waited and wondered, Who killed Kennedy? At 4:23 EST, NBC announced that a suspect had been arrested and soon identified him as Lee Harvey Oswald. All over America, conservatives checked their membership and donor lists. When they heard that Oswald had been a member of the Fair Play for Cuba Committee, a procommunist group, conservatives offered a prayer of thanks. Some liberals, like "TRB" in *The New Republic,* tried to obfuscate Oswald's background, but honest leftists like Dwight Macdonald quickly put an end to it:

> There may be "brooding Oswalds" of the right, but so far they have not taken action, which, as an old-fashioned believer in the Bill of Rights, I think is the important thing. The only Oswald we have had was of the left. . . . I agree it was a great pity that the assassin turned out to be not a lunatic Birchite, as we all assumed in that first hour of shock, but a lunatic "Marxist." But such was the fact. Oswald is our baby, not theirs.[4]

Goldwater's immediate and overwhelming impulse was to abandon any thought of running for president. As he later wrote, the central reason was his personal and political contempt for Lyndon Johnson, who would make it impossible to conduct the high-road, principled campaign that he and Kennedy had discussed. "Johnson was the epitome of the unprincipled politician," Goldwater said. "He would assume the Kennedy legacy" and manipulate "Jack's martyrdom" for his own political purposes. "I couldn't and wouldn't run against a man like that." LBJ had equally strong feelings about Goldwater, whom he once described as "a mean, vindictive little man."[5]

Second, Goldwater was convinced, as was almost every professional politician in America, that after the assassination no Republican, and particularly a conservative Republican, could win in 1964. As Goldwater put it, "the American people were not ready for three presidents in little more than one year."[6]

Third, there was the terrible personal burden that he would have to bear as a conservative candidate in the wake of Kennedy's death in Dallas, Texas. It did not matter that Oswald was a pro-Castro Marxist and not a conservative. What mattered was a public perception that it was Dallas's radical Right, ultraconservative climate of hate that had produced Kennedy's death.

Typical of the prevailing anticonservative bias in the media and elsewhere was Walter Cronkite's comment on the "CBS Evening News" that Goldwater was giving a political speech in Indiana and would not be present at Kennedy's wake and funeral. An angry Goldwater telephoned Cronkite to explain that he was in Indiana to bury his mother-in-law. An embarrassed Cronkite apologized on the air, but as Goldwater said, "Experience has shown that these corrections never undo the damage they cause."[7] Far from being indifferent to his friend's tragic death, Goldwater was deeply saddened, as his formal statement attested:

> The tragedy that struck down our president has struck also at the heart of our nation. It was a vile act. It embodied everything that America is against and against which all Americans should be united. . . .
>
> Let no man watching us now take twisted comfort from our plight and our pain. Let all men know that America and America's spirit will expiate this crime, will rise from prayerful knees and will face again, in new resolve and resolute knowledge, the future. . . .[8]

But Goldwater knew full well that the nation's future and his own had been irrevocably altered. All the old doubts and insecurities about himself as a presidential candidate and president came flooding back. Jay Hall told Clif White that Goldwater was in a state approaching deep depression. Goldwater later admitted that he had told his wife Peggy that he would "definitely not seek the nomination."[9] Yet he made no formal announcement, letting the question of 1964 drift as long as possible, encouraged by the thirty-day moratorium on public politics that had been declared on November 22.

At last, at Kitchel's insistence, he reluctantly agreed to talk things over with his closest friends and advisers. They met on December 8th in his Washington apartment. Present were Senators Norris Cotton of New Hampshire and Carl Curtis of Nebraska, former Senator William Knowland of California, Congressman John Rhodes of Arizona, Denny Kitchel, Bill Baroody, Peter O'Donnell, Jay Hall, Karl Hess, and John Grenier of Alabama, Southern field director for the draft committee.

Goldwater began by saying, "Our cause is lost," and enumerated the reasons: (1) With Kennedy dead and Johnson the certain Democratic candidate, the battle would not be of issues but of innuendos and lies; (2) the notion of running against Johnson was abhorrent to him—LBJ was a wheeler-dealer, a hypocrite, a dirty fighter, a man who "never cleaned [the] crap off his boots"; and (3) no Republican could win in 1964 because Americans did not want three different presidents in one year.

Separately, but repeating the same theme like a Greek chorus, the conservatives seated around the room told Goldwater that he had no choice but to run. This was the conservative hour—it was now or never; the party needed him; Rockefeller, Nixon, Romney, Scranton, and Lodge were not the answer but the problem. They urged him to think of all of the sacrifices made by the National Draft Committee and other conservative groups, to consider above all "the hundreds of thousands of young Republicans out there, the Young Americans for Freedom, the college students, all the young people who came to hear you speak over the last decade." *He could not let them down.*[10]

The final speaker, by design, was Cotton. He compared Goldwater with Charles DeGaulle and described how the French general had brought about a renaissance of postwar France through his inspirational leadership. America now urgently needed new conservative leadership, the New Hampshire senator declared, that would change the nation carefully, reasonably, prudently. No one else in the Republican party had Goldwater's "mass appeal—the vision, the character, the will to turn America in a conservative direction." This was the hour, said Cotton—if Goldwater would give the command.[11]

The heartfelt, eloquent appeal brought tears to the eyes of most in the room and left silence in its wake. They waited for Goldwater to respond, but he said nothing until at last he asked them to give him time "to sleep on it." He thanked them for coming and asked Kitchel to remain.

For a long time the two old friends sat silently, watching darkness fill the room, until at last Goldwater turned on a lamp and made a bourbon and water for Kitchel and a plain bourbon for himself. Pacing up and down, Goldwater recalled that he asked Kitchel, "What do you think?" to which his friend retorted, "What do *you* think?" Goldwater went over the same ground—the timing was wrong for a conservative Republican, the country would not accept a third president, the conservative cause could be badly hurt, he knew the kind of mean campaign Johnson would conduct. As he put it years later:

> I wasn't scared of a goddamned thing, but when you're faced with the fact that black is black, you don't try to change it to white. I knew that running against Johnson you're running against all the controlled political organizations in the country. He was president, he built bridges, he built roads, and that's the way you get elected.[12]

The two men sat silently, and then Kitchel, whom Goldwater trusted more than anyone else in the world because he knew that he would never mislead or lie to him, said bluntly, "Barry, I don't think you can back down." What was at stake, he went on, was not one man's personal feelings, not winning or losing an election, but "the millions of conservatives around the country who had made a stand in favor of Barry Goldwater." Goldwater admitted that he knew "the commitment—the bond I had made to so many conservatives and they to me—was virtually unbreakable at this point." He almost blurted the fateful words: "All right, damn it, I'll do it."[13]

Once again, duty and honor prevailed. The discipline and fidelity taught him by his family strengthened him. Although he had "no burning desire in his gut" to be president, he recognized that in running he assured conservatives of a strong, principled voice in the affairs of the nation. He knew he had no real chance of winning the election, but he hoped that by rallying conservatives, they would be able to take over the Republican party and help get the country back on the right course.[14]

It was an unprecedented act in American politics: never before had any presidential candidate run knowing beyond all reasonable doubt that he could not win the general election. That hard unyielding reality would affect Barry Goldwater in many different ways over the next eleven months, from his personal demeanor (his normal good humor was rarely seen) to the uncompromising, ideological content of his speeches (discussing TVA in Tennessee, farm subsidies in the Midwest, Social Security in Florida) to the composition of his campaign organization (he wanted to be surrounded by close friends). Almost all of what seems quixotic and even irrational in Goldwater's campaign becomes understandable and logical when seen through his reading of the political realities.

Goldwater ordered a poll, which showed that despite Kennedy's assassination, he was still very much in the running for the Republican nomination but he was far behind President Johnson, as was every other Republican. Following Kennedy's funeral, the Gallup Poll showed Johnson with 79 percent vs. 16 percent for Goldwater, with 5 percent undecided. By New Year's Day, the senator had improved slightly, 75 percent to 20 percent. As wide as the margin was, only Nixon did better against Johnson and only marginally: with 24 percent to the president's 69 percent.[15]

Even before Goldwater made up his mind, White and the Draft Goldwater Committee had made up theirs: they would continue to work toward their goal, confident, as they said publicly, that their efforts were in "the American tradition of the two-party system—a tradition which the late President Kennedy understood and supported." Privately, White reiterated their goal—"to make the GOP a conservative instrument in American politics."[16]

Nearly every liberal columnist in the nation had all but buried Goldwater's chances, but White and O'Donnell reported on December 11 to their steering committee that the nomination could still be theirs—especially if Johnson picked Robert Kennedy as his running mate, as widely predicted. Frank Kovac, the indefatigable director of the finance committee, reported one encouraging sign, fundraising had not collapsed. In fact a large number of checks had been written since November 22.

There was much to be done, such as keeping track of what other

Republicans were saying and doing during the so-called moratorium. Eisenhower made a statement in early December that was widely interpreted as meaning that he supported Henry Cabot Lodge for the Republican nomination, but he backtracked by explaining that Lodge was only one of several deserving candidates. Pressed by reporters, Scranton declined to say whether he would seek the nomination; he then met privately with Eisenhower, who, according to Scranton, urged him to give serious thought to seeking the presidency. "Draft Lodge" offices would be opened in Washington and Boston, next door to New Hampshire, the site of the nation's first primary. Supporters of Margaret Chase Smith disclosed that Senator Smith had authorized them to enter her name as a vice presidential candidate in the Illinois primary.

The one politician in America who did not set aside politics, privately or publicly, was President Johnson, who addressed a joint session of Congress on November 27, only two days after Kennedy was buried, and urged the "earliest possible passage" of a civil rights law, a tax cut, expansion of welfare programs, and foreign aid to communist nations. One conservative commented that it almost seemed as though LBJ "was vying with Walter Cronkite to see who could chalk up the most television coverage in a single month."[17]

Back in the Goldwater camp, the senator and the inner circle tried to put together a campaign plan and debated whether to keep the National Draft Goldwater Committee intact. Someone suggested that it operate as a citizens' group called "Americans for Goldwater" and cooperate with the new Goldwater for President Committee that would be launched after January 1 under Kitchel's command. But Kitchel and Goldwater decided that this would be "too cumbersome" and directed that the draft operation be turned over in its entirety to the official campaign organization.

Thus, some twenty-nine months after it had been conceived by Rusher, Ashbrook, and White at a series of meetings in Washington and New York City, the draft committee quietly died, but only after having accomplished its monumental mission—on a slim budget of only $750,000—of helping persuade Goldwater to run for the nation's highest public office. The three conservative activists were the founding fathers of the first authentic presidential nomination draft in the history of American political parties. While there were other important factors that led Goldwater to declare his candidacy, particularly his special feeling for the young conservatives who had cheered him on so many campuses and at so many political meetings, the senator would not have cast his hat into the presidential ring had not the National Draft Goldwater Committee laid a nationwide organizational and financial foundation for him. Goldwater put it flatly in his 1979 memoirs, "The Draft Goldwater movement was responsible for my nomination in 1964."[18]

STILL IN PAIN FROM SURGERY for a calcium deposit on the heel of his right foot, Barry Goldwater (a modern Achilles in a dark blue suit) hobbled out on crutches in front of his hilltop home in Paradise Valley overlooking Phoenix, on January 3, 1964, and promised to "offer a choice, not an echo" in his campaign for the Republican presidential nomination.

Declaring as he had in his first senatorial campaign twelve years earlier that he was *not* a "me-too" Republican, he let everyone know what kind of candidate he would be: "I will not change my beliefs to win votes. . . . This will not be an engagement of personalities. It will be an engagement of principles."[19] He intended to offer the nation a new direction based on greater respect for and support of individual initiative, fiscal responsibility by the federal and other governments, more power in the hands of local citizens, and a strong national defense.

He also revealed that it was the young people who had persuaded him to run. "I felt that if I didn't make myself available, they might become discouraged." His candidacy, he said, was pledged "to a victory for principle," giving the American people the opportunity to choose between a party that emphasized "individual liberty" and one that favored "the extension of government power."[20] But Goldwater's hopes for a principled campaign were almost immediately dashed by a skeptical political establishment, a resourceful Republican opposition, and his own mistakes.

Political professionals asserted that he was foolish to make his announcement in his home state of Arizona rather than Washington or New York where he would have attracted greater news coverage. But a stubborn Goldwater insisted that he would begin his presidential campaign where he had begun every one of his political campaigns, at home, sending an unmistakable message to his party, fellow conservatives, and the country: "I was going to be my own man, not packaged for the voters by Madison Avenue and a lot of other slick professionals who made me very uncomfortable."[21]

He warned the director of information for the Goldwater for President Committee that if the youthful publicist tried to generate "puff pieces" about his flying, photography, ham radio, electronic flag pole, Thunderbird car, and other personal hobbies and habits, he would throw him out the door and out of the campaign.[22] One of the major ironies of the 1964 campaign was that the master salesman of conservatism refused to present his human side, which would have helped to dispel at least some of the public fears about Goldwater as warmonger and destroyer of Social Security.

Stronger criticism was leveled at Goldwater for selecting an all-Arizona, all-amateur campaign staff: Denison Kitchel, general director; Dean Burch, assistant director; Mrs. Emory (Ann Eve) Johnson, director of the women's campaign; and Richard Kleindienst, director of field operations. The only one with any political experience was Kleindienst, who had served in the state legislature and had twice been elected chairman of the Arizona Republican party.

As he recounts in his memoirs, Kleindienst was literally dragooned into the campaign. He and his wife were returning from the New Year's Day Rose Bowl game when they were met at the California-Arizona border by a highway patrolman who told them "to proceed directly to Senator Goldwater's home in Phoenix." Puzzled and a little worried, they arrived at the senator's home to find television crews, vans, and reporters everywhere. In a back bedroom, Kleindienst saw Goldwater, Kitchel, and Burch, and asked worriedly, "What's going on, you guys?" They all laughed, and still grinning, Goldwater said, "In an hour or so, I'm announcing my candidacy for the Republican nomination."

"Great," replied Kleindienst, "but what does that have to do with me?"

Well, the senator told an amazed Kleindienst, he was to be the national director of field operations for the campaign.

"No kidding," said a bewildered Kleindienst. "What am I supposed to do as—what did you call it—director of field operations?"

"Get me 668 delegates on the first ballot," said Goldwater calmly. (The actual figure needed was 655.)

"You've got to be crazy, Barry!" blurted Kleindienst.

"You're right, Kleindienst. If I wasn't crazy, I wouldn't be doing it."

When Kleindienst suggested that a national organization should not have just Arizonans at the top but "loyal qualified persons from around the country," Goldwater immediately rejected the suggestion. "I'm not going to turn my life over to people I don't know and trust if I'm going to go through with this," he said grimly. "Either the four of you agree to go through this with me or I'm not going to do it."[23]

Given this ultimatum, Kleindienst and the others agreed. Kleindienst was often to defend the senator's insistence on loyalists. "You're a damned fool if you don't have around you the people you know and trust," he said. "If you have big names working for you, you wake up in the morning, and you don't know what deals they may have done in your name."[24]

The small band of Goldwater friends was quickly labeled the Arizona Mafia. None of the campaign veterans of the Draft Goldwater Committee, including Clif White and Peter O'Donnell, was initially included. But once in Washington and faced with the task of securing 655 delegates, Kleindienst insisted that White, the party's leading delegate hunter, be given a top post; they settled on the title of coordinator of field operations. But because no clear lines of authority were drawn, the two men worked in an atmosphere of tension and confusion until the results of the New Hampshire primary forced them to make some important adjustments.

Back in 1962 and 1963, Goldwater had reflected on how someone might go about winning the prize. He told Steve Shadegg, among others, that primaries were unimportant and, with the big exception of California, a waste of time and energy. To capture the nomination, he said, you should announce your candidacy, make a series of major speeches in various parts of the country, be represented at every state convention by skillful experienced politicians, and win California. Do all of this and the battle is over.

He was as aware as White, O'Donnell, and the other draft people that the great majority of delegates was chosen at state conventions by precinct committeemen and county chairmen, the very people whom he had been raising money for in his six years as chairman of the Republican Senatorial Campaign Committee. As he later reminded Dean Burch, "I know these people, they know me."[25] But he was wary of overexposure and the wounds that bitter primaries can leave and can be exploited by a resourceful opponent in a general election. John Grenier insists that when he joined the Goldwater group in November 1963, California was the only primary under serious consideration.[26]

In December, in one of his last acts as chairman of the Draft Goldwater Committee, Peter O'Donnell visited New Hampshire and submitted a report to Kitchel in which he warned, "There are serious weaknesses in organization, finance, public relations, and advertising, and in my opinion, we stand a great chance of being clobbered." Raymond Moley, the conservative political columnist for *Newsweek* and an old friend, privately urged Goldwater not to enter the New Hampshire primary. If, for some reason, Goldwater lost New Hampshire or did not do as well as the media said he should, it would be considered a significant defeat. If he won, Moley argued, the media would call it a predictable victory. William Loeb, the publisher of the powerful *Manchester Union-Leader* and a strong supporter of Goldwater, agreed: Stay out of New Hampshire!

But Kitchel and Burch, emulating the Kennedy strategy of 1960 and waving polls from the preceding October that showed Goldwater the choice of 65 percent of New Hampshire Republicans and independents, were confident that the senator would walk away with the nation's first primary.[27] They were encouraged too by the co-chairmen of the Goldwater effort in New Hampshire: Senator Cotton and Stuart Lamprey, the speaker of the state legislature. In all their enthusiasm, they neglected to brief their candidate on several important facts about the voters of New Hampshire. They were, for example, among the oldest in the nation and adamantly pro-Social Security. They were strong backers of the United Nations and its objectives. And they were reserved and liked to take their time about making up their minds. In 1952, they had resisted the strenuous personal campaign of Robert Taft and voted for General Eisenhower who, far off in Europe, never once visited the state.

On paper, Goldwater looked like a sure thing. But as he himself later admitted, the Goldwater for President Committee did not have an adequate campaign staff and no advance organization. The draft committee could have provided both, but it had been dissolved. Tony Smith, the senator's longtime press secretary, was thrust into the job of handling the press. Although Smith was a veteran newsman and familiar with the senator's positions, he had never worked in a major campaign and was not in good health. As incredible as it may seem, given the detailed preparation of today's presidential politics, Goldwater admitted that "there was no game plan, no rehearsal, no careful screening of what I would say or propose."[28] An experienced campaign manager like Shadegg or White would have warned the candidate that he was headed for a big fall.

Two other negative factors must be added: not fully recovered from his foot surgery, the senator was in constant pain during his first weeks in New Hampshire. Pain and illness can materially affect a candidate's physical and mental performance, as a far-from-well Richard Nixon, just released from a hospital, learned in his first television debate with John F. Kennedy in 1960. Goldwater's pain threshold was much higher than that of most people, but an absurdly full schedule (twenty-three days of campaigning, street tours, and handshaking with as many as eighteen appearances a day) combined with a heavy walking cast and constant pain in his right foot led him to say things that no healthy, mentally alert candidate would have. As he later remarked wryly, "I remember every footstep of that campaign."[29] Second, and more important, for the first several months of 1964, Barry Goldwater was not psychologically prepared to run for president. He was still looking back to the campaign that might have been against John Kennedy rather than to the campaign that now was: against Lyndon Johnson and liberal Republicans determined to do whatever was necessary to retain their control of the party.

On his first visit to New Hampshire, where the voters can be as granite-like as the ground, Goldwater said two things that provided his opponents, Republicans and Democrats alike, with the welfare-and-war themes they would use, and misuse, to destroy any chance he had of becoming president of the United States of America.

First, at a news conference in Concord on Tuesday, January 7, only four days after his formal announcement, Goldwater was asked whether he favored continuing the Social Security program. The senator had of course given his views about the program for years— although not in *The Conscience of a Conservative* as some careless writers have claimed—stating that it was actuarially unsound, a pseudoinsurance program inadequately funded, originally intended to do no more than "prevent stark privation," and in fact a tax levied against the nation's payroll "but collected and spent outside the government's annual budget." With that background in his mind, if not in the minds of those questioning him, he replied that he would like to suggest "one change"—that participation in the program be made voluntary. "If a person can provide better for himself, let him do it. But if he prefers the government to do it, let him." He pointed out that by 1970 the government would be taking 10 percent from a person's paycheck for Social Security and that for that amount of money people could "get a better Social Security program" through private insurance.[30]

As far as Goldwater was concerned all he was doing was being fiscally honest and philosophically consistent. But within a few hours, the *Concord Monitor* ran the banner headline: "GOLDWATER SETS GOALS: END SOCIAL SECURITY, HIT CASTRO." Within forty-eight hours, the Rockefeller organization had distributed a reprint of the misleading headline and article (which was generally accurate) to thousands of Republican households and later to every recipient of Social Security in New Hampshire.

Thus was born the myth of "Goldwater the Abolisher of Social Security," a myth that persisted over the next ten months because of the political propaganda of Republicans like Rockefeller and Democrats like Bill Moyers, who, from his command post in the White House, personally approved a television commercial in the fall that showed two hands, presumably Goldwater's, tearing a Social Security card in half.

At another New Hampshire news conference the same day a foreign policy paper that Goldwater had submitted to Eisenhower the previous September came up. While he did not want to create the impression that the former president had approved his foreign policy "in total," Goldwater said that when he asked Ike for criticism, "he had none and agreed with what I said. He was specifically drawn toward NATO and the Western problem." Then came this fateful exchange:

Q: How about nuclear weapons?
A: I have said, the commander should have the ability to use nuclear weapons. . . . Former commanders have told me that NATO troops should be equipped with nuclear weapons, but the use should remain only with the commander.[31]

The senator was clearly referring to *the* commander of NATO and to the use of *tactical* nuclear weapons. But several reporters wrote that Goldwater wanted to turn over the authority to use nuclear weapons to commanders in the field. The exception was the *New York Times'* Charles Mohr who reported that Goldwater specifically denied he favored this authority for local commanders of NATO.[32]

Spurred on by Rockefeller's disinformation machine, voters began asking: Did Goldwater mean that a captain or a colonel in the field could use such fearsome weapons? Under what circumstances would they be used—and against what targets? A column of tanks? An advancing army? A city? Although not asked publicly by the Rockefeller forces until the California primary, the seeds of an insidious question were planted in the minds of the New Hampshire voters: Who do you want in the room with the Bomb?

In fact, Goldwater had clearly stated his position about the use and control of nuclear weapons in a special article on foreign policy that appeared in *Life* magazine within the week. Arguing that the Johnson administration had nearly abandoned NATO, the senator declared that while authority over *strategic* weapons, such as Intercontinental Ballistic Missiles, should remain with the president, "I have suggested that the supreme commander in Europe be given authority over the tactical nuclear weapons appropriate to NATO's defenses. The best authorization ultimately must be worked out with NATO itself. I am convinced that it can be." "The question of 'nuclear sharing,'" he added, "revolves, actually, on a question of trust. Do we, in nuclear matters, trust the Soviets more than we trust our allies?"[33]

Six months later, *U.S. News & World Report* disclosed that what Goldwater had suggested in Concord, New Hampshire, in January had been established policy under both Presidents Eisenhower and Kennedy. Nixon later confirmed that during the Eisenhower administration, the NATO commander did have the authority "under certain carefully defined circumstances" to use "battlefield atomic weapons" without the express consent of the president. The "circumstances" included a communication breakdown in the event of a communist attack on Europe that would endanger the lives of European civilians and U.S. soldiers. General Lauris Norstad, a former NATO commander, revealed at about the same time that "the NATO military forces in Europe themselves depend to a considerable extent on nuclear weapons."[34]

In summary, what Goldwater proposed regarding nuclear weapons was not dangerous or radical but a realistic reading of what NATO needed to do to combat the superior conventional forces of the Warsaw Pact in the event of invasion.

Facts and reason notwithstanding, the image of Barry Goldwater as a trigger-happy warmonger was successfully implanted in the minds of New Hampshire voters by rival candidates in his own party and manipulated in the fall by a president obsessed with achieving the biggest victory ever in presidential politics. As Peter O'Donnell put it, Goldwater picked up "an atomic thorn in his foot," that harried him throughout his run for the presidency.[35]

THE TWIN distortions regarding Social Security and nuclear weapons had their inevitable impact. Goldwater later admitted that he should have realized that his every word and gesture would be minutely analyzed and picked apart. "I should have spelled out my proposals in elaborate detail with sufficient specificity to make misinterpretation extremely difficult. But I didn't."[36]

In Arizona, he had only to deal with pro-Republican newspapers like the *Arizona Republic* and the *Phoenix Gazette,* papers that tended to smooth over his inconsistencies and protect him from himself. He had come, naively, to expect similar treatment from every journalist. Years later he admitted as much to a *Washington Post* reporter, who had included all the profanity he had used in an interview. Conceding that he had uttered "every little bad word," Goldwater said that "reporters in the West eliminate those."[37] His old friend, John Kennedy, had foreseen this. "If [Goldwater is] the nominee," Kennedy told Ben Bradlee, "people will start asking him questions, and he's so damn quick on the trigger that he will answer them. And when he does, it will be all over."[38] It almost was.

By late January, Goldwater's own polls and canvasses revealed that he was in trouble, and his huge lead among Republicans had disappeared. An anxious Kleindienst, after a trip to New Hampshire, was convinced that he was going to be beaten. He recommended that Goldwater play the game of expectations by saying he expected to lose so that when the defeat came the impact would not be so serious.

White strongly disagreed, arguing that what the Goldwater campaign needed "was a healthy injection of confidence. Elections, particularly presidential elections, are not won with pessimism."[39] He counseled a lowering but not an abandonment of expectations. An uncertain Goldwater announced to the press that he would be happy to get 35 percent of the primary vote and then (with less than a week to go) raised the figure to 40 percent, enough, he said, to lead all five of his opponents.

For the senator, campaigning in New Hampshire was like trying to run through snow. The harder he tried—and he maintained a back-breaking, foot-aching, day-and-night schedule—the lower his approval ratings sank. His unhappiness with Rockefeller-style campaigning became more and more obvious. "I'm not one of those baby-kissing, handshaking, blintz-eating candidates. I don't like to insult the American intelligence by thinking that slapping people on the back is going to win you votes."[40]

At the same time, he became bored giving his stump speech as often as twelve times a day and began trying to make each talk a little different. One morning in Laconia, Goldwater said he would be inclined to withdraw from the United Nations if communist China were seated. One stop later, he said the United States must stay in the United Nations. At another stop, he said that if the mainland Chinese supplanted the Nationalist Chinese at the UN, it would blow U.S. participation in the United Nations to pieces. That evening, he stated, "I've never said, 'Let's get out of the UN.' I don't know how that rumor ever got started."[41]

Even when consistent, Barry Goldwater was a journalist's ticket to a byline. In one forty-five-minute talk in Wilton, New Hampshire, reported Theodore White, the senator explained that he wanted to go to the Republican convention to see that the good people of the party would not be kicked around as they were in 1952; advocated the elimination of the electoral college ("the big cities resist on that"); advocated "carrying the war to North Vietnam"; observed that he did not know a state in the union that had more discrimination than New York; defended his position on sending the Marines to Guantanamo by declaring that "a dictator was able to push the United States around and get away with it; sooner or later we must stop this, our embassies being burned up, our flag being torn down and scoffed at"; and ended by saying that he had been happy to visit with them—"it gave me a chance to find out what's on your mind and you to find out whether I have one."[42]

Goldwater knew he was being unpolitic, but he had always said what he wanted when he wanted where he wanted, and he did not intend to let anything, not even a national campaign for the presidential nomination of his party, change him. And, not so secretly, he enjoyed confounding the professionals and the press who expected him to play by their rules. Of course, his independence and stubbornness often made life difficult for those around him. He had, after all, told his new director of information, with a twinkle in his eye, "You don't know how much trouble I'm going to cause you this year."[43]

While Goldwater and Rockefeller were battling each other and trying to impress what one observer called the "hard-nosed, tight-spending, balanced-budget Yankees" who composed the majority of New Hampshire Republicans, two political newcomers, New England businessman Paul Grindle and Boston lawyer David Goldberg, had opened a Lodge for President headquarters in Concord, across from the state capitol. Lodge, U.S. ambassador to South Vietnam, was not on the ballot, and therefore his name would have to be written in. Using Grindle's direct mail expertise, the Lodge supporters sent six mailings to a statewide list of 96,000 registered Republicans, including a sample ballot explaining how to write in "Lodge." They produced, for only $750, a five-minute television program about Lodge's career, from his days as a lieutenant colonel in the U.S. tank corps to his years in the United Nations standing up to communists.

The Lodge operation was not as amateurish as it seemed: Robert Mullen, who had organized the successful write-in campaign for Eisenhower in New Hampshire in 1952, was quietly serving as chairman. And money was on hand to saturate the state with a TV program that featured Eisenhower introducing Lodge as the Republican candidate for vice president in 1960. But in this rendition a blast of trumpets obliterated the word "vice" in Ike's introduction, leading some New Hampshire voters to believe that the still-revered Eisenhower was supporting Henry Cabot Lodge in 1964. The press was amused and intrigued but skeptical that a write-in candidate ten thousand miles away, managed by non-New Hampshirites, could beat the well-organized, well-financed campaigns of Goldwater and Rockefeller.[44]

On March 10, 1964, in the middle of a blizzard that dumped fourteen inches of snow on New Hampshire, some 95,000 voters cast their ballots in the Republican primary. By 7:18 P.M., Walter Cronkite was able to tell CBS viewers that Henry Cabot Lodge had won the presidential preference primary. He received 33,521 votes, some 35 percent of those cast, while Goldwater was a distant second with 21,775 votes, 23 percent of the total vote. Rockefeller placed third with 19,496 votes, less than 21 percent. Nixon got 15,752 write-in votes, about 17 percent, a quite respectable showing.

Lodge's write-in victory was remarkable for a man who had never left Vietnam, but every Republican from Maine to California knew that Lodge was no Eisenhower, 1964 was not 1952, and Lodge was unlikely to be the nominee. Rockefeller's lackluster results confirmed that

Republicans had not forgiven him for his marital indiscretions and were uncomfortable with his big-spending, big-government proposals. As for Goldwater, his 23 percent showing was not even close to the 33 percent he had predicted as a worst case and about one-third of his approval rating back in October.

Typical was the seventy-two-year-old resident of Concord who told her neighbor that she was going to vote for Lyndon Johnson. "What do you mean?" asked her shocked friend. "You've voted solid Republican for fifty years." The woman replied that she was "afraid" to vote for Goldwater because "he will take away my TV." "No, no," her friend reassured her, "Goldwater's against the TVA, not *TV*." "Well," said the concerned woman, "that's good to know . . . but I don't want to take any chances."[45]

In any other year, and with any other candidate, Goldwater's dismal second place in the New Hampshire primary might have mortally wounded him as a presidential candidate. But in 1964, the great majority of delegates was selected through state and county conventions rather than through primaries. Thanks to the painstaking work of the draft Goldwater committee, on the same day he was losing badly in New Hampshire, Goldwater picked up forty-eight delegates at state conventions in Oklahoma and North Carolina and six at district meetings in Tennessee and Kansas. All Goldwater had to do was win the California primary to prove that he had popular appeal in the most populous state in the union, and he and his fellow conservatives would make political history.

In Washington, amid deflated spirits and half-eaten remains of an anticipated "victory" party, Goldwater candidly admitted over national television, "I goofed," and promised that he would not repeat the mistakes of New Hampshire.[46] He took steps, personally and organizationally, to keep his promise. Later that evening, White reminded the news media that New Hampshire was only the first primary and predicted that the senator would go on to win the nomination in San Francisco.

Many reporters dismissed his remarks as political rhetoric and concluded that Lodge was the all but certain Republican nominee. They grossly overestimated Lodge's public appeal and underestimated Goldwater's special standing among grassroots conservatives across the country who had been ignored and dismissed for so many years.

One of the first things Goldwater did was to elevate White to co-director of field operations and assign him the task of running the national convention. White and Kleindienst then divided the states between them, with Kleindienst taking the fourteen remaining primaries, except for Illinois where the two men agreed to work together, and with White assuming responsibility for the rest of the states in which delegates would be selected at conventions. As White laconically wrote, "this arrangement worked out quite well."[47] In fact, it produced a resounding nomination triumph for Goldwater.

The senator returned to his original strategy of focusing on a few important primaries, particularly California, making major speeches in key cities around the country, and letting the professionals go about their business at state and district conventions. As he put it, "pushing myself at people to shake hands for a vote just wasn't me—we'd do it only when it seemed natural."[48] Kitchel and Hess were assigned to travel with Goldwater whenever he went on the road: Kitchel as the close friend who could relax the candidate and tell him to do things he did not want to do (like meet with the press or a local group of wealthy supporters); Hess as his chief speechwriter.

In Washington, Burch efficiently coordinated the day-to-day operations of the Goldwater for President Committee, leaving the research and speechwriting to Baroody and his chief lieutenant, Ed McCabe. In short, Goldwater and his team did what all successful national campaigns do: took control rather than being dictated to by well-meaning but narrowly focused local politicians.

IT IS SOMETIMES written that Goldwater won only one major primary in 1964 (California) when in fact he won an important contest in the heart of the Republican Middle West—Illinois. Neither Rockefeller nor any other presidential candidate dared challenge Goldwater in the April 14 primary there, thanks to the superb grassroots organization built by Congressman Ed Derwinski, Charlie Barr, Patricia Hutar, and others, and galvanized by the senator's conservative message.

More than eight thousand Young Republicans jammed the amphitheater in downtown Chicago in early April to cheer Goldwater's pointed attack on the Johnson administration's foreign policy, roaring when he asked, "Where is the bright light of an American statement that can outshine Khrushchev's boast that our grandchildren will live under communism?"[49] A few days later, Goldwater received 509,000 votes, or 63 percent of the total, overwhelming Senator Margaret Chase Smith of Maine, who came in second with 209,000 votes.

Despite the decisive victory, many pundits spoke of Goldwater's showing as a setback and even a defeat arguing that he "should" have garnered 80 percent of the vote. They contrasted his "poor" showing in Illinois with that of Nixon, who got 782,849 votes in 1960, or that of Taft, who won 73 percent in 1952. But Nixon was unopposed while Taft was Mr. Republican from next door in Ohio.

In truth, Goldwater's Illinois win, coming one month after his disappointing showing in New Hampshire, gave his campaign important momentum toward his ultimate victory in San Francisco. Borrowing from Mark Twain, the senator wryly remarked to the American Society of Newspaper Editors later that week, "The published reports of my being out of the race are a bit premature." He then added, "I'm beginning to know exactly how Harry Truman felt as he read the polls and the papers in 1948."[50]

By the end of that same week, thanks to White's skillful maneuvering at the Kansas convention, plus earlier sweeps in Arizona and Louisiana, Goldwater could count on over two hundred delegates leaving all the other Republican candidates far behind. Over the next fortnight, he reaped another golden harvest of delegates, winning more than two hundred in seven primaries and six states. Highlights included eight publicly committed delegates in New Jersey, where Rockefeller had expected to collect all forty; 32,000 write-in votes in Pennsylvania, where Governor Scranton received only 58 percent of the total write-in vote (curiously, no reporter wrote that Scranton "should" have gotten 80 percent); and more than 75 percent of the votes in Texas's first Republican presidential preference primary.

On May 5, Goldwater had over four hundred delegates, or about four-fifths of all the delegates named to that date. At White's direction, however, the Goldwater Committee claimed fewer than 250, following a deliberate strategy of building slow in order to reach a climax just before the national convention in July. Hidden reserves of delegates might also be needed if the candidate suffered a major setback, particularly in California. If Goldwater lost all of California's eighty-six delegates in its primary, wrote White, they wanted to be able to "unveil two or three times that many the following day to send him back into the ring swinging haymakers after the press counted him out."[51]

How important was California? California was the megastate where the Goldwaters had had a second home for decades. It was the state of conservative Orange County and liberal Marin County, of Democratic Governor Pat Brown and the *Los Angeles Times* and Hollywood and Bob Gaston, the fiery Young Republican leader who openly acknowledged his ties with the John Birch Society; the home of conservative film and television stars like Efrem Zimbalist, Jr., Walter Brennan, John Wayne, Rhonda Fleming, Chill Wills, Chuck Connors, and an actor-union leader-TV host named Ronald Reagan. Everybody, especially the senator, agreed that if he won California, Goldwater would be the nominee.

But what if he lost California? Could he still win the nomination? William F. Buckley Jr. was so convinced of the essential nature of the California primary that he drafted a *National Review* editorial calling on Goldwater, if he lost, to pull out of the race to avoid a humiliating defeat. William Rusher insists that he would have resigned as publisher of *National Review* if the editorial had appeared, understanding, better than Buckley, that conservatives could only take control of the Republican party if Goldwater remained in the race.[52] He, White, and other delegate-counters were also convinced that it was mathematically possible for Goldwater to win the nomination without California.

But Kleindienst, Charles Lichenstein, and Dick Herman were as firm in their belief that Goldwater had to capture California to demonstrate conclusively that he had broad-based popular appeal. "If we had lost California," says Kleindienst, "Rockefeller would have won." "The California primary was *the* critical event," states Lichenstein. "We *had* to win California," argues Herman. "We were dead without California."[53]

Goldwater, the most important man in the equation, agreed. As he wrote in his 1988 memoirs, "I leaned toward dropping out if defeated in California."[54] That is a qualified statement, perhaps, but if he had lost California, Goldwater would probably have convinced himself that he did not deserve it. To Goldwater and the movement he led, California was crucial.

11

California, Here He Comes

CALIFORNIA IS A STATE OF NEWCOMERS, the last stop on the continuous move West that has helped shaped America since her discovery. The new Californians had left behind, they hoped, "the congestion of the Eastern cities, the clash of racial hatreds, the cramping of regulations, alien tongues, faiths and faces that overwhelmed their native neighborhoods."[1]

There was one other thing they never wanted to see again: big city machine politics. They venerated Hiram Johnson and his progressive legacy of no party conventions, no political patronage, no backroom deals. All of this made for unbounded, populist politics in which the people and not the bosses made the decisions.

It was in this anti-establishment, freedom-loving state that Barry Goldwater and Nelson Rockefeller engaged in the most expensive and bitter presidential primary fight in the history of American political parties. It was as close to life and death as politics can get, with some observers comparing it to the fight at the OK Corral. It was an epic battle fought at many different levels: between Goldwater volunteers and Rockefeller hired hands, the New Right and the California Establishment, the middle class of Los Angeles County and the upper class of San Francisco, the man who was not sure he should be president and the man who thought that only he should be president.

An ebullient Rockefeller came to California on the wings of a solid win in the Oregon primary (his only contested victory in 1964) where he received 94,000 votes, or 33 percent of the vote, while Henry Cabot Lodge placed second with 78,000 votes, 28 percent. Goldwater got 50,000 votes, or 18 percent; he stopped campaigning in Oregon with three weeks to go, deciding to concentrate on California and conceding the state to Rockefeller. Nixon came in fourth with 48,000.

Besides injecting new life into Rockefeller's candidacy, the Oregon results effectively eliminated Lodge and Nixon, who had allowed vigorous campaigns to be conducted on their behalf. Rockefeller knew that California was his last chance to secure the presidential nomination, and he gave his campaign organization carte blanche to defeat the one man who could deny him the prize he so desperately wanted.

In their biography of the Rockefellers, Peter Collier and David Horowitz state that Nelson Rockefeller officially spent $8 million, the bulk of it from his own and his family's funds, in the entire nomination campaign, of which $1.5 million was spent in California. But Stu Spencer of Spencer-Roberts, the campaign management team in charge of the Rockefeller effort, estimates they spent over $2 million, the most that any presidential candidate had ever expended in a single primary.[2] Clif White figures it must have been closer to $3.5 million given the extensive advertising, hundreds of professionals, and other expenses. During the primary, Rockefeller himself insisted that the cost of his California effort would not go "above $3 million."[3]

With the Rockefeller largess, Spencer-Roberts opened some fifty Rockefeller headquarters up and down the state, published a newsletter whose circulation reached 25,000, sent several mailings to all of California's 2.9 million registered Republicans, bought billboards, placed newspaper ads, and saturated television and radio with pro-Rockefeller and anti-Goldwater commercials. The latter were more numerous than the former because the Spencer-Roberts strategy from the beginning was to "raise Goldwater's negatives."[4]

As Frank Meyer of *National Review* wrote, Goldwater had been declared officially dead by political experts three times before: after Kennedy's assassination, after his second place finish in the New Hampshire primary, and after coming in third in Oregon. "Each time, like the fabled phoenix, [he] has risen from the ashes to confound" the prophets.[5]

Could he rise again in California? The answer lay in the resources he could bring to bear. First, he had Henry Salvatori, the wealthy, dynamic businessman, who raised a remarkable $1 million for the primary with the help of entrepreneurs like Patrick J. Frawley, chairman of the Schick Safety Razor Company; Cy Rubel of the Union Oil Company; Leland Kaiser of the shipbuilding family; Holmes Tuttle, the largest car dealer in the state; and other conservatives.

Second, the senator had a vast army of some fifty thousand conservative volunteers, many participating for the first time in politics, who comprised the largest and most enthusiastic group of volunteer workers in any state campaign. They demonstrated their effectiveness in March when they gathered more than 85,000 signatures, almost all of them valid, on filing petitions in just two days; only 13,000 were required.

By contrast, Rockefeller's paid workers took nearly four weeks to round up 44,000, 22 percent of which were found invalid. As a result, Goldwater occupied first place on the ballot, estimated by some politicians to be worth 5 percent of the vote. Many of the volunteers were organized under the United Republicans of California, headed by Rus Walton; others by the Young Republicans under its fiery leader, Bob Gaston; still others under the California Republican Assembly, founded by Earl Warren a generation earlier but now dominated by Goldwater partisans.[6] To this conservative army, Nelson Rockefeller was the Great Wrecker, not only of marriages, but of the Goldwater crusade by accusing the senator of extremism and creating doubts about his ability and stability.[7]

Third, there was Goldwater himself, a far different candidate in California from the tired, frustrated, uncertain man that the voters of New Hampshire had seen and rejected. Here in the West, he was calm, confident, at home. In early April, Goldwater met with former Senator Knowland, the official state chairman; Henry Salvatori; and other leaders in San Francisco. An old-style politician, Knowland had drawn up a crowded, morning to midnight schedule for the balance of the California campaign. He had shown what he intended to do in March, when he arranged twenty-four separate appearances for Goldwater in one day's campaigning in San Diego.

But Goldwater rejected Knowland's proposed schedule and laid down the following guidelines: (1) He would make no more than four or five appearances a day, preferably at large rallies that would be televised live or videotaped for telecast later; (2) the number of news conferences would be strictly limited; they too would be televised where possible so that "the people would not have to rely entirely on the interpretive accounts of reporters to determine [my] position on important issues"; (3) the number of days he would campaign would be limited so that he would not risk overexposure—California's Republicans already knew him well from his many years of residence and campaigning in the state—and (4) his speeches and remarks would concentrate on broad themes like freedom and prosperity and avoid divisive issues like Social Security and nuclear weapons that had so seriously damaged him in New Hampshire.[8]

The new strategy gave Goldwater a solid lead over Rockefeller in all of the California polls during April and the first half of May. But the Oregon primary changed everything, producing an eleven point margin for the governor of 47 to 36 percent, a dramatic twenty point shift. Signs of disarray had already surfaced in Goldwater's California organization, reflected in tension among conservative factions, delayed television and radio commercials, and a lack of coordination from the top.

Kleindienst moved his base of operations to Los Angeles and reported to the senator that if the primary election were held that day, May 15, he would lose California by at least 200,000 votes. He recommended that the senator's political team in Washington be brought out to California and that Burch be put in charge of the primary effort. The eleventh hour move was almost certain to offend Knowland and other Californians. But Goldwater took his cue from one of his military heroes, General George Patton, who invariably counseled, *"L'audace, toujours l'audace,"* and approved the leadership change (which Knowland graciously accepted).

The Goldwater team moved into Los Altos, an aging rococo stucco apartment house on Wilshire Boulevard, less than a mile from the official Goldwater headquarters. There, in a three-bedroom suite that the old night clerk insisted had been built to order for the legendary Greta Garbo, they directed what Shadegg described as "a political miracle" by reversing the Goldwater decline and engineering a historic victory by the slimmest of margins.[9]

Led by Burch and Kleindienst, the miracle workers included Lee Edwards, director of information for the Goldwater for President Committee; Chuck Lichenstein, on loan from the American Enterprise Institute; George Lyon, Cal Giegerich, Eugene Hooker, and Eunice Latham of Fuller, Smith and Ross, the Goldwater Committee's advertising agency; Ed Nellor, the senator's acting press secretary (Tony Smith remained in Washington, D.C.); Vern Stevens, the senator's first official advance man; Charlie Justice, Goldwater's security man and driver (in those days, the Secret Service did not assign agents to presidential candidates); Rus Walton of United Republicans of California; Ron Crawford, a young Los Angeles stockbroker who would become a close associate and fundraiser for the senator; Dick Herman, who as a Roman Catholic would play a particularly important role in the primary; and Shadegg.

On Monday morning, May 18th, only fifteen short days before primary day, the Goldwater team met for the first time with the leaders of the southern California operation and discovered, to their disbelief, that while adequate television and radio time had been purchased, no commercials or programs had been produced and no themes had been agreed upon.

The Los Altos gang sprang into action. Shadegg provided a master recording of radio spots, featuring Republican congressmen, which he had used in Oregon. The Fuller, Smith and Ross people began cutting up a thirty-minute TV film, *The Goldwater Story,* which they had produced for the Goldwater for President Committee, as well as a fifteen-minute panel discussion of the significance of the Goldwater candidacy, featuring Senators Curtis, Mundt, and others. Writers began drafting twenty-second, forty-second, and sixty-second radio and TV commercials, and Gene Hooker began laying out newspaper advertisements, taking extra care with the one that featured the entire Goldwater family (drawing a clear contrast with Nelson and Happy, who was very pregnant with their first child).

Calling upon his experience with Goldwater in their two senatorial campaigns, Shadegg proposed that in his final TV program Goldwater appear with his family in a living-room setting and explain why he was running and what he would do if he were elected president. Over Kitchel's and Hess's objections, the senator approved, saying, "Steve and I have done this a number of times, and it has always been effective."[10] The emphasis on the Goldwater family would have a decisive impact on the California electorate.

Lichenstein suggested that they send camera crews into the streets to ask citizens what questions they would like Goldwater to answer. The basic themes selected were limited government, lower taxes, and peace through strength.

Meanwhile the Goldwater army was distributing literature, canvassing neighborhoods, and readying its get-out-the-vote apparatus for the big day. In northern California, where Rockefeller was strongest, Goldwater volunteers took it upon themselves to give copies of Phyllis Schlafly's anti-establishment tract, *A Choice Not an Echo,* to voters. After the primary, Walton conducted a survey of the "book precincts" and discovered that among voters with the same economic, educational, and occupational backgrounds, the Goldwater vote was more than 20 percent stronger in the precincts where *A Choice Not an Echo* had been handed out. An estimated half million copies of the Schlafly book were distributed throughout the state.[11]

Goldwater workers engaged in more traditional politics in southern California. One Saturday, 8,000 volunteers took to the streets of Los Angeles County to canvass nearly 600,000 homes. Only about half the Republicans were contacted that day, but by election day the volunteers had compiled a list of 300,000 pro-Goldwater voters. Ten thousand workers helped get out the vote on June 3rd in an operation that nearly blanketed the largest county in California. In contrast, the Rockefeller organization had a maximum of about two thousand volunteers and was forced to limit its efforts to less than one-fifth of the precincts.[12]

Ten days after it began, although the polls still showed Goldwater behind Rockefeller by about nine points, the Los Altos operation had given a new sense of purpose and optimism to the Goldwater campaign. To retain their edge, the Rockefeller organization began swinging harder and lower. A mailing piece was sent to hundreds of thousands of California voters suggesting that Rockefeller had the endorsement of the other major Republican hopefuls. His picture appeared with smaller photographs of Nixon, Lodge, Romney, and Scranton under the headline, "These Men Stand Together on the Party's Principles." On the opposite page was a solitary photo of Goldwater with the headline, "This Man Stands Outside—by Himself." The text linked Lodge, Nixon, Romney, Scranton, and even Stassen to Rockefeller's candidacy, presenting them as a united Republican front against a far-out Goldwater. "Which Do You Want," the main headline asked, "A Leader? Or a Loner?"

In hundreds of precincts across California, Goldwater workers immediately began asking, "Do you want a leader or a lover?" Unlike the Rockefeller operation, the question was never turned into a political broadside in mailings and literature drops.[13]

But Rockefeller's attempt at disinformation backfired—first

Romney, then Nixon, and finally Scranton denied they were for or against anyone in California. Romney's pointed telegram to Knowland read: "I am neither supporting nor opposing any candidate." Nixon issued a similar statement: he was not "supporting or opposing either of the two candidates in the California primary" and urged Republicans to concentrate their fire on the Johnson administration "rather than on each other."[14] Goldwater personally sent one of the pamphlets to Scranton and asked him if Rockefeller "does in fact represent you in California." An emphatic response came swiftly from Harrisburg:

Dear Barry:

I have not been asked by anyone for permission to include my name or picture in this literature. Since I am not a candidate, no one "represents" me in California or anywhere else. . . .

My one overriding interest is for unity within the Republican party. Consequently, I have refused to join "Stop Goldwater, Stop Rockefeller, or Stop Anybody" movements. I believe that a unified Republican party can score a resounding victory this fall. . . . We cannot do this, however, unless we are unified and strong. With warm personal regards,

Most sincerely,

Bill /s/
William W. Scranton [15]

Two weeks later, after Goldwater had won California, Scranton would reverse himself and take the lead in a last-minute strident effort to deny the senator the Republican presidential campaign. But now, with Rockefeller the apparent winner, Scranton could afford to be magnanimous and an apostle of unity.

Meanwhile, the Eastern liberals left nothing to chance in their campaign to bury Goldwater, and conservatism, once and for all. Publisher Walter Thayer persuaded Eisenhower to sign a front-page article for the *New York Herald Tribune* in which the general described the kind of man he believed Republicans should nominate for the presidency. Under the headline, "A Personal Statement by Eisenhower: On the Republicans' Choice," the article endorsed civil rights; "true Republicanism"; "effective and humane government"; the need for firm prudent action in foreign affairs, not "impulsiveness"; and called for a nominee who would endorse "responsible, forward-looking Republicanism."

The language was unequivocal: it supported the things that Rockefeller stood for and appeared to reject Goldwater. To ensure that no one missed the point, the *Herald-Tribune* published an interpretive sidebar about the Eisenhower article by columnist Roscoe Drummond, which began: "If former President Eisenhower can have his way, the Republican party will not choose Sen. Barry Goldwater as its 1964 presidential nominee."[16]

Pressed for comment while campaigning in California, Goldwater responded that the Eisenhower statement was "most timely and most welcome," but his true feelings, and his puckish sense of humor, surfaced later that day. At a rally at Shasta Junior College, he tucked the feathered shaft of a long arrow under his arm so that it seemed to be imbedded in his back and said that it illustrated "some of the problems I've had in the last few days." The audience roared with laughter, and when newspapers from coast to coast ran a photograph of the "shafted" senator, most of the country joined in.[17]

One man who was not laughing was Ike, who had not intended that his article be used as anti-Goldwater propaganda. When George Humphrey, his former secretary of the treasury and one of his closest friends, telephoned him, Eisenhower was in a mood to set the record straight. Humphrey, a senior adviser to Goldwater, told his former boss that if he wished to maintain his neutral stance, he had better correct the widely held interpretation that his article opposed Goldwater.

It took several days but the following Monday, the day before the California primary, Eisenhower held a news conference in New York and sternly told the reporters: "You people tried to read Goldwater out of the party, I didn't." Any inference that his statement was intended to be anti-Goldwater was a "complete misinterpretation." As Clif White wrote: "The timing couldn't have been better. Instead of trooping to the polls under the illusion that the former president of the United States was supporting Nelson Rockefeller, the California voters were impressed at the most fortuitous possible moment that Eisenhower was doing no such thing."[18]

One final anti-Goldwater bomb was detonated on Sunday, May 24, nine days before the voting, when the senator appeared on ABC's "Issues and Answers" program with host Howard K. Smith. Since New Hampshire and the distortion of his remarks about the use of tactical nuclear weapons by the NATO commander, Goldwater had carefully stayed away from the subject. But during a discussion of the Vietnam War, Smith asked Goldwater how communist supply lines over jungle trails along the Laotian border into South Vietnam might be interdicted. At that moment, the candidate became the candid Goldwater of old and, adopting the casual tone of a reserve major general talking things over with his fellow officers, replied:

> Well, it is not as easy as it sounds, because these are not trails that are out in the open. I have been in these rain forests of Burma and South China. You are perfectly safe wandering through them as far as an enemy hurting you. There have been several suggestions made. *I don't think we would use any of them.* [Emphasis added.] But defoliation of the forests by low yield atomic weapons could well be done. When you remove the foliage, you remove the cover.[19]

ABC made the text of the program available to American Press and United Press International in advance of its broadcast, and, as if on cue, both wire services released stories suggesting that Barry Goldwater had "called" for the "use" of nuclear weapons in South Vietnam—a grossly inaccurate interpretation of his remarks. United Press International went so far as to report that Goldwater had "proposed" the use of low-yield atomic weapons to defoliate the forests along the borders of South Vietnam. The wire service later retracted its story, but as Goldwater remarked, "the retraction never caught up with the Sunday-morning headlines. It was a near-fatal blow."[20] He protested that he "would never use a nuclear weapon when a conventional weapon would do," but all his explanations were for naught.

This second nuclear flap branded Goldwater in the minds of many and probably most Americans as a careless advocate of nuclear warfare. Although the *New York Times* printed Goldwater's exact words, Rockefeller immediately branded his Republican opponent a nuclear extremist, commenting, "I do not believe that the answer to the failures of the present administration is to be found in a reckless belligerence typified by such *proposals* as . . . using nuclear weapons to clear the jungles of Viet Nam" [emphasis added].[21]

Hoping to capitalize on the public's fear of nuclear catastrophe, the Rockefeller organization mailed a poisonous brochure entitled, "Who Do You Want in the Room with the H-Bomb?" to all three million of the state's registered Republicans, at an estimated cost of $120,000. The pamphlet presented a collection of Goldwater quotes taken out of context and insinuated that if the senator were elected, nuclear war would almost surely follow.

But the pamphlet's shrill tone and obvious expense triggered a backlash among California Republicans, who were tired of being warned about a fellow Westerner whom they knew to be a good and decent man. At the last moment, Rockefeller canceled a half-hour television program, *The Extremists,* narrated by David Garroway, a savage indictment of right-wing hatemongers and, by association, Barry Goldwater. Even the governor was convinced that "McCarthyism-in-reverse" was a dangerous tactic for someone who liked to boast that he was the champion of responsible, forward-looking Republicanism.[22]

As time grew short, although detecting some upward movement by Goldwater in the final days, all pollsters still forecast a Rockefeller victory. The prestigious California Field poll gave Rockefeller 46 percent, Goldwater 37 percent, with 17 percent undecided. The Harris poll called it 49 percent Rockefeller, Goldwater 40 percent, and 11 percent undecided.[23] (Harris's last published poll, which appeared on the morning of the primary, gave the following figures: Rockefeller, 42 percent, Goldwater 40 percent, 18 percent undecided.) The Rockefeller camp was euphoric about their man's seemingly solid lead but should have noticed that the "undecided" vote was increasing rather than decreasing as election day neared.

Rockefeller personally brought on the climactic event. His wife Happy was so close to delivery that the governor flew back to New York every weekend to be with her—over the objections of his advisers who warned that the flights drew attention to the one issue that might defeat him. According to Theodore White, Rockefeller told his advisers that he would rather not be president if it meant leaving Happy to face the birth of their child alone. Publicly, he wisecracked, "I have a show opening on both sides of the continent the same weekend."[24]

This was too much for the Christian Right of the mid-1960s, and on Thursday, May 28, sixteen Protestant ministers, representing a wide segment of the Christian community, met in Los Angeles and issued a statement suggesting that Nelson Rockefeller should withdraw from the race because of his demonstrated inability to handle even his own domestic affairs.

The same week, Rockefeller was scheduled to speak at a leading

Catholic institution, Loyola University of Los Angeles, at the invitation of its students. Dick Herman, a prominent Roman Catholic
layman back in Nebraska, was sent by Burch to petition Francis
Cardinal McIntyre to cancel the invitation. Herman recalls that the
cardinal listened carefully to his arguments—that Rockefeller's appearance at a Catholic university so close to primary day could be
interpreted as the Church's endorsement of the governor—but made
no commitment.

Six hours before Rockefeller was scheduled to speak, however,
Loyola suddenly withdrew its invitation, explaining that the governor's
appearance on campus was being "generally interpreted" as an official
endorsement of his candidacy. Cardinal McIntyre drove the point home
by telling the press that he did not want anyone to think that the
Catholic Church was giving its blessing to the candidacy of someone
who had been divorced and then remarried.[25]

For the first time in California politics, Catholic and Protestant
leaders were united and vocal in strong opposition to a presidential
candidate. The denouement came on 4:15 P.M., Saturday, May 30, less
than 70 hours before the primary polls opened in California, when
Happy gave birth to a baby boy in New York Hospital. She named him
Nelson Rockefeller, Jr., and gave ministers and pastors throughout
California their Sunday sermon.

On Tuesday, June 2, a milestone in the history of the modern
conservative movement, thousands of volunteers fanned out across the
state with maps and information kits containing the names and addresses of known Goldwater supporters circled in red and got them to
the polls. The final tally was 1,120,403 votes for Goldwater, 1,052,053
for Rockefeller, a popular margin of 68,350 votes, 51.6 percent of the
votes cast. The senator received all eighty-six of California's delegates
and now had more than the 655 needed for nomination.

And where was Barry Goldwater on the occasion of the biggest
political victory of his life? Any normal politician would have been in
Los Angeles giving a victory speech, praising his workers and the
voters of California, joking with the press at a major news conference,
laying plans for the last six weeks until the Republican convention in
San Francisco. But the senator had taken the "red eye" midnight flight
from Los Angeles to Washington on election night when he was only
26,000 votes ahead and the networks were beginning to qualify their
earlier forecast of a Goldwater victory.

Henry Salvatori, a friend and Republican leader, claims that Goldwater was so unsettled by the prospect of winning California, and therefore the nomination, that he got drunk at a victory party and "we had to help him get on the plane for Washington."[26] Yet reporters accompanying the senator on the trip do not recall that he acted drunk, although one said that he fell asleep immediately. Did Goldwater try to drown his fears? That is too psychological an interpretation of a very basic man's actions. The senator probably had several drinks after dinner, and if he had more than usual the evening of June 2, it was because he felt he had earned them.

WHY DID Barry Goldwater win the most important primary of 1964? Because:

(1) he had the necessary money to mount a modern media-driven campaign;

(2) his army of volunteers simply overwhelmed the opposition (Rockefeller manager Spencer recalls with awe "the number of bodies they kept throwing at us" week after week)[27];

(3) Goldwater was an effective, energetic campaigner, clearly enjoying himself as he had not in New Hampshire and rarely on the defensive (Dean Burch said the senator never campaigned better)[28];

(4) as in the rest of the nation in 1964, the Republican party in California was undergoing a transformation from a me-too, establishment-led institution to a conservative, grassroots movement;

(5) Rockefeller conducted a strident, unrelievedly anti-Goldwater campaign that brought him close to victory but produced defeat because it galvanized the Goldwater volunteers; in a tight race, the key element may well be which candidate has the higher Intensity Quotient (IQ); among his supporters, and in the spring of 1964, Goldwater people rather than Rockefeller people unquestionably had the higher IQ;

(6) the Goldwater advertising, print, and broadcast, was skillful and timely; Spencer points to the impact of the full-page newspaper ads featuring the Goldwater family; Paul Grindle, director of the Draft Lodge effort in New Hampshire who worked for Rockefeller in California, felt that the single item which turned the tide was an ad containing quotes from respected, prominent Republicans praising the senator;

(7) the divorce-remarriage-birth issue unquestionably harmed Rockefeller and benefited Goldwater, although the senator ordered his staff never to mention his opponent's personal life;

(8) the Rockefeller campaign adopted a don't-rock-the-boat strategy in the final days, cutting back on newspaper advertising and TV-radio commercials and nearly closing down its field offices.[29]

In his 1988 memoirs, Goldwater states that he leaned toward dropping out of the presidential race if he did not win California, but "it was still a big if for two reasons": he wanted to "preserve conservative unity then and in the future," and he most emphatically did not want the nomination to go to Nixon. He expands on the latter point by saying that he "wouldn't have supported Nixon" in 1964 because the former vice president "was plotting behind closed doors to take over the convention and give all the current candidates [including Goldwater] the boot."[30]

This is post-Watergate revisionism by Goldwater. It is true that Nixon had been talking and meeting with old friends and aides, like Robert Finch, but he avoided any formal stop-Goldwater effort because he could not afford to alienate either Goldwater or his fervent backers. The *New York Times'* Charles Mohr, who had been covering Goldwater since before the Kennedy assassination, wrote a week before the California primary that if he failed to get the nomination, "Mr. Goldwater is privately determined to support the former vice president."[31] Goldwater states that if he had failed "completely," he planned to support Scranton because "he had not assailed the conservative movement" and therefore "we could live with him and fight another day." Clif White said that if Goldwater had tried to deliver his bloc of delegates to anyone other than Nixon "he would have had a major revolt on his hands. He might even have had great difficulty in turning them over to Nixon."[32]

But all that is beside the point, insisted White, for even without California's 86 delegates, Goldwater had 579 committed delegates on June 2 and would have picked up another 100 at the remaining state conventions for a total of 679, 24 more than the 655 needed to nominate. To those who argued that the declared delegates would have melted away, White said simply, "Our delegates were a brand-new breed. Nothing could shake them."[33]

12

Civil Rights and States' Rights

THE CIVIL RIGHTS ACT OF 1964 was the climax of a tense, often violent decade of black activism and white resistance in the South. It began in 1955 when Rosa Parks, a black, refused to comply with the law and move to the rear of a Montgomery, Alabama, bus. Black ministers, led by Martin Luther King Jr., and Ralph Abernathy, organized a bus boycott, and the South and American politics were never the same again. Because of the boycott, and a Supreme Court decision affirming that segregation on intrastate public transportation must end, the buses were integrated.

Civil rights activity continued, receiving national attention in 1960–1961 when young men and women conducted sit-ins at segregated restaurants. Although some restaurants desegregated, pressure built for a national public accommodations law. In March 1961, the Congress of Racial Equality (CORE) announced that it would sponsor "freedom rides" to desegregate waiting rooms and other facilities in bus stations in the South. The rides were marked by violence, beatings, and jailings of blacks, but the tide of black activism continued to roll across the South. Although concerned about the growing militancy on both sides, Goldwater publicly endorsed the goals of the freedom riders, stating that under the commerce clause of the Constitution, "bus companies, airlines, railroads, etc., engaged in interstate commerce, cannot deny any citizen the right to their facilities." The Constitution was his guiding star and not to be denied by anyone—North or South, white or black, liberal or conservative.[1]

Inspired by the success of CORE and other organizations, King and the Southern Leadership Conference planned a major, nonviolent campaign in the spring of 1963 (a century after the Emancipation Proclamation) in Birmingham, Alabama, "the most segregated city in the United States."[2] King and other black leaders calculated, correctly, that the national news media would publicize their sit-ins and freedom marches, which, in turn, would energize the nation to back their cause.

Birmingham's arch-segregationist chief of police, Eugene (Bull) Connor, ordered mass arrests, but the peaceful protests would not be halted. On May 7, confronted with several thousand student marchers who refused to disperse, an enraged Connor used firehoses, dogs, and nightsticks to break up the demonstration. Network television cameras carried the image of a snarling dog lunging at a terrified woman into the living rooms of millions of shocked Americans.

The Supreme Court nullified Alabama's segregationist laws, but white extremists would not be contained and bombed the home of King's brother. In response, Birmingham blacks rioted and stormed about the city. In June, President Kennedy went on national television to state that "a great change is at hand, and our task, our obligation, is to make that revolution, that change, peaceful and constructive for all." To that end, he asked Congress to enact a broad, sweeping civil rights bill committed to the premise "that race has no place in American life or law."[3]

It was an eloquent plea, but throughout that long hot summer of 1963, the race issue dominated the nation: 758 civil rights demonstrations broke out across the nation resulting in 13,786 arrests in seventy-five cities.[4] One demonstration, however, was entirely peaceful and produced a message whose power still resonates: it was the March on Washington on August 28, 1963.

More than 200,000 people, mostly black, marched down Pennsylvania Avenue and assembled on the Mall before the Lincoln Memorial to listen to union leader A. Philip Randolph, who had proposed the march twenty years before; Roy Wilkins of the National Association for the Advancement of Colored People (NAACP); UAW's Walter Reuther, CORE's Floyd B. McKissick; and Martin Luther King Jr. who intoned his memorable "I Have a Dream" speech in which he spoke of a day when people of all colors, creeds, and persuasions would join hands in brotherhood. In his stirring peroration, King declared:

> When we let freedom ring, when we let it ring from every village and every hamlet, from every state and every city, we will speed up that day when all God's children, black men and white men, Jews and Gentiles, Protestants and Catholics, will be able to join hands and sing in the words of the old Negro spiritual, "Free at last! Free at last! Thank God almighty, we are free at last!"[5]

Freedom. It was central to Barry Goldwater's political and personal philosophy, and he showed his understanding of black frustration when he told students at Phillips Academy three months before the March on Washington, "If I were a Negro, I don't think I would be very patient." More pointedly, he refused to join white Southerners in opposing the march, saying, "Anybody has the right to come to Washington and visit his congressman. I'll be in my office to receive people from my state."

The comment and the pledge were consistent with the Goldwater record, private and public. As Edwin McDowell, an early biographer, wrote, "Few men not deliberately courting minority bloc votes have expressed their sympathy for [blacks]—verbally and through action—more often than Goldwater."[6]

As a member of the Phoenix City Council, Goldwater had voted to desegregate the restaurant at Sky Harbor Airport. As chief of state for the Arizona Air National Guard, he had pushed for desegregation of the guard. As a businessman, he had opened his doors to everyone. As senator, he had desegregated the Senate cafeteria in 1953, insisting that his black legislative assistant, Kathrine Maxwell, be served along with every other Senate employee. As an individual citizen, he had donated generously to the Arizona NAACP, including a $200 check in 1952 to its legal defense fund to speed integration of the public schools. He was a member of both the Phoenix and Tucson chapters of the NAACP but withdrew when "they started attacking me politically."[7]

Goldwater was also a strong supporter of the Phoenix Urban League, particularly telling in the days when it was not fashionable for white businessmen to care about racial relations. He personally made up the league's operating deficit two years in a row when it was getting started. Moreover, along with Congressman John Rhodes, he obtained the $6 million needed to build the Urban League Manor, an adult complex for the handicapped. He also introduced Junius Bowman, the black president of the Phoenix Urban League, to the city's most important citizens. And through it all, Bowman recalled, Goldwater "never once asked me how I vote or what party I belong to—not once."[8]

In recognition of his many contributions, most of them unpublicized, Goldwater received the Humanitarian Award in December 1991 "for fifty years of loyal service to the Phoenix Urban League." When a few league members objected, Bowman said flatly that Barry Goldwater had saved the league more than once and that he preferred to judge a person on the basis of his daily actions rather than on his voting record.[9]

In October 1955, Goldwater addressed an NAACP convention in Tucson and compared promises made by candidate Eisenhower in 1952 with actions subsequently taken by his administration. The accomplishments ranged from ending segregation in the nation's capital and any remaining racial bias in the employment practices of the federal government to appointing Negroes to policy-making positions and strengthening the civil rights section of the Justice Department.

Along the way, he could not resist poking at organized labor by pointing out that the Republican administration had enforced the nondiscriminatory clauses of the Taft-Hartley Act, "which will break the grip of negrophobic labor unions." In short, Eisenhower had moved toward "the complete elimination of every vestige of segregation and discrimination in American life with first-class citizenship for all as a goal."[10]

Two accomplishments he did not mention were naming Earl Warren as Chief Justice of the Supreme Court and the Court's historic 1954 decision, *Brown v. Board of Education*. His omission of Warren was consistent. Back in September 1953, he had criticized Ike's appointment of the former California governor at a White House luncheon when the president asked his opinion. "I don't think much of it," Goldwater replied, and went on to explain that although he could overlook Warren's not practicing law for twenty-five years, he could not forget that, as governor, Warren had pushed programs of "the welfare state variety and I just don't like to see a man like that become Chief Justice."[11]

Regarding the *Brown* decision, Goldwater agreed with the objectives of the Supreme Court. "I believe that it is both wise and just for Negro children," he later wrote, "to attend the same schools as whites, and that to deny them this opportunity carries with it strong implications of inferiority." But, he maintained, the Tenth Amendment decrees that the actual matter of school integration be left to the states; to do otherwise was to subvert the Constitution. "Social and cultural change," he declared, repeating one of his fundamental principles, "should not be affected by the engines of national power."[12]

Goldwater the libertarian sided with the strict constructionists, insisting that the Constitution "is what its authors intended it to be and said it was—not what the Supreme Court says it is." If in the face of good intentions and passion and anger, he warned, "we condone the practice of substituting our own intentions for those of the Constitution's framers, we reject, in effect, the principle of constitutional government; we endorse a rule of men, not of laws."[13]

When racial unrest broke out in Little Rock, Arkansas, in the fall of 1957, Goldwater stuck by the Constitution. On that occasion, a handful of black students tried to enroll at previously all-white Central High School and were taunted and harassed by rabid segregationists. Governor Orval Faubus ordered in the National Guard, but when it was unable to maintain order, the White House stepped in and federalized the guard. When the black students returned to the school, surrounded by armed troops, violence erupted and engulfed Little Rock for months.

Goldwater criticized the use of federal troops. He accused the Eisenhower administration of violating the Constitution by assuming powers reserved for the states. While he agreed that under the law, every state should have integrated its schools, each state should integrate in its own way. "Leave them alone," he said. "They will eventually have integrated schools."[14] Law and society should move in tandem, he insisted. He knew that when law moves too quickly and too far in advance of society, violence and disruption ensue.

But black Americans declined to wait; they had been waiting for nearly a century for their basic civil rights and so they interpreted Goldwater's words as an endorsement of segregation and white political power. They were as unaware of his pro-civil rights record in Arizona as they were that in 1939, long before he had any thought of public office, he had written about the need for racial tolerance in an informal diary:

> I have always thought and have never lost sight of the thought that all men were and are created equal. . . . I can say that this is the one statement that I will make now that in the years to come I will not have to retract—I love my fellow man be he white or black or yellow and I am vitally interested in his well-being for that well-being is my well-being. . . .
>
> I cannot pass on to my son or sons any more valuable advice than to treat those with whom you associate as those people should be treated by a man that is good to all. . . .[15]

Goldwater's profound respect for the Constitution, as it was written, is the key to his position on the Civil Rights Act of 1964 and to his insistence that he would vote for its passage *if* Section II on public accommodations and Section VII on equal employment opportunity were removed. These sections, he believed, were unconstitutional and unenforceable without the creation of a huge federal police force more dangerous to the Republic than the wrongs they were supposed to right.

But even Goldwater could change his mind, as he did regarding the federal government's power to enforce school integration. It was Denison Kitchel, his longtime friend and a Harvard law graduate, who persuaded him to accept the government's authority in this area.

Even if he disagreed with it, Goldwater did not want to condone wanton disregard of the Supreme Court. When he was asked in 1963 how a state might resist the Court's school desegregation decisions, he said firmly, "The idea is not to resist it. There is nothing in our Constitution that says a person can violate the law. Neither is there anything that says a state can violate the law."[16] If a state felt that its rights had been tampered with, he argued it should use either the amendment or the electoral process. Furthermore, he went on, while still insisting that he would first use moral persuasion to integrate schools, he thought that a law should be passed giving the Attorney General the power "to use a very tightly drawn law aimed like a rifle at this precise problem in a school district."[17] And he would use whatever federal authority was legal, including federal troops or marshals, to carry out the courts' decisions.

This was far different from George Wallace's demagogic cry: "Segregation now! Segregation tomorrow! Segregation forever!"[18] Goldwater was not a segregationist but a constitutionalist. He was not a disciple of Jean Jacques Rousseau, giving in to the impulse of the moment, but a follower of Madison trying to ensure that no one faction would ever gain a permanent majority. He was a classical liberal in the Jeffersonian sense, concerned that the attempt to regulate private business as set forth by the civil rights bill was a giant step toward abolishing private property.

Yet many national leaders, from Walter Lippmann to Pat Brown to Roy Wilkins to Martin Luther King, called Goldwater a bigot, a racist, and even a Nazi, despite his Jewish heritage. They were blind to the fact that the nation's more rabid racists and segregationists attacked Goldwater. The National States Rights party labeled him a "kosher conservative" and linked him with "Jewish espionage artists." The American Nazi party picketed various Goldwater headquarters, carrying signs that read "Goldwater Is a Race Mixer" and "Goldwater Supported the Red NAACP."[19]

Part of the reason for the liberals' harsh criticism of Goldwater was crudely political: many of Goldwater's critics were Democrats who wanted to defeat the Republican nominee by any means at hand, including charges of racism. Part of it was philosophical: conservatism was a new way of looking at politics, and liberal critics dismissed its emphasis on individual responsibility and the principle of subsidiarity (allowing subordinate or local organizations to perform functions rather than a central authority) as an attempt to avoid dealing with deep-rooted problems like segregation.

Another part of the reason was racial: there were no blacks in 1964—no Thomas Sowell, no Walter Williams, no Clarence Thomas—to articulate the conservative point of view on civil rights. Blacks could claim, with some justification, that their views were not adequately represented within the emerging conservative majority of the Republican party.

Yet another reason why Goldwater was criticized so severely was the news media, which misrepresented or misreported Goldwater's views on civil rights and states' rights. For example, nearly thirty years later, in his best-selling work, *Chain Reaction: The Impact of Race, Rights and Taxes on American Politics,* Thomas Edsall presented Goldwater's position as being personally opposed to segregation but being "even

more deeply opposed on principle to federal intervention to end segregation." As proof, Edsall quoted, accurately, from *The Conscience of
a Conservative* that "the Constitution does not permit any interference
whatsoever by the federal government in the field of education."[20]

But Edsall fails to add that only three years later Goldwater publicly
changed his mind about the role of government in carrying out school
desegregation, and that during the 1964 campaign he stated repeatedly
that as president he would enforce the decisions of the Supreme Court,
regardless of his personal feelings about them.

Nor does Edsall mention the civil rights plank of the 1964 Republican platform, endorsed by Goldwater without reservation, that pledged
"full implementation and faithful execution of the Civil Rights Act of
1964, and all other civil rights statutes, to assure equal rights and
opportunities guaranteed by the Constitution to every citizen."

Finally Edsall omits Goldwater's statement to Southern delegates at
the Republican National Convention: that segregation was "wrong
morally, and in some instances, constitutionally" and that if elected,
he would use the "moral power" of the presidency to help end
discrimination.[21]

Consistent with his belief in federalism, Goldwater also opposed the
creation of a Fair Employment Practices Commission. He readily
agreed that it was "wrong, morally wrong," for employers to discriminate by hiring on the basis of color, race, or religion, and the Goldwaters stores were proof of it. When a picket carried a sign in a 1963
Phoenix march reading, "Goldwaters hires no Negro sales personnel,"
brother Bob Goldwater was quick to answer that the Goldwater stores
(which had been sold to a New York company) employed seventeen
blacks, several in supervisory jobs, out of a total of four hundred
employees. That amounted to just over 4 percent in a city where blacks
made up only .05 percent of the total population, a percentage far more
liberal than quotas demanded by the NAACP.[22]

For Goldwater, of course, what was at issue was not just discrimination, as reprehensible as that was, but also the proper role of government in eliminating it. He argued that if the government "can forbid
such discrimination, it is a real possibility that sometime in the future
the same government can *require* people to discriminate in hiring on
the basis of color or race or religion." He agreed with Milton Friedman
that it was no more desirable that momentary majorities decide what
characteristics are relevant to employment than what speech is appro-

priate.[23] That is, he made it perfectly clear that he was for equal opportunity, by which individuals are judged on their qualifications *without regard* to race, sex, and religion, but against preferential treatment (what came to be called "affirmative action") that required that individuals be judged *with regard* to their race, sex, and religion. Others were not so honest.

While guiding the Civil Rights Act of 1964 through the Senate, Senator Hubert Humphrey assured his colleagues that "it does not require an employer to achieve any kind of racial balance in his work force by giving preferential treatment to any individual or group." In this pledge he was joined by Democratic Senator Joseph Clark of Pennsylvania, another ardent advocate of the act, and Democratic Senator Harrison Williams of New Jersey who, for example, insisted that an employer could continue to hire "only the best qualified persons even if they were all white." One observer summed it up, "Congress declared itself in favor of equal opportunity and opposed to affirmative action."[24]

But Barry Goldwater believed that regardless of the rhetoric, the reality was that Title VII would lead to affirmative action. Events have proved him right. President Johnson created the Office of Federal Contract Compliance in the U.S. Department of Labor in 1965, which in 1968 spoke of "goals and timetables for the prompt achievement of full and equal employment opportunity." By 1970, under President Nixon, there was reference to "results-oriented procedures." Finally in December 1971, new guidelines made it clear that "goals and time-tables" were meant to "increase materially the utilization of minorities and women." The burden of proof, and remedy, was shifted to the employer, and affirmative action was "transformed into a numerical concept, whether called 'goals' or 'quotas.'"[25]

From almost his first day in the Senate, Goldwater placed himself on the side of states' rights, arguing that the fifty states are fifty laboratories in which citizens test the ways of civil government and find solutions to the problems of society. To those who questioned the competence of fifty state governments, so different in composition and resources, to operate effectively in our complex age, he replied, "How better to meet complexity than with a diversity of resources?"[26]

Goldwater's commitment to states' rights flowed from his abiding belief in federalism and the fifty states that comprise the federalist system. It rested on his regard for the practical wisdom of the people and their ability to solve their problems. "The federal system, with its base in the states," he said, "tolerates many differences without, of course, tolerating impairment of nationally agreed upon freedoms. It does not demand, in other words, that all citizens adopt a single best answer to any problem—but it does tend to prevent them from adopting any single worst answer."[27]

For Goldwater, the Tenth Amendment was not an afterthought but an essential safeguard to limit the federal government to its constitutional boundaries. The constitutional system does not thwart the will of the people, he stated, but subordinates *immediate* objectives to *long-range* objectives. He liked to quote approvingly the Senate Judiciary Committee, which concerning the 1937 court-packing plan by FDR, concluded that the preservation of the U.S. constitutional system is "immeasurably more important . . . than the immediate adoption of any legislation however beneficial."[28] He himself once remarked:

> The reason that the word "no" is used as a direct restraint on government twenty-six times in the original seven Articles of the Constitution, and five times more in the Bill of Rights, is to limit the scope and size of federal government, so it can't become tyrannical. If we expect to remain a free people, we have to see to it that states' rights are not permitted to disappear, even if sometimes we are perplexed at the actions of certain states.[29]

From the introduction of the Civil Rights Act on June 19, 1963— long before he committed himself to running for president—Goldwater stated that he wanted to vote for the legislation, as he had for the Civil Rights Acts of 1957 and 1960. But he as consistently opposed two of the act's eleven sections, those dealing with public accommodations (Title II) and fair employment (Title VII). He could find "no constitutional basis for the exercise of federal regulatory authority in either of these areas" and believed that the use of such power would be "a grave threat to our constitutional republic."

Title II, the so-called Mrs. Murphy clause, he found "particularly repellent" because it in effect stated that a landlord could not refuse rental to anybody. Goldwater put it bluntly, "I would not rent my home to a lot of whites for many reasons."[30] As for Title VII, he feared that it would create "a police state" that would dictate hiring and firing policy for seventy million working Americans. He shared the opinion of one observer who wrote that the House version, passed in February, "took the federal government further inside the private lives and customs of individual citizens than any federal legislation in American history."[31]

But, he approved the act's other major provisions that (1) prohibited vote registrars from applying different standards in disqualifying white and black voting applicants; (2) empowered the Attorney General to initiate suits or intervene on behalf of complainants in school desegregation and other discrimination cases; and (3) permitted halting funds to federally aided programs where racial discrimination persisted.[32]

One important Goldwater adviser (brought in by Bill Baroody) was Professor Robert H. Bork of the Yale University Law School. In the summer of 1963 Bork wrote in *The New Republic* that "the majority of the nation's moral and intellectual leaders" were practicing a kind of McCarthyism with regard to civil rights. In the early 1950s, he said, the issue was not whether communism was good or evil but whether men ought to be free to think and talk as they pleased. Now, asserted the legal scholar, the same leaders seemed to "be running with the other pack." The issue, he insisted, was not whether racial prejudice or preference was a good thing but "whether individual men ought to be free to deal and associate with whom they please for whatever reasons appeal to them." Bork argued:

One may agree that it is immoral to treat a man according to his race and religion and yet question whether that moral preference deserves elevation to the level of the principle of individual freedom and self-determination. If every time an intensely felt moral principle is involved, we spend freedom, we will sooner or later run out of it.[33]

When Bork was asked by the Goldwater staff for a legal analysis of the civil rights bill, he provided a seventy-five-page critique that was used in preparing the senator's position against the bill.

Another key legal adviser was William Rehnquist, then a member of Denison Kitchel's law firm in Phoenix, later Chief Justice of the Supreme Court.[34]

In the final days of the California primary, Goldwater told reporters that since he had voted for previous civil rights bills, "it wouldn't be out of character" if he voted for this one. A week later, he indicated that he might vote for the compromise fashioned by Senator Dirksen, particularly if coupled with three amendments suggested by Senator Bourke Hickenlooper of Iowa and other Republicans. Up to a few days before the final vote, he was still saying he hoped to be able to vote for final passage, but that it depended on whether the legislation was modified to meet his constitutional objections. But when common-sense amendments were brought up and bowled over "like a row of ninepins," Goldwater knew he had no choice but to vote no.[35]

He flew to Gettysburg on June 17th to inform Eisenhower of his intention to oppose the bill and was told, to his relief, that Ike would not hold this against him in the contest for the Republican nomination.[36] Later that same day, Goldwater went before the Senate and explained, with the eyes of the country upon him, why he felt compelled, albeit "reluctantly," to vote against the measure.

Stating his conviction that discrimination was "fundamentally a matter of the heart," he argued that it could never be cured by laws alone. Laws of course "can help—laws carefully considered and weighed in an atmosphere of dispassion, in the absence of political demagoguery, and in the light of fundamental constitutional principles." Unfortunately, he continued, the bill before the Senate was not such a law, and political pressure rather than persuasion or common sense had "come to rule the consideration of this measure."[37]

He did not flinch from the consequences of his vote, saying simply, "If my vote is misconstrued, let it be." His concern was not with himself or any single group but with the nation and "the freedom of all who live in it and all who will be born in it."[38] There was that quintessential Goldwater word again, "freedom." He would not give into the passion of the moment, no matter how fitting and proper it seemed, if it endangered individual freedom.

But he was not a radical libertarian indifferent to the needs of others; he was a constitutional conservative concerned with the individual and the nation. Individual freedom and the general welfare were harmoniously dependent on each other, he said, and would, if given sufficient time, work out their differences.

He disagreed with liberals that the federal government had to mandate the extremes of individual freedom and reduce the general welfare to the lowest common denominator of social welfare programs. Such federal intrusion would only create severe dysfunction between individuals and society unintended by the Founders and the Constitution.

The speech was not long—only five pages. And much of the language was taken from statements on civil rights that he had been making for a long time. But when Barry Goldwater finished speaking, the Republican party, conservatism, and American politics had been radically changed.

Although his opposition to the Civil Rights Act of 1964 was based on constitutional not political considerations, Goldwater's stand could not be separated from the politics of 1964 and beyond. Very much on every politician's mind that summer was the remarkable showing of Governor George Wallace of Alabama in the Northern as well as the Southern Democratic primaries.

It was not just how many votes Wallace got above the Mason-Dixon Line—34 percent in Wisconsin, 30 percent in Indiana, 43 percent in Maryland—but *where* he got them. As Theodore White pointed out, Wallace did extremely well in the ethnic blue-collar neighborhoods of Milwaukee, the mill town of Gary, Indiana, and among the steelworkers of Baltimore.[39] This white support of Wallace was called a "backlash" against civil rights, particularly where it affected jobs. If the Wallace vote in the North and South went to Goldwater in the general election, many thought President Johnson would be in for a far tougher race than the polls suggested. (Gallup gave the president 81 percent of the vote against Goldwater; Harris, 74 percent.) Such a projection, however, presumed that Goldwater was George Wallace in a cowboy hat and boots. But they were two very different men in philosophy, training, and temperament.

Goldwater was a self-taught intellectual who loved to play with ideas; Wallace was a fierce anti-intellectual who loved to mock the "pointy-heads" in the ivory towers. Goldwater was a constitutional conservative; Wallace was a calculating populist. Goldwater was an integrationist; Wallace, a segregationist. Goldwater wanted to limit the power of government everywhere; Wallace was willing to expand government spending and programs. Goldwater was an internationalist; Wallace, an isolationist. In sum, Goldwater was an American statesman; Wallace was a Southern pol.

That Goldwater would not join forces with Wallace was demonstrated conclusively when James Martin, a prominent Alabama Republican who had run for the Senate in 1962, presented the senator with an extraordinary offer during the GOP's national convention in San Francisco in July. The offer: Wallace might be willing to run on the Republican ticket with Goldwater. Back in Alabama, Wallace had intimated to Martin that he would change parties and become a Republican. One source insists that Goldwater's swift response was "Go to hell!" According to Martin, the senator said that a Goldwater-Wallace ticket was "not feasible" and turned down the governor's offer. Nevertheless, following Goldwater's nomination, Wallace announced that he would not be a candidate for president on a third party ticket, a decision that certainly helped Goldwater to carry the Deep South in the fall and Southern Republicans like Martin to win seats in the House of Representatives.[40]

The only way Goldwater could have ridden the backlash into the White House would have been to exploit the summer riots that began with the death of a fifteen-year-old black, James Powell, in New York City on July 16, 1964 (the same night Goldwater accepted his party's nomination for president in San Francisco), and raged up and down the Eastern seaboard in late July and early August. At this critical moment, with people mournfully wondering if the American presidency would be decided on the issues of race and violence between whites and blacks, Goldwater initiated a meeting with President Johnson in the White House.

Following a sixteen-minute talk in the Oval Office on July 24, the two nominees released a joint statement in which they agreed "to avoid the incitement of racial tensions" in the campaign.[41] The president was grateful because Goldwater's offer would reduce the possibility of more racial outbreaks—and because his opponent had just surrendered an issue that might have secured him, if not victory, at least a fighting chance at victory.

Goldwater kept his word, as he always did, down to the last frantic days of his campaign, when he vetoed "Choice," described by Theodore White as "the most electrifying campaign film of street violence ever prepared." "Choice" made the controversial Willy Horton commercial of 1988 look like *Rebecca of Sunnybrook Farm*. Goldwater's outright rejection of it confirmed his declaration that "I would never appeal to race, not for any reason."[42]

And yet that fall he became the first Republican since Reconstruction to carry all of the Deep South, winning Mississippi by 87.1 percent, Alabama by 69.5 percent, South Carolina by 58.9 percent, Louisiana by

56.8 percent, and Georgia by 54.1 percent. His sweep laid the foundation for Nixon's win in 1968 and a two-party South. At the same time, Goldwater's vote against the civil rights bill and his electoral success in the fall combined to alienate a generation of black Americans from the party that had overseen the freeing of black Americans a century earlier.

ON JUNE 19, 1964, after eighty-three days of debate that filled 2,890 pages of the *Congressional Record*, the Senate passed the Civil Rights Act of 1964 by 73–27, with twenty-one Democrats and six Republicans voting against it. (In his 1988 memoirs, Goldwater erroneously states, twice, that he cast the "only" vote against the measure, apparently confusing 1964 with 1958 when his was the only Senate vote against the Kennedy-Irvin labor bill, a forgivable lapse of memory after two decades.)

Among the "segregationist" Democrats who voted "nay" along with Goldwater were J. William Fulbright, Rhodes scholar and chairman of the Senate Foreign Relations Committee; Sam Irvin, noted constitutional scholar and later hero of the Watergate hearings; and Albert Gore, Sr., Tennessee liberal and father of Vice President Al Gore. The other Republicans in opposition were Norris Cotton of New Hampshire, Bourke Hickenlooper of Iowa, Edwin L. Mechem of New Mexico, Milward L. Simpson of Wyoming, and John Tower of Texas.

Perhaps Goldwater misstated that he was the only senator who voted against passage because he was the only senator who as a result of his vote was branded "the rallying point of the white resistance" (Walter Lippmann); "a rallying point for all the racists in America" (union official William Chester); and "a hopeless captive of the lunatic, calculating right-wing extremists" (Jackie Robinson). NAACP secretary Roy Wilkins later stated that a Goldwater victory "would lead to a police state" while Martin Luther King Jr., declared that there were "dangerous signs of Hitlerism" in Goldwater's programs, adding that if he were elected, the nation would erupt into "violence and riots, the like of which we have never seen before."[43]

Twenty-two years later, when emotions were not running so high, Roger Wilkins, Roy Wilkins' nephew and a fellow at the ultraliberal Institute for Policy Studies, wrote Goldwater on his retirement from the Senate that "your contribution to democratic institutions has been enormous" and praised him for the "character and integrity" that had marked his public career. "Thank you," Wilkins concluded, "for your service to our country."[44]

Many in the news media took their cue from Lippmann, labeling Goldwater an opportunist appealing to the segregationist South, but a few praised the senator for his principled stand. David Lawrence, editor of *U.S. News & World Report,* called his vote "the courageous act of a man who would rather risk the loss of a presidential nomination or even election than to surrender his convictions to political expediency." Arthur Krock of the *New York Times* agreed, writing that Goldwater "set an example of political and moral courage that was the more admirable because of the immediate circumstances." One of the most respected men in American journalism, John S. Knight, president and editor of the *Detroit Free Press,* became so disturbed at the one-sided media treatment of Goldwater that he took his colleagues across his knees. Although Knight did not support Goldwater, he wrote:

Some of the television commentators discuss Goldwater with evident disdain and contempt. Editorial cartoonists portray him as belonging to the Neanderthal age or as a relic of the nineteenth century. It is the fashion of editorial writers to persuade themselves that Goldwater's followers are either kooks or Birchers. This simply isn't so. The Goldwater movement represents a mass protest by conservatively minded people against foreign aid, excessive welfare, high taxes, foreign policy, and the concentration of power in the federal government.[45]

But Knight's rebuke was generally ignored by the news media that erred so badly in their coverage of Barry Goldwater that three decades later journalists like David Broder of the *Washington Post* were still apologizing for their mistakes. "It bothered me at the time," says Broder, "and it still bothers me in retrospect that we [the news media] were not able, even those of us who knew him very well, really to slow down that notion which Johnson and Democrats put out that this was in some sense a very dangerous and mean-minded person." People, he added, "had a fundamentally distorted picture of who Goldwater was or what he represented."[46] The electorate would have had a more accurate portrait if the mainstream media had listened to someone like Chuck Stone, editor of the national black weekly, the *Afro-American,* who after interviewing Goldwater in 1963, wrote that "in the area of civil rights . . . his deep feeling about racial equality again and again rises to the surface whenever he touches upon this critical subject." Stone added that if Goldwater became president, "one thing is certain: [black] people will have a sympathetic ear to their demands."[47]

Usually perceptive analysts erred badly in writing about Goldwater's opposition to the Civil Rights Act of 1964. The *New York Times'* James Reston stated that his vote jeopardized his chances of winning the Republican nomination, clearly not understanding that the overwhelming majority of Goldwater delegates supported the senator for his antigovernment, anticommunist positions, not his civil rights stances. Republicans did not separate and elevate civil rights, as Democrats did, but considered it within the framework of all issues.

There was also the matter of practical politics. The Democratic party had been receiving 70 to 90 percent of the black vote for thirty years. As Goldwater put it, Republicans should "stop trying to outbid the Democrats for the [black] vote." Instead, they should "go hunting where the ducks are." And for Republicans, the ducks were in the West, the Midwest, and the South.[48]

The character of the Goldwater movement was seriously distorted by Thomas Edsall when he wrote that the Goldwater nomination drive mobilized "a new breed of Republican." This breed, according to one observer, talked "boisterously" about "niggers" and "nigger lovers" at party meetings. Admitting that Clif White, Bill Rusher, John Ashbrook, and other architects of "the conservative revolution within the GOP" had not entered politics "because of racial issues," Edsall nevertheless stated that the backlash to the civil rights revolution provided the manpower for the takeover of the GOP, particularly in the South. But John Tower did not win his Senate seat in 1961 by running as a segregationist. And William E. Brock of Tennessee did not capture his congressional seat in 1962 by campaigning against civil rights.[49]

The true Goldwater was revealed in the mid-1970s when a member of the Church Committee, while investigating improper operations of the intelligence community inside the United States, proposed that transcripts of the FBI tapes about Martin Luther King's personal indiscretions be included in the public record. An outraged Goldwater declared that he would not be a party to destroying King's reputation and strode out of the committee room. The senator's protest "injected some common sense into the proceedings," and the electronic surveillance transcripts were not published.[50]

A quarter of a century later, Goldwater was still defending his opposition to the Civil Rights Act of 1964 as consistent with his belief that "more can be accomplished for civil liberties at the local level than by faraway federal fiat." He attacked what he called the "hypocrisy" of civil rights, charging that various people, black and white, "wanted the 1964 Act passed for their own ends. This was not a moral crusade in America. This was hard-nosed politics based on self-interest."[51]

But the act was also a rite of political passage for black Americans. To be opposed to it, in their eyes, was to be opposed to their acceptance as full and equal partners in the American polity. Blacks needed legislation in 1964, at a time when Mississippi was burning, to redress grievances and guarantee certain rights. Because the leader of the conservative movement voted against civil rights legislation at a defining moment in American history, although with the best of intentions and standing on constitutional ground, conservatives have been branded by most blacks as racists ever since. Jack Kemp and others have worked hard to build bridges to blacks, whose beliefs in family, church, and community parallel those of conservatives, but the memory of the Goldwater vote against civil rights lingers in the minds of many older American blacks.

There is a paradox, or a seeming paradox, in Goldwater's legalistic, constitutional approach to black Americans and his passionate concern for American Indians. He bluntly criticizes the government's treatment of the tribes, saying, "The biggest failure on our part to help the Indians has been our constant refusal to educate them right since the day we became a country."[52] The answer to the paradox lies in the fact that he grew up with Indians, studied their history and their culture, came to identify himself with them. But in his early life, he knew only a few blacks, a tiny minority in Arizona. He could not empathize with their needs as he did with those of his boyhood Indian friends.

In the end, whether addressing the problems of blacks, Indians, or any other minority, Goldwater always returned to the same premise: "Discrimination will not be abolished nor full equality of the races attained until it happens first in the hearts of men." The average American sensed what was needed in race relations—"Christian brotherhood"—and he resented being told by politicians how to achieve it. The whole question of "collective guilt," Goldwater asserted, "never did have validity with responsible citizens who performed their work, fulfilled their civic responsibilities, and added to the forces which add up to good in our society."[53] This was not what the liberal leaders of the Republican party wanted to hear, and they determined to launch one last attempt to save their party, and the country, from the man who was so out of touch, they insisted, with the realities of America and the world.

13

Extremism and Moderation

IN THE SIX WEEKS BETWEEN the California primary and the Republican National Convention in San Francisco, GOP liberals revealed that they were the true extremists by resorting to every Machiavellian trick to deny Barry Goldwater the presidential nomination he had fairly earned.

William Scranton, in announcing his candidacy, declared that the Republican party could not allow "an exclusion-minded minority [to] dominate our platform and choose our candidates," conveniently overlooking that Goldwater had received more than 2 million votes in the Republican primaries, twice as many as any other candidate and more than the total of all the other candidates. The primary percentages were Goldwater, 52.7 percent; Rockefeller, 29.6 percent; Henry Cabot Lodge, 7.5 percent; William W. Scranton, 5.7 percent; and Richard Nixon, 4.5 percent. Goldwater's 2.15 million votes were, in fact, 372,000 more than John F. Kennedy received in the same primaries in 1960.

Nelson Rockefeller, badly battered, withdrew from the race and threw his support behind Scranton whom he described, with less than full enthusiasm, as "in the mainstream of American political thought and action." The governor, however, did not release his delegates in

New York and Oregon because he knew that a good many of them would rush to declare for Goldwater.

Henry Cabot Lodge abruptly resigned as ambassador to Vietnam and hurried back to the United States to help Scranton's bid. Richard Nixon urged George Romney to become a candidate and lead the liberal forces within the Republican party, saying, "it would be a tragedy if Senator Goldwater's views, as previously stated, were not challenged and repudiated." Romney himself stated that a Goldwater nomination would be "suicidal" for the party but decided not to seek the nomination.

Dwight Eisenhower advised Scranton not to join any anti-Goldwater "cabal," but then hinted he would find it difficult to support Goldwater if he won the nomination. Ike, however, quickly reaffirmed his neutrality after another telephone call from George Humphrey.[1]

Amid all the liberal agitation, Goldwater remained calm, accumulating delegates and occasionally squeezing off a round when he felt like it. Of Nixon, he said, "He is sounding more like Harold Stassen every day." Of Romney and other liberal governors, he said, "A lot of them sound as if they were more intent on wrecking the Republican party than in winning an election." Of Lodge, "It is still difficult for me to believe . . . that anyone could leave such a post, at such a critical time, simply to pursue a personal, political course." Of Scranton, he reminded that the Pennsylvania governor had written him back in December, "I hope you decide to run." "Governor Scranton's persuasiveness," Goldwater added with a straight face, "is one of the major reasons I announced my own candidacy for the presidency."

Most important, as he had throughout the campaign, Goldwater focused on the Johnson administration, stating at the Texas Republican Convention in Dallas: "Maybe we can stand a Johnson monopoly in Texas when it comes to television. But this nation cannot stand a Johnson monopoly when it comes to fiscal responsibility and a responsible foreign policy." Texas Republicans enthusiastically gave Goldwater all fifty-six of its delegate votes for the presidential nomination.[2]

The last-minute challenge by Scranton was doomed to fail. The Eastern liberals should have agreed to back a single candidate. Instead, Romney, Lodge, Nixon, and the others hung back, hoping that the self-centered strategy each followed would lead to his nomination. Spurning the solid evidence that Goldwater had an excellent chance of being nominated, they thought they were only competing among themselves.

Thus they were defeated separately by a determined, unified conservative wing of the party they had once ruled so arrogantly.

Their belated maneuvering only served to divide the Republican
party and provide the Democratic opposition with the themes of extremism it would exploit so effectively in the fall. They did not listen to the
realistic counsel of Governor Mark Hatfield, a loyal Rockefeller supporter, who told Scranton and Romney at the Republican governors'
conference only days before Scranton entered the race: "Any stop-
Goldwater movement now by you eleventh-hour warriors is an exercise
in futility. My considered advice to both of you is to forget it."3

Scranton chose to plunge ahead with one of the most bitter and
ineffective campaigns in national politics. For five weeks he attacked Goldwater mercilessly, charging that he could not win, that his
foreign policy was "dangerously impulsive" and "reckless," that his
domestic policy was hopelessly out of date and "cruel." When told he
was not making any headway, he only escalated his attack, accusing
Goldwater of spreading "havoc across the national landscape." His
vicious campaign not only failed to win him delegates, it drove them
away.

As Clif White recalled, Scranton's "attacks exceeded even the vit-
riolic blasts that Nelson Rockefeller had fired at the Senator."4 He
estimated that during one week, Goldwater won twenty-one additional
delegates in states where Scranton campaigned. By late June, the
senator had over eight hundred first-ballot delegates, but Scranton kept
flying around the country, looking desperately for support.

The final curtain dropped on Scranton at a preconvention caucus in
Illinois, where he and Goldwater both addressed the delegates. The
senator was greeted ardently; the governor politely. When both men
were gone, Senator Dirksen, who had backed Taft over Dewey in 1948
and over Eisenhower in 1952 and who had urged Goldwater in 1951 to
run for the Senate, rose and said, "Too long have we ridden the gray
ghost of me-tooism. When the roll is called, I shall cast my vote for
Barry Goldwater!"5

When the delegation was polled, all but ten of the fifty-eight delegates voted for Goldwater—including Charles Percy, once he realized
that the senator had a majority. Later asked to explain how he could
support a man who had voted against the Civil Rights Act that he had
been so instrumental in guiding through the Senate, Dirksen replied
that any president was "mandated under the Constitution" to enforce

federal laws, and, to his mind, "If anyone would execute laws vigorously, it would be Barry Goldwater. He knows the value of an oath and he respects an oath."[6]

In the end, Scranton accomplished two things with his vainglorious pursuit of the nomination: (1) he eliminated himself as a possible running mate with Goldwater on the 1964 Republican ticket, and (2) he drove a gigantic wedge between the liberal and conservative wings of the GOP that ensured an overwhelming triumph for the Democrats in the fall.

Scranton and Goldwater had been amiable if not close political allies for several years. Goldwater had traveled to Pennsylvania on more than one occasion at the governor's invitation to raise substantial sums of money for its cash-strapped Republican party. Goldwater had been Scranton's senior officer in the 9999th Air Reserve Squadron on Capitol Hill, and the two men had gone overseas together on reserve duty for the NATO exercises in 1959. After announcing his candidacy in June, Scranton had sent a telegram to Goldwater saying that, while he disagreed with many of his positions, "I respect you as a man. I will say nothing in the weeks ahead to diminish that respect. On the issues I will be vigorous with all the power at my command. On personalities I will be silent."[7]

But now Scranton unleashed a barrage of anti-Goldwater diatribes, possibly encouraged by the mean-spirited columns written by such as Walter Lippmann, who solemnly warned the nation of the dire consequences of a Goldwater candidacy, let alone a Goldwater presidency. To make his point, the most respected columnist in America thought nothing of distorting Goldwater's positions. "We cannot afford," Lippman wrote shortly after the California primary, "to have a politician running for president who makes it his vocation to sharpen and to embitter the sectional, racial, class, ideological issues that we must learn to live with and to outlive. Nor can we afford the tom-toms and the flagpole sitting which he substitutes for serious consideration of the terrible issues of peace and war."[8]

Two weeks later, as Scranton faltered, Lippmann became even shriller, asserting that Goldwater wanted "to divide the country" and that his "kind of party" was not just a threat to Republicans but to the whole nation. "It is impossible to doubt," he wrote, in one of the most egregious statements of 1964, "that Senator Goldwater intends to make his candidacy the rallying point of the white resistance."[9]

James Reston of the *New York Times* chimed in dutifully. In a front page article for the *Times*, he solemnly stated that on the question of Goldwater, the Republican party faced an issue "that can be compared only to its past great struggles over slavery, the Reconstruction of the South, isolation, and industrial reform." Reston presented the nomination struggle as between progressives like Scranton and Rockefeller, and ultraconservatives like Goldwater. For many Republicans, as well as independents and Democrats, he wrote, Goldwater's policy toward "the Negro revolution" was "profoundly unjust, cynically expedient, and in the end probably politically disastrous."[10]

As it turned out, Goldwater's position on civil rights was not a political "disaster" for the GOP but a milestone in creating a genuine two-party system in the South that enabled Republicans to win the presidency in five of the next seven national elections. Reston's analysis was correct in one respect: Goldwater was challenging "the unwritten law of American politics" that the differences between the two major parties should be as few and modest as possible. From his first campaign for the U.S. Senate in 1952, Goldwater argued that the way for Republicans to win elections was to move to the right and emphasize their economic, social, and foreign policy differences with Democrats.

The "historic question" confronting the GOP, according to Reston, was whether it wanted to embark on Goldwater's "counterrevolution against the trend of social, economic, and foreign policies of the last generation."[11] Reston was again correct: Goldwater did want to reverse the trend toward the welfare state at home and to undertake an aggressive policy of victory over communism abroad. And he wanted to protect the Constitution by following a policy that honored both civil rights *and* states' rights, notwithstanding that such a position was cheered by the most prejudiced forces in the nation. Goldwater was a counterrevolutionary who challenged the statist revolution of the New Deal–Fair Deal–New Frontier.

THE LIBERAL LEADERS in the East did not fade away quietly at the Republican National Convention in San Francisco. In one last convulsive effort, they tried to prevent the conservative victory that they knew would signal the end of their thirty-year reign. They subjected the delegates to an unending barrage of propaganda, personal and public, ably assisted by newspaper columnists and television commentators who warned of the ominous consequences to party and country if Goldwater were picked. Letter-writing campaigns were launched in every state amid threats of political and financial reprisals. Through it all, as Clif White recounted, the Goldwater delegates "never wavered." A typical response came from a Kentucky delegate who wrote that he would cast his ballot for Goldwater "if my vote alone is the only vote you obtain."[12]

In their politics-as-usual campaign, the liberals revealed their essential misunderstanding of the depth, passion, and commitment of the Goldwater movement. The nomination campaign of 1964 was not a replay of 1952: the Goldwater forces had secured their delegates before the first gavel fell after three years of a painstaking grassroots campaign. Barry Goldwater was not a latter-day Robert Taft. Republicans respected Taft. They were prepared to work hard for him. They thought the country needed him. But conservatives idolized Goldwater. They were prepared almost, and maybe not almost, to die for him and what he represented. They were convinced that the country, facing socialism, and the world, facing communism, had to have him as president of the United States.

No CAMPAIGN organization ever prepared more thoroughly for a national convention than the Goldwater for President Committee. Its office manager, James Day, had been in San Francisco since early April, arranging for the housing and transportation of dozens of staff members and hundreds of delegates, working with the telephone company to install an intricate communications system between the Mark Hopkins Hotel and the Cow Palace, and, most important of all, setting up the nerve center of the Goldwater convention operation—a 55-foot trailer parked at the rear of the convention site. The trailer's communications were state-of-the-art with two direct telephone lines to the Mark Hopkins, one to the senator's suite on the seventeenth floor and the other to staff headquarters on the fifteenth floor; seventeen lines to floor managers in key delegations on the convention floor; and another thirteen private lines to the main Goldwater switchboard at the hotel and Goldwater regional posts at other hotels. As White writes, "By pushing a single white button on my console, I was instantly in touch with all our people manning the phones at all these locations."[13]

The Goldwater organization also had a shortwave radio network that linked the trailer with several dozen walkie-talkies carried by Goldwater leaders in delegations that had no telephones as well as in key sites in the galleries and at all entrances to the convention hall. This remarkable communications system (which served as the model for future national conventions) was designed by an "electronics genius," Nicholas J. Volcheff, who worked for the Pacific Telephone & Telegraph Company. Volcheff liked to solve seemingly impossible problems. Told that mobile radio equipment had failed at crucial times in previous conventions because of "mysterious jamming," Volcheff installed just under the roof of the Cow Palace a powerful, jamming-resistant antenna that produced a signal superior to that of the national radio and TV networks. A special frequency was assigned the Goldwater radio system by the federal government.

Nothing was left to chance. "Clif told me there could be no failures," remembers Day, who prepared backups for the backups to make sure that White and his assistants in the trailer could reach anyone they wanted any time they wanted. "I even had a train on standby to get our delegates to the Cow Palace if the streets were blocked," Day says.[14]

So that every Goldwater man and woman would receive reliable, up-to-date information, time was purchased on KFRC, a local radio station. Staff and delegates were instructed to carry transistor radios to monitor the sixty-second spots and five-minute programs that were broadcast every half-hour and every hour over what some aides informally called the "Goldwater Radio Network." In addition, three five-minute TV programs were produced and distributed every day. The messages were produced in a special radio-TV studio set up on the fifteenth floor of the Mark Hopkins Hotel.

The news media often tuned in to learn what the Goldwater camp was up to. Once the TV networks had to use a film clip of Senator Dirksen produced by the "Goldwater Television Network" because Dirksen gave the Goldwater organization an exclusive on why he was nominating, and backing, Barry Goldwater. Other prominent Republicans interviewed included Goldwater himself, John Tower, Clare Boothe Luce, Charlie Halleck, Bill Middendorf, Denison Kitchel, Senator Peter Dominick of Colorado, and assorted delegates.[15]

Another technique used to encourage solidarity among the delegates was the "buddy system," whereby delegates were paired off, preferably a strong delegate with one who might weaken in the face of political or other pressures. During June, the two-delegate teams were told to contact each other at least once a week; when they arrived in San Francisco, they lived, ate, and traveled with each other and usually shared the same room.

Locator boards with plastic overlays were used to keep track of staff members who told their supervisors when they went out. A closed-circuit TV camera was trained on the boards so that Kitchel, Kleindienst, Burch, and White, through TV sets in their private rooms, could tell instantly where anyone was. And a fleet of automobiles equipped with two-way shortwave radios was at the disposal of the Goldwater staff.

As White recalls, "The [six] regional directors were the key men in the whole convention operation."[16] Wearing a headset at all times, each director manned a position in the command trailer that linked him instantly by telephone or radio to the states for which he was responsible. Above each position, a television set enabled him to see what was happening on the convention floor. Behind him, an assistant was prepared to take over if a director had to leave the trailer to deal with a problem on the floor or in the gallery.

The six directors, all but one members of the Draft Goldwater Committee, were Lloyd Waring in Region One, which comprised New England plus New York; Edward Failor in Region Two, which covered the Middle Atlantic, plus Kentucky and the District of Columbia; Wayne Hood in Region Three, which contained the five Great Lakes States; John Grenier in Region Four, which included the states of the Confederacy plus Texas; Dick Herman in Region Five, which included the rest of the Midwest plus Oklahoma, Missouri, North and South Dakota, and Colorado; and Steve Shadegg in Region Six, which contained the Mountain States and the Far West, including California. Working directly under White as his administrative assistant was Tom Van Sickle, a young unflappable state senator from Kansas; cool, efficient Pamela Rymer was in charge of the delegate charts.

The White team went through a dress rehearsal on Saturday, July 11, and "everything worked perfectly." Although they were confident that the eight hundred-plus delegates for Goldwater would stick with the senator, everyone knew that the opposition would test and probe their commitment over the next five days until the first roll call on Wednesday night.

DESPERATELY SEEKING some "incident" that would dramatically, magically, stem the pro-Goldwater tide at the convention, the liberals first concentrated on the platform, hoping to win a fight on planks dealing with extremism, civil rights, and nuclear weapons. But they got nowhere with the platform committee because a majority of its hundred members (two from each state) was conservative, and because its chairman, Congressman Mel Laird of Wisconsin, was determined to give Goldwater a platform he could run on. In truth, Goldwater did not have to dictate the platform, as Nixon had in 1960; he and the committee were in agreement that the 1964 platform should offer a Republican choice and not a Democratic echo.

In the end, despite all the slings and arrows aimed at him by Rockefeller, Scranton, and other liberals, the senator did not seek to ride them out of the Republican party. In an unusual appearance before the platform committee, carried over national television and interrupted forty-one times by cheers and applause, a poised, confident Goldwater made an eloquent plea for party unity:

> I will not presume for a moment to tell you what should go into this platform in terms of specific planks or programs. You are Republicans. You know our Republican record. . . . You know the programs we have created and fought for. You know the ones we have resisted. You know where we have disagreed on this or that detail. . . . But most important you know the great basic principles on which we agree. . . .
>
> Let those meaningful principles guide your minds and hearts and reject the temptation to make this party's platform a bandstand for any factional cause. *You must seek a document that will unite us on principle and not divide us* [emphasis added].[17]

After this magnanimous statement, Goldwater took the unprecedented step of taking questions from committee members. No other leading presidential candidate to that time, including Nixon, Eisenhower, Taft, and Dewey, had ever engaged in such an act of popular democracy.

For starters, liberals jumped on his vote against the Civil Rights Act of 1964. Since he had voted no, he was asked, would he not try to repeal the act if he were elected president? Goldwater's response was firm and to the point, although it is not found in most histories of the 1964 campaign:

No. That's not in my opinion the duty of the president. . . . I think the legislative branch has now spoken for the majority . . . of the American people, and while I didn't agree and I represented the minority, I stand with the majority just as Harry Truman did when he vetoed the Taft-Hartley Act. He later used it six times even though he didn't like it.[18]

It was an honest, shrewd answer, but the only black member of the committee pressed the senator asking if he would "consistently, conscientiously, and in good faith use the powers and prestige" of the presidency to enforce the law. Goldwater patiently restated his position, that as president he would take an oath "to uphold all laws." It was the president's duty, he said, to "administer" the law, "not change it." He went on to state his lifelong opposition to segregation, stating that unlike some politicians he had "done more than just talk about it."

Goldwater was next questioned about the control of nuclear weapons by anyone other than the president, to which he replied that any decision regarding strategic weapons, like ICBMs and IRBMs, should rest with the president but that the NATO commander should have "closer supervision" over small tactical nuclear weapons in the event of a Soviet attack. He was next asked whether he would favor a plank supporting and strengthening Social Security, to which he answered, "Yes, I would. . . . I happen to think that there's a very grave responsibility that rests upon the president in relation to Social Security and this is to be found in fiscal soundness."[19]

After listening to testimony from the representatives of more than 170 organizations, including AFL-CIO President George Meany and civil rights leader Martin Luther King Jr., who surprised many by describing the Civil Rights Act of 1964 as a "cruel jest," the committee produced a platform that was conservative but not reactionary or extremist. In fact, it was a platform on which not only Barry Goldwater but almost "any other Republican," in *Time*'s words, could run.[20]

Unsuccessful in their attempt to provoke a fight within the platform committee, liberals next turned to "a certain general," hoping that if Eisenhower would not actually endorse Scranton, he would at least support the planks they intended to offer on the convention floor. Anti-Goldwater members of the platform committee visited Ike in his suite in the St. Francis Hotel and came away with the impression that he would back their changes at his scheduled news conference the next day. But they reckoned without Congressman Laird, who saw the former president next and persuaded him that it made sense to endorse the platform as written and approved by an overwhelming majority of the platform committee.

Eisenhower's decision was influenced by two other factors. He could not abandon the vow of neutrality he had steadfastly observed for more than eighteen months in the hope of promoting party unity.[21] And he could count delegates, which explains why just before his arrival in San Francisco he told intimates, for the first time, that Barry Goldwater would be a better president and better for the nation than President Johnson in the next four years. Until then, he would only say that "anybody would be better than what we've got [in the White House] now." Thus, at his news conference, Eisenhower expressed general approval of the platform, adding that if Goldwater campaigned on it, "I don't see how he can go far wrong."[22]

Even before this, the now frantic anti-Goldwater cabal manufactured the infamous Scranton letter that was hand-delivered to Goldwater in his Mark Hopkins Hotel suite at 6:47 P.M., Sunday, July 12, the eve of the convention. Scranton had long since abandoned any restraint in his attacks on the senator, charging, for example, that Goldwater's vote against the civil rights act would create "disruptive disorders, even violence"; that his foreign policy positions, such as "authorizing field commanders to use tactical nuclear weapons on their own initiative" (a wanton misrepresentation) were "reckless"; that his proposed "sale of TVA" (another misrepresentation) could only be ascribed to "ignorance."[23]

But the 1,200-word letter, drafted by his aide, William Keisling, and approved by his manager, Walter Alessandroni, but neither seen nor signed personally by Scranton, reached a new low. It characterized Goldwater as the leader of radical extremists, calling "Goldwaterism" a collection of absurd and dangerous positions" and Goldwater delegates a "flock of chickens whose necks will be wrung at will." It spoke of the "ill-advised attempts" to substitute Goldwaterism for Republicanism and presented an apocalyptic vision of the senator's positions:

Goldwaterism has come to stand for nuclear irresponsibility.

Goldwaterism has come to stand for keeping the name of Eisenhower out of our platform.

Goldwaterism has come to stand for being afraid to forthrightly condemn right-wing extremists.

Goldwaterism has come to stand for refusing to stand for law and order in maintaining racial peace.

In short, Goldwaterism has come to stand for a whole crazy-quilt collection of absurd and dangerous positions that would be soundly repudiated by the American people in November.[24]

Scranton challenged Goldwater to a debate before the entire convention on Wednesday evening before the nominating speeches. In one final insult, he stated that if his challenge were rejected, it would prove that the Goldwater philosophy could not stand "public examination— before the convention and before the nation."[25]

When he first read the letter, Goldwater was "boiling mad." He could not believe that a fellow Republican, a governor for whom he had raised money, a man who had served with him in the Air Force Reserve, could have written a letter that sounded like something out of the *Daily Worker.* White said tersely, "That ought to make it one thousand for you on the first ballot." But then, after some ribald banter, the inner circle agreed that a conciliatory tone would be the most effective reply. Harry Jaffa suggested that the letter should be distributed to every Republican delegate, along with a brief statement by Denison Kitchel quoting Abraham Lincoln's reply to a blistering attack on him by newspaper editor Horace Greeley: "If there be perceptible in [the editorial] an impatient and dictatorial tone, I waive it in deference to an old friend, whose heart I have always supposed to be right."[26]

White was right about the letter's impact: the Goldwater delegates were joined by a number from Oregon, Utah, and Colorado who were repelled by Scranton's intemperate attack. Scranton's remark that he had not written or read the letter but still took "full responsibility for it" only reinforced the conviction that the Pennsylvania governor was either a spoiler or a spoiled child.[27] Columnist Robert Novak wrote that it destroyed "the last hope for a Goldwater-Scranton *rapprochement.*"[28]

That is almost surely why it was written: to prevent any possibility of a Goldwater-Scranton ticket, which the senator favored until almost the last moment. With this letter, liberals burned all the remaining bridges between themselves and conservatives in the Republican party. They declared, in effect, that they wanted nothing to do with Goldwater or conservatism. They were writing off 1964 and preparing for 1968 in the belief that after Goldwater's certain defeat in the fall, they could pick up the pieces of the party and put them together as they wished.

Their rule-or-ruin philosophy produced the first but not the second result. On the first, as Theodore White writes, the Scranton letter and the deliberate liberal policy of seeking confrontation made "the Republican Convention the stage for the destruction of the leading Republican candidate." What Rockefeller began in New Hampshire, Scranton finished in San Francisco: the "painting for the American people of a half-crazed leader indifferent to the needs of American society at home and eager to plunge the nation into war abroad."[29]

More than any other event of the convention, the Scranton letter had a critical impact on Goldwater and his inner circle. It "shattered the customary icy calm" of Kitchel; it was the final insult, the "et tu Brute" for the senator in his reluctant pilgrimage toward the presidential nomination; it hardened the resolve of Baroody and others of the speechwriting team that the senator's acceptance speech would neither seek nor grant any quarter.[30]

The final futile attempt of the stop-Goldwater forces came on Tuesday night, July 14, with a roll call vote on a civil rights plank to the Republican platform offered by Scranton. The vote was preceded by a spirited address by Eisenhower, who dismayed liberals by sounding more than a little like Barry Goldwater. "Let us not be guilty," he said, "of maudlin sympathy for the criminal, who, roaming the streets with switchblade knife and illegal firearms seeking a helpless prey, suddenly becomes upon apprehension a poor, underprivileged person who counts upon the compassion of our society and the laxness or weaknesses of too many courts to forgive his offense." The delegates cheered.

Ike received his greatest approval, a deafening roar, when he urged the delegates to "particularly scorn the divisive efforts of those outside our family, including sensation-seeking columnists and commentators, because . . . these are people who couldn't care less about the good of our party." Suddenly, all the frustration and anger of those who had been vilified by the news media as extremists, right-wing radicals, and neo-Nazis burst, and a chorus of boos was directed at the press stands flanking the speaker's platform. Some delegates stood and shook their fists at the startled anchormen in the glassed-in television booths high above the convention floor. It was the first public expression of the people's deep-rooted dissatisfaction with the mass media in a national setting. An earnest and concerned Eisenhower went on to plead for unity, urging fellow Republicans not to "drown ourselves in a whirlpool of factional strife and divisive ambitions."

But the liberals quickly destroyed any hope of party unity.[31]

First came Rockefeller who, with a provocative smile, called on the convention to pass a Scranton amendment denouncing extremism (a deliberate swipe at Goldwater) and equating the John Birch Society with the racist Ku Klux Klan and the treasonable communist party (an application of McCarthyism, liberal-style). Rockefeller knew this would incite the conservatives, but his expectations were exceeded when he was interrupted by constant boos, catcalls, and thumps of a large bass drum. Standing patiently and smiling for the most part, he finally snapped, "Some of you don't like to hear it, ladies and gentlemen—but it's the truth," which brought more boos and shouts of "We want Barry!" The TV networks carried it all into the living rooms of tens of millions of fascinated, and revolted, Americans.

One of the enduring questions of the 1964 convention is, Who was doing the booing? White had given strict instructions to the floor: hear the governor out, then vote no. When the jeers started even before Rockefeller began to speak, White flashed the signal, *"Cut it."* But then, when the governor charged the John Birch Society with "infiltration and takeover of established political organizations by Communist and Nazi methods," the jeering became almost frenzied. By now, the regional directors in the Goldwater command trailer were pleading with floor leaders to silence the boos. And then they noticed over their TV monitors that the delegates were quiet, yet the booing continued in the spectator galleries.

James Day was in the galleries with a team of volunteers and reported to White that the booing spectators, many of them young, were "strangers" and had not gotten their tickets from the Goldwater organization. When they were asked to stop, they kept on shouting "We want Barry!" "In defying our orders," White said, "they were obviously carrying out someone else's."[32]

Were the booing, jeering people in the galleries hired hands of the Rockefeller-Scranton camp? Or out-of-control members of the John

Birch Society or Young Americans for Freedom? If they were the latter, where did they get their gallery tickets, a premium item at a national convention? And would they have fallen so easily and so noisily into the liberal trap?

Rockefeller's charade had little impact on the delegates, but it produced an indelible impression on TV viewers of conservatives as raving, ranting radicals and gave the Democrats another part of their script for the anti-Goldwater campaign in the fall.

During his speech, Rockefeller had asserted that "it's still a free country, ladies and gentlemen." And so it was. There followed a brief speech against the amendment by Congressman John W. Byrnes of Wisconsin, a respected senior member of the House Ways and Means Committee, who said that the proposal was "dangerous, demeaning, and it has no place in a Republican platform. . . . It is the essence of liberty that there be no bar to the unhampered clash of ideas, good or bad. If we do, we weaken individual freedom and endanger the liberty of all of us." When Senator Thruston Morton, the convention chairman, called for a vote, delegations from New York, Pennsylvania, and a few other states stood to say aye, but the overwhelming majority of the delegates roundly rejected the amendment.[33]

Next came Governor Romney of Michigan, as independent and self-righteous as ever, who offered his own amendment, denouncing extremism without naming any one group. Peter O'Donnell and several regional directors recommended that the Goldwater delegates support the innocuous proposal, but after consulting with Goldwater, it was decided that agreement would be interpreted as a sign of weakness, and the amendment was decisively rejected by voice vote.

Finally came Scranton's civil rights amendment that was intended to expose the Goldwater camp as a gang of "lily-white" antiblacks. But the liberals were again frustrated when Senator Dirksen and Congressman William M. McCullogh of Ohio, who had led the Republican support for the Civil Rights Act of 1964, announced that they would speak for the official platform plank on civil rights rather than the lengthy Scranton amendment.

After Congressman John Lindsay of New York presented the case for the liberal proposal, the delegates, by a margin of more than 2 to 1 (897 to 409), smothered the last liberal attempt to divide and conquer the convention's conservative majority. Led by Dirksen and McCullogh, they endorsed the official plank that called for "full implementation and faithful execution" of the Civil Rights Act of 1964 and all previous civil rights laws, putting the lie to Scranton's wild assertion that "Goldwaterism" refused "to stand for law and order in maintaining racial peace." As Clif White wrote, the landslide vote against the Scranton amendment foretold that Goldwater would win the presidential nomination "by more votes than any Republican candidate had ever received on the first ballot of a contested convention."[34]

GOLDWATER REFUSED to get caught up in all the political *Strum und Drang*. He had a portable shortwave radio installed in his hotel suite. "This is K7UGA, portable 6," he would say, "from the top of the Mark Hopkins Hotel, San Francisco, California. The handle is Barry—Baker Able Robert Robert Yankee." Holding hands, he and Peggy strolled along California Street on Sunday morning to Grace Episcopal Church, stopping traffic along the way. "Hello, Barry," shouted a man in his car. "Hi there, folks," he called back. Unable to control his restlessness, he went flying, exiting through a secret tunnel dug years before under the Mark Hopkins Hotel.[35]

On one occasion, he called Clif White and invited him up to the hotel suite to "go over this delegate business." A proud White arrived with all of his black looseleaf books and, beginning with Alabama, told the senator which delegates were for him and which for the other candidates. But less than halfway through the analysis, Goldwater "got up, went over, and turned on his ham radio and started fussing around." Dismayed but trying not to show it, White rushed through the rest of the list of delegates and stopped, at which Goldwater said, "Thanks."[36] That was the end of the delegate business for the senator who was not ungrateful or unaware of the work entailed—just uninterested in the details.

ON THE MORNING of his nomination, July 15, he got up at 5:30 A.M., cut himself shaving, had a larger breakfast than usual (fresh strawberries, bacon and eggs, milk but no coffee), and talked in Spanish with fellow radio hams in Venezuela and Mexico City.

He left the hotel to address a "captive nations" rally, and when asked by a reporter if the convention's refusal to strengthen its civil rights plank would not give the Democrats a good issue in November, he snapped, "After Lyndon Johnson—the biggest faker in the United States? He opposed civil rights until this year. Let them make an issue of it. I'll recite the thousands of words he has spoken down the years against abolishing the poll tax and FEPC [Fair Employment Practices Commission]. He's the phoniest individual who ever came around."[37]

That night, Goldwater watched the nominating and seconding speeches on television, lounging in a blue chair in his red and gold suite, his white shirt open at the collar, his blue-gray jacket put aside. Surrounded by Denny Kitchel, Bill Baroody, Tony Smith, Ed McCabe, and his brother Bob, he nibbled chocolates as the official roll call began. At 10:35 P.M., California time, with the Cow Palace echoing with cheers, South Carolina carried Goldwater over the 655 mark and gave him the Republican presidential nomination for 1964. The balloting, which gave him more than 883 votes, more than twice as many as were cast for all of the other seven candidates, lasted barely six minutes. "I didn't think it would come so fast," he said.[38]

It was an ironic comment about the climax of a long painstaking process that had started more than three years before with a luncheon meeting in Washington, D.C., and whose antecedents could be traced back as far as 1940 and the nomination of a me-too, one-worlder named Wendell Willkie.

SENATOR DIRKSEN began more than seven hours of speechmaking with his nomination of Goldwater, calling him a "peddler's grandson" who had based his political career on "blazing courage." Today, said the Senate Republican leader, it was the fashion "to sneer" at patriotism and "to label positions of strength as extremism, to find other nations' points of view right more often than our own." But through firmness and a sure hand, proclaimed Dirksen, Barry Goldwater could retrieve the self-respect of America. He described Goldwater's vote against the Civil Rights Act of 1964, of which he was a chief architect, as an example of "moral courage not excelled anywhere in any parliamentary body of which I have any knowledge." As for the swing of the GOP to an unabashed conservatism, which alarmed some in and out of the party, Dirksen declared, "Delegates to this convention . . . the tide is turning! . . . Let's give 190 million Americans the choice they have been waiting for!"[39]

It was also the moment the Goldwater delegates had been waiting for, and there followed one of the most impassioned demonstrations in convention history, almost messianic in its intensity, as gold tinsel fell like rain from the ceiling, a huge ticker tape six feet wide unraveled from the roof with the senator's name interwoven with the names and delegate totals of each state, and a Dixieland band played "When the Saints Come Marching In." Demonstrators filled the floor: Californians in gold bibs, Nevadans in red silk shirts, Texans carrying longhorn insignia. Signs danced above the crowd: "We Want Barry," "A Choice Not an Echo," "AU + H_2O = 1964."

It was a revival meeting as much as a political rally, an anointing as well as a Thanksgiving, New Year's Eve and the Fourth of July, the national birth on national television of a new national movement— American conservatism. The memory of that night of nights would sustain many a conservative through the bitter months of the fall campaign, the crushing defeat in November, and the often uncertain years that followed. When Senator Morton, the convention chairman, tried to gavel the demonstrators back into their seats after the allotted twenty minutes were up, they kept on marching and yelling and waving placards ("New York for Goldwater!" "La Louisiane Dit Allons Avec L'Eau d'Or!") for another fifteen minutes.

Then came the short seconding speeches by William Knowland; Clare Boothe Luce, who termed Goldwater a "fearless prophet" of "a fearless responsible America"; Senator Tower; and Congressman Halleck, the House Republican leader, who noted that the senator had had the good sense to marry a "Hoosier girl" from Muncie, Indiana, which brought an ovation for Peggy, who was in the hall.

The Goldwater delegates were ready to vote, but they had to endure several hours more of speeches as Nelson Rockefeller, Senator Hiram Fong of Hawaii (the first American of Chinese descent to be nominated by either major political party), Senator Margaret Chase Smith, William Scranton, George Romney, Dr. Walter Judd of Minnesota (that state's favorite son), and finally Henry Cabot Lodge were all nominated.

The final roll call tally was Goldwater, 883; Scranton, 214; Rockefeller, 114; Romney, 41; Smith, 27; Judd, 22; Fong, 5; and Lodge, 2. As soon as South Carolina put Goldwater over the top, the light signaling the senator's private line to the trailer flashed on Clif White's console, and he turned on the amplifier so that everyone could hear Goldwater say, "Clif, you did a wonderful job—all of you fellows. I can't thank you enough. See you down here a little later." In the senator's suite, the phone rang, and Kitchel announced that it was Rockefeller, to which Goldwater growled, "Hell, I don't want to talk to that son-of-a-bitch."[40]

One final scene was played that night. Scranton made his way to the podium and moved that Barry Goldwater's nomination be declared unanimous, setting off an earsplitting roar. The Goldwater delegates had been instructed to receive the governor graciously, and they applauded his plea for Republican unity. Scranton used almost the same language Goldwater had at the 1960 Chicago convention when he said that "this great Republican party is our historic house. This is our home; we have no intention of deserting it."[41] But even as Scranton spoke, some liberals were walking out of the hall, and the campaign to come. The next day, Congressman John Lindsay of New York stated that he was "searching" his conscience to see whether he could vote for Goldwater.[42]

At a midnight news conference at the Mark Hopkins Hotel, Goldwater was asked "why" he wanted "to be president of the United States" and almost blushed through his TV makeup. He gave a candid, revealing answer:

> Well, I don't know if it's a case of wanting to be. I think it's a case of responsibility that I felt, and I feel tonight, that the Republican cause needs a chance and the conservative cause needs a chance. And this is the only way that we can find these things out—is put them to the voter. If the voter says he agrees then I'll be elected; if he says he doesn't agree then I won't be elected, but I would have given it a chance.[43]

When asked if he thought that he could beat Lyndon Baines Johnson in November, he gave a predictable and, as he knew from his own polling, disingenuous response:

> Well, I wouldn't be in this thing if I thought I was going to lose because, as I've said, I'm too old to go back to work and I'm too young to get out of politics. . . . A Democrat has never defeated me, and I don't intend to start letting him at this late date.[44]

Earlier that evening, while watching himself being nominated, Goldwater was given the latest national poll from the Opinion Research

Organization in Princeton, New Jersey. It revealed that President Johnson was favored by almost 80 percent of the public. He was behind nearly four to one, not because the voters loved Johnson but because they feared Goldwater as an "extremist" who would abolish Social Security, oppose civil rights, and get America into war. The senator turned and joked to an adviser, "Christ, we ought to be writing a speech telling them to go to hell and turn it down, let someone else do it." Instead, he devoted more care to his acceptance speech than to any other speech in his political career. And with good reason: he would deliver it to the largest and most attentive audience of his life. No other statement of the 1950s and 1960s, including *The Conscience of a Conservative,* presents more truly Barry Goldwater's basic beliefs and his positions on current issues.

THE WRITING process began the preceding Saturday, July 11, with a buffet luncheon in Goldwater's hotel suite. Present, besides the senator, were Bill Baroody, Warren Nutter, Harry Jaffa, Richard Ware, and Karl Hess. Much of the discussion centered around a draft by Hess that had generated little enthusiasm. When the scurrilous Scranton letter arrived the following evening, the Hess draft was discarded, and it was decided to focus on one major point: "The conservative movement aimed to take the country in a new direction." As Goldwater later wrote, it seemed "politically illogical and personally contradictory" to offer any olive branches to Rockefeller, Scranton, and the other liberals after they had called him "every dirty name in politics." Rather, he would make it clear that his nomination was a "historic break," a signal that conservatives "were taking over the party from the Republican National Committee on down and setting a new course in GOP national politics."[45]

Goldwater was so impressed with Jaffa's Lincolnian suggestion on how to respond to the Scranton letter, as well as with a memorandum on extremism Jaffa had written for Congressman Rhodes during the platform hearings, that he asked the Ohio State political science professor to write his acceptance speech. Along with Warren Nutter, a professor of economics at the University of Virginia, Jaffa worked through the night and early morning on a draft that he presented to Goldwater the following morning. Jaffa, Nutter, and Baroody, acting as editor, continued to work all day Monday, Tuesday morning, and Wednesday afternoon. Goldwater was present at many of the sessions, listening carefully as

Baroody read aloud each line. Everyone agreed that the speech had to have "ringing rhetoric."[46]

It was Jaffa who wrote the most famous lines in the speech and perhaps in convention speechmaking history: "Extremism in the defense of liberty is no vice, and moderation in the pursuit of justice is no virtue." At any other national convention, these few words might have been uttered and then forgotten. But extremism had come to have a special meaning for every delegate, conservative or liberal, in San Francisco. For Rockefeller and the liberals, it was a scarlet word to be sewn on the breast of every conservative in the Republican party. For Goldwater and the conservatives, it was a badge of honor to be worn proudly, especially since to do so enraged the liberals. Rather than throwing the word away, the senator decided to turn his detractors' favorite epithet back on them. Jaffa provided a sound rationale for the word's use.

In *The Rights of Man,* published in 1791, Thomas Paine writes, "A thing moderately good is not so good as it ought to be. Moderation in temper is always a virtue; but moderation in principle is always a vice." As Jaffa has explained, Paine was rendering a major point of Aristotle's *Nicomachean Ethics* (Book II, Chapter 6)—that every virtue, while a mean of two contrary passions, is an extreme with respect to the opposite vice.

Other prominent Americans who counseled extremism included Patrick Henry, who vowed, "Give me liberty or give me death!"; Lincoln who in his famous "House Divided" speech in 1858 said that "this government cannot endure, permanently half slave and half free. . . . It will become *all* one thing, or *all* the other"; John Kennedy, who in his inaugural address said, "Let every nation know . . . that we shall pay any price, bear any burden, meet any hardship, support any friend, oppose any foe, to assure the survival and the success of liberty"; and Martin Luther King Jr., who wrote from the Birmingham jail in 1963 (only one year before Goldwater was nominated) that some clergymen saw his "nonviolent efforts as those of an extremist. . . . Was not Jesus an extremist for love? . . . Was not Paul an extremist for the Christian Gospel? . . . So the question is not whether we will be extremists, but what kind of extremists we will be."[47] (But, as Jaffa recalls, the words "originated entirely in my own head, without actually consulting anyone else or any book whatever."[48])

With Uncle Morris, who introduced him to politics.
(ARIZONA HISTORICAL FOUNDATION)

Standing (with brother Bob and sister Carolyn) beside the woman who molded him—his mother, Mun.
(ARIZONA HISTORICAL FOUNDATION)

At Staunton Military Academy, where he practiced duty, honor, country.
(ARIZONA HISTORICAL FOUNDATION)

Amid his beloved Arizona mountains in the 1930s. (BILL McCUNE)

Camping with Mike and Barry Jr. (ARIZONA HISTORICAL FOUNDATION)

An all American family: Barry and Peggy with Mike, Joanne, Barry Jr., and Peggy Jr. (ARIZONA HISTORICAL FOUNDATION)

A favorite subject of Goldwater the photographer: the American Indian.
(BARRY GOLDWATER)

In the cockpit of one of the more than 170 different planes he flew.
(J. WM. MIDDENDORF II ARCHIVES)

Vice chairman of the Phoenix City Council, 1949: his first political job.
(ARIZONA HISTORICAL FOUNDATION)

Riding in the annual rodeo in Prescott, before launching his presidential bid.

(ARIZONA HISTORICAL FOUNDATION)

Volunteers prepare for the July 4th draft Goldwater rally in 1963.

(J. WM. MIDDENDORF II ARCHIVES)

The official 1964 campaign photo—complete with crooked glasses.

(HIRO OF PHOENIX)

Accepting the presidential nomination in San Francisco, along with Peggy, vice presidential nominee Bill Miller, and Mrs. Miller. (N. Y. DAILY NEWS PHOTO)

On the boardwalk at Atlantic City, N.J., directly across from the Democratic Convention hall where LBJ was nominated. The idea for the billboard was developed by the author. (ARIZONA HISTORICAL FOUNDATION)

The author on the campaign trail with Goldwater and Miller.
(ARIZONA HISTORICAL FOUNDATION)

Matching smiles with General Eisenhower at the former president's Gettysburg farm.
(J. WM. MIDDENDORF II ARCHIVES)

With fellow conservative Ronald Reagan and Peggy at a 1964 rally.
(ARIZONA HISTORICAL FOUNDATION)

Shaking hands with President Lyndon B. Johnson in 1964, before LBJ approved the infamous "Daisy" commercial.
(ARIZONA HISTORICAL FOUNDATION)

With President Richard M. Nixon at Camp David in late 1972, discussing plans for the second term. Just 18 months later, he would tell Nixon it was time to resign. (ARIZONA HISTORICAL FOUNDATION)

With President Gerald Ford outside the Oval Office. Goldwater's strong support enabled Ford rather than Reagan to win the 1976 GOP presidential nomination. (ARIZONA HISTORICAL FOUNDATION)

At the Pentagon with General Colin Powell, chairman of the Joint Chiefs of Staff. Powell told Goldwater that his 1986 legislation reorganizing the Department of Defense was a major factor in the U.S. victory in the Persian Gulf War. (DEPT. OF DEFENSE)

With Susan in their home.
(CHESWICK, COURTESY *JEWISH NEWS OF GREATER PHOENIX*)

Today.
(GERRY SMITH, COURTESY OF THE U. S. AIR FORCE)

Unfortunately, Goldwater provided no such context in his acceptance address, and so his Republican opponents interpreted his reference to extremism as a deliberate counterattack against Rockefeller and other liberals while the media suggested that it was a call to extreme action by conservatives in the election.

Goldwater later insisted that all he was trying to do was to signal that freedom—"the single word [that] has expressed my political philosophy since entering public life"—would be the central theme of his campaign.[49] To the drafters, none of them practicing politicians, "extremism" was the appropriate word. They did not understand that the qualifying phrases would be ignored and all that would be heard would be: "Extremism . . . is no vice" and "moderation . . . is no virtue."

It was during one of the drafting sessions in the seventeenth floor suite that there occurred a foreshadowing of the extremist tactics of the Johnson White House in the fall. As Richard Ware recalls, Goldwater suddenly remarked, "What the hell is that?" and pointed to a piece of wire that snaked into the room under a window sash and ended behind an air-conditioner. Opening the window, Goldwater saw that the wire came up the outside of the hotel from a lower floor. Ware, Ed McCabe, and others were shocked and angry, but Goldwater laughed, took out his pocket knife, cut the wire, and dropped it out the window. "That'll take care of it," he said and went back to his acceptance speech as though he had not just discovered a bugging device in his campaign suite.[50]

At the time, an aide speculated that one of the TV networks, perhaps CBS, was trying to get a leg up on the competition or, more probably, that someone in the Scranton organization (headquartered on a lower floor) had decided that stopping Goldwater justified illegal electronic surveillance. But three months later, when it became clear that the White House knew what the Goldwater campaign was going to do almost before it did, the thought occurred that the FBI might have been involved.[51]

GOLDWATER WAS introduced to the convention and the country on Thursday evening, July 16, by Richard Nixon, who did his best to bind up the wounds of the party and put the campaign where it belonged—on the offensive. He predicted that when Barry Goldwater got through with him, Johnson would be singing "Home on the Range," and counseled the faithful to ignore the polls and the columnists, remarking that "Mr. Gallup isn't going to be counting the votes on November 3rd." Rather than being weaker, he said, the Republican party was stronger than in 1960 with more congressmen, more senators, more governors, and more state legislators. He encouraged unity by publicly recognizing Scranton and Rockefeller, and such was the power of his appeal that both of the men who had done so much to damage Goldwater received applause and cheers.

Nixon went on to capture the essence of his party's nominee by saying that America needed "new leadership," a man who would go up and down the length of the land crying out, "Wake up, America, before it is too late." And he warned that a vote for Johnson would be "a vote for the biggest spending spree of any president or administration in history," a vote for Johnson would continue a foreign policy "which means retreat, defeat, and war." It was a time, he declared, not for the New Deal of the 1930s or the Fair Deal of the 1950s or the "Fast Deal of Lyndon Johnson, but for the Honest Deal of Barry Goldwater."

And finally, Nixon urged those who watched and those who listened to put aside the "harsh criticisms of his critics" and "the complimentary compliments of his friends" and make their own decision about a man who had been called Mr. Conservative, a man who was now, by the action of the convention, Mr. Republican, a man who "after the greatest campaign in history" would be "Mr. President—Barry Goldwater."[52]

WHAT DID the people see when Goldwater stepped to the podium to accept his party's nomination for president? Theodore White, chronicler of presidential campaigns, provides a vivid portrait:

> Tall, six foot even; a muscular 182–185 pounds; not lithe, with dancing step, as was John F. Kennedy, but slow and dignified of walk; the face a deep tan, as is common among people who live in the sunlands; the frame of the face all sharp planes—the nose clean and sharp, the jaw pinch-pointed with one vertical dimple, the lips thin, the cheeks flat, no hint of the sagging jowl that normally overtakes men at his age, fifty-five. All this topped off by the silvery white hair set off by black horn-rimmed eyeglasses that made him instantly recognizable.[53]

And what did they hear? White reveals an empathy for his subject:

The dry voice of the Southwest, far lower pitched than the Eastern voices that have dominated American politics for so long. It drawls in private questioning, but becomes a snap when offended. . . . He is at his best in the formal public address where, with the audience booming applause, his voice rises to a rhythmic roar (Goldwater has a good ear for the cadence of English prose) and develops the pounding wrath of an Isaiah. And, altogether, all qualities combine to give a sense of hard virility and barely controlled tension.[54]

What the convention and the country saw that night was not John the Baptist (a comparison Goldwater detested and thought blasphemous) but a prophet out of the Old Testament. Like Isaiah or Jeremiah, he warned the people that they had been following "false prophets" and exhorted them to return to "proven ways—not because they are old, but because they are true." What the delegates and the enormous TV audience heard was not a me-too Republican but a conservative Republican who declared that Americans "must, and we shall, set the tide running again in the cause of freedom." Freedom, not extremism, was his central theme. Indeed, he invoked the word "freedom" twenty-five times in his address, but always a freedom properly understood:

This party, with its every action, every word, every breath and every heartbeat has but a single resolve, and that is freedom—freedom made orderly for this Nation by our constitutional government; freedom under a government limited by the laws of nature and of nature's God; freedom—balanced so that order, lacking liberty, will not become a slave of the prison cell; balanced so that liberty, lacking order, will not become the license of the mob and the jungle.[55]

A patriot as well as a prophet, Goldwater listed the failures of the Johnson administration at home:

Tonight there is violence in our streets, corruption in our highest offices, aimlessness among our youth, anxiety among our elderly, and there's a virtual despair among the many who look beyond material success toward the inner meaning of their lives. And where examples of morality should be set, the opposite is seen. Small men seeking great wealth or power have too often and too long turned even the highest levels of public service into mere personal opportunity.[56]

What is so striking is how these words apply to the America of today. Goldwater emphasized the "growing menace" to personal safety in homes, churches, playgrounds, and places of business and declared that a government that cannot provide elementary security against domestic violence "is one that cannot long command the loyalty of its citizens."[57]

IN A SHORT section little noted at the time, Goldwater called the "police action" in Vietnam what it really was:

Yesterday it was Korea; tonight it is Vietnam. Make no bones of this. Don't try to sweep this under the rug. We are at war in Vietnam. And yet the president, who is commander-in-chief of our forces, refuses to say, refuses to say, mind you, whether or not the objective over there is victory. And his secretary of defense continues to mislead and misinform the American people. . . .[58]

Written by the senator himself, the passage could have served as the opening salvo for a major attack on the Johnson administration's Vietnam policy in the general election. But guided by his commitment to duty, honor, and country, he was unwilling to make political capital of an issue so vital to national security.

Barely one week after he was nominated, he requested a private meeting with President Johnson. Sitting in the Oval Office, Goldwater began by saying that while they were divided by philosophy and party, they "shared a love of country." The president agreed: "That's right, Barry. You and I are not like some people around the country. We're Americans first." Goldwater went on to say that "there was already too much division in the nation over the war" and that neither he nor Johnson should contribute to it "by making Vietnam an issue in the campaign." According to Goldwater, Johnson took a deep breath and sighed in relief.

The president talked for several minutes about his difficulties in Vietnam and then thanked Goldwater for his pledge. "I interpreted that," said Goldwater, "to mean he agreed."[59] What politician would not agree to set aside an issue on which he was vulnerable and which weakened his bid for reelection?

The White House meeting took place just two weeks before two U.S. destroyers, the *Maddox* and the *C. Turner Joy,* were reportedly attacked by North Vietnamese patrol boats and before Congress passed the Tonkin Gulf Resolution, with Goldwater voting aye. The resolution was the equivalent of a declaration of war and strengthened the senator's determination to keep Vietnam "off limits" as a campaign issue.

At the time Goldwater accepted the facts of the attacks as they were presented by Johnson and McNamara, but he later concluded that (1) the attack on the *C. Turner Joy* never happened, and (2) McNamara misled Congress and the American people regarding the *Maddox,* particularly by not revealing that the ship was on a secret mission. "We voted on the Tonkin Gulf Resolution," Goldwater said, ironically echoing his liberal adversary in the Senate, J. William Fulbright, "with critical aspects of the situation withheld from us."[60]

If he had known in early August what he later learned, Barry Goldwater might have voted against the Tonkin Gulf Resolution. In that case, he might have reconsidered his pledge not to discuss Vietnam, and the war might have become a major issue in the general election. Such a change would not have reversed the final outcome of the presidential race, but it would have made it a closer race. It seems also fair to conclude that President Johnson would have been forced by an aggressive Goldwater to make certain assertions about what he would and would not do in Vietnam that would have prevented him from escalating the land war that ultimately cost 58,000 American lives and turned Indochina into a communist gulag.

BUT THAT JULY evening in 1964 Vietnam was far from the minds of the enraptured Republican delegates in the Cow Palace. They were waiting to hear how their chosen candidate proposed to reverse the failures of the incumbent administration and lead the nation and the world to peace and prosperity.

Leaving specific policy proposals for later, Goldwater dedicated his campaign to two basic conservative ideas (although he never used the word "conservative"): (1) individual responsibility and constitutional government are the best guarantors of a free, dynamic society, and (2) peace is only possible through strength, vigilance, and the defeat of those who threaten it.

Echoing Hayek, whom he had read as a young businessman in Phoenix almost twenty years before, Goldwater endorsed a government that "attends to its inherent responsibilities of maintaining a stable monetary and fiscal climate, encouraging a free and competitive economy, and enforcing law and order." Drawing on language suggested by newspaper publisher Eugene Pulliam, he underscored the failure of public officials "to keep the streets safe from bullies and marauders"— the law-and-order themes of Presidents Nixon, Reagan, and Bush. Never an isolationist in the Robert Taft mold, Goldwater argued that "we must look beyond the defense of freedom today to its extension tomorrow." And foreshadowing by nearly two decades Reagan's famous line about communism winding up on "the ashheap of history," Goldwater said that "the communism which boasts it will bury us will instead give way to the forces of freedom."[61]

As he spoke, he revealed his innate humility. His victory was not a personal one, he implied, but a victory for an idea: that conservatism deserved an opportunity to present its philosophy to the American electorate. Everyone knew that he had been reluctant to run for president and had almost withdrawn from the race. But now he spoke with the knowledge that a great political party had entrusted him with a grave responsibility—to be its standard-bearer.[62] Here was no wild-eyed radical or demagogue but a statesman offering a crusade at home and abroad of liberty, opportunity, and diversity. The delegates and the galleries liked what they heard very much, interrupting with applause and cheers some fifty-eight times. Then came the final paragraphs that would transfix the man and the campaign.

Normally, an acceptance speech is an instrument for reaching out, for binding up wounds, for bringing together. That had been Goldwater's way in 1960 when he went before the Republican National Convention in Chicago and urged conservatives not to walk away from but work within the party. Most politicians, including members of his own team, expected him to offer his hand to those who had opposed him during the bitter nomination campaign. But too many ugly things had been said and written about Goldwater and Goldwaterism to be so soon forgotten.

The Republican party, Goldwater declared, his voice turning harsh and unyielding, was a party for "free men," not "blind followers" or "conformists." It was a party committed to "preserving and enlarging freedom at home" and safeguarding it against "the forces of tyranny abroad." And he promised, "Anyone who joins us in all sincerity we welcome." But then came the words that anticipated and even invited liberals to defect: "Those who do not care for our cause, we don't expect to enter our ranks in any case." What was needed was a "focused" and "dedicated" Republicanism that rejected "unthinking and stupid labels."

The next lines are underlined in the original text:

I would remind you that extremism in the defense of liberty is no vice! And let me remind you also that moderation in the pursuit of justice is no virtue![63]

Inside the Cow Palace, conservatives roared, reveling in the stinging rebuff of Rockefeller, Scranton, Romney, and all the others who had taunted and reviled them for so long. Trent Lott, then a recent graduate of the University of Mississippi and now a U.S. senator, thought the lines were "an inspiration . . . a bugle call to arms." Vic Gold, who would shortly join the campaign as assistant press secretary, shouted, "Terrific!" when Goldwater used the word "extremism." John H. Buchanan, Jr., running for Congress from Alabama, enthused about the passage. "My heart skipped a beat when I read the 'extremism' line," recalls Carol Dawson, co-chairman of Youth for Goldwater. Richard Viguerie, sitting in the gallery, "loved" the extremism line and joined in the cheering.

But some conservatives were disappointed. Donald Devine, who would serve as director of the Office of Personnel Management in the Reagan administration, thought the lines were "insensitive" and "divided the party needlessly." Pat Hutar, who became co-chairman of the Republican National Committee in the fall, felt the words gave Goldwater's enemies the opportunity to say, in effect, "We told you he was an extremist." The word "extremism," she remembers, "chilled your bones." Patrick Buchanan later wrote that Goldwater "dealt the ace of trumps to a Democratic campaign that already had a fistful of trumps to play." Nixon felt "almost physically sick" as he listened to the words. "Not only did Goldwater fail to close the rifts in the party and heal its wounds," he said, "he opened new wounds and then rubbed salt in them." Conservative activist Sandy Scholte believes that "the liberal reaction to the 'extremism' speech was the beginning of Political Correctness."[64]

The two most experienced politicians on the Goldwater team, neither of whom saw an advance copy, agreed about the speech's harmfulness. Clif White wondered whether the crowd realized it was "hailing disaster and defeat," and Shadegg noted that the extremism phrase "ripped open old wounds and erected barriers which were never broken." In the senator's defense, Burch said, "If Goldwater had recited the Lord's Prayer there were certain people at the convention who were going to object to it."[65]

The next day, Rockefeller expressed his "amazement and shock" at the extremism statement, saying that it was "dangerous, irresponsible, and frightening."[66] He and other liberal Republicans used the speech to justify not helping the party's candidate in the fall, thereby breaking the "one cardinal rule of politics: You unite after the primaries."[67]

One of the few liberal Republicans who did not take a walk was Bill Scranton, for whom Goldwater had genuine affection. Goldwater wrote a magnanimous letter to him following the convention, concluding:

> I still maintain that there is not a vast canyon between you and me, but rather a relatively small ditch that either of us can jump back and forth over at the convenience of the party.
>
> Let me hear from you and in the meantime, give my very best to Mary and a very fond embrace for that delightful daughter who cried so hard for you, as my daughter did four years ago, and yet who cheered so lustily for me on the night of the nomination.[68]

The news media's initial reaction to Goldwater's nomination speech was almost rabid. It cast a pall over the important visit of Goldwater and Kitchel to General Eisenhower the next morning; they wanted and needed Ike on the team. "I sensed stormy weather ahead if the former president should follow [the media's] . . . lead," recalled Kitchel.[69] With his brother Milton sitting beside him, Ike began a "polite, jerky conversation" about everything but the coming campaign and his part in it.

At last, Eisenhower blurted that it seemed to him that in his acceptance speech Goldwater was giving the "right-wing kooks" a pat on the back and everyone else a slap in the face. Goldwater said that had not been his intention and explained that Rockefeller and the other liberals were trying to divide the party into extremists and moderates and suggesting that everyone who was for him was "a right-wing nut." Eisenhower interrupted, "What's all that got to do with saying that extremism is a good thing?" Milton Eisenhower, who had nominated William Scranton two nights earlier, chimed in, "I think it was a great mistake." Kitchel put in his oar: What "Barry was trying to put across, General, was that patriotism is not a vice. That defending the Constitution, opposing communism, trying to preserve our free enterprise system, that kind of thing, can't be made wrong by labeling it 'extremism.' " But Ike was adamant, his face was flushed red with anger, and the meeting seemed headed for disaster.

At this point Eisenhower suddenly revealed why he was taking the speech so personally. He turned to Goldwater and said, referring to one of Robert Welch's more dotty charges, "What you were saying, Barry, as I see it, was that there was nothing wrong, for example, in calling me 'a conscious agent of the communists.' " He continued, "Well, by golly, it is wrong—it's utter tommyrot. . . . People who say that kind of thing *are* nuts." Goldwater immediately countered, "General, I didn't say that and I didn't mean to say it." He leaned forward and said firmly, "General, I'm getting damn sick and tired of having people who love their country, who stand up for it, who fight for what it means, condemned by the phony use of words."[70]

The two men sat and looked grimly at each other, their jaws set. Kitchel could almost see the headline, "Ike Declines to Back Goldwater." But then Goldwater smiled and leaned even further toward his former commander-in-chief. "There's no more extreme action than war," he said. "General, in June 1944 when you led the Allied Forces across the English Channel, you were an 'extremist,' and you did it in defense of liberty." Ike looked puzzled for a moment and then rose excitedly to his feet, his blue eyes warm again, his famous smile filling his face. "By golly, I get it!" he said. "By golly, that makes real sense. . . . Barry . . . I'm glad you came to see me." He turned, beaming, toward his brother, who was not beaming, "By golly, Milton, I'm an extremist—and damn proud of it."[71] As they stood talking, smiling and relaxed, Eisenhower assured Goldwater that he would be happy to make some speeches for him and to do a television program with him.

But critics continued to charge that Goldwater's words were a blanket approval of extremism, and two weeks later, just before a GOP unity meeting in Hershey, Pennsylvania, Goldwater attempted a more public explanation. Responding to a letter from Nixon, who suggested that "it would be most helpful to clear the air once and for all" on the matter of extremism, Goldwater wrote: "If I were to paraphrase the two sentences in question in the context in which I uttered them I would do it by saying that wholehearted devotion to liberty is unassailable and that halfhearted devotion to justice is indefensible."[72]

But Goldwater's explanation failed to satisfy liberal Republicans who wanted a total repudiation of the extremism statement, and disturbed conservative Republicans who wondered if Goldwater was beginning to disavow what they had cheered so heartily at the convention. The clarification sank quietly from sight.

Nixon also encouraged Goldwater to take a conciliatory position at the summit meeting of Republican leaders in Hershey on August 12 so that he could "emerge as the leader and spokesman of a united party." In attendance were General Eisenhower, Nixon, Scranton, Rockefeller, Romney, and thirteen other Republican governors as well as Thruston Morton, chairman of the Senatorial Campaign Committee, and Bob Wilson, chairman of the Congressional Campaign Committee.

During the morning session, Nixon cautioned his fellow Republicans not to expect miraculous changes in attitudes as a result of the meeting. "Unity cannot mean and it does not mean unanimity" on all the issues, he said. "Unity means there has to be room for honest disagreement." Everyone nodded their heads, but when his turn came, Rockefeller insisted that Goldwater had to "repudiate" extremism, racism, and the use of nuclear weapons. Eisenhower said, "Nelson, that is *exactly* what Barry has said he *will* do," but Rockefeller was not satisfied.[73]

At the concluding news conference, Goldwater, flanked by Eisenhower, Nixon, and Scranton, denied that he had made any concessions on important issues during the meeting (closed to the media) and, among other things, reiterated his belief that the NATO military commander should have control over the use of tactical nuclear weapons. When asked about his policy toward Germany, Eisenhower winced when Goldwater replied, "I think it was the Germans that originated this modern concept of peace through strength." Nixon later learned that on the drive back to Gettysburg, Eisenhower said, "You know, before we had this meeting I thought that Goldwater was just stubborn. Now I am convinced that he is just plain dumb."[74]

Despite the best efforts of Eisenhower, Nixon, and Scranton, the Hershey "unity" meeting did not unite the party's leadership behind its presidential candidate. Rockefeller's attempt to dictate what Goldwater should say about extremism, racism, and nuclear weapons only served to reinforce the senator's belief that liberal Republicans would not campaign for him regardless of what he said.

IN THOSE early days, there were no spin doctors to descend en masse on the news media, depicting Goldwater's speech as one of the most brilliant in convention history, drawing attention to its Lincolnian and Churchillian accents, placing the extremism line in perspective with references to Aristotle, Paine, Henry, and Lincoln, emphasizing the theme of freedom at home and abroad. In those days, politicians proposed and the media disposed. Goldwater always stood by his assertion that "extremism in the defense of liberty is no vice," remarking, for example, to a TV interviewer nearly thirty years later, "I'd make that speech again any place any time—I think it's the best statement I ever made."[75] Still, he never again used the sentence in the 1964 campaign.

His uncompromising nomination speech signaled that Goldwater was determined to run as himself, regardless of what the professionals or the press or liberal Republicans said, no matter if it brought defeat. And the Democrats prepared to take full advantage of this magnificent stubbornness in the fall campaign.

Some six weeks later, in Atlantic City, Lyndon B. Johnson celebrated his fifty-sixth birthday by accepting the Democratic party's nomination for president and giving his poorest speech of the campaign. Outside the convention hall, where Miss America was annually crowned, an enormous lighted billboard, dominated by a photograph of a smiling Barry Goldwater, boldly proclaimed, "In Your Heart, You Know He's Right." Inside the hall, delegates openly wept at the conclusion of a moving memorial film about John F. Kennedy and cheered an ebullient Hubert Humphrey who chanted a litany of liberal proposals that most of Congress had voted for "but not Senator Goldwater!" Johnson and his several speechwriters tried too hard, and the result was an address that did not contain "a single memorable phrase, no tang or vault, little to pull the delegates or the television audience out of their evening lethargy."[76]

The president, however, had something more important than rhetoric on his side: a national poll that showed him to be ahead of his opponent, Goldwater, by 70 to 24 percent, with 68 percent of the women, 70 percent of voters aged 21 to 34, 73 percent of Catholics, 86 percent of blacks, and 97 of Jews favoring him. He was on his way to a landslide. But as Doris Kearns states, the man who had been haunted for years by the memory of his first senatorial margin of only 87 votes wanted not just any landslide, "but the largest landslide in history."[77]

14

Anything Goes

AND SO THE BATTLE WAS JOINED between a candidate for whom winning the presidency was not everything and a candidate for whom winning the presidency was the only thing. It would be difficult to find two men more diametrically opposite in their politics, philosophy, and personality. Goldwater came to Washington, D.C., not to pass laws but to repeal them; his commitment was to a free society. Johnson never met a federal program he did not like; his grandiose objective was the Great Society. Goldwater's favorite president was Thomas Jefferson; his political philosopher, F. A. Hayek. Johnson's favorite president was FDR, his philosopher, Niccolo Machiavelli (former LBJ aide Eric Goldman called LBJ "Machiavelli in a Stetson").[1] Goldwater believed in individuals; Johnson thought in electoral blocs—organized labor and minorities. Goldwater swore by the Constitution; Johnson, by the New Deal. Goldwater had many interests besides politics; Johnson had only one interest, politics. Even his enemies conceded that Goldwater was an honest man. Even his closest friends admitted that Johnson was a wheeler-dealer. Goldwater was content to be respected by his friends and peers; Johnson was desperate to be loved by everyone. As president, Goldwater would have followed Ike's policy of balancing economic stability and military strength. As president, Johnson's policy of guns and butter produced a tragic defeat in the war in Vietnam and a pyrrhic victory in the war on poverty.

But as different as these men were, they were bound by the same elements of a political campaign, beginning with money. In 1964, there was no federal underwriting. Goldwater calculated that he would need to raise approximately $13 million from the small individual contributor, more than any previous Republican nominee, because big business had defected to the Democrats. In 1964, Goldwater received more than one million contributions, as compared with 50,000 contributions in 1960 for Richard Nixon.

Ralph Cordiner, retired chairman of the board of General Electric, agreed to serve as Goldwater's finance chairman on the condition that no money would be spent or obligated until collected. A traditional conservative, Cordiner wanted a balanced budget and no deficit financing. Goldwater agreed but later admitted that he had "made a political mistake" because campaign money often arrives after it can be used most effectively. As a result of the Cordiner dictum, the Goldwater campaign wound up with more than $1 million in the black, a first in American politics. Much of the credit for the GOP's financial success must go to Frank Kovac, whose genius built a broad financial base of small contributors for the Republican party that has endured to this day.[2]

Challenging the usual Republican advantage in fundraising, the Democrats raised over $11 million while organized labor reportedly disbursed $3.67 million for all the campaigns, with the lion's share going to Johnson and Humphrey. A lucrative innovation, suggested by Johnson himself, was the President's Club, which grew to four thousand members, each donating at least $1,000 to the campaign. To avoid the Federal Corrupt Practices Act's restrictions on contributions, the President's Club formed state chapters. Members were photographed with the president, who also ladled out pens he used to sign bills and copies of the "First Family Photo Album." The most generous were given the ultimate honor: an invitation to swim naked with the president in the White House pool.[3]

Johnson took fundraising seriously. More than one wealthy person received a personal telephone call from the president who coined the phrase: "Money is the mother's milk of politics." Johnson even resorted to using confidential income tax information to force well-known conservatives to support him rather than Goldwater. Glenn

Campbell, former director of the Hoover Institution at Stanford University, knows of one conservative businessman who was told by the president, "The IRS is thinking about going over your return. They don't really want to do it but. . . ." The businessman got the message and publicly endorsed Johnson.[4] During the campaign, Goldwater knew of two Texans who had irregularities in their income tax returns. They were taking steps to correct the irregularities, "but were threatened by the president [with IRS action] unless [they] contributed to his campaign."[5]

At the organizational top, it was a contest between a Johnson-Kennedy team (Pierre Salinger was running for the U.S. Senate from California and Ted Sorensen had left the White House, but many of JFK's top aides worked for the Democratic ticket, including Kenny O'Donnell and Larry O'Brien) and the Arizonans, with a leavening of GOP professionals like Leonard Hall, Ray Bliss, and L. Richard Guylay. At the grass roots, it was unconditional war between the trained professionals of the AFL-CIO for the Democrats and fervent amateurs for the Republicans. An estimated 500,000 people helped canvass neighborhoods, escort voters to the polls, and engage in other activities for Goldwater, a record in American politics.

Departing from the usual practice, Goldwater ran his campaign through the Republican National Committee, although he ensured personal control by naming Burch as Republican National Chairman. But he passed over Clif White, the man who believed he had more than earned the job through his efforts for the Draft Goldwater Committee and at the national convention. In his 1988 memoirs, Goldwater admitted that "not selecting White was a mistake." If he had insisted on appointing White over the objections of his entire inner circle, Goldwater speculated that Buckley, Rusher, and other Easterners would have come back on board, adding "some professionalism to our ranks, and perhaps accelerat[ing] the political change that was taking place."[6]

Deeply depressed at not being named national chairman, White seriously considered dropping out of the fall campaign. But after receiving a very generous letter from the senator ("It was you who got this whole thing started and it was you who led the team on to victory in San Francisco"), White relented and went to work as national director of Citizens for Goldwater-Miller, a relatively minor role.[7]

But no matter what his position, White would not have been able to change Goldwater's determination to run his campaign the way he wanted. "Extremism in the defense of liberty is no vice" would still have been in his acceptance speech. Goldwater would still have addressed controversial issues like Social Security, TVA, farm subsidies, and the need for victory over communism where and when he wanted. He would not have manipulated the issues of civil rights and Vietnam for political impact. He would not have tried to build bridges to liberal Republicans who had burned their bridges to him.

In short, Goldwater believed that the most important thing was not trying to win an election that could not be won but building a political movement that could win the presidency and reinvigorate the country's principles in the future. As he put it in his 1988 memoirs:

> We were a bunch of Westerners, outsiders, with the guts to challenge not only the entire Eastern establishment—Republican and Democratic alike—but the vast federal apparatus, the great majority of the country's academics, big business and big unions, and a man with an ego larger than his native state of Texas, Lyndon Johnson.[8]

Goldwater campaigned as he had in California rather than New Hampshire, making two or three major speeches a day in heavily populated areas and depending on the news media to carry his message to the people beyond. Typically, he would arrive at an airport in his specially outfitted B–27, officially called "Yia Bi Kin" (Navajo for "House in the Sky"), and wave to the waiting faithful. A motorcade, including some fifty to sixty press, radio, and TV journalists, would proceed to the city five or ten miles away where a large, enthusiastic crowd would hear him speak on the steps of the city hall or courthouse or perhaps at a ballpark. The senator was relaxed, informal, and rarely indulged in the shouts and flourishes of political orators, as did Hubert Humphrey, but his honesty and conviction were palpable. Often, his dry sense of humor broke through, as at the Springfield (Illinois) State Fair. On the platform with the senator were Congressman Ed Derwinski, who at well over 200 pounds was literally the most prominent Polish-American in the House of Representatives, and Derwinski's tall, attractive, red-haired wife. Barry Goldwater, Jr., who loved being a bachelor, was struck by Mrs. Derwinski and asked his father whether he knew who she was. Goldwater replied, "Barry, she's just the girl for you—if you can get past 240 pounds of Polack."[9]

President Johnson was a far different candidate, restless, driven by his dream of an historic landslide. He conducted what one observer called "the most peripatetic campaign in the history of the Republic. Eighteen hours a day . . . twenty speeches a week . . . motorcades . . . dinners . . . handshakes. Andy Jackson in a jetliner." He mixed stump speeches with pressing the flesh at every opportunity. He wrapped himself in the flag and quoted the Bible and promised something for every city, town, and community he visited.[10]

Goldwater talked about the "forgotten American" (the central theme of his 1961 Senate speech), the citizen who was alarmed at his loss of identity and freedom in a society accelerating toward a welfare state. He addressed the millions of registered voters who had not voted in 1960 because they had seen no real choice between Nixon and Kennedy. The senator and his advisers believed that if he could arouse these forgotten Americans, he might manage "as staggering an upset as Harry Truman accomplished in 1948."[11]

He talked about "lawlessness and immorality" to awaken Americans to the sickness in society that had caused a 500 percent increase in crime in the past four years. He talked to those who, libertarian like himself, resented being told by politicians "how to behave, how to think, how to live, what to study, and even where or if to pray." He repeatedly cited Johnson's failure to recognize the real threat of communism and to fight to restore to the states their rightful power. These powerful broad-based issues, in a normal year, would have won votes across the country, not just in the South, and turned the 1964 campaign into a real contest between the two candidates.

But 1964 was anything but a normal year: John Kennedy had been dead less than a year, Goldwater had been cruelly caricatured by fellow Republicans for nearly seven months, and Lyndon Johnson was determined to do whatever necessary to win the presidency by the widest margin ever. For him, extremism in the pursuit of the presidency was no vice. To that end, Johnson ran one of the most deliberately negative campaigns in American political history.

Beginning with his acceptance speech in Atlantic City, LBJ condemned the tactics of "fear and smear" and warned the public about the danger of voting for an extremist. Borrowing directly from Nelson Rockefeller, he played on the people's dread of nuclear war. The Democratic platform, drafted with Johnson's approval, warned that "one rash act, one thoughtless decision, one unchecked reaction" could leave the world in ashes. The apocalyptic language anticipated the infamous "daisy" TV commercial. Again drawing from Republicans, Johnson contrasted Goldwater's alleged "intention" to eliminate Social Security, TVA, and other federal programs with his own commitment to a Great Society in which every American, especially the underprivileged, will have "a larger share of the growing pie."[12]

Although Goldwater had looked forward to debating Kennedy, a Goldwater-Johnson debate never took place because the Democratic Senate killed legislation that would have temporarily suspended Section 315 of the Communications Act and allowed joint TV appearances by the two presidential candidates in prime time. NBC invited both candidates to meet in a series of hour-long programs; the Republicans promptly accepted, the White House had "no comment." In the fall, Burch and other Republican leaders occasionally criticized the president for his unwillingness to face his opponent, but the Senate's action had effectively settled the issue for 1964.[13] As a result, discussion of the issues was limited to a daily ritual of long-distance charges and countercharges.

The sixty-odd journalists accompanying Goldwater in his political travels were nearly unanimous in their personal liking of the senator and as unanimous in their hostility to his political beliefs. As one reporter said, "How can such a nice guy *think* that way?"[14] Robert MacNeil, co-host of the PBS program, "The MacNeil-Lehrer News-Hour," covered Goldwater for NBC-TV and recalls that those who spent a lot of time with him found him "irresistible." MacNeil, Charles Mohr of the *New York Times*, and Walter Mears of the Associated Press were the only national correspondents who traveled with Goldwater prior to the Kennedy assassination. They once asked themselves, "If you were climbing a mountain, who would you rather be roped to—Jack Kennedy or Barry Goldwater?" They all agreed—Barry Goldwater.[15]

At the time, MacNeil was convinced that Goldwater would not have made a good president because he "seemed too casual in his judgments, too careless about words and facts, too indifferent to complexity, a man of too little intellectual discipline." But in retrospect, he wondered whether Goldwater's qualities "might not have served the nation better" than Johnson's—whether Goldwater's "decency and common sense had not been undervalued and his belligerent rhetoric taken too literally."[16]

David Broder of the *Washington Post,* the most respected political reporter in Washington, conceded that reporters failed to convey "the essential decency of this guy." While not arguing that the American people made "a terrible mistake" in the election, Broder nevertheless insisted that they had a "fundamentally distorted picture of who Goldwater was."[17]

In 1964, political advertising was still evolving, and for the most part, there was nothing remarkable about the shorter Goldwater commercials. But Goldwater's half-hour programs, including "Brunch with Barry" and "Conversation at Gettysburg" (with General Eisenhower), anticipated the half-hour infomercials of Ross Perot in 1992. Also, as political scientist Kathleen Hall Jamieson notes, the Goldwater organization "elevated to an art form the process of using media to raise money for media."[18] Every one of the longer programs included an appeal for funds, usually by a well-known film star like John Wayne or Raymond Massey. Goldwater's ads showed him delivering calm, controlled speeches, to demonstrate that he was not the reckless warmonger and welfare destroyer portrayed by his Democratic opponents.

The harsh negative tone of Johnson's spot ads precluded his direct association with them. But the president personally approved an all-out media attack, saying he would be willing to add as many as fifteen additional fundraising dinners, if necessary, to purchase air time.[19] In sum, Goldwater spent $6.4 million on television while Johnson spent $4.5 million with another $500,000 on radio. One reason the Democrats did not have to match the Republicans dollar for dollar was that all the networks constantly showed the anti-Goldwater "daisy" commercial on their news programs after it was pulled by the Johnson organization—an example of how being "banned in Boston" can boost public interest.

Then there were the paperback books that, for the most part, argued the case against Lyndon Johnson and for Barry Goldwater. Never before had any paperbacks been printed and distributed in such volume, between 15 and 17 million copies, in so short a time. The top three best-sellers were written by conservatives: *A Texan Looks at Lyndon* by J. Evetts Haley (about six million copies bought); *None Dare Call It Treason* by John A. Stormer (an estimated five million copies); and *A Choice Not an Echo* by Phyllis Schlafly (approximately three million copies sold, mostly in bulk sales of one thousand or more at 20 cents each).

The most popular book was *A Texan Looks at Lyndon*, subtitled *A Study in Illegitimate Power*, by Haley, a widely respected historian and biographer of the Southwest, described by the liberal *Austin American-Statesman* (before he looked critically at LBJ) as "the region's Tom Paine, a brilliant historian and a provocative pamphleteer." A self-described constitutional Democrat, Haley stated in the introduction that Johnson was a compulsive wheeler-dealer and political fixer.[20] The *New York Times* criticized Haley for his heavy reliance on rumor, but in his multivolume biography of Lyndon Johnson, begun twenty years later, Robert Caro substantiated many of Haley's assertions, particularly Johnson's blatant abuse of political power.[21]

None Dare Call It Treason was vintage John Birch Society propaganda (although Stormer was not a member): heavily documented (802 footnotes), action-oriented (suggesting books to read, radio programs to listen to, organizations to join), and conspiratorial from the first page to the last. "The future of Americans as a free people is threatened," wrote the youthful Stormer, chairman of the Missouri Young Republicans, because elected officials had refused to rid the government of communists like Owen Lattimore and John Stewart Service. There were, he charged, communists everywhere—in the schools, the churches, the news media, organized labor, foundations, and international organizations like the United Nations.[22] Their goals were a socialized economy and one world government.

None Dare Call It Treason was hopelessly simplistic as geopolitical analysis. Stormer suggested that John Foster Dulles, the apostle of brinkmanship, really believed that the communists were "mellowing," that the CEOs of U.S. Steel and General Motors wanted socialism, that Time-Life founder Henry Luce, who steadfastly stood by Whittaker Chambers throughout the two Hiss-Chambers trials, was a liberal anti-anticommunist. For Stormer, it was very simple: treason explained why America continued to aid the communist enemy, to disarm in the face of danger, and to bow before communist dictators in every corner of the earth.

In *A Choice Not an Echo* (specifically intended to help Goldwater win the presidential nomination), Phyllis Schlafly, president of the Illinois Federation of Republican Women, argued that a small group of "secret kingmakers" in the Eastern wing of the Republican party had selected the Republican nominees since 1936. After naming many of the secret kingmakers (including Republicans Dwight D. Eisenhower, Thomas E. Dewey, David Rockefeller, Nelson Rockefeller, and Senator Alexander Wiley; and Democrats Dean Rusk, J. William Fulbright, George F. Kennan, Paul H. Nitze, Dean Acheson, and Walter Lippmann), Schlafly explained that she spoke out "to help grass-roots Republicans face the realities of 1964" and avoid "an unnecessary defeat" in the fall. Half a million copies of *A Choice Not an Echo* were distributed in the California primary, where, according to Gardiner Johnson, the state's Republican national committeeman, they were "a major factor in bringing victory to Barry Goldwater" over Nelson Rockefeller.[23]

In the face of such controversial assertions, the Republican National Committee stated that it was "the official policy of the committee . . . not to recommend or endorse publications prepared outside the committee," but conceded, "we have no way of controlling people out in the field."[24] Two blocks away, the national headquarters of Citizens for Goldwater-Miller referred the "thousands" of inquiries it got about the Haley, Stormer, and Schlafly books to a distribution company in Houston that also offered copies of the virulently anti-Goldwater work, *Barry Goldwater: Extremist on the Right* by Fred J. Cook.

The Democratic National Committee admitted in early October that it not only had sold fifty thousand copies of the Cook paperback, but received a commission from the publisher for each sale, a fundraising gimmick the Republicans rejected for the anti-LBJ books.[25] In fact, although Goldwater campaign offices in many states promoted *A Texan Looks at Lyndon* and *None Dare Call It Treason*, the conservative paperbacks did not really need much help. These best-sellers were prominently displayed at general bookstores, department stores, drug store chains, supermarkets, and newsstands.

ANOTHER KEY factor in any political race is the attitude of the journalists. The media elite in Washington were fascinated by Johnson, who had an "ambition and appetite for power unmatched by any other politician."[26] Philosophically liberal, they agreed with his progovernment, Great Society plans, and believed him when he said there would be no escalation of the conflict in Vietnam ("We are not going to send American boys nine or ten thousand miles away from home to do what Asian boys ought to be doing for themselves").[27]

Convinced that Goldwater would be dangerous for the country and the world, the media elite tilted their coverage in favor of Johnson, looking the other way when the president was out of control—rhetorically or physically. For example, CBS's George Herman recounted that in Evansville, Indiana, Johnson "came reeling out of the [campaign] plane" and made "a rambling, incoherent speech." Herman asked a Secret Service agent, "Is that man drunk?" to which the agent replied, "If aged Scotch will make you drunk, he's drunk." Every reporter knew that a central Johnson theme was, in the president's words, "Whose finger do you want to mash that [nuclear] button?" As Herman later admitted, "Here was the man whose finger *was* on the button as drunk as can be in a campaign that was centered around responsibility. But none of us reported it."[28]

Confronted with such monumental bias, Goldwater took refuge in humor, saying, "I wonder where Christianity would be today if some of these reporters had been Matthew, Mark, Luke, and John."[29] For his part, Johnson was aware that television seemed to magnify his "political" nature—what others called his deviousness—and he did not spend a lot of time or money on programs featuring himself.[30] But he kept pressing Bill Moyers and other White House aides to come up with the hardest hitting anti-Goldwater TV commercials possible. They succeeded beyond Johnson's greatest expectations.

GOLDWATER AND HIS strategists decided to apply the same mathematics for the fall campaign that had brought them victory in the nomination drive: write off the big Northeastern states like New York, New Jersey, Pennsylvania, and Michigan that are traditionally contested by presidential candidates; carry almost all of the South; hold on to the Middle West, the heartland of the GOP; and sweep the Mountain States and most of the far West. One formula showed that the Midwest without Michigan and Minnesota, the Border States without West Virginia, and the South without Arkansas, Georgia, or Texas would produce 257 likely electoral votes for Goldwater. Then he would have to carry either California or Texas to be able to win without a single Eastern state, which suited the senator and his aides just fine.[31]

As outlined in an August memorandum of the senator's steering committee, four primary issues needed to be stressed: (1) the shocking decline in political morality and increase of moral decay in the nation; (2) the breakdown in law and order that led to crime and violence, "terrorizing our people"; (3) the weakening of the nation's defense and alliances that allowed communism to "make gains all over" the world while the "Johnson administration flounders"; and (4) the failure of the present national leadership to inspire the nation or the world. Johnson "is a wheeler-dealer, not a leader," concluded the memorandum. "And his running mate is a creature of the ADA [Americans for Democratic Action], which has goals dangerous to our best interests."[32]

There was no mention of the economy because America was enjoying widespread prosperity and growth as a result of Kennedy's decision (in the face of considerable congressional opposition) to cut taxes. The gross national product grew at an annual rate of 5 percent under JFK, reaching $622 billion in 1964. There was minimal inflation and unemployment of just 5 percent; over 70 million Americans had jobs. While the national debt topped $1 trillion for the first time, the Kennedy era was a time of sustained economic growth.

The Democratic strategy was a "model of orthodoxy" that relied on incumbency, the halo effect resulting from Kennedy's assassination that prolonged Johnson's honeymoon with Congress and the media, and his leadership of what was, after all, the majority party.[33] The White House set out to create an image of Goldwater as a dangerous, reckless man while presenting Johnson as a thoughtful, sensible man of the center, the president of all the people. As White House aide Clifton Carter put it shortly before Labor Day, "The big issue, I think, is peace—peace or war. I think what most people want to know is whose hand is next to that nuclear panic button. We are going to stress responsibility versus irresponsibility in high office."[34]

IN THE OPENING speech of his formal campaign, drafted by Karl Hess and delivered in his good luck city, Prescott, Arizona, on September 3, Goldwater was tough and conciliatory. He pledged to stop "the cancerous growth of the federal government" and to let the people "use more of your money for yourselves." At the same time, reflecting what some called the Spirit of Hershey (which had emerged from the Republican unity meeting in Hershey, Pennsylvania), he promised to act

compassionately and gradually in implementing conservative principles. All present social-welfare and economic commitments to the
public, he said, "whether explicit or implicit," would be honored.
Republicans would never "abandon the needy and the aged, we shall
never forsake the helpless."

The vow was not new or a retreat from conservatism as some
suggested. It was consistent with the language of his first senatorial
campaign in 1952 and with *The Conscience of a Conservative*, which
proposed that those who could not help themselves should be helped,
first by private agencies and then by government if necessary. What
must be kept in mind, he insisted that bright sunny September day, was
that *lasting* solutions of the underprivileged's problems "cannot be
found in degrading, capricious, and politically motivated handouts."[35]
Goldwater was offering a fusion of classical liberalism and traditional
Republicanism, borrowing from Jefferson and Hayek on the one hand
and Theodore Roosevelt and Robert Taft on the other.

Turning to foreign policy, he noted that Johnson had not mentioned
communism once in his acceptance speech and yet communism was
"the only great threat to the peace . . . [and] to every free man. It can't
be ignored!" He promised not war ("I do not intend to be a wartime
president") but peace through preparedness and strength. He would
return to the Eisenhower-Dulles policy of the "flexible, balanced
weapons systems [that] give us the vital options of controlled, graduated deterrence—rather than only a capacity for all-out nuclear confrontation," i.e., Robert McNamara's MAD (Mutual Assured
Destruction) policy. Revealing his libertarian side, Goldwater criticized the "outmoded and unfair military draft system" and promised
to end Selective Service "as soon as possible."[36]

Goldwater then showed his traditionalist side by turning to two
related themes that deeply troubled him and a growing number of
Americans: law and order and public morality. It was, he said, the
responsibility of the national leadership "to enforce the law not let it be
abused or ignored. . . ." Choose the present administration, he warned,
"and you have the way of mobs in the street, restrained only by the plea
that they wait until after the election to ignite violence again." Putting
his finger on a problem that was to escalate for years to come, he
asserted that "those who break the law are accorded more consideration than those who try to enforce the law."[37]

Critics charged that Goldwater was referring subtly to the civil rights movement and appealing to white resentment against it. But Goldwater was no George Wallace. He was Robert Taft, Dwight Eisenhower, and even Governor Rockefeller (who called in troops to put down the Attica prison riots), in insisting that laws must be obeyed until and unless they were changed by the courts or Congress.

Regarding morality, he said that "the tone of America" was too often being set "by the standards of the sick jokes, the quick slogan, the off-color drama, and the pornographic book." In a clear reference to Bobby Baker, who had become a millionaire as secretary of the Senate when Johnson was Senate majority leader, Goldwater said that "the shadow of scandal falls, unlighted yet by full answers, across the White House itself." Public service, he added, "has become for too many at its highest levels, selfish in motive and manner. Men who preach publicly of sacrifice, practice private indulgence."[38]

Reporters knew that Goldwater was referring to Johnson's considerable fortune, which he had built by amassing broadcast properties in Texas, and of his many adulterous affairs in and out of the White House. But this was 1964, pre-Vietnam, pre-Watergate, pre-Gary Hart, pre-Bill Clinton, before the press had adopted an adversarial stance toward the presidency and its aspirants. Besides, to investigate the Johnson White House would have aided Goldwater. Although in his later years, he often expressed his scorn for the Moral Majority and the Christian Right, that day Goldwater declared on the steps of the Yavapai County Courthouse that "when men use political advantage for personal gain we can understand the decline of moral strength generally."[39]

Drawing on his libertarian roots, the senator concluded with an ode to the individual:

This is a challenge to the overwhelming majority of Americans who share these basic beliefs with us:

That each man is responsible for his own actions.

That each man is the best judge of his own well-being.

That each man has an individual conscience to serve and a moral code to uphold.

That each man is a brother to every other man.

America's greatness is the greatness of her people. Let this generation, then, make a new mark for that greatness. Let this generation light a lamp of liberty that will illuminate the world. Let this generation of Americans set a standard of responsibility that will inspire the world. We can do it! And God willing, together, we will do it.[40]

The speech was partly reassuring (to those who thought he might start launching missiles at Moscow the day after he was inaugurated), partly provocative (to goad Johnson into saying something he should not), and partly philosophical (to educate the people about conservatism). The politicians on the second floor of the Republican National Committee at 1625 I Street, N.W., in Washington, D.C. (men like Shadegg, Wayne Hood, Sam Hay, and Robert Mardian) wanted the senator to spell out specifically what he would do as president, but Goldwater preferred to take the high road, although he sometimes detoured when his urge "to give the Democrats, all those liberals and Lyndon Johnson hell" got the better of him.[41]

The crowds in his first week of campaigning were good to excellent: 53,000 in Los Angeles, 15,000 with a 3,000 overflow in Seattle, and 11,000 with 5,000 left outside in Minneapolis. What set the Goldwater audiences apart was an enthusiasm and fervor quite unlike the customary partisan roars of political meetings. When Goldwater remarked that he sensed a "revival" in the land, he did not use the word in an evangelical sense, but the gatherings nevertheless showed "elements indicative of a religious mood."[42]

Another novel feature was that in Los Angeles and Seattle, more than seventy thousand people paid $1 each for admission, whereas political rallies are usually free and even offer entertainment to attract a full house. Most of the men and women who came were in the lower middle-age group, age thirty to fifty, and often brought their teenaged sons and daughters with them. The next largest group was made up of young men and women in their twenties, and then there were the senior citizens. They were average Americans, conservatively dressed and orderly, which contrasted with the small bands of pickets that showed up at each meeting. The protestors were in the main bearded young men and straggly haired young girls in tight-fitting jeans with banners labeling Goldwater "racist" and "bigot." Police invariably confirmed they were from out of town.[43]

Goldwater was encouraged not only by the enthusiastic response, but by the evidence that the man in the White House was paying close attention to him. His frequent references to the Bobby Baker scandal energized the Senate Rules Committee to repopen the case and look into an alleged $35,000 payoff by Matthew McCloskey, a Philadelphia contractor. His call for an end of the draft prompted a favorable response from the Pentagon. And his charges that national defense had been dangerously reduced evoked sharp replies from high-ranking Department of Defense officials.[44]

One Goldwater proposal (drafted by Milton Friedman) was received in silence: "As one of my first actions in the White House," he promised at Dodger Stadium in Los Angeles, "I shall ask the Congress to enact a regular and considered program of tax reduction of 5 percent per year in all income taxes, both individual and corporate." As private incomes increased and the economy grew, he explained, the tax decrease would prevent government expenditures from increasing. Here was the first public expression of what would become supply-side economics in the late 1970s and one of the biggest issues in the Reagan decade of the 1980s.[45]

At the end of his first week of campaigning, Goldwater could truthfully say that he had had a good week, but he was still behind 30 to 70 percent in most of the polls, with a little more than six weeks to go.

Goldwater decided not to campaign in Mississippi because of the continuing racial tension there, and he bypassed Virginia because of his longtime friendship with Democratic Senator Harry F. Byrd and his conviction that Byrd Democrats would vote against Johnson anyway (he was wrong: Virginia went for LBJ by 53.5 to 46.2 percent). All the other Southern states and the border state of Tennessee were made key targets, subject to one proviso: Goldwater never stayed in the South overnight so that he could avoid sleeping in a segregated hotel.[46]

Sam Claiborne, who was responsible for the political operations of the Southern region, worked for hours with Chuck Lichenstein in the "think tank" (located on the third floor at 1625 I Street) to ensure that Goldwater would discuss cotton in Memphis, reassure the elderly about Social Security in Florida, and clarify his stand on TVA in Knoxville. They might as well have gone to the movies.

In Winston-Salem, North Carolina, the senator attacked McNamara and the administration's policy in South Vietnam and never mentioned cotton, peanuts, or tobacco. In St. Petersburg, he spoke of the rising crime rate, terror in the streets, and the evils of Medicare and not one word about Social Security. In Knoxville, he appealed for Democratic support and ignored the TVA statement Claiborne and Lichenstein had labored over. In Memphis, he made a partisan Republican speech and passed over cotton, and in Montgomery, Alabama, he repeated his proposals to end the draft and cut personal and corporate income taxes by 5 percent per year.

According to Shadegg, "The slow fuse which had been smoldering among the politicians on the second floor since early August suddenly exploded."[47] The sabotage seemed deliberate to most of the regional directors: Kitchel and Baroody were apparently ignoring every single opportunity to counteract the Democrats and garner support for Goldwater.

Herman and Claiborne, with Wayne Hood's approval, began working on a radical plan to change the composition of the think tank and make the speechmaking more effective. What they did not realize was that Goldwater, not Kitchel or Baroody, was deciding the course of the campaign, and he was determined to discuss what he saw as important national issues and not pander for votes by focusing on local interests.

In mid-September, the senator received a tremendous boost in South Carolina and the rest of the South when Senator Strom Thurmond, who had run for president in 1948 as a "Dixiecrat," decided to switch parties and become a Republican. To make certain that Goldwater liked the idea, Thurmond personally called on him. Goldwater was delighted: "I very much want you to come out for me, and I want you to go all the way and change parties." Standing before a giant poster of Goldwater, Thurmond declared over statewide television that the national Democratic party had "abandoned the people" and that to protect freedom and constitutional government, he would "do everything in [his] power" to help elect Barry Goldwater president of the United States of America.[48] That fall, Thurmond made dozens of campaign speeches for Goldwater, which helped him to sweep the Deep South.

ATTENTION SHIFTED to a region Goldwater had to carry if he were to have any chance at all of winning the election: the Midwest and the Plains states, the historic core of the Republican party. There were indications that the nation's farmers would respond favorably to a reasonable alternative to the administration's liberal program of subsidies and controls; they had, for example, rejected Agriculture Secretary Orville Freeman's wheat proposal in a national referendum. But Democrats kept warning farmers that electing Goldwater would mean an immediate end to the subsidy program (misquoting *The Conscience of a Conservative* and other Goldwater statements on agriculture). It was imperative to state the truth—that the senator's goal was the gradual elimination of government price supports and an ultimate return to the free market.

Senators Karl Mundt of South Dakota and Milton S. Young of North Dakota were convinced that Goldwater's showing in the Midwest depended upon his delivering the right speech at the annual plowing contest at Fargo, North Dakota, and they persuaded the inner circle to let him come. For nearly ten days, the two Republican senators worked closely with Goldwater people on a statement, with the understanding that it would deny that Goldwater intended to make "immediate and drastic changes" in farm policy.

But once again Goldwater refused to compromise with principle. He roundly condemned the administration's farm program, reminded his farmer audience that 17 percent of their income, amounting to $2.1 billion annually, was a federal subsidy, and asked, "Do you want that to continue?" That was a fair and acceptable criticism, even to farmers. But Goldwater did not come out concretely with what his administration would do or would not do in the area of agriculture. He gave his audience three short paragraphs filled with generalities and concluded: "We know in our hearts that you are plagued with your special problems, and we know they are serious problems. We will work with you toward solutions, not schemes." He did depart from the text to say, "I have no intention of stopping supports overnight." Goldwater supporters crowded close to the speaking stand and applauded his remarks, but most of the crowd was silent.[49]

It took another whole month, until mid-October, at the annual corn-picking contest in Sioux Falls, South Dakota, before Goldwater said specifically that he would honor "commitments already made by the federal government" and "move slowly in making changes so that the citizens of this nation and indeed the economy itself can make smooth adjustments."[50] It was a clear, forthright statement that might have reassured the farmers of the Midwest if they had been listening, but by then almost all of America had made up its mind about Barry Goldwater, helped along by the attack commercials of the Johnson campaign.

In late September, following the national broadcast of what most observers agreed were three ineffective TV programs, Finance Chairman Ralph Cordiner and Finance Director Bill Middendorf joined the frustrated regional directors in an attempt to reorganize the campaign and, among other things, put Shadegg in charge of the speechwriting.

The television programs that failed to generate much public interest or Republican enthusiasm were (1) a filmed address in which the senator answered the charges that he was impulsive, imprudent, and trigger-happy by denying that he was impulsive, imprudent, and trigger-happy—a tactic that delighted Democrats; (2) an appearance with General Eisenhower, entitled "Conversation at Gettysburg," in which the former president declined to give an unequivocal endorsement of Goldwater but did say, finally, "Certainly the country recognizes in you a man of integrity, good will, honesty, and dedication to his country"; and (3) a question-and-answer format that had been used to great effect in the California primary, but that now, because of Madison Avenue editing, came across as stilted rather than spontaneous.[51]

There followed an intense game of "Catch the Senator," in which various people—Cordiner, Middendorf, Hood, and others—tried to talk privately with Goldwater on the campaign plane. But Kitchel, Baroody, or some other member of the inner circle was always present, and no one could break through to talk about so sensitive a matter as the direction of the campaign. At last, during the first week of October, Bob Mardian, an old, personal friend from Arizona, was dispatched with firm instructions not to return until he had talked to the senator.

Mardian boarded the "House in the Sky" in Portland for the flight to Salt Lake City and found a seat near Goldwater, who was in a relaxed mood. But before Mardian could open his mouth, the senator gripped his arm tightly with one of his big hands and said, "You've been a very busy boy, Robert, and I want you to stop it."

"I've been doing nothing more than trying to help you win this election," Mardian protested.

Accounts vary as to the senator's answer. According to Shadegg, the senator growled, "Well, whatever it is you say you're not doing, I want you to stop it. It's too late."

Mardian himself recalls that Goldwater said, "You go back and tell your crowd that I'm going to lose this election. I'm probably going to lose it real big. But I'm going to lose it my way."[52]

Either way, the message was clear. Friends and politicians stopped trying to turn the campaign in a more pragmatic direction. In effect, they accepted the advice of Peter O'Donnell, who after listening to them commented, "Well, we knew what we were getting when we nominated him. We knew he'd speak his mind. I thought that's why we backed him. Now let's try to help him instead of bitching all day long."[53]

The irony is that the Goldwater strategy of speaking his mind (plus the Goldwater charisma) doubled his position in the polls from around 20 percent in mid-July when he was nominated to just under 39 percent in the first week of November. Among the voters who changed their minds between August and election day, Goldwater bested Johnson by nearly 2 to 1. But they were a small minority of the public.[54] Even if Goldwater had done a brilliant job of articulating his positions on Social Security, TVA, nuclear weapons, and farm subsidies, he would not have been able to improve his standing significantly, particularly given what the Democrats were doing to him.

FROM THE VERY beginning, LBJ was determined to portray Goldwater as a right-wing extremist who could not be allowed to sit in the White House. Right after the Republican convention, Johnson called his aide, Bill Moyers, and told him, "Barry is making a headlong race for respectability. He's trying to shed himself of all the convictions, beliefs, images, and the extremism that [have] surrounded him all of his career in the Senate and characterized his speeches to the right wing." The Democrats, he instructed Moyers, had to "remind people of what Barry Goldwater was before he was nominated for president."[55]

Moyers dutifully passed the word to their advertising agency, Doyle Dane Bernbach. It turned to the outpourings of Rockefeller, Scranton, and other liberal Republicans for "proof" that Goldwater was too dangerous to vote for. The ad agency also combed the voluminous Goldwater files provided by the Democratic National Committee for statements that could be twisted or turned to its client's advantage. The starting date of the anti-Goldwater advertising was moved up after the Republican unity meeting in Hershey to prevent him, as White House aide Lloyd Wright put it, from "appearing to moderate his stands and assume the offensive in the campaign."[56]

Ironically, while the White House was approving the brutal ads that would stigmatize Barry Goldwater as a warmonger and extremist, the senator was asking the White House for a meeting with the president to discuss how to keep civil rights and Vietnam out of the campaign.

As Kathleen Hall Jamieson points out, the most controversial ad of 1964—and perhaps of all political advertising—does not mention Barry Goldwater, or anything he ever said. It begins with a small girl standing in a sun-speckled field, plucking petals from a daisy as she childishly counts, "1, 2, 3, 4, 5, 7, 6, 6, 8, 9, 9. . . ." When she reaches "9," a deep bass voice overrides her voice and ominously begins a countdown, "10, 9, 8, 7, 6, 5, 4, 3, 2, 1, zero." At zero, the camera, which has been closing in on the child's face, dissolves from the pupil of her eye to an atomic bomb that explodes and expands and fills the screen. Like a doomsday prophet, President Johnson's voice solemnly intones: "These are the stakes—to make a world in which all of God's children can live, or to go into the dark. We must either love each other, or we must die." On a black screen are the words, "Vote for President Johnson on November 3," which an announcer repeats and then adds, "The stakes are too high for you to stay home."[57]

The ad was aired commercially only once, on CBS's "Monday Night at the Movies," on the evening of September 7 to an audience of approximately 50 million Americans. To this day, people insist that they heard Goldwater's name and an attack on his alleged pronuclear weapon policies.

Tony Schwartz, the creator of the Daisy commercial and an admitted liberal Democrat, has since explained that he deliberately played off the public's memories, vague and otherwise, of the senator's many statements, and his opponents' distortions, about atomic bombs and weapons. "It was comparable to a person going to a psychiatrist and seeing dirty pictures in a Rorschach pattern," he said. "The Daisy commercial evoked Goldwater's probomb [sic] statements. They were like the dirty pictures in the audience's mind."[58] That Schwartz would equate dirty pictures and Goldwater's statements reveals his state of mind.

The response to the TV spot was electrifying. The switchboard of the White House lit up, and Johnson called Moyers excitedly, "Jesus Christ, what in the world happened?" Moyers said, "You got your point across, that's what." After a pause, the president said, "Well, I guess it did what we Goddamned set out to do, didn't it?" Moyers: "I would think so."[59]

The Johnson campaign reportedly planned to run the ad on all three networks, although Moyers insists that the plan had been to air "Daisy" only once, which seems improbable. But Republicans, led by

Republican National Committee Chairman Burch and Senator Dirksen, protested so vehemently that all three networks, CBS, NBC, and ABC, picked up on the story and showed the commercial on their evening newscasts, giving the spot millions of dollars of free air time. *Time* followed with a cover story about "The Nuclear Issue," using the "daisy girl."

Burch filed a complaint with the Fair Campaign Practices Committee and called on Johnson "to halt this smear attack on a United States senator and the candidate of the Republican party for the presidency," but news and commentary programs showed the ad over and over again, until it became the most discussed political commercial of that or any other year.[60]

Even so, the Democratic campaign to vilify Barry Goldwater was far from over. Five nights later, viewers of "Saturday Night at the Movies" saw an ad that showed a young girl happily licking an ice cream cone. This time the child was threatened, not by an exploding atomic bomb, but by a radioactive poison called Strontium 90. Thanks to the nuclear test ban treaty, the warm maternal voice of a woman announcer said, such poisons "started to go away." But now "there is a man who wants to be president of the United States, and he doesn't like this treaty. . . . He wants to go on testing more bombs. His name is Barry Goldwater, and if he's elected, they might start testing all over again." The ad ended with an authoritative male voice proclaiming: "Vote for President Johnson on November 3. The stakes are too high for you to stay at home."[61]

Like the Daisy spot, the Ice Cream Cone ad appeared only once on network television, but, again like Daisy, that sufficed. As Moyers proudly proclaimed several years later, the commercials "hung the nuclear noose around Goldwater and finished him off."[62]

In retrospect, several of America's leading journalists concede they should have challenged the anti-Goldwater fear campaign. James "Scotty" Reston of the *New York Times* says, "I wish the media had kicked the stuffing out of LBJ and the White House on the TV ads issue. . . . [T]he press was remiss in letting that garbage get out without nailing them." Ben Bradlee of the *Washington Post* describes the two Moyers nuclear ads as "a fucking outrage." The *Post*'s David Broder calls the Johnson White House's attacks "highly irrational because they were so heavily favored to win." Catholic writer Michael Novak, who publicly supported Johnson in articles for *Commonweal* and the *New Republic,* recalls that he "reacted with revulsion to the caricature of Goldwater."[63] By the middle of September, the Harris Poll reported that 53 percent of women and 45 percent of men believed that Goldwater, if elected, would involve the country in war.[64]

A third attack commercial that appeared in September became the most heavily aired Democratic TV spot of the campaign. It charged that Goldwater would "destroy" Social Security, something the senator had never said or implied. To get around that rather large impediment, it was alleged that his running mate, William Miller, "admits that Senator Goldwater's voluntary plan would *destroy* [emphasis added] your Social Security." Meanwhile the video showed a pair of large masculine hands going through a stack of photos, IDs, and cards until it reached a Social Security card. The hands (implicitly Goldwater's) ripped the Social Security card in two, dropped the pieces on the table, and disappeared. The announcer said: "President Johnson is working to strengthen Social Security. Vote for him on November 3."[65]

To drive home the point, another Democratic commercial stated that "on at least seven different occasions, Barry Goldwater has said he would drastically change the Social Security System."

Again, for the record, Goldwater never said he would "drastically" change Social Security. What he suggested was that it might be made voluntary, but only *over time* in order not to disrupt the program or hurt those who depended on it. In defense of the torn-card commercial, Moyers has argued that a "substantial and distinguished body of opinion had concluded that making it voluntary would wreck Social Security." But political scientist Benjamin Page disagrees, pointing out that "experts were not all agreed, and the consequences would have depended upon what kind of voluntariness was provided."[66]

In truth, Goldwater was deeply disturbed, as were others in Congress, about the fiscal soundness of the system. In 1964, about 21 million Americans were receiving Social Security while some 55 million people were paying into the plan. But the Social Security trust fund of $21 billion was in the form of U.S. securities, not cash, and the government had borrowed the money and spent it. As the senator later put it, "How would any employee like to be part of a pension fund that had spent their contributions for other purposes?"

Goldwater was also worried about the rapidly declining ratio of worker to retiree. In the 1930s, when Social Security was launched, there were thirty-five workers for every retiree; in 1964 the ratio was five to one. It was clear to him that the "federal government was playing games with the money and that the system was financially overextended."[67]

In 1977, thirteen years after his warning, Congress finally passed what was then the largest peacetime tax increase in history to give Social Security a critically needed financial transfusion. It was not enough. In 1983, payroll taxes were raised to put the system on a "sound actuarial basis." But it was not enough. Most analysts agree that at the present rate of increase the Social Security system will break apart by the year 2020 or earlier.

Using the Social Security issue, Moyers and other White House aides produced a radio commercial that broke the truth-in-advertising scale by asserting: "Barry Goldwater's plan means the end of Social Security, the end of widow's pensions, the end of the dignity that comes with being able to take care of yourself without depending on your children. On November 3, vote for keeping Social Security."[68]

In response to what he called "electronic dirt," the senator used every possible medium—campaign speeches, print, radio, and TV ads—to stress that he did not want to wreck but to strengthen Social Security, pointing out that he had voted for every Social Security measure that had come before Congress. He persuaded Senator Margaret Chase Smith, the prickly Republican from Maine who had sought the presidential nomination herself, to make a TV commercial in which she testified that she had been present in the Senate when Goldwater had voted "time and again" for Social Security. One campaign aide estimated that Goldwater issued twenty-two major statements on Social Security and emphasized the point in most of his campaign stops. The Sunday before election day, full-page ads describing his stand on Social Security appeared in major papers across the country.

It was all for naught, as Kathleen Hall Jamieson wrote: "Many millions of voters—particularly the elderly and union families—held to their conviction that Goldwater was a foe of the Social Security system."[69]

After the election, Goldwater said that liberal Republicans had created a cruel caricature of him and Democrats had run with the distortion. He was the "trigger-happy" fellow, "the man who is going to drop the bomb," "the man who would tear up Social Security cards." "Try as I would," he said, ruefully, "[they] could not be erased."[70]

ANY NORMAL politician who was greeted by cheering crowds everywhere he went, enjoyed the backing of 70 percent of the daily press, was ahead by thirty points in the polls, and had his opponent on the ropes would have been content to coast a little. But Lyndon Johnson was obsessed with the idea of winning by the biggest margin ever. Weary of the Kennedy legend, he wanted to make John F. Kennedy's 118,000 victory of 1960 look "like a pathetic peep."[71] The attack commercials kept coming.

There was the TV spot in which the Eastern seaboard of the United States was slowly sawed off while the announcer reminded viewers of Goldwater's "belief" that the country would be better off if the East were allowed to float out to sea. That the senator had said it in the 1930s while a young Phoenix businessman made no difference.

There was the "outside the mainstream" commercial in which a camera panned a confetti-littered floor topped by placards of Rockefeller, Scranton, and Romney. The announcer repeated what each liberal Republican had said about the senator—"disaster for the party and the country," "a crazy-quilt collection of absurd and dangerous positions," "suicidal destruction of the Republican party"—and concluded, "So even if you're a Republican with serious doubts about Barry Goldwater, you're in good company."

There was the Ku Klux Klan commercial that, although it never aired, was preliminarily cleared for regional showing. It showed Klansmen, played by actors, marching in hooded robes. A burning cross was superimposed over the images as was a picture of the Klan wizard. Robert Cleal of the Alabama KKK was quoted as saying: "The majority of people in Alabama hate niggerism, Catholicism, Judaism. . . ." The announcer then quoted Cleal's endorsement: "I like Barry Goldwater. He needs our help." The announcer did not mention that the senator had twice repudiated Klan support or that he was half Jewish. The KKK ad was such a flagrant example of "guilt by association" that Democrats at the last moment canceled it, but reluctantly.[72]

The campaign's strident tone was set by the president himself, who told the United Steelworkers of America at their annual convention in late September that "you know it takes a man who loves his country to build a house instead of a raving, ranting demagogue who wants to tear down one."[73] With these spiteful words, Johnson sent an unmistakable signal to the White House, the Democratic National Committee, and every other campaign worker: Anything goes.

THE WHITE HOUSE turned to the Central Intelligence Agency to get advance inside information about the Goldwater campaign, although Barry Goldwater could hardly be described as a "domestic enemy." E. Howard Hunt, later convicted for his part in the Watergate break-in, was then serving as chief of covert action for the CIA's Domestic Operations Division. He told a congressional committee more than a decade later that he was ordered by his superior, C. Tracey Barnes, to spy on Goldwater's headquarters in the fall of 1964. Hunt set up a special unit (under the cover of Continental Press, located in the National Press Building) and arranged for a daily pickup of "any and all information" about the senator and his campaign plans, including advance copies of speeches not yet released to the media. Hunt confessed his shock at the intrusion into Goldwater's affairs but was told that President Johnson "had ordered this activity and that [Chester L.] Cooper would be the recipient of the information."[74]

Cooper, a former CIA official, was a White House aide. In testimony before the House Select Committee on Intelligence in November 1975, CIA Director William Colby admitted that Cooper prepared campaign material for Johnson and obtained advance texts of Goldwater's speeches through a "woman secretary." Colby's testimony suggests that in addition to the Hunt effort, the CIA planted someone inside the Goldwater campaign organization. Goldwater, who had his own excellent intelligence sources, was aware that he was under surveillance. "I just assumed it was one man or two men assigned at the direction of the president. . . . It never bothered me. I never got upset about it. Oh, I guess [I] should have, but knowing Johnson as I did, I never got upset about it."[75]

The senator had every right to get upset, and more. Time and again, the Democrats used the covertly obtained information to undercut a Goldwater initiative. On September 9, for example, the Goldwater campaign announced the formation of a Task Force on Peace and Freedom, headed by former Vice President Nixon and including Herbert Hoover, Jr., former undersecretary of state; General Lucius D.

Clay, one-time commander-in-chief of U.S. forces in Europe; Senator Bourke Hickenlooper of Iowa, ranking minority member of the Senate Foreign Relations Committee; Representative Mel Laird of Wisconsin, a ranking member of the House Armed Services Committee; Adolph W. Schmidt, a financial and foundation executive; and Professor Gerhart Niemeyer of Notre Dame University. The Associated Press described the task force as one of the most "unusual tactics in the history of American politics."

Three hours *before* the news release about the Goldwater task force was released, the White House announced that President Johnson had created a sixteen-member panel of distinguished citizens to consult with him on international problems.[76] The White House release trumped the Goldwater plan. The Democrats' preknowledge of Goldwater's speeches was later confirmed by John Roche, a speechwriter for the Johnson-Humphrey campaign, who wrote, "We used to get advance texts of Senator Goldwater's key speeches. The consequence of this was that before Goldwater had even opened his mouth, we had five speakers primed to reply. . . . When I innocently inquired how we got them, the reply was 'don't ask.' "[77]

One of the Democrats' sources was the Washington press corps itself. A copy of the confidential transcript of the August 12th Republican unity conference in Hershey can be found in the files of White House political aide Clifton Carter at the LBJ Presidential Library; printed in large letters on the cover page of the transcript is the name "Ben Bradlee," then Washington bureau chief of *Newsweek*. Bradlee has no recollection of giving the transcript to the White House and does not know how it wound up in Carter's files.[78]

George Reedy, who succeeded Bill Moyers as White House press secretary, later commented that he was "bored and sick" at the dirty tricks operation coordinated by Moyers, who loved intrigue. Reedy said the "espionage was silliness because we had the race won."[79] In another twist, Hal Pachios, deputy White House press secretary, revealed that Johnson was so upset by anti-LBJ or pro-Goldwater signs at his rallies that he ordered them to be removed. A dutiful Marvin Watson, another Johnson aide, reportedly had Democratic operatives sprinkle itching powder behind the necks of people holding the signs.[80]

Essential to the White House's dirty tricks was the Anti-Campaign, a political operation conceived by and watched over by Johnson himself. Run by about a dozen experienced Washington-based Democrats, the

Anti-Campaign churned out clandestine "black propaganda." No minutes or notes were kept of the meetings, held in a small conference room on the second floor of the West Wing of the White House, almost directly above the Oval Office. Its members included Myer Feldman, the president's special counsel; Daniel Patrick Moynihan, then an assistant secretary of labor; Leonard Marks, an old friend of Johnson who later became director of the U.S. Information Agency; James Sundquist, an assistant secretary of agriculture and former speechwriter for Truman; and Hyman Bookbinder, a former labor lobbyist and future Washington representative of the American Jewish Committee.

Typical of the Anti-Campaign's black politics tactics was their habit of scheduling anti-Goldwater speakers before and after a Goldwater appearance to suggest strong anti-Goldwater sentiment in the area. Advance knowledge of the senator's travel schedule was provided by the spy within Goldwater headquarters. The central mission of the Anti-Campaign operation was to encourage "frontlash," LBJ's own word for the phenomenon of Republican voters defecting to him because of Goldwater's "extremism." As Evans and Novak summed up, the Anti-Campaign was LBJ's "unique contribution to presidential campaigning."[81]

But the Anti-Campaign was only one part of the massive anti-Goldwater operation. The Democrats had many tricks up their sleeves. By the middle of September, Goldwater's regional directors were convinced that the telephones at the Republican national headquarters were bugged. All the important offices were periodically swept for listening devices, but information, often important, still leaked to the Democrats. Once, at a private meeting in John Grenier's office, several directors were discussing the possibility of a campaign stop by the senator in the Chicago area. Sam Hay suggested that East St. Louis, Illinois, be added to the itinerary and called the Republican chairman of Cook County who agreed. Within the hour, a *Chicago Tribune* reporter called Hay to say that he had heard Goldwater would be coming to town, and he wanted the details.[82]

To protect themselves, many of the regional directors began to make their confidential calls from a pay telephone outside the building. As Shadegg pointed out, these tactics fostered a feeling "of uncertainty and mutual distrust which was not beneficial to the campaign"—and was precisely what the Johnson White House hoped to create.[83] Goldwater recalls that once two correspondents questioned him about a proposal he had not yet made publicly—that if elected, he would send Eisenhower to Vietnam to examine the situation and report back to him. The senator insists that he discussed the Eisenhower visit with only two members of his personal staff, yet the two reporters swear they heard about it at the Johnson White House.[84]

STILL, JOHNSON was not satisfied. He ordered the nation's premier police organization—the Federal Bureau of Investigation—to engage in illegal political activity. Presidents had long used the FBI to investigate enemies or suspected enemies of the government and the nation.[85]

Serious abuse of the FBI's investigatory power began during the Kennedy administration, which initiated as many as one hundred wiretaps of reporters, professors, businessmen, and others for alleged "national security" purposes. Ben Bradlee, John Kennedy's close friend, once remarked, "My God, they wiretapped practically everyone else in this town."[86]

Although FDR ordered the FBI to wiretap and surveil a high-ranking member of his own administration (probably Joseph P. Kennedy, then U.S. ambassador to Great Britain) and told the IRS to examine Charles Lindbergh's tax returns (Lindbergh opposed America's entry into the European war), Lyndon Johnson was the worst abuser of the FBI for *electoral* purposes. Johnson was the only president to direct the bureau to surveil his political opponent in a presidential campaign. He had no excuse whatsoever—Barry Goldwater was not engaged in espionage, sabotage, or subversion. But he was standing in the way of a historic presidential landslide for LBJ. That was enough. In the fall of 1964, Johnson directed J. Edgar Hoover and the FBI to bug the Goldwater campaign plane and to conduct security checks of Goldwater's staff.

That was not Johnson's first violation of the civil liberties of those who opposed him. That summer, he had ordered the FBI, bypassing Attorney General Robert F. Kennedy, to set up a special "security" squad at the Democratic National Convention in Atlantic City to surveil civil rights leaders. Johnson feared that picketing by Martin Luther King Jr., and others to unseat "Regular" Mississippi delegates would mar the image of Democratic unity. He also suspected that the civil rights leaders favored Bobby Kennedy for vice president, an option he had definitely ruled out. The information on the civil rights leaders was transmitted to Cartha "Deke" DeLoach, the FBI's liaison with the

White House, who was located in a control center on the second floor of the old Post Office Building in Washington, D.C. A former agent, Leo Clark, later recalled that he overheard DeLoach "speaking on the telephone to President Johnson and to Director Hoover, giving them summary information from the technical surveillance."[87]

When the facts of the unlawful FBI operation became public more than a decade later, the *New York Times* editorialized:

> If the strong inferences to be drawn from the former agent's disclosure are correct, the 1964 incident is an even graver offense than the original Watergate break-in, for it represented the turning of a police instrument of Government to illegal activities for political purposes.[88]

After the Democratic convention, Bill Moyers sent a note to De-Loach thanking him and his fellow FBI agents for their "fine" work, to which DeLoach responded, "I'm certainly glad that we were able to come through with vital tidbits from time to time which were of assistance to you and Walter [Jenkins]. You know you have only to call on us when a similar situation arises."[89]

A potentially damaging "situation" arose in the last two weeks of the general campaign when Jenkins, longtime political aide of the president, was arrested on a morals charge involving homosexuality. Here was dramatic corroboration of a major Goldwater theme: the sharp decline of morality in government.

Although Goldwater ordered his campaign staff not to make political capital of the Jenkins affair, Johnson came storming into Moyers' office, claiming that J. Edgar Hoover had informed him that "Goldwater's people" may have "trapped" Walter Jenkins. The president told his aide to have the FBI "find those bastards"—i.e., the Republicans who had "set up" the homosexual rendezvous for Jenkins.[90]

Moyers immediately called DeLoach, who initiated an illegal file check of fifteen people employed in Goldwater's Senate office, including Edna Coerver, his executive secretary, and Ted Kazy, his administrative assistant, neither of whom had been involved in the campaign, plus one non-Senate aide, a veteran GOP publicist who had been filling various Goldwater campaign posts since early in the year.

A memorandum dated October 23, 1964, and directed to DeLoach (who initialed it to indicate he had read it), reported that "no derogatory information was located concerning any" of the people in Goldwater's office. The memo stated, irrelevantly, that in October 1956 a prostitute had advised the bureau's Washington Field Office that she had had at least "six dates" with the GOP publicist and that on one occasion he had become "drunk and abusive." A search of fingerprint cards uncovered no arrest records except for one traffic violation by the senator's legislative assistant. No evidence of Goldwater or Republican complicity in the Jenkins scandal was uncovered because there was none. Hoover personally approved the Moyers request as shown by the following addendum: "According to instructions from the Director, there is attached a letterhead memorandum containing the results of a check of our files on employees in Senator Goldwater's office."[91]

Far more disturbing was the FBI's bugging of the Goldwater campaign plane where the senator and his inner circle often made their most confidential decisions. The bureau's illegal surveillance was discovered by Robert Mardian, when he was assistant attorney general for the internal security division in the first Nixon administration.

During a two-hour conversation with Hoover in early 1971, Mardian asked about the procedures of electronic surveillance. To Mardian's amazement, Hoover revealed that in 1964, the bureau, on orders from the Oval Office, had bugged the Goldwater plane. In explanation, Hoover said, "You do what the president of the United States orders you to do." William C. Sullivan, the FBI's number two man, confirmed to Mardian the spying operation against the Goldwater campaign. "It was mind-boggling to me," admitted Mardian. "The reason Sullivan told me about it," he added, "was that he was a Goldwater man."[92] Because it was a warrantless tap, with the request coming directly from the president and bypassing the attorney general, the Goldwater bugging was not included in the Justice Department's index of wiretaps.

A decade after it happened, DeLoach publicly denied the illegal FBI operation. In testimony before the Senate Select Committee on Intelligence Activities in December 1975, DeLoach was asked by Senator Howard Baker whether he had any personal knowledge "of FBI surveillance of Senator Goldwater or his staff during the 1964 convention." DeLoach replied that he had no "personal recollection whatsoever" of it, that he would have "known about it if it had happened," and, extraordinarily, added:

> The request was made of me to make so-called name checks of Senator Goldwater's staff. I came back and told Mr. Hoover about it and Mr.

Hoover said, what do you recommend, and I told him I recommended we do nothing, and he said, I agree with you. *And that's exactly what we did, nothing. I told the White House nothing* [emphasis added].[93]

When Senator Philip Hart, a liberal Democrat, also brought up the question of name checks of Senator Goldwater's staff, DeLoach again denied the charge:

HART: I think the record is left hanging a little with respect to the Bureau's reaction to requests made by the White House for name checks on Senator Goldwater's staff. It is my impression—-

DELOACH: Well, Senator, we felt that to be purely political and that's why I made the recommendation to Mr. Hoover.

HART: I'm told the next day he went ahead and did it.

DELOACH: We did no name checks, Senator. We furnished no information, as far as I know, to the best of my recollection.

HART: I stand corrected. You are correct.[94]

But DeLoach was not correct: he was either trying to protect the FBI (although he was no longer a bureau employee at the time of his 1975 testimony) or to cover up his own role in an illegal act. A Hart aide quickly passed a note to his boss, who quoted to DeLoach an FBI memorandum indicating that a check of the Goldwater staff had been made and that DeLoach himself had reported the results to Moyers (as indeed he had). DeLoach repeated his denial of any bureau action for the third time:

DELOACH: To the best of my recollection, Senator, as I recall the incident, no information was given to the White House concerning Senator Goldwater's staff. Not because of the fact that we did not have information in the Bureau's files, but simply because the Bureau did not desire to be involved in such a request.[95]

Although Goldwater has forgiven the FBI for its illegal, unethical conduct and President Johnson for instigating it, he has nothing but scorn for Bill Moyers, who, he says, has made a career of lecturing "us on truth, the public trust, a fairer and finer America."

Goldwater recounts a meeting between Moyers and Johnson the night the Daisy ad aired, during which Moyers told the president that he had ordered the commercial to be shown only once. As he went out of the room, Johnson asked, "You sure we ought to run it just once?" "Yes, Mr. President," Moyers replied. The twisted logic behind Moyers' remark, Goldwater pointed out, is that it is okay to stab someone in the back once, but it is immoral "if you get caught stabbing someone five or ten times." When Goldwater, who watches a lot of television, catches Moyers on one of his frequent PBS appearances, his reaction is to the point: "Every time I see him, I get sick to my stomach and want to throw up."[96]

DESPITE THE depressing polls, the savage TV commercials, and the defection of prominent Republicans like Romney and Rockefeller, who pocketed Goldwater buttons when offered them, Goldwater campaigned hard throughout September, determined to spread his message of "peace through preparedness, progress through freedom and purpose through constitutional order."[97] He shrugged off an extraordinary Senate speech by Senator J. William Fulbright—"Goldwater Republicanism is the closest thing in American politics to an equivalent of Russian Stalinism"—and a remark by Roy Wilkins, NAACP executive secretary—"a Goldwater victory . . . would bring about a police state."[98]

Paradoxically, it was Johnson who campaigned as the "conservative," the representative of the status quo, seeking to conserve and expand the big government philosophy of the New Deal, while it was Goldwater who crisscrossed the country as the "radical," the apostle of change, urging the people to return to their roots of political liberty and individual responsibility.

Goldwater's address before the annual meeting of the American Political Science Association (APSA) in Chicago on September 11, drafted by Harry Jaffa with the help of William Rehnquist, was a brilliant examination of the uses and abuses of political power. He was interrupted by applause twelve times and received a standing ovation from about half the audience, no mean accomplishment for a conservative speaking to a venerable institution of the liberal establishment. Prior to the meeting, reflecting the emotional but illogical position of many academicians, a distraught professor at the University of Chicago had circulated a letter urging members to boycott the senator's appearance.[99]

In his speech, the senator praised the American system of federalism with its genius for combining "the size and power of a great empire with the freedom of a small republic." But the system was endangered, he cautioned, by the prevailing Democratic party doctrine that the Constitution "is now widely held to mean only what those who hold power for the moment choose to say that it means." The union, he warned:

> is a union only so long as the states are states. Federal power, indefinitely extended to any limit that a temporary majority in control of the central government may wish, crushes the concurrent powers of the states in one field after another, until the states have no will, and finally no resources, moral or financial, of their own.

To drive home the point, he added:

> Let us be clearer than we have been in this country in these recent years: That the concentration of all the powers of government, in the same hands, either by the breakdown of the separation of powers, or by the breakdown of the lines separating states from nations, will mean a breakdown of liberty.[100]

The federal system, he declared, is "our great political achievement. It is the very foundation of our greatness—yesterday, today, and tomorrow."[101]

It was a persuasive, carefully reasoned address. And yet within three days, Martin Luther King Jr. claimed that there were "dangerous signs of Hitlerism" in the Goldwater program. The *Saturday Evening Post* a week later called Goldwater "a wild man, a stray, an unprincipled and ruthless political jujitsu artist." And Walter Lippmann, who must have read at least excerpts of the APSA speech, wrote ten days later, "In Barry Goldwater we have a demagogue who dreams of arousing the rich against the poor."[102]

When Vic Gold once asked him how he was able to maintain his apparent equanimity amid such gratuitous criticism, Goldwater replied that campaigning was "like a bullfight and every once in a while, you get gored—don't worry about it."[103]

Goldwater campaigned bravely on through the sunny days and crisp nights of September, proposing (in Montgomery, Alabama) a system of unconditional state grants rather than the present programmatic grants; attacking (in Charleston, West Virginia) the Great Society where no one will fall below the average because no one will be permitted to rise above it; defending (in Boston) the rights of law-abiding citizens first and those of criminals second; attacking (in Louisville) Robert "Yo-Yo" McNamara for his constantly contradictory reports about the war in Vietnam; and advocating (in Toledo) two kinds of education tax credits: (1) a credit on federal income taxes based on the share of local property taxes allocated to public school costs, and (2) a credit, graduated in favor of low- and middle-income families, to help parents meet the ever-growing tuitions of schools, colleges, and universities.[104]

In short, for the first time in thirty years, a presidential candidate was challenging the basic assumptions of the liberal welfare state. Theodore White wrote, "One could not question the conscience of this conservative. Here was no ordinary politician pitching for votes; he was on a crusade to free America from enslavement."[105]

The Democratic response was to run TV ads about little girls and nuclear bombs, radioactive ice cream cones, ripped-in-half Social Security cards, and the Eastern seaboard being sawed off. The leading organ of the liberal press greeted his remarks with titles like "Some New Ways to Slice the Old Baloney."[106]

There were a few encouraging moments, like the whistle-stop tour of the Midwest in late September. Goldwater had to win in Ohio, Indiana, and Illinois if he were to add the Midwest to his Southern base. The polls, public and private, were still running heavily against him (Gallup: 65 percent for Johnson, 29 percent for Goldwater), and he had said privately that if there were no upturn by October, it was all over.

For five days and 2,500 miles, the seventeen-car Goldwater train rambled through the Midwest, while high school bands played and curious people crowded around the rear platform of the Baltimore and Ohio observation car to hear the Republican nominee decry riots in the cities, the rising crime rate, and the "flood of pornographic literature that corrupts our youth." He rode through the America of Booth Tarkington and Norman Rockwell, of Main Streets and Union Memorials, of ice cream parlors and barber shop quartets.

"You got trouble right here in River City," he said in effect in every small town he stopped in, "and it's spelled Lyndon."[107] When a ten-year-old boy climbed up on the back platform and asked for an autograph in the middle of the senator's speech, Goldwater gladly interrupted himself. "Hi, boy," he said, signing the piece of paper thrust at him. "You never get anything unless you ask for it. That's why I'm asking to be president."

Goldwater was comfortable among these people and in good humor. "There's so much dirt under the White House rug," he told farmers, "it would qualify for the soil bank." To the women he said, "You housewives will be interested to know that in Washington in the stores now they have a new measure. It's called the Bobby Baker dozen. You get thirteen, but you have to kick back two."[108]

The crowds were good, the people enthusiastic, the media coverage voluminous, and the local politicians eager to ride a stop or two with a would-be president. Everyone had a good time, including Moira O'Connor, a pretty twenty-three-year-old brunette who said she was a freelance reporter but turned out to be a Democratic agent passing out copies of a newsletter, "Whistlestop," which made fun of the Goldwater tour. She was caught slipping the newsletter under compartment doors in the predawn hours by Vic Gold, Goldwater's assistant press secretary. "I think you may have made your last delivery, my dear," said Gold, a graduate of the University of Alabama and a devotee of old Hollywood movies.

The Goldwater staff put out a final edition of "Whistlestop" which reported gleefully that by purchasing the $225 ticket, the Democrats had been "contributing to the operation of the Goldwater campaign train."[109]

But all too soon the train ride was over, and it was time to leave the friendly Midwest behind and jet back to Washington and face the probability of a crushing defeat by a man for whom Goldwater had little affection and less respect.

15

Waiting for the Landslide

BARRY GOLDWATER HAD NEVER LOST an election, but with one month to go in this campaign, he had to confront the certainty that he was about to receive the political trouncing of his life, going down in history as one of the biggest losers in presidential politics. Although he was climbing slowly in the Gallup and other public polls (up from the low twenties in July to the low thirties by early October—his own confidential polls showed him a few points higher), it was unlikely he would reach 40 percent by election day. He could, in fact, fall short of hapless Alf Landon, who received 36.5 percent against FDR in 1936, or James M. Cox, with his 34 percent against Warren Harding in 1920.

Grimly, he recalled that when he was considering whether to challenge John Kennedy, he had said that rather than risk hurting the burgeoning conservative movement, he would not declare his candidacy unless he believed he could win at least 45 percent of the popular vote. Now it seemed that he would be fortunate to win 40 percent, and the polls foreshadowed an even worse beating in the electoral college.

He had hoped to enlist the forgotten American, "the man who pays taxes, the man who works, the man who stays out of trouble," in his crusade for freedom at home and abroad. Instead, he wound up running not against Johnson but against himself, or, rather, against the cruelly

316

false image created by Rockefeller and Scranton in the primaries and magnified by Johnson in the general election. His theme, "In Your Heart, You Know He's Right," was turned inside out by his opponents to read, "In Your Gut, You Know He's Nuts." At every rally, taunting placards proclaimed: "Goldwater in 1864" and "Back to the Store in '64." Hoots and jeers greeted him everywhere, some spontaneous, some planned by the Anti-Campaign in the White House. As Theodore White wrote, so efficient was the dirty tricks operation that sometimes refutations of a Goldwater speech appeared in local papers before he had delivered it.[1]

Johnson constantly played on public fears that Goldwater would propel the nation into war, as at a New Orleans rally when he echoed the words of Rockefeller's H-bomb brochure in the California primary. "By a thumb on a button," Johnson warned, "you can wipe out 300 million lives in a matter of moments." This was no time and no hour and no day, he declared, "to be rattling your rockets around or clicking your heels like a storm trooper. . . . Whose thumb do you want edging up that way?"[2]

This was uttered when plans were under active consideration in the Pentagon to enlarge U.S. participation in a war that Johnson kept insisting did not need a greater American presence. As *The Pentagon Papers* later revealed, high-level officials of the Johnson administration reached a "general consensus" in the first week of September that direct air attacks against North Vietnam would probably have to be launched early in 1965—the very policy Goldwater was advocating and Johnson was denouncing. On September 28, 1964, Johnson said, "We are not going North and drop bombs at this stage of the game," knowing that the operative phrase was "at this stage of the game." Among the other measures being actively considered by the administration were deploying American ships in Vietnamese waters, using air reconnaissance over Laos, instigating "deliberately provocative actions," and enlisting the help of Southeast Asian allies to isolate North Vietnam.[3]

Because he and Johnson had agreed not to make a partisan political issue out of Vietnam at their White House meeting in July, Goldwater said little about the war, beyond urging the president to give the American people a complete picture of what was happening in Southeast Asia. In retrospect, he regretted making the agreement: "Had Johnson and I squared off on the issue, the president might have revealed his intention to escalate the conflict without a military plan or diplomatic policy to win it. We might have saved many American lives."[4]

When it seemed that the anti-Goldwater campaign could sink no deeper in calumny, the September-October issue of *Fact* magazine appeared, with its cover trumpeting in large black letters: "1,189 Psychiatrists Say Goldwater Is Psychologically Unfit to Be President!" A questionnaire had been sent to 12,356 psychiatrists in the United States asking, "Do you believe Barry Goldwater is psychologically fit to serve as president of the United States?"

As it turned out, nearly ten thousand psychiatrists refused to participate in such a farce, but 2,417 responded, with 571 saying, properly, that they did not know enough about Goldwater to answer the question. That left 1,189 who said they thought Goldwater was not psychologically fit—without having questioned him or followed any of the other normal procedures in a physician-client relationship. Another 657 respondents said the senator was psychologically fit.[5] In its analysis of the poll, *Fact* liberally quoted psychiatrists who compared Goldwater with Hitler and Stalin, described him as "paranoid," "megalomaniacal," "unstable," "dangerous," and "a mass murderer at heart."[6]

To their credit, the president and the medical director of the American Psychiatric Association wrote jointly that "by attaching the stigma of extreme political partisanship to the psychiatric profession as a whole in the heated climate of the current political campaign, *Fact* has in effect administered a low blow to all who would advance the treatment and care of the mentally ill of America." The president of the American Medical Association, Dr. Donovan F. Ward, described the *Fact* attack as an "exercise in yellow journalism and scientific irresponsibility."[7]

The news media, however, did not exhibit the same professionalism. The *New York Times* and other major newspapers published full-page *Fact* ads trumpeting that Goldwater was "psychologically unfit to be president." They were well aware that Ralph Ginzburg, editor and publisher of the grotesquely named *Fact,* had been convicted in a federal court of printing and distributing pornography and was currently out on bail.[8]

Some journalists used the *Fact* "survey" as an excuse to bring up Goldwater's "nervous breakdown" in the 1930s, when he was the very young president of Goldwaters and working night and day to keep the family store going during the Depression. Holmes Alexander, a veteran syndicated columnist, traveled to Phoenix where he examined Goldwater's past medical record, interviewed his personal physician, and concluded that the senator had never suffered any kind of mental problem. His most convincing evidence was Goldwater's Air Force medical report. "No man with a history of mental instability or a tendency toward a nervous breakdown," Alexander wrote, "is certified by the Air Force to fly a Mach 2 aircraft, and each year the senator had passed with flying colors the intensive medical and psychometric examination given to Air Force pilots."[9]

Although he put behind him most of the distortions of the 1964 campaign, Goldwater did not forget *Fact* magazine's political pornography. He filed a suit for libel against Ginzburg and his magazine, describing the article as "false, scandalous and defamatory." A libel judgment of $1 in compensatory damages and $75,000 in punitive damages was awarded by a U.S. District Court jury in southern New York in 1968 and upheld by the U.S. Circuit Court in New York City the following year. In 1970, the Supreme Court, by 5–2, denied a request by Ginzburg to review the case. The judgment was rare, for under Supreme Court libel standards, a public figure has to prove actual malice to win a judgment against a newspaper or magazine; i.e., prove that an article was printed with reckless disregard of its truth or falseness or with the knowledge that the article was false.[10]

Throughout 1964, the Goldwater team debated how to handle the nuclear issue, and never came up with a solution. Said Denison Kitchel, "When I went to bed, if ever I could have just a few hours sleep, I would lie awake asking myself at night, how do you get at the bomb issue? My candidate had been branded a bomb-dropper—and I couldn't figure how to lick it. And the advertising people, people who could sell anything, toothpaste or soap or automobiles—when it came to a political question like this, they couldn't offer anything either."[11]

Although the television program with Eisenhower was supposed to eliminate these fears, Ike only said that talk of Goldwater's desire to use an atomic bomb was "tommyrot." What was needed was a convincing response by Goldwater himself, akin to John Kennedy's dramatic confrontation with the Protestant ministers in Houston in 1960, following which the nation knew "where he stood on Church and State."[12] The nation was far from reassured by speeches in which Goldwater mentioned nuclear weapons, war, destruction, and "holocaust" twenty-six times in as many minutes.[13]

The false charges about his psychological unfitness, racism, and nuclear brinkmanship deeply hurt Goldwater. The long days and nights seemed even longer when faced by this unrelenting hostility. In his 1988 memoirs, Goldwater talks about the life of a presidential candidate:

> Denny Kitchel used to sit down with me at 2 A.M., and we'd begin battling over the same old subject—the daily schedule. I was going from a 7 A.M. television interview to an 8 A.M. breakfast and speech to a 9 A.M. outdoor rally and speech in the center of downtown Billings, Montana, to a 10 A.M. flight to Cheyenne, Wyoming, with a noon rally and speech on the state Capitol grounds followed by a 12:30 lunch with leading towns-folk, with a news conference to follow. We were to take off for Denver at 1:30 with an airport rally and news conference before heading to Albuquerque for a 4 P.M. news conference, a 6 P.M. dinner speech, and an outdoor speech at the University of New Mexico at 8 P.M. A strategy session would begin at 9 P.M., followed by finance, advertising, and speechwriting conferences. As I told Kitchel a few dozen times, "You guys are killing me." [14]

With some four weeks to go, it was clear that Goldwater could not overcome: the emotional attachment of the people to the martyred John Kennedy and his successor Lyndon Johnson, the bitterly divided Republican party, the juggernaut efficiency of the Johnson campaign, and the distorted coverage of the news media. As Goldwater said years later, "If I didn't know Goldwater in 1964 and I had to depend on the press, I'd have voted against the son of a bitch myself." [15]

That Goldwater was a different kind of politician was definitively demonstrated in his handling of the Walter Jenkins scandal. If any other presidential candidate had been speaking for weeks about the corruption in Washington and the need for morality in government, and his opponent's longtime personal assistant was arrested for committing a homosexual act in the YMCA, two blocks from the White House, he would have taken full and prompt advantage of the incident. Any other candidate would have pointed an accusing finger, called for a congressional investigation, ordered up a couple of TV commercials, and told his staff to squeeze the issue dry. In truth, Dean Burch and others in the inner circle wanted to do just that. But Goldwater had known Jenkins as a member of the Air Force Reserve Unit on Capitol Hill he commanded, and he refused to add to the pain of Jenkins' family. He remained silent, leaving the occupants of the White House deeply puzzled. As he later wrote ironically:

> Here was the cowboy who shot from the hip, the Scrooge who would put the penniless on the street with no Social Security, the maniac who would blow us and our little children into the next kingdom in a nuclear Armageddon. If he would kill a million men and women, why wouldn't he destroy one individual? Why was the extremist pursuing moderation?[16]

Jenkins was arrested on a charge of "disorderly conduct" on Wednesday, October 7, but no reporter checked the police blotter, and forty-eight hours passed before someone leaked the story to the Republican National Committee. Monday, five days later, Goldwater was informed, but he said nothing, and instructed his campaign organization to do likewise. Sometime on Monday, the story reached the *Chicago Tribune* and the *Cincinnati Enquirer* (both supporters of Goldwater), which decided (in those pre-Watergate days) not to publish it. But the *Washington Star* (an anti-Goldwater paper) learned of the arrest on Tuesday and on Wednesday morning, October 14, a full week after the arrest, called the White House to check the story.

Jenkins immediately contacted Abe Fortas, an old friend of his and the president's, who telephoned Clark Clifford, Truman's former top political aide. Together, Fortas and Clifford visited the offices of three Washington newspapers, begging editors not to publish the story on compassionate grounds, to spare the forty-six-year-old Jenkins, his wife, and six children. The two Democrats insisted that they were not speaking on behalf of the White House, but such well-known loyalists could not be separated from their party and their president. Reluctantly, the editors agreed to delay the story, but it was too late for a coverup— too many people now knew about the episode. During the day, Fortas and Clifford discovered that Jenkins had been arrested for a similar act in 1959; the earlier charge read, succinctly, "pervert."[17]

Learning of the Fortas-Clifford interventions with newspaper editors, an angry Dean Burch persuaded Goldwater to let him issue a one-sentence statement late in the afternoon: "The White House is desperately trying to suppress a major news story affecting the national security." At 8 P.M., Wednesday, October 14, the United Press finally broke the news logjam with a story about the arrest. As Theodore White put it, "the nation, in mid-campaign, had to face the fact that the president's personal assistant, an attendant at National Security Council meetings, master of the inner chambers of the White House, was a sexual deviant."[18]

There was no immediate statement from President Johnson, who was campaigning in New York City, but the following day, the White House announced Jenkins' resignation as special assistant to the president and the appointment of Bill Moyers as his successor. It was later revealed that one of Johnson's first actions when he heard the startling news about his longtime aide and friend was to order Oliver Quayle, his personal pollster, to conduct an overnight public survey. After Quayle reported on Thursday morning that the scandal would have little bearing on the election, Johnson issued a statement of sympathy for Jenkins, who "has worked with me faithfully for twenty-five years" with "dedication, devotion and tireless labor."[19] Johnson always kept his political priorities in order.

But Quayle might have been wrong. Officials of both parties agreed that it was "a severe setback to the Democratic campaign." As one leading Republican put it, the arrest of Johnson's aide "accented the whole Bobby Baker corruption mess, which is Barry Goldwater's strongest issue."[20] Although not enough to overturn Johnson's wide lead (an October Harris poll showed 60 percent for Johnson, 34 percent for Goldwater, 6 percent undecided), the hard evidence of immorality in the White House could have swung many voters.

But within forty-eight hours the Jenkins case was swept from the front pages by the sensational news that Nikita Khrushchev had been replaced as dictator of the Soviet Union, Communist China had exploded its first nuclear bomb, and the Conservative party of Great Britain had been defeated after thirteen years in power. As always in a time of external crisis, the nation rallied around its president who responded with an impressive televised address to the nation on Sunday, October 18, only three days in ordinary time since Walter Jenkins had resigned, but a light year in political time.

Speaking somberly but reassuringly, Lyndon Johnson told the American people what they wanted to hear—that regardless of the great and dramatic changes, the United States was capable of holding "the balance firm against danger." He had told the Soviet ambassador, he said, that "the quest for peace in America" had never been more determined. He concluded by repeating what he had said eleven months before when he had assumed the presidency:

> We must be ready to defend the national interest and to negotiate the common interest. That is the path that we shall continue to pursue. Those who test our courage will find it strong, and those who seek our friendship will find it honorable. We will demonstrate anew that the strong can be just in the use of strength, and the just can be strong in the defense of justice.[21]

It was a masterful performance, Kennedy-like in its rhetoric, subtle in its reference to a nuclear test ban that Goldwater had voted against, shrewd in its mixture of strength-keeping and peace-making, and inspired in its marriage of force and justice. After this speech by Johnson, the campaign, for all practical purposes, was over. Rising to the occasion, Johnson had eschewed partisanship and presented himself as a firm but not belligerent president and commander-in-chief. All that remained in question was the margin of victory.

IN THE FINAL two weeks of the campaign, Johnson was in turn evangelist, master of ceremonies, salesman, cheerleader, and demagogue as he exhorted every audience to vote Democratic on November 3. On a six-mile motorcade into Denver from the airport, he yelled to crowds along the road, "Come on down to the speakin'. I want you all there. There's gonna be a hot time in the old town tonight. It's Democrats all the way. We're going to have a party. You don't have to dress. Just bring your kids and your dogs and anything." To a predominantly black crowd at one stop, Johnson shouted, "This is the most important decision of your life. You look after me at the polls November 3 and I'll look after you for the next four years." In New Orleans, he revealed his affinity for Huey Long, commenting, "The things that I am talking about from coast to coast are the things that he talked about thirty years ago." After equating Long and John F. Kennedy—as unlikely a couple as can be found in American politics—the president continued, "Their voices are still tonight but they have left some to carry on, and as long as the Good Lord permits me, I am going to carry on." In Peoria, he urged the Illinois State Federation of Labor to get out the vote: "You and I have a job to do on November 3, and we are going to do that job. The first job is to get back home, quit our big talk and bragging, get down to work, and get our friends and our uncles and our cousins and our aunts to the polls and elect Lyndon Johnson by the greatest landslide in history!"

Wherever he saw people assembled, Johnson would shout, "Vote Democratic on November 3. Vote to save your Social Security from going down the drain. Vote to keep a prudent hand which will not mash that nuclear button. I want you all to come to my inauguration next January."[22]

Once, although he insisted that he never campaigned on Sunday or in an opponent's state, he stopped off in Phoenix on Sunday to "go to church." The president made nineteen speeches on the way from the airport to the church, arriving two hours late to find the minister standing in front of the church and the congregation waiting inside. As the presidential limousine pulled to a stop, Johnson yelled through a bullhorn at the crowd: "Sorry, I've got to go now, folks, I'm late for church." As Kenneth O'Donnell says, "If it hadn't been for Goldwater, [the press would] have just murdered him."[23]

Johnson was most two-faced when talking about Vietnam. "There are those that say," he charged, obviously referring to Goldwater, "you ought to go North and drop bombs to try to wipe out the supply lines. . . . We don't want our American boys to do the fighting for Asian boys." That Goldwater had never proposed the use of U.S. troops made no difference. Again, only ten days before the election, Johnson, who would send more than half a million U.S. servicemen to Vietnam, vowed, "We are not about to send American boys nine or ten thousand miles away from home to do what Asian boys ought to be doing to protect themselves."[24]

GOLDWATER WAS fatalistic as he waited for the landslide. One observer described the mood of his campaign jet as "a jolly wake." His seat on the B-27 plane faced forward against a bulkhead with three clocks (showing the different time zones) and two signs: "Re-Elect Goldwater in 1968" and "Better Brinkmanship than Chickenship."[25] For the last two weeks of his campaign, he scheduled a swing through California and Texas, a speech in Madison Square Garden, a tour through the South and the Midwest, a day in Pennsylvania, a closing rally in San Francisco where he had been nominated, and a final last speech in Fredonia, Arizona, where he had wound up his two winning Senate campaigns. He also took time to thank personally the staff of the Republican National Committee and Citizens for Goldwater-Miller for all they had done for him and for the conservative cause.

Early Monday morning, October 19, Goldwater shook hands with about six hundred workers and then, after watery scrambled eggs and salty bacon, gave an amusing, confident report. He looked tanned and trim and, despite a slight hoarseness, which he doctored with frequent sips of water, sounded fine. He described the enthusiastic and youthful crowds that, in the last ten days, he said, had been growing significantly. He spoke of the first egg thrown at him and reported that Johnson had a new radio program, "Me, the People." He promised to send LBJ back to "his little ole farm to drive his little ole Continental and throw those little ole beer cans around." He described the crowds at Youngstown and Lubbock and the five thousand volunteers in Los Angeles "we don't know what to do with," and he concluded, "We are going to win." The workers cheered and he smiled, although he knew and some of them knew they were not. But defeat was the one thing an honorable candidate did not talk about or try to think about, except perhaps at three o'clock in the morning.[26]

There were still many miles to travel and many speeches to give. In a nationally televised address, he discussed the "terrifying" deterioration of the home, the family, and the community, of law and order, and of good morals and manners, and blamed it on thirty years of modern liberalism. After all, he said, revealing his traditionalist rather than libertarian side:

It is the modern "liberal" who supports education for "life-adjustment" and fosters permissiveness in the school and the home.

It is the modern "liberal" who regards discipline and punishment as barbaric relics of a discredited past.

It is the modern "liberal" who seeks to eliminate religious sentiment from every aspect of public life.

It is the modern "liberal" who is concerned for the criminal and careless about his victims . . . who frowns on the policeman and fawns on the social psychologist.

It is the modern "liberal" who regards our children as educational guinea pigs. . . .[27]

Down to the very last day, Goldwater remained an Old Testament prophet, warning the people to change their ways, urging the government "to let my people go." He knew full well the political price of his rhetoric, but he would not change his message.

Speaking in East St. Louis, he wondered aloud whether people thought he did not know what views would be most popular, "what housewives and diplomats and white collar workers want to hear." He knew, of course, what to say to get votes, but he would not say it for two reasons. First, "if I just went around telling people what they wanted to hear, I'd sound like Lyndon Baines Johnson. And I still think the American people are entitled to a choice." But more important, "if I had to cater to every special interest in the country to get elected, I wouldn't want the job."[28]

Instead, he chose to present his vision of America. He wanted to see a nation and a people "prosperous, free, secure, and progressive" through "the free enterprise and individual liberty upon which this nation was founded." Once before, he pointed out, a great, self-governing people gave up their liberty and placed themselves in the hands of their leader, trading their votes for "bread and circuses," trading their Senate for an emperor. The Romans, he said, "lost their nation when they traded away their freedom." He reminded his audience that there was one freedom, and *only one freedom*, on which America had been founded—"freedom from government—from too much, oppressive government."[29] It was to preserve that freedom that he was offering his candidacy.

GOLDWATER'S IDEAS and programs deserved to be discussed and debated, but Johnson preferred to warn against people who went around "rattling their rockets" or clicking their heels "like a storm trooper," all the while piously proclaiming, "I don't believe in muckraking or slanderous comments or mudslinging." In Columbia, South Carolina, he recalled the presidential campaigns from Woodrow Wilson to John F. Kennedy and Richard Nixon, and added, "But none of these men tried to split our country wide open, none of these men preached hate."[30]

Even the pro-Johnson *New York Times* was moved to complain about the president's adamant refusal to address the issues: "Rarely in modern times and never in recent years has there been such a campaign in which the issues facing the nation have been so inadequately discussed by the two leading candidates."[31] The object of the *Times'* criticism was clear; no one could fault Goldwater for not trying to engage Johnson in a debate.

Goldwater took presidential politics into previously unexplored territory by listing categories of people whose votes he did *not* want— bigots, communists, and radical left-wingers. Nor, he told an Illinois crowd, did he want "the lazy, dole-happy people who want to feed on the fruits of somebody else's labor" or "the socialist, ADA-type followers of Hubert Horatio Humphrey," or those "who don't care if the Social Security system goes bankrupt as long as it keeps making more and more unkeepable promises," or those "who are willing to believe that communism can be accommodated."

As a conservative and an American, Goldwater wanted the votes of people who believed in the Declaration of Independence and the Constitution, who rejected promises of something for nothing, whose votes couldn't be bought.[32] Most of all, he said, he wanted those who knew that "*something must be done*" about an America in which the federal government "will tell you what business you can be in," whether your children can pray in school, and what to charge "for the things you sell." "Let's get our country back!" he snapped, and the faithful cheered, and the band played one last chorus of "The Battle Hymn of the Republic," and the TV cameras were turned off, and there were only four days left in a campaign that everyone, except perhaps Lyndon Johnson, wanted over.

POLITICAL CAMPAIGNS, especially losing campaigns, do strange things to people. Normally rational men and women, frustrated and fatigued, begin acting irrationally. They eat the wrong things, they drink too much, they rarely get a good night's sleep. They lose their temper, they contradict themselves, they make mistakes. They keep saying they can win when they know in their hearts they will lose. Their minds are on automatic pilot, and their reflexes are like mashed potatoes, but they cannot stop until election day, no matter what the polls say. When the presidency is at stake, the highest stake of all, and it becomes clear that the candidate is going to lose more badly than any other presidential candidate in history, the candidate and his coterie are profoundly affected.

Denison Kitchel, who was a corporate lawyer and not a politician of any kind, doggedly stuck to the first rule of law: when in doubt, say no.

Sometimes he was right, as when he opposed the showing of the documentary film "Choice," and sometimes he was wrong, as when he raised questions about airing Ronald Reagan's electrifying TV address, "A Time for Choosing." Although he was supposed to act as a bridge between the politicians and the eggheads at national headquarters, Kitchel was almost always with the candidate, preventing him from blowing up at people, places, and things. As he explained, "Barry's a difficult man to handle . . . he has a short fuse." One of the very few people Goldwater did not jump on was Kitchel because "I'd come right back at him." Kitchel was usually the last one to see him at the end of a campaign day—"we'd spend an hour or two and he'd blow off steam and I'd tell him to go to hell."[33] But unfamiliar with Washington as well as national politics, Kitchel depended heavily upon William J. Baroody.

On leave from the presidency of the American Enterprise Institute, Baroody controlled the speechwriting and the content of the national television programs. An intellectual who reveled in the Washington power game, he had never before participated in, let alone managed, a political campaign. He not only agreed with Richard Weaver that ideas have consequences but believed they were all that were needed to win a campaign. Paul Wagner, the campaign press secretary, said about the speeches produced by Baroody and his team, "They were exceptionally good as classical documents, but not as political speeches to the American people."[34]

Many years later, Kitchel described Baroody as a "Svengali," so possessive about his position that he contrived to exclude prominent conservatives from the campaign. But Kitchel and Goldwater allowed Baroody to play almost any role he wanted in 1964. In his 1988 memoirs, Goldwater protests that there was never "any effort" on his part to keep Bill Buckley or other conservatives out. But, among other instances, Buckley was prevented from speaking at a rally during the Republican convention in San Francisco, and Robert Bauman, the national chairman of the Young Americans for Freedom, was rejected as the head of Youth for Goldwater-Miller because he and YAF were perceived as too far right.[35]

Baroody, in short, was a brilliant idea merchant and think tank president but a woefully inexperienced politician. Busy with managing the candidate, Kitchel and Baroody turned over the day-to-day running of the campaign to Dean Burch.

Although he too had no previous national political experience, Burch turned out to be a superb manager who transformed the old headquarters of the Republican National Committee into a model of modern communications and organization. He set up a map-and-chart room to rival the Map Room of the White House, teletype machines that could transmit up to eight thousand words an hour, a "Go-out" chart to track the location of anyone leaving the office, biweekly national polls by Opinion Research, Sunday afternoon strategy meetings, and more.

Unfortunately, neither Goldwater nor Miller ever attended any of the strategy meetings, creating a "critical gap."[36] Burch tried so hard to fill this and other gaps that by the end of the campaign, he was numb with fatigue and angry at the analyses (based on local newspaper reports and political observers) prepared by Jay Hall and Pam Rymer that showed Goldwater losing in state after state by larger and larger margins. Burch had traveled with the candidate, he had seen the large enthusiastic crowds, and he refused, point-blank, to believe they meant nothing. Richard Thompson, an assistant to Hall and Rymer, recalls that Burch came into their office in mid-October and declared, "I know we are on the verge of victory."[37] Shortly thereafter, he halted the circulation of the negative and, to him, misleading Hall-Rymer reports.

Clif White watched the presidential race from the sidelines. Only once did he attempt seriously to affect the course of the campaign, with the documentary film called "Choice." He was inspired by Goldwater's continuing argument that there was a "sickness of spirit" in America and that "when morals collapse, they don't collapse upward, they collapse downward."

Goldwater charged that lack of national leadership had "turned our streets into jungles, brought our public and private morals into the lowest state of our history, and turned out the lights even at the White House itself."[38] He spoke of the climbing divorce rates, juvenile delinquency, and street violence, and insisted that civil rights was fundamentally a moral issue, not a legal issue. "I charge with a sincerely heavy heart," he said in Minneapolis, "that the more the federal government has attempted to legitimate morality, the more it has incited hatreds and violence."[39]

In response to a query from White about "Choice," Goldwater sent the following message from his campaign plane: "Agree completely

with you on morality issue. Believe it is the most effective we have
come up with. Also agree with your program. Please get it launched
immediately."[40] "Choice" was filled with beer cans (Johnson's favorite), speeding black limousines (another LBJ favorite), white women in
topless bathing suits, drunken college students, and blacks rioting and
looting in the streets. Rus Walton, who produced the film along with
Robert Raisbeck, forthrightly explained the purpose of the film:

> To portray and remind the people of something they already know exists,
> and that is the moral crisis in America, the rising crime rate, rising
> juvenile delinquency, narcotics, pornography, filthy magazines. . . . We
> want to just make them mad, make their stomachs turn. . . . They will see
> all this on television, and there is only one way they can go, and that is
> with Goldwater. . . .[41]

"Choice" was scheduled to be shown nationally over NBC-TV at
2 P.M. Thursday, October 22. Dean Burch had not yet seen the film, but
journalists who had attended a preview arranged by the Democratic
National Committee were sharply critical of "Choice." Walton admitted that the documentary was "shocking" but "we believe what is
happening today in America is shocking."

On the day of its scheduled appearance, the Citizens Committee
announced that it was withdrawing the film temporarily at the senator's
request. That same day, while campaigning in Philadelphia, Goldwater
finally saw "Choice" and said flatly, "It can't be used." Although
there were an equal number of scenes of whites and blacks rioting, the
more violent scenes featured predominantly inner-city blacks.

On the morning of October 23, Goldwater publicly repudiated
"Choice," saying, "It's nothing but a racist film."[42] White and Walton
strongly protested that the film was about immorality in the United
States, but Goldwater, sensitive to charges of racism and bigotry, decided he could not offer their kind of "choice" to the American people.

In 1981, at a Washington breakfast reunion of the original Draft
Goldwater Committee, White announced that he wanted to show
"Choice." Goldwater, who was a special guest, said, "Okay, let's look
at that dirty movie." Afterward, he remarked, "I still think we were
right" not to show it.[43]

And then there was the vice presidential nominee, Congressman
William E. Miller of New York, personally picked by Goldwater be-

cause he believed Miller would "drive Johnson nuts" with his sarcasm and partisan attacks. But neither Johnson nor anyone else paid any attention to Miller, who soon decided that the most sensible thing he could do was to enjoy himself. At times, his campaign plane, "The Niagaran," resembled an airborne "Animal House." In his 1988 memoirs, Goldwater writes, almost wistfully, that "no campaign crew in history" (referring to Miller, his staff, and the news media covering him) "drank more booze, lost more laundry, or bet more money on card games."[44]

Miller was a skillful bridge player who won hundreds of dollars from reporters. Toward the end of the campaign, one of them said to Miller, "I'll bet you a hundred bucks you guys lose the election—and give you five to one odds." The never-to-be vice president never hesitated: "I may be a gambler, but I'm not crazy enough to bet on *this* election."

The one thing that everyone on the Bill Miller plane took seriously was the pursuit of pleasure. In between the singing and the drinking and the card-playing, Miller would occasionally get off the plane to make a short speech to a small crowd in an obscure town and then eagerly hop back on the plane.

The day after the election, Miller delivered these final telling words over the cabin microphone before flying back to Washington: "What we have said apparently was little noted by the electorate, and certainly will not be long remembered. But it is for us the living, not the dead drunk, to here resolve: that this government, of the birds, by the birds, and for the birds shall not continue on this earth."[45]

AND WHAT OF Goldwater himself as the campaign neared its end, and the Gallup Poll reported, with five days to go, that it was 64 percent for Johnson, 29 percent for Goldwater, and 7 percent undecided?[46] He often piloted "Yai Bi Kin," his official Boeing 727 campaign plane, "because it relaxed me." One day, flying back from Texas, he donned a magnificent white sombrero, draped a huge black-and-yellow-striped Mexican blanket over his shoulder, and gave away both items in a drawing to a lucky reporter. When the winner turned out to be Frank Cancellare, a very small Italian-American, who looked like a "Mexican Kewpie doll" in the enormous hat and brightly colored serape, Goldwater roared with laughter and rushed for his camera.[47]

Sometimes, he refused to make a speech or shake hands until Kitchel, the only one who could talk to him that way, would say sharply, "Damn it, Barry, you're a presidential candidate. Act like one!"[48] But Barry Goldwater could not and would not pretend that he was enjoying his own hanging. He remarked that it might be nice if "we could change this crazy system in this country whereby we have to campaign for months and months and months. How nice it would be if we could run a [six-week] campaign like they do in England and get it over with."[49] Goldwater compared his running for the presidency to flying with no wings or engine, gliding along on "the currents of public opinion—the cheers, the handshakes, the deafening roar in a big stadium." It was also like a "helluva bumpy ride with all four engines pumping, clouds behind and a storm ahead." He admitted that he popped off and shot from the lip, but he "was not about to let conservatism die of sleep and boredom."[50]

Indeed he was not. In Pikesville, Maryland, he said that four years of drift in foreign policy had led the nation "into Lyndon Johnson's war in Vietnam. . . . American sons and grandsons are being killed by communist bullets and communist bombs. And we have yet to hear a word of truth about why they're dying."

In New York City's Madison Square Garden (where Nelson Rockefeller was conspicuously absent), he accused "Lyndon Johnson and his curious crew" of "political Daddyism [which is as] old as demagogues and despotism." Some eighteen thousand conservatives clapped, cheered, chanted, stamped, and whistled for almost a half hour. In Pittsburgh (where William Scranton conspicuously introduced him), he charged that the State Department and Secretary Dean Rusk had "coddled the liars, the wiretappers, the brutal abusers of government power who tried to railroad" Otto F. Otepka, the department's chief of security who gave information to a congressional committee about lax State security.

In San Francisco, where several hundred thousand people filled downtown streets to cheer him on his way to the Cow Palace, he warned that a continuing shift of power to the federal government would result "in the ultimate destruction of American freedom."[51]

And in Columbia, South Carolina, during that final week, he discussed civil rights standing side-by-side with Strom Thurmond, the 1948 Dixiecrat candidate for president. Goldwater's words were the same he had used in his Chicago address, where he had condemned segregation and declared that government must treat "all men as equal in the areas of law and civil order." His forthright speech was televised on eighty-seven stations throughout the South. As John H. Kessel put it, the senator "never did yield to Southern pleas that he take a segregationist stand."[52]

ONE OF THE most curious, and revealing, actions taken by Goldwater in the entire campaign was when he tried to block what he himself described as "the best speech of the campaign."

Ronald Reagan first met Goldwater in the early 1950s at the home of his wife Nancy's parents in Phoenix and saw him often thereafter although they never became close friends. In truth, the two men had little in common beyond their beliefs: strong anticommunism, a profound dislike of government bureaucracy, and the intrinsic worth of the individual.

Goldwater came from a wealthy privileged background; his father owned department stores. The Reagans lived on the other side of the tracks; his father sold shoes. Goldwater was a Westerner and had all the outdoor qualities. He was energetic, individualistic, physically strong, stoic, tough, and rebellious. Reagan was a Midwesterner, also strong, determined, and independent, but more cautious, more controlled, more willing to listen and reflect before speaking or acting. Both men were reserved, even shy, but Reagan wanted people to like him while Goldwater did not care whether they did or not. Both were intelligent, intuitive men who could grasp the essence of a problem or a situation quickly; but Goldwater learned by reading while Reagan preferred to learn by listening.

Goldwater worked his way up the political ladder, from city council member to presidential candidate after years of hard work; Reagan started at the top, running for governor of California without ever having held public office. Goldwater's idea of a good time was a lively party with lots of booze and old friends; Reagan preferred to put on pajamas and watch a patriotic movie with his wife Nancy. Goldwater was from the start a Jeffersonian Republican; Reagan was an FDR Democrat turned conservative Republican. Goldwater was a political fissionist; Reagan a political fusionist.

In 1964, because of the circumstances that prevailed, Goldwater campaigned as though he preferred to be right rather than president; by

1980, after the failures of the Great Society and détente, Reagan proved it was possible to be both. In several respects, Reagan was Goldwater without the rough edges and the unrestrained rhetoric.

Whatever their personal differences, Reagan, as he writes in his autobiography, always admired Goldwater "greatly" and actively supported his candidacy for the presidency. *The Conscience of a Conservative*, he says, "contained a lot of the same points I'd been making in my speeches, and I strongly believed the country needed him."[53]

Reagan had become increasingly disillusioned with the Democrats. He finally registered as a Republican in 1962, although he had campaigned for every Republican candidate for president since 1952. "I thought we sorely needed Goldwater," Reagan wrote, ". . . I said I'd do anything I could to get him elected."[54] For Reagan, that meant making speeches, and he did, including one at the national convention in San Francisco when he was the master of ceremonies at a YAF rally for Goldwater.

During the late summer and fall, Reagan, now co-chairman of California Citizens for Goldwater-Miller, spoke at many fundraising functions. The most important of all, as it turned out, was to nearly one thousand Republicans at the Ambassador Hotel in Los Angeles. He gave essentially the same speech he had given for years as a spokesman for General Electric, altering it where necessary to fit 1964. Several prominent California Republicans, including oil businessman Henry Salvatori, asked if he would repeat his speech on national television if they could raise the money. "Sure," Reagan replied, "if you think it would do any good."[55] This was the genesis of the best speech of 1964, a speech that made Reagan a national political star overnight.

Reagan suggested that rather than repeating his remarks to a camera in a television studio, he deliver them to an audience in a campaign setting. Within a few days the money was raised for a half hour on NBC, and he filmed his speech before a group of invited Republicans, with Robert Raisbeck as the producer.

Then, a few days before the program was scheduled to be aired—on Tuesday, October 27, one week before election day—he received a telephone call from an "uneasy" and "uncomfortable" Goldwater. Some of his advisers, the senator said, were concerned about references in Reagan's speech to Social Security and wanted to rebroadcast in its place the Goldwater-Eisenhower program, "Conversation at Gettysburg." In fact, Kitchel and Baroody opposed the Reagan telecast because they felt it was too "emotional" and "unscholarly," revealing how little they understood about the art of politics. Here is the passage about Social Security that so agitated the inner circle:

> Now are we so lacking in business sense that we cannot put this program on a sound actuarial basis, so that those who do depend on it won't come to the cupboard and find it bare, and at the same time can't we introduce voluntary features so that those who can make better provisions for themselves are allowed to do so?[56]

Reagan's suggestions almost exactly paralleled Goldwater's long-held positions about Social Security. "Barry," said Reagan in a reassuring voice, "I've been making the speech all over the state for quite a while and I have to tell you, it's been very well received, including whatever remarks I've made about Social Security. I just can't cancel the speech and give away the airtime; it's not up to me. These gentlemen raised the money and bought the airtime. They're the only ones who could cancel or switch it."

"Well," said Goldwater, "I haven't heard or seen the speech yet. They've got a tape here, so I'll run it and call you back."

According to Reagan's older brother, Neil Reagan, who was traveling with Goldwater, the senator and members of his staff sat down and listened to an audiotape of the disputed speech. When it was over, Goldwater looked at everybody and said, "What the hell's wrong with that?" He immediately called Reagan and gave him the okay to go ahead.[57]

Yet Baroody and Kitchel (encouraged by the campaign's advertising agency that would realize no commission from its telecast) persisted in trying to derail the Reagan half hour, now suggesting that a more suitable substitute would be "Brunch with Barry," which featured Goldwater and half a dozen women talking about high prices and the growing dangers of the war in Vietnam. Baroody kept up the pressure until three hours before airtime on the evening of October 27, at which point Walter Knott, chairman of the Goldwater TV Committee, called from California and said, politely but firmly, that the national committee had better approve the Reagan telecast or find the money for their own program. Baroody reluctantly granted permission to air the television program that made political history.[58]

The program shifted tens, perhaps hundreds of thousands of votes. In addition to bringing in over \$600,000 immediately for the national campaign, it raised several million more dollars from constant rebroadcasts in the following week. It was called the "one bright spot in a dismal campaign" by *Time*. After it aired, General Eisenhower called the Republican National Committee from Walter Reed Hospital where he was undergoing routine tests to say it was "the best thing" he had seen in the campaign and to ask for a copy. David Broder and Stephen Hess called the speech "the most successful national political debut since William Jennings Bryan electrified the 1896 Democratic convention." But, according to Nancy Reagan, Goldwater never wrote her husband a thank-you note.[59]

Even further, although Goldwater praised the Reagan address in his 1988 memoirs, he also subtly undercut it, and its author, by writing:

> Reagan had already delivered ["A Time for Choosing"] in California. When our staff suggested I make a national fund-raising address like it, I didn't want to do it. The words just weren't me. I watched a film of Reagan delivering it and immediately phoned him and said, "That was an eloquent speech. You're more eloquent than I am. You do it."[60]

Reagan does not recall any such conversation with Goldwater. The reference to the speech as a "fund-raising address," moreover, is puzzling: "A Time for Choosing" was intended to stir viewers to vote for Goldwater, not to send money. The appeal for funds was tacked on at the end and not made by Reagan.

Goldwater has suggested on other occasions that the most important political speech Reagan ever gave was not of his own making. On the Saturday before Reagan's inauguration as president in January 1981, the senator told a luncheon meeting of the original Draft Goldwater group: "Now you fellows can see what happens when you give a speech away." Smiling, he implied that the Reagan speech had originally been written for him "but some of those damn words were just too long for me so I said give it to Ron Reagan."[61]

Why has Goldwater consistently given a misleading picture of one of the most significant events in Reagan's life? Perhaps because Reagan's address was extravagantly praised while his own speech-making efforts were often criticized for being flat and ineffective. Perhaps because more than a few conservatives, after seeing "A Time for Choosing," said that more televised speeches like it should have been delivered and maybe the wrong man had been nominated. Perhaps because if he had not delivered The Speech, Reagan would not have run for governor of California and begun the meteoric career that made him, not Barry Goldwater, the leader of the conservative movement within a decade. The telecast's impact on the politics of California has been confirmed by Henry Salvatori, who says flatly that he and other leading Republicans would not have approached Reagan to run for governor had it not been for "A Time for Choosing."[62]

In short, for one of the very few times in his life, Goldwater displayed jealousy. The man who did not give a damn what people thought cared deeply when it came to the leadership of the movement he had done so much to build.

Over the next two decades, the Goldwater-Reagan relationship alternated between cooperation and confrontation, with the senator doing much of the confronting, as when he endorsed Gerald Ford over Reagan in their bitter contest for the Republican nomination for president in 1976. According to General William Quinn, the senator's closest friend in Washington, Nancy Reagan was so angered by Goldwater's decision that she never invited him to an official function at the White House during the Reagans' years there.[63]

IN THE LATE afternoon of November 2, Goldwater delivered his last campaign speech in the small village of Fredonia, population three hundred, located on the Arizona-Utah border. There before people who knew and understood him—men in worn boots, Navaho and Paiute Indians with black hats—the senator talked softly about America and Americans and freedom. He talked about simple virtues and hardworking people like those who lived in Pipe Springs just down the road. He said:

> I think of the courage of those people who came here not knowing that the federal government could help them, but doing it on their own, standing off all kinds of abusive action, standing off the weather, but finally triumphing in raising cattle where cattle probably shouldn't have been raised, and living their lives as they felt God wanted them to. These are the things, the simple things that I have talked about, and I will continue to talk about as long as I live. . . .[64]

16

The Meaning of Defeat

ON NOVEMBER 3, 1964, Lyndon Johnson achieved his deepest wish. He won the presidency by the largest margin in history, receiving 43,126,218 votes to Barry Goldwater's 27,174,898. That was 61.05 percent of the popular vote; it beat the previous record of 60.79 percent set by FDR in 1936. (Both Gallup and Harris gave Johnson 64 percent of the vote in their closing estimates.)

The president carried 44 states for a total of 486 electoral votes; Goldwater won just 6 states (Alabama, Georgia, Mississippi, Louisiana, South Carolina, Arizona) and 52 electoral votes. Johnson carried with him 28 Democratic senators, for a total of 68 out of 100, a gain of 2 (although Paul Fannin retained Goldwater's seat in Arizona), and 295 Democratic congressmen, as against only 140 Republican congressmen, for a gain of 37 seats. It produced the biggest Democratic majority in the House of Representatives since the high point of the New Deal in 1936.

Among the staunch Goldwater conservatives who lost in the House were Katharine St. George and Steven B. Derounian of New York, Donald Brotzman of Colorado, Gene Snyder of Kentucky, George Goodling of Pennsylvania, Bruce Alger and Ed Foreman of Texas, Lou Wyman of New Hampshire, and Jack Westland of Washington. (Of fifty-four congressmen who formally endorsed Goldwater in June 1964, eighteen were defeated for reelection.)

In the upper house, incumbent Senator Kenneth Keating of New York (who disavowed Goldwater) lost to Democratic challenger Robert Kennedy, and Robert Taft, Jr. (who refused to disavow Goldwater) lost to incumbent Democratic Senator Stephen Young of Ohio. One Goldwater Republican did capture a Democratic Senate seat—former Hollywood actor George Murphy beat short-term incumbent Pierre Salinger.

Republicans advanced in only one area; they added one governor to their previous sixteen for a total of seventeen. But they lost over five hundred seats in the state legislatures and control of both houses in twelve states.

Johnson carried every geographical region, and decisively, except the Deep South, and every voting group except Republicans. Men and women, white and nonwhite, high school and college graduate, blue collar and white collar, under thirty and over fifty years, all voted for LBJ by generally wide margins. In the 108-year history of the Republican party, only two presidential candidates received a lower percentage of the popular vote than Goldwater's 38.5 percent—John C. Fremont, the GOP's first standard-bearer in 1856, and Alf Landon in 1936.

Although all three networks predicted a landslide victory for Johnson by 9 P.M. Eastern Standard Time (NBC first declared Johnson the winner at 6:48 P.M., four hours and twelve minutes before the polls in California closed) it was well after 1 A.M., Texas time, before a triumphant president stood with his wife and two daughters before a cheering crowd in Austin and said that his overwhelming election was "a mandate for unity, for a government that serves no special interest . . . but a government that provides equal opportunity for all and special privileges for none." Of the size of his historic victory, Johnson said only, "I doubt that there has ever been so many people seeing so many things alike on decision day."[1]

That morning, Goldwater had voted at the Phoenix Country Day School and when asked by reporters whether he had split his ticket, replied, "I always split it"—independent to the end.[2] That night, he watched the early returns with his family and a few friends (including Kitchel, Hess, and Fannin) in his home, not at the official headquarters at the Camelback Inn. He had indicated that he would have an election night statement, but he changed his mind and went to bed at eleven o'clock when it was obvious he had been trounced. Hess recalls that everyone but the senator was crying.[3]

A press aide told reporters that Goldwater would have nothing to say until the next day because "he wants to analyze the vote." Goldwater's silence was disappointing. Losing presidential candidates are expected to make gracious, timely concession speeches, not brood in their mountaintop homes. But Goldwater ended the campaign as he began it— doing things his way, regardless of what others thought.

The following morning, he got up early as usual and began building a color television set. He also sent the president a nominally congratulatory but still defiant telegram:

> Congratulations on your victory. I will help you in any way I can toward achieving a growing and better America and a secure and dignified peace. The role of the Republican party will remain in that temper but it also remains the party of opposition when opposition is called for. There is much to be done in Vietnam, Cuba, and [about] the problem of law and order in this country, and a productive economy. Communism remains our No. 1 obstacle to peace and I know that all Americans will join with you in honest solutions to these problems.[4]

By the time he held a news conference that afternoon, he had regained his composure. He said he intended to devote his time to strengthening the Republican party and that he did not think his defeat had hurt the conservative cause. This exchange followed:

> QUESTION: Have the Republican voters not shared in repudiating this philosophy you say the party must cling to?
> GOLDWATER: Well, unfortunately I think you're right—that my defeat to some degree, although, I would not say a major degree, was occasioned by Republicans in this country who did not vote for the—or work, I should say—for the top of the ticket. Now this is in direct contrast to times when the conservatives did not win at the convention, when we would go out and work our hearts out for the more liberal or moderate members of the Republican party.
> But I don't—this is not a repudiation. This was announced. They announced as soon as the convention was over, and I think they're entitled to do what they want, but I don't think we can build a Republican party on their concepts, which in my opinion have no difference with the Democratic concepts.[5]

Goldwater was understandably tired and not too precise in his language. But his fundamental point was clear: notwithstanding his defeat, he still believed that the future of the Republican party lay with conservatism, not liberal me-tooism.

To understand how he could say something that seemed absurd to most political observers and why most conservatives agreed with him, it is necessary to understand why he lost.

First, a political fact: *no* Republican could have defeated Johnson after the assassination of John F. Kennedy. The American people wanted to give the new president a chance to carry out his and the martyred president's programs. They were in no mood to put another new man in the White House, especially when times were good. As Bill Buckley wrote, "The Archangel Gabriel running on the Republican ticket probably could not [have won]."[6] Goldwater might have defeated Kennedy, but he could not defeat his ghost.

Second, Johnson and his team conducted a highly effective campaign; the Goldwater organization did not. From the beginning, the senator campaigned defensively because of the extremist label pinned on him by fellow Republicans. He was a warmonger; Johnson was a peacekeeper. He was a radical; Johnson was a moderate. When Goldwater insisted on trying to set the record straight, he only called attention to the fact that something was apparently wrong. In the end, he decided to run a nonpolitical campaign against the most political campaigner in modern history.

Third, unlike the election of 1952, when Taft conservatives worked hard for Eisenhower in the fall, liberals who wanted Rockefeller or Scranton in 1964 did not unite behind Goldwater. Accustomed to getting their way for nearly three decades, liberals could not bring themselves to accept a conservative nominee. Rockefeller usually found he had to be somewhere else when Goldwater came to New York, and Scranton campaigned alongside Goldwater only within the boundaries of Pennsylvania. Only Nixon campaigned extensively for the party's standard-bearer, calculating that he would earn the gratitude, and support, of conservatives when he himself ran again. The political ostracism was extreme: in some states, including New York, Goldwater-Miller literature was never unpacked, let alone distributed.

Fourth, the news media were tilted decisively against Goldwater and etched into the minds of Americans a distorted image of the Republican challenger. While reporters like Charles Mohr of the *New York Times* and Robert Pierpoint of CBS have argued that the media were fair, Dave Broder (then of the *Washington Star)* and Ben Bradlee (then of *Newsweek)* have spent hours debating "why we didn't do justice to Goldwater's run for the presidency." Columnist James Jackson Kilpatrick has suggested that journalists speak more reasonably about conservatives today "because the conservative movement has risen to respectability and power" in America. Broadcaster Howard K. Smith said that the media treated Goldwater better once he had lost because he was "no longer a threat to the liberal establishment."[7]

Fifth, and perhaps most important, the American people were not ready to admit that the New Deal, the Fair Deal, the New Frontier, and the Great Society were fundamentally flawed concepts of modern government. In fairness, the premise that for every societal problem there is a governmental solution seemed reasonable in 1964. It took years for the failures of the Great Society and its successors to become evident.[8] To the voters of 1964, Barry Goldwater seemed a lonely, some said loony, voice ordering progress to stop.

One of the best analyses of campaign mistakes was made by Deputy Campaign Director John Grenier in a letter to the senator two months after the debacle. Candid as the candidate, he made the following points:

(1) Goldwater should not have entered the New Hampshire primary because he had not yet made the psychological adjustment from running against Kennedy to running against Johnson. After making several verbal errors in New Hampshire, which gave credence to the liberal charge that he was "trigger happy," he overreacted by restricting himself too much to speeches written by others. The result "was that you tended to be withdrawn, which gave an impression of being cold, and unfeeling."

(2) The failure to offer an olive branch at the national convention "was an error." Specifically, the Romney amendment on extremism should have been adopted and the acceptance speech should have stressed the theme that the Republican party was "a tent big enough for all." A quarter of a century later, Lee Atwater, another young, tough Southern politician, would urge Republicans to adopt a Big Tent policy.

(3) Although the final tally could not have been "altered substantially," a more effective campaign could have carried several more

states. The principal mistakes were as follows: First, the failure "to designate any one person to act as a campaign manager." As a result, there was no real coordination between public relations and finance until October. Second, the "nonpolitical," issues-led campaign placed too large a burden on the voter to perceive "your true position" on things like Social Security and nuclear weapons, given the hostile news media. That the voters never understood where Goldwater truly stood on the issues was proven by their "unreasoning fear"—the primary factor in his defeat. Third, the public relations effort "was almost a total failure" because Lou Guylay and the advertising people were inadequately directed and did not understand the "dynamic forces underlying the conservative movement."

For all the mistakes and the sharp pain of defeat, Grenier concluded, a "tremendous service" had been rendered to the conservative movement and to the nation. He spelled out the benefits that would be felt for decades to come:

> The conservative forces of the nation have finally been rallied into a cohesive force as a result of your defining the principles for which they stand. Also, the two-party system is now a reality in the South; history will not be concerned with motives of the Southern vote, only that from 1964 onward a Republican can run equally with a Democrat without the insurmountable obstacle of prior party prejudice. This was an essential step in positioning the GOP to win nationally in view of its decline in the East and Middle Atlantic over the past thirty years.[9]

Such far-sighted analysis was rare in the days following Goldwater's defeat. Most of the talk circled around the enormity of the president's victory. Johnson won every category of voter by margins ranging from a whopping 94–6 percent among blacks to a surprisingly narrow 52–48 percent among college graduates. He carried Catholics by 76–24 percent, Independents by 56–44 percent (closer than many expected), voters under thirty years of age by 64–36 percent, and manual workers (heavily influenced by organized labor) by 71–29 percent.

Johnson won seven of eight geographical regions, excepting only the deep South. The ten states of the old Confederacy were the only regional group to go for Goldwater, but by the narrowest of margins, 49 to 48.9 percent. Even in the Mountain States, Goldwater's home base, the president won 56.5 percent of the vote.

Theodore White concluded that "the elections of 1964 had left the Republican party in desperate condition."[10] He was far from alone in his doomsday analysis of the GOP and his implied interment of conservatism:

• Walter Lippmann wrote that "the returns prove the falsity of the claim ... that there is a great silent latent majority of 'conservative' Republicans who will emerge as soon as the Republican party turns its back on 'me-tooism' and offers them a 'choice.' The Johnson majority is indisputable proof that the voters are in the center."

• Tom Wicker of the *New York Times* argued that Republicans can win only as a "me-too" party.

• Author-journalist Robert J. Donovan wrote bleakly: "If the Republicans are to be, or merely seem to be, the voice of right-wing radicalism or extremism, advocating reactionary changes at home and adventures abroad that might lead to war, they will remain a minority party indefinitely."

• Political scientists Nelson W. Polsby and Aaron B. Wildavsky went even further, writing that if the Republican party continued "to nominate conservatives like Goldwater" it would continue to lose so badly that "we can expect an end to a competitive two-party system."

• Richard Rovere, a *New Yorker* staff writer, wrote in *Commentary* that "the election had finished the Goldwater school of political reaction."

• Even the *Wall Street Journal*, editorially sympathetic to Goldwater, conceded that because of his overwhelming defeat, "conservatism has been given a black eye it will be a long time recovering from."[11]

• The *Times'* James Reston summed up that "Barry Goldwater not only lost the presidential election yesterday but the conservative cause as well."

Conservative leaders vehemently disagreed. Conservatism had not been repudiated, because it had not really been tested. They were, in truth, remarkably feisty. "A party that polls over 25 million votes," said Bill Knowland, who had helped manage Goldwater's primary win in California, "is neither bankrupt nor on its deathbed."

In its postelection analysis, *National Review* displayed a striking prescience by presenting the views of two future U.S. presidents—Ronald Reagan and George Bush. Reagan wrote, "The landslide majority did not vote against the conservative philosophy, they voted against a false image our liberal opponents successfully mounted." Bush, defeated in his try for a U.S. Senate seat from Texas, sounded very much as he did in the 1980s, urging Republicans to "repackage our philosophy, emphasize the positive, eliminate the negative, warn of the dangers from the Left but do so without always questioning the patriotism of those who hold liberal views. Let's present an image of workability and reason and common sense."

In an unsigned *National Review* editorial, William F. Buckley Jr. and James Burnham wrote that "it is only safe to say that [conservatism] is dead if one assumes that otherwise the senator would have been elected. . . . One year's landslide loss . . . is not necessarily a permanent thing in a dynamic society, and there is no reason for American conservatives to believe either that their hearts deceived them in telling them he was right, or that the time will never come again when the American people can correct our public policies."[12]

As Frank Meyer, *National Review*'s most politically shrewd editor, put it, "Despite the caricature of Goldwater's position, despite the fact that everything was done to make it appear that the conservative course is extremist, radical, nihilist, anarchic—still two-fifths of the voters saw through the distortions and solidly voted for the unthinkable proposition that there is an alternative to liberal domination."

The effectiveness of the Democratic distortions was demonstrated by *National Review* itself when it suggested, in its postelection analysis, that Goldwater should have been more specific in his proposals, endorsing, for example, a constitutional amendment reaffirming the right of the public schools to permit public prayers. Apparently, America's leading conservative magazine did not realize that the senator had frequently called for such an amendment in his campaign speeches. If *National Review* was not aware of what Goldwater was saying, how could the general public be expected to know? In the face of this widespread public misunderstanding and deliberate Democratic disinformation, Meyer was emboldened to say that the Goldwater campaign was but "a few months of the first opportunity on a broad national scale to confute thirty years of liberal indoctrination." In fact, he insisted, "conservatives stand today nearer to victory than they ever have since

Franklin Roosevelt. A shift in the vote of 12 percent of the electorate is the goal of the next four years."[13]

Meyer's words struck most analysts as silly. Among a very select few in the Establishment, Theodore White grasped that Goldwater had made a unique contribution to the American political debate although he did not comprehend the nature of that contribution. He wrote that "one cannot dismiss Goldwater as a man without meaning in American history. Again and again in American history it has happened that the losers of the presidency contributed almost as much to the permanent tone and dialogue of politics as did the winners." Casting about for comparisons, White considered and then rejected Adlai Stevenson and Al Smith, whom he called "creative losers," and finally settled on William Jennings Bryan as the best parallel.[14]

White was right about Goldwater's extraordinary impact on American politics but wrong to compare him with Bryan or any other presidential loser, creative or otherwise. Barry Goldwater was *sui generis*. He was not so much the candidate of a political party as the personification of a political movement. He was, in fact, the first ideological presidential candidate. To him, ideas, not voting blocs, were of primary importance. To him, principle, not power, should be the core of the presidency. To him, politics was a means, not an end. He was like no other losing presidential candidate, because no other had a more permanent impact on American politics.

Goldwater, with his nationwide grassroots appeal, enabled the GOP, through direct mail and television, to broaden its financial base by a factor of 30 to 1. In 1960, there were between forty thousand and fifty thousand individual contributors to the Nixon campaign; in 1964, the number was estimated as 661,500, nearly half in response to the various TV programs, especially the Reagan telecast.[15] No longer did the Republican National Committee have to cater to the wishes and whims of wealthy satraps who might, and often did, veto candidates and programs they disliked.

The Goldwater candidacy gave the Republican party broad-based financial independence for the first time in its history. As Goldwater put it later, "We needed true believers, not just accommodaters like the elite who wanted to wheel and deal and narrow the party's agenda to their special interests."[16]

Based on their experience with the Draft Goldwater and Goldwater for President Committees, Jerry Milbank and Bill Middendorf encouraged Frank Kovac to pursue the small contributor in the general election. The result was boxes piled high with thousands of wrinkled dollar bills and small checks, even Social Security checks, made out to Barry Goldwater. Attached to many were handwritten letters with a common theme: "I only wish I could give more. But you can be certain you'll get my vote in November." Surveying the stacks of mail one day, Kovac commented, "From where I sit, watching these letters and checks rolling in, I can tell you that this movement is the wave of the future."[17]

In 1994, the Republican National Committee estimated that it would raise $60 million, essentially through direct mail techniques spawned by the 1964 election. Republican National Committee chairman Haley Barbour stated that the committee would have 1.3 million donors in the 1994–95 cycle, the highest ever.[18]

POLITICS IS PEOPLE, and thousands of young conservatives entered and stayed in politics because of Barry Goldwater's run for the presidency. As Robert Bauman, a Goldwater delegate and future member of Congress from Maryland, said, "We were young and we didn't want to live the rest of our lives under [liberalism] and we didn't want communism to destroy the world. . . . I remember reading *The True Believer* at the time and saying, 'Yeah, that's us.' "[19]

Young conservatives loved Goldwater's independence: he would "not be hogtied by anything—not even the conservative movement."[20] And they were given more responsibility in 1964 than ever before. Besides their energy and idealism, there was a practical reason for their presence: "many old-timers, who belonged to the liberal wing of the party, had simply deserted" the GOP.[21] As Mary Elizabeth Lewis, then executive director of Michigan YAF, now head of her own direct mail and communications company, put it, "We learned how to organize, how to motivate, how to run campaigns. We learned that to make a change, you have to start at the grass roots." [22]

Today, those young conservatives sit in Congress, manage campaigns, conduct national polls, head think tanks, edit magazines, host talk shows. Senator Trent Lott of Mississippi, elected Senate Republican whip following the watershed 1994 elections, stated that Goldwater "inspired a whole generation of young people to get involved," among them his Senate colleagues, Connie Mack of Florida, Dan Coats of Illinois, and Thad Cochran of Mississippi.[23]

As a young man, Senator Larry Presler of South Dakota carried a copy of *The Conscience of a Conservative* in his hip pocket. When he was a law student a quarter century ago, freshman Senator Fred Thompson of Tennessee worked the night shift in a motel sitting at the front desk reading Russell Kirk's *The Conservative Mind*. Senator Phil Gramm of Texas, who as chairman of the Senate Republican Campaign Committee masterminded the 1994 GOP takeover of the Senate, reveals that "my first political thoughts, in the eleventh grade, came from reading *The Conscience of a Conservative*." The conservatives who will "lead America into the twenty-first century," says Gramm, "got involved in politics in 1964. Sometimes you win by losing on principle."[24]

In the House of Representatives Goldwater conservatives include James Sensenbrenner of Wisconsin, Philip Crane of Illinois, and John Duncan of Tennessee, who sent his first paycheck to the Draft Goldwater Committee. Yet another congressman who cut his political teeth on the 1964 campaign is Duncan Hunter of California, former chairman of the House Republican Conference, who said that the seventy-three Republican freshmen entering the 104th Congress live by the Goldwaterite message, sent loud and clear by the American people in 1994: "Government is too big and spends too much!"[25]

James L. Buckley, who served as senator from New York from 1971 through 1976 and is now a judge of the U.S. Court of Appeals for the District of Columbia Circuit, says flatly, "But for Goldwater and 1964, I wouldn't be sitting here." The 1964 campaign made him realize the profusion of conservatives out there, "a cadre of troops," which helped persuade him to run for the Senate in 1970 as a conservative. What astounded New York reporters about his Senate campaign, he recalls, is that "we drew more students, high school and college students, more young volunteers, than the other two candidates combined. . . . That was Barry Goldwater's doing."[26]

Paul Laxalt, invariably described as "President Reagan's closest friend in the Senate" during the 1980s, ran for the U.S. Senate from Nevada in 1964 against incumbent Democrat Howard Cannon and proudly appeared with Goldwater at a rally in Las Vegas the weekend before the election. He lost by a mere forty-nine votes, a victim of the Johnson landslide. Laxalt liked Goldwater and what he stood for. He had read *The Conscience of a Conservative* and admired its "common sense and simplicity."

In 1973, after one term as governor, Laxalt was urged to run again for the Senate when Alan Bible retired. When he declined, Goldwater immediately called him and said, "What's the shit about not running? If you and I are going to chicken out of politics, what's going to happen to this country of ours?" Laxalt changed his mind and won.

Laxalt can recall many other political leaders "who were turned on" by Goldwater, including Governor, later Senator, Henry Bellmon of Oklahoma; Governor James Edwards of South Carolina, later secretary of energy in the Reagan administration; Governor Don Samuelson of Idaho; and Governor Tim Babcock of Montana. "Clearly, Goldwater changed the course of American politics," says Laxalt. "He was the pioneer. . . . He brought the Sunbelt into political prominence."[27]

William E. Brock of Tennessee was an architect of the new GOP in the South. Brock, an independent "nominal" Democrat in 1960, became a Republican after reading *The Conscience of a Conservative*. "I loved the clarity of *Conscience*," Brock remembers. "It turned on the lights." He was elected to Congress in 1962 and became Tennessee chairman of the Draft Goldwater Committee.

For Brock, Laxalt, and many others, the *combined* appeal of Goldwater the author of *The Conscience of a Conservative* and Goldwater the presidential candidate drew them into politics. Initially attracted by the philosophical vision in Goldwater's book, they were galvanized by his unapologetic conservatism as a candidate. Goldwater "took my breath away," recalls Brock, "he was so daggoned honest. There was no question in my mind," he adds, that "we could win the nomination and the election. Jack Kennedy was not popular. Questions were being raised about his leadership."

But Brock and other members of the "new wave" of Southern Republicans realized that with Kennedy's assassination, Goldwater's "chances were tougher, a lot tougher. The country would be reluctant to change presidents again so soon." The reality, says Brock—who went on to become U.S. senator, chairman of the Republican National Committee, and to hold various cabinet positions in the Reagan administration—was that Goldwater could not have won the election with a "10-foot 2×4." Too many things were going against him, like the media "who loved him personally but still cut his throat." And yet, Brock states, "1964 was the salvation of conservatism . . . it broke the Solid South."

In 1966, the Republicans elected forty-six new members to the

House of Representatives, most of them Goldwater conservatives, many from the South. "The 1964 loss was the kickoff for a resurgence of the GOP," says Brock. "No one looked back, and election politics has never been the same since."[28]

Brock's Tennessee Republican colleague, Howard Baker, agrees. A shrewd, pragmatic politician who became Senate Republican leader and later White House chief of staff under Reagan, Baker calls 1964 a "watershed time" in America's two-party system. Goldwater, he says, was the first Republican "to make an overt and successful appeal to Southern Democrats" through issues. Because of Goldwater, "the GOP changed from regional party strength to national party strength for the first time."[29]

LONG BEFORE she was nominated as associate justice of the Supreme Court by President Reagan in 1981, Sandra Day O'Connor was a neighbor of Barry Goldwater in Scottsdale; in fact, she stuffed envelopes for him in his 1958 senatorial campaign. She rose in Arizona Republican politics from a member of the Young Republicans to precinct committeewoman to Senate majority leader in the state legislature.

Justice O'Connor has always admired Goldwater for his "very strong character. He knows who he is and what he is. He has a system of values that has guided him all his life." Goldwater's early, enthusiastic support of her nomination to the Supreme Court "made a difference . . . it was very important." In Justice O'Connor's opinion, the senator's notion of conservatism "was economic conservatism." "He was against tax and spend politics," she says. "He emphasized individual initiative and independence. He didn't see as large a role for government in the social policy of the nation." His 1964 candidacy, she believes, had "a ripple effect" on the Republican party and every Republican president since.[30]

Political pollster-strategist Richard B. Wirthlin did his first survey in 1964 for a gubernatorial candidate in Utah. Although he did not work for Goldwater in his presidential campaign, he handled the senator's polling in 1968 and all his subsequent senatorial campaigns. In 1980, when Wirthlin joined Reagan's presidential campaign team, the only other client he kept was Barry Goldwater.

A strategist as well as a pollster, Wirthlin says that "there is no doubt that Barry Goldwater's message was Ronald Reagan's message. . . . Goldwater really forged American politics for the next thirty years." "He was not a politician who played politics," marvels Wirthlin, "but who played principle." It took a man with "tremendous self-confidence," he reflects, to present conservatism in 1964 when it was not popular to criticize the Great Society and talk about the danger of communism. But for Goldwater, says Wirthlin, "the message was more important than the presidency." And it was necessary to speak bluntly, even harshly, "to cut through the media."

Goldwater was "the forerunner" of conservatism, in Wirthlin's opinion, while Reagan was "the consolidator." Both were criticized for their intellectual "simplicity," but both had "a very clear vision of America," a vision that changed the perceptions and lives of millions of Americans.[31]

In mid-October 1964, the future president of the Heritage Foundation was seated on the stage of an auditorium at the University of Pennsylvania, watching as a couple of tomatoes and eggs were being thrown at Barry Goldwater. Edwin J. Feulner, a graduate student at the Wharton School, had become a Goldwaterite a few years earlier after reading *The Conscience of a Conservative:* "He was the political embodiment of what I believed."

Like so many young conservatives of the day, Feulner never accepted the notion that "our ideas were wrong," despite the size of Lyndon Johnson's victory. Rather, Goldwater's candidacy was "absolutely critical" for the conservative movement, proving that "we could mount a national campaign, albeit thin in spots." Goldwater's and therefore conservatism's showing "proved our political maturity. . . . [1964] was our political bar mitzvah, our confirmation in a political sense."

Asked to speculate on what a President Goldwater might have accomplished, Feulner, head of Washington's most influential conservative think tank, responded that in Vietnam "there would have been a Curtis LeMay rather than a Robert McNamara approach." That essential difference in foreign policy might have prevented "the radicalization of a whole generation on campus. . . . There would not have been the ugliness of 1968." Goldwater, Feulner argues, "was absolutely essential in defining conservatism."[32]

The America First columnist-commentator who ran for the Republican nomination for president in 1992 was an editorial writer for the conservative *St. Louis Globe-Democrat* in 1964 and a fierce Goldwater partisan. When his newspaper declined to endorse either candidate, Patrick J. Buchanan was astounded. "The fighting *Globe-Democrat* was taking a dive," he later wrote, probably because President Johnson had called owner Sam Newhouse, who had called publisher Richard H. Amberg, who had personally written the nonendorsement editorial.

Because Barry Goldwater would never do such a craven thing, Buchanan attests, he "touched our minds and hearts. He brought whole new classes and groups of people into the GOP. He was the wedge— the man who brought the South and West, the young and energetic into Republican circles." He was "the political champion of the conservative movement of the 1950s and 1960s, the first great modern conservative in the modern era."

Goldwater's historic importance, argues Buchanan, can be measured by the actions of the shrewdest politician of our times, Richard M. Nixon, who always knew where the political power was. In 1960, Vice President Nixon went to Nelson Rockefeller, the leader of the Eastern liberal Republicans, and cut a deal to ensure his nomination. In 1968, candidate Nixon went to Goldwater and other prominent conservatives because he knew that the power of the Republican party had shifted from East to West and South and from liberal to conservative.[33]

Ironically, it was ultraliberal Dalton Trumbo writing in the radical left *Nation* who snapped editor-author M. Stanton Evans out of his postelection depression in early 1965. Trumbo warned that the defeat of Goldwater did not mean the end of conservatism. How could it, he pointed out, when never before had conservatives "been able to carry [their] program to the whole people from the platform of a national party; never had a candidate of the Right been so attractive, or aroused such profound devotion; never before had hundreds of thousands of dollars—perhaps even millions—flowed to [their] cause from the 'grass roots.'"[34]

In 1964, at age twenty-nine, Evans was one of the most influential young conservatives in America having been a leader in Young Americans for Freedom and Young Republicans and written *Revolt on the Campus*, which documented the burgeoning growth of conservatism in the nation's colleges and universities. Inspired by Trumbo's "paranoid" analysis, he reviewed conservatism's assets and liabilities and concluded that "we could win on the issues if we didn't make the mistakes we did in 1964." For all the mistakes, insists Evans, "Ronald Reagan would never have become president" in 1980 without the Goldwater campaign of 1964. It was Goldwater who "threw his body on the barbed wire" and prepared the way for Reagan. Barry Goldwater, emphasizes Evans, "was absolutely central to the subsequent success of conservatism."[35]

David R. Jones, former vice chancellor of Vanderbilt University, former president of the National Federation of Independent Business Foundation, and now president of the Fund for American Studies, was a Florida high school teacher when he first met Goldwater in March 1962. Like so many other young conservatives, Jones had read *The Conscience of a Conservative*, "the one book that politically brought the pieces together for me." He flew to New York City for the YAF rally in Madison Square Garden and joined in the fervent cheers for the senator, attracted not by his oratory but his honesty. "He matched what he said with what he did wherever he was," says Jones, who observed Goldwater firsthand when he was administrative assistant to Senator James Buckley of New York in the 1970s.

Jones was a disciple of Frank Meyer and his fusionism and saw Goldwater as combining the traditionalist and libertarian strains of conservatism—"personal freedom *and* personal responsibility." "If it hadn't been for Goldwater in 1964," he sums up, "there probably wouldn't have been a President Nixon in 1968 or a President Reagan in 1980."[36]

J. A. Parker, born and raised on the south side of Philadelphia, is one of the most influential black conservatives in America, most strikingly through *The Lincoln Review,* a quarterly published by his Lincoln Institute. Among many others, Supreme Court Justice Clarence Thomas credits Parker for making him realize that he too was a conservative. Parker sees in Goldwater a white male version of Zora Neal Hurston, the gifted Harlem novelist who has greatly influenced him. Goldwater was "fiercely independent, a libertarian," he says, "but he was tempered by a belief in God and the Constitution, which provides limits."

Parker applauded Goldwater's antigovernment stance. "Selling TVA made sense to me," he admits. "I was fearful of government— so were the Founding Fathers. I just want the federal government to protect me and my property." A strong admirer of Reagan—"he finished what Goldwater started, beating liberals across the nation as Goldwater beat liberals in the Republican party"—Parker refuses to compare Goldwater with anybody. "It's almost sacrilegious," he states, "he was one of a kind."[37]

Ironically, almost all the leaders of the New Right, which Goldwater criticized time and again in the 1970s and 1980s, were drawn into politics because of him. Direct mail pioneer Richard A. Viguerie memorized passages of *The Conscience of a Conservative* for his debates in the early 1960s when he was a high-ranking YAF official. For him, Bill Buckley, the intellectual, and Barry Goldwater, the politician, were the "co-fathers" of the conservative movement. Ronald Reagan, says Viguerie, was "the product" of the movement while Goldwater and Buckley "created" the movement.

Viguerie explains that in 1976, when he wrote a critical article about Goldwater in his magazine, *Conservative Digest,* he was trying to hold "Goldwater's feet to the fire he had set" a decade before. He now realizes that "we wanted him to do more than he could reasonably do." In truth, says the man who created a national direct mail network for the Right, "conservatives will never be able to repay their debt to Goldwater."[38]

The man who, along with Howard Phillips, persuaded Jerry Falwell in 1978 to start the Moral Majority and thereby helped elect Ronald Reagan president, was a young reporter for the *Milwaukee Sentinel* in 1964. Paul Weyrich, one of only four *Sentinel* reporters for Goldwater, "was mesmerized by Goldwater." Like many young Midwestern conservatives, "we thought he was going to win and save the country." Even when Goldwater lost so badly, Weyrich kept saying, like others, "Twenty-seven million Americans can't be wrong."

Regarding the possible "Balkanization" of conservatism, Weyrich suggests that "if you had a leader like Goldwater or Reagan all these divisions wouldn't come to the surface." What is needed, says Weyrich, is the "conservatism based on common sense" that Reagan articulated so well in 1980—and the conservatism centered on the "whole man" that Goldwater talked about so eloquently in 1964.

Comparing the two men, Weyrich believes that Goldwater had strengths that Reagan lacked, at least in part. Reagan was inclined to avoid confrontation while Goldwater liked it. Reagan had "compassion," an ability to forgive, to "deal with" and win over his enemies.

Weyrich believes that Goldwater was scarred, even embittered, by the experience of 1964 and "was never the same." Goldwater once remarked to a fellow senator, after he had been criticized by conservatives, "My attitude is, 'Screw 'em.'" But, Weyrich speculates, Goldwater's natural combativeness would have served him well if he had been elected president in 1964. Like Harry Truman, Goldwater "would have taken on Congress, gone to the people, and probably won."[39]

The youngest elected delegate at the 1964 National Republican Convention in San Francisco was twenty-three-year-old Morton Blackwell of Baton Rouge, Louisiana, who went on to serve in the Reagan White House and has introduced several thousand young men and women to practical politics through his Leadership Institute. Goldwater's message to him and other young conservatives was simple and to the point: "Do what you know is right." Goldwater "catalyzed a national youth movement" through his many appearances on college campuses all over the country up to 1964. Blackwell echoes Weyrich that the 1964 campaign changed Goldwater, who felt "he had been used by conservatives."[40]

Thomas L. Phillips, who would launch a publishing empire that in 1994 numbered more than one hundred publications and grossed an estimated $160 million, was a senior at Dartmouth College and chairman of New Hampshire Young Americans for Freedom in 1964. Like many others, he read and was profoundly affected by *The Conscience of a Conservative*, which "articulated what I felt" about the dangers of big government and the importance of the individual.

Conservatives, particularly young conservatives like Phillips, did not quit after Goldwater's loss in the fall of 1964 because "we believed it was a tactical defeat." They were convinced that "our beliefs were correct and the fact that other people didn't agree with them was their problem, not ours." Besides, many already saw "a new leader" in Ronald Reagan. Still, says Phillips, as electrifying as was Reagan's televised speech, "Barry Goldwater was the most important political figure in my formative years. You can triumph if you stand by your principles."[41]

Charlton Heston is best known for his moving performances in such epic films as *The Ten Commandments* and *Ben Hur*, for which he received an Academy Award. But in recent years he has more often used his talents as an articulate spokesman for *National Review*, the National Rifle Association, and other conservative causes.

How did someone whose first serious political involvement was on behalf of Adlai Stevenson become a conservative? According to an interview with the Media Research Center, the answer was Barry Goldwater. As Heston described it:

> During the 1964 campaign, I was making a film near Sacramento. I was driven to location every morning, and there was only one traffic light on the whole trip. At that intersection was a big billboard, and on it was a head portrait of Goldwater, and the text was, "In your heart, you know he's right." Whenever we stopped at that intersection for a red light, I'd look at that, and then one morning, I thought, "Son of a bitch, he *is* right." It was like Paul on the road to Damascus.[42]

The Goldwater campaign produced its share of ironies. George F. Gilder and Bruce K. Chapman, who became prominent members of the conservative movement in the 1980s, co-authored in 1966 a scathing criticism of Goldwater's failed candidacy, describing him and those around him as "extreme rightists," "ultraconservatives," and "demagogues." Their work, *The Party That Lost Its Head,* urged Republicans to adopt a "progressive" ideology, to "insist that Medicare and other social-security and welfare programs are properly and economically administered."

The Gilder-Chapman thesis was an early form of Irving Kristol's neoconservative argument—that the welfare state is here to stay, and the only debate is whether it will be liberal or conservative.

The two young liberals, founders of the Ripon Society with significant financial support from Nelson Rockefeller, did propose reforms— a revitalized federalism, the regeneration of metropolitan areas, the conservation of natural resources, greater concern for the problems of youth, and a "conservative approach" to technological progress. But in almost every case, they gave government, especially the federal government, a primary role. They wrote, "In areas where the state cannot or will not act, [the Republican party] must urge federal intervention, first through the provision or new incentives for private and state action, then, if necessary, through direct federal intervention."[43]

This of course was not the philosophy of Goldwater, Reagan, or the later Gilder, who in 1981 wrote the widely acclaimed work, *Wealth and*

Poverty, an attempt to fuse supply-side economics with traditional values.

ONE OF THE young Southern conservatives elected to the House of Representatives in November 1964 was John H. Buchanan, Jr., of Birmingham, Alabama. He had read *The Conscience of a Conservative* and found it "compelling." He campaigned as a Goldwater Republican because "to me he represented fiscal responsibility, commitment to the free enterprise system, limited government, protection of the basic constitutional rights and liberties of American citizens, devotion to the Constitution and the Bill of Rights." During his sixteen years in Congress, he gradually shifted to a liberal position on social and racial issues. Labeled a "progressive" by many of his conservative constituents, he was defeated in the 1980 Republican primary by a member of the Moral Majority.

Buchanan recalls that despite his "progressive" label, Goldwater came to Birmingham in the late 1970s and campaigned for him, saying that Congress needed men of "integrity" and "ability" and "fine progressive Republicans like John Buchanan." The Arizona conservative and the Alabama progressive have remained allies and friends. Indeed, says Buchanan, who became president of People for the American Way, "Barry Goldwater has been a consistent friend of People for the American Way because of [its support] for constitutional rights and liberties."[44]

FOR JEANE KIRKPATRICK, Michael Novak, Midge Decter, Ben Wattenberg, and others who broke with the Democratic party and became leading neoconservatives a decade later, Barry Goldwater and his run for the presidency in 1964 were in the main irrelevant. Kirkpatrick recalls that the "biggest reason why I didn't support [Goldwater] was that he was a Republican." Novak "was very relieved when Johnson won," he remembers, although he was struck by how many of his ethnic, working-class friends voted for Goldwater. To Decter, the landslide "seemed perfectly predictable."[45] Indeed, most liberals understood it to signal the end of what they called "the right wing" in American politics.

Liberal opinion notwithstanding, Goldwater's campaign positions were the positions of a significant part of the electorate. A Harris poll found that 88 percent of the people agreed with Goldwater that prayer should be restored in the schools; 94 percent believed the government had been lax in security matters; and 60 percent said the federal government should be trimmed, that some of its welfare and relief programs had a demoralizing effect on their beneficiaries, and that a federal right-to-work law should be enacted.[46]

In 1964, like many others, Ben Wattenberg accepted that Goldwater was an extremist. By 1970, when he wrote *The Real Majority* with Richard M. Scammon, his sensibility to the issues the senator had raised had been sharpened by the 1968 Democratic convention and the anti-Vietnam War movement. For Wattenberg and similar Henry "Scoop" Jackson Democrats, "Goldwater became a guy who was right—both on foreign and on social and value issues."[47] But in 1964, he and every other Jackson Democrat pulled the lever for Lyndon Baines Johnson.

Irving Kristol, the founding father of the neoconservatives, on the other hand, has never understood the political or philosophical importance of Goldwater. Nearly thirty years later, analyzing Patrick Buchanan's 1992 run for the presidency, he wrote that if Buchanan were to assume leadership of the American conservative movement (his true ambition, according to Kristol), the movement "will have suffered its greatest defeat since the election of 1964, which set the liberal tone for American politics for the next fifteen years."[48]

It would be difficult to write a more inaccurate summary of the 1964 election and its meaning for the conservative movement and for American politics. The year 1964 was not the movement's "greatest defeat" but its greatest triumph. It provided the electoral foundation for a string of political victories from the presidency on down that reached its apex in a burst of triumph in the remarkable elections of November 1994. Rather than shifting "the tone" of American politics (that is, its philosophical content) to the left, the election of 1964 provided many of the major issues (limited government, law and order, anticommunism, a strong national defense) that led conservative Republicans to victory, starting in the congressional elections of 1966.

THE MOST DRAMATIC turnabout of all Goldwater partisans was executed by Karl Hess, his favorite speechwriter. In a passionate defense of Goldwaterism in 1967, Hess predicted that "the cause in which [Goldwater] put his political life on the line is one which ultimately will triumph." But the triumph would not be for Goldwater or conservatism—"that weary and not terribly meaningful word"—or for the Republican party but for "every American who wants to be left alone long enough to do his job, who asks no favors or favoritism, who helps or is helped only when truly needed."[49]

Hess's idiosyncratic interpretation led him somehow to join the anti-Vietnam War movement, praise the Black Panthers, champion the legalization of drugs, refuse to pay income taxes, and, finally, describe himself as an "anarcho-syndicalist."

Yet the two men stayed friends. In 1969, after he returned to the Senate, Goldwater was making his way through a group of antiwar protestors on Capitol Hill when a policeman said to him, "Say, Senator, there's a former aide of yours here." A little startled, he waded through the seated men and women and found Hess. Grinning broadly, Goldwater said, "Karl, where the hell have you been? I haven't seen you for months."

"Well, Senator," Hess said, "I didn't want to bother you and I didn't think your staff would care to have me see you."

"Piss on them. You're my friend. Give me a call as soon as you're free."

Hess is one of many who say, "The older I get the more I revere that man. He's remarkable—there is no one else like him in American politics."[50]

GOLDWATER'S IMPACT as a presidential campaigner was twofold. First, he provided a national political platform for a future presidential candidate, Ronald Reagan. The day after Reagan won the California Republican gubernatorial primary in June 1966 (easily defeating George Christopher, the former mayor of San Francisco), he called Denison Kitchel in Phoenix to say, "Had it not been for you and Barry I would not have won this nomination." He then wrote Goldwater: "You set the pattern. . . . I have tried to do the same and have found the people more receptive because they've had a chance to realize there is such a thing as truth." Reagan was responding, in part, to a letter from Goldwater, who had predicted his victory, which, he said, "will bring me great personal joy."[51]

Second, Goldwater's structured campaigning (limiting appearances to two or three big speeches a day in places where "the ducks are") was adopted by presidential winners Ronald Reagan and George Bush; even Nixon in 1968 did not try to repeat his foolhardy attempt in 1960 to visit all fifty states.

In the realm of ideas, Goldwater prepared the way for future candidates like liberal George McGovern in 1972, conservative Ronald Reagan in 1980, "New Democrat" Bill Clinton in 1992, and the 1994 "Contract With America." Goldwater insisted on addressing the issues that have dominated the national debate for the past three decades: *Social Security* (it is in actuarial trouble—strengthen it, perhaps by introducing some voluntary option); *government subsidies* (work toward reducing and even eliminating them, as in agriculture); *privatization* (start selling government-owned properties, like parts of the TVA, to the private sector); *law and order* (the rights of victims should take precedence over the rights of criminals); *morality in government* (the president and all in public office must avoid scandal and corruption and set a good example for society); *foreign aid* (stop propping up governments and regimes that spit in our face); and *communism* (why not victory?).

His articulation of private solutions to public problems laid the foundation for Nixon's appeal to the "silent majority" in 1968 and Reagan's openly conservative themes of less government and stronger national defense in 1980. As campaign strategist John Sears put it, Goldwater changed "the rhetoric of politics" by challenging the principles of the New Deal, "something no Democrat or Republican before him had dared to do." In the field of foreign policy, political scientist Harry Jaffa says, it was with the Goldwater candidacy that "the Republican party became the hawks."[52] The college dropout who had doubts about his intellectual ability turned out to be a great teacher.

The most lasting legacy of the Goldwater campaign in the mass media was the unprincipled use of the negative TV commercial. The devastating success of various Johnson White House inspirations—the Daisy, Ice Cream Cone, and Social Security spots—convinced future presidential candidates and managers that the most effective advertising was negative advertising, and accelerated the debasement of the electoral process. As a positive contribution, Goldwater's half-hour TV programs that focused on a single issue were copied nearly thirty years later by independent candidate Perot in his infomercials. One Goldwater practice was not adopted, although several future presidential candidate wished they could have: he never held a formal news conference.

In addition to the above impacts on politics, Goldwater prepared the way (coming from a state with only five electoral votes) for outsider presidential candidates like George McGovern, Jimmy Carter, and Bill Clinton, none of whom represented a big state or had a large power base within their party.

In his 1988 memoirs, Goldwater stated that his campaign helped to broaden and deepen the conservative movement beyond "any other movement of our times." Today, he said, "conservatives come from all regions, every social class, every creed and color, all age groups. The new GOP was forged in the fires of the 1964 presidential campaign."[53]

And it emerged triumphant in the historic 1994 elections. The 1964 campaign transformed the Republican party into the Conservative party—the anti-big government party—that won the presidency in five of the next seven national elections and captured both Houses of Congress in 1994; and the Democratic party into the Liberal party—the pro-big government party—that won national elections in the ensuing years only when it rejected liberalism and nominated moderates.

Democrats went down to crashing defeat in 1994 not because the voters were in a "temper tantrum" like "an angry two-year-old," as ABC News's anchor Peter Jennings argued, but because they finally realized that only a Republican Congress could ensure less government. Haley Barbour, chairman of the Republican National Committee, stated: "This election was an election of ideas. Voters clearly understood what they were doing when they voted for us."[54]

Every exit poll in 1994 confirmed the prevailing conservative, anti-liberal mood of the American electorate. One national poll reported that 43 percent of voters considered themselves "conservative," 33 percent "moderate," and only 16 percent "liberal." Polls in key states corroborated the conservative trend: 36 percent identified themselves as conservative in California, 39 percent in Michigan (home of Walter Reuther's United Auto Workers), 40 percent in New Jersey, and 46 percent in Texas.[55]

And to be conservative was to be highly skeptical about government. In 1964, when Goldwater was nominated for president, 76 percent of Americans thought you could trust the government to do what was right always or most of the time. By 1984, at the peak of President Reagan's popularity, only 44 percent agreed. In 1994, the figure was down to a mere *19 percent*, with 9 percent saying that you can *never* trust the government to do what's right.[56]

Liberal economist Robert J. Samuelson summed up the 1994 elections well: "The terms of political debate have fundamentally and, in my view, irreversibly changed." The elections, as conservative columnist George Will wrote, were "a resounding ideological statement."[57]

Almost thirty years to the day after Goldwater was roundly defeated, a *USA Today*–CNN Gallup poll found that 64 percent of Americans agreed with the Republicans' Contract with America. The people wanted smaller government, lower taxes and spending, tougher anticrime measures, and less Washington meddling in their lives.

Every one of these ideas was first proposed by Barry Goldwater in his 1964 campaign. He was simply thirty years too early.

17

Vindication

MOST LOSING PRESIDENTIAL CANDIDATES disappear quickly from sight. One week they are waving to thousands of cheering supporters, quoted daily in the *New York Times* and the *Washington Post* and over the TV networks, surrounded by aides and reporters, courted and cosseted like a visiting chief of state, and the next week they are driving themselves to the grocery store. It is as though they had never existed. Some reappear from time to time, hovering on the edges of a campaign or convention like black sheep cousins at a family reunion. Sometimes they run again, but they are shadows of their former solid selves. The public ignores them or turns away embarrassed. A very select few are rehabilitated by circumstance or accomplishment.

Of all the men who have run for and lost the presidency in modern times, only Barry Goldwater and the central themes of his campaign were vindicated in four short years. Reviled and rejected in 1964 as no other presidential candidate in the twentieth century, Goldwater was easily reelected to the U.S. Senate in 1968 while the president who buried him in a historic landslide dared not seek reelection.

The immediate reason for Johnson's defeat was the Vietnam War, the war that Goldwater had warned the American people about, the war that Johnson had promised he would not send American boys to fight, the war that ended with over 58,000 American dead, 303,000 wounded. By 1967, from one end of America to another, conservatives were grimly joking: "I was told that if I voted for Goldwater, we were going to war in Vietnam. Well, I did, and damned if we didn't."

Goldwater's criticisms of the overinflated promises and understated costs of the Great Society would take longer, but in the end they too were proven correct. Still, it was Johnson's gross mishandling of the Vietnam War that brought him crashing down in the spring of 1968 and raised Goldwater up as a prophet with honor in his own land. It was put succinctly in a giant billboard along the Eisenhower Expressway in Chicago. In the fall of 1964, it read: "In Your Heart, You Know He's Right." Following the election and for nearly two years, it read: "In Time, You Will Know He Was Right." Just before the 1966 elections, it read: "Now You Know He Was Right."[1]

Coming from a generation that believed that partisan politics should stop at the water's edge, Goldwater did his best to warn Johnson of the terrible consequences of the war policy he was pursuing. In the spring of 1965 he had an opportunity to speak privately with the president. He was in the White House as a member of a Republican policy group, formed at Eisenhower's instigation shortly after the 1964 election. Eager to unite the country behind his programs, Johnson frequently invited the Republican group to meet with him.

Sitting in the Oval Office with his former rival, Goldwater as usual got right to the point. "I urged him to replace Robert McNamara as secretary of defense," he later wrote. He restated his belief that McNamara was "deliberately pursuing a policy of parity with the Russians" and in consequence the United States was losing its military advantage. Johnson listened intently, occasionally nodding his head in agreement, but when Goldwater had finished, he said, "Barry, I just can't do that." According to Goldwater, the president neither contradicted him nor offered a defense of McNamara.[2] Goldwater concluded that because McNamara was one of Kennedy's most celebrated cabinet appointments, Johnson did not dare dismiss him.

Goldwater kept trying to convince Johnson that he was badly off course in his direction of the war. As a brigadier general in the Air Force Reserve, he was able to tell the president what he saw firsthand during his five visits to Vietnam over the next four years as well as what he was hearing from American troops through the shortwave telephone calls patched through the ham radio shack next to his home. His message to Johnson and colleagues on Capitol Hill was the same: "We had two clear choices: Either win the war in a relatively short time, say within a year, or pull out all our troops and come home."[3]

Goldwater never discussed or advocated the use of nuclear weapons; he supported a conventional air, ground, and sea war because he was convinced that conventional weapons would get the job done. As commander in chief, he would have warned the North Vietnamese that either they halt the conflict or "we would wipe out all their installations—the city of Hanoi, Haiphong harbor, factories, dikes, everything. . . . If they did not respond, we would literally make a swamp of North Vietnam." He would have also sent South Vietnamese troops north and used U.S. sea power "to mine and blockade North Vietnamese ports."[4]

Goldwater's plan to win the war rested on two crucial points: it would have been launched in 1965 "when we were a credible adversary," and it would have been carried out quickly and across the board. "To this day," he wrote in his 1988 memoirs, "I believe the North Vietnamese would have stopped the war if we had carried it to them by land, sea, and air over a three- to six-month period."

He dismissed the notion, raised by some Asian experts, that such an escalation would have brought mainland China into the war. He pointed out that (1) China was protected by massive mountains north of Vietnam and would not have been affected by the U.S. air strikes; (2) for all their communist comraderie and cooperation (China allowed the transport of Soviet arms across their territory into Vietnam), China and Vietnam had a long history of conflict and did not really trust each other; and (3) Beijing was beginning to move toward Washington "as its confrontations with Moscow continued."[5] A fourth point can be made: Mao Tse-tung was already considering the radical purification of China that erupted as the Cultural Revolution in the summer of 1966. For the next decade, China's military was too preoccupied with its internal security to attempt any major external operations.

Second only to Richard Nixon, Robert McNamara is the public official for whom Barry Goldwater has the most contempt because McNamara also lied deliberately and publicly about important matters of state. When he first became secretary of defense, McNamara lied about the decline of U.S. missile strength to support the false claim made by Kennedy during the 1960 campaign that the Soviets had surpassed the United States in missile power. It was early in 1961 that an exasperated Goldwater, aware of U.S. missile superiority, told a New Jersey audience, "We've got one that can hit the men's room in the Kremlin."[6] Democratic propagandists in 1964 twisted that comment around too: Goldwater, they implied, wanted to launch a missile at Moscow.

A few months before Kennedy was assassinated, McNamara assured the president that with sufficient support, the Vietnam conflict could be won by the end of 1965. Throughout 1964, McNamara and Johnson recognized the dangers of announcing a large-scale, open-ended commitment in an election year, and "hid their escalation of the war in hopes of an early victory."[7] Goldwater warned the American people that such a plan would not work, but too few listened to the "warmonger" from Arizona.

Goldwater also faulted McNamara for persuading Kennedy and Johnson to accept nuclear parity with the Soviet Union—the policy of Mutual Assured Destruction. "It was MAD all right," Goldwater said. "McNamara would deliberately abandon our policy of nuclear superiority, the greatest defense not only against a surprise Soviet nuclear attack but against the massive Russian army, which could launch a sneak assault with conventional weapons."[8] Ironically, because of MAD, the Soviets took a missile lead over the United States during McNamara's stewardship of the Defense Department, a fact the CIA reported to President Nixon in 1969.[9] This dramatic shift in strategic power forced the adoption of détente and America's departure from the peace through strength strategy of Harry Truman.

Goldwater frequently contrasted McNamara's public optimism about the Vietnam War with his private pessimism. In January 1962, the secretary of defense told the president and the people that the situation in Vietnam was "encouraging"; in September 1963, it was "getting better and better"; and in March 1964, it had "significantly improved." By November 1965, with American troop strength up to some 184,000, we had "stopped losing the war," and by July 1966, with more than 300,000 American men in Vietnam, he was "cautiously optimistic." But in January 1966, after completing the largest troop buildup of the war, he admitted at a Georgetown party that the conflict could not be won militarily.[10]

Despite McNamara's belated apology in the spring of 1995 (*In Retrospect: The Tragedy and Lessons of Vietnam*), Goldwater's statement about the architect of U.S. military policy in Vietnam is stern but just: "No honorable man can walk away from a war to which he has sent hundreds of thousands of men"—too many of whom died.[11]

GOLDWATER'S INVOLVEMENT in Vietnam was not limited to personal visits and policy recommendations to the president. He used one of his oldest hobbies to boost the morale of American servicemen thousands of miles from home. In 1967, he "loaned" his ham radio station and its equipment to a group of local hams, all in the Air Force MARS (Military Affiliate Radio System), to let our fighting men in the Pacific area communicate with their families in the United States. The radio-telephone hookups produced thousands of "I love you" or "It's a boy, honey" or "I'm not where there's any danger so don't worry" messages.

AFA7UGA became the largest amateur MARS station in the world, handling 179,593 phone patches and thousands of teletype messages from August 1967 through February 1977. One ironical episode occurred when Pat Nugent, a young U.S. serviceman stationed in Cam Ranh Bay in South Vietnam, wanted to talk to his wife, Lucy Baines, in Texas. Via shortwave radio, he contacted AFA7UGA in Phoenix and was patched through to Johnson City for a twenty-minute telephone conversation. When asked what President Johnson's son-in-law said, the operator replied, "Aw, we told the boy to go ahead and say he loved her."

The operation was quintessentially Goldwater: he personally paid for the upkeep of the equipment and all of the telephone calls (about $20,000 a year) within the state of Arizona; he and a group of about thirty volunteers manned the operation, without any bureaucratic supervision; they did it night and day for a decade without any thought of publicity or reward.

There was a bonus for the volunteers and the occasional visitor: being surrounded by Goldwater memorabilia, including an autographed photograph from President Kennedy that read: "To Barry Goldwater, who I urge to follow the career for which he has shown so much talent—photography." There were also signed pictures from Eisenhower and Hubert Humphrey, covers of *Time* and *Newsweek* featuring Goldwater, and a certificate that Goldwater had traveled 146 hours and ten minutes, for a distance of 79,250 miles, in his official 727 jet during his 1964 presidential campaign.[12]

ALTHOUGH THEY HAD lost the election, Goldwater and the conservatives still controlled the Republican National Committee through its chairman, Dean Burch. Conservative strategists like *National Review*'s Frank Meyer wanted Goldwater to fight to retain control of the committee. But that was asking Goldwater to devote as much energy to party politics as to spreading the conservative gospel, something he had never done.

Disturbed by the growing dissension within the party that he loved so much, he requested a private meeting with Eisenhower and Nixon in New York City. With Burch left waiting outside the door, the three men agreed that if Burch could not achieve a "broad base of support within the party" before the national committee meeting on January 22, he should step aside as chairman.

While the Waldorf Towers agreement was not another "surrender" on Fifth Avenue, it gave Burch an impossible task. Eisenhower suggested that the leadership crisis could be resolved by selecting Ray C. Bliss of Ohio as national chairman. Within a few days, liberal Republicans began to coalesce behind Bliss, the Ohio party chairman, to oust Burch.[13]

The pressure on Goldwater to compromise intensified. The end came at a briefing for Republican leaders, including Goldwater, after a poll revealed that "fewer than 25 percent of the Republican voters now wanted Goldwater to continue at the party's helm." That was all the senator needed to hear; he was not about to lead a suicide mission or fracture the GOP. On January 12, on the same patio of his Phoenix home where he had declared his candidacy for the presidency a year before, Goldwater announced that Burch would resign on April 1st and Bliss would succeed him. Goldwater, Miller, Burch, and Bliss all smiled, shook hands and, while cameras flashed, read unity statements.

His action revealed that when it came to issues and ideas, Goldwater was usually a conservative first and a Republican second. He would not compromise his beliefs. But when it came to party politics, Goldwater was usually a Republican first and a conservative second, believing, as he said at the 1960 Republican National Convention, that the Republican party was the "historic home" of conservatives. He would never knowingly divide and thereby damage the party. He would use this rationale to explain his support of incumbent President Ford over challenger Ronald Reagan in 1976. In the fall of 1965, he went so far as to suggest that in the interests of party unity, he might not have competed for the 1964 presidential nomination, telling a news-magazine:

I'm not sorry I made the race, but in view of what happened—[a preconvention fight that] left the party just completely torn with no way in the world it could be put together—in all probability I might have withdrawn my name and let Rockefeller and Scranton fight it out.[14]

When the Republican National Committee met in late January 1965 to ratify the Bliss for Burch compromise, Goldwater accepted full responsibility for his defeat and said, "I'm sorry I couldn't produce better results. I'm sorry that so many good men . . . went down with me." He also made it clear whom he considered the frontrunner for the 1968 nomination—Richard Nixon, the man "who worked harder than any one person for the ticket." Turning to the former vice president, Goldwater added, "Dick, I will never forget it. I know that you did it in the interests of the Republican party and not for any selfish reasons. But if there ever comes a time I can turn those into selfish reasons, I am going to do all I can to see that it comes about."[15]

Goldwater's apology to his fellow Republicans was appropriate, but in 1966 the GOP, led by Goldwater conservatives, made one of the most remarkable comebacks in modern politics: it gained forty-seven in the House of Representatives and three in the Senate. The Democratic casualties were, almost without exception, strong supporters of LBJ's Great Society and Vietnam policy. The GOP's gains were national, not regional. Among the Goldwater Republicans outside the South who returned to the House were Peter Garland of Maine, Steven Derounian of New York, George Goodling of Pennsylvania, Henry Schadeberg of Wisconsin, and Gene Snyder of Kentucky. John Tower of Texas and Strom Thurmond of South Carolina, Goldwater's strongest supporters in the Senate, were reelected.

The first scorecard of Americans for Constitutional Action for this 90th Congress showed that all but two of the twenty-five Republicans from the South (including thirteen new members) had conservative ratings higher than 80 percent, with the two exceptions scoring 79 percent. These new and not so new Republicans were not Rockefeller or Scranton "moderates," as *The Reporter,* a liberal magazine, attempted to suggest, but Goldwater conservatives.[16] The most significant conservative victory outside Congress was, of course, the election of Ronald Reagan as governor of California.[17]

One Republican in particular had anticipated and helped bring about the conservative comeback in 1966—Richard Nixon. Gone were his days of kowtowing to Eastern liberals, of negotiating demeaning compacts in Fifth Avenue townhouses. Nixon not only campaigned widely for Goldwater in his presidential bid, he sharply attacked Rockefeller and other liberals, accusing Rockefeller of "dragging his feet" during the 1964 campaign and calling him "a spoilsport . . . a party divider."[18]

That was sweet music to conservatives' ears, and when Nixon asked Tower and Thurmond to support him for the Republican presidential nomination in 1968, they looked around, saw no viable conservative alternative, and said yes. As early as June 1965, in an appearance on NBC's "Meet the Press," Goldwater implied that he too favored the former vice president: "I would say if the convention were held tomorrow that Dick Nixon would be the man." On the same broadcast, he said he would run for the Senate in 1968 if there were an opening—"I'm too old to go back to work and I'm too young to get out of politics."[19] An opening seemed probable: an increasingly frail Carl Hayden would be ninety-one years old in the fall of 1968.

GOLDWATER HAS DESCRIBED the years from 1965 through 1968 as among "the most satisfying" he had known as an adult. There was time to "become reacquainted with my family," as he put it, and to explore his beloved Arizona, especially Monument Valley, the mile-high desert located in the middle of Navajo country. On one trip, Harry Goulding, the owner of a lodge in the valley for nearly forty-five years, told Gordon Greer, a magazine writer accompanying the senator, about the winter that Goldwater came to the rescue of the Navajo when the snow was "two Indians high":

> The winter was the worst I've ever seen here. Our Navajo friends in the valley were starving. We could see them from up here on the mesa. But we couldn't get down there to share our food with them. The snow was too doggone deep. I tell you, we were getting pretty desperate. Then one

day there's all this noise in the sky, and here comes Barry with his airplanes. When I saw them start dropping those bundles of supplies . . . well, there's just no way to tell you how I felt. Barry had to show the other pilots where to go because the rest of them weren't familiar with the valley. They had to drop their packages right next to the hogans so the Indians could reach them. One fell too close and hit a roof. It went through and killed a Navajo inside. Barry has never forgotten. "But think of all the people you *saved*," I tell him. That's what our valley remembers."[20]

During their explorations of Monument Valley, Greer saw no evidence of the famed Goldwater temper, despite provocations like the busloads of tourists who swarmed around and insisted that he sign autographs and pose for their cameras. Quite the opposite; he tossed off jokes right and left. When all the tourists insisted that none of them had voted against him, Goldwater murmured, "Hell, *somebody* must have." Later, a flock of dirty sheep wandered by and someone observed that the sheep would stay dirty until the valley had its next heavy rain. Goldwater grinned and said, "Don't worry about it. In their hearts they know they're white."

Upon reflection, Greer hit upon a reason for the senator's easy mood—the harmony between himself and the valley that was, in every sense, Goldwater country. "It is a land," he wrote, "of glaring sunlight and well-defined shadows where the problems men encounter are equally clear and can be surmounted only by those pioneering virtues Barry Goldwater best understands—courage, truthfulness, teamwork, sacrifice, strength."

Toward the end of their stay, Goldwater, Greer, and Goulding were watching a lingering sunset that had painted the sky blood red when the old lodge owner interrupted the silence: "Barry, I'm glad you didn't make it. That job is so big I'm afraid it might have killed you; you're just too good a friend for us to lose." Goldwater's matter-of-fact response was revealing: "Yes, I probably would have been assassinated. There were a good many threats, you know. For my own sake, it wouldn't have mattered that much, but what a terrible effect it would have had on the country to have it happen again so soon after Jack died."[21]

The crucible of the 1964 election seemingly changed Goldwater very little. According to close friends like Sally Quinn, there were no scars, no trauma. "I never heard a bitter word about 1964," she says. He did not take the defeat personally but saw it as a temporary ideological setback. Never one to look back or to speculate needlessly, he told his friends, "Let's move on."[22] But occasionally, his guard slipped, as when he told a visiting reporter, "Rockefeller and Scranton cut me up so bad there was no way on God's green earth that we could have won." He also criticized the news media, particularly the columnists and editorial writers, for caricaturing him as someone who was "going to push the button." "I don't care," he said, "if I had walked around with wings on, there's nothing that could have been done."[23]

Along with pleasure trips around the state and overseas, often with Peggy, he found time for politics. In the fall of 1965, he volunteered to endorse William F. Buckley Jr., who was running for mayor of New York City against John Lindsay, a liberal Republican congressman, and Democrat Abe Beame. Buckley wisely responded that while such an endorsement "would greatly increase my vote," critics would be given an opening to compare his showing with Goldwater's 1964 total of 800,000 in the city. Inasmuch as it was almost impossible for Buckley to do that well, liberals "would announce a great falling off in conservative strength." Goldwater agreed, and in the end Buckley received a very respectable 341,226 votes, 13.4 percent of the total, far more than any previous Conservative candidate in New York City.[24]

A deep shadow fell across the carefree days in late December 1966 when his seemingly indomitable mother, Mun Goldwater, died at the age of ninety. Although she had been silenced by a stroke, Goldwater wrote that he could see through her eyes "into a happy and contented heart and mind, backed by a spirit and courage I will never know again. Her eyes again spoke of the things she had taught us and smilingly said, 'Do your best.' "[25]

GOLDWATER WAS PULLED into a public quarrel with Governor George Romney in late 1966 when a private exchange of letters between the two men following the 1964 campaign was leaked to the news media. The dispute began when Romney said on a national TV program on December 6, 1964, that before the election Goldwater "was never willing to meet" with him in an effort to "bury what differences we had." Goldwater shot back with a three-page, single-spaced letter that began: "George, that statement was just not true." He charged that Romney's real goal, along with other liberal governors, was not to remove Dean Burch as chairman of the Republican National Committee but "to see [me] out of the party." Romney's twelve-page, single-spaced reply attempted to explain why he had refused to support his party's national ticket. In summary, he was disturbed over "extremism" and the Goldwater strategy to win votes in the South. A sarcastic Goldwater riposted:

> I don't claim for one moment that had you, Governor Smylie, Governor Rockefeller, Senator Keating, Senator Javits, etc., supported me, I would have won. But I can tell you that many rank and file Republicans got a bad taste in their mouths when they saw leaders of their own party failing to support a national ticket. . . .
>
> I doubt if you will ever see a united party when one element of that party refuses to cooperate 1 hundred percent with the top of the ticket.[26]

The exchange served to remind every prospective delegate to the 1968 Republican National Convention who had been a loyal Republican in 1964, and who had not. Goldwater went public with his preference in March 1968, announcing at a Phoenix news conference that he supported Nixon for the presidential nomination. (A year earlier, he had written Ed McCabe, among others, that "I am supporting Richard Nixon as long as he wants that support in the primary.")

But he endorsed Nixon only after he had satisfied himself that Reagan would not be a candidate. He called on Reagan in his Pacific Palisades home in the hills above Los Angeles and asked him directly, "Do you want the presidency?" As Goldwater recalls the conversation, Reagan replied, "No." "Well," said Goldwater, "I wanted to know because Nixon wants me, and if you don't—if you decide to run for the presidency, I'm with you." Reagan repeated, "I don't want it."[27]

That was that so far as Goldwater was concerned until Reagan changed his mind, causing the senator to write to selected delegates and wealthy contributors about the California governor's last-minute challenge. Goldwater said that Reagan had "told me time and again that he would not seek the presidency but that he would not turn it down if it were offered him." He now sensed "a desire" in Reagan for the office and predicted that "every effort" would be made at the convention "to influence delegates to switch to Reagan after the first ballot." Reagan's campaign in Miami, he said, "will be well financed and he will have some talented people with him," but "waiting until the last two or three weeks before a National Convention is not the way, in my opinion, to win the nomination." In fact, "Nixon will win on the first ballot."

Goldwater went so far in his pro-Nixon politicking as to write Reagan as "a very cherished and valued friend" to suggest that he release California's delegates to Nixon. He proposed the action "to make sure that Rockefeller does not go to the convention with any possible chance of being nominated."[28]

The ploy did not work, and when he arrived in Miami, Goldwater discovered that the Nixon forces were uncertain whether they had enough delegates to nominate their candidate on the first ballot. They were particularly concerned about Reagan's strong appeal to Southern delegations. If Nixon did not win on the first roll call, many observers agreed, convention sentiment would begin to shift shortly to Reagan.

A little nervous about his reception, Goldwater made the opening address on Monday night, and as he had in 1960, made an appeal for party unity, eliciting what NBC's David Brinkley described as "the most spontaneous, emotional, enthusiastic Republican response of the entire convention." When he returned to his hotel, there was a note to call Nixon, who, ever the opportunist, asked him to remain in Miami and meet with delegates on Tuesday and Wednesday. Goldwater agreed and over the next forty-eight hours talked with hundreds of delegates and alternates who were being importuned from the left by Rockefeller, from the right by Reagan, and from the center by Nixon. Thurmond and Tower also "shored the Southern dike against Reagan's rising waters."

The day before the balloting, Nixon spent much of his time reassuring restless Southern delegations that he opposed school busing, would appoint "strict constitutionalists" to the Supreme Court, and was critical of federal intervention in local school board affairs. He won the nomination on the first ballot with 692 votes, just 25 more than necessary.

The Nixon forces had had every right to be nervous. Goldwater was shown an independent survey after the convention that revealed that 20.7 percent of the delegates said "they were influenced to vote for Nixon as a result of their meetings with me."[29] Nixon went out of his way during the convention to express his appreciation for Goldwater's "determining influence." In a letter to the author, he was more explicit, stating: "Senator Goldwater's support for me . . . played a decisive role in assuring my nomination for president. It is possible that I could have won the nomination without his support. But his support made it possible for me to win on the first ballot."[30] And Nixon needed to win on the first ballot.

Goldwater's central part in Nixon's success that year did not end in Miami; many of Nixon's top aides were graduates of the 1964 campaign, including Richard Kleindienst, who served as national director of field operations for the Nixon presidential campaign under John Mitchell. In October, when Nixon was steadily losing ground to Humphrey, he called Goldwater almost every day. Each time, Goldwater urged Nixon to "exploit the mismanagement of the Vietnam War."[31]

Despite a last-minute bombing halt in Vietnam by President Johnson and an eleventh-hour surge by Hubert Humphrey, Nixon won the presidency by a popular vote of just 510,000. His margin in the electoral college was more decisive: Nixon carried thirty-two states with 302 electoral votes to Humphrey's 191 votes. Third-party candidate George Wallace received nearly ten million popular votes and five states with forty-five electoral votes.

In his 1979 memoirs, Goldwater says that if he were again allowed to choose "between the policies and programs of my friend Hubert Humphrey and the promises and policies of Richard Nixon, I would still support Nixon." But Watergate, he acknowledges, left a bitter taste in his mouth. He does not offer the same endorsement in his 1988 memoirs in which he describes Nixon as "a two-fisted, four-square liar."[32]

In November 1968, Goldwater easily won reelection to the Senate over Roy Elson, a longtime aide to Carl Hayden, receiving 232,939 votes to his opponent's 175,114, a larger plurality than in 1952 or 1958. He was delighted with Republican gains in the Congress and elsewhere: a pickup of sixteen seats in the Senate, seventeen in the House of Representatives, and the election of thirty-one Republican governors—the greatest number of state chief executives since the Harding landslide of 1920. "All of this," he noted with satisfaction, "took place just four years after the pundits had written that my defeat at the hands of Lyndon Johnson signaled the end of the Republican party as a viable, political instrument."

In a letter to Kitchel, he contrasted his and the then-president's fortunes: "Here is Lyndon Johnson sitting at his ranch a total disgrace and here am I having just won the biggest election of my life four years after he clobbered me." Healthy and vigorous at sixty, he looked forward to rejoining the Senate where he had spent so many productive years and working with the new Republican president, whom he believed would move to end the Vietnam War and "to take immediate charge of the federal establishment."[33]

PART IV

Legislator

18

The Making and Unmaking of Presidents, I

WHILE IT IS UNUSUAL for the ideas and positions of a losing presidential candidate to be as quickly vindicated as Goldwater's were, it is unprecedented in American politics for a presidential loser to have a continuing major impact on the presidential politics of his party. Yet, so strong was his hold on the hearts of millions of grassroots conservatives, that Barry Goldwater played a decisive part in the nomination of Richard Nixon in 1968, the resignation of President Nixon in 1974, the nomination of Ford rather than Reagan in 1976, and the nomination of Vice President George Bush rather than Senate Republican leader Bob Dole in 1988—twenty-four years after his presidential bid and two years after he had left the Senate.

Bush and Dole were locked in a tight race in 1988 in the always important New Hampshire primary, and in the waning days of the campaign, Bush telephoned Goldwater to say, "I may need you," and asked him to stand by. The following Monday morning, the day before Republicans went to the polls, the senator, along with Joanne Goldwater and Michael Goldwater's fifteen-year-old son, Mike, was flown from Phoenix to the Granite State for a day of campaigning, returning home late that evening. Goldwater warmly endorsed Bush and put Dole down by stating that "running the political affairs of forty-seven [Republican senators] is not like running or helping in running the lives of 250-odd million." Asked why he was not endorsing a more conservative candidate than Bush, he said, "Who in the hell is it? I'm not running." In a five-minute paid broadcast, Goldwater called Bush "the most qualified candidate of my lifetime," and then added, "except me, George."[1] Goldwater's eleventh-hour visit, along with an advertising blitz by the Bush organization, helped overcome Dole's apparently safe lead and gain a critical victory for Bush.

Goldwater had a respect-contempt relationship with Nixon. The dichotomy is reflected in his 1979 memoirs, which describe Nixon critically yet often sympathetically, while in his 1988 memoirs the pendulum swings far to the contempt side. In the later book, he portrays Nixon as a habitual liar and schemer who deliberately betrayed his family, his party, and his country.

In this respect it should be remembered that in 1979 Goldwater was still a prominent Republican senator who faced reelection in 1980; he could not afford to be too critical of the former head of his party and the country. In 1988, Goldwater had retired from the Senate; he could say whatever he wanted with impunity. Also, Goldwater became even more outspoken, more uninhibited, more opinionated as he grew older.

Goldwater's 1979 collaborator was his longtime adviser and campaign manager, Steve Shadegg, who had managed many Republican campaigns and had a natural empathy for his adopted party and its leaders. Goldwater's 1988 coauthor was Jack Casserly, a veteran journalist who was quite willing to bring out the most caustic in the senator about one of the media's favorite targets, Richard Nixon.

Describing his meeting (along with Senator Hugh Scott and Congressman John Rhodes) with Nixon in the Oval Office on August 7, 1974, two days before the president resigned, the 1979 Goldwater was filled with sorrow over the disgrace and discredit that Nixon had brought on himself; he had tears in his eyes. He described a "serene, confident, cheerful" Nixon who reminisced about the past and how he and Goldwater had campaigned together for over twenty years. Rhodes remembered the president as calm and composed, but tired and gray.

"Almost casually," recalled Goldwater, Nixon "asked me how things stood in the Senate. I told him he could count on about twelve votes, perhaps as many as fifteen. No more." As both men knew thirty-four votes were needed to defeat the impeachment charges in the Senate. Scott confirmed that "maybe" there were fifteen votes in the Senate, but "they're not very firm." Asked for his estimate, Rhodes replied, "About the same, Mr. President." Goldwater observed that a good lawyer might be able to beat Articles I and III (Obstruction of Justice and Defiance of Committee Subpoenas) in a Senate trial. How about Article II? (Abuse of Presidential Power) asked the president. Goldwater answered, "I'm leaning that way myself, Mr. President."

Goldwater revealed that he had always had "reservations" about Nixon. "Despite our long association, I never felt that I truly knew him." To Goldwater, who never dissembled and never calculated, Nixon "always seemed to be too well programmed, to be carefully calculating the ultimate effect of everything he did or said"—a carefully rendered judgment with which even Nixon's friends would agree.

When Goldwater, Scott, and Rhodes left the Oval Office, Nixon, according to Goldwater, was smiling. He believed that at the end the president "was putting the welfare of the nation ahead of every other consideration." He summed up the dramatic thirty-minute meeting: "Whatever else I may say or think about Richard Nixon, he displayed a quality of courage I have rarely encountered on that Wednesday afternoon."[2]

When Nixon met with a selected group of senators and congressmen in the Cabinet Room the following evening, just before his televised farewell address to the nation, he said, tears streaming down his face, "I just hope . . . I haven't let you down." A visibly moved Goldwater hugged Nixon as he passed. One observer wrote, "Now almost all were crying, as if at a death in the family."[3]

In 1988, however, Goldwater described a far different Oval Office meeting and Nixon. Nixon still had his feet up on the desk and still reminisced about the past, but "I didn't buy it," recounted a scornful Goldwater, "not one bit." Gone was the "serene, confident, cheerful Nixon," replaced by a hard-edged, narrow-eyed, sarcastic Nixon who demanded to know what support he had in the Senate. Goldwater replied in kind: "I took a nose count in the Senate today. You have four firm votes. The others are really undecided. I'm one of them."

Goldwater was close to tears, but they were tears of humiliation at what Nixon had done to the nation, not of sorrow at the sight of a falling president. Disgusted by Nixon's desperate attempts to find some way out and determined to force him to resign, Goldwater wrote that "I hit him as directly and as hard as I could." The 1988 Goldwater made no mention of Nixon's "courage," merely saying: "Nixon now knew beyond any doubt that one way or another his presidency was finished. None of us doubted the outcome. He would resign."[4]

BACK IN JANUARY 1969, Goldwater's first face-to-face meeting with the new president after his inauguration was at an Alfalfa Club dinner in Washington. He warned Nixon that unless he moved quickly to appoint Republicans to the more than three thousand executive positions in the government, "Kennedy-Johnson holdovers would frustrate" his efforts to take charge of the bureaucracy. Nixon said that he intended to act as soon as he had selected his cabinet. But his appointments never satisfied Goldwater and other conservatives.

Their first private meeting in the White House came in March when Goldwater sat down with Nixon who greeted him warmly in the living room on the second floor; Bryce Harlow, a senior White House aide, was the only other person present. After various pleasantries, Nixon got to the point: "Where do you see the problems, Barry?"

Goldwater reiterated that Nixon should remove all the Kennedy-Johnson holdovers, especially those in the State Department who had been responsible for the no-win policy in Vietnam. The president said that he intended to give the peace process another six months, but if no progress were made in Paris, he might "have to order a resumption of bombing" in Vietnam.

On the home front, Goldwater urged Nixon to implement the Republican platform by reducing inflation and waste in government. The voters of Arizona had made it clear to him that they wanted "lower taxes, less federal spending, and a reduction in federal interference" in their lives. Nixon replied by implying that Arizona voters were "atypical" and Goldwater "too blunt" in his prescriptions.[5]

It was to be the last private meeting between the two men for more than two years. Goldwater blamed this on what he called the White House's "inner guard"—John Ehrlichman and Robert Haldeman, "administrative types with little sensitivity for political reality" who moreover had "never been identified with the Republican party."[6]

In June 1971, Goldwater spent an hour with the president discussing a wide range of issues including the 1972 presidential campaign, "Red"

China, and the economy, particularly inflation, which was running a worrisome 6 percent per year. Nixon said it was essential that he win reelection by an overwhelming plurality so that he could carry out his campaign promises. Goldwater agreed, particularly if it should increase Republican membership in Congress.

Nixon went on to explain that he wanted to improve U.S. relations with mainland China in order to exploit the "natural animosities" between Moscow and Peking, but reassured Goldwater he would never do anything to injure America's relationship with the Republic of China on Taiwan (long and ardently supported by Goldwater). Nixon was confident that the United Nations would not admit Communist China to membership that fall. At that very moment Nixon was making serious overtures to Peking that would change the political map of Asia and the world.

On the subject of inflation, Nixon vowed that his administration would never resort to wage and price controls. At that very moment he and Treasury Secretary John Connally were discussing just such a step.

Goldwater was given the full Nixon treatment—telling his visitor only what he wanted to hear.[7] On August 15, Nixon announced over national television that standby wage and price controls were being imposed on a "temporary" basis; they remained in effect for nearly two years. On July 15, Secretary of State Kissinger called Goldwater to inform him that the president would announce that day that he was going to Peking. Kissinger asked Goldwater to delay any public comment or criticism until he could brief him. It was the first of many times that Kissinger was directed by the White House to "handle" Goldwater.

Three weeks later, on August 5, at a breakfast meeting in his White House office, Kissinger thanked Goldwater for his silence and went on to report that Nixon's projected visit to China was already "having a profound effect on Moscow." Both he and the president had been invited to visit the Soviet Union, and there were indications that Hanoi might release the American POWs they were holding. Kissinger predicted that if the Peking talks went well, "we could expect an early and satisfactory end to the war in Vietnam." When Goldwater expressed concern that the tilt toward Peking might damage seriously the U.S. relationship with Taiwan, Kissinger "assured me this was not going to happen."[8]

Satisfied that he had pacified his visitor, Kissinger proceeded to take up a major concern: conservative support of the president. He lamented the "lack of vigor" among conservative Republicans in Congress to defend the president. Goldwater replied that conservative Republicans "were disappointed" in Nixon and his administration, which appeared "to us" to be "drifting left."

Denying the charge, Kissinger pointed out that the *New York Times* and the *Washington Post* were praising Nixon for his détente-like foreign policy and added that "the president wants to cultivate this new climate."[9] The idea that praise by the *Times* and the *Post* would persuade Goldwater that Nixon was on the right track shows how little Kissinger understood conservatives. Nevertheless, Goldwater was impressed by Kissinger's encyclopedic grasp of foreign issues and flattered by his appreciation of "my viewpoint." They agreed to meet at least once a month.

At their November 1971 meeting, following the admission of Communist China to and the expulsion of Taiwan from the United Nations, Kissinger said that he did not think the president's announced visit to China had been a deciding factor in the UN's actions.[10] He knew better. Although the U.S. delegation to the United Nations, led by George Bush, insisted that the United States was 100 percent behind the Republic of China, the UN delegates took their cue from Nixon's actions— his travel plans—and expelled Taiwan.

Despite his doubts about and frustrations with Nixon, Goldwater continued to be a good Republican soldier. In June 1971, he agreed to be a last-minute replacement for the administration on an ABC-TV program examining the *New York Times'* publication of the Pentagon Papers. White House aide John Scali described his performance as "superb." The following month, Goldwater appeared on the "Dick Cavett Show" as "an administration spokesman."

In September, Nixon wrote Goldwater commending him for his "perceptive and generous" speech in Boston supporting the administration. The president went on to assure him that the economic controls he had just imposed were "temporary" and that his trip to China "will not be taken at the expense of old friends [i.e., Taiwan] and I have no intention of weakening our defense posture."[11]

By the fall of 1971, Nixon had decided that in his reelection effort, Goldwater should be scheduled "in as many events as possible throughout the country." He emphasized to aides that "Barry should only accept invitations that were presidential in nature" and should be provided logistical support. H. R. Haldeman wrote Goldwater confirming the special relationship and offered "whatever advance help you may require in order to make your schedule the kind that will 'make the difference.' "[12] By agreeing to campaign for Nixon, Goldwater, still "Mr. Conservative" to many Republicans, helped to undercut the challenge of conservative Congressman John Ashbrook in the New Hampshire primary.

When the Shanghai Communiqué, setting forth a new and more formal relationship between the United States and China, was issued on February 28, 1972, the White House called Goldwater to endorse it, but he said he would wait until Nixon returned so he could learn the full details. He was disturbed by Communist China's insistence in the communiqué that Taiwan was a part of China and the United State's apparent concurrence, as suggested by the following language in the American part of the communiqué:

The United States acknowledges that all Chinese on either side of the Taiwan Strait maintain there is but one China and that Taiwan is a part of China. The United States government does not challenge this position.[13]

Several newspapers interpreted this to mean that the Nixon administration was prepared to abandon Taiwan to improve relations with the mainland—an interpretation Nixon angrily denied at a White House briefing for Goldwater and other congressional leaders. He insisted that he had released a statement in Shanghai that the United States would maintain and respect all its treaties with Taiwan. Kissinger, looking directly at Goldwater, said, "I can see Chou En-lai with his Chinese Goldwaters having the same trouble the president is having with Barry right now."[14]

On returning to his office, Goldwater dictated a personal ten-page memorandum covering the briefing and exploring his options. Should he criticize the communiqué? Was he duty-bound to support the president? His inclination was to refuse comment, reasoning that "if I speak favorably, my conservative friends will accuse me of having abandoned Nationalist China. This is not true, and I must not let anyone gain that impression." His memo concluded: "To sum it up, if I cannot believe my president, then I have lost all my faith in men and friends and in my leadership."[15]

Subsequently, Goldwater admitted that he "might" have made the wrong decision. As he wrote in his 1979 memoirs, the Shanghai Communiqué became the basis for President Jimmy Carter's recognition of mainland China, derecognition of Taiwan, and abrogation of the mutual defense treaty between the United States and the Republic of China.[16] Despite the reversal—even betrayal—on an issue that meant so much to him, Goldwater in 1979 still avoided the anti-Nixon rhetoric that suffuses his later memoirs.

In July 1972, Nixon invited Goldwater to the White House to discuss his campaign plans for reelection and the senator's role at the convention. Looking at the coming contest between the president and ultra-liberal Senator George McGovern, Goldwater stated that all Nixon had to do was "stay in the White House, be presidential, and pursue an honorable peace in Vietnam." A couple of weeks later, the White House asked Goldwater to make one of the opening convention speeches.

He began working on a typical Goldwater address with several well-chosen words about deserters, draft-dodgers, and former Attorney General Ramsey Clark, who had recently been spending more time in North Vietnam than the United States. When Fred LaRue, who had worked for him in 1964 and was now assigned to the Committee to Re-elect the President (CRP), asked him to delete the references to Clark and the deserters, Goldwater replied that if CRP insisted on the deletions, he would cancel his speech and return to Washington. CRP and the White House backed down, and Goldwater delivered his remarks unexpurgated. CBS's Walter Cronkite noted that the references to draft-dodgers and Ramsey Clark evoked the greatest audience response on opening night.[17]

It was the fourth straight Republican national convention at which Goldwater demonstrated that he, and what he stood for, echoed the feelings of a majority of the delegates.

Following his monumental victory over McGovern (60.7 percent of the popular vote, only .4 percent behind LBJ's landslide win in 1964; forty-nine out of fifty states, with only Massachusetts and the District of Columbia voting Democratic; 520 electoral votes to McGovern's 17), Nixon asked Goldwater to Camp David to talk about his second administration.

Oozing hubris, Nixon told Goldwater that he intended to implement a conservative agenda: he would reduce the size and cost of government, reinvigorate federalism by giving the states more authority, and force North Vietnam to come to the peace table. Goldwater again urged the president to take quick hold of the federal bureaucracy. He believed that Democrats like Senate Majority Leader Mike Mansfield would help "to make the upper-echelon government employees subject to presidential appointment and removal."[18]

Anticipating his crowning legislative effort of more than a decade later—the reorganization of the Department of Defense—Goldwater told Nixon that the United States had four tactical air forces (Army, Navy, Air Force, and Marines) all doing the same job. The result was needless competition, waste, and duplication. He also mentioned the separate communications systems maintained by the Army, Navy, and Air Force. In the past, the three services had used compatible frequencies but now each insisted on having its own. "It seemed to me," Goldwater recalled telling Nixon, that this could "prevent proper cooperation between the military branches in time of crisis."[19] (There was, in fact, just such a communications foul-up in the 1983 Grenada invasion when an officer had to use his private credit card to place a telephone call regarding the disposition of forces.)

Switching to his own future, Goldwater told the president that he was inclined not to run for reelection in 1974. (Goldwater would go through a similar "Should I run?" debate with himself, his family, and his friends in 1980. Each time, he could not bring himself to leave the Senate, which had become his purpose in life in so many ways; each time he won reelection.) Nixon said that if Goldwater did retire, he would consider appointing him ambassador to Mexico, which would have caused cardiac infarctions throughout the State Department and might have been part of Nixon's new plan finally to clean out the department.

At the end of their lengthy one-on-one conversation, Goldwater was "convinced the second Nixon administration would be vastly different from the first."[20] This time Nixon would deliver on his conservative promises.

His conviction was borne out in December when the president ordered twelve days of intense bombing of North Vietnam and the mining of Haiphong Harbor. A month later, representatives of North and South Vietnam, the United States, and the Vietcong signed a treaty ending the longest (and most unsuccessful) war in American history. Yet Goldwater could not help but reflect that "those of us who urged an all-out drive to win the war were proved right. . . . Limited war is a brutal,

reckless sacrifice of lives and treasures. Once hostilities commence
there is no substitute for victory."[21]

BUT IN THE AREA OF DOMESTIC POLICY, days became weeks, which
became months, and still Nixon did not take the steps he and Goldwater
had discussed at Camp David. A major reason, of course, was Watergate. At the time, Goldwater accepted assertions that the White House
was not involved because (1) he did not believe the president would lie
to him and/or the American people and (2) the burglary seemed to him
to be "pointless," "amateurish," and "naive," three things Nixon had
never been guilty of. But when Watergate continued to preoccupy (and
thereby impede) the administration, Goldwater decided to go public
with his discontent in a newspaper interview.

On April 11, 1973, Goldwater called on the president "to speak up
now and come out in the open and get rid of Watergate once and for
all." He added some hyperbole: "It's beginning to be like Teapot
Dome. I mean there's a smell to it. Let's get rid of the smell." He
warned that if Watergate were not settled, it would put Republican
candidates all over the country on the spot in 1974. He repeated his
belief that Nixon was not personally involved.[22]

The White House did not dare ignore criticism from Goldwater and
other Republicans. Less than three weeks later, Nixon announced over
national television that he had accepted the resignations of Robert
Haldeman and John Ehrlichman and had fired John Dean. He also said
that Richard Kleindienst was leaving as attorney general because of his
personal relationships with some of those involved in Watergate, and
named Elliot Richardson in his place.

Goldwater was incensed at the coupling of Kleindienst with the
innermost circle of the White House. Goldwater knew Kleindienst to be
an experienced politician who would have spurned the Watergate caper
and cussed out anyone "stupid enough to suggest such a thing."
Kleindienst moreover had been a loyal Nixon man, heading his
delegate hunt in 1968. "He didn't deserve this cruelty," Goldwater
wrote, "at the hands of the man he had supported, befriended, and
defended."[23]

On May 16, still angry over Nixon's treatment of Kleindienst and his
failure to deliver on his postelection promises, Goldwater released a
statement that America's ability to govern at home and to lead abroad

was being hampered by Watergate. On June 20, he personally typed a long private letter to Nixon, urging him to end his preoccupation with Watergate, come out of his shell, meet with members of Congress, and "push the reforms he had promised to make at our Camp David meeting." Ever the party loyalist, he praised Nixon for his foreign accomplishments and concluded with a pledge of support.[24]

Publicly, he accused the news media of a "shameless double standard" regarding Nixon and other politicians. He compared the journalistic outcry over a Watergate "coverup" with the coverup of Senator Edward Kennedy and Chappaquidick. "If I had run that girl off the bridge," Goldwater remarked, "you wouldn't have heard the end of it."[25]

Five weeks later, Bryce Harlow called to say that the president would like to see him, but Goldwater wound up talking only with Harlow. Many Republicans, Goldwater reported, were beginning to question the president's veracity. There was already talk of impeachment, and while Nixon might finish his term, "he would be an impotent president, a rejected party leader." Harlow promised to relay the message, as unpleasant as it was.[26]

In August, while Goldwater was vacationing in Newport Beach, California, Henry Kissinger, who had just been named secretary of state following Bill Rogers' resignation, invited him to San Clemente. During a brief discussion of Watergate, Kissinger conceded that the president had suffered "almost irreparable damage but would probably survive." Nixon, Goldwater said, would survive "if he now took hold of the government and began doing the things he had promised me he would do." Both men were wrong, but neither would learn until almost a year later that Nixon had lied all along about his central role in the attempted coverup of the Watergate break-in.

Kissinger went on to say that Nixon favored either Connally or Nelson Rockefeller as his successor. There was, he admitted, the possibility that Reagan might also run, but if he did, Goldwater gathered from Kissinger's remarks, he would not have Nixon's support. "Apparently Reagan's abortive attempt in 1968 had never been forgiven."[27] Kissinger did not mention Vice President Spiro Agnew as a 1976 possibility, probably because the *Wall Street Journal* had just published an exclusive story that Agnew was under federal investigation for allegations of conspiracy, extortion, bribery, and tax fraud. Agnew, it was alleged, while governor of Maryland, had taken money in return for state contracts and had continued to receive money for favors as vice president.

Kissinger's omission disturbed Goldwater, who had become a good friend of Agnew. The senator and the vice president had a number of things in common. Both were of immigrant stock. Agnew was a World War II decorated army officer and had also served in the Korean War. And like Goldwater, Agnew had worked his way up the political ladder, in his case to the govenorship of Maryland. He too was tall and handsome, a beautiful dresser, exuding confidence and charm. He was the GOP's best fundraiser. He was in the Goldwater mold: a patriot and a candid politician.

In the late fall of 1971, Agnew asked Goldwater to visit him in his office and revealed that he thought the "palace guard"—Ehrlichman and Haldeman—wanted him off the ticket in 1972. Proud and hurt, as only a successful, self-made man can be, Agnew said that he was contemplating making an early announcement of his withdrawal. "I urged him not to do this," Goldwater later wrote. "I said Republicans throughout the country had more confidence in him than they had in Nixon." Agnew complained bitterly that Nixon excluded him from White House decisions, that what he learned came to him secondhand—he had not known, for example, about the overtures to China until Nixon made his televised announcement. When Goldwater remarked that Kennedy had isolated Johnson, and Hubert Humphrey in turn had felt isolated by Johnson, Agnew rejoined that Nixon had discussed his frustrating years as vice president under Eisenhower and vowed in Miami that things would be different in his presidency.[28] But Goldwater persisted—Agnew had a duty to his party and country— and the vice president finally agreed to remain on the ticket.

Two years later, on the evening of September 9, 1973, Goldwater received another urgent invitation from Agnew to meet with him at his Kenwood home. An angry Agnew said that after months of rumors about a Justice Department investigation of him concerning alleged payoffs by contractors while he was governor, he had been told that Attorney General Elliot Richardson was taking the case to the grand jury and asking for an indictment. He was upset that the attorney general had not contacted him personally and that Nixon "had permitted the matter to go this far without any effort to discover [his] side of the story."[29]

In his 1988 memoirs, Goldwater called the White House's conduct "purely and obviously political. They should have been concerned—unless someone wanted to use Agnew, perhaps even force him to leave his post." Agnew had not been able to learn the exact nature of the charges against him or the names of his accusers, apparently three or four Maryland businessmen who were being investigated by the Internal Revenue Service. He wanted to know what Goldwater thought about his going to Carl Albert, the Speaker of the House, and requesting the House of Representatives, rather than the Justice Department, investigate and determine if the charges were true.[30] Agnew thought that Richardson was out to get him and that he could not expect fair treatment from him or the Justice Department, which had been leaking information about the investigation for months.

Goldwater liked the idea and suggested that Agnew immediately visit Albert, along with two Republican and two Democratic congressmen, but without telling the White House. Agnew "thanked me for my sympathy and for the advice and indicated he intended to follow it."[31]

Goldwater was touched by Agnew's plight because they were friends. And because he had some experience with baseless charges and believed that someone was innocent until proven guilty. He noted in his private "Alpha File" that the move "to get Ted Agnew might have originated close to the White House. It was representative of the same mentality which had spawned the Watergate." He carried his defense of Agnew to the extreme, writing, "Whether Agnew was innocent or guilty was not my immediate concern. It was, rather, the motives of Richardson and the White House."[32]

He did not seem to care whether his friend was telling the truth, nor about the potentially serious damage to the Republican party and the nation if the vice president had been breaking the law.

Five days later, on September 14, Goldwater met again with Agnew, who told him that Nixon had asked him to resign and "was making it impossible for him to go to the House of Representatives." Goldwater learned much later that Agnew had lied to him. He had met with Speaker Albert and others, but the Democratic leadership did not want to become part of a Republican dispute already in the courts, a dispute that could only redound to the advantage of the Democrats. But despite the lie, Goldwater continued to make excuses for Agnew, particularly in his 1988 memoirs.

At the September 14 meeting, Agnew admitted to Goldwater that as governor he had accepted political contributions, sometimes from people who did business with the state, but they had been "small contributions." (This too was a lie: the "small contributions" totaled tens of thousands of dollars.) The contracts, Agnew insisted, had been awarded on merit. All he had done was to follow "the pattern" established by his predecessors. This was Agnew's basic defense: every other governor of Maryland—paid one of the smallest salaries in the country—accepted "contributions" from contractors as an income supplement. Why should he say no when everyone else had said yes?

Agnew told Goldwater that he thought he could win acquittal, "even with the president and the attorney general against him," but a long trial would be "a burden" for the administration. He believed that the press, the public, and "perhaps some of the judges" were in "a vengeful mood" because of Watergate. Therefore, he informed Goldwater, he intended to resign. Goldwater pointed out that simply resigning "might not block prosecution" and that Agnew would be in a strong legal position as vice president. Agnew countered that he would not resign until he had "absolute guarantees there would be no prosecution."[33]

Later that day Goldwater flew home to Phoenix, but was not able to leave the Agnew affair behind. White House aides Fred Buzhardt and Bryce Harlow followed him to Phoenix that evening and briefed him on the latest developments. Sending two of his top aides across the country to fill Goldwater in personally showed how important Nixon felt the senator was to his political future. The deal was seemingly simple: the attorney general would drop prosecution of the alleged bribes if the vice president resigned and entered a plea of *nolo contendere* (no contest) to one charge of failure to pay income tax. An upset Goldwater thought the bargain was "shameful" and told his visitors that he was "sick" of the whole dirty business. He saw inherent drawbacks in the agreement for both sides and serious damage to the Republican party in either case. It could persuade the public that the White House had forced Agnew to resign "with threats of prosecution on the alleged bribery charges." On the other hand, if Agnew pleaded no contest, the public would conclude that he had in fact accepted the payments (which of course he had).

Goldwater warned that if Agnew resigned and Nixon appointed either Connally or Nelson Rockefeller, "it would provoke a split in the party." The senator recalled that Harlow was "sensitive" to the political implications of Agnew's resignation while Buzhardt was more concerned "with getting rid of Agnew lest his continued presence complicate the president's personal problems with Watergate."[34]

In his 1988 memoirs, Goldwater wrote that many people had told him he was wrong to offer Agnew "any consolation" because he was a crook. But though the evidence that Agnew had accepted payoffs over a number of years was convincing, Goldwater would only say, "Perhaps he was [a crook]. But I do not lightly view abandoning anyone under fire." That is commendable and consistent with Goldwater's frontier code.

Less commendable and certainly inconsistent is the double standard he applied—one to Agnew, who lied to him and received his support and sympathy the other to Nixon, who lied to him and was condemned by him.[35] The wide variance in Goldwater's treatment of the two men stemmed in large part from a simple fact: Goldwater counted Agnew as a friend, but he was never able to connect personally with Nixon. Friendship, for Goldwater, could cover a multitude of sins.

Goldwater's constant references to Nixon as "the most dishonest man" he had ever known ring hollow. Was Nixon more dishonest than Robert McNamara, who lied that America could win a war that cost more than 58,000 Americans lives? More dishonest than Lyndon Johnson, who promised not to send American boys to fight an Asian war and wound up dispatching nearly 700,000 men? More dishonest than Nelson Rockefeller, who charged that Goldwater wanted to end Social Security and was too dangerous to have in the room with the H-bomb? More dishonest than Bill Moyers, who personally approved television commercials that planted an indelible picture of Goldwater in the minds of millions of Americans as a man who would destroy the nation and the world?

When the White House canvassed Republican members of Congress for their recommendation to replace Agnew in the fall of 1973, they came up with four names: John Connally, Nelson Rockefeller, Ronald Reagan, and Gerald Ford, leader of the House Republicans. In so doing, they disregarded a Gallup Poll of Republicans, who, when asked who they thought should succeed Agnew, divided as follows: Connally, 24 percent; Goldwater, 19 percent; Senator Howard Baker, 15 percent; Rockefeller, 14 percent; Elliot Richardson, 5 percent; and Congressman Rogers Morton, 4 percent.[36]

Although he was the number two choice of the party, Goldwater was not interested in the job; his personal choice was George Bush because of his political experience (he was then chairman of the Republican National Committee) and his age (he was under fifty and could serve as vice president and then run for the presidency). He felt that Connally would be opposed by Democrats who resented his switch to the Republican party and by Republicans who considered him to be a newcomer to the GOP. Conservatives would resist Rockefeller for all the obvious reasons. Significantly, he did not say one word, pro or con, about Reagan, the very successful governor of California. Subsequently, he stated that "Nixon made a wise political choice when he selected Jerry Ford."[37]

IN THE FALL of 1973 and the spring of 1974, Goldwater urged, almost begged, Nixon to take the initiative on Watergate. He suggested that he appear before the Senate Watergate Committee, arguing that unless the president answered the committee's questions he would be unable to recoup public support. At times, in frustration, he even considered calling on Nixon to resign, but always drew back—remembering how Nixon had stumped the country for him in 1964.

But the letters and telephone calls imploring him to do something poured in, so that in late November he made a plea for "a moment of tranquillity." "If we can have such a moment to quiet the hysteria that grips us," he said, "we may be able to proceed to the task ahead, to put in order our house of government, to eliminate the incompetent, punish the guilty, and to make sure that what has happened may not happen again. But all this in an orderly, deliberate fashion."[38]

When the president did not respond to his and other Republicans' suggestions to act, but continued to insist that his administration was not sinking, Goldwater became more outspoken.

One month later, acknowledging his sharp disappointment, he told the *Christian Science Monitor* that Nixon had ignored his advice to open up on Watergate. "He chose to dibble and dabble and argue on very nebulous grounds like executive privilege and confidentiality when all the American people wanted to know was the truth." Americans, he said, wanted to know how honest their president was, adding, "I hate to think of the old adage, 'Would you buy a used car from Dick Nixon?'—but that's what people are asking around the country."[39] That wisecrack got him an immediate invitation to dinner at the White

House with the president and Mrs. Nixon and a few other guests in the family quarters.

Even before they sat down to eat, Nixon acted erratically, jumping from subject to subject. Recalling the president's strange behavior years later, Goldwater wondered whether he "was witnessing a slow-motion collapse of Nixon's mental balance." The explanation, as recounted by Pat Buchanan, one of the other guests, was far less dramatic. Nixon's capacity for alcohol was quite limited; two drinks was one drink too many. The night of his dinner with Goldwater, he had two drinks plus several glasses of wine.[40] In his 1988 autobiography, although not in his 1979 recollections, Goldwater asserts that the sight of a "jabbering," "incoherent" Nixon convinced him that the "presidency was crumbling," and he would "not stand idly by if the situation worsened."

Ironically, Goldwater once commented that Nixon was "really a wonderful fellow when he drinks. I wish he'd done more drinking when he was president." But now, deeply concerned about Watergate's effect on the nation and the party, he predicted that there would be a confrontation between them, boasting that Nixon had remarked that "he feared only one man in Congress—Barry Goldwater. If no one in the Republican party would stand up to Nixon, I would."[41]

That is tough talk worthy of a Goldwater, a Teddy Roosevelt, or a John Wayne, but it is misleading. While Goldwater certainly was a major player in the Watergate drama, he was not the only, or even the first, prominent member of the Republican party to challenge Nixon. Senator James Buckley of New York was the first conservative senator, on March 19, 1974, to suggest that President Nixon should resign. Other senators, including Goldwater, did not join Buckley although they expressed their sympathy with his stand.

When the president continued to avoid disclosing the contents of the incriminating Oval Office tapes, his position swiftly deteriorated. John Tower, as strong a Nixon backer as could be found in the Senate, admitted that the "atmosphere of confrontation" Nixon had created had seriously damaged his cause. Even Vice President Ford, who rarely displayed any emotion, revealed his frustration by telling a meeting of Midwestern Republicans in Chicago: "Never again must Americans allow an arrogant elite guard of political adolescents like CREEP to bypass the regular Republican party organization."[42]

Goldwater still hesitated to call directly for Nixon's resignation. But by late May, he said flatly that he would have "no qualms" about asking Nixon to resign if it were clear that by remaining president, Nixon would harm the party and the country.[43]

Yet Goldwater still believed that Nixon had not known about the Watergate break-in nor been involved in any coverup. Former Senator Charles Percy recalls that he and Goldwater visited Nixon in the White House in the late spring to discuss the Watergate "mess." They laid out a strategy for the president to go on national television and apologize to the public for the breakdown in governmental institutions and for the excesses of Watergate. Nixon replied, "The only thing wrong with that is that I knew *nothing* about Watergate."[44] Thus, when he finally realized that Nixon had lied to him and everyone else about his involvement, Goldwater was furious. He controlled his anger in his 1979 reflections but in his 1988 memoirs the dam finally broke:

> President Nixon lied to his wife, his family, his friends, longtime colleagues in the U.S. Congress [including Barry Goldwater], lifetime members of his own political party, the American people, and the world. . . . No lie is intelligent, but his were colossal stupidity because they involved the presidency of the United States. . . .
>
> Nixon's masquerade was . . . a long and tortuous trail of deceit that squandered the generosity and goodwill of millions of Americans who wished desperately to believe that their president was not a liar. It was the manipulation and misuse of the vast American storehouse of bighearted-ness that history will condemn.[45]

Goldwater listed all the times Nixon had (1) lied to him, (2) lied to others, and (3) failed to keep his promises, dating back to 1960 when he promised he would advocate a right-to-work plank in the party platform and then reneged after his Fifth Avenue meeting with Nelson Rockefeller. At the time, Goldwater wrote of Nixon in his private "Alpha File": "The man is a two-fisted, four-square liar."

Most damning of all the lies was the "smoking gun"—the June 23, 1972, tape, in which Nixon's own words proved his direct involvement in the coverup—which was about to become public. In late July of 1974, even before the June 23 tape came to light, the senator was beginning to lean toward impeachment.[46]

The pressure on Goldwater, from inside and outside Washington, was unrelenting. Letters and phone calls poured into his office—from political and military friends, from people who had shaken his hand

and voted for him in 1964, from people he had never met but who looked to him as "the conscience of the Senate"—all with one message: *Do something.* At times the wave of emotion was frightening. Some callers were almost hysterical, he recalls, warning of "a military coup with possible bloodshed in the streets."[47]

Now convinced that impeachment would come before the Senate, he wrote his longtime friend, Denison Kitchel, asking him to serve as an informal counsel during the proceedings. "This vote that I will face," he said somberly, "will undoubtedly be the most difficult one and the most important one that I have ever had before me."[48]

Late in the afternoon of Monday, August 5, Dean Burch, now a special assistant to the president, personally delivered to his old boss a copy of Nixon's statement in which he admitted he had used the FBI and the CIA to cover up the break-in and had discussed how to limit the political consequences of Watergate. Nixon conceded that he had held back these facts from the House Judiciary Committee, kept them from his lawyers, and not disclosed them in his public statements. Goldwater had desperately wanted to believe Nixon—"Every man deserved a final say," he had written. And it turned out that Nixon's final word was that he had lied.

Goldwater went home to brood, answering no calls for the rest of the evening. He was outraged at what Nixon had done to those who around him, particularly to his two "wonderful" daughters. "He lied to his family," he kept repeating then and in the following days. Remembering the stern injunction of his mother, Goldwater could not understand how a husband, how a father could lie so baldly to his wife and children. That night, he decided that on Article II of the impeachment, Abuse of Power, he would vote to convict.[49]

The following day, August 6, the Senate Republican Policy Committee met for lunch; Vice President Ford attended. When Ford reported that at the cabinet meeting that morning Nixon had said he was not guilty of an indictable offense, Goldwater exploded. The best thing he could do for the country and the party, snapped Goldwater, "was to get the hell out of the White House—the sooner the better." The senator was interrupted to take an urgent call from the White House—Alexander Haig, the White House chief of staff, wanted to speak with him. When Goldwater picked up the phone, he was certain he heard a second click—"I guessed it was Nixon."

Haig asked how many votes the president had in the Senate; Goldwater estimated not more than a dozen. It was all over, he said, the president was finished: "Al, Dick Nixon has lied to me for the very last time. And to a hell of a lot of others in the Senate and House. We're sick to death of it all."[50]

Later that day, at a meeting of the Republican Senate leadership, it was decided that Goldwater alone should go to the White House and, speaking for his fellow Republicans, ask Nixon to resign. It was a signal honor from his peers. That evening, he told Peggy that maybe he ought to change his mind about seeking reelection. If he called for Nixon's resignation, it would infuriate the people back home who had "backed Nixon through thick and thin."

Calm and sensible as usual, Peggy disagreed: "No, Barry, they will respect your truthfulness and honor. You do what you think is right, but don't retire. It's just not the way to leave after so many years."[51]

The next day, Wednesday, August 7, Burch invited Goldwater to have lunch with him and Haig before he met with the president. He reported that Nixon wanted Senator Scott and Congressman Rhodes to accompany Goldwater so that he could have as broad a picture as possible of what Republicans on the Hill might do.

As he did in so many ways throughout the last two weeks of the Nixon presidency, Haig skillfully orchestrated the Goldwater-Nixon meeting. The senator and the others, he asserted, could not demand that Nixon resign—that would be "a banana-republic solution"—and he mentioned the separation of powers and due process. Rather, said Haig, Goldwater should lead the president to conclude that there were no more alternatives, no more options, "there was no way out except to quit or lose a long, bitter battle that would be good for no one—the country, Nixon, his family, or the party."

Goldwater was in no mood to forgive Nixon, but the appeal to the Constitution hit home. "You're right on every count," he asserted. "Don't worry, Al. We won't say a word about resignation to Nixon or anyone else."[52]

By the time he returned to his Senate office, Bob Clark of ABC was reporting (someone at the Senate Republican leadership meeting had leaked the story) that Goldwater had said Nixon would resign. Afraid that Nixon might be driven to insist that he would not quit, Goldwater picked up the phone and told Clark that he had said no such thing. ABC broadcast a retraction, but NBC refused to withdraw a false report that

Goldwater had been refused entrance to the White House the previous evening.

As his temperature rose, along with his anxiety about his meeting with the president, Goldwater rushed to the floor of the Senate and announced that both the NBC and ABC stories were totally false. Looking up at the press gallery, filled to capacity, he declared loudly, "You are a rotten bunch!"[53] Visitors in the other galleries cheered and clapped, even senators on the floor applauded.

Goldwater believed that he helped avert the agony of impeachment and insured Nixon's resignation in one other way. Benjamin Bradlee, the executive editor of the *Washington Post*, called the senator on Wednesday, August 7, to ask if he had been deputized by the Republican leadership to go to the White House and ask Nixon to resign. Goldwater refused to answer the question, adding that if the *Post* published any such speculation, it might get Nixon's "back up" and he would refuse to step down. Bradlee promised to keep quiet and kept his word.

In his 1988 memoirs, Goldwater embellished the story by stating that he telephoned Katherine Graham, the owner of the *Washington Post*, and told her that Nixon was "wobbling and could go off in any direction," depending on how the media, particularly the *Post*, played the story. "Could they play it cool for just one day, refrain from saying Nixon was finally finished, and let the president resign?" As things stood, he told Mrs. Graham, he believed that Nixon would.

Goldwater called the *Washington Post*'s self-discipline its "finest hour," adding, "I will never forget their recognition of responsibility as long as I live."[54]

WHEN A VERY SOLEMN TRIO, Goldwater, Scott, and Rhodes went before reporters and cameras after their Oval Office meeting with Nixon, they said, truthfully, that they had not asked the president to resign ("That subject didn't even come up," Goldwater stated) or discussed when the president would make and announce his decision. But Goldwater dissembled when asked about Nixon's support on Capitol Hill by saying, "We have no way of making nose counts" and "I myself have not made up my mind." Since he was still uncertain how Nixon would react if he admitted publicly that the president was certain to lose in both Houses, he merely said that "whatever decision he makes, it will be in the best interest of the country."[55] (On their way to the press briefing, Goldwater said to Rhodes, "Here's the first time that this has ever happened, and who was sitting there with the president? Two guys from one of the smallest states."[56])

Goldwater has never forgiven Nixon for failing to ask the forgiveness of the American people for what he had done to them and to the nation. When President Ford called him in September just after granting a pardon to Nixon but before announcing it, Goldwater said bluntly: "Mr. President, you have no right and no power to do that. Nixon has never been charged or convicted of anything. So what are you pardoning him for? It doesn't make sense."

"The public has the right to know that, in the eyes of the president, Nixon is clear," Ford said.

Goldwater was stunned, and growled, "He may be clear in your eyes, but he's not clear in mine."[57]

In January 1975, Goldwater visited Nixon at his home in San Clemente, and the two men talked about oil, Congress, the CIA, politics, and at last Watergate. Nixon admitted that mistakes had been made and that it was his fault for waiting too long before acting. He then asked Goldwater if he should go ahead with his plans to write a book, and the senator replied, "Yes, by all means, write it. Tell the truth. Tell everything." When they parted, Goldwater repeated, "Tell the truth."[58]

Although that was their last private meeting, the senator tried one last time to persuade Nixon to make a public confession, urging him, in a confidential letter, to "waive your Pardon and offer to appear before any court in the Capital City to, in effect, stand trial for whatever charges might be brought against you." In so doing, Goldwater argued, Nixon would show himself "as a man of courage, as a man of decency, as a man of respect for the law, and as a man who is determined to allow justice to clear his name."[59]

Nixon never responded. Goldwater is still so deeply disappointed in Nixon that when asked to comment about the former president, he will often reply, "I don't want to talk about him."[60]

19

The Making and Unmaking of Presidents, II

ON AUGUST 11, 1974, two days after Nixon resigned, Goldwater was invited to meet with President Ford at the White House to consider a "very serious problem of public policy"—the selection of his vice president. Since there could be a problem with Senate confirmation, Ford said he intended to choose someone who would be acceptable to the Senate but also to the country. He invited Goldwater's suggestions, but hoped they could discuss kinds of candidates rather than specific individuals.

As he had done when asked about Agnew's successor, Goldwater said it was important (assuming Ford's 1976 election) to pick someone young enough to serve six years as vice president and then potentially run for the presidency. "To my mind," he later recalled, "that ruled out anyone who was much over fifty."

Ford then asked what Goldwater thought about appointing a black man. The senator replied that if the president could find a competent man, he would support him, but he did not think that Senator Edward Brooke of Massachusetts "properly represented the blacks or the Republican party. [Ford] agreed with me."[1] They also discussed the possibility of a woman (Goldwater said he had no objection to someone "highly qualified"). The president said that if he selected someone from Congress, "it might be easier to gain prompt confirmation," but added that before making up his mind, he would have to know if the person were willing to serve. After the two politicians had talked about the frustrations and disappointments of the vice presidents they had known, Ford at last came to the point: he asked Goldwater if he would accept the vice presidency if it were offered. After a pause, Goldwater replied that he was too old and carried "too many scars from the 1964 campaign." He could think of several younger men who would be more suitable, who could add strength to the ticket in 1976.

Somehow the conversation switched to Goldwater's recent knee surgery. He pulled up one trouser leg to show his scar, prompting the president to show the scar he carried from an old football injury. "It would have made a great memento for both of us had there been a photographer present," Goldwater later wrote, "two political warriors displaying their wounds."[2]

Did Ford seriously consider offering the vice presidency to Gold- water, or was this just a set piece of political stroking? In his Ford biography, Richard Reeves says that Ford wanted someone who would bring stature and a national constituency to an administration short on both. Ford had also always believed in a balanced ticket and had privately recommended New York liberal John Lindsay as Nixon's running mate in 1968. Reeves states that Ford made his vice president decision alone—"the discussions with friends were essentially information-gathering."[3]

In his autobiography, Ford says that he had one overriding crite- rion: "He had to be a man fully qualified to step into my shoes should something happen to me." Ford describes how White House aide Bryce Harlow, using a mathematical formula, narrowed the list of potential candidates from sixteen to five, based on their national stature, executive experience, and "ability to broaden my political base."

The five finalists, in descending order, were George Bush, chairman of the Republican National Committee; Congressman Rogers Morton of Maryland; Congressman John Rhodes of Arizona; Senator Bill Brock of Tennessee; and Governor Nelson Rockefeller. Harlow listed Rockefeller's strengths as (1) proving Ford's self-confidence by naming so well-known a person as his number two, (2) making available "superb [intellectual] resources" to the administration, and (3) broadening Ford's political base. Rockefeller's weaknesses included his age (sixty-six), his being an "anathema" to conservatives, and his probable distaste at being number two.[4]

Strangely, Ford does not mention that he also asked a top aide, Robert M. Hartmann, to canvass several hundred prominent Republicans for their opinions on the vice presidency. A total of 911 recommendations were received from about three hundred Republican governors, senators, representatives, the cabinet, the Republican National Committee, personal friends, and senior staffers (each person was asked to list his first, second, and third choices).

The leading candidate of the Republican establishment was George Bush, with 255 mentions, followed by Rockefeller with 181, Goldwater, 83, and Reagan, 52. Senator Jesse Helms of North Carolina attempted a minicampaign in support of Goldwater, but had marginal success; most conservative leaders wanted Goldwater to stay in the Senate.

In addition, the White House received 11,782 unsolicited telegrams and letters (many of them from local Republican leaders). The people's choice was clear—Goldwater was the winner by a wide margin, receiving 2,280 "votes," almost three times as many as the second-place choice, Bush, with 887. Reagan came in third with 690, and Rockefeller a distant fourth with just 544. Rockefeller did lead in one category: 3,302 people opposed the New York governor, thirty times as many negative mentions as Goldwater received.[5]

When Ford was asked in November to list the achievements of his first hundred days as president, he said, "Number one, nominating Nelson Rockefeller." Goldwater did not agree. He made it quite clear that he was not pleased with Ford's choice—his 1964 adversary who was so "acceptable to the Eastern establishment and to the liberals of both parties."

On December 10, when the U.S. Senate confirmed Rockefeller's nomination by ninety to seven, Goldwater voted no. He later told his friends in the White House and the party that he "would do everything in my power to block his nomination on the Republican party ticket in 1976."[6] In his 1979 memoirs, Goldwater writes he had been told by several insiders that his adamant opposition kept Rockefeller off the ticket. "If so," he said, "I am glad," because "I am certain the presence of Nelson Rockefeller as a Republican nominee for vice president in 1976 would have split the party."[7] He used the same argument to explain his support of Gerald Ford rather than Ronald Reagan as the Republican nominee for president in 1976.

GOLDWATER HAS STATED that 1976 presented him with "the most painful political dilemma of my public life." On the one hand, Ford was the incumbent Republican president; the senator's longtime friend and former campaign manager, Dean Burch, was a close adviser to the president; and Goldwater agreed with Ford on his political objectives, if not all of his tactics. On the other hand, Reagan was a fellow conservative. His support in 1964, Goldwater wrote, "is something I will always cherish." If Reagan was interested in running for president, Goldwater owed him, at the very least, a hearing.

On May 4, 1975, the two men had dinner at the Madison Hotel in Washington, D.C. Goldwater claims that Reagan did not discuss the presidency and did not ask for his support should he decide to run. "I wasn't sure then," Goldwater wrote later, "and I'm not sure now, that he had made up his mind." But according to John Sears, Reagan told Goldwater that supporters were going to start an exploratory committee in a month or so, to which Goldwater said that Reagan should "just announce" his intentions. After explaining that he was not ready for a formal announcement (fundraising had just begun), Reagan switched to other subjects.[8]

He was interested in finding out what Goldwater would do if Ford insisted on having Rockefeller as his running mate. Goldwater assured Reagan that he was firmly opposed to a Ford-Rockefeller ticket. In a memorandum for his private "Alpha File" (dictated later that evening), Goldwater stated that his endorsement of such a ticket "would let down a large block of the 27,000,000 people who voted for me."

While criticizing Ford for not providing "consistent" leadership, Goldwater did not indicate a preference for Reagan. Rather, he would "play this very cool" and "then at the proper time make my move."[9] Reagan later spoke of Goldwater "as lukewarm on the whole idea" of his running for the presidential nomination. Neither Reagan nor his advisers expected Goldwater to wind up on their side in a Ford-Reagan context.[10]

One month later, Goldwater told Max L. Friedersdorf, head of congressional liaison for the White House, that he would support Ford for the presidential nomination in 1976. He declined to sign a letter that Friedersdorf was circulating among Republican senators (eighteen out of thirty-eight initially signed) to that effect.[11] From the very beginning, everyone knew how important Goldwater's support was to a nonelected president who had no natural constituency within his own party. Over the next twelve months, Goldwater advised, encouraged, and defended Ford, finally and formally endorsing him on June 30, 1976.

Like an anxious suitor, the White House constantly checked to see if Goldwater still supported the president. The White House, for example, was disturbed by an Associated Press story that quoted Goldwater as saying that he "might" endorse Reagan if he made a bid, although he also admitted that such a move would put him "on the horns of a dilemma." Tony Smith, who had worked for the senator since 1961, explained to Friedersdorf that Goldwater felt compelled "to not put Reagan down at this time because of Barry Goldwater, Jr.'s interest in the California Senate race. . . . Barry Sr. did not want to alienate Reagan supporters in the event that Barry Jr. decides to run."[12]

The White House tried hard to persuade Goldwater to come out publicly for the president before Reagan formally announced his candidacy. Richard Cheney, the White House chief of staff, sent two memos to Ford prior to his private meeting with Goldwater on November 13, 1975. Based on his conversations with Bryce Harlow and Bill Baroody, Cheney recommended that the president begin by soliciting the senator's advice on whom he should appoint to the Supreme Court (Justice William O. Douglas had just resigned) and then press "him for a firm commitment to publicly endorse your candidacy."

The arguments to be used against Reagan were simple: (1) his candidacy "simply" could not succeed, and (2) he could only win "after a primary struggle which would make it impossible to win in November." The most likely outcome of a serious Reagan challenge would be that "the president is renominated but presides over a weakened party." Cheney's erroneous use of the word "renominated" confirms the incumbent mindset of the White House. For all their confidence, the Ford team knew they urgently needed Barry Goldwater to counterbalance the conservative appeal of Ronald Reagan. Cheney wrote Ford on November 13, 1974:

It is more important than ever that Senator Goldwater indicate now his commitment to a united Republican party and to the candidacy of Gerald Ford. That commitment should be public, it must be firm, and it must occur in the next few days. The senator is in a position to make a decision which is essential for the health of the Republican party and the good of the nation.[13]

In a second memorandum written the same day, Cheney repeated that Ford must be "very firm" with Goldwater and let him know "that you need him now, not later, and that you need him publicly, not just privately." If the senator raised the matter of his son's potential candidacy in California, Cheney suggested that the president pledge "to do whatever you can to help Barry Jr., capture the Republican nomination and defeat Senator [John] Tunney in the general election." Aware of the president's tendency to be too accommodating, Cheney sternly told Ford, "We cannot afford to let [Goldwater] off the hook, and you should be very tough and very forceful in seeking his commitment. This is no time to be understanding or sympathetic with respect to his perceived problems."[14]

We do not know how firm or soft President Ford was (Goldwater does not refer to the meeting in his memoirs, nor does Ford), but Goldwater did not publicly endorse Ford for another seven months. He did, however, agree to join the Advisory Committee of the President Ford Committee, which met privately later in November to discuss campaign organization, activities, and issues.

Goldwater was on the agenda, but was asked to address organization, not issues—a somewhat surprising assignment, as he was not the best organized man in the political world. But he took the opportunity seriously. He cautioned the fieldmen not to become overconfident (in response to their optimistic reports) but then stated that the Reagan organization "is not as strong as generally thought"; he declared that Ford should not "worry" about New Hampshire and Florida (where Reagan led the president in the polls) because Reagan "does not have strength in the big states"; he said that a candidate should go where the votes were, like the big states of the Midwest and the Northeast, where Ford was strongest; and he stated that in his opinion "the key issue will be the economic issue and it should break to *our* advantage."[15]

Neither he nor anyone else in the Ford and Reagan camps anticipated that the Panama Canal would turn out to be the most important and emotional issue of the campaign.

Reagan's impending entry into the nomination race made a significant difference in the polls. In a mid-October Gallup survey, Ford had led Reagan by 58 to 36 percent. By December, Gallup revealed a sharp shift: Reagan now led among Republicans by 40 to 32 percent and among independents by 27 to 25 percent. In a trial presidential heat, a Harris Poll showed Ford losing badly to Hubert Humphrey by 52 to 41 percent.[16]

GOLDWATER DID NOT HESITATE to use his special status with the White House to further a particular interest, such as the relationship between the United States and Taiwan. Following one of his monthly luncheons with Henry Kissinger in early December 1975, Goldwater wrote the president, who had just returned from an Asian trip and meetings with Communist China's Mao Tse-tung and Deng Tsiao-ping. Notwithstanding the assurances of the secretary of state, Goldwater was bothered by press speculation that the administration was considering a change in its recognition policy. Did the president, he wanted to know, intend to keep his promise, made privately to him, that he "would never call for the dropping of formal recognition of the government of Taiwan in favor of the government of Peking"?

It took two months and several memos among the State Department, the National Security Council, and the White House to agree on a response, but there was never any doubt about the bottom line: the president did not dare alienate Goldwater. The language in Ford's February 12, 1976, reply was careful and diplomatic ("I continue to believe that the strengthening of our ties with the nearly one-quarter of mankind which inhabits the People's Republic of China [PRC] should continue to be an essential element of our foreign policy") but concluded with, "We will continue to be mindful of the interests of our friends and allies, including the Republic of China on Taiwan."[17]

An unexpected trip by Nixon to China in late February, just before the New Hampshire primary, led Goldwater to make a memorable remark about the former president on ABC's "Good Morning America": "I don't think Mr. Nixon's visit to China did anything, and if he wanted to do this country a favor he might stay over there." When Reagan was asked to comment on Nixon's China trip, he quipped, "Don't ask me . . . ask the man who pardoned him."[18]

Goldwater and other Ford partisans were pleased by the president's strong showing in the early primaries: a narrow but unexpected victory in New Hampshire, a 53–47 percent win in Florida, and a decisive

59–41 victory in Illinois, Reagan's home state. As Ford wrote, "I had 166 delegates; Reagan had 54 and many in both camps expected him to quit."[19] Reagan might have withdrawn (his campaign manager, John Sears, was privately hinting to Ford people, without authorization, that the governor might drop out) if he had not discovered an issue that touched a raw nationalist nerve among Republicans and made it the centerpiece of his campaign in the next primary, North Carolina, where the president had a twelve-point lead.

The issue was the Panama Canal, and Reagan's position was simple: "We built it, we paid for it, it's ours, and we should tell Torrijos and Company that we are going to keep it."[20] Backed by the formidable organization of Senator Jesse Helms, Reagan stepped up his attacks on the Ford administration, adding the dangers of détente and the mess in Washington to his list of charges. He crisscrossed the state half a dozen times, purchased time for a half-hour program on fifteen of North Carolina's seventeen television stations, and campaigned hard down to the last hour.

To the surprise of most pollsters and the consternation of the White House, Reagan narrowly won the North Carolina primary by 52–48 percent. It was only the third time in American history that a challenger had defeated an incumbent president in a primary state. Ford and his people realized they were in a race all the way to the national convention in Kansas City, and needed all the help they could get.[21]

Until now, Goldwater had not publicly criticized Reagan, but with the nomination uncertain, he changed his tactics. Making an unexpected appearance at the Arizona Republican convention on April 24, he denounced the campaign tactics used by Reagan supporters (they denied Senator Paul Fannin, a Ford supporter, a place on the Arizona delegation) and all but endorsed the president. While proclaiming his "love and affection" for Reagan, Goldwater declared, "I have worked with President Ford at the national level of government for over twenty-five years and I have every faith in his ability to continue to lead this country, and lead it along the paths that will be best for America and best for the prospects of a peaceful world."[22]

The President Ford Committee immediately distributed his statement to Republicans across the country. A week later, after Reagan stunned Ford by decisively winning the Texas primary, carrying all twenty-four congressional districts and winning all ninety-six delegates, Goldwater appeared on NBC's "Meet the Press." Although he still refused to endorse any candidate formally, he stated that President Ford was as conservative as Reagan, adding, "I don't know why he should be denied the nomination."[23]

On May 4, the day of the critical Indiana primary, Goldwater aimed his hardest punch yet at his fellow conservative, suggesting that Reagan's recent statement about the Panama Canal reflected "a surprisingly dangerous state of mind." Reagan had said, in response to a question whether his Panama Canal policy was worth the risk of guerrilla warfare, "We would have to [risk it] just as we would have to protect Alaska or any other sovereign territory of the United States. I think it's time we stand firm and start trying to make people respect us instead of love us."

In a statement broadcast over radio (and drafted at least in part by Mel Laird, the president's longtime political ally), Goldwater charged that "my old friend Ronald Reagan" had made "gross factual errors" in his statements about the Panama Canal and had represented himself "in an irresponsible manner on an issue that could affect the nation's security." "Ron's attacks" on President Ford's policy, Goldwater said, "reflect a surprisingly dangerous state of mind which is that he will not seek alternatives to a military solution when dealing with complex foreign policy issues."[24]

Goldwater's reference to Reagan's "dangerous state of mind" was eerily reminiscent of the 1964 attacks on Goldwater that he was psychologically unfit to be president. Conservatives lamented that the Cold Warrior who had always urged a policy of victory over communism should now be willing to accommodate a third-rate Latin American dictator.

In *Why Not Victory?* Goldwater had opposed concessions to the Panamanians because they might be considered "weaknesses," asking, "Does anyone seriously suppose, for instance, that our generous decision to permit the Panamanian flag to fly over American territory in the Canal Zone will placate the Panamanian nationalists? The gesture is bound simply to whet the mob's appetite and transfer its sights to bigger targets."[25]

And in 1964, when campaigning for president, Goldwater had used language about Panama that anticipated Reagan's twelve years later: "I hope and pray the president doesn't back down one inch. The canal is ours. . . . The United States can't afford having governments taking our property away from us. . . . There is no reason to change [the treaty]."

And in March 1975, Goldwater had sponsored S. Res. 97, introduced by Strom Thurmond, which urged "retention of undiluted United States sovereignty over the Canal Zone."[26]

Now, perplexed conservatives asked why Goldwater was excoriating Reagan for taking the same position he had held for so many years. They did not know of course that Goldwater had given his word to Ford that he would support him for president.

Stuart Spencer, a top Ford campaign aide, urged the President Ford Committee to exploit the criticism by Goldwater and "present Ronald Reagan as a dangerous warmonger on the Panama Canal and other international issues." He recommended that permission be obtained from Goldwater to use the audio tape of his news conference for commercials "to begin *immediately* in all primary states." Spencer, who had been responsible for producing the anti-Goldwater brochure in the 1964 California primary that asked the loaded question, "Who Do You Want in the Room with the H-Bomb?," reverted to type: "The one big weapon left to us is fear. Fear of a President Reagan with his bellicose statements, as a commander-in-chief and with his finger on the nuclear button."[27]

Over the next two weeks, the Ford Committee, with Goldwater's permission, flooded the airwaves of Nebraska and several other primary states with a radio commercial featuring the senator's comment about Reagan's "dangerous state of mind." An upset Nancy Reagan called Goldwater to complain, and a contrite senator wrote Committee Chairman Rogers Morton that "you are not going to win a Reagan vote by using that approach so call it off." The Ford campaign quickly complied and pulled the commercial. Goldwater later said he did not realize that the Ford people would distribute his anti-Reagan statement so widely, but he had set no conditions when he allowed its use.[28]

On June 30, 1976, with only six weeks until the national convention and with neither candidate having a majority of the delegates, Goldwater formally endorsed Gerald Ford. In a letter to the 2,259 convention delegates, he said he felt impelled to come out for the president even though it was "the most difficult [decision] I have ever had to make in my life." Calling the philosophies of Ford and Reagan "almost identical," he chastised his fellow Republicans for risking defeat in November by engaging in a bitter intraparty fight for the nomination. His decision, he asserted, rested "solely on the fact that at this time in our history I do not believe that our government can suffer through months and months of reorganization that would be necessary if we had a change in office."[29]

It was one of the most deceptive remarks ever made by Goldwater. First, it was not a difficult decision: he had been helping the president in every way he could, short of a formal endorsement, for more than a year. Second, he had extraordinarily mixed feelings about Reagan, often far removed from the "great admiration" he proclaimed. Although Goldwater always praised Reagan's rhetorical efforts on his behalf in 1964, he resented his swift ascension to the leadership of the conservative movement, that he, more than anyone else, had made into a national political force.

Particularly after he left the Senate, Goldwater frequently and openly expressed disdain for his fellow conservative. Invited to make a comment for a 1987 commemorative film about President Reagan, Goldwater repeated, over and over, "He's just an actor."[30]

On another occasion, when President Bush presented the Presidential Medal of Freedom to Reagan in January 1993, Goldwater and columnist James Jackson Kilpatrick were seated in the audience of former medal recipients. As Bush recited Reagan's personal and political accomplishments, Goldwater leaned toward Kilpatrick and muttered, "What a lot of shit." Asked about his first recollections of Reagan, Goldwater responded, "He was as far to the left as you can get in his politics. . . . He never was what I would call a complete conservative." He recalled that one time when he and Hollywood actor George Murphy were visiting Reagan in his Pacific Palisades home, Reagan called them "a couple of Fascist bastards."[31]

In late 1993, Goldwater suggested that what most disturbed him about Reagan was that as president he "never really cut down spending. Didn't stop welfare. Didn't diminish the bureaucracy. . . . Had I been in Reagan's place, this country never would have gone $3 trillion in debt."[32]

This was the senator who never met a domestic program he did not try to trim or eliminate if possible. But he also sounded like liberal critics who insist that the Reagan 1980s were a decade of excess and greed and nothing more. While it is true that the national debt tripled during Reagan's eight years in the White House, there were two extraordinary benefits: the longest economic expansion in peacetime history and the peaceful end of the Cold War. According to the *Wall Street Journal*'s Robert Bartley, America's gross national product (GNP) grew by a third (equal to the entire GNP of West Germany), per capita income increased by nearly a fifth, 18.4 million jobs were created, and the "misery index" (the sum of the inflation and unemployment rates) fell by almost half to just over 10 percent during the Reagan 1980s.[33]

Perhaps Goldwater got around to reading Bartley's book, for in an interview after the remarkable 1994 election, he praised Reagan as a president "who brought to life the free enterprise economic system that made this country great. . . . It remade this country."[34]

Sally Quinn, whose mother and father were Goldwater's closest friends in Washington, sees more similarities than differences in the two men: "Reagan is really a clone of Barry. I think Barry is the real Ronald Reagan, that Reagan didn't say or do anything that Barry hadn't already said and done. It's just that [Reagan's] timing was better. Barry came along too early."[35]

While there is truth in these observations, particularly the matter of timing, the key to Goldwater's anti-Reagan outbursts is that the senator, who always personalized his politics, never connected personally with Reagan (as he had not with Nixon). They shared the same political platform, but little else. They had even come to conservatism by different paths, Reagan because he had been mugged by the reality of high income taxes and his struggle against communists in Hollywood, Goldwater because he rejected liberal fantasies that the government could solve most of life's problems and that the Cold War was America's fault.

Goldwater liked to measure people by what they did with their hands. He would sit and talk for hours with someone about ham radio or classic automobiles or flying. But not with Reagan. Goldwater liked to do things for himself, flying his own plane to campaign appearances, even when he ran for president. Reagan accepted a large retinue that got him to a speech carefully briefed, well rested, and on time. Goldwater was an individualist, a maverick, an antihero; Reagan was a communitarian, a team player, a Hollywood hero. Goldwater used the Protestant "I," Reagan the Catholic "we." Goldwater hated what he called "phonies," people who pretended to be something they were not. Reagan was not so judgmental, accepting the foibles and flaws of those around him, whether actors or politicians. Goldwater was Arizona adamantine, Reagan was California mellow.

These personality differences led the two conservatives to approach the practice of politics differently. Goldwater operated from bedrock beliefs and principles that *he* held. He wanted to influence voters, not have voters influence him. Reagan too had a central core of convictions from which, in the experience of Howard Baker when he was his White House chief of staff, he would not deviate. But Reagan also had "a set of invisible antennae" that enabled him "to understand the ordinary American" and play back his beliefs "in language that would resonate."[36]

Goldwater proudly called himself a Republican and a politician; Reagan straddled the two parties and presented himself as a citizen-politician. Goldwater liked playing the role of curmudgeon; Reagan was "a thoroughly charming human being who, with very little preparation, could make anybody feel like he'd known them all their life."[37] Goldwater constantly ripped into friends and foes alike; Reagan never said an unkind word about anybody. Goldwater became a Washington insider; Reagan remained an outsider. Goldwater ran for the presidency in 1964 because he felt he had to; Reagan ran in 1976 and again in 1980 because he wanted to.

Clif White, who worked closely with Goldwater and Reagan in their presidential bids, has suggested that their relationship was star-crossed because both could not be the leader of the conservative movement. In 1964, Goldwater was the unquestioned star, Reagan the understudy. But by 1975, Goldwater was sixty-six and not in the best of health; every one of his joints, and especially his hips, were as stiff as a board. Perhaps, he reflected, it was time to let someone else take the lead.

In a speech at the National Press Club in November 1975, Goldwater declared, "I don't want those 27 million to think I'm trying to lead them. . . . I never for any moment assumed I had a position of leadership over anybody." Writing in *Conservative Digest* in January 1976, Richard Viguerie argued that Goldwater should be taken at his word and that conservatives should "look for someone else to lead the new majority of the 1970s and 1980s and to take advantage of the swelling conservative sentiment in America."[38] In late 1975 that "someone" could only be Ronald Reagan, a political fact that, despite his seeming indifference, bothered Goldwater greatly.

Evidence of Goldwater's difficulty to talk objectively about Reagan can be found in his 1979 memoirs when he offers this bizarre explanation of why he backed Ford in 1976: "There is a very simple answer. I believed the incumbent would be a stronger candidate."[39] Not even Jerry Ford believed he was a stronger or better candidate than the man who was well on the way to becoming the Great Communicator.

In his 1988 book, Goldwater tries again, stating that he backed Ford because he was "the incumbent president." This argument makes sense for a traditional Republican like Bob Dole, George Bush, or Jerry Ford. But not for the author of *The Conscience of a Conservative* and *Why Not Victory?*—the slayer of liberal dragons, the businessman who came to Washington to repeal, not pass, laws, the presidential nominee who talked about Social Security in Florida, TVA in Tennessee, and farm subsidies in South Dakota.

Columnist John Kolbe of the *Phoenix Gazette* has suggested that Goldwater was not a "fearless man of principle often doing battle with his own party," but "first, last, and always a Republican."[40] Yet Goldwater was willing in 1964 to do battle with his own party when he saw it falling once again into the hands of Eastern liberals. William Rusher, for his part, has described Goldwater as "a devout economic conservative of the traditional Republican variety" who was "never entirely comfortable with the conservative ideologues who made him their standard-bearer in 1964."[41]

This is partially true. Goldwater is certainly an economic conservative, but he is of the Hayek-Friedman libertarian school rather than the Taft-Dole-Bush variety. As for ideologues, he was comfortable in 1964 with conservative intellectuals like Russell Kirk, Harry Jaffa, Gerhart Niemeyer, Stefan Possony, and Warren Nutter, and, judging by his correspondence, with William F. Buckley Jr., Milton Friedman, Frank Meyer, and other "ideologues" in the years following.

In justifying his endorsement of Ford over Reagan to Republican delegates—describing both as "bona fide conservatives"—Goldwater ignored the real philosophical differences between them. Goldwater knew very well that a President Reagan would not have nominated Nelson Rockefeller as his vice president, kept Henry Kissinger as his secretary of state, offered amnesty to draft-dodgers and deserters from the Vietnam War, proposed a $60 billion deficit in the annual budget, laid the foundation for a SALT II agreement that confirmed Soviet nuclear superiority over the United States, and refused to meet with the famed Russian exile, Alexander Solzhenitsyn.

Why, then, did Goldwater back Ford? In addition to his jealousy of him, Goldwater regarded Reagan's bid for the presidential nomination in 1976 as he had Dean Burch's attempt to remain national chairman in 1965—as harmful and divisive to the party. A Republican loyalist, Goldwater had built the Republican party out of nothing in his own state and over the years made thousands of speeches across the country for Republican candidates. Asking him to stop putting the Republican party first was like asking the Pope to stop putting Catholicism first. Forced to make a choice, Goldwater endorsed his old congressional friend, Jerry Ford.

There were rumors at the time that the president expressed his gratitude for the endorsement in a very practical way. Goldwater himself later admitted that Ford "promised both John Rhodes and me that we'd have the solar energy research laboratories in Arizona. Then he double-crossed us and gave them to California and Colorado. I never got over that."[42] But no evidence suggests that Goldwater demanded this favor as the price of his support. That kind of political quid pro quo would have been totally out of character for him.

How important was Goldwater's endorsement? At the time he made it, there were 135 uncommitted delegates who held the balance of power in the Republican presidential race. Rogers Morton, chairman of the Ford Committee, predicted that Goldwater's backing "will have a profound effect on many delegates to the convention." Peter Kaye, the Ford Committee's spokesman, contended that "you're not dealing with large numbers. If it's helpful with ten delegates, then it's a hell of a help. . . . Goldwater is one of the few people who is truly influential with the delegates and in the party."[43]

The presidential roll call in Kansas City was Ford, 1,187 votes; Reagan, 1,070 votes; Commerce Secretary Elliot Richardson, 1 vote; and 1 abstention. A switch of just fifty-nine delegates, or less than 3 percent of the total number, would have given the nomination to Reagan. With so narrow a winning margin, it is clear that President Ford would have been denied the nomination without Goldwater's early private and later vocal public support. His backing was all the more crucial because prominent conservatives like Strom Thurmond and Paul Laxalt were committed to Reagan.

THE 1976 NATIONAL CONVENTION was the last at which Goldwater was a major player. In 1960, he had burst onto the national scene with his "Let's grow up, Conservatives" speech. In 1964, he had captured the presidential nomination over the fierce opposition of the liberal establishment that had dominated the party for nearly thirty years. In 1968, he helped hold the Southern line for Richard Nixon against Ronald Reagan. And in 1976, he helped persuade his party to pick a moderate conservative rather than the bold conservative, the emotional favorite of the convention.

But in 1976, many conservatives did not forgive Goldwater for what they perceived as an inexplicable compromise with principle. When Ford narrowly lost to Jimmy Carter—receiving only 29 electoral votes less than the needed 270—conservatives declared that Reagan would have won. *Human Events* theorized that because of Reagan's ability to challenge Carter in the South and in the border states, Reagan probably would have carried nine more states with their 112 electoral votes than Ford.[44] Conservatives asked: What if Goldwater had kept his word and not backed either candidate? Tom Winter, the editor of *Human Events,* says that 1976 was the year "when Goldwater and the conservative movement parted."[45]

The platform of the 1976 convention marked another division between conservatives and Barry Goldwater. For the first time, in addition to the usual limited government, anticommunist language, the Republican platform included a plank on abortion, declaring that "the Republican party . . . supports the efforts of those who seek enactment of a constitutional amendment to restore protection of the right to life for unborn children."[46] Unlike Jesse Helms, who insisted on the right-to-life plank, and Ronald Reagan, who warmly endorsed it, Goldwater had ambivalent feelings about abortion and the other social issues that meant so much to the New Right, the Moral Majority, and other newly active elements of the Republican party and the conservative movement, as well, of course, to the old conservatives.

Goldwater never accepted the critical importance of social issues to the forging of a national political coalition that could capture the White House. His inability to adjust to the new conservatism led him to (1) fail to distinguish between principled political preachers like Jerry Falwell and Pat Robertson and TV charlatans like Jim Bakker and Jimmy Swaggart, and (2) accuse New Right leaders Viguerie, Weyrich, Blackwell, and Terry Dolan of being a "wrecking crew of special interests" when they helped lay the foundation for Ronald Reagan and George Bush's presidential triumphs in the 1980s.[47]

20

Coping with the New Conservatism

ALTHOUGH HE KNEW MOST OF ITS LEADERS (indeed, they were inspired to enter politics because of his 1964 presidential campaign), Goldwater was uncomfortable with the New Right almost from the beginning. It seemed to him that it "preached little or no spirit of compromise," that its social agenda often compromised constitutional rights, that it stressed single interests too much. He called Viguerie and his associates "narrow but gifted men" who were convinced of "their absolute rightness." And he warned that their zealous approach to politics could splinter the Republican party that, as he grew older, became more important to him than any ideology. In effect, he was accusing the New Right of being what he had been branded in 1964—extremist.

Goldwater was even more critical of the Moral Majority. It had no right, he declared, to "dictate" its moral and political beliefs to the rest of the country. He even spoke grimly of "holy wars" in America similar to those that afflicted Northern Ireland and Lebanon.[1] The Old Testament prophet who had thundered about the need for morality in government in 1964 had become a New Age libertarian proclaiming the strict separation of church and state.

417

But the truth is that the state, not the church, started the war. The Moral Majority came into being because of President Jimmy Carter, the born-again Christian elected in 1976 with the strong support of fundamentalist Christians. In August 1978, Jerome Kurtz, Carter's director of the Internal Revenue Service, stated that any private school started after 1953 was presumed to be discriminatory and would lose its tax-deductible status, which of course would almost surely force it to close. Because the great majority of private schools in the South are Christian, the Southern Baptists and other Protestant denominations viewed the IRS ruling as a direct threat to their existence. This forced them to organize politically, to protect what they saw as their constitutional right to practice, not discrimination (many of their schools were integrated), but their faith.

The National Christian Action Coalition, headed by Bob Billings, led the campaign that defeated the IRS attempt to tax the Christian schools that would not set racial quotas for their student bodies.[2] Ironically, it was Howard Phillips, a Jew and head of the Conservative Caucus, and Paul Weyrich, a Melkite Catholic and head of the Free Congress Foundation, who persuaded Falwell, an ordained Baptist minister, to organize the Moral Majority and launch what has come to be called the Christian Right. And it was Ed McAteer, a business executive and lifelong Christian lay leader, who in early 1979 brought Phillips and Weyrich together with Falwell, who was reaching an estimated fifteen million Americans weekly with his "Old Time Gospel Hour" TV and radio program.

McAteer recalls the meeting in Lynchburg, Virginia, at which Weyrich, while offering an overview of American politics, remarked that "there's a moral majority in this country." McAteer interrupted Weyrich, asked him to repeat himself, and then said, "That's a great name." Falwell agreed: "I like that."[3]

The Moral Majority was born. It immediately jumped into domestic issues like abortion, school prayer, the Equal Rights Amendment, and homosexuality, and foreign issues like SALT II, and soon became a formidable political force. Evangelists like Falwell, Pat Robertson, and Jim Robison were an imposing force themselves, reaching over twenty million Americans by television each week. Separation of church and state, they constantly reminded their audiences, did not mean separation of God and government.

The Moral Majority and similar groups have since concentrated their help on Republican candidates. Over the years, the Christian Right has become to the Republican party what blacks have been to the Democrats—an indispensable part of a winning coalition. Ronald Reagan acknowledged the vital contribution of the Moral Majority and similar organizations to his 1980 and 1984 presidential campaigns, as did George Bush in his 1988 victory. According to the ABC News–Lou Harris survey, "The white followers of the TV evangelical preachers gave Ronald Reagan two-thirds of his 10-point margin in the [1980] election." McAteer estimates that Bush received "80 percent" of the Christian evangelical vote in 1988.[4]

In contrast, Goldwater actively worked against the Christian Right's candidates, endorsing, for example, a liberal Democrat rather than a conservative Republican for an Arizona congressional seat in 1992 because the Republican was backed by evangelical Christians.

IN 1964, CONSERVATISM was a tripartite movement, made up of traditional conservatives, libertarians, and anticommunists. The traditionalists were defenders of order, community, religion, and virtue. The libertarians were classical liberals who stood for individual liberty, a market economy, and private property. Anticommunists stressed the pervasive character of the red menace at home (represented by Alger Hiss) and abroad (coordinated by Nikita Khrushchev).

Twenty years later, nourished by Reagan's continuing political success, there were almost as many strains of conservatives as stars in the American flag, ranging from paleoconservatives to cultural conservatives to even (oxymoron of oxymorons) big-government conservatives.

The most important additions were the neoconservatives, who added intellectual credibility to the movement, and the New Right conservatives, who brought with them tens of thousands of foot soldiers. The neoconservatives were one-time liberals who, in Irving Kristol's famous phrase, had been mugged by reality. But they still endorsed the idea of the welfare state, albeit with a conservative face. The New Right were middle-class populists who attacked the four bigs of America—Big Government, Big Business, Big Labor, and Big Media. They were the forerunners of today's powerful Christian Right.

In his 1988 memoirs, Goldwater describes himself as "a traditionalist" who believes in individual freedom, free enterprise, limited government, a strong national defense, and religious principles—a careful mix of the different strains of conservatism. But he asserts there were strong differences between himself and other traditionalists like Jerry Falwell, whom he linked with Jesse Jackson—an odd coupling.

Goldwater traces his concern about Falwell and other "political preachers" to their "heavy-handed, continuing attempt to use political ends to obtain moral ends," describing it as "one of the most dangerous trends in this country." Goldwater refused to concede that Falwell and other Protestant preachers were forced to enter politics by the actions of others, including the federal government. And he conveniently ignored the fact that in 1964 he constantly called for "morality in government" and once asked, "If the Christian church is not to fight . . . then who on Earth is left to resist this evil [of communism] which is determined to destroy all virtue, all decency?"[5]

One issue in particular became a dividing line between Barry Goldwater and the New Right and the Christian Right—abortion. The senator did not like the rising number of abortions, but he did not like pro-life extremists either. In his 1988 memoirs, he stated that while he opposed abortion, as did groups like the New Right and the Moral Majority, "in [our] pluralistic society the issue is not ours to decide alone. . . . The truth is—and no one in the country appears to have the courage to say it—that the American people want it both ways on abortion. Most people are privately horrified by it, but they are either victims of peer pressure or favor it only in limited circumstances." He also admitted that his wife Peggy believed that "each woman had the moral and legal right to choose for herself whether she was capable of continuing her pregnancy and then raising the child." He, however, disagreed with her and that, he said, is the way "it is and must be, in a free and pluralistic America."[6]

This is far from the whole story. His wife was a founder of Planned Parenthood of Arizona in 1937 and continued to play a leadership role in the organization. She planned and hosted a major fundraising banquet in 1965 that honored birth-control guru Margaret Sanger, a close personal friend. As she liked to put it, "Planned Parenthood is my baby."[7]

When his daughter Joanne, not yet twenty and still in school, became pregnant with the child of her intended husband and told her father that she did not want to have the child, Goldwater said, "I'll take care of it." He arranged for Joanne to fly back to Washington and have a then-illegal abortion (it was 1955) in the converted dining room of a large three-story house in the suburbs. "I just want to prevent anyone from going through that," says Joanne Goldwater, who admits that all three of her daughters have had abortions.[8]

Given this family pattern, it is not surprising that Goldwater ultimately assumed a pro-abortion position.

Yet he vacillated throughout the 1970s between being pro-life and pro-choice. In September 1973, only seven months after *Roe v. Wade*, he wrote that "the rights of the unborn should be protected" and that he "strongly" respected the "medical and religious reasons" for the proposed Right to Life Amendment. But he did not endorse the amendment. Several months later, in a letter to a constituent, he said flatly that he was not and never had been "pro-abortion." Then, in June 1974, he admitted that while he supported the work of Planned Parenthood in Arizona, he opposed "abortion on demand" and was in favor of legislation that would "return jurisdiction over abortion to the states and remove the Supreme Court from the field. This would permit the states to protect all human life from the moment there is a separate life until natural death." He did not explain what he meant by "separate life." About the same time, he wrote that he did not favor a constitutional pro-life amendment "as a practical matter," preferring "the legislative route."[9]

In the fall of 1980, in the most difficult reelection campaign of his political life, Goldwater abruptly changed his position and endorsed the Human Life Amendment, naming the Supreme Court as the main reason for his shift. He cited the Court's recent rulings that a husband had no say if his wife wanted to abort their child and that parents had no right to prevent an abortion by their unwed, minor daughter living in their home. Previously, he admitted, "I was not persuaded of the need for a constitutional amendment," but because of the Court's rulings and proposed government funding of abortion, he endorsed S. J. Res. 22, the Human Life Amendment introduced by Senator Dennis DeConcini of Arizona. At the same time, he drastically reduced the number of exceptions for abortion, mentioning only "the very few pregnancies resulting from rape, which includes by definition incest involving a minor."[10]

The same year, Goldwater filed an *amicus curiae* brief with the Supreme Court, urging the Court to uphold the Hyde amendment that prohibited the use of federal funds to pay for abortions. As a result, Goldwater received the endorsement of Arizona Right to Life and

groups like the Pro Family Action Committee. His Democratic opponent, William Schulz, opposed a constitutional ban on abortions and
favored making federal funds available to poor women seeking an
abortion.

In his eagerness to stress the difference between himself and his
opponent on abortion, Goldwater misrepresented his past. Appearing
before a Tucson church group just ten days before election day, he
stated baldly, "I have always felt that we should try to introduce a life
amendment." He also said that he believed that human life begins "at
the moment of conception," a shift from his earlier position.

Mary Tucker, head of Arizona Right to Choose, quickly accused him
of taking contradictory and misleading positions and produced letters
Goldwater had written to members of her group declaring his opposition to a human life amendment. Tucker asserted, "He claims he has
always been for an amendment, in which case his letters are a lie, and
he supports exceptions for abortion not included in the Human Life
Amendment." She also pointed out that in early October, Goldwater
and his wife Peggy held a reception at their home for Planned Parenthood of Arizona, which offered, among other services, abortions.[11]

Goldwater's reversal on the Human Life Amendment was the most
blatantly political act of his Senate career. But it was also the right
political decision. He won by 51 percent to 49 percent, receiving just
nine thousand votes more than his pro-choice opponent.

Once back in the Senate, Goldwater shifted yet again, causing some
pro-lifers to accuse him of being just another opportunistic politician.
He told Terry Emerson, his legislative assistant, that a woman had a
right to say what happened to her body and that he did not accept the
argument that the embryo was a viable being. His position was inescap-
ably pro-choice, as set forth in this October 1985 letter to a constituent:
"I believe that the decision to have or not to have an abortion is one for
the mother herself to make in consultation with her attending physician. . . . The choice should remain with the mother in all cases of rape
or incest, in situations where the life of the mother is in danger, and in
those instances where the health of the mother is put at serious risk, as
verified by her physician."[12] He told another constituent in November
1985 that "until the fetus is capable of surviving birth, I think that the
mother's right of personal liberty prevails."[13]

Goldwater now allowed his libertarian side to determine his position
on social issues ranging from abortion to prayer in the schools to gay

rights, moving sharply away from the traditional conservatism of *The Conscience of a Conservative* and his statements in the 1964 presidential race.

Goldwater's pro-choice stance even led him to modify his previous opposition to federal funding of abortion. When the District of Columbia appropriations bill came before the Senate in 1985, he voted against an amendment that would have prohibited the use of any federal funds to perform abortions. As he explained to a constituent, he supported exceptions where the life of the mother was "in danger" and for "victims of rape and incest."[14]

GOLDWATER RARELY ADDRESSED the issue of homosexuality during his thirty years in the Senate, usually saying that the civil rights of homosexuals "is a matter for judicial determination . . . under the equal protection or due process clauses of the Fourteenth Amendment."[15] In 1980, Congressman Robert Bauman, whom Goldwater had known for two decades, was arrested for committing a homosexual act with a young male prostitute. Bauman expected minimal sympathy and understanding from his fellow conservatives. To his surprise, the Moral Majority's Jerry Falwell response was, "I don't know anything about the particulars. His record has been foursquare with ours. We support him." Goldwater, however, only said, "I don't think they'll like that kind of thing on the Eastern Shore of Maryland."[16]

In September 1985, he assured a constituent that he opposed a "so-called Gay Bill of Rights," explaining that "the kind of laws Congress should be working on are those that would strengthen traditional American family life, not weaken it."[17] In a related area, he co-authored a bill imposing penalties against exploiting minors in producing pornographic films or magazines which was narrowly defeated in the Senate. But, as he told a constituent, he would continue "to oppose this outrage."[18]

But that was then. In June 1993 Goldwater wrote an op-ed article for the *Washington Post* supporting the lifting of the ban on gays in the military. And that same year he granted an interview to *The Advocate,* the national homosexual magazine, in which he stated:

> The Republican party should stand for freedom and only freedom. Don't raise hell about the gays, the blacks, and the Mexicans. Free people have

a right to do as they damn well please. To see the party that fought communism and big government now fighting the gays, well, that's just plain dumb.[19]

Leaving aside the remarkable statement that the Republican party should "only" stand for freedom (what happened to responsibility?), a major reason for Goldwater's sudden, outspoken, pro-gay campaign was, as so often in his life, personal: his grandson, Ty Ross, was a homosexual (and HIV positive); a grandniece was a lesbian.

Ross revealed that he brought his boyfriends to the house and helped his grandfather realize "that there are normal people out there who are gay." When his grandfather speaks out, he said, he "shows his love and respect for his family. . . . This is a way for him to do what's right for me and for his family."[20] The grandson related how he introduced Goldwater to a former Air Force staff sergeant, discharged for being gay, and that his grandfather took up the young man's cause and was later honored for his stand by a gay rights group in Arizona.

It is significant that the revelations about Goldwater's gay relatives only came to light after the publication of his *Post* article and his appearance on "Larry King Live." That information might have undercut the homosexuals' argument that if as conservative a man as Barry Goldwater could support the idea of gays in the military, it ought to be acceptable to everyone.[21] Goldwater understood this: neither in the *Post* nor with Larry King did he reveal that he had a gay grandson or gay grandniece.

A year later, Ty Ross told a reporter for *POZ,* a magazine for HIV positive people, that he could tell by the way his grandfather looked at him that "he's proud of me for hanging in there. I can see it all in his eyes."[22] What Goldwater could not have been proud of (and could not have been aware of) was that the cover article in *POZ* ended with a description of the author getting into bed with Ross and having sex with him.[23]

In July 1994, Goldwater insisted that "as long as they're not doing things that are harmful to anyone else," they can be as gay as they want to be. The interviewer did not bring up, nor did the senator discuss, the North American Man-Boy Love Association, the Catholic-smashing tactics of Act-Up, and other extremist actions of the gay-lesbian community in America.

Goldwater's enthusiasm for gay rights led him that summer to become honorary co-chairman of a campaign to pass a federal law preventing job discrimination against homosexuals. The effort was called Americans Against Discrimination and was organized by the Human Rights Campaign Fund, a gay lobbying group. Goldwater argued that there was no gay exemption in the right to "life, liberty and the pursuit of happiness" in the Declaration of Independence and that his action was based on constitutional principles.[24]

Conservatives groaned. Where was the Goldwater who promised to repeal, not pass, federal laws? Where was the Goldwater who voted against the Civil Rights Act of 1964 because it was unconstitutional and unenforceable without the creation of federal regulations more dangerous to the Republic than the wrongs it was supposed to right?

Liberals tried to co-opt him. In December 1994, the Arizona chapter of the American Civil Liberties Union named Barry Goldwater its "Civil Libertarian of the Year" for his support of the "constitutional rights" of gays and lesbians and his commitment to the "reproductive rights" of women. The senator insisted that all he was doing was sticking to the Constitution, which "tells you and tells me the way we should live in a country that's dedicated to freedom." He mentioned only in passing the responsibility of a society to protect those whose rights are violated or denied in the pursuit of freedom, reproductive, homosexual, or otherwise.[25]

Although Goldwater continued to attack conservatives (suggesting, for example, that Jesse Helms was "off his rocker"), most conservatives turned the other cheek. Typical was a comment by Senator Helms, who declared that he would "always be grateful" to Goldwater. "The fact that he now attacks some of us," said Helms, "who have admired, respected, and stood with him through the years does not diminish my recognition that there wouldn't have been a 'conservative movement' in the United States had it not been for him."[26]

THAT THE SENATOR could not adjust to the emerging new conservatism of the post-Watergate era was demonstrated by his roller-coaster positions on the Panama Canal treaties. Goldwater omitted any discussion of the issue in both his 1979 and 1988 memoirs, presumably because it would have been almost impossible to rationalize his many contradictory statements. On the one hand, in March 1975, he cosponsored S. J.

Res. 97, which said, in effect, that turning over the Panama Canal to the government of Panama would be "a clear and present danger to the hemispheric security." Along with thirty-seven other senators, Goldwater condemned the attempt "to cede, dilute, forfeit, negotiate, or transfer any of these sovereign rights, power, authority, jurisdiction, territory, or property" of the canal.

Scarcely a year later, in May 1976, he attacked Reagan for opposing the transfer of American sovereignty over the Canal Zone to Panama. In a 180-degree change of a public position he had held for approximately fourteen years, Goldwater stated, "I fully support the policies of the Ford administration"—that is, America did not have sovereignty in the zone and had to make concessions to Panamanian dictator Omar Torrijos in order to avoid guerrilla attacks and sabotage. At the same time, Goldwater insisted that the United States would not "surrender" its interests in the canal but somehow preserve them "through the process of negotiation."[27]

The emotional debate over the Panama Canal widened the gap between Goldwater and the New Right. As Patrick J. Buchanan wrote, "A political war to the death over the canal treaty could realign American politics, reinvigorate a weakened spirit of nationalism, and if lost, do for those who surrendered the canal what Yalta did for the Democratic party." Richard Viguerie called it a "no-loss" issue for conservatives, pointing out that while the establishment, including the Democratic leadership of both Houses of Congress, favored the treaties, some 70 percent of the American people, and perhaps 80 percent of registered Republicans, opposed any "giveaway" of the canal.[28]

Given Goldwater's unequivocal statements in 1976, Jimmy Carter had good reason to count on the senator's support when he submitted the Panama Canal treaties to the Senate for ratification in the fall of 1977. Carter urgently needed Goldwater because (1) the administration's margin of victory was very thin in the Senate and (2) his backing would offset the opposition of Jesse Helms and other conservatives.

The president did his best to win Goldwater's support. He invited the Goldwaters to a formal White House dinner on September 7th, following the signing of the treaties by himself and General Torrijos. Other guests included congressional leaders of both parties and several undecided senators.

Two days later, when Goldwater's administrative assistant, Jack

Murphy, was quoted erroneously by CBS as saying that the senator now opposed the treaty, a representative of the treaty negotiating team, then the White House, and finally President Carter himself tried to contact Goldwater that same evening. But it had been a long day, and the senator did not feel like speaking to anyone.

The next day, Saturday, Goldwater drove to Bill Quinn's farm on the Eastern Shore of Maryland for a quiet weekend, only to find eight telephone messages waiting for him, including one from the president and another from Rosalyn Carter. He finally reached Frank Moore, head of congressional liaison for the White House, and told Moore that he had *not* made up his mind about the treaties. He conceded that he had objections but hoped that they and those of other senators could be met through changes in committee and on the Senate floor.[29]

On March 16 and again on April 18, 1978, Barry Goldwater was one of thirty-two senators who voted against the two Panama Canal treaties. He described them as "poorly conceived, poorly negotiated, and consummated in a manner, in my opinion, that is not going to help Panama."[30] In that one sentence, Goldwater dismissed the multiyear efforts of President Ford, who conceived the treaties, President Carter, who negotiated the treaties, and the U.S. Senate, which ratified them.

But few conservatives, and no one in the New Right, cheered his votes or his words. They remembered his sharp criticism of Reagan in 1976 when the Republican presidential nomination had hung in the balance. They complained that Goldwater had been a follower, not a leader, for the antitreaty side in the Senate debate. They did not deny that Goldwater usually voted correctly on important issues, from the antiballistic missile system to the Jackson amendment prohibiting U.S. trade with the Soviet Union to the Panama Canal treaties. But they were looking for a resolute man who would eagerly grab the reins and lead the new conservatism.

They were yearning for the Barry Goldwater of 1964, the uncompromising conservative who had brought them into politics. But even if he could have been resurrected, the Goldwater of 1964 would have been unable to lead the conservative movement of the late 1970s because the movement, and the country, had been transformed by epochal social events like *Roe v. Wade,* school busing, the decline of the family, and the emergence of gay rights. The Goldwater of the 1970s thought that these new issues should be handled in a libertarian way—by individual action. He could not accept the argument that collective action, even federal government action in the form of constitutional amendments and federal statutes, might be needed to counteract the mischievous decisions of the Supreme Court and acts of Congress that had weakened the social fabric of America.

How poorly Goldwater understood what was happening was made plain in his 1988 memoirs when he wrote:

> The great danger in the new conservative movement is that, instead of broadening its base, the movement may tear itself and the GOP apart. Its real challenge in the years ahead is to broaden the Republican base and accommodate many new aims without weakening the party's foundations and pulling the whole house down.[31]

The "danger" he refers to lay in groups like the Moral Majority that helped Republicans win Senate seats and presidential victories throughout the 1980s. Here is a disquieting example of Goldwater's tendency to preach inclusion ("broaden" the party's base) but practice exclusion (keep out Christian activists).

Whereas in the 1960s he shot from the hip at the Left, he now fired without aiming at the Right. Informed that Falwell had announced that all good Christians should be concerned by Arizona Judge Sandra Day O'Connor's nomination to the Supreme Court (O'Connor declined to take a firm enough anti-abortion position for many pro-life advocates), Goldwater growled that "every good Christian ought to kick Falwell right in the ass."[32]

As it turned out, Falwell had been misquoted, but Goldwater neither recanted nor apologized. One liberal colleague clapped him on the back and said, "Barry, you old bastard, that was magnificent." Another rejoiced that "the old Goldwater we know and love is back, full of life. He has that old spark in his eye."[33]

If conservatives were disappointed in Goldwater, liberals now constantly praised him. Starting in 1974, they applauded him for his critical role in ridding the nation of President Nixon, and they rarely stopped cheering for the next two decades. In April 1974, Roy Reed wrote of Goldwater in the *New York Times* that "the man who was the villain in 1964 has become a hero. In fact, he is one of the few political heroes left alive in the United States." He had become the "liberal's favorite conservative."[34] And this, quite simply, because he was a man of the right who attacked others on the right—Nixon, Reagan, Falwell,

Viguerie, William Rusher, anyone who angered or even irritated him. For the media, he was the political equivalent of man bites dog, and they discovered that he delighted in taking large chunks out of the rear ends of conservatives.

Goldwater was also the liberals' favorite conservative because they could praise him without fear of the consequences. He was a U.S. senator, one of one hundred, effectively limited in his influence; he was not a president, the leader of America and the Free World, with the power to make life and death decisions.

In 1964, liberal strategists had delighted in disparaging Goldwater, calling him a bigot and a Nazi. These same liberals now embraced Goldwater because he no longer thought of himself as Mr. Conservative. "My personal feeling," he told the *New York Times,* "is, I no longer feel that a Republican *has* to be a conservative. I can live with [ultraliberal] Jack Javits."[35] In a sense, he was echoing what he had said many times as chairman of the senatorial campaign committee when he was raising money for Republicans of all philosophical hues, including Javits.

But such a stance was far removed from the Goldwater who proudly authored *The Conscience of a Conservative*, urged conservatives at the 1960 convention to work to take over the Republican party, and offered a conservative choice not a liberal echo in his presidential campaign.

Which Goldwater was the real Goldwater? In the realm of politics, there were two Goldwaters. There was the Republican loyalist who put his party first and was willing to help almost anyone so long as he called himself a Republican. He even ended up by saying that Nelson Rockefeller "was a great American and would have made a great President"—a startling evaluation given Rocky's fondness for big government, bigger budgets, and party disloyalty.[36] This Republican Goldwater was most visible in the 1970s and 1980s in his final terms as U.S. senator.

Then there was the uncompromising conservative of 1957–1964 who challenged President Eisenhower, sparked a political revolution with books like *The Conscience of a Conservative* and *Why Not Victory?*, and captured the Republican presidential nomination over fierce liberal opposition. This conservative Goldwater prevailed for less than a decade, but he cast a brilliant light that has not faded in the minds of millions.

What accounted for the change? Unstinting praise from former enemies can be intoxicating, even for a seasoned professional like Barry Goldwater, who in 1974 appeared on the Gallup Poll list of the most admired men in the world, finishing tenth, right behind Pope Paul VI. CBS's Walter Cronkite, invariably described as "the most trusted man in America" in the 1970s, offered this tribute to the senator in the midst of Watergate:

> If Goldwater now sounds like the voice of moderation and reason, in this current crisis of public confidence, perhaps it's because on Watergate he seems to be one of the few outspoken individuals who belong to no faction. Whether you agree with him on specifics, he seems to plead no special cause, right now, except for frankness and honesty.
>
> No wonder he seems like such a loner in Washington these days. Once, his many critics told us Goldwater's approach to government was overly simplistic. He was ridiculed as an anachronism. But now, without fundamental change, he seems to strike a responsive chord in wider circles than just those right-wing groups which always venerated his name. Is Goldwater catching up to changing times? Or, asked more properly, are the times catching up to Barry Goldwater? [37]

In part, the times *were* catching up to the Goldwater who had warned the nation about the dangers of a protracted conflict in Vietnam, called for morality in government and its leaders, and pointed out that "a government big enough to give you all you want is big enough to take it all away." But the times were also moving swiftly *beyond* Goldwater, who did not appreciate the extraordinary power of the new political forces in America (mobilized by issues like abortion, school busing, feminism, homosexuality, and criminal rights) and who could not bring himself to welcome the New Right, the Moral Majority, and the other groups that molded the new conservatism.

The man who had begun the conservative revolution almost seemed to be repudiating it, at least in its new form. In 1979, as he contemplated a possible fifth term in the Senate, he looked back over his career and contented himself with saying that he and others had had "some influence" in changing the direction of government. He did not seem to realize what he had accomplished, commenting, "The country is becoming not conservative but responsible."[38]

His remarks reflected the reality that in the realm of ideas, as in politics, there had always been two Goldwaters—the Brent Bozell–

Russell Kirk–Edmund Burke conservative and the F. A. Hayek–Milton Friedman–Thomas Jefferson libertarian. The conservative and the libertarian blended during his early Senate career and in his presidential campaign. Sometimes the traditional prevailed when he talked about "the laws of God and of nature" and decried the decay of American values and the lack of morality among the nation's leaders. Sometimes the libertarian dominated when he called for a swift end to government subsidies and programs and pointed out the pernicious effect of "welfarism" on the state and the individual citizen. Throughout the 1950s and 1960s, these two philosophical sides of Goldwater were generally in balance, neither achieving a lasting dominance.

But when the social issues of the 1970s and 1980s came to the fore, Goldwater usually assumed a libertarian stance, extolling individual rights above almost all else. He said, in effect, the woman has a right to an abortion—never mind the fetus, because it is a fetus, nothing more. Every man, even a gay, has the right to live as he wants, as long as he does not infringe on the rights of others—never mind public schools presenting homosexuality as an acceptable lifestyle to little children and infringing on their parents' rights. Voluntary prayer in the public school, even when sanctioned by the federal government through a constitutional amendment, is an invasion of individual rights—and never mind the Constitution.

Gone was the earlier traditional-libertarian balance, or fusionism. It had been replaced by a commitment to the all but unbridled freedom of the individual.

21

Final Flight

DURING HIS THIRTY YEARS IN THE SENATE, Goldwater consistently argued that the best legislator was the one who repealed rather than passed laws. But he stopped short of being a radical libertarian who sought to eliminate all aspects of government, particularly the Department of Defense; he preferred the role of a constitutional conservative who recognized the need for limited government. If and when laws were needed, he wanted the best possible laws consistent with the Constitution.

Acting from this principle (which both Hayek and Burke would have approved), Goldwater was instrumental in passing "libertarian" measures that gave the vote to eighteen-year-olds; abolished state residency restrictions to allow citizens on the move (approximately ten million in the 1970s) to vote for president; and ended the military draft and instituted the volunteer army.

In the area of economics, he constantly sought the counsel of Milton Friedman, whom he had met through Bill Baroody in the late 1950s and who served as a key adviser in his 1964 presidential campaign. They maintained an extensive correspondence on such topics as taxation, the gold standard, block grants to states, and inflation. In April 1975, Goldwater informed Friedman that he believed it was time "I advocate an end to Social Security." He was not worried about the political consequences as he had just been reelected to the Senate and did not intend to run again. "I think," he said, "this is one of the things I can do for my country."

Friedman, who if anything was more skeptical about Social Security than Goldwater, wrote the senator a carefully reasoned three-and-a-half page letter, urging him not "to undertake that particular crusade as your final parting shot in the public arena." In the first place, if Social Security were ended, "the major result would be simply to divert those expenditures into another governmental channel." It could be argued that the funds "drained off by Social Security" were doing less harm there than spent on other government projects like "socialized medicine." A better approach to limiting government spending, he suggested, would be to introduce, at the federal level, legislation similar to the Proposition 1 that "Ronald Reagan tried to get through in California." Proposition 1 was an amendment to the state constitution setting a maximum limit on government expenditures as a percentage of the income of the state. "Here," Friedman said to Goldwater, "is a cause which would be worthy of your greatest efforts."[1]

Goldwater took Friedman's advice on both issues; he remained silent on Social Security and co-sponsored a balanced budget amendment in Reagan's first term.

Goldwater also supported "conservative" legislation such as saving Radio Free Europe and Radio Liberty from extinction for lack of funds (the two services had been secretly funded by the CIA) and making it a crime to print and send pornographic literature through the mails.

Above all else, he could be depended upon to vote money for a strong national defense, convinced that freedom and peace needed a military second to none, especially the Soviet Union's, and to ensure that the United States stood by its old friends and allies, such as the Republic of China (ROC) on Taiwan. Although he never publicly criticized either the Nixon or Ford administrations for their diplomatic openings to the People's Republic of China (PRC), he made quite clear that he would resist any attempt to abandon Taiwan to appease Beijing. His steadfastness drew him into a constitutional battle against President Carter and his administration.

GOLDWATER HAD BEEN A FRIEND of Nationalist China since his tour of duty in the China-Burma-India theater during World War II. In Burma, he helped train Chinese pilots to fly the P-40, the United States' pursuit plane, and formed many close friendships. Throughout his Senate career, he frequently took the floor to praise the economic and political progress of Taiwan in contrast to the totalitarian regime of Mao Tse-tung on the mainland.

In April 1977, Goldwater traveled to Taiwan to deliver a talk at Tamkang College, where, in a departure from normal protocol, he openly criticized President Carter for not granting the request of the ROC ambassador in the United States to meet with officials at the State Department or the White House. By contrast, Carter had invited the PRC representative to a lengthy visit in the Oval Office. Goldwater stated grimly that "an honorable people like the United States had been acting dishonorably and show every sign of continuing to do that relative to our treaties and obligations to friends that we have had for many, many years."[2]

He was right. The Carter administration was indeed planning to make a dramatic change in U.S.-PRC relations. In a major foreign policy address at Notre Dame in May, the president stressed the importance of continuing to normalize relations with China. A worried Goldwater talked with Senator John Sparkman, chairman of the Senate Foreign Relations Committee, and reported to Bill Buckley that the committee had no plans and Sparkman knew of no plans "to recognize Red China or discontinue relations with the Republic of China." Goldwater pointed out that Carter had recently stated that "as long as Taiwan has an ambassador in this country, there would be no demand for the formal recognition of Red China." But the president's statement notwithstanding, Goldwater wrote Buckley, "I intend to keep a very strong outlook on this . . . to keep our treaties [with Taiwan] intact and operational."[3]

Goldwater did not know that Carter had already decided to accede to Peking's demands that the United States (1) terminate the U.S.-Taiwan defense treaty, (2) establish U.S. diplomatic relations with the government in Peking rather than Taipei, and (3) withdraw U.S. military forces from Taiwan.

As outlined in his memoirs, Carter's conditions for these significant concessions were that the United States would be able to continue selling "some" defensive weapons to Taiwan, maintain trade and other relations on an unofficial basis, end the defense treaty on one year's notice "as that treaty provided," and state publicly that the dispute between the mainland and Taiwan "would be resolved peacefully." Carter's realpolitik revealed that he, the erstwhile apostle of principle in foreign affairs, finessed at will such questions as the integrity of America's word in international agreements and the future of the seventeen million people on Taiwan.[4]

Following his first visit to the mainland, Secretary of State Vance reported to Carter that the Chinese communist leaders were more cautious than expected and preoccupied with internal politics because of the recent deaths of both Mao Tse-tung and Chou En-lai. Carter decided to put China "on the back burner," aware that any public move would alert Goldwater and the rest of what the president called the "Taiwan lobby."[5] That Carter would describe Goldwater as a "lobbyist" for Taiwan suggests why he was so unsuccessful in working with Congress throughout his presidency.

In October 1977, Goldwater set forth his basic position regarding the president's limited authority to abrogate treaties in an op-ed article for the *New York Times,* arguing that "a treaty cannot be revoked without some role for Congress." He quoted James Madison, who foresaw "the same authority, precisely, being exercised in annulling as in making a treaty."[6] The president, Goldwater contended, did not have the "untrammeled power . . . to annul any treaty he wishes." He offered a general rule: "As the president alone cannot repeal a statute, so he alone cannot repeal a treaty." And he added a warning should Carter attempt unilaterally to abrogate treaties with the government on Taiwan: "Any president who would violate the Constitution on such a major matter as breaking faith with the nation's treaty obligations would run the risk of impeachment."[7]

The following May, the Heritage Foundation published a forty-page monograph (written by the senator's legislative assistant, Terry Emerson) in which Goldwater presented an extended historical and constitutional argument against a president withdrawing from or ending a treaty "without the approval or ratification of two-thirds of the Senate or a majority of both Houses of Congress."

The timing of the monograph (warmly praised by Eugene V. Rostow of the Yale University Law School, among others) was deliberate: National Security Adviser Zbigniew Brzezinski was scheduled to go to China that month to discuss further normalization of relations between the United States and the PRC. Goldwater was angry that the visit coincided with the inauguration of Chiang Ching-kuo, Taiwan's new president—"an historic occasion which President Carter saw fit to ignore." Always sensitive to hypocrisy, Goldwater pointed out that the constant "flirting with a communist regime which is notorious in the history of murderous human repression does nothing but destroy any semblance of sincerity in Carter's constant lip service to a humane foreign policy."[8]

Over the next six months, Goldwater made speeches, released statements, wrote letters to the editor, and even introduced a Senate resolution (on October 10, the anniversary of the founding of the Republic of China), declaring that the Senate or both Houses of Congress should give approval before the United States abrogated any of the post-World War II mutual defense treaties. Historical usage and international law, he said, permitted the president to suspend a treaty all by himself only if circumstances were changed by the *other* government, in this case, the Republic of China. It was clear, he stated, that Carter "could not present his own action as the basis of a presidential decision that the defense treaty with Taiwan had lapsed."[9]

But the president pushed ahead with his dual goal—to recognize Peking and derecognize Taipei—driven, among other things, by the need to lift his slumping public popularity. On the evening of December 15, 1978, over national television, Carter announced that the United States would formally recognize the People's Republic of China on January 1, 1979, ambassadors would be exchanged in March, and the U.S. defense pact with Taiwan would be abrogated in one year.

The president had briefed congressional leaders (excluding Barry Goldwater) at the White House only a few hours before his dramatic announcement. During the meeting, an aide had interrupted to say that an important telephone hookup had come through. Carter left the room to talk with the leader of an island nation in Asia that had counted for decades on the United States for its security, but the call was to Japan, not Taiwan. There was no direct contact at all between the president and the Republic of China, a faithful friend and ally of the United States for more than four decades.[10]

Although Carter later claimed that no "serious opposition" to his diplomatic move materialized in Congress, and the press treated him favorably, there was widespread criticism, and not only from the "Taiwan lobby." The president had in fact acted against the wishes of a majority of the American people and their representatives.

In midsummer, the Senate voted unanimously that the president should not abrogate a treaty without first seeking the advice and consent of the Senate. (The State Department had rubber-stamped the resolution.) Carter ignored the Senate. A poll of the House of Representatives showed that only a handful favored recognition of Peking on its terms. Carter agreed to all of the PRC's demands. A Harris-ABC survey recorded that by more than a 3–1 majority, the U.S. public was opposed to withdrawing recognition from Taiwan; by a similar 3–1 margin, Americans said they did not want the president to abrogate the defense treaty with Taiwan. Carter stubbornly persisted.[11]

Eight days after Carter's national TV address, Goldwater assailed the president's decision and his China policy in a special ten-minute broadcast over CBS-TV, in accordance with the network's policy of providing free time for opposition speakers following presidential telecasts. Carter's brief China speech, he said, might be recorded in history "as ten minutes that lived in infamy," harking back to FDR's denunciation of the Japanese attack on Pearl Harbor as "a day that will live in infamy." At another point, Goldwater likened Carter's actions to the "doctrine of might and size make right," a reference to the operating principle of Nazi Germany. The treatment of Taiwan, he stated, "calls into question the honor—the very soul—of America's word in the field of foreign relations."

Using sharp language, Goldwater announced that, along with seven other senators, retired Senator Carl Curtis, and seventeen congressmen, including Dan Quayle of Indiana, he had brought suit in federal court against President Carter to prevent him from terminating the Taiwan defense treaty unless Congress approved. He promised, "We will pursue the case all the way to the Supreme Court, if necessary."[12]

In seeking support for his challenge to the president, Goldwater began to doubt his 1976 decision regarding the Republican presidential nomination. Gerald Ford immediately approved Carter's action; in contrast, Ronald Reagan accused the Carter administration of "outright betrayal of our close friend and ally, the Republic of China on Taiwan." An irritated Goldwater wrote Ford that he was "flabbergasted" at his taking Carter's side. "I want to stop the precedent Carter has established of any president stopping any treaty he wants to. This is bad and dangerous," Goldwater said, "and you should know it."[13]

Republican Senators Howard Baker of Tennessee and Robert Dole of Kansas endorsed Goldwater's legal efforts, as did Democratic Senators Robert Morgan of North Carolina and Richard Stone of Florida, who led the Senate in passing the Taiwan Relations Act, which cemented all but diplomatic relations between the United States and Taiwan.[14] Even Richard Nixon, while maintaining that the normalization of relations with the PRC was "indispensable" to building "a structure of peace in Asia and around the world," stated that the "Taiwan issue" had to be handled in a way that would reassure other nations "that it is safe to rely on America's word and to be America's friend"—one of Goldwater's central arguments.[15]

Among Goldwater's strongest supporters in his legal battle was the distinguished legal scholar, Eugene V. Rostow, former undersecretary of state from 1966 to 1969 and former dean of the Yale Law School. Rostow was counsel, along with Charles E. Rice, J. Daniel Mahoney, Daniel J. Popeo, Paul D. Kamenar, and Robert F. Pietrowski, to Goldwater's fifty-page legal brief (drafted by Terry Emerson), which was filed with U.S. District Court Judge Oliver Gasch, a respected jurist.

After hearing arguments from both sides (the administration revealed how seriously it regarded the Goldwater petition by having former Attorney General Griffin Bell personally argue its case), Judge Gasch on June 6 dismissed the senator's suit as premature but said he would allow it to be refiled later. Within hours, the Senate approved by 59–35 a resolution (introduced by Independent Harry Byrd of Virginia) that "approval of the United States Senate is required to terminate any mutual defense treaty between the United States and another nation." A week later, Goldwater resubmitted his suit. On October 17, 1979, Judge Gasch made legal history by ruling that President Carter could not terminate the U.S. defense treaty with Taiwan without the consent of Congress and said he was blocking Secretary of State Vance from ending the treaty on January 1, 1980, as scheduled.

"While the president may be the sole organ of communication with foreign governments," the judge stated, "he is clearly not the sole maker of foreign policy."[16] He agreed with Dan Popeo, Goldwater's attorney, that while the treaty did allow either "party" to cancel the treaty on one year's notice, the "party" in the case of the United States included the president *and* the Senate.

Goldwater was elated, accurately describing the ruling as "the first time in this nation's almost two hundred years of constitutional history that a federal judge has ruled directly on the power of treaty termination and it means that no American, not even the president, can break the law of the land."[17]

Attorney General Benjamin Civiletti said that the Justice Department would immediately appeal Gasch's ruling to the U.S. Court of Appeals in the District of Columbia. In doing so, the administration revealed its unwillingness to take the treaty termination to Congress, where it might be defeated, and its determination to avoid any precedent that might bind the executive branch.

At this critical point, Goldwater offered Carter an alternative to their legal impasse, suggesting that the president submit a treaty termination notice to the Senate. Addressing his colleagues, Goldwater explained that he had filed his suit to make the president obey the law, and the Constitution, not just to save the Taiwan treaty. He told his colleagues:

> The president of the United States is not an emperor. He does not possess all the powers of the national government in the making of foreign policy. . . . We are a government of divided and checked powers. The president cannot make a law on his own and he cannot repeal a law by himself. The president cannot make a treaty on his own and neither can he terminate a treaty unilaterally.[18]

Yet even on so fundamental an issue, Goldwater was uncomfortable confronting a president. He had challenged Eisenhower, criticized Kennedy, rebuked Johnson, and dismissed Nixon, but he had not enjoyed it, so great was his respect for the office of the presidency, if not always its occupant.

On October 20, Goldwater wrote a conciliatory letter to Carter, suggesting that the president ask the Senate Foreign Relations Committee to report out a bill or resolution giving "the necessary consent" of the Senate or Congress to ratify the termination of the Mutual Defense Treaty with Taiwan. Although not revealing how he might vote, Goldwater predicted, "I am convinced you could reach agreement with the Senate or Congress so that this could be accomplished swiftly."[19] In a November 10th response that began "Dear Barry," Carter politely declined the senator's suggestion, stating that he had been informed that the Court of Appeals would render a "prompt decision" and that, if necessary, the case could still be reviewed by the Supreme Court "by the year-end."[20]

On November 30, by 4–1, the U.S. Court of Appeals for the District of Columbia overturned Gasch and ruled that Carter's termination of the defense treaty was legal, stating that the president must have the power "to conduct our foreign policy in a rational and effective manner."

The unsigned majority opinion insisted that its decision did not mean that the president's authority to end treaties was absolute, commenting, "History shows us that there are too many variables to lay down any hard-and-fast constitutional roles." But the court noted the "novel and somewhat indefinite relationship" between the United States and Taiwan and stated, "The subtleties involved in maintaining amorphous relationships are often the very stuff of diplomacy, a field in which the president, not Congress, has responsibility under our Constitution."[21]

Goldwater received one consolation. Judge George E. MacKinnon, although indicating that he concurred in part with the majority, dissented from the ruling, saying that Carter would need the approval of both Houses to end the treaty on January 1, 1980.

For Goldwater, the opinion was based on bad history (there was nothing "indefinite" or "amorphous" about the relationship between the two countries, which had signed more than fifty bilateral treaties over the years) and bad constitutional law (the Founders gave the Senate explicit authority in the realm of diplomacy through its power to approve or disapprove not only treaties but ambassadorships as well). He quickly appealed the U.S. Court of Appeals' decision to the Supreme Court, knowing that the odds against reversal were extremely high.

On December 13, by a vote of 7–2 (the votes of four justices being needed), the Court refused to hear *Goldwater v. Carter*, with Justice Lewis Powell holding that the case was "not ripe for judicial review." Neither the Senate nor the House, he reasoned, despite the Byrd Resolution, had taken any *final* action against Carter's termination of the defense treaty. "If Congress chose not to confront the president," Powell wrote, "it is not our task to do so." (Ironically, Justice William Rehnquist, who had helped write speeches for Goldwater in his 1964 presidential campaign, stated that the senator's challenge was a "political question" not suitable for the judiciary.) In a partial victory for the plaintiffs, the Supreme Court vacated the judgment of the Court of

Appeals and sent the case back to the District Court with instructions to dismiss the complaint. In so acting, as Goldwater pointed out, the Court removed "a judicial basis for unilateral action by the president to break all of the country's treaty commitments."[22]

The two dissenters, Byron A. White, a moderate appointed by John F. Kennedy, and Harry A. Blackmun, one of the most liberal members of the Court, said that Goldwater should be given the opportunity to argue his case. The Court's decision not to hear arguments sorely disappointed Goldwater, who told his colleagues on the Senate floor: "The internal division in the Court, reflected by five different opinions, would seem to have cried out for an opportunity to have the case decided after the thorough study it only could have received by allowing a submission of briefs and oral arguments. . . . The Supreme Court," he added, "has avoided its responsibility. . . ."[23]

On the surface unsuccessful, Goldwater's legal challenge of President Carter had three measurable impacts on American policy: one, it signaled that Congress was determined to be not merely a junior but an equal partner in the making of foreign policy; two, it reminded the executive branch that the principle of checks and balances applied to foreign as well as domestic affairs; and three, it strengthened the determination of Congress to pass the strongest possible Taiwan Relations Act (TRA) over the objections of the State Department and the White House. In the end, the TRA established more than one hundred different "treaties" between the United States and Taiwan, covering trade, military assistance, education, and culture.

WHILE HE WAS CHALLENGING CARTER in the courts, seventy-year-old Goldwater was pondering a contest of a different kind: Should he seek a fifth and certainly final term in the Senate? There were good reasons why he should not. Although not old by senatorial standards (his former colleague, Carl Hayden, had sought and won reelection at the age of eighty-four), he was not a healthy seventy. The artificial hip, inserted in 1976, caused him serious problems and constant pain. He found it more and more difficult to walk, even to get in and out of a chair. One journalist recalls watching Goldwater take several minutes just to get out of his car and then slowly hobble up the steps of the Senate office building, leaning heavily on a cane. "Why," the reporter wondered, "was he clinging to the Senate?"[24]

But independent as always, Goldwater adamantly refused any help from friends or staff. Once, on the way to testify before a congressional committee about a bill to help the Zunis, a Pueblo tribe in New Mexico, he was hit by such a wave of pain that he almost fell against the wall. When his legislative assistant, Phyllis "Twinkle" Thompson, instinctively reached out, he waved her off, saying, "Don't touch me. I'll handle this myself." After a minute, he drew himself up and walked very slowly to the hearing. "You would never have known how much pain he was in while he was testifying," Thompson recalled. He would not let the pain "stop him," added Ellen Thrasher, another legislative aide.[25]

But his increasing physical incapacity coupled with his lifelong impatience with routine and what he considered unimportant things affected his conduct. He would often stay in his office operating his shortwave radio during a roll call vote. When asked why, he would tell fellow senators, "We vote on too many damn things in this body." That was true, but it was also true that the effort to go back and forth between his office and the Senate floor several times in an afternoon was often more than he could manage. He would usually leave the Senate at 5 P.M. unless there was a scheduled vote on an issue that mattered to him, like a military appropriation or the American Indian. But domestic issues, especially social conservative concerns like busing or abortion, did not spark a similar interest.

Goldwater's attendance record in the years leading up to his last reelection campaign was poor. He made only 55 percent of the Senate's roll call votes in 1972, 56 percent in 1973, and 76 percent in 1974; the average senator in 1974 answered 86 percent of such votes.[26] His attendance six years later was no better.

And then there was his drinking. He had always had a couple of bourbons late in the afternoon with Senate colleagues or with his staff. He now drank, and not just after the close of business, to help dull the pain of his hip and the arthritis that plagued his knees and other joints. Senators and government officials soon learned that the earlier in the day they did business with the senator the better.[27]

His moods became even more mercurial. Once, at a late night session, a young Senate page went to the Marble Room where Goldwater was sleeping and woke him, for about the eighth time, for a quorum call. Goldwater came padding out in his socks, tie pulled down, hair tousled, and was counted present. On his way back, he stopped at the steps of the podium where the pages sat and snarled at the young man who had awakened him, "You little son-of-a-bitch, if you ever do that to me again, I'll kill you!" Other senators recall that the boy nearly fainted and, for a very long time, refused to enter the Marble Room when Goldwater was there.[28]

Another evening, Goldwater came hobbling on his cane onto the Senate floor, hopeful that action would at last be taken on a communications bill of his that Senator Howard Metzenbaum of Ohio had been holding up. Informed by a Senate clerk that there would be no vote that night because of another Metzenbaum delaying tactic, an enraged Goldwater lifted a telephone off a desk and hurled it across the Senate chamber, yelling, "That goddamn son-of-a-bitch!"[29]

Yet he continued to treat his office staff, male and female, with respect and thoughtfulness, giving them maximum responsibility and independence to do their jobs and sharing with them his many trips and experiences. After being invited to the British Embassy to meet Prince Charles and Princess Diana, for example, he called in the staff and described the evening in minute detail, down to the color of Princess Di's dress. He sent an audio tape of his "briefing" to Peggy back in Phoenix so that she too could enjoy the evening. He bought muumuus for Thompson, Thasher, Eisenhower, and the other woman aides when he visited Hawaii and necklaces for them when he was in Greece.

But far more important to his aides was the knowledge that he cared about them and would take the time to show it, as when he personally drove to Mary Vinovich's wedding and reception in Baltimore. As one aide said, he cast "a giant shadow, and you either blossomed or withered in the shade."[30]

In considering whether he should run for reelection in 1980, Goldwater had to give extraspecial thought to Peggy. She too was not well and was spending more and more time back home in Phoenix. Conscious that he had frequently put the Senate before his wife and children, he had written Peggy at least three letters over the years, promising that this term would be the last.

In July 1979, he wrote his younger son Mike and asked for his "candid advice" about running again. "I'm receiving all kinds of pressure," he said, from personal friends, Senate colleagues, the military, and Republicans in Arizona and across the country that "my word is more respected now than ever and I cannot give up the ship." Republican senators, for example, had signed a letter urging him to run, stating that the party had a good chance in 1980, or no later than 1982, to gain control of the Senate. For once, Goldwater's political antenna failed him. "I wouldn't bet a lot of money on it," he commented skeptically.[31] He was not in any case, he insisted, impressed by such an argument, for "if a political party, such as the Republican party in Arizona, has gotten down to the place where if I quit the whole thing collapses, then it had better collapse." On the other hand, "there are some things here in Washington and around the world that maybe I can do." He also emphasized that if he retired from the Senate, "I can no more stay at home day after day after day than fly to the moon."[32] He needed a job, "not just to keep from driving myself up the wall and dying" but for the income.[33] Like his father, Barry Goldwater always lived like a millionaire no matter what money he earned.

Mike answered his father's letter in full. He argued that his father was a statesman and a model to the younger generation; that the future of the country and not the Arizona Republican party should be his major consideration; that while his mother was "sick and tired of politics" she was "a lot stronger . . . than you think she is"; and that if he did not seek reelection "I see a severe case of atrophy setting in. . . . You'd wither and die." A grateful Goldwater replied, "I agree with everything . . . in your letter," but reiterated his concern about Peggy's health and "what she would do with me being here for another six years."[34]

Joanne Goldwater shared his concern. She is convinced that her father's prolonged absences over the years contributed significantly to her mother's poor health (and heavy drinking) as well as to the Goldwater children's feelings of insecurity and other emotional problems. But Goldwater could not retire. He telegraphed his decision by recalling what his old Staunton instructor, Sandy Patch, had often said: "Gentlemen, you are soldiers; you can always take one more step forward." Patch's dictum, he said, had been "pretty much a guiding light for me down through my life."[35]

On New Year's Day, 1980, with his family grouped around him in young Peggy's home in Newport Beach, California, Barry Goldwater listened to his wife say, "I won't hold you to your promise, Barry. Whatever you decide is all right with me. I want you to be happy." For Goldwater, as he readily admitted, happiness had become the Senate:

> Arizona was my home, but the Senate had become my life. I couldn't give it up. . . . The Senate and Washington had become me. . . . I could not climb down from Capitol Hill.[36]

In his 1988 memoirs, Goldwater writes that from the beginning the 1980 campaign "did not go well," although most political observers thought he would be reelected. He had an experienced campaign organization headed by Steve Shadegg, who had been his campaign manager in his successful 1952, 1958, and 1974 races. He had adequate financing led by his old friend, Harry Rosenzweig. He had a voting record on most state and national issues that reflected the conservative temperament of Arizona. And he was one of the most respected politicians in Washington and the nation, instantly recognized wherever he went. His Democratic opponent was William Schulz, a wealthy real estate developer who had never held public office.

But there were weaknesses in the Goldwater campaign, starting with an often-arrogant candidate, who indicated that it was up to his supporters to get him elected. "I've served the state for twenty-four years," he said to Shadegg. "Damn it, they know me."[37] But many Arizonans did not. An estimated 400,000 new voters had moved into the state since 1974, and many who would be voting for the first time were too young to remember his historic presidential campaign of 1964. They would not automatically accept his campaign slogan: "Barry Goldwater, NOW, More Than Ever." Newcomers and first-timers wanted to know *why* he should continue to be their senator. Money was another concern. Schulz was a multimillionaire prepared to spend whatever was necessary to win. He wound up spending nearly $2 million, including $1.7 million of his own money, to Goldwater's $863,398.

As the campaign developed, the central issue became not what Goldwater had done for Arizona (everyone agreed he had served the state well) but what he could do in the future. Schulz hammered away at the senator's spotty attendance and voting records, nearly the worst in the Senate. In 1980, Goldwater participated in only 58 percent of the Senate roll-call votes. Schulz's slogan was "Energy for the '80s," a not very subtle suggestion that Goldwater was no longer able to handle the job.

The senator also had difficulty adjusting to the demands of the new political groups that had formed around single issues like abortion. He wanted the support of the influential Arizona Right to Life organization, which deliberately delayed a decision, in part because of the contest for the Republican presidential nomination. Ronald Reagan was openly anti-abortion; George Bush was ambivalent about it. Arizona Right to Life leaders were explicit: they would remain silent about

Goldwater until he publicly declared he was pro-life and stated his preference for president.

The senator did not like ultimatums, but after Reagan decisively won the New Hampshire primary, he bowed to political reality and released a brief ten-line endorsement of the former California governor, stating that Reagan was "the man best equipped to lead the nation." Shortly thereafter, Arizona Right to Life endorsed Barry Goldwater's bid for reelection.[38]

Slowly, Goldwater began to realize that he was being seriously challenged by the constantly campaigning Schulz. But his Senate duties prevented him from campaigning back home, and he was confined to his Washington apartment for all of July and most of August because of serious complications resulting from hip surgery. In fact, he almost died from internal hemorrhaging. When he was finally able to return to Arizona, he was hobbled by painful knees, two aching arthritic hips, and serious physical weakness for the first time in his life.

Shadegg assured Goldwater that he would easily win, but the campaign manager, like the candidate, had lost touch with much of the new Arizona. Their outmoded approach was reflected in the dull, defensive TV commercials. A pro-Goldwater advertising expert described one ad as showing "Barry Goldwater sitting in a parlor, talking with a group of elderly ladies with blue hairdos, discussing Social Security. Schulz was right. He looked old, weak, and tired."[39] Symptomatic was the incident at a campaign stop when a man asked Goldwater about American soldiers still missing in Vietnam, and the senator, whose hearing had declined, gave him a long answer about the hostages in Iran.

All the while, Schulz kept pounding away on three points: Goldwater was not working full time in the Senate; he was out of touch with the people of Arizona; and the United States was paying a disproportionately large amount of the free world's defense costs.

By early October, it was clear that younger Arizonans were shifting to Schulz. The race had significantly tightened.[40]

The first week of October, a worried Goldwater phoned Richard Wirthlin and asked him to conduct a statewide poll. It revealed that Schulz had actually moved ahead of the senator—by 46 to 44 percent, with 10 percent undecided. Wirthlin said bluntly that Shadegg was mismanaging the campaign; he had failed to identify Goldwater with the people and problems of the state. He summed up the public's mood as, "We still love Barry, but we're not sure he loves us."[41]

With less than three weeks to go, "we completely revamped the campaign," Goldwater later said. Ron Crawford, a longtime Washington friend and political consultant, and Judy Eisenhower, his administrative assistant in his Senate office, were placed in charge. The old commercials were dumped, and Jay Taylor, a skilled advertising executive, was called in to produce an entirely new TV-radio campaign. In the closing weeks, Goldwater spent nearly $370,000, most of it on new TV ads that showed the candidate wearing a cowboy hat and talking to Indians beside a pickup truck, or Goldwater talking about Arizona problems and how an experienced hand was needed to solve them. Was it hypocritical of Goldwater, who always scorned Madison Avenue image makers, to rely on TV now that he was in trouble? A somewhat defensive Goldwater later insisted that "the commercials were real—not baloney—since I had given my life to the state."[42]

Goldwater was helped when Schulz's criticism turned personal and intemperate, and a number of prominent Democrats reacted by forming "Democrats for Goldwater." Despite his hips, knees, and other sore parts, and the advice of his doctors, Goldwater campaigned hard in the final weeks. "I told myself," he later said, "I would win or die trying. . . . All I had to do was hang tough for three weeks. Hell . . . Big Mike and Uncle Morris hung tough most of their lives."[43]

In their only one-on-one confrontation of the campaign, a luncheon commemorating the centennial of the *Phoenix Gazette,* Goldwater and Schulz traded barbs, not blows. They differed over inflation (Goldwater wanted to cut spending, Schulz did not), abortion (Goldwater favored the Human Life Amendment, his opponent opposed it), and the new Department of Education (Goldwater wanted to abolish it, his opponent to retain it). In answer to a question about his poor Senate attendance record, a central Schulz theme, Goldwater said candidly, "I'm not going to try to tell you I have a good voting record—I don't. I'm not proud of my voting record, but I've given service to this state, and that's the important thing." Both men agreed on one thing: taking on a Goldwater in Arizona was an awesome task.[44]

In the closing days, the Goldwater organization issued a pamphlet, listing over three hundred bills that the senator had introduced since 1953 and that had been signed into law, including key Arizona projects like the Central Arizona Project, the Navajo-Hopi land dispute, expansion of the Grand Canyon National Park, and an interagency committee on Mexican-American Affairs. Goldwater boasted that his eyes were better than ever, he swam a mile a day, he had just passed his fifty-first annual Air Force pilot's physical exam, and he was "tougher than hell." His TV and radio commercials constantly intoned, "Arizona has clout, because Barry Goldwater speaks for us."[45]

On election day, November 4, 1980, the hallowed Goldwater name and a Reagan landslide were together just enough to give Barry Goldwater the narrowest of victories, 430,101 votes to Schulz's 420,871 votes—a 49 to 48 percent margin. Reagan swept Arizona by nearly 61 percent, receiving 529,688 votes to Carter's 246,843. Included in Goldwater's paper-thin plurality of 9,320 votes were about 7,600 absentee ballots from Pima County that were tallied the next day, thanks to Shadegg, who had allotted about $15,000 of Goldwater's campaign funds to the Arizona Republican party for this very purpose.

As he had done in 1964, an aloof Goldwater remained in his Paradise Valley home with family and aides all election day and evening, unavailable to reporters. At a news conference the next morning, the ungracious side of Goldwater was in full view. He sourly agreed that the Reagan landslide "definitely had an effect on every race" and said sarcastically, "I wanted to see what he could do for me." Unable to resist a jab at the president-elect, he added, "He'd still be chasing cows over the horizon if it hadn't been for me." Asked if he perceived any message from the voters in the extremely narrow margin, Goldwater said shortly, "I don't know and I don't particularly care." And then to the question would he make an effort "to improve your voting record," he replied, "I won't break my back at it."[46]

Even before the angry telephone calls and letters began pouring in, Goldwater realized he had made a mistake. The man who titled his 1979 memoirs *With No Apologies* now offered a public one in a letter to the editor of the *Arizona Republic* (later published as a full-page advertisement). He explained that it had been "a difficult campaign and a few hours of sleep made me abrasive, instead of responsive. . . . I do care what the people of Arizona think" he added, and "Yes, I intend to work hard."[47]

It was not an empty promise. In his last years in the Senate, which then had a Republican majority, Goldwater, first as chairman of the Select Committee on Intelligence and then chairman of the Armed

Services Committee, accomplished his most effective and enduring work as a national legislator.

SINCE HIS TEENAGE YEARS at Staunton Military Academy, Goldwater had had a love affair with the U.S. military, extending through his service as a pilot in World War II, his decades as an officer in the Air Force Reserve (from which he retired as a two-star general), and his service on the Senate Armed Services Committee. It was said that he never met an airplane he did not want to fly or fund. While the former was true, the latter was not. He would oppose a new plane (as he did the T-46A trainer pushed by New York Republican Alphonse D'Amato) if he felt a senator wanted it more than the Pentagon did. Nevertheless, a sign on his desk read, "Air Force Spoken Here."

But he was not blind to the flaws and mistakes of the military, which he acknowledged was "the most tradition-minded, conservative institution in America."[48] Sometimes, it was too conservative, even for him.

In 1958, when he was a colonel in the Air Force Reserve, he wrote a seventy-five-page monograph, "A Concept for the Future Organization of the United States Armed Forces," in which he stated that "the weak spot in our [military] is in our scheme of organization." He proposed the creation of a new command structure that would enable lower echelons to perform "commensurate with the fast weapons with which they will be associated in wars of the future." And he suggested a guiding principle based on the signs at NORAD headquarters: "Our mission is to defend the United States, Canada, Alaska, and the northeast area from an attack: NOT TO DEFEND THE ROLES OF THE RESPECTIVE SERVICES."[49] Turf wars among the services, Goldwater later concluded, had botched the attempted rescue of American hostages in Iran in 1980 and had produced excessive confusion and casualties in the 1983 intervention in Grenada.

In his 1958 paper, Colonel Goldwater also urged the creation of a permanent standing military, i.e., a volunteer army, a measure that he successfully championed in the Senate in the early 1970s. A more unified command structure, he argued, would save billions of dollars; there was "no excuse" for "the different budgetary procedures and classifications now existing" in the services. This criticism anticipated the infamous $640 toilet seat of the Reagan Pentagon. Goldwater charged that the military leaders who planned and conducted a war "are so enmeshed in committees, conferences, study groups, congressional investigations, and civilian counterparts that the time from decision to accomplishment is longer than it was in World War II." He concluded:

> The maintaining of a complex command structure on top of a complex operating structure just won't work in this age. It worked when we spoke of speed as miles per hour, but since Mach has become our judgment of speed, reorganization and streamlining should become the daily goal of everyone connected with the military, the Congress, and the executive.[50]

Goldwater was therefore eager to reorganize the Pentagon (for the first time in nearly forty years) when he became chairman of the Senate Armed Services Committee in 1985. Military reform had not been discussed since the late 1950s when President Eisenhower spoke out for more effective coordination of our armed forces, stating, "We must free ourselves of attachments to service systems of an era that is no more"[51] (the central point of Colonel Goldwater's monograph). But the Pentagon bureaucracy delayed any serious action until General David Jones, the incumbent chairman of the Joint Chiefs of Staff (JCS), dropped the equivalent of a nuclear bomb in February 1982—a scorching 6,500-word critique of the nation's military command structure and its problems.

Over the strong objections of Defense Secretary Caspar Weinberger and other Pentagon officials, the air force leader focused on the JCS: "By law, if we cannot reach unanimous agreement on an issue, we must inform the Secretary of Defense. We are understandably reluctant to forward disagreements, so we invest much time and effort trying to accommodate differing views of the chiefs."[52]

Jones recommended that the military abolish the current system in which each service (Army, Navy, Air Force, and Marines) had a virtual veto on every issue at every stage of a routine staffing process. "We need," said Jones, echoing NORAD's slogan, "to spend more time on our war fighting capabilities and less on an intramural scramble for resources." The JCS chairman called for (1) common missions during which the services would work together but retain their service identity, (2) more JCS time and effort on strategic planning, (3) strengthening the role of unified commanders in the field, and (4) a vice chairman to help the JCS chairman become a more effective and timely adviser to the president.[53] Every one of Jones's recommendations would be included in what came to be called the Goldwater-Nichols Pentagon Reorganization Act of 1986.

General Jones could not be ignored, and in response, the House Armed Services Committee, spurred by Congressman Richard White of Texas, held hearings and then passed a bill to reform the Joint Chiefs of Staff system. But the Senate dithered until Senator John Tower of Texas, chairman of the Senate Armed Services Committee, with the backing of Democratic Senator Henry (Scoop) Jackson, decided in June 1983 to examine not just the JCS but all aspects of the Department of Defense. He assigned James R. Locher III, a brilliant young member of the committee staff, to direct the effort. Tower intended the study to serve as the legislative basis for "comprehensive reform at the Pentagon," but his decision to retire from the Senate again delayed Senate action.[54]

In the late fall of 1984, when Goldwater was preparing to assume the duties of chairman of the Senate Armed Services Committee, he was briefed by two conservative think tanks—the Center for Strategic and International Studies and the Heritage Foundation—on defense reorganization. Their presentations helped convince him to make Pentagon reform his number one concern for the next two years.[55]

Aware that he would run up against extraordinary resistance from Defense Secretary Weinberger, several if not all of the Joint Chiefs, some of his colleagues on the Armed Services Committee and in the Senate, and many in the military, Goldwater took several important steps. First, he made sure that reorganization would not become a partisan issue by setting up a task force with himself and Sam Nunn, the ranking Democrat on the committee, as co-chairmen and appointing Locher as the senior staff person who would report to both of them. Second, knowing that he could overcome the formidable opposition only by a carefully orchestrated and sustained effort, he laid out a thirteen-month campaign, with the staff study as the centerpiece.

For the first few months of 1985, Goldwater and Nunn went through each chapter of the study with Locher, digesting its contents, suggesting revisions and changes. In May, the co-chairmen expanded the task force, adding four Republicans and three Democrats, and began holding weekly two-hour and three-hour meetings at which Locher would

discuss chapters or parts of chapters. They also held task force breakfasts at which former secretaries of defense James Schlesinger and Mel
Laird and former JCS chairman David Jones gave their views.

In late September and early October, just before the release of the
645-page staff study, Goldwater and Nunn made a series of speeches on
the Senate floor about different aspects of reorganization—the Joint
Chiefs of Staff, unified commands, military procurement—to build
media and public support. Drew Middleton, the distinguished military
correspondent of the *New York Times,* endorsed the Goldwater-Nunn
initiative, declaring that if the two senators were not successful, "the
services will continue policies that can only weaken America's ability
to deter war."[56]

What concerned Middleton and other experts most was the "unified" command structure under which all branches were equal and no
one was in charge, which resulted in war by committee with all too
predictable results. The 1983 Grenada invasion was a case in point.
Army and navy forces could not talk to each other over their incom-
patible radios. It led to the ridiculous situation mentioned earlier of an
army officer on the beach in Grenada having to use his personal
AT&T credit card to call North Carolina to coordinate naval fire
support.[57]

A key event in the yearlong Goldwater campaign was a weekend
retreat for the reorganization task force at Fort A. P. Hill near Rich-
mond, Virginia, on October 11–13, 1985. Determined to present a broad
spectrum of opinion, Goldwater invited fifteen experts, including former Defense Secretaries Harold Brown and Schlesinger, who supported reorganization, and Admiral Thomas Moorer, former JCS
chairman, who opposed it, to brief the nine members of the task force.
Except for Goldwater and Nunn, the other senators were not ready to
commit themselves to reform because of the perceived opposition of
the military. But after they heard authorities like Schlesinger, Brown,
and Jones endorse reorganization, they began to support some if not all
of the reforms.

The following week the staff study, recommending ninety-one ways
to streamline the military, was finally released. Part of the strategy was
to include some rather extreme staff recommendations (like eliminating the Joint Chiefs of Staff) so that Goldwater and Nunn could counter
with a more moderate position (like creating a vice chairman of the
JCS) and thereby achieve their real objective.[58] After a series of public

hearings in November and December, Locher and other staffers, working closely with Goldwater and Nunn, prepared a bill for consideration by the Armed Services Committee.

In his 1988 memoirs, Goldwater recounts how he and Nunn were "invited," indeed almost summoned, to the Pentagon on February 3, 1986, to meet with the Joint Chiefs of Staff the day before the committee was scheduled to begin marking up the reorganization bill. "It was obvious," the senator writes, "that those opposing military reform were trying to maneuver us into an early, full-blown confrontation." General John A. Wickham, Jr., army chief of staff; General P. X. Kelley, commandant of the Marine Corps; and Admiral James D. Watkins, chief of Naval Operations, "launched a direct, frontal attack on the bill," arguing that it would destroy the independent judgment and professional integrity of the JCS by placing each chief under the civilian secretary of his military department. Goldwater was shocked at the sharp, emotional attack by men whom he respected but who had badly misinterpreted "the meaning and intention of our plan." The Joint Chiefs would indeed lose power, but to the JCS chairman and commanders in the field.

Now it was Locher's turn, and he presented the legislation's central theme: "to have U.S. air, sea, and ground forces fight as a team through a series of organizational and command changes within the services." Wickham, Watkins, and Kelley skipped over the objective and got to the core of their discontent—the increased authority the bill would give commanders leading troops into combat. These commanders, they asserted, would be diverted from the combat itself because they would become bogged down in allocating resources and other administrative details, including contracting. Nunn jumped in and explained in detail that these charges were simply not true. The JCS stood hard.[59]

The JCS raised nine major objections, and Goldwater and Nunn answered all of them—but not to the satisfaction of the Joint Chiefs. Their message was clear: "They didn't believe in reorganization, and they were telling us to go to hell."[60] Such tactics might have cowed a less secure man or less knowledgeable chairman, but Goldwater was convinced of his cause. He would not be stopped by the Joint Chiefs fighting for turf or by senators beholden to this or that service or by anyone else. When Locher asked whether he wanted to regroup and reconsider the next step, Goldwater gave a simple answer: "Proceed as planned."[61]

As the Armed Services Committee began formal consideration of military reorganization, ten members, including Strom Thurmond, supported the plan while nine were against or leaning against the plan, including Republicans John Warner and Dan Quayle. Warner, a former secretary of the navy, was the stiffest opponent, backed by Secretary of the Navy John Lehman, who set up a crisis management center in the Pentagon to fight reform. Once asked which elements of the Defense Department were resisting reorganization, Goldwater answered, "That portion of the organization that sails ships," and Nunn chimed in, "We haven't been serenaded with 'Anchors Aweigh' lately."[62]

When Warner introduced the first of fifteen amendments, Goldwater worried that the legislation might suffer death by amendment, and he decided to send a signal to opponents within and outside the committee. He announced that the reform bill would take precedence over all other committee business, including military promotions, budget hearings, presidential nominees, and new weapons. Essentially, Goldwater told his colleagues, "If we have to stay here all year debating this bill, we're going to do it." Everyone realized he was serious when late one afternoon, Goldwater grew so angry at the desultory pace that he ordered the doors of the meeting room locked and, waving his cane at them, warned his fellow senators that no one would be allowed to leave until he had voted on a particular amendment.[63]

The first few committee votes were decided by 10–9 margins, but gradually the margin widened to 11–8 and then 12–7 until, a month later, all opposition collapsed. In the end, all nineteen members of the Armed Services Committee voted for and reported out the reorganization bill in early March.

But the fight took its toll, and sometimes Goldwater, suffering from painful hips and other ailments, was unable to chair a session. He would tell Nunn to go ahead, but in almost every instance Nunn insisted that "if Barry can't run the show then we'll put it off."[64] He knew that Goldwater's personal involvement as Mr. Defense was crucial to passage of the bill.

Goldwater was also burdened by Peggy's serious illness—and his guilt at not being able to be with her. He recalled that the preceding year, shortly before they celebrated their fiftieth wedding anniversary, Peggy had remarked that "all" she had done for most of their fifty years together was "to say goodbye."[65] She underwent several operations for circulatory problems, including the amputation of her left leg, but on December 11, 1985, at the age of seventy-six, she died in Good Samaritan Medical Center in Phoenix after her heart, lungs, and kidneys failed. The senator was with her. The obituary in the *Arizona Republic* described her as "a modest retiring woman" who preferred to stay in the background during her husband's long political career.[66]

Goldwater's tears, his obvious grief at the funeral (attended by dozens of senators and other top Washington officials), caused some to wonder when and even if Goldwater would return to Washington. But shortly thereafter, he walked slowly onto the Senate floor, leaning heavily on his cane. His old friend, Alan Simpson of Wyoming, offered his condolences and then asked, "What are you doing here?" After a second, Goldwater said simply, "This is where I have to be right now, in the Senate. This is my family."[67] As much as he loved his Arizona family, he needed his Washington "family"—the Senate—more in order to cope with the grief of Peggy's death. As he wrote Joanne, "I don't know how many times a day I reach for the phone just to call her and then realize that she is not there. . . . I don't know if I will ever get over it, but I have a long time to go and I'll just work it out."[68] He preferred to "work it out" in the Senate, which, he was determined, would act on his bill to reform the Defense Department.

ON MAY 7, 1986, after seven hours and ten minutes of deliberation, the U.S. Senate by a vote of 95–0 approved the most sweeping reorganization of the military establishment in nearly four decades. Goldwater neatly undercut any potential opposition by framing the debate as one "between those who seek a truly unified defense effort and those who would cling to traditional service prerogatives."

The Senate overwhelmingly endorsed the two major reforms of the year-long Goldwater-Nunn effort: designating the chairman of the Joint Chiefs of Staff as the president's "principal military adviser" and granting the seven commanders-in-chief (or CINCs) responsible for military operations in specific geographic areas around the world "full operational command" over units assigned to them.

During the debate, senator after senator rose to praise Goldwater for his leadership and dedication in bringing the bill to the floor and shepherding its passage. John Exon, a Nebraska Democrat, teased him for not having "reorganized the U.S. Senate as I think it should be reorganized." Goldwater retorted, "I would remind my friend that it has taken over two hundred years to screw this place up. I do not think I am going to live long enough to get it turned the other way. But it would be a lot of fun trying."[69]

In a rare gesture, the Senate adopted an amendment offered by Nunn to name the bill after Goldwater, prompting the genuinely touched seventy-seven-year-old senator to growl, "The hell with it. You get to the point when you get old that you can't say thank you." Congressman Les Aspin, chairman of the House Armed Services Committee, called the measure "one of the landmark laws of American history." Senator Joseph Biden commented accurately that "only Goldwater" could have produced the measure. "If anybody else had been the one who had been advocating this reorganization," Biden said, "every military man and woman at the Pentagon would have been down on our backs as 'communist sympathizers.' "[70]

Five days later, President Reagan awarded Goldwater the Presidential Medal of Freedom in the East Room of the White House, describing him as "a prophet" and "an American legend." As he presented the medal to Goldwater, Reagan said, "Here you go, Mr. Conservative." After the ceremony, the senator remarked, "This is the highest award I've ever gotten and probably ever will get in my life."[71]

THE HISTORIC IMPACT of the Goldwater-Nichols Act was proven conclusively by the remarkable success of the Persian Gulf War of 1991. Major General Gus Pagonis, chief of logistics for the ground forces of Desert Shield, told Nunn that without the authority granted him by the Goldwater reorganization he could not have moved "the unprecedented amount" of goods, food, medicine, fuel, and other material that made possible the famous flanking ground attack of the Gulf War. "Every one of the other commanders," says Nunn, including Lt. General Charles Horner, who ran the air campaign against Iraq, "has said virtually the same thing." From an operational point of view, in Nunn's opinion, Goldwater-Nichols "was the most important reform that has occurred since World War II, other than the creation of [the Department of Defense] itself."[72]

In the late summer of 1992, on one of his periodic trips to Washington, D.C., Goldwater was invited to the Pentagon one morning by General Colin Powell, chairman of the Joint Chiefs of Staff, who warmly thanked him for his bill and asked him to sign his copy of it.

"Goldwater was truly thrilled," remembers Gerry Smith, a former defense aide for the senator, that "one of the most powerful generals since World War II" would take the trouble to thank him personally.[73]

At a news conference held in the Senate Press Gallery on May 7, minutes after passage of his bill, Goldwater told reporters, "It's the only goddamn thing I've done in the Senate that's worth a damn." Plopping down in his wheelchair before making his exit, he added, "I can go home happy, sit up on my hill, and shoot the jackrabbits."[74]

And off he went to Phoenix although he did not have to. He received offers from leading defense contractors and airplane manufacturers to remain in Washington as their "representative" for fees totaling more than a million dollars. He could have used the money. Large bills from Peggy's illness were waiting to be paid, but the life of a lobbyist, no matter how it was dressed up, was not for him. As he told a friend who asked whether he was going to accept any of the lobbying offers, "I'm too old to be a pimp."[75]

22

A Summing Up

OLD POLITICIANS, like old soldiers, usually fade away, but in 1993, seven years after he had retired from the Senate, eighty-four-year-old Barry Goldwater appeared on CNN's "Larry King Live," was interviewed by Hugh Downs on ABC's "20/20," was a guest on Jay Leno's "The Tonight Show" (with TV sitcom superstar Roseanne Barr), and was featured on the cover of the weekly Sunday supplement, *Parade*. Goldwater got the media's and everyone else's attention by stating that opposition to lifting the ban on gays in the military was "just plain dumb" and declaring (in the *Washington Post*), "You don't need to be 'straight' to fight and die for your country. You just need to shoot straight."

To his many military friends, Goldwater's endorsement of President Bill Clinton's plan to lift the ban on homosexuals in the armed forces was like John Paul II approving a NOW demand to ordain woman priests. Gary Bauer, president of the Family Research Council, pointed out that 84 percent of active duty personnel opposed the Clinton plan. He suggested that while Goldwater knew a lot about flying military jets, he knew little about the impact of "placing gays in close quarters with heterosexual service members on submarines, on ships, and in armored, artillery, and infantry units."[1]

Undeterred by such criticism and flattered by the media attention, the senator reared back and let go, like Harry Truman in his last years, with comments on *abortion*: "Women have been aborting ever since time began and they are going to be aborting when time ends—so forget about it." The *religious Right*: "These gentlemen who profess to run a political effort through the church, I think they're doing a disservice to the church and a disservice to politics. I hope they'll quit." *Tattoos*: "I'm looking for a model," Goldwater said, reaching over and pursing Roseanne's mouth. "I want a pair of red ruby lips right on my ass."[2]

Roseanne, Jay, and Barry all laughed merrily, but many conservatives were dismayed that the man who had challenged liberal opinion on TVA, Social Security, and Vietnam had become "politically correct" on social issues like homosexuals and abortion.

In the spring of 1994, at the height of media and political interest in the Whitewater affair, Goldwater further confounded partisans of both parties by calling on "my Republican friends" in Washington "to get off" President Clinton's back and "let him be president." Summoning reporters to his home in Paradise Valley, the senator read a brief statement that he had drafted after a "night of agonizing." Of the Whitewater real estate venture, he said, "I haven't heard anything yet that says this is all that big of a deal." Goldwater admitted that he talked occasionally by phone with Clinton, who once called him "a saint," but emphasized that the decision to speak out about Whitewater was entirely his own.

Some Arizona Republicans demanded that his name be removed from the front of the Barry Goldwater Center in downtown Phoenix. "The idea that he's Mr. Republican is a bunch of baloney," said the angry executive director of the leading pro-life organization in the state. "He's really becoming a joke."[3] Conservative columnist John Kolbe of the *Phoenix Gazette* was equally harsh, writing that while Goldwater was "as plain-spoken as ever . . . there's no conviction left. His beliefs seem to flap with the breeze. It's as if he is only parroting someone else's views."

At the same time, however, Goldwater was sharply challenging the president's health care plan. He felt so strongly about the proposed "health alliances" that he asked voters in some twenty congressional districts to contact their congressmen about the suggested "health care bureaucracies" that would cost "billions of dollars" and turn "a lot of your freedom of choice over to the government."[4] He told a reporter that "if you made [the Clinton proposal] law, it would cost as much as the whole country is worth . . . you know that's not going to happen."

The open unhappiness of some conservatives with Goldwater misled *New York Times* columnist Russell Baker to write that Republicans were "entering the Robespierre phase of their conservative revolution" by wanting to send Goldwater to the guillotine. A more perceptive George Will wrote that Goldwater delighted in his role as "the Republicans' leading curmudgeon." While the senator's views understandably exasperated conservatives, Will added, they should not have surprised anyone familiar with his lifelong message about government: "When in doubt, get it out of people's lives."[5]

GOLDWATER ALSO CREATED CONTROVERSY in the summer of 1992, when, just before Republicans convened in Houston, he declared that if the GOP included an anti-abortion plank in its platform "the Republican National Convention will go down in a shambles as will the election." In a letter to Mary Dent Crisp, head of the liberal National Republican Coalition for Choice, he said that "abortion is not something the Republican party should call for the abolition of, by legal means or by any other means. . . ."[6] Goldwater and Crisp notwithstanding, the Republican platform committee stood firm. And Goldwater's dire prediction lay fallow; most analysts agreed that abortion was not a determining issue in the Bush-Clinton campaign.

The senator carried his anti–Christian Right crusade to extreme lengths that fall when he publicly endorsed liberal Democrat Karan English over conservative Republican Doug Wead for a new congressional seat in Arizona. It was not the first time Goldwater had split his ticket, but never before had he advertised his reasons quite so loudly.

In an unusually harsh statement, Goldwater described former White House aide Wead, strongly pro-life and supported by evangelical Christians, as a hybrid of "an Amway salesman and Jerry Falwell." State Senator English, whom he supported, was a vigorous backer of abortion on demand and an opponent of state tax limitations. Both sides confirmed that the Goldwater endorsement was decisive: English defeated Wead by 52–48 percent.[7]

Why was Goldwater saying and doing things that seemed to be at such odds with his conservative philosophy and career? To begin with, Barry Goldwater was being what he had always been—provocative and unpredictable. As William F. Buckley Jr. put it, Goldwater "was born with an inclination to keep his listeners on their toes."[8]

He had been firing before aiming his whole life, beginning when he fired a cannon at the church across the street as a boy. And he usually got away with it because he was Barry Goldwater. One sunny afternoon in 1992, for example, police received a disturbing report of gunfire in the hills around the Goldwater home. When the sheriff arrived, he found the senator happily firing a .22 rifle into the sky. "Come on, Barry," the sheriff said, reprovingly, "you can't be doing that." As Goldwater tells the story, he said, "Oh, hell, well, okay," and then roared with laughter.[9]

Being outrageous and in your face got him headlines and invitations to appear on leading TV programs and make speeches. No other retired politician, aside from former presidents, was more sought after. Judy Eisenhower remembers that when she and the senator were closing down the Senate office in December 1986, he said with a smile, "Now, I'll get to say what I really feel."[10] To put it in political terms, Goldwater now had a constituency of just one—himself. He could finally lay down the heavy burden of being the conscience of the conservative movement.

Some conservatives wondered whether Goldwater was being unduly influenced by his vivacious new wife, Susan, thirty-one years his junior and openly liberal. At a testimonial dinner in his honor, *Arizona Republic* editorial cartoonist Steve Benson said publicly what many were thinking privately when he acknowledged the presence of "Senator Goldwater and his lovely ventriloquist wife, Susan."[11] When the senator's criticism of the Clinton health plan was repeated to her, she said, "He's so ill-informed about it, and he shouldn't even talk about it."[12] Friends, however, scoffed at the suggestion that Goldwater could be molded by anyone. "I've known him well for thirty years," states Dodie Londen, chairwoman of the Arizona Republican party. "He has never been afraid to speak his mind"—and to admire those who did likewise.

Following his statement that Republicans ought to get off Clinton's back, Londen publicly stated that Goldwater was entitled to his opinion but did not speak for the Republican party. Shortly thereafter, she was invited to the Goldwater home for a charitable fundraising event. As she was leaving, Goldwater took Londen aside and said, "You keep speaking your mind even if it's negative about me."

"That's one thing I have learned" about politics, says Londen, "be honest about your feelings—that's the only way to be. Barry Goldwater is certainly a good teacher in that."[13]

Susan Goldwater laughs when asked about her supposed Svengali-like influence over her husband. "You should see me around the house," she comments, "trying to get him to pick up his dirty clothes or comb his hair a certain way. . . . He goes in the other direction if you try to make him do something." In truth, she says, "he enjoys his stubbornness."[14]

While she has views that are to the left of those of her legendary husband on most social issues, Susan Wechsler Goldwater's most telling contribution has been to give new vitality to Barry Goldwater, who had been in physical and mental decline since Peggy's death and his retirement from the Senate. Visitors to his home, Be-Nun-I-Kin, in the late 1980s came away with the impression of a man who had lost much of his zest for life, who talked incessantly about his aches and pains.

Friends and family noted an immediate change after his marriage to Susan, a health care manager, in February 1992. Soon he was walking as much as a mile every day or riding a three-wheeled bicycle; the wheelchair was put away. The sprawling glass, stone, and wood home high above Phoenix was once again filled with laughter and company and good times.

Susan Goldwater describes her husband as a rugged individualist who can be contrary, "an incisive thinker who can get to the heart of almost any matter." He has, she says, "a true pioneer spirit"; he once remarked to her that he would "be on the shuttle to the moon tomorrow" if he could.[15]

Second, social issues like abortion and homosexuality were not debated when Goldwater published *The Conscience of a Conservative* and ran for president. He made his mark and coalesced a national political movement on positions of limited government and anticommunism. What would he have said in 1964 if asked about the rights of gays and abortion? Which Goldwater would have prevailed—the libertarian or the traditionalist? Some argue that Goldwater would have been pro-choice and pro-gay rights then as he was now, that the Goldwater of the 1990s was the Goldwater of the 1960s—the apostle of freedom and individual choice. They insist that he has always presented a "totally consistent message."[16]

As we have seen, this was not always true. While Goldwater was extremely consistent on economic issues (opposing big government and federal spending, favoring the elimination of government agencies, advocating a balanced budget), he changed course several times on the most controversial social issue of all—abortion. In the wake of

Roe v. Wade, as mentioned, he adopted a moderate pro-life stand (against "abortion on demand"), then opposed a constitutional amendment preventing abortions, then endorsed a Human Life Amendment (in the middle of his 1980 reelection), and finally settled on a strong pro-choice position after leaving the Senate. (He also shifted on voluntary prayer in public schools; he supported a constitutional amendment in the 1960s but opposed one in the 1980s.) As he once put it, "I'm not *for* abortion, but it's something that's up to the individual, not the government—like praying."[17]

And then there is the religious Right. Goldwater has not always insisted, as he did in August 1993, that "there is no place in this country for practicing religion in politics."[18] In his most irfluential book, he wrote: "The laws of God and of nature have no dateline. . . . These principles are derived from the nature of man and from the truths that God has revealed about His creation."[19] He developed the theme of the natural place of religion in politics in his 1970 book, *The Conscience of a Majority,* in which he attacked the liberal notion that change for the sake of change is good:

> I am struck with the unhappy realization that the concept of "change" as it is advocated by today's liberals is becoming a sickness. It no longer looks to the consequences. It no longer respects the confines of decency and taste. No institution, be it church, school, or the United States Capitol, is sacred or even respected.[20]

As one conservative journal put it, "no member of the religious Right could have said it better."[21] Examples of Goldwater's acknowledgement of the importance of religion in public life are abundant. In 1964, Goldwater told the graduating class of the Pennsylvania Military College that "it is impossible to maintain freedom and order and justice without religious and moral sanctions." In a 1962 article for *Human Events,* he denied that churches had no role to play in the struggle against totalitarianism, asking, "If the Christian church is not to fight . . . then who on Earth is left to resist this evil which is determined to destroy all virtue, all decency?"[22]

Most significantly, there was his eloquent call for "morality in government" throughout his 1964 presidential bid. Even in the 1990s, when asked about his faith, Goldwater said, "I'm a very great believer in the fact that God created everything. . . . It's reassuring that something, somebody—I can call him God—has His hand in things."[23]

Ed McAteer, who played a central role in forming the Moral Majority and heads the Religious Roundtable, praises Goldwater as a political leader who "was head and shoulders above his peers in the 1960s" but "got off track" in later years. Goldwater, he says, reminds him of King Saul of the Old Testament, whose last words are, "I have played the fool" rather than the Saul (or Paul) of the New Testament, whose last words are, "I have stayed the course."[24]

Biographer Jack Casserly believes that Barry Goldwater became more libertarian during his last term in the Senate because of his constant association with *Washington Post* executive editor Ben Bradlee, his wife, Sally Quinn, and their circle of liberal friends. Goldwater's philosophical balance between traditionalist and libertarian that prevailed in the 1950s and 1960s gradually tilted toward libertarianism, but not always. He does not, for example, favor decriminalizing drugs, although most libertarians and even some conservatives like Bill Buckley do. And he is uncomfortable with the widespread distribution of condoms by the government in public schools, commenting, "When I was younger, even the discussion of a condom was forbidden."[25] He opposes "mandatory birth control devices" like Norplant but worries that the world's population "seems to be exploding."[26] Not a smoker himself, he would not ban public smoking although he once co-sponsored a Senate bill to prohibit smoking in public buildings.[27]

Never a model of consistency, Goldwater, at the age of eighty-six and depending upon the issue, is sometimes a traditionalist and sometimes a libertarian. It may be confusing, but the *Washington Post* errs badly when it declares that Goldwater has taken "a late left turn" by emphasizing his libertarian position on gay rights and downplaying his hard right opinions about Clinton's health plan, foreign policy ("he doesn't know a goddamn thing about it"), and national security policy ("the thing that worries me right now is Clinton. I don't think he understands the military").[28] When asked to describe himself, he says simply, "I'm a conservative."[29]

Even the most exasperated conservatives are reluctant to criticize, let alone condemn him. As Richard Viguerie says, "Conservatives will never be able to repay their debt to Goldwater." Of his libertarian comments about abortion, gay rights, and other social issues, Phyllis

Schlafly counsels conservatives, "Let him enjoy his retirement. . . . [His] legacy is the way the 27 million, who braved the vitriol of Big Media in 1964, lived to grow into the 54 million that validated the Reagan Revolution in 1984 and 1988."[30] Dick Armey asserts, "No one today who calls himself a conservative can do so without paying implicit tribute to Barry Goldwater."[31]

Even so, when Goldwater remarked, only three weeks after the November 1994 elections, that Gingrich "talks too much" and Senator Jesse Helms is "off his rocker," and tells a student that the Vietnam War was "a useless war," friends and admirers of the senator wish he would take his own advice and stop talking so much and so carelessly. He harms himself as well as the cause of freedom for which he has fought all his life when he argues that the United States was wrong to pour so much money and energy into fighting communism. The more than 500 million people who used to live behind the Iron Curtain would emphatically disagree.[32]

As the culture war rages on all sides, many on the right applaud the social conservatism of William J. Bennett, who argues that "every serious student of American history, familiar with the writings of the Founders, knows the civic case for religion. It provides society with a moral anchor—and nothing else has yet been found to substitute for it."[33]

Goldwater has long been conscious of the growing gap between himself and the conservative movement. As early as February 1983, he wrote plaintively to Bill Buckley: "What the heck did I do to bring down the wrath of Young Americans for Freedom and, I might as well throw in, most conservative organizations? It's been quite a few years since I was invited to even attend one of the functions here in Washington. . . . Where did I mess up? I'm just as conservative as I ever was."

Gently, Buckley explained that while his admiration and affection for Goldwater had not diminished "by a whisker," he disagreed with the senator on a number of positions he had taken. "No doubt," he wrote, "the accumulation of these positions is the cause of the disenchantment you finger," adding, "The young conservatives are very adamant . . . on the subject of abortion. So, as a matter of fact, am I: so, indeed, should everyone be if they are convinced that the unborn child is a human being."[34]

A second issue was the Supreme Court, which "has been engaged in writing its own constitution," Buckley pointed out. "Your resolute opposition to any legislative efforts to cure the usurpations of the Court

I know has distressed a lot of people." Having let his old friend know why there was considerable conservative disaffection about their one-time champion and hero, Buckley imparted a far greater truth: "Your own place in history is very secure."[35]

WHAT IF THERE HAD BEEN NO BARRY GOLDWATER? Or, more precisely, no Senator Barry Goldwater? To begin with, there would have been no *Conscience of a Conservative,* bought by more than 3.5 million Americans and read, probably, by as many as ten million Americans, making it the most popular political manifesto of twentieth-century America. Without *The Conscience of a Conservative* (still read by college students more than thirty-five years after its publication), thousands of young men and women would not have been persuaded to enter politics and help lay the foundation for the modern conservative movement in America.

If there had been no Senator Goldwater, there would have been no presidential bid by candidate Goldwater in 1964. There would have been no creation, through direct mail, of an army of grassroots contributors who helped the Republican party become a truly national party. No conservative cadre would have emerged to dominate the organization of the GOP at the national, state, and local levels for the ensuing three decades.

Without Goldwater in 1964, the Republican party would have continued to be dominated by its Eastern liberal wing and remained a regional minority party. There would have been no decisive electoral breakthrough in the South, no development of a two-party system in the South, and no emerging Republican majority.[36]

Without Goldwater, there would have been no President Reagan, for there would have been no opportunity for Reagan to deliver a nationally televised address on behalf of the party's presidential nominee. Without such a political jumpstart, Reagan would have remained on what he calls the mashed potato circuit for the rest of his public life.

Without Goldwater there might well have been no President Nixon because Scranton or Rockefeller would have been the Republican presidential nominee in 1968, not two-time-loser Nixon. Nixon was able to win the nomination in 1968 because he could call upon the conservative forces created by Goldwater's run four years earlier. If there had been no President Nixon, there would have been no Watergate, certainly a reason for celebration, but without the catalyst of Watergate, there would have been no New Right, no Moral Majority, and no winning conservative coalition at the national level.

Finally, without Goldwater in 1964, the conservative movement would have remained the intellectual plaything of a group of writers and academics revolving around *National Review, Human Events,* and similar publications.

If there had been no Goldwater in the Senate, there would have been no one to tell Ike that he was spending too much money, Kennedy that he had not been a profile in courage at the Bay of Pigs, Johnson that he should not play politics with Vietnam, Nixon that it was time for him to go, Carter that he was violating the Constitution, and Reagan that he should stop trying to cover up covert operations. Without Goldwater in the Senate, there would have been no reorganization of the Pentagon (and no textbook triumph in the Persian Gulf War) and no great champion of the American Indian. Without Goldwater, the Senate would have been far quieter and more predictable—which is why so many senators agree that the Senate could use another outspoken, curmudgeonly Goldwater today.

On the other hand, if there had been a President Goldwater in 1965, we can be certain that: first, the Vietnam War would have been brought to a successful conclusion through the extensive use of air and sea power in no more than six months, or American forces would have been brought home. Second, the nation would not have launched a vainglorious, multi-trillion-dollar experiment in welfarism, initially called the Great Society, that not only failed to end poverty, hunger, homelessness, and assorted ills of the modern world, but opened a Pandora's box of other ills—drugs, broken families, illegitimacy, crime, and more.

WHO, THEN, was Barry Goldwater? He was a cradle conservative who opposed the Bigs of America—Big Government, Big Business, Big Labor, Big Media. He defended the entrepreneur, the dreamer, the man and the woman who asked only to be given the opportunity to go as far and as high as their talent and ambition could take them. He called himself a Jeffersonian republican, with a small "r." He believed in custom, tradition, the Constitution. He lived by the words of the old Cole Porter song, "Don't fence me in," battling against economic regulations or social rules.

He was as paradoxical a politician as ever came to Washington. He had deep-rooted reservations about some of the new members of the conservative movement, particularly the Christian Right, whose leaders seemed to him to be more interested in this life than in the afterlife. But their support was indispensable to his narrow victory in the California primary, without which he would not have been nominated in 1964.

He was a man of his word who could not abide someone who failed to keep his. Because Richard Nixon lied to his friends and his family, Goldwater called the former president "the most dishonest individual" he had ever met. Yet Goldwater excused Vice President Spiro Agnew, who brazenly lied to friends and supporters about his acceptance of bribes, and forgave Nelson Rockefeller, who cruelly distorted Goldwater's positions in their 1964 battle for the Republican presidential nomination.

He was as American as bourbon and water, cheeseburgers and milkshakes, cowboys and Indians, Thunderbird cars and jet airplanes. As one conservative remarked, "Everything he did was unrehearsed even when it was rehearsed."[37] He was the envy of every politician because when it came down to it, he invariably did and said exactly what he wanted to—whatever the consequences. He was forgiven inconsistencies, inaccuracies, and non sequiturs that would have ruined any other public figure. Friend and adversary alike invariably would smile and shake their heads at the latest Goldwaterism and say, "Oh, that's just Barry." In his own phrase, he just liked to poop along, but often someone else—an aide, a colleague, a friend—had to clean up after him.[38]

He grew up on the old frontier, in a desert city that was still a town, in a state that was still a territory when he was born. He was the product of Mun, his fiercely independent, iconoclastic mother; Uncle Morris, his Jeffersonian Democrat uncle; and Sandy Patch, his disciplined, demanding instructor at Staunton Military Academy. He was molded by his many hours among the stoic Navajos and Hopis and by danger-filled flights over the Atlantic and the Himalayas during World War II. He was influenced by the ideas he found in books like *The Road to Serfdom* and *The Conservative Mind* and by mentors like Steve Shadegg, Jay Hall, Bill Baroody, and Denny Kitchel. He was inspired by the lives of heroes like Charles Lindbergh and Jimmy Doolittle. He was fortunate to have steadfast, loyal friends like Harry Rosenzweig, Bill Quinn, and Trapper Drum, and the unqualified love of wives like Peggy and Susan. He deeply loved his four children, but he was not always there when they wanted him. He tried to make it up to them with long letters and generous gifts, but they wanted more of the father and less of the senator.

WHO WAS Barry Goldwater? He said about himself, "I would like to be remembered as an honest man who did his best." He was a patriot who loved his country passionately and without apology. As a 1964 campaigner put it, "He shot from the heart, not the hip."[39] He had been willing to give his life for his country in war, and he continued to give his life for his country in peace. He set a new standard of political courage by going through the crucible of crushing defeat and national humiliation in 1964 without uttering a single word of public complaint.

He was a prophet, an Old Testament Jeremiah, who sternly warned the people to repent of their wasteful ways or reap a whirlwind of debt and deficits. He was a pioneer who led the Republican party out of the barren east and into a verdant south and west where milk and honey and victory awaited them. He was, in George Will's words, "a man who lost forty-four states but won the future."[40] He did not seek greatness, but quietly accepted it when it was thrust upon him. A man of seemingly boundless energy, he inspired more people, especially young people, to enter politics than any other losing presidential candidate in modern history—more than Eugene McCarthy, more than George McGovern, more than Jesse Jackson. There was a grandness about him; as a friend remarked, "He would look good on Mount Rushmore."[41]

He was the first ideological presidential candidate of a major political party, placing issues and ideas at the center of his campaign. He was not so much the candidate of a political party as the personification of a political movement. His candidacy for president marked the true beginning of a tectonic shift in American politics—from East to West, from the cities to the suburbs, from big government to limited government, from containment to liberation, from liberal to conservative—that continues to shape the nation, as the historic elections of 1994 attest.

Acknowledgments

FOR A CURMUDGEON, Barry Goldwater is one of the most accommodating people in the world. He gave me unrestricted access to his papers, granted me interviews early and often, answered my letters of inquiry promptly and candidly, and told his family, friends, and colleagues whom I wanted to interview that he was cooperating with me. I am especially indebted to his longtime assistant, Doris Berry, for her unfailing efficiency and good humor. Demonstrating again how rare a politician he is, the senator did not seek to approve the manuscript before its publication.

The Goldwater papers are maintained by the Arizona Historical Foundation in the Carl Hayden Library on the campus of Arizona State University in Tempe, Arizona. I wish to express my special thanks for the foundation's help to Dr. Evelyn Cooper, its director, as well as Dennis D. Madden and Susie Sato. The nation's presidential libraries are a great national resource. In researching this book, my wife Anne and I visited the Eisenhower, Kennedy, Johnson, Ford, and Carter libraries. All contained important information, but the collections of the Johnson and Ford libraries were particularly revealing.

Among the other collections consulted, the Steve Shadegg Papers located at the Texas Historical Society at the University of Texas in Austin and the Clarence Manion Papers at the Chicago Historical Society in Chicago were most important.

One of the reasons why I determined to write this book is that there has been no biography of Barry Goldwater for nearly thirty years, and there has never been any in-depth examination of his influence on

471

American politics. Of the early works, the best by far is *Barry Gold-water: Portrait of an Arizonan* by Edwin McDowell. Dean Smith's *The Goldwaters of Arizona* is an excellent short history of the Goldwater family. The senator's two autobiographies (the 1979 one written with Steve Shadegg, the 1988 one with Jack Casserly) are invaluable resources.

I conducted 174 interviews for this book, nearly all of them in person and audiotaped. I want to thank in particular the following who gave me a special measure of their wisdom and time: Denison Kitchel, friend and colleague of the senator for fifty years; Terry Emerson, for eighteen years Goldwater's legislative director; Jack Casserly, collaborator of the 1988 autobiography; Dean Smith, a true Arizonan; F. Clifton White, who, unhappily, did not live to read this work; Susan Goldwater and all four of the Goldwater children—Joanne, Barry Jr., Michael, and Peggy—for their candid comments about the husband and father; Harry Jaffa, for his recollections about the most famous sentence in presidential acceptance addresses; Robert Mardian, for his revelations about Lyndon Johnson and the FBI; Bill Middendorf, for his memories about the Draft Goldwater Committee and giving me access to his personal archives; Sally Quinn, for her special insights into Goldwater, the man and the friend; William A. Rusher, without whom there would not have been a rise of the Right; Theodore Sorensen, for recollections about John Kennedy and Barry Goldwater; Gerry Smith, head of the Barry M. Goldwater Scholarship Foundation; and filmmaker Bill McCune for sharing his insights and his interviews of the senator and his family and friends.

For their research assistance, I thank Mark Petersen, Susan Bishay, and Michael H. DeThomas.

I express my special gratitude to the following institutions for their generous financial support: the Historical Research Foundation, the Fund for American Studies, the Earhart Foundation, and the Wilbur Foundation.

This book has been a project of the Edwards family. My wife Anne conducted research at the Eisenhower and Carter libraries and the Nixon archives; our younger daughter Catherine did research at the Catholic University of America, where she is a graduate student in the School of Philosophy; our older daughter, Elizabeth Edwards Spalding, read every line of the manuscript in between defending her doctoral dissertation at the University of Virginia and settling into a new house.

I am grateful to Mike Giampaoli at Paragon House for initially accepting the book and thankful that my agent, Leona Schecter, persuaded Al Regnery to publish my biography. Trish Bozell is not only a treasured friend but the best book editor I have ever had.

The longer I live the more I realize how much all that we do depends upon others. I am fortunate in having so many good and generous people on whom I can depend—first, last, and always, my wonderful wife Anne.

Lee Edwards
Alexandria, Virginia
April 1995

Notes

Introduction

1. LBJ's percentage of the total vote cast was a historic 61.1 percent to Goldwater's 38.5 percent, higher even than FDR's 60.8 percent in 1936 and Warren G. Harding's 60.3 percent in 1920.

    I have depended on a number of sources for the statistics in the Introduction, including *Congressional Quarterly's Guide to U.S. Elections,* 2nd ed., *Congressional Quarterly,* 1985; Theodore White, *The Making of the President—1964* (New York: Signet Books, 1965); Paul F. Boller, Jr., *Presidential Campaigns* (New York: Oxford University Press, 1984); Richard M. Scammon and Ben J. Wattenberg, *The Real Majority* (New York: Primus, 1992); Kevin P. Phillips, *The Emerging Republican Majority* (New Rochelle, N.Y.: Arlington House, 1969).
2. James B. Reston, *New York Times,* November 5, 1964.
3. "Dr. Fell's Election," *New York Times*, November 10, 1994; "The Sea Change," *Washington Post National Weekly Edition*, November 14–20, 1994.
4. Richard Brookhiser, "Reagan Revolution Redux," *New York Times*, November 11, 1994; David Brooks, "Meet the New Establishment," *Wall Street Journal*, November 17, 1994; Pat Buchanan, "Flight of the Liberals," *Washington Times*, November 2, 1994.
5. David S. Broder, "Vote May Signal GOP Return as Dominant Party," *Washington Post*, November 10, 1994; George Will, "Reagan's Third Victory," *Washington Post*, November 10, 1994.
6. Barry Goldwater: Letter to the author, December 6, 1994.
7. Ralph Hallow, "Supports a line item veto even if it benefits Clinton," *Washington Times*, November 14, 1994.
8. Richard Armey: Fax to the author, December 19, 1994.

9. Lee Edwards, *Reagan: A Political Biography* (Houston, Texas: Nordland Publishing, 1981), p. 235.
10. Morton Kondrake, "Leapfrog Opportunity," *Washington Times*, November 21, 1994.
11. Edwards, *Reagan*, p. 237; "The Sea Change," *Washington Post National Weekly Edition*, November 14–20, 1994, p. 26.
12. Barry Goldwater, *The Conscience of a Conservative* (Shepherdsville, Kentucky: Victor Publishing Co., 1960), pp. 42, 74.
13. Sam Nunn: Interview with the author, September 15, 1992.
14. Theodore White, *The Making of the President—1964* (New York: Signet Books, 1965), p. 411.
15. Barry M. Goldwater with Jack Casserly, *Goldwater* (New York: Doubleday, 1988), p. 388.
16. "Inside Politics: Goldwater Unloads," *Washington Times*, March 18, 1994; Timothy Egan, "Goldwater Defending Clinton: Conservatives Feeling Faint," *New York Times*, March 24, 1994.

Chapter 1   Peddler's Grandson

1. William Safire, *Safire's Political Dictionary* (New York: Random House, 1978), p. 286.
2. William Manchester, *The Glory and the Dream: A Narrative History of America 1932–1972,* vol. 1 (Boston: Little, Brown and Company, 1973), p. 509.
3. Friedrich A. Hayek, *The Road to Serfdom* (Chicago: University of Chicago Press, 1944), pp. xx, 70.
4. George Nash, *The Conservative Intellectual Movement in America Since 1945* (New York: Basic Books, 1976), p. 7. I am indebted for my analysis of Hayek and other conservative intellectuals of this period to Nash, whose book remains definitive.
5. Ibid., p. 26.
6. Dean Smith, *The Goldwaters of Arizona* (Fallstaff, Ariz.: Northland Press, 1986), p. 8. Smith's book is invaluable for its careful research and lively writing about the early Goldwaters. I have also drawn upon Edwin McDowell, *Barry Goldwater: Portrait of an Arizonan* (Chicago: Henry Regnery, 1964), and Stephen Shadegg, *Barry Goldwater: Freedom Is His Flight Plan* (New York: Fleet Publishing Corporation, 1962). Historian Bert Fireman did extensive research on the Goldwater family, but unfortunately never finished what promised to be an outstanding work about a remarkable family.
7. Smith, p. 13.
8. Ibid., p. 17.

9. Ibid., p. 23.
10. Ibid., p. 24.
11. Ibid., pp. 43–44.
12. Edwin McDowell, *Barry Goldwater: Portrait of an Arizonan* (Chicago: Henry Regnery, 1964), p. 45.
13. Ibid., p. 43.
14. Rob Wood and Dean Smith, *Barry Goldwater* (New York: Avon Books, 1961), p. 30.
15. McDowell, p. 45.
16. Smith, p. 93.
17. Shadegg, p. 65.
18. McDowell, p. 58.
19. Smith, p. 140.
20. Ibid., p. 134.
21. Ibid., p. 146.
22. Jack Bell, *Mr. Conservative: Barry Goldwater* (New York: Doubleday & Company, 1962), p. 42.
23. Robert Goldwater: Videotape interview with Bill McCune, June 27, 1991.
24. McDowell, p. 49.
25. McDowell, p. 52.
26. "Salesman for a Cause," *Time,* June 23, 1961, p. 14.
27. Smith, p. 149.
28. Wood and Smith, p. 60.
29. Shadegg, p. 38; Wood and Smith, p. 61.
30. Shadegg, p. 86.
31. Smith, pp. 144–150.
32. Shadegg, p. 89.
33. James M. Perry, *Barry Goldwater: A New Look at a Presidential Candidate* (Washington, D.C.: National Observer, 1964), p. 24.
34. Barry M. Goldwater with Jack Casserly, *Goldwater* (New York: Doubleday, 1988), p. 55.
35. Perry, p. 25.
36. Wood and Smith, p. 47.
37. *Goldwater,* p. 44.
38. Stewart Alsop, "Can Goldwater Win in 64?" *Saturday Evening Post,* August 24, 1963, p. 21.
39. Shadegg, p. 99.
40. Smith, pp. 166–167.
41. *Goldwater,* p. 85.
42. Shadegg, pp. 109–115.
43. Peggy Goldwater's response to a letter from Beatrice L. Rowland, an editor at Coward, McCann & Geoghegan, January, 11, 1980, Barry Gold-

water Papers, Arizona Historical Foundation, Arizona State University, [hereafter BMG.]

44. Ibid., p.121.
45. Smith, p. 176.
46. *Goldwater,* p. 28.
47. Ibid., p. 58.
48. Smith, p. 2.
49. McDowell, p. 79.
50. Wood and Smith, p. 57.
51. Ibid., p. 58.
52. *Goldwater,* pp. 65–66.
53. Andrew Kopkind, "Older, Wiser But Still Prickly as a Saguaro, Barry Goldwater Remembers When Right Was Wrong," *People,* February 13, 1989, p. 68.
54. "Goldwater: His Life and Legacy," *Arizona Republic,* January 18, 1987, p. 18.
55. Wood and Smith, p. 51.
56. Perry, pp. 35–36.
57. Barry Goldwater to Lyda Hardin, May 4, 1940, William Saufley collection, Arizona Historical Foundation, Arizona State University, Tempe, Arizona.
58. Wood and Smith, pp. 51–52.
59. Ibid., p. 53.
60. Barry Goldwater, *With No Apologies* (New York: William Morrow and Company, 1979), pp. 31–32.
61. Ibid., p. 35.
62. Wood and Smith, p. 72.
63. Barry Goldwater Diary, July–August 1943, BMG.
64. Ibid.
65. Ibid.

Chapter 2   In the Ring

1. James M. Perry, *Barry Goldwater: A New Look at a Presidential Candidate* (Washington, D.C.: National Observer, 1964), p. 23.
2. Edwin McDowell, *Barry Goldwater: Portrait of an Arizonan* (Chicago: Henry Regnery, 1964), McDowell, p. 66.
3. Perry, p. 51.
4. McDowell, p. 164. Accused of hypocrisy because he opposed parts of the Tennessee Valley Authority (TVA) but favored the Central Arizona

Project (CAP), Goldwater pointed out that the two were unrelated in concept and practice. TVA, he said, produced and sold power and fertilizer that were heavily subsidized by the federal government and were exempt from federal taxes; CAP was truly a reclamation project. "The purpose of the CAP," he said, "is to conduct this additional water into central Arizona, not for the purpose of expanding agricultural production in the state, but for the purpose of preserving an existing economy."

5. Barry Goldwater to Norman Hull and the Board of Directors, Phoenix Chamber of Commerce, December 26, 1946, William Saufley Collection, Arizona Historical Foundation (AHF).

6. Ray Busey to Barry Goldwater, July 5, 1947, with enclosed Goldwater ad, William Saufley Collection, AHF.

7. Perry, pp. 39–40.

8. Barry Goldwater, *With No Apologies* (New York: William Morrow and Co., 1979), p. 42.

9. Barry Goldwater with Jack Casserly, *Goldwater* (New York: Doubleday, 1988), p. 88.

10. Barry Goldwater, letter to the author, December 6, 1994; *With No Apologies,* pp. 43–45.

11. *With No Apologies,* p. 45.

12. Later versions of this letter have smoothed out the grammar, carefully adding apostrophes to all the "don't"s. This is the original version from *Barry Goldwater* by Rob Wood and Dean Smith (New York: Avon Books, 1961), p. 78, although I have subdivided what was a one-paragraph letter to make for easier reading.

13. Wood and Smith, p. 79.

14. Ray Schultze, "Courtship with voters began in 1949," *Phoenix Gazette,* December 3, 1986, p. 16 of special section, "Goldwater."

15. McDowell, p. 89.

16. *Goldwater,* p. 90.

17. Perry, p. 42.

18. Ibid., p. 43; *Arizona Republic,* February 14, 1951.

19. Stephen Shadegg, *Barry Goldwater: Freedom Is His Flight Plan* (New York: Fleet Publishing Corp., 1962), pp. 137–139; *With No Apologies,* p. 45; *Goldwater,* p. 93; Marc Ramirez, "Pyle: Barry Goldwater started snowball of conservatism rolling," *Phoenix Gazette,* December 3, 1986, p. 22 of special section, "Goldwater."

20. Wood and Smith, p. 80.

21. *Goldwater,* pp. 93–94.

22. *With No Apologies,* p. 48.

23. From a 1964 memorandum, "Ronald Reagan Speaks Out on Barry Gold-water," in the author's campaign files. According to Rosalie Crowe, Goldwater rendered the same "airline" service to her father and other servicemen stranded in San Francisco during Christmas of 1945. Rosalie Crowe, "Making holiday wishes come true," *Phoenix Gazette,* December 3, 1986, p. 17 of special section, "Goldwater."

24. *Goldwater,* p. 94.

25. Ibid., p. 95.

26. Ibid., p. 95.

27. Wood and Smith, p. 82.

28. Perry, p. 44.

29. Ibid., p. 45.

30. Sean Griffin, "The man who helped elect Goldwater," *Phoenix Gazette,* December 3, 1986, p. 19 of special section, "Goldwater."

31. Wood and Smith, p. 85.

32. *With No Apologies*, p. 52.

33. Ibid.; *Goldwater,* p. 96.

34. McDowell, p. 92.

35. Barry Goldwater, *Why Not Victory?* (New York: Macfadden Books, 1962), p. 9.

36. Shadegg, pp. 187–188.

37. George Nash, *The Conservative Intellectual Movement in America Since 1945* (New York: Basic Books, 1976), p. 58.

38. *Goldwater,* p. 255.

39. Goldwater to Shadegg, July 10, 1952, Stephen C. Shadegg Papers, Center for American History, University of Texas at Austin [hereafter UTA].

40. Wood and Smith, p. 85.

41. McDowell, p. 95.

42. Wood and Smith, p. 86.

43. *Arizona Republic,* August 4, 1952.

44. Wood and Smith, p. 87; Jack Bell, *Mr. Conservative: Barry Goldwater* (Garden City, N.Y.: Doubleday & Company, 1962), p. 67.

45. Shadegg, pp. 192–193.

46. Ibid., pp. 151–152.

47. *Arizona Republic,* September 19, 1952.

48. Jerry Kammer, "Campaign '52 and '58: Burma Shave and Stalin," *Arizona Republic,* January 18, 1987, p. 20.

49. *Arizona Republic,* October 30, 1952.

50. Perry, p. 46.

51. Advertisements published November 1, 1952, and November 3, 1952, Shadegg Papers, UTA.

52. *Arizona Republic,* October 28, 1952.

53. Wood and Smith, p. 88.
54. McDowell, p. 98; Dean Smith, *The Goldwaters of Arizona* (Falstaff, Ariz.: Northland Press, 1986), p. 201.
55. *Goldwater,* p. 98.

Chapter 3   Mr. Goldwater Goes to Washington

1. Barry M. Goldwater with Jack Casserly, *Goldwater* (New York: Doubleday, 1988), p. 98.
2. Barry Goldwater, *Conscience of a Conservative* (Washington, D.C.: Regnery Gateway, 1990), p. 17. Originally published by Victor Publishing Company, Shepherdsville, Ky., 1960.
3. Jack Bell, *Mr. Conservative: Barry Goldwater* (New York: Doubleday & Co., 1962), pp. 74–75; Barry Goldwater, *With No Apologies* (New York: William Morrow and Co., 1979), p. 58.
4. John Kolbe, "Talking with an Arizona 'legend,' " *Phoenix Gazette,* December 3, 1986, p. 8 of special section, "Goldwater."
5. Bell, p. 78.
6. Barry Goldwater: Interview with the author, December 17, 1991.
7. I am indebted to Matthew Spalding of the Heritage Foundation for the analysis of Jeffersonian principles.
8. Robert T. Patterson, *Mr. Republican: A Biography of Robert A. Taft* (Boston: Houghton Mifflin Company, 1970), p. 556.
9. *Congressional Record*, May 12, 1953, pp. 4766, 4778, 4780–4792.
10. Eisenhower quote, *Goldwater,* p. 99; Theodore Sorensen: Interview with the author, March 8, 1993; Bell, pp. 71–73.
11. Edwin McDowell provides an excellent analysis of this now-neglected constitutional amendment in *Barry Goldwater: Portrait of an Arizonan* (Chicago: Henry Regnery, 1964), pp. 99–101.
12. McDowell, p. 101.
13. Ibid., pp. 101–102.
14. Bell, p. 144.
15. Edmund Burke, Speech to the Electors of Bristol, November 3, 1774, as reprinted in Russell Kirk, *Edmund Burke: A Genius Reconsidered* (New Rochelle, N.Y.: Arlington House, 1967), p. 90.
16. *Congressional Record*, July 31, 1953, pp. 10632–10633.
17. Rob Wood and Dean Smith, *Barry Goldwater* (New York: Avon Books, 1961), p. 93.
18. Much of the following is taken from the reportage and personal files of my father, Willard Edwards, who as a reporter for the *Chicago Tribune* not only covered Senator McCarthy but became one of his closest confidants. Of the many books written about McCarthy, one of the most balanced is

The Life and Times of Joe McCarthy by Thomas C. Reeves (New York: Stein and Day), 1982.

19. Bell, pp. 100–101; *With No Apologies* (New York: William Morrow and Co., 1979), p. 61.
20. *Goldwater*, p. 129.
21. Bell, pp. 96–98.
22. Thomas C. Reeves, *The Life and Times of Joe McCarthy*, pp. 658–659.
23. Bell, p. 102.
24. *Memorial Services Held in the Senate and House of Representatives of the United States, Together with Remarks Presented in Eulogy of Joseph Raymond McCarthy, Late a Senator from Wisconsin,* 85th Congress, First Session (Washington, D.C: U.S. Government Printing Office, 1957), p. 39.
25. William F. Buckley Jr. and L. Brent Bozell, *McCarthy and His Enemies* (Chicago: Henry Regnery Co., 1954), p. 335.
26. *Human Events*, April 14, 1973, p. 117.

Chapter 4 Big Labor and Big Government

1. Robert T. Patterson, *Mr. Republican: A Biography of Robert A. Taft* (Boston: Houghton Mifflin Co., 1970), p. 365.
2. Archie Robinson, *George Meany and His Times* (New York: Simon & Schuster, 1981), p. 183.
3. Jameson G. Campaigne, *Checkoff: Labor Bosses and Working Men* (Chicago: Henry Regnery Company, 1961), p. 13.
4. Edwin McDowell, *Barry Goldwater: Portrait of an Arizonan* (Chicago: Henry Regnery, 1964), pp. 111–112.
5. Ibid., p. 114.
6. F. Clifton White: Interview with the author, April 6, 1992.
7. Re the Hall-Baroody-Goldwater association, William Baroody, Jr.: Interview with the author, October 27, 1992; re "Secret Agent X-9," Darrell Coover: Interview with the author, November 24, 1992; Carl Curtis: Telephone interview with the author, February 4, 1993. Stephen Shadegg makes several references to Hall in *What Happened to Goldwater?* (New York: Holt, Rhinehart and Winston, 1965) but always under the pseudonym, "Charles Wiggamore Kelly."
8. Willard Edwards, "The Senator Is Jet Propelled," *Chicago Tribune,* January 24, 1960, p. 29.
9. Barry M. Goldwater with Jack Casserly, *Goldwater* (New York: Doubleday, 1988), p. 114.
10. Ibid., pp. 115–117.

11. Ibid., pp. 76, 79.
12. Ibid., p. 74.
13. Darrell Coover: Interview with the author, November 24, 1992.
14. Richard L. Gilbert, Jr., "Barry Goldwater: The Admonitions of an Older Man," *Esquire,* October 1962, p. 171.
15. Ibid., p. 172.
16. Peter Carlson, "A Goldwater Family Crisis," *People,* June 20, 1983, p. 37.
17. Ibid.
18. Barry Goldwater, Jr.: Telephone interview with the author, April 2, 1993.
19. *Congressional Record*, February 4, 1955, pp. 1179–1188.
20. Ibid., April 23, 1955, pp. 5221–5224.
21. Ibid., June 20, 1955, pp. 8784–8786.
22. Barry Goldwater on ABC's "20/20," July 23, 1993.
23. *Congressional Record*, June 30, 1955, pp. 1955–1956.
24. Ibid., July 26, 1955, p. 11466.
25. Ibid., March 7, 1956, pp. 4238–4239.
26. Rob Wood and Dean Smith, *Barry Goldwater* (New York: Avon Books, 1961), p. 97.
27. Jack Bell, *Mr. Conservative: Barry Goldwater* (New York: Doubleday & Co., 1962), p. 118.
28. *Congressional Record*, April 21, 1955, p. 5208.
29. Senator Carl T. Curtis and Regis Courtemanche, *Forty Years Against the Tide: Congress and the Welfare State* (Lake Bluff, Ill: Regnery Gateway, 1986), pp. 174–175.
30. McDowell, p. 119.
31. Ibid., p. 120.
32. Wood and Smith, p. 98.
33. Walter Reuther, "How Labor and Management Can Cooperate To Preserve Freedom Around the World," speech before the Economic Club of Detroit, November 1953.
34. Wood and Smith, p. 100.
35. McDowell, p. 120.
36. Ibid., pp. 120–121.
37. Bell, p. 120.
38. Ibid., p. 121.
39. "Caucus Room's Use Arouses Senators," *Arizona Republic,* February 27, 1958.
40. Goldwater Challenges Reuther," *Arizona Republic*, March 17, 1958.
41. Robert F. Kennedy, *The Enemy Within* (New York: Harpers & Brothers, 1960), pp. 294–295; Jerry Kammer, "Slinging with Reuther," *Arizona Republic*, January 18, 1987, p. 25.

42. "Goldwater and Reuther Hold Tempers at Quiz," *Arizona Republic*, March 28, 1958.
43. McDowell, pp. 121–122; Bell, pp. 122–123.
44. McDowell, pp. 122–123.
45. Kennedy, p. 298.
46. Barry Goldwater, *With No Apologies* (New York: William Morrow and Co., 1979), p. 63.
47. Kammer, p. 25.
48. "Post Article Praises Goldwater Potential," *Arizona Republic*, June 3, 1958.
49. Bell, pp. 135–136.

Chapter 5   Becoming a National Leader

1. Edwin McDowell, *Barry Goldwater: Portrait of an Arizonan* (Chicago: Henry Regnery, 1964), pp. 137–138.
2. Rob Wood and Dean Smith, *Barry Goldwater* (New York: Avon Books, 1961), p. 109; McDowell, pp. 137–138.
3. Jack Bell, *Mr. Conservative: Barry Goldwater* (New York: Doubleday & Co., 1962), pp. 138–139.
4. Bell, p. 140.
5. *Congressional Record*, April 8, 1957, pp. 5258–5265.
6. Ibid., p. 5259.
7. *Public Papers of the Presidents: Dwight D. Eisenhower*, The President's News Conference of April 10, 1957, pp. 270–272.
8. For a description of modern Republicanism by one of its architects, see Paul G. Hoffman, "How Eisenhower Saved the Republican Party," *Collier's*, October 26, 1956, pp. 44–47.
9. Wood and Smith, p. 111.
10. Barry M. Goldwater with Jack Casserly, *Goldwater* (New York: Doubleday, 1988), p. 109.
11. Goldwater to Shadegg, February 27, 1956, Shadegg to Goldwater, March 5, 1956, Steven Shadegg Papers, Center for American History, UTA.
12. Goldwater to Shadegg, June 11, 1956, Shadegg Papers.
13. John Spanier, *American Foreign Policy Since World War II, 8th edition* (New York: Holt, Rinehart and Winston, 1980), p. 87.
14. Goldwater telephone conversation with Shadegg, January 4, 1957, Shadegg Papers, UTA.
15. For the following account of the 1958 campaign, I have depended in large part upon Stephen Shadegg's *Barry Goldwater: Freedom Is His Flight*

Plan (New York: Fleet Publishing Corp., 1962), pp. 207–232, and Wood and Smith's *Barry Goldwater,* pp. 116–122.

16. Wood and Smith, p. 117.
17. Robert Welch, *The Politician,* privately printed for Robert Welch, Belmont, Mass., 1963, pp. 276–279.
18. *Goldwater,* p. 126.
19. Ibid., p. 127.
20. Wood and Smith, p. 117.
21. Ibid., p. 117.
22. Shadegg, p. 222.
23. "Goldwater Tells TV Audiences," *Phoenix Gazette,* October 24, 1958.
24. Shadegg, p. 223.
25. McDowell, p. 130.
26. Shadegg, pp. 225–227; statement by Bert Fireman, approximately November 3, 1958, Shadegg Papers; "Goldwater Aide Linked to 'Stalin' Handbills," *Arizona Daily Star,* November 4, 1958.
27. "Smear Diabolical Plan—Goldwater," *Arizona Republic,* November 4, 1958.
28. Shadegg, p. 229; McDowell, p. 132; *Arizona Republic,* November 4, 1958.
29. Barry Goldwater, *With No Apologies* (New York: William Morrow and Co., 1979), pp. 92–93.
30. Wood and Smith, p. 118.
31. Ibid., p. 122.
32. Statement by Barry Goldwater, June 10, 1958, BMG.
33. Bell, p. 182; *With No Apologies,* pp. 74–75.
34. *With No Apologies,* p. 75.
35. McDowell, p. 124.
36. Shadegg, p. 240.
37. Michael Baroody: Interview with the author, April 14, 1992; Barry Goldwater: Interview with the author, December 17, 1991.
38. *With No Apologies,* pp. 97–98.
39. Ibid.

Chapter 6   *The Conscience of a Conservative*

1. William Manchester, *The Glory and the Dream: A Narrative History of America 1932–1972, Volume Two* (Boston: Little, Brown and Company, 1974), p. 1034.
2. Confidential Memorandum, May 15, 1959, Clarence Manion Papers, Chicago Historical Society [Hereafter CHS].

3. Manion to C. S. Hallauer, May 25, 1959, Manion Papers, CHS.
4. Manion to D. B. Lewis, May 27, 1959, Manion Papers, CHS.
5. Frank Cullen Brophy to Manion, June 1, 1959, Manion Papers, CHS.
6. Brophy to Goldwater, June 18, 1959; Brophy to L. Brent Bozell, June 18, 1959; Manion Papers, CHS.
7. Manion to Frank R. Seaver, June 25, 1959, Manion Papers, CHS.
8. *Human Events,* July 1, 1959, Vol. XVI, No. 26, p. 1.
9. Robert Welch to William J. Grede, July 8, 1959, Manion Papers, CHS.
10. Manion to Mrs. Marion J. Pritchard, July 17, 1959, Manion Papers, CHS.
11. Manion to Frank C. Brophy, July 28, 1959; Manion to Earl Pratt, August 11, 1959, Manion Papers, CHS.
12. Bozell to Manion, August 17, 1959, Manion Papers, CHS.
13. L. Brent Bozell: Interview with the author, March 9, 1992.
14. Manion to William F. Buckley Jr., September 28, 1959; Buckley to Manion, October 2, 1959, Manion Papers, CHS.
15. Buckley to Manion, September 24, 1959, Manion Papers, CHS.
16. Manion to Russell, November 16, 1959; Russell to Manion, December 2, 1959; Manion to Russell, December 4, 1959; Manion to Fellers, December 16, 1959, Manion Papers, CHS.
17. L. Brent Bozell: Interview with the author, January 10, 1992, Washington, D.C; Judy Eisenhower: Telephone interview with the author, May 23, 1994.
18. Roger Milliken to Manion, December 29, 1959; G. D. Shorey, Jr., to Manion, January 20, 1959, Manion Papers, CHS.
19. L. Brent Bozell: Interview with the author, January 10, 1992, Washington, D.C.
20. Barry M. Goldwater with Jack Casserly, *Goldwater* (New York: Doubleday, 1988), p. 120.
21. Barry Goldwater, *Why Not Victory?* (New York: Macfadden Books, 1962), pp. 12–13; Barry Goldwater, *With No Apologies* (New York: William Morrow and Co., 1979), p. 99; *Goldwater,* p. 120.
22. Neal Freeman: Conversation with the author, May 18, 1993.
23. Abstract of Minutes Taken at Goldwater Meeting, January 23, 1960, Chicago, pp. 2–3, Manion Papers, CHS.
24. Abstract, Goldwater Meeting, pp. 3, 5, Manion Papers, CHS.
25. Ibid., pp. 8–10.
26. Ibid., p. 16.
27. Ibid., p. 18.
28. Manion to Brophy, February 15, 1960; Manion to Milliken, February 18, 1960; Shadegg to Goldwater, February 22, 1960; Goldwater to Bozell, February 24, 1960; Bozell to Manion, March 5, 1960, Manion Papers, CHS.

29. Barry Goldwater, *The Conscience of a Conservative* (Shepherdsville, Ky.: Victor Publishing Company, 1960). All citations are from the thirtieth anniversary edition published by Regnery Gateway, Washington, D.C., in 1990, with an introduction by Patrick J. Buchanan. See pp. xxiv–xxv.
30. *Conscience,* pp. 5–8.
31. Ibid., p. 17.
32. Ibid., pp. 22, 24, 26–28.
33. Ibid., pp. 30–31.
34. Ibid., pp. 36, 48.
35. For an extended discussion of a flat tax, see Milton Friedman, *Capitalism and Freedom* (Chicago: The University of Chicago Press, 1962), chapters V and X.
36. *Conscience,* pp. 60–61.
37. Ibid., pp. 67–69.
38. Ibid., p. 78.
39. Ibid., pp. 84, 93, 99, 100, 104, 108, 110, 111, 112.
40. Ibid., pp. 116–117.
41. George Morgenstern, "Harsh Facts, Hard Sense on the Perils to Liberty," *Chicago Sunday Tribune Magazine of Books,* April 17, 1960; "Old Guard's New Spokesman," *Time,* May 2, 1960; "The Conscience of a Conservative," Westbrook Pegler, *New York Journal American,* April 29, 1960; John Chamberlain, "The Humane Base of Conservatism," *Wall Street Journal,* June 2, 1960; Russell Kirk, "Conscience of a Conservative," *Chicago Daily Calumet,* May 3, 1960; "Conscience of a Conservative," *Barron's,* May 2, 1960; *Pravda,* March 21, 1960.
42. *With No Apologies,* p. 102.
43. Stephen Shadegg, *Barry Goldwater: Freedom Is His Flight Plan* (New York: Fleet Publishing Corp., 1962), pp. 248–249.
44. Memoranda to Manion, April 12 and 13, 1960, Manion Papers, CHS.
45. Manion to Brophy, May 3, 1960; Manion to Roger Milliken, May 6, 1960; Brophy to Raymond Moley, June 9, 1960; "Best Seller List," *New York Times Book Review,* June 26, 1960, Manion Papers, CHS.
46. R. L. Duffus, "One Senator's Manifesto," *New York Times Book Review,* June 26, 1960, Manion Papers, CHS.
47. Manion to V. M. Haldiman, June 22, 1964, Manion Papers, CHS.

Chapter 7 "Let's Grow Up, Conservatives"

1. *Human Events,* May 19, 1960, p. 2. Goldwater called the health care plan proposed by Arthur Fleming, Secretary of Health, Education and Welfare, "socialized medicine" and asked, "What is voluntary about a plan which will entail participation of every taxpayer whether he wants to or not?"

2. "Suggested Declaration of Principles," presented by Barry Goldwater, July 19, 1960, before Republican Platform Committee, Chicago; Stephen Shadegg, *Barry Goldwater: Freedom Is His Flight Plan* (New York: Fleet Publishing Corp., 1962), pp. 295–299.

3. Barry Goldwater, *With No Apologies* (New York: William Morrow and Co., 1979), pp. 110–111.

4. Ibid.

5. Ibid., p. 112.

6. Ibid., p. 112; Jack Bell, *Mr. Conservative: Barry Goldwater* (New York: Doubleday & Co., 1962), p. 21.

7. Guest article in *Newsweek,* August 1, 1960, as reprinted in Shadegg, pp. 299–302.

8. Richard Nixon, *Six Crises* (New York: Doubleday & Company, 1962), pp. 314–316.

9. Theodore White, *The Making of the President 1960* (New York: Atheneum Publishers, 1961), pp. 203–204.

10. Robert F. Croll: Interview with the author, October 2, 1993.

11. Bell, p. 27.

12. Ibid., p. 23.

13. Shadegg, p. 255.

14. Ibid., pp. 256–259.

15. *With No Apologies,* pp. 114–115.

16. Ibid., p. 115.

17. Bell, p. 29.

18. Ibid., pp. 14–15.

19. Ibid., p. 15.

20. Bell, pp. 14–15; Shadegg, p. 270; Barry M. Goldwater with Jack Casserly, *Goldwater* (New York: Doubleday, 1988), p. 119.

21. *Goldwater,* p. 119; David Broder: Interview with the author, August 25, 1992.

22. Walter Trohan, *Chicago Tribune,* July 30, 1960.

23. Dan Smoot to Paul H. Talbert, August 25, 1960, Manion Papers, CHS; Barry Goldwater: Interview with the author, December 17, 1991.

24. "Conservative Crusader," *Time,* October 17, 1960, p. 23.

25. Bell, p. 153.

26. Ibid., p. 154.

27. Ibid., pp. 154–155.

28. Nixon, p. 413.

29. *With No Apologies*, p. 125.

30. Ibid.

31. Willard Edwards, "Did Biased Reporters Cost Nixon the Election?" *Human Events*, April 7, 1961, pp. 213–216.

32. *With No Apologies*, p. 134.
33. "Salesman for a Cause," *Time*, June 23, 1961, p. 16.

Chapter 8 A Genuine Draft

1. Robert D. Novak, "Conservative Senator Softens Views, Offers a Plan To Build GOP," *Wall Street Journal*, January 11, 1961, pp. 1, 10.
2. Willmoore Kendall, "Quo Vadis, Barry?" *National Review*, February 25, 1961, pp. 107–108, 127.
3. Goldwater to William F. Buckley Jr., March 8, 1961, Buckley Papers, Sterling Library, Yale University.
4. F. Clifton White with William J. Gill, *Suite 3505: The Story of the Draft Goldwater Movement* (New Rochelle, N.Y.: Arlington House, 1967), p. 35.
5. Rita Bree: Telephone interview with the author, May 10, 1993.
6. "Salesman for a Cause," *Time,* June 23, 1961, p. 12.
7. William A. Rusher, *The Rise of the Right* (New York: William Morrow and Co., 1984), p. 99.
8. White, p. 32.
9. Ibid., p. 33.
10. Ibid., pp. 25–26.
11. Ibid., p. 34.
12. Ibid., p. 24.
13. Tower remained one of Goldwater's closest political friends for more than a quarter of a century until his untimely death in an airplane crash in April 1991.
14. Senator Ted Stevens: Interview with the author, September 25, 1992, Washington, D.C.
15. James M. Perry, *Barry Goldwater: A New Look at a Presidential Candidate* (Washington, D.C.: National Observer, 1964), p. 74.
16. "Salesman for a Cause," pp. 12–13.
17. Ibid., p. 16.
18. "Conservatism in the U.S. . . . and Its Leading Spokesman," *Newsweek,* April 10, 1961, pp. 28, 30.
19. "The Goldwater Story—How It Is Growing," *U.S. News & World Report,* August 7, 1961, pp. 57–59.
20. William F. Buckley Jr., "If Goldwater Were President," *Coronet,* July 1961, pp. 156–162.
21. Robert Sheehan, "Arizona Fundamentalist," *Fortune,* May 1961, pp. 137–140, 246, 251, 252, 254.
22. "The Goldwater-McCarthy Debate: Does a Big Federal Government Threaten Our Freedom?" *CBS Reports,* January 26, 1961, pp. 6, 23, 27–28, 41, 55.

23. "Washington Conversation," CBS-TV, April 2, 1961, p. 9.
24. *Issues and Answers,* ABC News, August 6, 1961, pp. 5, 23.
25. White, p. 40.
26. Ibid., p. 41.
27. Ibid., pp. 45–46.
28. Ibid., p. 46.
29. Rusher, p. 108.
30. Ibid., p. 109.
31. Ibid.
32. "We'll Take Manhattan, the Bronx, and . . ."; and "Why," *The New Guard,* March 1961, pp. 3, 4.
33. George O. Porter, "YR's Stay Right," *The New Guard,* August, 1961, p. 8.
34. "Victory Over Communism," *The New Guard,* April 1962, pp. 6–7; also excerpts from an unpublished manuscript by the author.
35. Peter Kihss, "18,000 Rightists Rally at Garden," *New York Times*, March 8, 1962.
36. White, pp. 61, 75.
37. Judy Lewis: Interview with the author, April 29, 1993.
38. White, pp. 73–74.
39. Barry Goldwater to Wirt Yerger, September 19, 1962, F. Clifton White Papers, Carl A. Kroch, Library, Cornell University.
40. White, p. 89.
41. Joseph Fisher, political editor, Rockford, Illinois, newspapers, to Albert Fay, September 17, 1962, F. Clifton White Papers, Cornell; White, p. 78.
42. White, pp. 96–97.
43. Ibid., pp. 97–99.
44. J. William Middendorf II Notes, Part 1 [undated], Middendorf Archives, Washington, D.C.
45. White, p. 105.
46. Ibid., p. 111.
47. Kitchel Memorandum, December 23, 1962, Kitchel Papers, Hoover Institution Archives, Stanford University.
48. Dean Burch to Barry Goldwater, January 14, 1963, Dean Burch Papers, Center for American History (CAH), University of Texas at Austin Library.
49. Goldwater to Burch, January 21, 1963, Burch Papers, CAH.
50. Barry M. Goldwater with Jack Casserly, *Goldwater* (New York: Doubleday, 1988), pp. 189, 162.
51. Rusher, p. 141.
52. White, p. 117.
53. Ibid., p. 118.
54. Ibid.

55. Some eighty years earlier, General William Tecumseh Sherman was being enthusiastically promoted as a Republican presidential candidate when he destroyed his supporters' hopes with the famous words: "I will not accept if nominated, and will not serve if elected." William Safire, *Safire's Political Dictionary* (New York: Random House, 1978), p. 643.

56. William A. Rusher to Barry Goldwater, January 18, 1963; Barry Goldwater to Rusher, January 22, 1963, F. Clifton White Papers, Cornell.

57. William A. Rusher, "Crossroads for the GOP," *National Review,* February 12, 1963, p. 112.

58. Frank Meyer to Barry Goldwater, February 11, 1963, F. Clifton White Papers, Cornell; Barry Goldwater to Meyer, February 20, 1963, Kitchel Papers, Hoover Institution Archives, Stanford.

59. White to Barry Goldwater, January 31, 1963, F. Clifton White Papers, Cornell.

60. White, p. 121.

61. White to Barry Goldwater, January 31, 1963, F. Clifton White Papers, Cornell; White, pp. 121–122.

62. White, p. 123.

63. Ibid., pp. 124–126.

Chapter 9   Making Up His Mind

1. " 'Draft Goldwater' Move Starts—Its Meaning," *U.S. News & World Report,* April 29, 1963, pp. 42–45; F. Clifton White, *Suite 3505: The Story of the Draft Goldwater Movement* (New Rochelle, N.Y.: Arlington House, 1967), pp. 132–133.

2. White, pp. 133–134.

3. Cabell Phillips, "Goldwater Acts Like '64 Aspirant," *New York Times,* April 15, 1963.

4. Barry Goldwater, *With No Apologies* (New York: William Morrow and Co., 1979), p. 161.

5. "The President Thing," *Time,* June 14, 1963, pp. 26–31.

6. Barry M. Goldwater with Jack Casserly, *Goldwater* (New York: Doubleday, 1988), p. 139.

7. *Goldwater,* p. 140.

8. George Gallup, "Kennedy Way Ahead of Rockefeller in Poll," *Boston Globe,* March 17, 1963.

9. *Goldwater,* p. 135.

10. Ibid., p. 136.

11. Ibid., pp. 136–137.

12. Ibid., p. 137.

13. Ibid.

14. Ibid., p. 138.
15. Anne L. Edwards: Interview with the author, May 1, 1992; Alsop as quoted in Peter Collier and David Horowitz, *The Rockefellers: An American Dynasty* (New York: Holt, Rinehart and Winston, 1976,) p. 350.
16. *Congressional Quarterly* provided further proof of how badly Rockefeller had been hurt by his marital decision by publishing the results of two polls of the delegates to the 1960 Republican convention. Before the wedding, nearly 65 percent voted for Rockefeller with only 26 percent for Goldwater. After the wedding, 46 percent of the delegates preferred Goldwater while Rockefeller dropped thirty points, to 34.5 percent. George Gallup, "Rockefeller's Remarriage—Boost for Goldwater," *New York Herald Tribune,* May 25, 1963; "The Public Record of Barry Goldwater," *Congressional Quarterly,* September 20, 1963, p. 1598.
17. *Goldwater,* pp. 141–142; White, p. 162; *With No Apologies*, p. 156.
18. "Text of Rockefeller's Statement Criticizing 'Radical Right' of the Republican Party," *New York Times,* July 15, 1963.
19. "Barry Goldwater Talks About 'Liberals' and 'Liberalism,' " *U.S. News & World Report,* July 8, 1963, pp. 44–45; Lawrence E. Davies, "Young G.O.P. Group Hails Goldwater," *New York Times,* June 28, 1963.
20. Michael Kramer and Sam Roberts, *I Never Wanted to Be Vice-President of Anything* (New York: Basic Books), 1976, as quoted in *The Rise of the Right* by William A. Rusher, pp. 148–150.
21. *Goldwater,* pp. 143–144.
22. Ibid., pp. 144–145.
23. Howard Norton, "6,000 at D.C. Rally Launch Draft-Goldwater Drive," *Baltimore Sun,* July 5, 1963.
24. George Gallup, "Not-So-Solid South Turns Republican," *New York Herald Tribune,* August 18, 1963.
25. Stephen Shadegg, *What Happened to Goldwater?* (New York: Holt, Rinehart and Winston, 1965), p. 105; Gilbert A. Harrison, "Way Out West: An Interim Report on Barry Goldwater," *The New Republic,* November 23, 1963, p. 17; Kitchel to Robert Welch, June 8, 1960, Kitchel Papers, Hoover Institution Archives, Stanford University.
26. White, p. 205.
27. Ibid., p. 202.
28. Ibid., p. 205.
29. William F. Buckley Jr.: Interview with the author, April 13, 1992.
30. *Goldwater,* pp. 147–148.
31. John B. Judis, *William F. Buckley Jr.: Patron Saint of the Conservatives* (New York: Simon and Schuster, 1988), pp. 223–224.
32. Ibid., p. 224.
33. White, p. 210.

34. Remarks by Barry Goldwater, Young Republican Rally, Dodger Stadium, Los Angeles, September 16, 1963, *Human Events* Library; James M. Perry, *Barry Goldwater,* Washington, D.C.: National Observer, 1964, p. 76.
35. "Will It Be Goldwater, Rockefeller, or —?" *U.S. News & World Report,* October 7, 1963, pp. 46–48.
36. Wallace Turner, "Goldwater Reserves 51 Rooms in Hotel for GOP Convention," *New York Times,* September 6, 1963.
37. Walter Lippmann, "The Goldwater Movement," *Newsweek,* August 5, 1963, p. 13.
38. Stewart Alsop, "Can Goldwater Win in '64?," *Saturday Evening Post,* August 24, 1963, pp. 19–24; White, p. 225.
39. White, p. 226.
40. Edward A. McCabe: Interview with author, March 23, 1992.
41. *Time,* October 3, 1963, pp. 34–35.
42. *Public Papers of the Presidents,* "John F. Kennedy, 1963," Presidential Press Conference, October 9, 1963, p. 405.
43. Arthur M. Schlesinger, Jr., *A Thousand Days: John F. Kennedy in the White House* (Boston: Houghton Mifflin Company, 1965), p. 981; James Reston, *New York Times,* October 12, 1963.
44. Pierre Salinger: Telephone interview with author, February 4, 1993.
45. Theodore Sorensen: Interview with author, March 8, 1993; Schlesinger, p. 1018.
46. White, pp. 236–237.
47. Richard Reeves, *President Kennedy: Profile of Power* (New York: Simon & Schuster, 1993), pp. 655–656.
48. White, p. 215.
49. *Goldwater,* pp. 180–182; White, pp. 228–229.
50. Theodore Sorensen: Interview with the author, March 8, 1993, New York.
51. *Goldwater,* p. 139.
52. *Arizona Republic,* October 17, 1963.
53. William Manchester, *The Glory and the Dream, Vol. 2* (Boston: Little, Brown and Company, 1973) p. 1219; *Time,* November 22, 1963.

Chapter 10   A Choice, Not an Echo

1. William Manchester, *The Death of a President: November 20–25, 1963.* (New York: Harper & Row, 1967) pp. 243–244.
2. F. Clifton White: Interview with the author, April 6, 1992.
3. Unpublished diary of the author, November 22, 1963.
4. Edwin McDowell, *Barry Goldwater: Portrait of an Arizonan* (Chicago: Henry Regnery, 1964), p. 185.

5. Richard N. Goodwin, *Remembering America: A Voice from the Sixties* (Boston: Little, Brown and Company, 1988), p. 302.
6. *Goldwater*, p. 150.
7. Ibid.
8. F. Clifton White, *Suite 3505: The Story of the Draft Goldwater Movement* (New Rochelle, N.Y.: Arlington House, 1967), pp. 250–251.
9. *U.S. News & World Report,* December 21, 1964.
10. Goldwater, pp. 151–152. Grenier reported that the South was still solid and predicted the senator would capture 285 Southern delegates at the national convention (the actual number was 283). John Grenier: Telephone interview with the author, May 31, 1994.
11. *Goldwater,* p. 152.
12. Barry Goldwater: Interview with the author, December 6, 1991.
13. *Goldwater,* pp. 153–154.
14. Ibid., p. 154.
15. George Gallup, "Gallup Poll Rates the GOP," *New Herald Tribune,* January 3, 1964.
16. White, *3505,* p. 251; Charlotte-Anne Lucas, "Doing his 'duty': the primary trail," *Arizona Republic,* January 18, 1987, p. 28.
17. White, *3505,* p. 259.
18. Barry Goldwater, *With No Apologies* (New York: William Morrow and Co., 1979), p. 165.
19. "Transcript of Goldwater's News Conference on His Entry into Presidential Race," *New York Times,* January 4, 1964.
20. Ibid.
21. *Goldwater,* p. 156.
22. Barry Goldwater: Conversation with the author, April 1964.
23. Richard Kleindienst, *Justice: The Memoirs of an Attorney General* (Ottawa, Ill.: Jameson Books, 1985), p. 30.
24. George V. Higgins, *The Friends of Richard Nixon* (Boston: Little, Brown and Company, 1974), p. 191.
25. Stephen Shadegg, *Barry Goldwater: Freedom Is His Flight Plan* (New York: Fleet Publishing Corp., 1962), pp. 92–93; Dean Burch: Interview with Stephen Shadegg, early 1965, Shadegg Papers, University of Texas at Austin Library.
26. John Grenier: Telephone interview with the author, May 31, 1994.
27. Shadegg, pp. 93–94; *With No Apologies,* p. 165.
28. *With No Apologies,* p. 166.
29. Theodore White, *The Making of the President—1964* (New York: Signet Books, 1965), p. 131.
30. White, *3505,* p. 289; Lionel Lokos, *Hysteria 1964: The Fear Campaign*

Against Barry Goldwater (New Rochelle, N.Y.: Arlington House, 1967), pp. 63–69.

31. White, *3505*, p. 290.
32. Charles Mohr, *New York Times*, January 8, 1964, p. 26.
33. Barry Goldwater, "My Proposals for a 'Can-Win' Foreign Policy," *Life*, January 17, 1964; *Congressional Record*, January 14, 1964, pp. 435–437.
34. *New York Times*, October 8, 1964, p. 30; *Time*, September 25, 1964, p. 18.
35. Dean Burch: Interview with Stephen Shadegg, early 1965, Shadegg Papers, UTA.
36. *With No Apologies*, p. 170.
37. Barry Goldwater to Fred Hiatt, December 12, 1984, Barry Goldwater Papers, Arizona Historical Foundation, Arizona State University.
38. Ben Bradlee, *Conversations with Kennedy* (New York: Pocket Books, 1976), p. 179.
39. White, *3505*, p. 291.
40. Charles Mohr, *New York Times*, March 7, 1964, p. 9.
41. Walter H. Mears, "Last of the Freewheelers," *Goldwater: His Life and Legacy, Arizona Republic*, January 18, 1987, p. 33.
42. White, *Making*, pp. 132–133.
43. From the unpublished diary of the author, March 1964.
44. White, *Making*, pp. 135–137.
45. William F. Buckley Jr., "The One and Only Barry Goldwater," *Family Weekly*, December 30, 1984, p. 5.
46. *Goldwater*, p. 162.
47. White, *3505*, p. 304.
48. *Goldwater*, p. 162.
49. David Halberstam, "8,000 in Chicago Hail Goldwater," *New York Times*, April 11, 1964.
50. Arthur Krock, "In the Nation," *New York Times*, April 16, 1964; David Lawrence, *Washington Star*, April 16, 1964.
51. White, *3505*, pp. 313–319.
52. William A. Rusher: Interview with the author, February 22, 1992.
53. Richard Kleindienst, Charles Lichenstein, Richard Herman: Interviews with the author: March 5, 1992; May 26, 1992; April 26, 1993.
54. *Goldwater*, p. 170.

Chapter 11   California, Here He Comes

1. Theodore White, *The Making of the President—1964* (New York: Signet Books, 1965), p. 145.
2. Stu Spencer: Telephone interview with the author, July 16, 1993. Of the

$2 million plus, says Spencer, only $100,000 was raised in California; the rest came from the Rockefeller family.

3. Peter Collier and David Horowitz, *The Rockefellers: An American Dynasty* (New York: Holt, Rinehart and Winston, 1976), pp. 352–353. Rockefeller quote, Wallace Turner, "Rockefeller Plans to Step Up Drive," *New York Times,* May 24, 1964.

4. Stu Spencer: Telephone interview with the author, July 16, 1993.

5. Frank S. Meyer, "Why Goldwater Can Defeat Johnson," *National Review,* July 14, 1964, p. 581.

6. F. Clifton White, *Suite 3505: The Story of the Draft Goldwater Movement* (New Rochelle, N.Y.: Arlington House, 1967), pp. 335–336; White, *Making of the Presidency—1964,* pp. 147–148.

7. Collier and Horowitz, p. 354.

8. White, *Suite 3505,* p. 339.

9. Stephen Shadegg, *What Happened to Goldwater?* (New York: Holt, Rinehart and Winston, 1965), p. 116.

10. Ibid., p. 123.

11. Shadegg, p. 124; Phyllis Schlafly: Telephone interview with the author, May 17, 1994.

12. John H. Kessel, *The Goldwater Coalition: Republican Strategies in 1964* (Indianapolis: The Bobbs-Merrill Company, 1968), p. 87.

13. White, *3505,* p. 341; Shadegg, p. 123.

14. "Goldwater Gains Neutrality Vows," *New York Times,* May 28, 1964.

15. White, *3505,* p. 341.

16. Dwight D. Eisenhower, "A Personal Statement by Eisenhower": Roscoe Drummond, no title, *New York Herald Tribune,* May 25, 1964.

17. Charles Mohr, "Goldwater Says Blueprint by Eisenhower Is Timely," *New York Times,* May 26, 1964.

18. Robert Trumbull, "Eisenhower Denies He Wanted to Drive Goldwater from Party," *New York Times,* June 2, 1964; White, *3505,* p. 343.

19. "Goldwater Poses New Asian Tactic," *New York Times,* May 25, 1964.

20. Barry Goldwater, *With No Apologies* (New York: William Morrow and Co., 1979), p. 176

21. "Goldwater Poses New Asian Tactic," *New York Times,* May 25, 1964.

22. Michael F. Keating, "Goldwater Victory Key: Los Angeles," *New York Herald Tribune,* June 4, 1964; White, *The Making of the Presidency—1964,* p. 153.

23. Michael F. Keating, "Goldwater Victory Key: Los Angeles," *New York Herald Tribune,* June 4, 1964.

24. White, *Making,* p. 123.

25. R. L. "Dick" Herman: Interview with the author, April 26, 1993;

Shadegg, p. 125; Wallace Turner, "University Bars Rockefeller Talk," *New York Times,* May 28, 1964.

26. Henry Salvatori: Interview with the author, December 21, 1991.
27. Stu Spencer: Telephone interview with the author, July 15, 1993.
28. Shadegg, p. 126.
29. Stu Spencer: Telephone Interview with the author, July 15, 1993; Michael F. Keating, "Goldwater Victory Key: Los Angeles," *New York Herald Tribune,* June 4, 1964.
30. Barry Goldwater: Interview with the author, December 17, 1991; Barry M. Goldwater with Jack Casserly, *Goldwater* (New York: Doubleday, 1988), pp. 169–170.
31. Charles Mohr, "California Primary—Can Goldwater Be Stopped?" *New York Times,* May 24, 1964.
32. *Goldwater,* p. 170; White, *3505,* p. 350.
33. White, *3505,* p. 350.

Chapter 12   Civil Rights and States' Rights

1. Jack Bell, *Mr. Conservative: Barry Goldwater* (New York: Doubleday & Co., 1962), p. 310.
2. Not only the city's schools but its public toilets, drinking fountains, theaters, parks, playgrounds, restaurants, and even churches were segregated. Once, when Theodore White asked a Mississippi state official, a Democrat, whether it bothered him that blacks could find no place in the downtown of his capital to sit and eat like human beings, he replied, "Not one god-damned bit." Theodore White, *The Making of the President—1964* (New York: Signet Books, 1965), p. 203.
3. William Manchester, *The Glory and the Dream: A Narrative History of America, 1932–1972* vol. 2, (Boston: Little, Brown & Co., 1973), p. 1202.
4. White, p. 207.
5. Manchester, p. 1203; Clarence B. Carson, *The Welfare State 1929–1985 (A Basic History of the United States, Volume 5)* (Wadley, Ala.: American Textbook Committee, 1986), pp. 239–240.
6. Edwin McDowell, *Barry Goldwater: Portrait of an Arizonan* (Chicago: Henry Regnery, 1964), pp. 169–170.
7. Ibid.
8. Junius Bowman: Interview with the author, March 4, 1992.
9. Ibid.
10. *Congressional Record,* January 12, 1956, pp. 488–489.
11. Bell, pp. 143–144.

12. Goldwater, *The Conscience of a Conservative* (Washington, D.C.: Regnery Gateway, 1990), p. 31.
13. Ibid., p. 30.
14. Rob Wood and Dean Smith, *Barry Goldwater* (New York: Avon Books, 1961), p. 112.
15. Ibid., p. 113.
16. McDowell, p. 177.
17. McDowell, p. 181.
18. Manchester, *The Glory and the Dream*, p. 1198.
19. McDowell, p. 181.
20. Thomas Byrne Edsall with Mary D. Edsall, *Chain Reaction: The Impact of Race, Rights and Taxes on American Politics* (New York: W. W. Norton and Company, 1992), pp. 40–41.
21. *National Party Conventions 1831–1984* (Washington, D.C.: Congressional Quarterly, Inc., 1987), p. 111; *New York Times,* July 13, 1964.
22. McDowell, p. 174.
23. Ibid., p. 178.
24. Thomas Sowell, *Civil Rights: Rhetoric or Reality?* (New York: William Morrow and Co., 1984), pp. 39–40.
25. Ibid., p. 41.
26. McDowell, p. 179.
27. Ibid.
28. Ibid., p. 181.
29. Ibid.
30. Barry M. Goldwater with Jack Casserly, *Goldwater* (New York: Doubleday, 1988), p. 173.
31. Barry Goldwater, "Civil Rights," *Congressional Record,* June 18, 1964, p. 14319; White, p. 211.
32. Ibid.
33. James M. Perry, *Barry Goldwater: A New Look at a Presidential Candidate* (Washington, D.C.: National Observer, 1964), p. 125.
34. Charles Lichenstein: Interview with the author, February 12, 1992; Denison Kitchel: Interview with the author, December 16, 1991.
35. Lionel Lokos, *Hysteria 1964: The Fear Campaign Against Barry Goldwater* (New Rochelle, N.Y.: Arlington House, 1967), pp. 87–88; Andrew J. Glass, "Goldwater Now 'Thinks' He'll Vote for Final Version of Rights Bill," *New York Herald Tribune,* June 9, 1964.
36. Charles Mohr, "Eisenhower Stand on Bill Reported," *New York Times,* June 20, 1964.
37. Barry Goldwater, *Congressional Record,* June 11, 1964, p. 14319.
38. Ibid.

39. White, p. 281.
40. James Martin: Telephone interview with the author, March 29, 1994.
41. Charles Mohr, "Goldwater Joins in a Ban on Inciting Races," *New York Times,* July 25, 1964.
42. White, pp. 283–284; *Goldwater,* p. 174.
43. Walter Lippmann, *New York Herald Tribune,* June 30, 1964, p. 18; William Chester, *New York Times,* July 12, 1964, p. 58; Jackie Robinson, *New York Herald Tribune,* July 24, 1964, p. 15; Roy Wilkins, *New York Times,* September 7, 1964, p. 6; Martin Luther King, *New York Times,* September 13, p. 66.
44. Roger Wilkins to Barry Goldwater, November 18, 1986, Barry Goldwater Papers, Arizona Historical Foundation, Arizona State University.
45. Barry Goldwater, *With No Apologies* (New York: William Morrow and Co., 1979), p. 181; David Lawrence, "Goldwater Stand Seen as a 'Courageous' Act," *New York Herald Tribune,* June 20, 1964.
46. David Broder: Interview with the author, August 25, 1992.
47. McDowell, p. 174.
48. Stewart Alsop, "Can Goldwater Win in '64?," *Saturday Evening Post,* August 24, 1963, pp. 23–24.
49. Thomas Byrne Edsall with Mary D. Edsall, *Chain Reaction*, pp. 39–44.
50. John G. Tower, *Consequences: A Personal and Political Memoir* (Boston: Little, Brown and Company, 1991), p. 137.
51. *Goldwater,* p. 173.
52. Barry Goldwater: Interview with the author, December 17, 1991.
53. Barry Goldwater, *The Conscience of a Majority* (Englewood Cliffs, N.J.: Prentice-Hall, 1970), pp. 63, 66.

Chapter 13   Extremism and Moderation

1. Earl Mazo, "Gov. Scranton's Call to Battle," *New York Herald Tribune,* June 13, 1964; Joseph Lelyveld, "Rockefeller Gives Up Race; Aids Scranton," *New York Times,* June 16, 1964; Michael F. Keating, "Lodge Reported Resigning Post to Aid Scranton in GOP Battle," *New York Herald Tribune,* June 15, 1964; Peter Grose, "Lodge Denies Plan to Quit as Envoy," *New York Times,* June 16, 1964; Earl Mazo, "Nixon Urges Romney Race to Block Goldwater Drive," *New York Times,* June 10, 1964; Felix Belair, Jr., "Eisenhower Hints He'll Refuse to Support a Goldwater Race," *New York Times,* June 12, 1964; Joseph A. Loftus, "Curb on Scranton Is Laid to a Shift by Eisenhower," *New York Times,* June 9, 1964.
2. Cabell Phillips, "Goldwater Likens Nixon to Stassen," *New York Times,* June 11, 1964; Charles Mohr, "Goldwater Attacks Lodge for Resigning 'at

a Critical Time,' " *New York Times,* June 26, 1964; "I Am a Candidate," *Time,* June 19, 1964, p. 15; "Bring LBJ Back to His Range, Goldwater Urges Texas GOP," *New York Daily News,* June 16, 1964.

3. "Bring LBJ Back to His Range, Goldwater Urges Texas GOP," *New York Daily News,* June 16, 1964.

4. "I Am a Candidate," *Time,* June 19, 1964, p. 14; F. Clifton White, *Suite 3505: The Story of the Draft Goldwater Movement* (New Rochelle, N.Y.: Arlington House, 1967), p. 364.

5. Richard H. Parke, "Scranton Asserts Goldwater Stirs 'Havoc' in Nation," *New York Times,* June 14, 1964; White, *3505,* pp. 368–374.

6. White, *3505,* p. 374.

7. Ibid. p. 374; Charles Mohr, "Dirksen Asserts That Goldwater Can't Be Stopped," *New York Times,* July 2, 1964.

8. Bill Scranton to Barry Goldwater, June 12, 1964, Papers of William W. Scranton, Pattee Library, Pennsylvania State University.

9. Walter Lippmann, "Goldwater After California," *New York Herald Tribune,* June 9, 1964; Lippmann, "A Choice but a Bad One," *New York Herald Tribune,* June 30, 1964.

10. James Reston, "A Fortnight of Decision: G.O.P. Faces Hard Choice, "*New York Times,* June 29, 1964.

11. Ibid.

12. White, *3505,* p. 379.

13. Ibid., p. 382.

14. James M. Day: Interview with the author, May 12, 1992.

15. Unpublished diary of the author.

16. White, *3505,* p. 384. For another insider's view of the Goldwater convention operation, see pp. 136–151 in Stephen Shadegg, *What Happened to Goldwater?* (New York, Holt, Rinehart & Winston, 1965).

17. White, *3505,* p. 387; Anthony Lewis, "Goldwater Asks a Tougher Stand Against Red Bloc," Excerpts from Goldwater Remarks at G.O.P. Platform Session," *New York Times,* July 11, 1964.

18. *New York Times,* July 11, 1964.

19. Ibid.

20. *Time,* July 17, 1964. The plank on civil rights pledged "full implementation and faithful execution of the Civil Rights Act of 1964 and all other civil rights statutes, to assure equal rights and opportunities guaranteed by the Constitution to every citizen." Official Report of the Proceedings of 28th Republican National Convention, July 13–16, 1964, published by the Republican National Committee, p. 274.

21. Felix Belair, Jr., "Eisenhower Shuns a Role as Convention Kingmaker," *New York Times,* July 11, 1964.

22. Felix Belair, Jr., "Eisenhower Would Favor Goldwater Over Johnson,"

New York Times, July 12, 1964; Felix Belair, Jr., "Eisenhower Sees No Party Crisis," *New York Times,* July 14, 1964.

23. Robert D. Novak, *The Agony of the GOP 1964* (New York: Macmillan Company, 1965), p. 455.

24. Scranton to Goldwater, July 12, 1964, Scranton Papers, Pattee Library, Pennsylvania State.

25. Ibid.

26. Walter R. Mears, "The Story Behind 8 Days in History," *Arizona Republic,* January 18, 1987, p. 32; White, *3505,* p. 392.

27. Handwritten notes of Scranton about his letter to Barry Goldwater, July 12, 1964, Scranton Papers, Pattee Library, Pennsylvania State; White, *3505,* p. 392; Joseph A. Loftus, "Scranton Denies Writing Letter but Stands Behind It," *New York Times,* July 14, 1964.

28. Robert Novak, *Agony of the GOP,* p. 457.

29. White, *Making,* p. 239.

30. Shadegg, p. 155.

31. Felix Belair, Jr., "Eisenhower Plea; He Calls on Factions to Unite— Warns Against Split," *New York Times,* July 15, 1964.

32. White, *3505,* p. 398.

33. Tom Wicker, "Goldwater Backers Vote Down Scranton's Anti-Bircher Plank and Stronger Civil Rights Stand," *New York Times,* July 15, 1964; Willard Edwards, "Hectic Session Is Called G.O.P. Turning Point," *Chicago Tribune,* July 15, 1964.

34. Wicker, *New York Times,* July 15, 1964; White, *3505,* p. 399.

35. Mears, *Arizona Republic,* January 18, 1987, p. 32.

36. F. Clifton White: Interview with the author, April 6, 1992.

37. Charles Mohr, "Senator Charges That President Changed Civil Rights Stand," *New York Times,* July 16, 1964.

38. Mears, *Arizona Republic,* January 18, 1987, p. 32.

39. Tom Wicker, "Goldwater Is Nominated on First Ballot," *New York Times,* July 16, 1964; Honorable Everett McKinley Dirksen Nominating Honorable Barry Goldwater for President, *Official Proceedings of the Twenty-Eighth Republican Convention,* Washington, D.C.: Republican National Committee, 1964, pp. 301–305.

40. White, *3505,* p. 404; unpublished dairy of the author.

41. William W. Scranton, *Official Proceedings of Twenty-Eighth Republican National Convention,* p. 368.

42. Anthony Lewis, "Lindsay Ponders Bolt from Ticket," *New York Times,* July 17, 1964.

43. "Goldwater's Remarks to the Press," *New York Times,* July 17, 1964.

44. Ibid.

45. *Goldwater,* pp. 185–186.

46. Richard Ware: Telephone interview with the author, January 25, 1993; Harry Jaffa: Interview with Matthew Spalding, August 3, 1993.
47. Harry V. Jaffa, "Goldwater's Famous 'Gaffe'," *National Review*, August 10, 1984, p. 36.
48. Jaffa to Denison Kitchel, March 11, 1969, Kitchel Papers, Hoover Institution Archives, Stanford University.
49. *Goldwater*, pp. 186–187.
50. Richard Ware: Telephone interview with the author, January 25, 1993; Ware letter to the author, February 19, 1994.
51. Author Victor Lasky reports that Goldwater also discovered a "bug" in the living room of his Washington apartment. According to Lasky, Goldwater "yanked" the bug out from behind a piece of furniture. The senator mentioned the episode to aides but soon dismissed it as something done "in the heat of the campaign." If there were two separate bugging incidents, the most likely perpetrator would have been the FBI rather than a TV network or the Scranton organization. See pp. 170–171 of Victor Lasky, *It Didn't Start with Watergate* (New York: Dial Press, 1977).
52. Richard M. Nixon, *Official Proceedings of the 28th Republican National Convention*, pp. 408–412.
53. White, *Making*, p. 251.
54. Ibid.
55. Official Proceedings, p. 413.
56. Ibid., p. 414.
57. Ibid.
58. Ibid., p. 416.
59. *Goldwater*, pp. 192–193.
60. Ibid., p. 232.
61. *Official Proceedings*, pp. 416–418.
62. Willard Edwards, "Family Stands with Him in Cow Palace," *Chicago Tribune*, July 17, 1964.
63. *Official Proceedings*, pp. 418–419.
64. Trent Lott, March 22, 1993; Victor Gold, February 10, 1992; John H. Buchanan, Jr., September 3, 1993; Carol Dawson, February 1, 1992; Richard A. Viguerie, February 5, 1992; Donald Devine, February 7, 1992; Patricia Hutar, August 15, 1993: Interviews with the author; Patrick J. Buchanan, *Right from the Beginning* (Boston: Little, Brown and Company, 1988), p. 307; Richard Nixon, *RN: The Memoirs of Richard Nixon* (New York: Grosset & Dunlap, 1978), p. 260; Sandy Scholte, December 3, 1992: Interview with the author.
65. White, *Suite 3505*, p. 15; Shadegg, p. 167; *Goldwater*, p. 187.
66. Earl Mazo, "Goldwater View Is 'Frightening' to Rockefeller," *New York Times*, 1964.

67. Edward J. Derwinski: Interview with the author, May 7, 1993.

68. Barry Goldwater to Scranton, dictated in Arizona, July 18, 1964, Scranton Papers, Pattee Library, Pennsylvania State University.

69. Denison Kitchel, "Explaining Things to Ike," *National Review*, April 30, 1976, p. 447.

70. Ibid.

71. Ibid., p. 448.

72. "Goldwater Seeks to End G.O.P. Rift Over 'Extremism,' " *New York Times,* August 10, 1964.

73. From a private memorandum by the author, August 12, 1964.

74. Charles Mohr, *New York Times,* August 13, 1964; Nixon, p. 262.

75. Barry Goldwater on ABC's "20/20," with interviewer Hugh Downs, July 23, 1993.

76. Eric F. Goldman, *The Tragedy of Lyndon Johnson* (New York: Dell, 1968), p. 257.

77. Doris Kearns, *Lyndon Johnson and the American Dream* (New York: Harper & Row, 1976), p. 206.

Chapter 14 Anything Goes

1. Eric F. Goldman, *The Tragedy of Lyndon Johnson* (New York: Dell, 1968), p. 619.

2. Barry M. Goldwater with Jack Casserly, *Goldwater* (New York: Doubleday, 1988), p. 191.

3. Herbert E. Alexander, "Financing the Parties and Campaigns," Milton C. Cummings, Jr., ed., *The National Election of 1964* (Washington, D.C.: The Brookings Institution, 1966), pp. 159, 161, 170–171; Alfred Steinberg, *Sam Johnson's Boy: A Close-Up of the President from Texas* (New York: The Macmillan Company, 1968), p. 684; J. William Middendorf II, "Report of the Republican National Finance Committee," January 21, 1965, Middendorf Archives.

4. Glenn Campbell: Interview with the author, January 9, 1993.

5. Fendall W. Yerxa, "Goldwater Calls Military Power the Key to Peace," *New York Times,* September 24, 1964.

6. *Goldwater,* pp. 188–189.

7. F. Clifton White, *Suite 3505: The Story of the Draft Goldwater Movement* (New Rochell, N.Y.: Arlington House, 1967), p. 18.

8. *Goldwater,* p. 191.

9. Edward J. Derwinski: Interview with the author, May 7, 1993.

10. James Reston, *New York Times,* May 8, 1964.

11. Willard Edwards, "Barry Sets His Sights on Nonvoters," *Chicago Tribune,* September 6, 1964.

12. Anthony Lewis, "The Issues: Civil Rights, Extremism and Nuclear Policy Are the Major Themes Now," *New York Times,* August 30, 1964.

13. Charles A. H. Thompson, "Mass Media Performance," pp. 127–134, Milton C. Cummings, Jr., ed., *The National Election of 1964,* (Washington: The Brookings Institution, 1966).

14. Willard Edwards, "Goldwater's Tours Stir Enthusiasm," *Chicago Tribune,* September 13, 1964.

15. Robert MacNeil: Interview with the author, March 8, 1993.

16. Robert MacNeil, *The Right Place at the Right Time* (Boston: Little, Brown and Company, 1982), p. 226.

17. David Broder: Interview with the author, August 25, 1992.

18. Kathleen Hall Jamieson, *Packaging the Presidency: A History and Criticism of Presidential Campaign Advertising* (New York: Oxford University Press, 1992), pp. 174–175.

19. Ibid. p. 175.

20. J. Evetts Haley, *A Texan Looks at Lyndon: A Study in Illegitimate Power* (Canyon, Tex.: Palo Duro Press, 1964), p. 10.

21. Robert Caro, *The Years of Lyndon Johnson: Means of Ascent* (London: The Bodley Head, 1990), for its definitive treatment of the 1948 senatorial campaign.

22. John A. Stormer, *None Dare Call It Treason* (Florissant, MO: Liberty Bell Press, 1964), p. 210.

23. Phyllis Schlafly, *A Choice Not an Echo* (Alton, Ill.: Pere Marquette Press, 1964), pp. 102–116, 120–121; Schlafly: Telephone interview with the author, May 17, 1994.

24. Statement by Lee Edwards, deputy director of public relations, Republican National Committee, October 3, 1964, as reported in the *New York Times,* October 4, 1964.

25. Donald Janson, "Extremist Book Sales Soar Despite Criticism in G.O.P.," *New York Times,* October 4, 1964.

26. Robert MacNeil: Interview with the author, March 8, 1993.

27. Steinberg, p. 690.

28. Larry Sabato, *Feeding Frenzy: How Attack Journalism Has Transformed American Politics* (New York: The Free Press, 1991), p. 44.

29. William L. Rivers and Cleve Mathews, *Ethics for the Media* (Englewood Cliffs, N.J.: Prentice Hall, 1988), p. 63.

30. Tom Wicker, "The Candidates: Two Men from the West Offer Radically Different Political Philosophies," *New York Times,* August 30, 1964.

31. Harold Faber, ed., *The Road to the White House: The Story of the 1964 Election* (New York: The New York Times, 1965), p. 141.

32. Faber, p. 235.

33. Nelson W. Polsby and Aaron B. Wildavsky, *Presidential Elections: Strat-

egies of American Electoral Politics, 2nd ed. (New York: Charles Scribner's Sons, 1968), p. 200.

34. Faber, p. 153.
35. Charles Mohr, "Goldwater Vows Gradual Change If He Is Elected," *New York Times,* September 4, 1964.
36. Ibid.
37. Ibid.
38. Ibid.
39. Ibid.
40. Ibid.
41. *Goldwater,* p. 192.
42. Willard Edwards, "Goldwater's Tours Stir Enthusiasm," *Chicago Tribune,* September 13, 1964.
43. Ibid.
44. Ibid.
45. Stephen Shadegg, *What Happened to Goldwater?* (New York: Holt, Rinehart & Winston, 1965), p. 207.
46. According to campaign aide Jack Buttram, who traveled extensively with Goldwater throughout the South. Interview with the author, February 12, 1993.
47. Shadegg, p. 219.
48. Nadine Cohodas, *Strom Thurmond and the Politics of Southern Change* (New York: Simon & Schuster, 1993), pp. 358–361; address of Senator Strom Thurmond, September 16, 1964, reprinted by the Republican National Committee, author's private files.
49. Shadegg, pp. 232–236; Charles Mohr, "Goldwater Says 'We Are at War,' " *New York Times,* September 20, 1964.
50. Shadegg, p. 237.
51. Jamieson, pp. 205–207.
52. Shadegg, p. 241; Charlotte-Anne Lucas, "Doing His 'Duty': The Primary Trail," *The Arizona Republic,* January 18, 1987, p. 29; Robert Mardian: Interview with the author, December 19, 1991.
53. Karl Hess, *In a Cause That Will Triumph* (Garden City, N.Y.: Doubleday & Company, 1967), p. 21.
54. The precise figures, as reported by the Opinion Research Corporation, were undecided to Goldwater, 6.0 percent; undecided to Johnson, 4.9 percent; Johnson to Goldwater, 7.3 percent, and Goldwater to Johnson, 2.6 percent. Totals: Goldwater, 13.3 percent; Johnson, 7.5 percent. "Exhibit 27, Change in voting choice from August to Election Day," *Public Opinion Trends . . . Their Meaning for the Republican Party,* presented to the Republican National Committee in Chicago, January 22–23, 1965, by the Opinion Research Corporation, Princeton, N.J.

55. Jamieson, p. 186.
56. Ibid.
57. Jamieson, pp. 198–199; Edwin Diamond and Stephen Bates, *The Spot: The Rise of Political Advertising on Television* (Cambridge, Mass.: The MIT Press, 1988), pp. 128–129.
58. Jamieson, p. 200.
59. Ibid.; Diamond and Bates, p. 129.
60. Jamieson, p. 200.
61. Ibid., p. 201. At the time, mothers were marching against the dangers of Strontium 90, and the dairy industry had expressed its concern. "That issue," Moyers recalls, "played into our hands because Goldwater had called for more nuclear testing"—although not, as the commercial implied, for more radioactive poison in milk and ice cream.
62. Victor Lasky, *It Didn't Start with Watergate* (New York: The Dial Press, 1977), p. 181.
63. Reston, Bradlee, and Broder quoted in *Goldwater,* pp. 200–201; Michael Novak: Interview with the author, April 15, 1992.
64. *New York Times,* September 14, 1964.
65. Diamond and Bates, p. 137.
66. Jamieson, p. 192.
67. *Goldwater,* pp. 194–195.
68. Edward H. Crane, "Give Me Liberty, Not Utopia," *Washington Post,* January 11, 1995.
69. Jamieson, p. 192.
70. *U.S. News & World Report,* December 21, 1964, p. 47.
71. Lasky, p. 180.
72. Jamieson, pp. 187–189, 197; Diamond and Bates, pp. 135–137.
73. Goldman, p. 272.
74. E. Howard Hunt, *Undercover: Memoirs of an American Secret Agent* (New York: Berkley Publishing Corp., 1974), p. 133.
75. Hunt, p. 133; Lasky, pp. 171–173.
76. Shadegg, p. 215.
77. Lasky, p. 171; also *Philadelphia Bulletin*, September 29, 1972.
78. Ben Bradlee: Interview with the author, October 9, 1992.
79. *Goldwater,* p. 200; George Reedy: Telephone interview with the author, February 15, 1993.
80. *Goldwater,* p. 200.
81. Rowland Evans and Robert Novak, *Lyndon B. Johnson: The Exercise of Power* (New York: The New American Library, 1966), pp. 468–469.
82. Sam Hay: Telephone interview with the author, August 24, 1993.
83. Shadegg, p. 238.

84. Theodore White, *Breach of Faith — The Fall of Richard Nixon* (New York: Atheneum Publishers, 1975), p. 100.

85. In the 1930s, FDR directly ordered the FBI to investigate "subversive activities being conducted in the United States by Communists, Fascists," and others advocating the overthrow of the government by illegal methods. Truman (in July 1950 right after the invasion of South Korea) and Eisenhower (in December 1953) reaffirmed the domestic intelligence gathering responsibilities of the bureau. In June 1962, in National Security Memorandum 161, Kennedy placed all internal security operations, including foreign counterintelligence and domestic security investigations, under the attorney general. The attorney general subsequently stated that the FBI should remain in "charge of investigative work in matters relating to espionage, sabotage, subversive activities, and related matters." *Hearings before the Select Committee to Study Governmental Operations with Respect to Intelligence Activities*, U.S. Senate, 94th Congress, First Session, Volume 6, Federal Bureau of Investigation (Washington, D.C.: Government Printing Office, 1975), pp. 562, 575.

86. Lasky, p. 71.

87. Ibid., pp. 164–167.

88. *New York Times,* January 29, 1975.

89. *Senate Hearings,* Vol. 6, p. 510.

90. Lasky, p. 179.

91. M. A. Jones, FBI Memorandum Re: Senator Barry Goldwater, October 23, 1964, Robert Mardian Papers, Hoover Institution Archives, Stanford University.

92. Robert Mardian: Interview with the author, December 19, 1992. In his memoirs, Richard Nixon reveals that President Johnson did the same thing to him, stating that "Hoover told me that in 1968 Johnson had ordered my campaign plane bugged." See p. 629 of *RN: The Memoirs of Richard Nixon* (New York: Grosset & Dunlap, 1978).

93. *Senate Hearings,* Vol. 6, p. 190.

94. Ibid., p. 192.

95. Ibid., pp. 194–195.

96. *Goldwater,* pp. 199–200.

97. Cummings, *The National Election of 1969,* p. 68.

98. E. W. Kenworthy, "Fulbright Scorns G.O.P. Candidates," *New York Times,* September 9, 1964; "Wilkins Says Goldwater Victory Might Bring About Police State," *New York Times,* September 7, 1964.

99. Charles Mohr, "Goldwater Sees Presidency Peril," *New York Times,* September 12, 1964.

100. Campaign speech before the American Political Science Association, Chicago, September 11, 1964, Middendorf Archives.
101. Ibid.
102. King, *New York Times,* September 13, 1964; *Saturday Evening Post,* September 19, 1964, p. 80; Lippmann, *New York Herald Tribune,* September 22, 1964.
103. Vic Gold: Interview with the author, February 10, 1992.
104. Campaign speech at Civic Center, Charleston, West Virginia, September 18, 1964; Campaign speech, Montgomery, Alabama, September 16, 1964; Campaign speech at Fenway Park, Boston, September 24, 1964; Campaign speech to the National Federation of Republican Women, Louisville, Kentucky, September 25, 1964; Campaign speech at Toledo University Field House, Toledo, Ohio, September 30, 1964, Middendorf Archives; Yerxa, *New York Times,* September 24, 1964.
105. Theodore White, *The Making of the President—1964* (New York: Signet Books, 1965), p. 389.
106. James Reston, "Some New Ways to Slice the Old Baloney," *New York Times,* September 4, 1964.
107. David Wise, "And a Nostalgic Glimpse at Politics Past," *New York Herald Tribune,* October 4, 1964.
108. Ibid.
109. Charles Mohr, "The Spy on the Goldwater Train," *New York Times,* September 30, 1964.

Chapter 15   Waiting for the Landslide

1. Theodore White, *The Making of the President—1964* (New York: Signet Books, 1965), p. 416.
2. Ibid.
3. Edward Jay Epstein, *Between Fact and Fiction: The Problem of Journalism* (New York: Vintage Books, 1975), pp. 82–85.
4. Barry M. Goldwater with Jack Casserly, *Goldwater* (New York: Doubleday, 1988), p. 197.
5. Warren Boroson, "What Psychiatrists Say About Goldwater," *Fact,* September–October 1964, p. 24.
6. Ibid., pp. 25–64, for these and many other similar comments. One board-certified psychiatrist in Stamford, Connecticut, wrote that "any psychiatrist who does not agree with the above [that Goldwater was "a mass murderer at heart" and "a dangerous lunatic"] is himself psychologically unfit to be a psychiatrist," p. 63.
7. *Goldwater,* p. 205; statement by Dr. Donovan F. Ward, president, American Medical Association, September 30, 1964, author's private files.

8. Stephen Shadegg, *What Happened to Goldwater?* (New York: Holt, Rinehart and Winston, 1965), pp. 257–258.
9. Ibid., p. 258.
10. "Goldwater's Libel Judgment Stands," *Phoenix Gazette,* January 26, 1970.
11. White, p. 393.
12. Ibid., p. 392.
13. Charles Mohr, "Goldwater Hunts a Winning Tactic," *New York Times,* October 6, 1964.
14. *Goldwater,* p. 206.
15. Richard Charnock, "Drawing the Battle Lines," *Goldwater: His Life and Legacy, Arizona Republic,* January 18, 1987, p. 31.
16. *Goldwater,* pp. 203–204.
17. White, pp. 436–437.
18. Ibid., p. 437.
19. Burch statement: "White House: Aide Out, Aide In," *New York Journal American,* October 15, 1964; Johnson statement: Victor Lasky, *It Didn't Start with Watergate* (New York: Dial Press, 1977), p. 191.
20. "Issue of Security Is Raised by G.O.P.," *New York Times,* October 16, 1964, p. 20; Earl Mazo, "G.O.P. Hopes Rise, But Jenkins Effect on Race Is Cloudy," *New York Times,* October 16, 1964.
21. "Text of Johnson's Address to the Nation," *New York Times,* October 19, 1964.
22. Willard Edwards, " 'Come to the Speakin',' " October 13, 1964; "Johnson Switches Personalities When Not on TV," October 19, 1964; "Johnson's Ego Masks Underlying Concern Over Election Outcome," October 11, 1964; *Chicago Tribune.*
23. Kenneth P. O'Donnell: Interview for the oral history project of the LBJ Library, July 23, 1969.
24. Rowland Evans and Robert Novak, *Lyndon B. Johnson: The Exercise of Power* (New York: The New American Library, 1966), p. 532.
25. White, p. 399.
26. Lee Edwards: Unpublished campaign diary, October 19, 1964.
27. Barry Goldwater, "The Real Job of the Presidency," address over ABC-TV, October 9, 1964, Middendorf Archives.
28. Campaign speech at East St. Louis, Illinois, October 28, 1964, Middendorf Archives.
29. Ibid.
30. "President Finds G.O.P. 'Smearlash,' " *New York Times,* October 22, 1964. Charles Mohr, "Johnson, in South, Decries 'Radical' Goldwater Ideas," *New York Times,* October 27, 1964.
31. "The Campaign Ends," *New York Times,* November 1, 1964.

32. Barry Goldwater campaign speech at East St. Louis, Illinois, October 28, 1964, Middendorf Archives.

33. Denison Kitchel: Interview with the author, December 16, 1991.

34. *Goldwater*, p. 190.

35. James Harff: Interview with the author, September 2, 1993.

36. White, pp. 378–379.

37. Richard Thompson: Interview with the author, July 7, 1992.

38. Charles Mohr, "Goldwater Has a Virtual Monopoly on the Morality Issue in the Campaign," *New York Times,* October 29, 1964.

39. Ibid.

40. Barry Goldwater to Cliff [sic] White, October 13, 1964, F. Clifton White Papers, Cornell.

41. Charles A. H. Thomson, "Mass Media Performance," Milton C. Cummings, ed., *The National Election of 1964* (Washington, D.C.: The Brookings Institution, 1966), p. 125.

42. Thomson, pp. 125- 126; Karl Hess, *In a Cause That Will Triumph* (Garden City, N.Y.: Doubleday & Company, 1967), p. 140.

43. F. Clifton White: Interview with the author, April 6, 1992.

44. *Goldwater,* p. 208.

45. Ibid.

46. Earl Mazo, "Polls Predicting a Johnson Sweep," *New York Times,* October 28, 1964.

47. *Goldwater,* p. 209; White, p. 403.

48. Denison Kitchel: Interview with the author, December 16, 1991.

49. John D. Pomfret, "The Senator's Fervor Seldom Matches His Audience's," *New York Times,* November 2, 1964.

50. *Goldwater,* pp. 205–206.

51. E. W. Kenworthy, "Goldwater Says Johnson 'Doesn't Understand' Job," *New York Times,* October 21, 1964; Peter Kihss, "Goldwater Exhorts 18,000 in Garden 'Victory' Rally; Hits Johnson 'Daddyism,' " *New York Times,* October 27, 1964; "Goldwater Charges Rusk Is Lax," *New York Times,* October 30, 1964; John D. Pomfret, "Goldwater Hailed on Coast," *New York Times,* November 3, 1964.

52. John H. Kessel, *The Goldwater Coalition: Republican Strategies in 1964* (Indianapolis: The Bobbs-Merrill Company, 1968), p. 216.

53. Ronald Reagan, *An American Life* (New York: Simon and Schuster, 1990), pp. 138–139.

54. Ibid., p. 139.

55. Ibid., p. 140.

56. Reagan, p. 140; Lee Edwards, *Ronald Reagan: A Political Biography* (Houston, TX: Nordland Publishing, 1981), p. 69.

57. Reagan, pp. 140–141.

58. Edwards, pp. 69–70.
59. Lee Edwards: Unpublished campaign diary, October 28, 1964; Edwards, p. 70; Stephen Hess and David Broder, *The Republican Establishment: The Present and Future of the G.O.P.* (New York: Harper & Row, 1967), pp. 253–254; William F. Buckley Jr.: Interview with the author, April 13, 1992.
60. *Goldwater,* p. 209.
61. F. Clifton White and William J. Gill, *Why Reagan Won: The Conservative Movement: 1964–1981* Chicago: Regnery Gateway, 1981), p. 20.
62. Henry Salvatori: Interview with the author, December 21, 1991.
63. William Quinn: Interview with the author, October 2, 1992.
64. White, pp. 406–407.

Chapter 16   The Meaning of Defeat

1. Harold Faber, ed., *The Road to the White House: The Story of the 1964 Election* (New York: New York Times, 1965), p. 268.
2. Ibid., p. 264.
3. Karl Hess: Interview with the author, June 22, 1992.
4. Faber, p. 268.
5. Ibid., p. 279.
6. *Quotations from Chairman Bill: The Best of William F. Buckley Jr.,* compiled by David Franke (New Rochelle, N.Y.: Arlington House, 1970), p. 96.
7. Barry M. Goldwater with Jack Casserly, *Goldwater* (New York: Doubleday, 1988), pp. 216–218.
8. For example, in 1993, after the nation had spent $5.1 trillion fighting the War on Poverty (more than the cost of battling Germany and Japan in World War II), the Census Bureau announced that there were still more than 30 million "poor" Americans, as many as when Johnson declared his War on Poverty in 1964. (Robert Rector, "The Poverty Paradox," October 5, 1993, a "Point of View" distributed by the Heritage Foundation, Washington, D.C.) Such discouraging results were all far in the future.
9. John E. Grenier to Barry Goldwater, February 8, 1965, Shadegg Papers, Texas Historical Society, University of Texas at Austin Library.
10. Theodore White, *The Making of the President—1964* (New York: Signet Books, 1965), pp. 453–457.
11. Walter Lippmann, *Washington Post,* November 5, 1964; Wicker, Faber, p. ix; Robert J. Donovan, *The Future of the Republican Party* (New York: Signet Books, 1964), p. 124; Nelson W. Polsby and Aaron B. Wildavsky, *Presidential Elections: Strategies of American Electoral Politics, 2nd ed.* (New York: Charles Scribner's Sons, 1968), p. 208; Reston, Faber, p. 273;

Richard Rovere, "The Conservative Mindlessness," *Commentary,* March 1965, p. 39; *Wall Street Journal,* Donovan, p. 68.

12. Knowland, Donovan, p. 66; Rickenbacker, *National Review,* November 17, 1964, p. 1001; Niemeyer, ibid., p. 1056; Reagan, ibid., p. 1055; Bush, ibid., p. 1053; Kirk, ibid, p. 1055; Buckley and Burnham, ibid., p. 1000.

13. Frank Meyer, "What Next for Conservatism?" *National Review,* December 1, 1964, p. 1057.

14. White, pp. 409–411.

15. Barry Goldwater, *The Conscience of a Majority* (Englewood Cliffs, N.J.: Prentice-Hall, 1970), p. 42.

16. *Goldwater,* p. 211.

17. Richard Harwood, "Goldwater's Camp Lining Up Broad Support," *Louisville Times,* July 28, 1964.

18. Remarks by Haley Barbour before the Frank Meyer Society, Washington, D.C., September 14, 1994.

19. Robert Bauman: Interview with the author, September 11, 1993.

20. David Franke: Interview with the author, May 28, 1992.

21. *Goldwater,* p. 214.

22. Mary Elizabeth Lewis: Interview with the author, March 24, 1992.

23. Trent Lott: Interview with the author, March 24, 1992.

24. Phil Gramm: Conversation with the author, November 30, 1994.

25. J. Jennings Moss, "104th's freshmen tilt way to right," *Washington Times,* November 11, 1994.

26. James L. Buckley: Interview with the author, May 19, 1992.

27. Paul Laxalt: Interview with the author, March 10, 1992.

28. William E. Brock: Interview with the author, October 28, 1992.

29. Howard Baker: Interview with the author, November 10, 1993.

30. Sandra Day O'Connor: Interview with the author, June 16, 1993.

31. Richard B. Wirthlin: Interview with the author, June 10, 1992.

32. Edwin J. Feulner, Jr.: Interview with the author, April 20, 1993.

33. Patrick J. Buchanan, *Right from the Beginning* (Boston: Little, Brown and Company, 1988), p. 291; *Goldwater,* pp. 132–133; Patrick J. Buchanan: Interview with the author, May 5, 1993.

34. M. Stanton Evans, *The Future of Conservatism* (New York: Holt, Rinehart & Winston, 1968), p. 135.

35. M. Stanton Evans: Interview with the author, March 20, 1992.

36. David R. Jones: Interview with the author, May 16, 1992.

37. J. A. Parker: Interview with the author, January 30, 1992.

38. Richard A. Viguerie: Interview with the author, February 5, 1992.

39. Paul Weyrich: Interviews with the author, February 18, 1992, April 16, 1992.

40. Morton Blackwell: Interview with the author, January 13, 1992.
41. Thomas L. Phillips: Interview with the author, June 11, 1993.
42. *TV. etc.*, Media Research Center, Alexandria, Va., Vol 5, No 4, April 1993.
43. George F. Gilder and Bruce K. Chapman, *The Party That Lost Its Head* (New York: Alfred A. Knopf, 1966), pp. 24–26, 295, 323–324.
44. John H. Buchanan, Jr.: Interview with the author, September 3, 1993.
45. Jeane Kirkpatrick, Michael J. Novak, Midge Decter: Interviews with the author, May 29, 1992; April 15, 1992; March 31, 1992.
46. David Danzig, "Conservatism After Goldwater," *Commentary,* March 1965, pp. 31–37.
47. Ben J. Wattenberg: Interview with the author, April 29, 1992.
48. Irving Kristol, "A Letter from Irving Kristol," *National Review,* March 16, 1992, p. S–17.
49. Karl Hess, *In a Cause That Will Triumph: The Goldwater Campaign and the Future of Conservatism* (Garden City, N.Y.: Doubleday & Company, 1967), p. 162.
50. Karl Hess: Interview with the author, June 22, 1992, Martinsburg.
51. Denison Kitchel: Interview with the author, December 16, 1991; Barry Goldwater to Ronald and Nancy Reagan, June 2, 1966; Reagan to Barry Goldwater, June 11, 1966, Barry Goldwater Papers, Arizona Historical Foundation, Arizona State University.
52. John Sears: Interview with the author, June 9, 1992; Harry Jaffa: Interview with Matthew Spalding, August 3, 1993.
53. *Goldwater,* p. 220.
54. Peter Jennings, as quoted in "Inside the Beltway," John McCaslin, *Washington Times*, November 25, 1994; Richard Benedetto, "Poll: Most view GOP favorably," *USA Today*, December 2, 1994.
55. Morton Kondracke, "Leapfrog opportunity," *Washington Times*, November 21, 1994; Cal Thomas, "Requiem in the graveyard," *Washington Times*, November 22, 1994.
56. Stephen Chapman, "Demons of disillusionment," *Washington Times*, October 30, 1994.
57. Robert J. Samuelson, "Changing the Mainstream," *Washington Post*, November 30, 1994; George Will, "Reagan's Third Victory," *Washington Post*, November 10, 1994.

Chapter 17   Vindication

1. Mark Rhoads: Interview with the author, June 17, 1993.
2. Barry Goldwater, *With No Apologies* (New York: William Morrow and Co., 1979), pp. 200–201.

3. Barry M. Goldwater with Jack Casserly, *Goldwater* (New York: Doubleday, 1988), p. 222.
4. Ibid.
5. Ibid., p. 224.
6. Carl Albert, "The Goldwater Record on Foreign Policy," *Congressional Record,* September 23, 1964, p. 22673.
7. *Goldwater,* p. 230.
8. Ibid., p. 231.
9. Ibid., pp. 230–231.
10. Marie Smith, "Barry Calls Him 'Irresponsible,' " *Washington Post,* May 6, 1966.
11. *Goldwater,* pp. 239–240, 246.
12. Don Dedera, "Barry Tours Viet MARS Stations," *Congressional Quarterly,* September 1970, pp. 56–57; Maxine Goodman, "'Nam' Hams place 100,000th radio call," *Scottsdale Daily Progress,* December 15, 1971; Bill Anderson, "Back Home with Senator Goldwater," *Dots and Dashes,* April-May-June 1974; Sisley Barnes, "Barry's 'Ham' Station Makes Big Contribution," *Arizona Republic,* April 2, 1977.
13. Harold Faber, ed., *The Road to the White House: The Story of the 1964 Election* (New York: New York Times, 1965), p. 284.
14. "No Remorse, No Grudges," *Newsweek,* November 15, 1965, pp. 41–42.
15. Faber, p. 286; Stephen E. Ambrose, *Nixon: The Triumph of a Politician: 1962–1972 Volume Two* (New York: Simon & Shuster, 1989), pp. 60–61.
16. M. Stanton Evans, *The Future of Conservatism* (New York: Holt, Rinehart and Winston, 1968), p. 154.
17. Ibid., p. 143.
18. Faber, p. 282.
19. Transcript of "Meet the Press," NBC television and radio, June 13, 1965.
20. Gordon Greer, "Barry Goldwater's Very Special Place," *Venture,* circa 1967, pp. 27–33.
21. Ibid.
22. Sally Quinn: Telephone interview with the author, October 29, 1993.
23. "No Remorse, No Grudges," *Newsweek,* November 15, 1965, pp. 41–42.
24. William F. Buckley to Barry Goldwater, October 15, 1966, William F. Buckley Jr. Papers, Yale; John B. Judis, *William F. Buckley Jr.: Patron Saint of the Conservatives* (New York: Simon & Shuster, 1988), p. 255.
25. Barry Goldwater to his brother Bob and sister Carolyn, January 17, 1967, Josephine Goldwater Collection, Arizona Historical Foundation.
26. Barry Goldwater to George Romney, December 6, 1964, Romney to Goldwater, December 21, 1964, Barry Goldwater Papers, Arizona Historical Foundation, Arizona State University; Ted Lewis, Goldwater's 'Dear George' Letter Bared," *New York Daily News,* November 30, 1966.

27. Barry Goldwater to Edward A. McCabe, February 1, 1967, BMG; Barry Goldwater: Interview with the author, December 6, 1991.

28. Form letter to Admiral Lewis Strauss and others from Goldwater, July 22, 1968; Goldwater to Ronald Reagan, June 19, 1968, BMG.

29. *With No Apologies,* p. 207; Richard Nixon, *RN: The Memoirs of Richard Nixon* (New York: Grosset & Dunlap, 1978), p. 309; *National Party Conventions 1831–1984* (Washington, D.C.: *Congressional Quarterly,* 1987), p. 113.

30. Richard Nixon to the author, November 4, 1992.

31. *With No Apologies,* p. 208.

32. Ibid., p. 207, *Goldwater,* p. 256.

33. Barry Goldwater to Kitchel, November 12, 1968, Kitchel Papers, Hoover Institution Archives, Stanford University.

Chapter 18　The Making and Unmaking of Presidents, I

1. Gerald Boyd, "The Vice President Tries to Cope with a Troubled Campaign," *New York Times,* February 16, 1988; E. J. Dionne, Jr., "Bush in Struggle with Surging Dole in New Hampshire," *New York Times,* February 16, 1988.

2. Barry Goldwater, *With No Apologies* (New York: William Morrow and Co., 1979), pp. 267–268; Bob Woodward and Carl Bernstein, *The Final Days* (New York: Simon & Shuster, 1976), p. 415; Theodore White, *Breach of Faith,* (New York: Atheneum Publishers, 1975), p. 28.

3. White, p. 31.

4. Barry M. Goldwater with Jack Casserly, *Goldwater* (New York: Doubleday, 1988), pp. 277–279.

5. *With No Apologies,* pp. 214–215.

6. Ibid., p. 215.

7. Ibid., pp. 231–232.

8. Ibid., p. 234.

9. Ibid.

10. Ibid., pp. 234–235.

11. John A. Scali memorandum, June 29, 1971, Box 12, President's Office Files, Nixon Presidential Materials; Al Snyder to Charles Colson, July 1971, Bruce Oudes, ed., *Richard Nixon's Secret Files* (Cambridge, Mass.: Harper & Row, 1989), p. 288; Nixon to Goldwater, September 17, 1971, Box 13, President's Handwriting File, Nixon Presidential Materials.

12. The President to Bob Haldeman, November 12, 1971, *Richard Nixon's Secret Files,* p. 334; Haldeman to Goldwater, October 8, 1971, President's Office Files, Nixon Presidential Materials.

13. *With No Apologies,* p. 240.

14. Ibid., p. 241.
15. Ibid., p. 242.
16. Ibid.
17. Ibid., pp. 245–247.
18. Ibid., p. 248.
19. Ibid.
20. Ibid., p. 249.
21. Ibid.
22. Ibid., p. 251.
23. Ibid., p. 252.
24. Ibid., p. 254.
25. *Human Events*, July 7, 1973, p. 2.
26. *With No Apologies*, pp. 252–254.
27. *With No Apologies*, p. 255.
28. *With No Apologies*, pp. 235–236; *Goldwater*, p. 258.
29. *With No Apologies*, p. 256.
30. Ibid., pp. 256–257; *Goldwater*, p. 263.
31. *With No Apologies*, p. 257.
32. Ibid., pp. 257–258.
33. Ibid., p. 264.
34. *Goldwater*, p. 265; *With No Apologies*, pp. 258–259.
35. *Goldwater*, p. 265.
36. Ron Zeigler to the President, September 23, 1973, Box 22, White House Special Files, Nixon Presidential Materials.
37. *With No Apologies*, p. 259.
38. *Human Events*, December 1, 1973, p. 9.
39. *Goldwater*, pp. 266–267.
40. Patrick J. Buchanan: Interview with the author, May 5, 1993.
41. *Goldwater*, pp. 267–271.
42. Clark R. Mollenhoff, *Game Plan for Disaster: An Ombudsman's Report on the Nixon Years* (New York: W.W. Norton & Company, 1976), p. 342.
43. *Human Events*, December 29, 1973, p. 2; February 2, 1974, p. 2; June 1, 1974, p. 2.
44. Charles H. Percy to Barry Goldwater, March 27, 1987, Personal Papers of Percy; Charles Percy: Interview with the author, December 9, 1993.
45. *Goldwater*, p. 255.
46. Ibid., p. 274.
47. Woodward and Bernstein, p. 333; *Goldwater*, p. 272.
48. Barry Goldwater to Denison Kitchel, July 23, 1974, Barry Goldwater Papers, Arizona Historical Foundation, Arizona State University [hereafter BMG].
49. White, pp. 21–22; Woodward and Bernstein, p. 389.

50. *Goldwater*, pp. 275–276.
51. Ibid., pp. 276–277.
52. Alexander M. Haig, Jr., with Charles McCarry, *Inner Circles: How America Changed the World, A Memoir* (New York: Warner Books, 1992), pp. 498–499; *Goldwater*, p. 277.
53. *Goldwater*, p. 277.
54. *With No Apologies*, p. 266; *Goldwater*, pp. 279–280. Benjamin Bradlee: Interview with the author, October 9, 1992. Bradlee confirms that Goldwater called him to say that "Nixon's going to leave if you don't beat him over the head. So, we fudged [our story] a little bit."
55. "The White House Press Conference of Senator Hugh Scott, Congressman John J. Rhodes, and Senator Barry Goldwater, The North Lawn," August 7, 1974, Box 169, Gerald R. Ford Library, Ann Arbor, Michigan.
56. Woodward and Bernstein, p. 416.
57. *Goldwater*, p. 280.
58. Goldwater, p. 282.
59. Goldwater to Nixon, January 30, 1975, BMG.
60. Barry Goldwater: Interview with the author, December 17, 1991.

Chapter 19   The Making and Unmaking of Presidents, II

1. Barry Goldwater, *With No Apologies* (New York: William Morrow and Co., 1979), pp. 270–271.
2. Ibid., pp. 271–272.
3. Richard Reeves, *A Ford, not a Lincoln* (New York: Harcourt Brace Jovanovich, 1975), p. 149.
4. Gerald R. Ford, *A Time to Heal* (New York: Harper & Row, 1979), pp. 142–143.
5. Robert M. Hartmann Files, Box 21, Gerald R. Ford Library, Ann Arbor, Michigan [hereafter GRF].
6. *With No Apologies,* p. 272.
7. Ibid., p. 275.
8. John Sears: Telephone interview with the author, March 18, 1994; *With No Apologies*, p. 275.
9. Memo for the Alpha File, May 5, 1975, Barry Goldwater Papers, Arizona Historical Foundation, Arizona State University [hereafter BMG].
10. *With No Apologies*, pp. 275–276; John Sears: Telephone interview with the author, March 18, 1994.
11. Memorandum of Max L. Friedersdorf to the President, June 11, 1975, Box 36, Presidential Handwriting File, GRF.
12. Goldwater to Howard Callaway, July 21, 1975, Box 18, Richard Cheney Files; Ford to Goldwater, October 6, 1975, Box 101, John Marsh Files;

Friedersdorf to the President, October 10, 1975, Box 101, John Marsh Files, GRF.

13. Memorandum of Richard B. Cheney to the President, November 13, 1975, Box 16, Richard Cheney Files, GRF.

14. Cheney to the President, November 13, 1975, Box 16, Richard Cheney Files, GRF.

15. Memorandum of Jerry Jones to Richard B. Cheney regarding the President Ford Advisory Committee meeting, November 18, 1975, Box 18, Richard Cheney Files, GRF.

16. Ford, p. 344.

17. Goldwater to Ford, December 10, 1975, Box B1, Kissinger-Scowcroft Files; Ford to Goldwater, February 12, 1976, Box B1, Kissinger-Scowcroft Files, GRF.

18. Clark R. Mollenhoff, *The Man Who Pardoned Nixon* (New York: A Giniger Book, 1976), p. 264.

19. Ford, p. 374.

20. Robert Keatley, "The Big Flap Over the Canal," *Wall Street Journal,* April 29, 1976.

21. Ford, pp. 374–375.

22. Grace Lichtenstein, "Goldwater, at Arizona Meeting, Critical of Reagan," *New York Times,* April 25, 1976.

23. UPI dispatch, May 2, 1976, Box 16, Michael Raoul-Duval Papers, GRF; transcript of Barry Goldwater appearance on "Meet the Press," May 2, 1976.

24. Daniel P. Hose, May 4, 1976, UPI dispatch, Box B6; Press Conference by Barry Goldwater, May 4, 1976, Box B6, President Ford Committee Records, GRF.

25. Barry M. Goldwater, *Why Not Victory?* (New York: MacFadden Capitol Hill Book, 1962), p. 34.

26. "Goldwater's Curious Stand on Panama Canal Issue," *Human Events,* p. 3, May 15, 1976.

27. Memorandum of Stu Spencer and Peter Kaye to Rogers C. B. Morton, May 5, 1976, Box B10, President Ford Committee Records, GRF.

28. Barry Goldwater to Rogers Morton, May 18, 1976, Box B6, President Ford Committee Records, GRF; Spencer Rich, "Goldwater Bars Use of Remarks on Canal," *Washington Post,* May 14, 1976.

29. Edward Walsh, "Goldwater Endorses President," *Washington Post,* July 1, 1976.

30. Tom Edmonds: Conversation with the author, October 9, 1993.

31. James J. Kilpatrick: Telephone interview with the author, July 15, 1993; Ann Devroy, "As Vans Load Up, Republicans Bid Farewell to Two Presidents," *Washington Post,* January 14, 1993; Barry Goldwater: Inter-

view with the author, December 6, 1991. Burton Bernstein, "AuH$_2$O," *New Yorker,* April 25, 1988, p. 67; Roger Rosenblatt, "Our National Buzzard," *Men's Journal,* August 1994, p. 48.

32. Dotson Rader, " 'This Country Has to Make a Decided Change,' " *Parade,* November 28, 1993, pp. 4–6.

33. Robert L. Bartley, *The Seven Fat Years: And How To Do It Again* (New York: Free Press, 1992), pp. 3–15.

34. David Pittman, "He's still kicking at 85," *Tucson Citizen,* November 15, 1994.

35. Sally Quinn: Telephone interview with the author, October 29, 1993.

36. Howard Baker: Interview with the author, November 10, 1993; Robert Merry: Interview with the author, June 17, 1992.

37. Robert Bauman: Interview with the author, September 11, 1993.

38. F. Clifton White: Interview with the author, April 6, 1992. Richard A. Viguerie and Lee Edwards, "Goldwater: Leader or Legend?" *Conservative Digest,* January 1976, pp. 6–10.

39. *With No Apologies,* p. 276.

40. Barry M. Goldwater with Jack Casserly, *Goldwater* (New York: Doubleday, 1988), p. 29; John Kolbe, "Nation's Conservatives Sadly See Goldwater's No Longer Their Man," *Phoenix Gazette,* May 17, 1976.

41. William A. Rusher, *The Rise of the Right* (New York: William Morrow and Co., 1984), p. 281.

42. Steve Neal, "Goldwater: A Man Ahead of His Time," *Arizona Republic,* December 16, 1979.

43. Edward Walsh, "Goldwater Endorses President," *Washington Post,* July 1, 1976.

44. "Could Reagan Have Beaten Carter?" *Human Events,* November 20, 1976, p. 3.

45. Tom Winter: Interview with the author, February 4, 1992.

46. *National Party Conventions 1831–1984* (Washington, D.C.: Congressional Quarterly, 1987), p. 132.

47. See pp. 384–387 of *Goldwater* for the senator's most extended discussion of the New Right and other manifestations of social conservatism.

Chapter 20 Coping with the New Conservatism

1. Barry M. Goldwater with Jack Casserly, *Goldwater* (New York: Doubleday, 1988), pp. 384–387.

2. Paul Weyrich: Interview with the author, April 16, 1992; Richard A. Viguerie, *The New Right: We're Ready to Lead* (Falls Church, Va.: Viguerie Company, 1980), p. 157; Lee Edwards, *You Can Make the Difference* (Westport, Conn.: Arlington House, 1980), p. 276.

3. Ed McAteer: Telephone interview with the author, May 3, 1994.
4. Viguerie, p. 230; McAteer: Telephone interview with the author, May 3, 1994.
5. "Goldwater's U-Turn on Religion, Morality, and Politics," *Human Events*, September 18, 1994, pp. 5–6.
6. *Goldwater*, p. 387.
7. Peggy Goldwater, "Why I believe in planned families," *The Arizonian*, April 14, 1967.
8. Joanne Goldwater: Interview with the author, January 6, 1993.
9. Form letter, September 5, 1973; Barry Goldwater to Dayra Gordon, April 16, 1974; form letter, August 7, 1974; Barry Goldwater to Dexter Duggan, May 9, 1974; Barry Goldwater to Barbara Hartz, May 2, 1974; Barry Goldwater to Norma Matheson, June 5, 1974, Correspondence, 93rd Congress, Barry Goldwater Papers, Arizona Historical Foundation, Arizona State University [hereafter BMG].
10. Barry Goldwater to Nancy Woodling, October 30, 1980; memorandum regarding abortion for *Phoenix Gazette* luncheon, October 28, 1980, BMG.
11. "Goldwater Creates Confusion with Backing of Abortion Ban," *Arizona Republic*, October 22, 1980; Jerry Hickey, "Goldwater's Abortion Views Called Misleading," *Arizona Republic,* October 24, 1980; Don Harris, "Goldwater Affirms Support of Anti-abortion Amendment," *Arizona Republic,* November 1, 1980.
12. Barry Goldwater to Karen Harvey, October 1, 1985, BMG.
13. Barry Goldwater to Jean Ronquillo, November 13, 1985, BMG.
14. Terry Emerson: Interview with the author, May 27, 1992; Barry Goldwater to Karen Harvey, October 1, 1985; Barry Goldwater to Jean Ronquillo, November 13, 1985; Barry Goldwater to Margaret C. McNamara, December 10, 1985, BMG.
15. Barry Goldwater to Mr. and Mrs. Jerome Oliver, April 5, 1977, 95th Congress, BMG.
16. Robert Bauman: Interview with the author, September 11, 1993.
17. Goldwater to Eva L. Duffus, September 20, 1985, BMG.
18. Goldwater to A. Mark Branes, September 30, 1985, BMG.
19. "Goldwater's Grandson Is Homosexual," *Lambda Report,* September 1993, p. 6.
20. Kevin Sessums, "Ty Ross Comes Clean," *Poz*, April-May 1994, pp. 20–24.
21. "Goldwater's Kin Come Out of Closet," *Human Events*, October 2, 1993, p. 18.
22. Sessums, pp. 20–24, et seq.
23. Ibid.

24. Barry Goldwater, "Job Protection for Gays," *Washington Post,* July 13, 1994. Lloyd Grove, "Barry Goldwater's Left Turn," *Washington Post,* July 28, 1994.

25. "Goldwater Given Honor by State ACLU," *Arizona Republic*, December 12, 1994.

26. Jesse Helms to Hoover Adams, October 28, 1985, BMG.

27. Barry Goldwater, *Why Not Victory?* (New York: Macfadden Books, 1962), p. 34; Barry Goldwater statements in January and February 1964; column by John D. Lofton, Jr., "Goldwater Changes Tune," May 1976, BMG; "Goldwater's Turnabout," *Arizona Republic*, May 7, 1976; M. Stanton Evans, "Strange Reversal," *Los Angeles Times,* May 1976, BMG; Barry Goldwater press release, May 4, 1976, BMG.

28. Viguerie, pp. 83–84.

29. Barry Goldwater to President Carter, August 26, 1977, White House Name File; President Carter to Barry Goldwater, September 10, 1977, Box 48, Staff/Office of Secretary, Jimmy Carter Library, Atlanta, Georgia [hereafter JCL].

30. Barry Goldwater, "Statement on the Panama Canal Treaty," *Congressional Record,* April 18, 1978, p. 10577.

31. *Goldwater,* pp. 387–388.

32. "Barry Goldwater Tastes New Life," *Time,* July 27, 1981, p. 24.

33. Ibid.

34. Roy Reed, "The liberals love Barry Goldwater now," *New York Times Magazine*, April 7, 1974, p. 23.

35. Ibid., p. 53.

36. Barry Goldwater, *With No Apologies* (New York: William Morrow and Co., 1979), p. 97.

37. William F. Buckley Jr., "Tribute to Goldwater," *National Review*, November 9, 1973, p. 1265.

38. Steve Neal, "Goldwater: A Man Ahead of His Time," *Arizona Republic*, December 16, 1979.

Chapter 21   Final Flight

1. Barry Goldwater to Milton Friedman, February 4, 1972; Friedman to Barry Goldwater, February 21, 1972; Barry Goldwater to Friedman, April 7, 1975; Friedman to Barry Goldwater, May 19, 1975, Personal Papers of Milton Friedman.

2. "Goldwater Address at Tamkang College of Arts and Sciences," *Congressional Record*, April 20, 1977, pp. 11370–11371.

3. Barry Goldwater to William F. Buckley Jr., April 26, 1977, Box 147, Buckley Papers, Sterling Library, Yale University.

4. Jimmy Carter, *Keeping Faith: Memoirs of a President* (Toronto: Bantam Books, 1982), pp. 189–191.
5. Ibid., p. 192.
6. Barry Goldwater, "Abrogating Treaties," October 11, 1977, *New York Times*. Goldwater also referred to Thomas Jefferson, who wrote in his manual of rules and practices of the Senate: "Treaties being declared, equally with the laws of the United States, to be the supreme law of the land, it is understood that an act of the legislature alone can declare them infringed and rescinded."
7. Ibid.
8. Barry M. Goldwater, *China and the Abrogation of Treaties* (Washington, D.C.: The Heritage Foundation, 1978), p. 39; Press release of Barry Goldwater, May 23, 1978.
9. Statement by Barry Goldwater regarding his "Concurrent Resolution Reaffirming the Constitutional Role of Congress in Terminating Defense Treaties," October 10, 1978, Barry Goldwater Papers, Arizona Historical Foundation, Arizona State University [hereafter BMG].
10. John Maclean, "Questions about Taiwan's Future," *Chicago Tribune*, December 24, 1978.
11. John Franklin Copper, "Opportunistic China Move Typical of Carter Mistakes," *Commercial Appeal*, December 21, 1978.
12. Text of remarks by Barry Goldwater over CBS-TV, December 23, 1978.
13. Barry Goldwater to Gerald Ford, October 23, 1979, BMG.
14. "Ford, Kennedy Endorse Move; Goldwater Bitter," *New York Times*, December 16, 1978; "Reagan Rips 'Betrayal of Taiwan,' " *Independent Press-Telegram*, December 17, 1978; Advertisement of Committee for a Free China, *Human Events*, January 20, 1979, p. 8.
15. Richard Nixon to Lester L. Wolff, chairman, subcommittee on Asian and Pacific Affairs, House Foreign Affairs Committee, February 14, 1979, BMG.
16. Henry S. Bradsher and Allan Frank, "U.S. Will Appeal Court Ruling on Taiwan Treaty," *Washington Star,* October 18, 1979.
17. Ibid.
18. Barry Goldwater, "Barry Goldwater Supports an Early Vote to Uphold the District Court's Decision Requiring Legislative Approval to Terminate the Mutual Defense Treaty with Taiwan," *Congressional Record*, October 23, 1979, p. 14926.
19. Barry Goldwater to President Carter, October 18, 1979, BMG.
20. Jimmy Carter to Barry Goldwater, November 10, 1979, Box 246, C-Track, Name File, Jimmy Carter Library, Atlanta, Georgia [hereafter JCL].

21. *Facts on File,* December 7, 1979, p. 919.
22. Barry Goldwater, "Supreme Court Opinions in Taiwan Treaty Case," *Congressional Record*, December 14, 1979, pp. 36141–36144.
23. Ibid.
24. Robert Merry: Interview with the author, June 17, 1992.
25. Phyllis "Twinkle" Thompson: Interview with the author, August 4, 1992; Ellen Thrasher: Interview with the author, August 7, 1992.
26. Richard A. Viguerie and Lee Edwards, "Goldwater: Leader or Legend?" *Conservative Digest,* January 1976, p. 7.
27. Bobby Ray Inman: Interview with the author, October 6, 1992.
28. Howard Baker: Interview with the author, November 10, 1993.
29. John Tuck: Interview with the author, November 10, 1993.
30. Phyllis Thompson: Interview with the author, August 4, 1992; Mary R. Vinovich: Interview with the author, October 22, 1992; Ellen Thrasher: Interview with the author, August 7, 1992.
31. Barry Goldwater to Michael Goldwater, July 21, 1979, Private Papers of Michael Goldwater.
32. Ibid.
33. Don Harris, "A Reluctancy to Run," *Arizona Republic,* January 18, 1987, p. 47.
34. Michael Goldwater to Barry Goldwater, September 20, 1979; Barry Goldwater to Michael Goldwater, September 26, 1979, Private Papers of Michael Goldwater.
35. Joanne Goldwater: Interview with the author, January 6, 1993; Barry Goldwater to Michael Goldwater, Sept. 26, 1979. Private Papers of Michael Goldwater.
36. Barry M. Goldwater with Jack Casserly, *Goldwater* (New York: Doubleday, 1988), p. 375.
37. Harris, "A Reluctancy to Run," *Arizona Republic.*
38. William A. Rusher: Interview with the author, February 22, 1992; statement by Barry Goldwater, March 4, 1980, BMG.
39. *Goldwater,* pp. 377–378.
40. Ibid; Tom Fitzpatrick, *Arizona Republic,* October 15, 1980.
41. *Goldwater,* p. 378.
42. Ibid., p. 379.
43. Ibid., p. 380.
44. John Kolbe, "Goldwater, Schulz Spar in Debate," *Phoenix Gazette,* October 29, 1980; Don Harris, "Goldwater, Schulz Cross Swords over Inflation and Abortion Funding," Arizona Republic, October 29, 1980.
45. Harris, "A Reluctancy to Run."
46. Don Harris and Randy Collier, "Absentee Ballots Seal Goldwater Win,"

Arizona Republic, November 6, 1980; John Kolbe, "Goldwater's Magic Just Enough to Shatter Democrats' Dream," *Phoenix Gazette,* November 6, 1980.

47. Harris, "A Reluctancy to Run."
48. *Goldwater,* pp. 83, 336.
49. Barry M. Goldwater, Col., USAFR, "A Concept for the Future Organization of the United States Armed Forces," 1958, pp. 1, 11, 64, 69, BMG.
50. Ibid., pp. 73, 75.
51. *Goldwater,* p. 342.
52. Ibid., p. 351.
53. Ibid., pp. 351–352.
54. John G. Tower, *Consequences: A Personal and Political Memoir* (Boston: Little, Brown and Company, 1991), pp. 247–248.
55. I am indebted for most of the following details to James Locher, who was the principal author of the staff study and an indispensable aide to Goldwater and Nunn during their thirteen-month campaign to win Senate approval of Pentagon reorganization.
56. Drew Middleton, "Senators Fighting Uphill Battle for Unified Military Strategy," *Arizona Republic,* October 1985.
57. "Deadly Bureaucratic Inertia," *Arizona Republic* editorial, October 1985.
58. James Locher: Interview with the author, October 2, 1992.
59. *Goldwater,* pp. 334–338. General Kelley would later go so far as to declare publicly that enactment of the bill would degrade the Pentagon's efficiency "to the point where I would have deep concerns for the future security of the United States." (Pat Towell, "Pentagon Reorganization Bill Approved by Goldwater Panel," *Congressional Quarterly,* March 8, 1986, p. 573.)
60. *Goldwater,* p. 338.
61. Ibid., p. 339.
62. Walter Andrews, "Senate Committee Votes to Reorganize Pentagon," *Washington Times,* March 7, 1986.
63. Ibid.; Sam Nunn: Interview with the author, September 15, 1992.
64. James Locher: Interview with the author, October 2, 1992.
65. Barry Goldwater to Mrs. Barry Goldwater, May 11, 1985, Private Papers of Michael Goldwater.
66. "Senator's Wife Dies; Is Praised," *Arizona Republic,* December 12, 1985.
67. Alan Simpson: Interview with the author, July 28, 1993.
68. Barry Goldwater to Joanne Goldwater, October 6, 1986, Private Papers of Joanne Goldwater.
69. Pat Towell, "Senate Backs Major Changes in Organization of Pentagon," *Congressional Quarterly,* May 10, 1986, pp. 1030–1033; Exon quote,

L. Edgar Prina, "Realization of a dream," *Arizona Republic,* January 18, 1987, p. 48.

70. George C. Wilson, "Goldwater Has Finest Hour of Senate Career," *Washington Post,* May 8, 1986; Aspin quote, *Facts on File,* September 21, 1986, p. 771.
71. Anne O. Hoy, "Goldwater and 6 Others Who 'Made America Better' Get Freedom Medal," *Arizona Republic,* May 13, 1986.
72. Sam Nunn: Interview with the author, September 15, 1992.
73. James Locher: Interview with the author, October 2, 1992; Gerry Smith: Interview with the author, October 1, 1992.
74. George C. Wilson, "Goldwater Has Finest Hour of Senate Career," *Washington Post,* May 8, 1986.
75. Jack Casserly: Interview with the author, January 3, 1992.

Chapter 22   A Summing Up

1. Barry Goldwater, "The Gay Ban: Just Plain Un-American," *Washington Post,* June 10, 1993; Gary L. Bauer, "Gays Don't Belong in the Military," *Washington Post,* June 26, 1993, p. A23.
2. Barry Goldwater on CNN's "Larry King Live," June 10, 1993; ABC's "20/20," July 23, 1993; NBC's "The Tonight Show" with Jay Leno, November 12, 1993; Dotson Rader, "This Country Has to Make a Decided Change," *Parade,* November 28, 1993, pp. 4–6.
3. Timothy Egan, "Goldwater Defending Clinton; Conservatives Feeling Faint," *New York Times,* March 24, 1994; "Inside Politics: Goldwater Unloads," *Washington Times,* March 18, 1994.
4. John Kolbe, "Comic Ritual, No Convictions," *Phoenix Gazette,* March 21, 1994; transcript of Barry Goldwater radio broadcast for USA Health Network, airing in late February 1994.
5. Lloyd Grove, "Barry Goldwater's Left Turn," *Washington Post,* July 28, 1994; Russell Baker, "Ashes in Phoenix," *New York Times,* March 26, 1994; George Will, "Goldwater: A Man Who Won the Future," *Washington Post,* March 27, 1994.
6. Barry Goldwater to Mary Dent Crisp, July 29, 1992, Barry Goldwater Papers, Arizona Historical Foundation, Arizona State University. "Goldwater Warns Abortion Plank May Wreck GOP," *Washington Post,* August 7, 1992.
7. "Goldwater Sinks Conservative House Hopeful," *Human Events,* November 14, 1992, pp. 3–4; Laura Laughlin, "Some in Arizona GOP Angry at Elder Statesman Goldwater," *Los Angeles Times,* December 9, 1992.
8. William F. Buckley Jr., "Love-fest on the Right Side," *Washington Times,* May 7, 1994.

9. Michael Leahy, "I'd Have Ended the Vietnam War in a Week or Two," *New Choices,* December 1992-January 1993, p. 44.

10. Judy Eisenhower: Telephone interview with the author, May 23, 1994.

11. John Kolbe: Conversation with the author, November 9, 1994.

12. Lloyd Grove, "Barry Goldwater's Left Turn," Washington Post.

13. Dodie Londen: Telephone interview with the author, April 19, 1994.

14. Susan Goldwater: Telephone interview with the author, May 23, 1994.

15. Susan Goldwater: Interview with the author, January 4, 1993.

16. William McCune, "Mr. Conservative: Goldwater remains totally consistent in his views," *Arizona Republic,* June 1992.

17. Burton Bernstein, "AuH₂0," *New Yorker,* April 25, 1988, p. 71.

18. Interview with Barry Goldwater, *The Advocate,* August 1993.

19. Barry Goldwater, *The Conscience of a Conservative* (Washington, D.C.: Regnery Gateway, 1990), p. xxv.

20. Barry Goldwater, *The Conscience of a Majority* (Englewood Cliffs, N.J.: Prentice-Hall, 1970), pp. 21–23.

21. "Goldwater's U-Turn on Religion, Morality, and Politics," *Human Events*, September 18, 1993, pp. 5–6.

22. Ibid.

23. Barry Goldwater: Interview with the author, December 17, 1991.

24. Ed McAteer: Telephone interview with the author, May 3, 1994.

25. Barry Goldwater: Letter to the author, February 22, 1994.

26. Ibid.

27. Ibid; Goldwater to Imogene K. Bryan, September 30, 1985, re S. 1440. BMG.

28. Lloyd Grove, "Barry Goldwater's Left Turn," *Washington Post.*

29. Barry Goldwater: Interview with the author, December 6, 1991.

30. Phyllis Schlafly: Telephone interview with the author, May 17, 1994; "25th Anniversary of *A Choice Not an Echo,*" *The Phyllis Schlafly Report,* August 1989, Vol. 23, No. 1, Section 1.

31. Dick Armey: Fax to author, December 19, 1994.

32. Lynn Rosellini, "A Conservative Hero Surveys His Heirs," *U.S. News & World Report,* December 26, 1994/February 2, 1995, pp. 35, 36.

33. William J. Bennett, "Getting Used to Decadence: The Spirit of Democracy in Modern America," December 7, 1993, lecture celebrating the twentieth anniversary of The Heritage Foundation, delivered in Washington, D.C.

34. Barry Goldwater to William F. Buckley Jr., February 24, 1983; Buckley to Barry Goldwater, March 17, 1983, Buckley Papers, Sterling Library, Yale University.

35. Ibid.

36. John Grenier: Telephone interview with the author, May 31, 1994. As Alabamian John Grenier puts it, the 1964 campaign was the catalytic event that "absolutely broke the back of the Democratic party in the South."

37. Margo Carlisle: Interview with the author, June 29, 1992.

38. The author's paraphrase of a Robert Bauman remark in an interview: Goldwater "pooped along an awful lot . . . and quite often we had to clean it up," September 11, 1993.

39. Barry Goldwater: Interview with the author, December 17, 1991; Elizabeth Bowen: Interview with the author, November 12, 1992.

40. George Will, "Goldwater: A Man Who Won the Future," *Washington Post,* March 27, 1994.

41. Sally Quinn: Telephone interview with the author, October 29, 1993.

Bibliography

Author's Interviews

Howard Baker, Jr., Washington, D.C. · Michael E. Baroody, Washington, D.C. · William J. Baroody, Jr., Alexandria, Virginia · Robert E. Bauman, Washington, D.C. · Doris Berry, Phoenix, Arizona · Morton C. Blackwell, Springfield, Virginia · Elizabeth Bowen, Washington, D.C. · Junius Bowman, Phoenix, Arizona · Anna Chennault, Washington, D.C. · L. Brent Bozell, Washington, D.C. · Patricia B. Bozell, Washington, D.C. · Benjamin Bradlee, Washington, D.C. · Rita Bree, New Haven, Connecticut (via telephone) · William E. Brock, Washington, D.C. · David S. Broder, Washington, D.C. · Anne Brunsdale, Washington, D.C. · John H. Buchanan, Jr., Bethesda, Maryland · Patrick J. Buchanan, Washington, D.C. · James L. Buckley, Washington, D.C. · William F. Buckley Jr., New York, New York · Jack Buttram, Washington, D.C. · Glenn Campbell, Palo Alto, California · Margo Carlisle, Washington, D.C. · Jack Casserly, Tempe, Arizona · Peggy Goldwater Clay, Newport Beach, California (via telephone) · Darrell Coover, Washington, D.C. · Edward H. Crane, Washington, D.C. · Philip M. Crane, Washington, D.C. · Robert Creighton, Phoenix, Arizona · Ronald Crawford, Washington, D.C. · Robert F. Croll, Detroit, Michigan · Carl T. Curtis, Lincoln, Nebraska (via telephone) · Carol B. Dawson, Bethesda, Maryland · James Day, Alexandria, Virginia · Midge Decter, Washington, D.C. · George Dennison, Bethesda, Maryland · Edward J. Derwinski, Washington, D.C. · Donald J. Devine, Alexandria, Virginia · Maria Downs, Washington, D.C. · James H. Drum, Washington, D.C. · Earl Eisenhower, Scottsdale, Arizona · Judy Eisenhower, Scottsdale, Arizona · Terry Emerson, Washington, D.C. · Carolyn Erskine, Scottsdale, Arizona · M. Stanton Evans, Washington, D.C. · Paul Fannin, Phoenix, Arizona · Edwin J. Feulner, Jr., Washington, D.C. · David Franke, Potomac,

Maryland · Neal B. Freeman, Washington, D.C. · Milton Friedman, Palo Alto, California (via telephone) · Jack Germond, Washington, D.C. · William J. Gill, Washington, D.C. · Vic Gold, Washington, D.C. · John Goldsmith, Washington, D.C. · Barry Goldwater, Jr., Los Angeles (via telephone) · Joanne Goldwater, Scottsdale, Arizona · Michael Goldwater, Phoenix, Arizona · Robert Goldwater, Phoenix, Arizona · Susan Goldwater, Phoenix, Arizona · James Harff, Washington, D.C. · Sam Hay, Milwaukee, Wisconsin (via telephone) · R. L. "Dick" Herman, Washington, D.C. · Karl Hess, Martinsburg, West Virginia · Stephen Hess, Washington, D.C. · James Hinish, Washington, D.C. · James Hobson, Washington, D.C. · John Howard, Chicago, Illinois · Patricia Hutar, Chicago, Illinois (via telephone) · Bobby Ray Inman, Washington, D.C. · Harry Jaffa, Claremont, California (conducted by Matthew Spalding) · Virginia Kadell, Bethesda, Maryland · Ted Kazy, Tucson, Arizona · David Keene, Alexandria, Virginia · James Jackson Kilpatrick, Charleston, South Carolina (via telephone) · Russell Kirk, Washington, D.C. · Jeane Kirkpatrick, Washington, D.C. · Denison Kitchel, Scottsdale, Arizona · Richard Kleindienst, Tucson, Arizona · John Kolbe, Phoenix, Arizona · Frank Kovac, Beaumont, Texas (via telephone) · David R. Jones, Nashville, Tennessee · Donald Lambro, Washington, D.C. · Reed Larson, Springfield, Virginia · Paul Laxalt, Washington, D.C. · Judy Lewis, Washington, D.C. · Mary Elizabeth Lewis, Alexandria, Virginia · Charles Lichenstein, Washington, D.C. · Marvin Liebman, Washington, D.C. · Leonard Liggio, Fairfax, Virginia · James R. Locher III, Arlington, Virginia · Dodie Londen, Phoenix, Arizona (via telephone) · Trent Lott, Washington, D.C. · Robert Mardian, Phoenix, Arizona · James Martin, Birmingham, Alabama (via telephone) · Edward E. McAteer, Memphis, Tennessee (via telephone) · Edward A. McCabe, Washington, D.C. · William McCune, Phoenix, Arizona · Forrest McDonald, Philadelphia, Pennsylvania · George McDonnell, Rosslyn, Virginia · James P. McFadden, New York, New York · Robert MacNeil, New York, New York · Walter Mears, Washington, D.C. · Robert Merry, Washington, D.C. · Edwin Meese III, Washington, D.C. · J. William Middendorf II, Alexandria, Virginia · Jeremiah Milbank, Jr., New York, New York · Lynn Mote, Kensington, Maryland · Daniel Patrick Moynihan, Washington, D.C. · Hugh C. Newton, Washington, D.C. · Gerhart Niemeyer, Chicago, Illinois · Lyn Nofziger, Washington, D.C. · Michael Novak, Washington, D.C. · Robert D. Novak, Washington, D.C. · Sam Nunn, Washington, D.C. · Sandra Day O'Connor, Washington, D.C. · J. A. Parker, Washington, D.C. · Charles Percy, Washington, D.C. · James M. Perry, Washington, D.C. · Howard Phillips, Vienna, Virginia · Kevin Phillips, Bethesda, Maryland (via telephone) · Thomas L. Phillips, Potomac, Maryland · Daniel Popeo, Washington, D.C. · Sally Quinn, Washington, D.C. (via telephone) · William W. Quinn, Washington, D.C. · Thomas Reed, San Francisco, California · George Reedy, Milwaukee, Wisconsin (via telephone) · Mark Rhoads, Washington, D.C. · Cokie Roberts, Bethesda, Maryland (via telephone) · Harry Rosenzweig, Phoenix, Arizona · Lester (Budge) Ruffner, Prescott, Arizona · William Rickenbacker, Chicago, Illinois · William A. Rusher, Washington, D.C. · Pamela Rymer, Washington, D.C. · Allan Ryskind, Washington, D.C. · Donald Saltz, Washington, D.C. · Phyllis Schlafly, Alton, Illinois (via telephone) · Sandy Scholte, Manassas, Virginia · William Schulz, Washington, D.C. · John Sears, Washington, D.C. · Denny Sharon, Rosslyn, Virginia · Ivan Sidney, Flagstaff, Arizona · Alan K. Simpson, Washington, D.C. · Dean Smith, Tempe, Arizona · Gerry Smith, Washington, D.C. · Theodore C. Sorensen, New York, New York · Stu Spencer, Los Angeles, California (via telephone) · Ted Stevens, Washington, D.C. · Pierre Salinger, London (via telephone) · James Streeter, Washington, D.C. · John and Priscilla Stringer, Washington, D.C. · Richard Thompson, Washington, D.C. · Ellen Thrasher, Washington, D.C. · Phyllis (Twinkle) Thompson, Washington, D.C. · Strom Thurmond, Washington, D.C. · William E. Timmons, Washington, D.C. · Ralph de Toledano, Washington, D.C. · John Tuck, Washington, D.C. · Richard A. Viguerie, Falls Church, Virginia · Mary R. Vinovich, Cheverly, Maryland · Earl Voss, Washington, D.C. (via telephone) · Paul Wagner, Washington, D.C. · Richard Ware, Intervale, New Hampshire (via telephone) · John Warner, Washington, D.C. · Ben Wattenberg, Washington, D.C. · Barbara Wells, Manassas, Virginia · Paul Weyrich, Washington, D.C. · F. Clifton White, Greenwich, Connecticut · Margita White, Washington, D.C. · Jack Williams, Phoenix, Arizona · Garry Wills, Chicago, Illinois (via telephone) · Thomas S. Winter, Washington, D.C. · Richard Wirthlin, Alexandria, Virginia · Henry Zipf, Tucson, Arizona.

Unpublished Sources

Papers of Barry Goldwater, Carl Hayden Library, Arizona State University, Tempe, Arizona

Papers of Jimmy Carter, Jimmy Carter Library, Atlanta, Georgia

Papers of Dwight D. Eisenhower, Dwight D. Eisenhower Library, Abilene, Kansas

Papers of Gerald R. Ford, Gerald R. Ford Library, Ann Arbor, Michigan

Papers of Lyndon B. Johnson, Lyndon Baines Johnson Library, Austin, Texas

Papers of John F. Kennedy, John F. Kennedy Library, Boston, Massachusetts

Papers of Richard B. Nixon, Nixon Presidential Materials, Alexandria, Virginia

Papers of William F. Buckley Jr., Sterling Library, Yale University, New Haven, Connecticut

Papers of Dean Burch, University of Arizona, Tucson, Arizona

Private Papers of Joanne Goldwater, Scottsdale, Arizona

Private Papers of Michael Goldwater, Phoenix, Arizona

Papers of Denison Kitchel, Hoover Institution Archives, Stanford University, Palo Alto, California

Papers of Robert Mardian, Hoover Institution Archives, Stanford University, Palo Alto, California

Papers of Clarence Manion, Chicago Historical Society, Chicago, Illinois

Private Papers of J. William Middendorf II, Washington, D.C.

Papers of William A. Rusher, Library of Congress, Washington, D.C.

Papers of William W. Scranton, Pattee Library, Penn State University, College Station, Pennsylvania

Papers of Stephen Shadegg, Center for American History, University of Texas at Austin Library, Austin, Texas

Papers of F. Clifton White, Carl A. Kroch Library, Cornell University, Ithaca, New York

Oral History Transcripts

Clifton C. Carter (Johnson Library), Larry O'Brien (Kennedy Library), Kenneth P. O'Donnell (Kennedy Library), Richard M. Scammon (Johnson Library), John G. Tower (Johnson Library), Jack Valenti (Johnson Library)

Other Library and Archival Sources

Arizona Republic Library, *Human Events* Library, J. William Middendorf II Archives · National Archives, Washington, D.C.

Published Sources

Official Publications

Congressional Record

Defense Organization: The Need for Change. Staff Report to the Committee on Armed Services, U.S. Senate, October 16, 1985. U.S. Government Printing Office.

Hearings before the Select Committee to Study Governmental Operations with Respect to Intelligence Activities of the United States Senate: Federal Bureau of Investigation, 94th Congress, First Session, November 18–19,

Bureau of Investigation, 94th Congress, First Session, November 18–19, December 2–3, 9–11, 1975. Volume 6. Washington, D.C.: U.S. Government Printing Office.

Memorial Services Held in the Senate and House of Representatives of the United States, Together with Remarks Presented in Eulogy of Joseph Raymond McCarthy, Late a Senator from Wisconsin, 85th Congress, First Session, Washington, D.C.: U.S. Government Printing Office.

Official Report of the Proceedings of the Twenty-Eighth Republican National Convention, San Francisco, California, July 13–16, 1964. Published by the Republican National Committee.

Public Papers of the Presidents: Jimmy Carter 1977–1981, Washington, D.C.: Government Printing Office.

Public Papers of the Presidents: Gerald R. Ford 1974–1977, Washington, D.C.: Government Printing Office.

Public Papers of the Presidents: Dwight D. Eisenhower 1953–1961, Washington, D.C.: Government Printing Office.

Public Papers of the Presidents: Lyndon B. Johnson 1963–1969, Washington, D.C.: Government Printing Office.

Public Papers of the Presidents: John F. Kennedy 1961–1963, Washington, D.C.: Government Printing Office.

Public Papers of the Presidents: Richard M. Nixon 1969–1974, Washington, D.C.: Government Printing Office.

Public Papers of the Presidents: Ronald Reagan 1981–1989, Washington, D.C.: Government Printing Office.

Books

Ambrose, Stephen E. *Nixon: The Triumph of a Politician 1962–1972, Volume Two.* New York: Simon & Schuster, 1989.

Bartley, Robert L. *The Seven Fat Years: And How To Do It Again.* New York: The Free Press, 1992.

Bell, Jack. *Mr. Conservative: Barry Goldwater.* New York: Doubleday & Company, 1962.

Boller, Paul F., Jr. *Presidential Campaigns.* New York: Oxford University Press, 1984.

Bradlee, Ben. *Conversations with Kennedy.* New York: Pocket Books, 1976.

Broder, David S. and Stephen Hess. *The Republican Establishment: The Present and Future of the G.O.P.* New York: Harper & Row, 1967.

Buchanan, Patrick J. *Right from the Beginning.* Boston: Little, Brown and Company, 1988.

Buckley, William F. Jr. and L. Brent Bozell. *McCarthy and His Enemies.* Chicago: Henry Regnery Company, 1954.

Campaigne, Jameson G. *Checkoff: Labor Bosses and Working Men.* Chicago: Henry Regnery Company, 1961.

Caro, Robert. *The Years of Lyndon Johnson: Means of Ascent.* London: The Bodley Head, 1990.

Carson, Clarence B. *The Welfare State 1929–1985 (A Basic History of the United States, Volume 5).* Wadley, Alabama: American Textbook Committee, 1986.

Carter, Jimmy. *Keeping Faith: Memoirs of a President.* Toronto: Bantam Books, 1982.

Cohodas, Nadine. *Strom Thurmond and the Politics of Southern Change.* New York: Simon & Schuster, 1993.

Collier, Peter and David Horowitz. *The Rockefellers: An American Dynasty.* New York: Holt, Rinehart and Winston, 1976.

Cook, Fred J. *Barry Goldwater: Extremist of the Right.* New York: Grove Press, 1964.

Cummings, Milton C., ed. *The National Election of 1964.* Washington, D.C.: The Brookings Institution, 1966.

Curtis, Carl T. and Regis Courtemanche. *Forty Years Against the Tide: Congress and the Welfare State.* Lake Bluff, Illinois: Regnery Gateway, 1986.

Diamond, Edwin and Stephen Bates. *The Spot: The Rise of Political Advertising on Television.* Cambridge, Massachusetts: The MIT Press, 1988.

Dionne, E. J., Jr. *Why Americans Hate Politics.* New York: Simon & Schuster, 1991.

Donovan, Robert J. *The Future of the Republican Party.* New York: Signet Books, 1964.

Edsall, Thomas Byrne with Mary D. Edsall. *Chain Reaction: The Impact of Race, Rights and Taxes on American Politics.* New York: W.W. Norton and Company, 1992.

Edwards, Lee. *Ronald Reagan: A Political Biography.* Houston, Texas: Nordland Publishing, 1981.

———*You Can Make the Difference.* Westport, Connecticut: Arlington House, 1980.

Epstein, Benjamin R. and Arnold Foster. *The Radical Right: Report on the John Birch Society and Its Allies.* New York: Vintage Books, 1967.

Epstein, Jay Edward. *Between Fact and Fiction: The Problem of Journalism.* New York: Vintage Books, 1975.

Evans, M. Stanton. *The Future of Conservatism.* New York: Holt, Rinehart & Winston, 1968.

Evans, Rowland and Robert Novak. *Lyndon B. Johnson: The Exercise of Power.* New York: The New American Library, 1966.

Faber, Harold, ed. *The Road to the White House: The Story of the 1964 Election.* New York: The New York Times, 1965.

Ford, Gerald R. *A Time to Heal.* New York: Harper & Row, 1979.

Franke, David, ed. *Quotations from Chairman Bill: The Best of William F. Buckley Jr.* New Rochelle, New York: Arlington House, 1970.

Gaddis, John Lewis. *Strategies of Containment: A Critical Appraisal of Postwar American National Security Policy.* New York: Oxford University Press, 1982.

Gilder, George F. and Bruce K. Chapman. *The Party That Lost Its Head.* New York: Alfred A. Knopf, 1966.

Goldman, Eric F. *The Tragedy of Lyndon Johnson.* New York: Dell, 1968.

Goldwater, Barry M. with Jack Casserly. *Goldwater.* New York: Doubleday, 1988.

Goldwater, Barry. *An Odyssey of the Green and Colorado Rivers.* Privately printed by Barry Goldwater, 1941.

——*The Coming Breakpoint.* New York: Macmillan Publishing Company, 1976.

——*The Conscience of a Conservative.* Shepherdsville, Kentucky: Victor Publishing Company, 1960.

——*The Conscience of a Majority.* Englewood Cliffs, New Jersey: Prentice-Hall, 1970.

——*With No Apologies.* New York: William Morrow and Company, 1979.

——*Why Not Victory?* New York: Macfadden Books, 1962.

Goodwin, Richard N. *Remembering America: A Voice from the Sixties.* Boston: Little, Brown and Company, 1988.

Gottfried, Paul and Thomas Fleming. *The Conservative Movement.* Boston: Twayne Publishers, 1988.

Haig, Alexander M., Jr., with Charles McCarry. *Inner Circles: How America Changed the World, A Memoir.* New York: Warner Books, 1992.

Haley, J. Evetts. *A Texan Looks at Lyndon: A Study in Illegitimate Power.* Canyon, Texas: Palo Duro Press, 1964.

Hayek, Friedrich A. *The Road to Serfdom.* Chicago: University of Chicago Press, 1944.

Hess, Karl. *In a Cause That Will Triumph: The Goldwater Campaign and the Future of Conservatism.* Garden City, New York: Doubleday & Company, 1967.

Higgins, George V. *The Friends of Richard Nixon.* Boston: Little, Brown and Company, 1974.

Hunt, E. Howard. *Undercover: Memoirs of an American Secret Agent.* New York: Berkley Publishing Corporation, 1974.

Jamieson, Kathleen Hall. *Packaging the Presidency: A History and Criticism of Presidential Campaign Advertising.* New York: Oxford University Press, 1992.

Johnson, Lyndon Baines. *The Vantage Point: Perspectives of the Presidency 1963–1969.* New York: Holt, Rinehart and Winston, 1971.

Judis, John B. *William F. Buckley Jr.: Patron Saint of the Conservatives.* New York: Simon & Schuster, 1988.

Kearns, Doris. *Lyndon Johnson and the American Dream.* New York: Harper & Row, 1976.

Kennedy, Robert F. *The Enemy Within.* New York: Harper & Brothers, 1960.

Kessel, John H. *The Goldwater Coalition: Republican Strategies in 1964.* Indianapolis: The Bobbs-Merrill Company, 1968.

Kissinger, Henry. *White House Years.* Boston: Little, Brown and Company, 1979.

———*Years of Upheaval.* Boston: Little, Brown and Company, 1982.

Kleindienst, Richard. *Justice: The Memoirs of an Attorney General.* Ottawa, Illinois: Jameson Books, 1985.

Kirk, Russell. *The Conservative Mind: From Burke to Santayana.* Chicago: Henry Regnery Company, 1953.

Kramer, Michael and Sam Roberts. *I Never Wanted To Be Vice-President of Anything.* New York: Basic Books, 1976.

Lasky, Victor. *It Didn't Start with Watergate.* New York: The Dial Press, 1977.

Liebman, Marvin. *Coming Out Conservative.* San Francisco: Chronicle Books, 1992.

Lokos, Lionel. *Hysteria 1964: The Fear Campaign Against Barry Goldwater.* New Rochelle, New York: Arlington House, 1967.

MacNeil, Robert. *The Right Place at the Right Time.* Boston: Little, Brown and Company, 1982.

Manchester, William. *The Glory and the Dream: A Narrative History of America 1932–1972.* Vol 1. Boston: Little, Brown and Company, 1973.

McDowell, Edwin. *Barry Goldwater: Portrait of an Arizonan.* Chicago: Henry Regnery, 1964.

Meyer, Frank S. *The Conservative Mainstream.* New Rochelle, New York: Arlington House, 1969.

Mollenhoff, Clark R. *Game Plan for Disaster: An Ombudsman's Report on the Nixon Years.* New York: W.W. Norton & Company, 1976.

———*The Man Who Pardoned Nixon.* New York: Giniger Book, 1976.

Murray, Charles. *Losing Ground: American Social Policy, 1950–1980.* New York: Basic Books, 1984.

Nash, George. *The Conservative Intellectual Movement in America Since 1945.* New York: Basic Books, 1976.

Nixon, Richard. *RN: The Memoirs of Richard Nixon.* New York: Grosset & Dunlap, 1978.

———*Six Crises.* New York: Doubleday & Company, 1962.

Nofziger, Lyn. *Nofziger.* Washington, D.C.: Regnery Gateway, 1992.

Novak, Robert D. *The Agony of the GOP 1964*. New York: The Macmillan Company, 1965.

Oudes, Bruce, ed. *Richard Nixon's Secret Files*. Cambridge: Harper & Row, 1989.

Patterson, Robert T. *Mr. Republican: A Biography of Robert A. Taft*. Boston: Houghton Mifflin Company, 1970.

Perry, James M. *Barry Goldwater: A New Look at a Presidential Candidate*. Washington, D.C.: The National Observer, 1964.

Petro, Sylvester. *Power Unlimited: The Corruption of Union Leadership*. New York: The Ronald Press Company, 1959.

Phillips, Kevin. *The Emerging Republican Majority*. New Rochelle, New York: Arlington House, 1969.

Podhoretz, Norman. *Breaking Ranks: A Political Memoir*. New York: Harper & Row, 1979.

Polsby, Nelson W. and Aaron B. Wildavsky. *Presidential Elections: Strategies of American Electoral Politics, 2nd edition*. New York: Charles Scribner's Sons, 1968.

Reagan, Ronald. *An American Life*. New York: Simon & Schuster, 1990.

————*Speaking My Mind*. New York: Simon & Schuster, 1989.

Reeves, Richard. *President Kennedy: Profile of Power*. New York: Simon & Schuster, 1993.

————*A Ford, Not a Lincoln*. New York: Harcourt Brace Jovanovich, 1975.

Reeves, Thomas C. *The Life and Times of Joe McCarthy*. New York: Stein and Day, 1982.

Rivers, William L. and Cleve Mathews. *Ethics for the Media*. Englewood Cliffs, New Jersey: Prentice-Hall, 1988.

Robinson, Archie. *George Meany and His Times*. New York: Simon & Schuster, 1981.

Rusher, William A. *The Making of the New Majority Party*. New York: Sheed and Ward, 1975.

————*The Rise of the Right*. New York: William Morrow and Company, 1984.

Sabato, Larry. *Feeding Frenzy: How Attack Journalism Has Transformed American Politics*. New York: The Free Press, 1991.

Safire, William. *Safire's Political Dictionary*. New York: Random House, 1978.

Scammon, Richard M. and Ben J. Wattenberg. *The Real Majority*. New York: Primus, 1992.

Schlafly, Phyllis. *A Choice Not an Echo*. Alton, Illinois: Pere Marquette Press, 1964.

Schlesinger, Arthur M., Jr. *A Thousand Days: John F. Kennedy in the White House*. Boston: Houghton Mifflin Company, 1965.

Shadegg, Stephen. *Barry Goldwater: Freedom Is His Flight Plan.* New York: Fleet Publishing Corporation, 1962.

——*What Happened to Goldwater?* New York: Holt, Rinehart and Winston, 1965.

Smith, Dean. *The Goldwaters of Arizona.* Flagstaff, Arizona: Northland Press, 1986.

Sowell, Thomas. *Civil Rights: Rhetoric or Reality?* New York: William Morrow and Company, 1984.

Spanier, John. *American Foreign Policy Since World War II, 8th edition.* New York: Holt, Rinehart and Winston, 1980.

Stegner, Wallace. *Where the Bluebird Sings to the Lemonade Springs: Living and Writing in the West.* New York: Penguin Books, 1992.

Steinberg, Alfred. *Sam Johnson's Boy: A Close-Up of the President from Texas.* New York: The Macmillan Company, 1968.

Stormer, John A. *None Dare Call It Treason.* Florissant, Missouri: Liberty Bell Press, 1964.

Tower, John G. *Consequences: A Personal and Political Memoir.* Boston: Little, Brown and Company, 1991.

Viguerie, Richard A. *The New Right: We're Ready to Lead.* Falls Church, Virginia: The Viguerie Company, 1980.

Welch, Robert. *The Politician.* Privately printed for Robert Welch. Belmont, Massachusetts, 1963.

Whalen, James R. *Hunters in the Sky: Fighter Aces of World War II.* Washington, D.C.: Regnery Gateway, 1991.

White, F. Clifton with William J. Gill. *Suite 3505: The Story of the Draft Goldwater Movement.* New Rochelle, New York: Arlington House, 1967.

——*Why Reagan Won: The Conservative Movement: 1964–1981.* Chicago: Regnery Gateway, 1981.

White, Theodore. *Breach of Faith—The Fall of Richard Nixon.* New York: Atheneum Publishers, 1975.

——*The Making of the President 1960.* New York: Atheneum Publishers, 1961.

——*The Making of the President 1964.* New York: Signet Book, 1965.

Wicker, Tom. *One of Us: Richard Nixon and the American Dream.* New York: Random House, 1991.

Wills, Garry. *Nixon Agonistes: The Crisis of the Self-Made Man.* Boston: Houghton Mifflin Company, 1970.

——*Reagan's America: Innocents at Home.* London: Heinemann, 1988.

Wood, Rob and Dean Smith. *Barry Goldwater.* New York: Avon Books, 1961.

Woodward, Bob and Carl Bernstein. *The Final Days.* New York: Simon & Schuster, 1976.

Articles

Alsop, Stewart. "Can Goldwater Win in 64?" *Saturday Evening Post,* August 24, 1963.

Bernstein, Burton. "AuH$_2$O," *The New Yorker,* April 25, 1988.

Buckley, William F. Jr. "If Goldwater Were President," *Coronet,* July 1961.

——"Tribute to Goldwater," *National Review,* November 9, 1973.

Carlson, Peter. "A Goldwater Family Crisis," *People,* June 20, 1983.

Chamberlain, John. "The Humane Base of Conservatism," *Wall Street Journal,* June 2, 1960.

Danzig, David. "Conservatism After Goldwater," *Commentary,* March 1965.

Duffus, R. L. "One Senator's Manifesto," *New York Times Book Review,* June 26, 1960.

Edwards, Willard. "A New Look at Joe McCarthy," *Human Events,* April 14, 1973.

——"Did Biased Reporters Cost Nixon the Election?" *Human Events,* April 7, 1961.

Evans, M. Stanton. "Can a Conservative Be a Radical?" *The New Guard,* September 1961.

Friedman, Milton. "The Goldwater View of Economics," *New York Times Magazine,* October 11, 1964.

Gilbert, Richard L., Jr. "Barry Goldwater: The Admonitions of an Older Man," *Esquire,* October 1962.

Goldwater, Barry. "Abrogating Treaties," *New York Times,* October 11, 1977.

——"My Proposals for a 'Can-Win' Foreign Policy," *Life,* January 17, 1964.

——"The Gay Ban: Just Plain Un-American," *Washington Post,* June 10, 1993.

——"Unified Commands," *Phoenix Gazette,* November 25, 1985.

Greer, Gordon. "Barry Goldwater's Very Special Place," *Venture,* 1967.

Harrison, Gilbert A. "Way Out West: An Interim Report on Barry Goldwater," *The New Republic,* November 23, 1963.

Hoffman, Paul G. "How Eisenhower Saved the Republican Party," *Collier's,* October 26, 1956.

Jaffa, Harry V. "Goldwater's Famous 'Gaffe,' " *National Review,* August 10, 1984.

Kendall, Willmoore. "Quo Vadis, Barry?" *National Review,* February 25, 1961.

Kitchel, Denison. "Explaining Things to Ike," *National Review,* April 30, 1976.

Kolbe, John. "Nation's Conservatives Sadly See Goldwater's No Longer Their Man," *Phoenix Gazette,* May 17, 1976.

Kopkind, Andrew. "Older, Wiser But Still Prickly as a Saguaro, Barry Goldwater Remembers When Right Was Wrong," *People,* February 13, 1989.

Kristol, Irving. "A Letter from Irving Kristol," *National Review,* March 16, 1992.

Lawrence, David. "Goldwater Stand Seen as a 'Courageous' Act," *New York Herald Tribune,* June 20, 1964.

———"What Goldwater Said on A-Bomb," *New York Herald Tribune,* May 28, 1964.

Leahy, Michael. " 'I'd Have Ended the Vietnam War in a Week or Two,' " *New Choices,* December 1992–January 1993.

Lewis, Ted. "Goldwater's 'Dear George' Letter Bared," *New York Daily News,* November 30, 1966.

Lippmann, Walter. "A Choice but a Bad One," *New York Herald Tribune,* June 30, 1964.

———"Goldwater After California," *New York Herald Tribune,* June 9, 1964.

———"The Goldwater Movement," *Newsweek,* August 5, 1963.

McCune, William. "Mr. Conservative: Goldwater Remains Totally Consistent in His Views," *Arizona Republic,* June 1992.

Mears, Walter R. "The Story Behind 8 Days in History," *Arizona Republic,* January 18, 1987.

Meyer, Frank S. "What Next for Conservatism?" *National Review,* December 1, 1964.

———"Why Goldwater Can Defeat Johnson," *National Review,* July 14, 1964.

Morgenstern, George. "Harsh Facts, Hard Sense on the Perils to Liberty," *Chicago Sunday Tribune Magazine of Books,* April 17, 1960.

Neal, Steve. "Goldwater: A Man Ahead of His Time," *Arizona Republic,* December 16, 1979.

Novak, Robert D. "Conservative Senator Softens Views, Offers a Plan to Build GOP," *Wall Street Journal,* January 11, 1961.

Oakes, John B. "America's Loss of Face," *New York Times,* December 29, 1978.

Porter, George O. "YRs Stay Right," *The New Guard,* August 1961.

Prina, L. Edgar. "Realization of a Dream," *Arizona Republic,* January 18, 1987.

Quinn, Sally. "Goldwater Assailed as Critic of Reagan," *Washington Post,* May 21, 1976.

Rader, Dotson. " 'This Country Has to Make a Decided Change,' " *Parade,* November 28, 1993.

Reed, Roy. "The Liberals Love Barry Goldwater Now," *New York Times Magazine,* April 7, 1974.

Reston, James. "A Fortnight of Decision: G.O.P. Faces Hard Choice," *New York Times,* June 29, 1964.

——— "Some New Ways to Slice the Old Baloney," *New York Times,* September 4, 1964.

Ritchie, Robert. "A Look into the Future," *The New Guard,* November 1961.

Rovere, Richard. "The Conservative Mindlessness," *Commentary,* March 1965.

Rubinoff, Michael W. "At Odds with Reagan," *Arizona Republic,* January 18, 1987.

Rusher, William A. "Crossroads for the GOP," *National Review,* February 12, 1963.

Sheehan, Robert. "Arizona Fundamentalist," *Fortune,* May 1961.

Towell, Pat. "Pentagon Reorganization Bill Approved by Goldwater Panel," *Congressional Quarterly,* March 8, 1986.

——— "Senate Backs Major Changes in Organization of Pentagon," *Congressional Quarterly,* May 10, 1986.

Viguerie, Richard A. and Lee Edwards. "Goldwater: Leader or Legend?" *Conservative Digest,* January 1976.

Will, George. "Goldwater: A Man Who Won the Future," *Washington Post,* March 27, 1994.

Magazines and Journals Consulted

Commentary · Congressional Quarterly · Conservative Digest · Fortune · Human Events · Life · Look · National Review · New York Times Magazine · Newsweek · People · Reader's Digest · Saturday Evening Post · The New Guard · The New Republic · The New Yorker- · Time · U.S. News & World Report

Newspapers Consulted

Arizona Daily Star · Arizona Republic · Chicago Tribune · Los Angeles Times · Manchester (NH) Union-Leader · New York Daily News · New York Herald Tribune · New York Times · Phoenix Gazette · USA Today · Wall Street Journal · Washington Post · Washington Star · Washington Times

Index